THE ULTIMATE ILLUSTRATED GUIDE TO

DREAMS, SIGNS
& SYMBOLS

THE ULTIMATE ILLUSTRATED GUIDE TO

DREAMS, SIGNS
& SYMBOLS

IDENTIFICATION AND ANALYSIS OF THE VISUAL VOCABULARY AND SECRET LANGUAGE THAT
SHAPES OUR THOUGHTS AND DREAMS AND DICTATES OUR REACTIONS TO THE WORLD

MARK O'CONNELL
RAJE AIREY AND
RICHARD CRAZE

Published by World Publications Group, Inc.
140 Laurel Street, East Bridgewater, MA 02333
www.wrldpub.net

Produced by Anness Publishing Ltd, Hermes House,
88–89 Blackfriars Road London SE1 8HA
tel. 020 7401 2077; fax 020 7633 9499
www.annesspublishing.com

If you like the images in this book and would like to investigate
using them for publishing, promotions or advertising, please visit
our website www.practicalpictures.com for more information.

Publisher: Joanna Lorenz
Editorial Director: Helen Sudell
Executive Editor: Joanne Rippin
Designer: Adelle Morris
Production Controller: Wendy Lawson

ETHICAL TRADING POLICY
Because of our ongoing ecological investment programme, you,
as our customer, can have the pleasure and reassurance of
knowing that a tree is being cultivated on your behalf to
naturally replace the materials used to make the book you are
holding. For further information about this scheme, go to
www.annesspublishing.com/trees

A CIP catalog record for this book is available from
the British Library.

ISBN-10: 1-57215-520-5
ISBN-13: 978-1-57215-520-6

Printed and bound in China

Previously published as two separate volumes;
The Complete Encylopedia of Signs & Symbols,
and *Dictionary of Dreams and their Meanings*

Publisher's Note:
Although the advice and information in this book are believed to
be accurate and true at the time of going to press, neither the
authors nor the publisher can accept any legal responsibility or
liability for any errors or omissions that may be made.

CONTENTS

INTRODUCTION

ABOVE Dreams can be messages from the subconcious, which can bring about life changes.

The word "symbol" is derived from the ancient Greek *symballein*, meaning to throw together. Its figurative use originated in the custom of breaking a clay tablet to mark the conclusion of a contract or agreement: each party to the agreement would be given one of the broken pieces, so that when they reconvened the pieces could be fitted together like a jigsaw. The pieces, each of which identified one of the people involved, were known as *symbola*, so that a symbol not only represents something else but also hints at a missing "something", an invisible part that is needed to achieve completion or wholeness. Whether consciously or unconsciously, the symbol carries the sense of joining things together to create a whole greater than the sum of its parts, as shades of meaning accrue to produce a complex idea.

A sign, on the other hand, may be understood as something that stands for, or points to, something else in a more literal way. A sign exists to convey information about a specific object or idea, while a symbol tends to trigger a series of perceptions, beliefs and emotional responses. For example, as a sign, the word "tree" means a particular type of plant that develops a permanent woody structure with a trunk and branches, roots and leaves. As a symbol, the tree may have many meanings: it can represent fruitfulness and the bounty of nature, endurance and longevity or the web of family relationships; as a Christian symbol it can refer to the cross, and in many traditions it represents the "tree of life" that links the everyday world with the world of spirit.

Neither signs nor symbols have intrinsic meaning. The same tree can be described by many different words in different languages, and its meanings as a symbol are formed through human interaction with it. Both signs and symbols have become part of human social and cultural identity, changing and evolving as we do. They are vehicles for information and meaning, operating on many different levels – the universal and particular, intellectual and emotional, spatial and temporal, spiritual and material. They are a way of making sense of experience, including our dreams. If we could not classify the world using symbolic codes and structures we would be overwhelmed by sensory data. We need a way of describing what happens to us in order to understand it.

As well as being an essential part of human society, signs and symbols appear in nature, and may refer to pre-conscious information, as in the case of smoke signifying a fire nearby, or

tracks signposting the presence of a particular animal. This book is primarily concerned with signs that have a conscious or unconscious meaning for humans, but as we are rooted in nature, we will see that there may be deeper connections between natural phenomena and the symbols that are meaningful to us. It is also concerned with the more personal world of dreams, in which the interpretation of symbolic themes are much more individual.

Part of the book is a guide to making sense of dreams. It recognizes that no two people are exactly alike and therefore no two dreams are the same. When interpreting dreams the book takes the view that it is experience rather than theory that counts: you can become your own dream expert.

ABOUT THIS BOOK

The book is divided into five main sections. Part One provides an overview of the uses, meaning and development of signs and symbols as seen from a number of different perspectives: historical, cross-cultural, sociological and psychological. Part Two looks at the applications of symbols in many areas of life, and includes chapters on culture and communication, abstract symbols, myth and the cosmos, plants and animals, the human life cycle, and the earth. Part Three contains chapters on the history, nature and sense of dreams as well as one on working with dreams. This section is intended to give an overview of dream theories, past and present, and to provide information that can help you recognize different types of dream and dream symbols. It also offers practical suggestions for how to programme your dreams and to improve dream recall, as well as techniques to help you unravel the mystery of your dreams.

Part Four is the Dream Lexicon. Divided thematically, it begins with an exploration of the world we live in – its abstract qualities and the natural environment. It then looks at our own development through the cycles of life, and aspects of mind, body and spirit. Other people and how we engage with them and with the world at large are discussed in the following chapters, along with a section on motion and mechanics. Lastly we see how magic and fantasy figure in our dreams. The book ends with Part Five, a directory of more than 1,000 signs and symbols, each with its own ideograph and a brief explanation of its meaning and application.

It is hoped that the information in this book will stimulate readers' interest in this profound and complex subject, prompting them to look beyond the superficial meaning of everyday objects and ideas to arrive at a greater understanding of the ways in which so much of daily life, the way we communicate with each other, and what we process and experience in our personal dream worlds, is informed by the richness of signs and symbols.

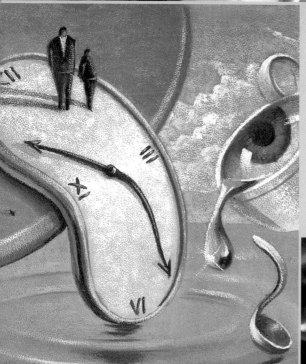

ABOVE Fire has been one of the most ancient and primal of signs for thousands of years. It's symbolism has grown and changed through the centuries.

LEFT The complex or surreal content of many dreams can sometimes obscure or confuse their significance and meaning.

BELOW The six-pointed star has great symbolic significance in many cultures, but is perhaps best known as the Star of David, an important symbol in the Jewish faith.

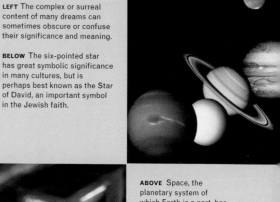

ABOVE Space, the planetary system of which Earth is a part, has had great symbolic meaning over the centuries. This is subject to change as science finds out more about the universe we exist in.

PART ONE

SIGNS OF LIFE

ANCIENT
SYMBOLS

The power and meaning of some of the world's oldest symbols are still available to us today. Found in the surviving art and artefacts of the world's early civilizations, they speak clearly of our ancestors' physical, social and spiritual concerns, and represent ideas that remain fundamentally important to modern humanity.

RIGHT The pyramids of ancient Egypt symbolized for their architects the creative power of the sun and the immortality of the pharaohs who were buried inside them.

PRIMORDIAL BEGINNINGS

ABOVE This Palaeolithic cave painting in Lascaux, France, was probably intended to create a symbolic link between the hunter and the bison, connecting him with the spirit of the animal.

LEFT The San Bushmen of the Kalahari desert still create rock paintings as symbolic visualizations of successful hunts.

Between the era of *Australopithecus*, the "Southern Ape" (from about 3.6 million BC) to *Homo sapiens sapiens* (25,000–10,000 BC), humans began to make tools, learned to use and then make fire, and constructed homes with hearths. They also began to use language, ritual and symbols.

What we know of our early ancestors comes from archaeological evidence such as cave paintings, artefacts and the traces of possible ritual practices, as well as comparisons with primitive peoples of later eras. Evidence of the development of symbol and ritual comes mainly from the Paleolithic people who emerged about two million years ago. They were hunters, and much of their industry involved working with chipped stone.

During this era, the mythic imagination was stirred, and art began to be created. The dawn of mythology and symbolism meant that people were beginning to relate to concepts deeper than just their daily existence. It is easy to imagine that their relationship with nature, the seasons and weather, the animals they hunted, the birth of their children and the inevitability of death led them to ponder the source and meaning of events in their lives. The primitive symbols of the cave, fire, the hand-axe, and the representation of animal figures, may serve as foundation metaphors for the complex human mythologies that have subsequently evolved. The symbols and rituals of primordial human beings may have served to align these people with the rhythms of their bodies and in nature, and to honour the forces influencing them.

THE MAKING OF FIRE

The ability to make fire and harness its energy was a highly significant development, achieved by *Homo erectus* (around 1.6 million–300,000 BC), and gave fire important symbolic qualities. The act of making fire represents the spark of imagination and creativity, and the energy of fire is in itself a symbol of power: harnessing and using nature to control other aspects of the natural world, bringing life-sustaining warmth, and frightening away threatening animals. Fire enabled people to extend the day after dark, creating a social time around a campfire or hearth, sharing myths and stories. At this early stage fire also became a symbol of transformation through the process of cooking.

CAVES AND CAVE ART

To primitive humans, caves were sacred places. People appear to have lived around or just inside the entrance, but ventured deeper into a cave only for religious or magical purposes.

Painting animals on the walls of caves may have been a means of connecting with their spiritual qualities. Boys were taken into the caves to be initiated as hunters – a rite that probably involved a symbolic death and rebirth, and which must have been a powerful experience, deep within a dimly lit, womb-like place surrounded by animal images.

To early humans a cave may have symbolized the leaving of everyday reality, as they went inside to find where their deeper nature connected with and honoured the spirits of other animals; a place of transformation where they ritually died and were reborn in a new form.

Many early cave paintings, such as those of the Trois Frères cavern, in southern France, depict beings who are part-animal and part-human in form. A bearded male figure, with the ears of a bull, antlers and a horse's tail, may have represented either a divinity or a magician.

It is hard to differentiate between images of human magicians and divine figures in Palaeolithic art, as both appear to share this mixture of human and animal features. The magician was an important member of the community, and was probably considered a god in human form, with influence upon the gods and animal spirits.

HUNTING MAGIC

Palaeolithic humans certainly used magic to help in hunting animals. The principal form of magic was mimetic: they would imitate an animal they were hunting to connect to its spirit and ensure success. However, they also used sympathetic or homeopathic magic, in the belief that an act upon an object representing the animal would literally have an effect on the animal itself. Thus clay figures and drawings of animals that have been cut and slashed have been found, which were presumably to aid success in hunting.

A constant supply of game for the hunt was crucial, and fertility magic was performed to ensure it. This usually involved depicting a mating pair of animals, or females with offspring. Clay models of bison in couples and a bull following a cow have been found in France; at La Madeleine a drawing shows a doe with a fawn.

MAKING OFFERINGS

The earliest evidence of probable offerings to supernatural powers was found in the Drachenloch, in the Tamina Valley, in Switzerland. Bear bones had been placed there with some flesh still attached to the skulls, brains intact, and some leg bones, in a state as if to be eaten. They are thought to have been offerings to appease animal spirits, to thank them for a successful hunt, and seek favour for future hunting expeditions.

BURIAL

Palaeolithic finds include the first evidence of burial for sacred

THE HAND-AXE

The stone-age hand-axe appears wherever early humans existed (except the very far east of Asia) and has been the most popular form of tool during the last two million years. It is a multi-purpose tool used for scraping animal skins, cutting meat, digging holes, cutting wood, and possibly as a weapon of self-defence against animals or other humans. The making of these tools involved chipping flakes from a "core" stone, signifying spiritual and psychological renewal of the core essence. Early two-faced axes are also thought to represent the repairing of interpersonal conflict.

purposes. The dead were believed to gain supernatural powers, and would have been respected and referred to for guidance. Red ochre was sprinkled over the bodies; this may have represented blood and symbolized life and strength for the journey into the other world.

In Les Hoteaux, in Ain, France, a late Palaeolithic skeleton was found in a small trench, covered with red ochre. There was a large stone behind its head, and buried with it were flint tools and the staff of a chieftain made from horn and engraved with a stag. Numerous other examples of bodies have been found in stone tombs or shallow graves, together with valuable jewellery, tools and other ritual objects. It seems the

dead were being given food and tools, perhaps symbolically, to equip them for their existence in the next world.

Sometimes buried bodies have been found to have been tied up in a doubled-up position. This may have been intended to stop the dead from returning and tormenting their living descendants. In China the remains of human beings at an evolutionary stage halfway between *Pithecanthropus* and Neanderthal humans were found: apart from their skulls and lower jawbones, the other bones of the bodies had been placed to represent the animals they would have eaten. Did this ancient funerary ritual mean "You are what you eat"?

ABOVE Depictions of the sun and moon are centred on a human figure in this Venezualan engraving.

ABOVE Early people made ritual use of red ochre, used to stain this stone found in Bevoc, Bohemia, from 250,000 years ago.

LEFT As a symbol, fire is associated with creativity, destruction and imagination.

THE CRADLE OF CIVILIZATION

ABOVE We can only imagine what the early cities of ancient Mesopotamia looked like. This artist's impression shows a city's towering ziggurat to the left of the picture.

BELOW The law code of Hammurabi, 18th century BC, is an example of cuneiform script, the first written signs to replace pictorial representations.

fairly simple mud-brick constructions, decorated with cone geometrical mosaics and frescoes with human and animal figures. A rectangular shrine, known as a "cella", had a brick altar or offering table in front of a statue of the temple's deity. Public rituals, food sacrifices and libations took place on a daily basis, as well as monthly feasts and annual celebrations of the New Year.

As early hunter-gatherer societies found ways to work the land, more permanent settlements began to appear, particularly in areas where crops would flourish. One such area was in Mesopotamia, the "Fertile Crescent" of land between the Tigris and Euphrates rivers in what is now southern Iraq. From around 5000 BC small farming villages in the region were gradually developing into towns and cities, giving birth to some of the earliest civilizations – the word "civilization" comes from the Latin civis, which means "citizen of a city". People were inventing written languages, building temples, palaces and dwellings, and creating complex societies in which signs and symbols were interwoven with the fabric of daily life.

RECORD KEEPING

The ancient civilization of Sumer had thriving agriculture, trade and industry and was one of the first civilizations to develop a system of writing. Initially pictographs or icons were used, with one of the earliest

dictionaries containing about 2,000 graphic symbols, each one meant to resemble that which it represented. However, as society developed and the need to record complex matters increased, the limitations of pictorial representation became apparent. Gradually people realized that written signs could be used to represent sounds rather than things, and so pictures were replaced by cuneiform script, a written code based on a series of wedge-shaped characters, usually inscribed on to a soft surface, such as clay.

RELIGIOUS LIFE

The flooding of the Tigris and Euphrates was violent and unpredictable: from one day to the next, life-giving rain could change into an agent of devastation. It was believed the gods controlled these powerful forces, with humans little more than slave subjects to the whims of fate. This put religion firmly at the centre of daily life, with a temple dedicated to one of the major gods at the heart of each town or city. Initially these were

ZIGGURATS

These early temple complexes gradually evolved into ziggurats, towering pyramid-like structures, some reaching as high as 90m (300ft). One of the earliest examples from the region is the White Temple of Uruk (Erech in the Old Testament), dedicated to the Sumerian god An, lord of the heavens, dating back to the late 3000s BC.

Mesopotamian ziggurats were built in a series of three, five or seven increasingly narrow terraces, with steps for climbing to the next level. The seven terraces are said to correspond to the seven planetary Heavens. According to a Sumerian tradition, the bottom level was linked with Saturn and was painted black; the second level was white and corresponded to Jupiter; the third was brick-red and symbolized Mercury, while the fourth, blue level was associated with Venus. The sixth level, Mars, was yellow, while the seventh level was grey or silver to represent the moon, upon which the golden light of the sun would shine. Sacrifices were usually

RIGHT A winged bull with a human head, one of the hybrid mythological creatures known as lamassu that were carved into important public buildings in Assyrian cities.

made at the top level. The symbolism of the ziggurat has also been compared with the cosmic mountain alleged to lie at the centre of the world, as well as with temples built in the shape of mountain. Symbolically, ziggurats are similar to ladders, joining Heaven and Earth and creating a passageway for mortals to ascend and the gods to descend. Ziggurats were allegedly the inspiration for the Tower of Babel, which in the Old Testament was interpeted as a symbol of pride built by humans attempting to equal God's splendour.

THE GODDESS ISHTAR

Arguably the most important deity in ancient Mesopotamia was the moon goddess, Ishtar, also known as Inanna, Astarte or Ashtar (and later, in ancient Egypt, as Isis). Ishtar personifies the forces of nature that can give and destroy life, and, like the moon, her form is ever-changing. Sometimes she was represented as a large-breasted, round-bellied fertility goddess. She is the goddess of sexual love, and in the homes of ancient Babylon little shrines containing her image showed her nude, seated in a window frame – the typical pose of the prostitute.

Ishtar is also the goddess of war, and in this aspect she could be depicted standing on a lion (symbolizing ferocity) and with the talons and wings of an owl. She was also shown wearing a three-tiered crown of stars, blue lapis lazuli stones and a rainbow necklace, symbolizing her connection with the sky. As queen

of the heavens, each night she rides across the sky in a chariot drawn by lions or goats. The zodiacal constellations were known to the ancient Arabs as the Houses of the Moon, and the whole zodiacal belt was known as the "girdle of Ishtar", a term that referred to the moon calendar of the ancients.

BABYLON

In ancient Babylon, the lion was a popular symbol of royal power, while the dragon was associated with the supreme god, Marduk. The laws and customs of the land were unified under Hammurabi (r.1792–1750 BC), and the city of Babylon became a renowned centre for learning, especially in science, mathematics and astronomy. Babylonian scholars developed a numbering system, based on groups of 60, which led to our 60-minute hour and 360-degree circle. The ancient Greek historian Herodotus declared that Babylon "is so splendid, that no city on earth may be compared with it". Its walls and famous hanging gardens were among the seven wonders of the ancient world, and Babylon became synonymous with excellence and attainment. In the Judaeo-Christian tradition, however, it became the antithesis of paradise and the heavenly Jerusalem, and symbolized the profane.

LAMASSU

Symbols of power and protection, massive winged sphinxes, or lamassu, have their roots in Babylonian magical traditions, although they are more usually

associated with Assyrian culture (c.1000–600 BC). With the body of a bull or lion, sometimes with five legs, winged, and with bearded human heads, these sculptures were incorporated into important civic structures, such as the royal palace or city gateways. Some stood as high as 5m (16ft) and weighed as much as 30 tons. The lion and the bull symbolized masculine power, virility and sovereignty, although both animals were also associated with the moon goddess: the spectacular Ishtar Gate that led into the city of Babylon was decorated with lions, while the bull's horns on Ishtar's headdress denoted the crescent moon. The head of the lamassu symbolized the power of the sovereign to protect his people, the wings denoted the ability to fly, while the legs represented vigilance against both human and supernatural enemies who could attack from any direction.

ABOVE This artist's impression of Babylon shows the popular sport of lion hunting. The lion was a symbol of royal authority and power for the Babylonions.

BELOW An impression of one of the towers of the Ishtar Gate of the city of Babylon, which was elaborately decorated with golden lions.

ANCIENT EGYPT

PYRAMIDS

The pyramid is a symbol of ascension: erected in alignment with the sun and stars to create a passageway between Earth and the Heavens by which the dead pharaoh could cross to the afterlife. In the Western hermetic tradition, the pyramid combines the symbolism of the square with the triangle. The symbolism of the pyramid is also linked with the mound (and cosmic mountain), thought to resemble the hill that emerged from the primeval waters when the earth was created, so a symbol of the power of life over death.

In its prime, the civilization of ancient Egypt was arguably the most spectacular on earth. It emerged about 5,000 years ago and continued to flourish for three millennia, giving us a fascinating array of symbols, many of which were rooted in the land and nature. Ancient Egypt existed in a landscape of extremes, referred to in symbolic terms as Red and Black. The Red Land (Deshret) was the Saharan side of the country, made scorched and barren by the fierce heat of the sun; the Black Land (Kemet) was the fertile area in the Nile valley, darkened by the river's seasonal floods and shaded by its vegetation. In this way, the land of Egypt came to symbolize a marriage of opposites, a synthesis. This view informed the Egyptians' belief systems and lay at the heart of their culture.

ORDER AND CHAOS

The relationship between order (*maat*) and chaos (*isfet*) was at the crux of ancient Egyptian thought. The god Horus was associated with all that was right and ordered, and Seth with chaos, as well as infertility and aridity.

Similarly Kemet was a place of order – at the same time each year the Nile, Egypt's lifeblood, flooded the land, ensuring bountiful harvests – while Deshret was associated with infertility and disorder. Harmony was achieved when these two forces were held in equilibrium, neither gaining control at the expense of the other, and was personified by the goddess Maat, daughter of Re, the creator god and pre-eminent solar deity.

Maat was represented wearing an ostrich feather, symbol of truth and an ideogram of her name, on her head. She maintained order on Earth and in Heaven, ruling over the seasons, day and night and the movement of the stars, she also decided the fate of the dead in the underworld, weighing the deceased's heart against the feather of truth in her scales of justice. When the scales balanced, paradise was the reward; when they tipped, the deceased was devoured by a monster, part-lion, part-hippopotamus, part-crocodile. Maat also presided over decrees, legal acts and social relationships, and regulated religious rites.

DIVISION AND UNIFICATION

Politically, the kingdom was divided into two parts: Upper and Lower Egypt, with Upper Egypt being in the south, and Lower Egypt in the north in the Nile Delta region – a division represented by the white and red crowns. The red crown of Lower Egypt had a tall, thin back and a narrow coil at the front, while the white crown of Upper Egypt was shaped like a tall cone with a bulbous tip. It was sometimes adorned with two plumes in a form called the atef-crown, which was associated with Osiris, lord of the underworld. Sometimes both crowns were combined to form the Double Crown.

It was believed that the origins of the state of Egypt could be traced to an act of unification of Upper and Lower Egypt by a ruler named Menes (for whom there is no actual archaeological evidence), around 3100 BC. The hieroglyphic sign used to express this notion of unification was a

THE SCARAB

The dung or scarab beetle symbolized new life and resurrection. It was called the dung beetle because of its practice of rolling a ball of dung in which it has laid its eggs. This was thought to symbolize the journey of the sun making its way through the sky. The beetles emerging from the mud were associated with life emerging from the primeval mound, and symbolized spontaneous creation.

THE ANKH

Formed by a loop over a T-cross, the ankh was the ancient Egyptian hieroglyph for life and immortality and was often used in the iconography of opposites. The loop, a form of circle, may stand for the universe (the macrocosm), and the T-cross for man (the microcosm). Alternatively, it combines the male and female symbols of the god Osiris (the T-cross), and the mother goddess Isis (the oval), sister and wife of Osiris, and symbolizes the union of Heaven and Earth. In Egyptian wall paintings, gods (particularly Isis) and kings are depicted holding the ankh, to symbolize their powers over life and death. The ankh is also associated with death and funerary rites: carried by the dead, it signals a safe passage between this world and the next, while held upside down, it is the key that unlocks the gates of death into eternity. Sometimes it is seen placed on the forehead between the eyes, linking it with clairvoyance.

stylized rendering of a pair of lungs, with a windpipe extending straight upwards from between them. In artistic representations, this emblem might be flanked by two deities, sometimes Horus and Seth, or on other occasions two Nile gods, one with a papyrus plant (the heraldic emblem of the Delta) on his head, and the other with the lotus (or waterlily) plant (the emblem of the Nile Valley). The figures on each side are often depicted tying the papyrus and lotus stems in a knot around the hieroglyph. It was the role of the king, or pharaoh, to unite these two lands, with his titles of "Lord of the Two Lands" and "King of Upper and Lower Egypt".

THE PHARAOH

The term pharaoh (*per-aa*) literally means "great house". In the New Kingdom period (c.1550–c.1069 BC) it was used to describe the king, but before that time it referred to the king's palace or the royal court. In ancient Egypt the king, or pharaoh, was believed to be a living manifestation of divinity, associated with both Horus, the falcon-headed sky god, and Re,

sometimes represented as a winged sun disc. This god-like status gave the pharaoh absolute power, having control over the army and all civil appointments, as well as the priesthood. Everywhere they went, ordinary people were reminded of the pharaoh's status, symbolized by massive stone statues of the king in the guise of Re, as well as the majestic pyramids – the funerary monuments of the kings and queens of ancient Egypt.

THE AFTERLIFE

Death and burial had many symbolic associations in ancient Egypt, where the existence of an afterlife was at the heart of religious belief. The practice of mummification reveals the strongly held belief that the body was required to be intact for life after death, while funerary texts show that the dead were believed to ascend to the heavens, the realm of the sun and place of the afterlife. There were several methods of ascent, including riding on the back of a falcon, goose or other bird; being wafted upwards with burning incense; or travelling on a reed float or barque that was sailed, rowed or towed. The journey was hazardous, and spells and recitations were uttered to help

the deceased on their way, while protective funerary amulets were positioned on the dead body.

Two of the most widely used amulets were the protective Eye of Horus (also known as the udjat or wadjat eye), which in one version of the myth of Osiris is used by Osiris's son, Horus, to bring his father back to life, and the scarab, which was placed over the heart. The scarab beetle was associated with Khepri (an aspect of the solar deity, Re) and was therefore a symbol of new life and resurrection. Sometimes scarabs were depicted with falcon's wings, as a symbol of transcendence and protection.

ABOVE The practice and ritualistic elements of mummification were full of symbolic meaning.

BELOW The Eye of Horus (wadjat) gives protection to a funerary barge on its way to the afterlife.

THE CLASSICAL AGE

ABOVE The Acropolis symbolizes the glory of the classical world.

ABOVE In antiquity, a laurel wreath was a symbol for victory, as well as a sign of status worn by the ruling classes.

Both the classical Greek civilization and the mighty Roman Empire have had an enormous impact on Western society, influencing its laws and customs, its art and science, its philosophy and way of life. The belief systems of these Mediterranean peoples can be seen in their mythologies, which were characterized by a vivid, dramatic vitality that enshrined the moral principles, natural laws and the great contrasts and transformations that determine both cosmic and human life. The gods and goddesses of the Greco-Roman pantheon acted out archetypal themes such as birth, death and renewal, war and peace, love and marriage, and governed all aspects of daily life.

The highest peak in the landscape of ancient Greece was Mount Olympus, home to the gods. From here they presided over the world and helped or hindered humans according to their whims. All the gods were thought to be descendants of Gaia (the Earth) and Uranus (the sky), and their lives were thought of in human terms – they fell in love, had children, played music, quarrelled and had affairs. Each of the gods had their own sphere of influence – Aphrodite (Roman Venus) governed love, and Ares (Mars) war, for example – and all the major deities had temples and sanctuaries dedicated to them.

CENTRE OF THE WORLD
One of the most important sanctuaries was the main shrine of Apollo at Delphi on the slopes of Mount Parnassus. Apollo, who in one of his aspects was associated with the sun, had the power of prophecy and divination, and at Delphi he would reply to questions about the future through his priestess. Delphi was thought to be the centre of the world, the point where two birds flying from opposite ends of the earth met. A huge stone, known as the *omphalos* or navel-stone, was placed there to symbolize this.

THE SUPREME GOD

The greatest god was Zeus (Jupiter to the Romans), who was the supreme ruler of Heaven and Earth as well as dominating the lesser Olympian gods. He was married to his sister Hera, but had many other sexual liaisons, father-ing offspring of both goddesses and mortal women, typically while in disguise – taking such forms as a swan, a bull, a horse or a shower of gold. His symbols were the thun-derbolt and eagle, although he was also depicted in human form wear-ing a crown of laurel leaves, seated on a throne and holding a sceptre.

TEMPLES

The earthly homes of the gods were their temples, and no expense was spared in their construction. Early wooden structures gave way to stone, especially marble, and they were decorated with brightly painted friezes showing the exploits of gods, goddesses and heroes. Most temples were dedicated to a particular deity, whose cult was centred on the location.

One of the most famous temples of ancient Greece, the Parthenon, was built on the Acropolis ("the high city") in Athens between 447 and 432 BC. It was dedicated to the city's patron deity, Athene, goddess of wisdom and warfare, and housed a huge gold and ivory statue of her. The owl, symbolizing wisdom, was her emblem and can be found on silver coins issued in Athens after the Greeks won decisive victories against the Persians in 479 BC.

The Romans' custom of deifying dead emperors meant that many temples were built to worship them, including that of Augustus and his wife Livia, which still stands in Vienne, France. Such temples were symbols of both divine and worldly power, testimony to the cultural and political achievements of the Romans.

SEASONS AND CYCLES

Greek life was dominated by religion, and this was inherently bound up with nature's cycles. The annual death and rebirth of the Earth's vegetation took symbolic form in the myth of Persephone (whom the Romans called Proserpine), the virgin daughter of Zeus (Jupiter) and Demeter (Ceres) the Earth Goddess. According to the myth of Persephone, Hades (Pluto, lord of the underworld) spied the beautiful maiden picking poppies and abducted her to be his queen in the realm of the dead. Consumed by grief, Demeter neglected the land while she searched for her daughter. The earth became barren as crops withered and died, and the result was perpetual winter.

To help humanity, Zeus intervened and sent Hermes (Mercury), the messenger god, to bring Persephone back. Meanwhile, however, she had eaten the food of the dead (in the form of six pomegranate seeds) and so was bound to Hades: she could be restored to Demeter for only part of the year. Her annual arrival is marked by the rebirth of spring but at the end of summer, she must return to Hades and the earth once again becomes barren.

GAMES

Not just for entertainment, sport was a way of training for warfare and of honouring the gods. National festivals attracted athletes from all over the Greek world, the most important being the Olympic Games, held every four years in honour of Zeus.

The Games were so important that wars were suspended to allow people to travel in safety to and from Olympia. The first Olympics were held in 776 BC and continued into Roman times, coming to an end in the late 4th

THE MYSTERIES OF ELEUSIS

At the heart of Greek religion were the Mysteries of Eleusis, secret annual rituals that were believed to hold the human race together. Initiates maintained their secrecy so securely that we do not know for certain exactly what they experienced, but they seem to have had a threefold revelation: a beatific vision of the maiden Persephone; knowledge that Persephone had given birth in fire to the Aeon, a divine child; and the sight of an ear of wheat, with its promise of new life and fertility. The Mysteries were observed for 2,000 years, coming to an end with the sack of Eleusis by the Goths in AD 396.

century AD. They were revived in the modern era in 1896. One of the symbols associated with the Olympic Games is a runner bearing a torch, harking back to the time when relay races took place after dark, and the runners carried torches to light the way. The winning team used them to light fires on altars dedicated to Zeus or Athene. Winners wore laurel wreaths sacred to Apollo and a symbol of victory.

ABOVE The five rings that make up the symbol for the modern Olympic Games represent the five continents of the world.

BELOW Triptoleme, a prince of Eleusis, being initiated into the Eleusian Mysteries by Demeter and Persephone.

LAUREL

Through its
association with
Apollo, the aromatic
leaves of laurel, or
bay, were the
crowning emblem of
the Greco-Roman
world for both
warriors and poets.
It was a symbol of
truce, victory, peace,
divination and
purification.

BELOW The caduceus, a
rod or staff entwined by
two serpents, is a symbol
of the god Hermes. It is
used as an emblem for
homeopathic medicine.

BELOW A she-wolf
suckling the twins,
Romulus and Remus, is
one of the symbols for the
ancient city of Rome.

MEDICINE AND HEALING

To the ancient Greeks, illness was
seen as a punishment sent by the
gods, to whom they also prayed
for a cure. Sanctuaries dedicated
to Asclepius (a Greek physician
deified as the god of medicine)
were set up all over the Greek
world, the most famous being at
Epidaurus. The sick made
pilgrimages to such temples,
where they practised a healing
process known as incubation.
They slept in the temple and used
their dreams as a channel for
communication with Asclepius, in
the hope that he could show
them how to get well. The priest
would then carry out the
recommended treatment. It was
customary to leave some kind of
symbolic representation of the
afflicted part of the body, both
when asking for healing and as an
offering of thanks afterwards.

The emblem of Asclepius was
his staff, a rough-hewn branch
entwined with a serpent, whose
shedding of skin symbolizes the
renewal of youth. The staff is still

a familiar symbol of healing, and
is used by medical bodies such as
the World Health Organization.

The Romans also believed that
illness could be caused by the
gods, as well as by witchcraft and
curses, and also left offerings to
the gods in the shape of body
parts. This practice continues in
churches in some Mediterranean
countries today, where embossed
metal tokens are used.

THE FOUNDING OF ROME

According to legend, Rome was
founded in 753 BC by the twin
brothers, Romulus and Remus,
sons of the Roman war god Mars.
As babies, the twins were thrown
into the river Tiber and left to die
but were carried ashore and cared
for by a female wolf. When they
grew up, they decided to build a
city on the Tiber. To decide where
to build the city, each brother
climbed a hill (Remus the
Aventine and Romulus the
Palatine) and sought omens from
the gods. In the Greco-Roman
tradition, the vulture was sacred

to Apollo and was a bird of
augury. So when Romulus saw 12
vultures, while Remus saw only 6,
the Palatine hill was chosen, and
Romulus ploughed a furrow to
mark out the city's limits. When
Remus tried to take the initiative
from his brother, Romulus killed
him. Once Rome was established,
Mars carried Romulus away in his
chariot to become a god.

With its valour and predatory
nature, the wolf was held sacred
to Mars and became a totem
symbol of Rome, one of the
world's greatest superpowers. The
Roman empire was built on the
strength of its army.

POWER AND VICTORY

Based on rigorous discipline, iron
will and courage, the Roman
army became synonymous with
the might of Rome. The army not
only extended the empire's
frontiers but also was responsible
for its protection, building
impenetrable hilltop fortresses to
defend Roman gains. The goddess
Nike, a winged aspect of Athene,
became the symbol of military

victory. She was often shown with a globe and a victor's wreath, and sacrifices were made to her before and after battles to ensure victory and give thanks for success.

The eagle was adopted as the Roman standard. Known as the *aquila*, the standard itself became an emblem of imperial power. The eagle's wings sheltered the peace of the empire, while the bird's capacity to fell its victim in one deadly swoop was a reminder of Rome's warrior-like virtues.

Slaves were one of the spoils of war, and some (including women) trained as gladiators, who fought each other, often to death, in amphitheatres erected all over the empire. Public architecture of this kind, a powerful symbol of Roman domination, culminated in the building of the spectacular Colosseum in Rome. Opened in AD 80, it held about 50,000 people, and it has been estimated that 500,000 combatants died there. Gladiatorial fights had a religious origin, having been held at funerals to honour the dead, but by the time of the emperors

they were a bloodsport. The victors could win their freedom, and some gladiators achieved celebrity status – a graffiti inscription at Pompeii describes one called Celadus as "the man the girls sigh for". When a gladiator was wounded he could appeal for mercy. If the crowd (and the emperor) favoured him, the thumbs-up sign spared his life, while a thumbs-down sign signified a brutal death.

THE CULT OF MITHRAS

Originally a Persian sun god, Mithras achieved cult status with the Roman army, which spread his worship throughout Roman society and the empire. As creator and controller of the cosmos, Mithras was usually depicted slaying a bull, symbolizing man's victory over his animal nature, as well as Rome's political power over her enemies. Mithras was

worshipped in subterranean temples where the *taurobolium* (ritual sacrifice of a bull) took place, and initiates into the cult were baptized in its blood. Sometimes Mithras is depicted spanned by the circle of the zodiac, possibly alluding to the end of the age of Taurus and the beginning of the age of Aries pertinent to the time.

ABOVE Winged Victory – or Nike, an aspect of Athena to the Greeks – holds two of the most important Roman symbols of power and victory, a staff with an eagle on top and a wreath made of laurel leaves.

ABOVE LEFT The standard of a Roman legion was the ultimate symbol of its pride and military honour.

RIGHT In the ancient Roman empire, the cult of Mithras was open to men only. This frieze depicts the god slaying a white bull, symbolizing male sexual potency and power in its purest form.

PAGAN EUROPE

When Rome and its western
empire fell to barbarian invaders
in AD 476, northern Europe
entered a period of instability. The
influence of Roman civilization
receded, though classical learning
was preserved in Christian
monasteries, and the old Celtic
culture was interwoven with the
Germanic and Scandinavian
traditions of the incoming forces.

In the 6th century the Anglo-
Saxons reached Britain from
Scandinavia and Germany,
displacing Roman, Celtic and
Christian culture from what now
became the "land of the Angles",
or England. Later, between 800
and 900, the Vikings raided
mainland Europe and Britain. By
the 11th century, however, the
new cultures had been assimilated
and Europe rose re-formed out of
the Dark Ages into the Middle
Ages, with the flourishing Roman
Christianity as the dominant faith,
blended with elements of the
older, pre-Christian cultures.

THE CELTS

Celtic myths and symbols were
passed down by the bards, who
blended the roles of priest,
teacher and entertainer and kept
the culture alive. The Celts had a
deep affinity to nature, and
natural patterns feature strongly
in Celtic art.

In County Galway in Ireland
stands an ancient standing stone,
known as the Turoe stone. It is
carved with stylized patterns
suggestive of plants and animals,
and is a symbol of regeneration. It
may have been a place where
ageing kings were sacrificed for
cultural renewal.

ABOVE The Gundestrup cauldron
displays a magnificent array of
Celtic nature symbolism, including
the horned god Kernunnos, an
animal deity.

The Celtic cauldron was an
important symbol of abundance,
rebirth and sacrifice: an unending
supply of food or knowledge,
often associated with the supreme
Celtic god Dagda. The dead,
thrown into the cauldron, were
said to be reborn the next day.
The Celtic cauldron may be a
precursor of the Holy Grail of the
Arthurian legends. A magnificent
gilded silver and copper cauldron
of the 1st or 2nd century BC, the
Gundestrup cauldron depicts
Kernunnos, the "Horned God", a
male animal deity, in a sacred
marriage with Mother Earth, or
nature. He bears the antlers of a
stag, symbolizing renewal (as
stags shed their antlers and grow
new ones). He appears also with a
boar, which the Celts admired for
its speed and willingness to fight;
they believed it had magical
qualities and direct links to the
underworld. Kernunnos holds a
ram-headed serpent, symbol of
sexuality and regeneration.

There are many examples in
Celtic art of the triple goddess,
appearing in her three aspects:
maiden, mother and crone. Brigid
was the triple goddess commonly
associated with the Celtic spring
festival of Imbolc, celebrated at
the time of lambing. She inspired

the bards and was a deity of
healing who also protected
women in childbirth.

Another triple goddess was
Morrigan, who was associated
with the crow. The consort of
Dagda, she was a goddess of
battle, strife and fertility. She had
the power to make men
completely helpless, in particular
when they did not recognize their
feminine qualities. Dagda's name
means "the all-powerful god". He
was a protective father-figure,
often pictured holding a club, or
with an erect penis, symbolizing
virility and the creation of life.

The Celts worshipped their
gods in sacred groves of trees.
They began to build temples only
when influenced by the Romans.
The oak tree symbolized power
and protection, and oak groves
were sacred spaces.

THE ANGLO-SAXONS

Around AD 450 the Anglo-Saxons
began their migration to Britain
from Denmark and northern
Germany. They were a proud
warrior society, with polytheistic

beliefs, and worshipped animals such as the boar, horse and stag.

The Anglo-Saxons believed in a fixed destiny or fate, known as *wyrd*. The concept was embodied in the three Wyrd Sisters, or Norns, who wove the web of fate (rather like the Greek Fates who were believed to spin, measure and cut the thread of each human life).

Horses were sacred to the Anglo-Saxons, and represented great wealth and rank. Legends tell of Hengist ("stallion") and Horsa ("horse"), the twin gods who were said to have led the invasion of Britain. Huge chalk horses carved into the hillsides of southern England, such as those at Uffington and Westbury in Wiltshire, are thought to be Anglo-Saxon in origin.

The boar was an Anglo-Saxon symbol of protection and royalty. It was associated with Frô, a god of kingship and fertility. Warriors bore its image on their helmets, in the belief that this would make the power of the boar accessible to the wearer. At Yuletide, to mark the shortest day of the year, solemn vows were made over the Yule Boar, which was then sacrificed: it was thought to go straight to the gods, taking the vows with it, while its carcass was roasted and served with an apple in its mouth, symbolizing the rebirth of the sun goddess.

The stag was a noble symbol for the Anglo-Saxon king and his leadership. A stag-pole, mounted with the head of a stag facing the sun, was customarily erected to curse or insult an enemy.

The festival of the fertility goddess Eostre was celebrated in spring, and she gave her name to the Christian festival of Easter. Her animal was the hare or rabbit – the origin of the modern Easter Bunny: according to one legend she transformed a bird frozen in a winter storm into a rabbit, which continued to lay eggs each spring in gratitude.

THE VIKINGS

The Norse people of Scandinavia, worshipped a pantheon of gods and goddesses led by Odin. The Vikings were seafaring Norse warriors and traders who flourished from the 8th to the 11th centuries, raiding Europe from the sea in their mighty, longships, taking first belongings, and then territory, from the native Saxons.

Odin, or Wotan, the chief Norse deity, was the god of thought and memory, two mental faculties esteemed by the Norse peoples. Thor was the god of lightning and thunder, and thus of power, wielding a mighty hammer to protect humans and gods from giants. Freya was the goddess of love and beauty, but was also a warrior goddess; her sacred animal was the cat. Freya's twin brother was Freyr, a horned fertility god, god of success, and also a warrior god, fighting with a horn or an elk.

BELOW Viking longships were symbols of terror and ferocity to the unfortunate people who suffered the incursions of the Norsemen.

ABOVE The Anglo-Saxons associated the boar with kingship, plenty and protection in battle.

VIKING SHIPS

The Vikings were master ship builders and saw their sea vessel ("horse of the waves") as a symbol of power and speed. The ships were also potent symbols for safe passage to the afterlife, with ships used in burials, securely moored and anchored, protecting the corpse's body.

HELM OF AWE

Thought to make the wearer magically invincible and terrifying to his enemies, the Helm of Awe is a Viking symbol of protection. As well as being a physical helmet worn between the eyes, the Helm of Awe also probably refers to a form of magic practice used to create delusions in the minds of others.

THE MIDDLE EAST

Sometimes referred to as the
crossroads of history – the
meeting point of East and West –
the Middle East saw the
beginnings of civilization and was
the birthplace of Judaism, Islam
and Christianity. Its cultural
complexity reflects its long
history of human migration,
conquest and trade.

THE PERSIAN EMPIRE

From the late 6th century BC the
Persian Empire, the largest and
best-organized empire the ancient
world had hitherto seen,
dominated the Middle East,
embracing lands from the
Mediterranean coast to the
borders of India. The Persians
unified for the first time the
Iranian plateau, which became
the new power centre of the
region – an area that had been
dominated culturally and
politically by Mesopotamia and
Egypt for most of the preceding
2,500 years.

A vast and mountainous area,
the Persian empire contained
many different peoples who often
rebelled against Persian control.
To keep order, the Persians had a
very effective army of 10,000
specially trained men, bodyguards
to the king and keepers of law
and order who were feared
wherever they went, moving
quickly to put down rebellions.
The members of this elite warrior
force were known as the
"immortals" because when one

soldier died, he was immediately
replaced. Mosaics of the
immortals carrying spears
decorated the royal palace at
Susa, the capital city.

ZOROASTRIANISM

In AD 247, the Sassanid dynasty
established Zoroastrianism as the
official religion of the Persian
Empire, and it is still practised in
Iran and other parts of the world.
It is founded upon the teachings
of the prophet Zarathustra (called
Zoroaster by the Greeks), in
which the opposing forces of
good and evil are symbolized by
Ahura Mazda, the supreme deity
responsible for truth and light,
and the evil Ahriman. The two
represent the duality of the
cosmos: unlike Satan, Ahriman is
not a creation of the supreme god
but his equal.

The universal conflict between
good spirits (*ahuras*) and bad
ones (*daevas*) will ultimately
result in the triumph of Ahura
Mazda, and the faithful are
encouraged to follow Ahura
Mazda through "good thoughts,
good words and good deeds".

These three ideals are represented
by the three wing feathers of the
faravahar, a central Zoroastrian
symbol. Zoroastrians believe that
the first animal to be created was
a white bull, the progenitor of all
other animals and plants, while
the focal point of the religion is
fire, seen as the purest
manifestation of Ahura Mazda.
Perpetual fires were set up all
over Persia, some in the open air,
others enclosed in fire temples,
and tended by priests known as
magi (from which comes the
word "magic"). Depictions of fire
altars are found on ancient coins.

Because Zoroastrians consider
fire to be sacred, cremation is
disallowed because it would
contaminate it; instead, bodies are
exposed at the top of "towers of
silence" for their bones to be
picked clean by scavengers.

THE BEDOUIN

The Bedouin are the desert-
dwelling nomads of the Middle
East, many of whom preserve
their traditional lifestyle to this
day. Their name comes from an
Arabic word meaning "inhabitant

BELOW The camel is
central to the survival of
the Bedouin, and is
celebrated by Arab poets
as the "ship of the
desert", transporting
people and goods across
vast oceans of sand.

RIGHT This winged device is the
faravahar, a symbol of the human
desire to achieve union with Ahura
Mazda, the supreme deity of the
Zoroastrian faith.

CARPETS

Throughout the Middle East, carpets are much more than functional objects, being used to symbolize important elements of tribal, family and personal life. Their patterns are rich in symbolic meaning. For instance, camels, the wealth of the Bedouin, signify happiness and riches for the weaver and owner of the carpet, while the peacock's wheel-like tail is a symbol of the sun and the cosmic cycle. It is customary for a carpet to contain a deliberate flaw, as only God can create perfection.

of the desert". They wear long, flowing robes to stay cool, but probably the most important aspect of a Bedouin man's attire is his headgear. This consists of a cloth held in position by the *agal* (rope), which indicates the wearer's ability to uphold his honour and fulfil the obligations and responsibilities of manhood. Bedouin women also signify their status with their headgear – married women, for instance, wear a black cloth, known as *asaba*, about their foreheads.

Traditionally the Bedouin are divided into related tribes, each led by a sheikh. Moving from place to place according to the seasons, and living in tents, they herd camels, sheep and goats, riding highly prized horses, famous for their grace and speed.

In such a harsh environment, any violation of territorial rights is viewed with severe disfavour:

BELOW Incense resins are precious substances with many different symbolic properties. Frankincense is used for purification.

small piles of stones are traditionally used to mark property boundaries. On the other hand, in the silence and solitude of the desert, encountering another person can be an unusual and noteworthy event. This has led Bedouin culture to place great value on hospitality and social etiquette: visitors are greeted with music, poetry and dance. Throwing frankincense pellets on the fire is a traditional greeting.

PRECIOUS INCENSE

One of the best-kept secrets of antiquity was the location of the trees that produced myrrh and frankincense, valued more highly than gold. Fantastic stories surrounded their whereabouts: the Greek historian Herodotus wrote that they were guarded by winged serpents who would kill any who tried to take their resins, and the wealth of the legendary Queen of Sheba was said to have been built on these substances. In the desert lands of Arabia,

frankincense and myrrh were rich in symbolic associations. Together with gold, they have always been associated with royalty and divinity. Incense has a long tradition of use in sacred ceremonies, its swirls of fragrant smoke viewed as a flight path for prayers and communion with the gods. Frankincense is associated with masculinity and the spirit of the heavens myrrh is feminine and linked with the earth.

ABOVE The black head-cloth worn by Bedouin women is a sign of their married state.

TOP Many of the everyday trappings of Bedouin life have symbolic meaning, including this man's tent and clothes.

TRADITIONAL TENTS

The tent is the abode of the desert nomad and has many symbolic associations. In the Old Testament, the wandering tribes of Israel set aside a tent (or tabernacle) for God, which became the prototype for the temple. Like the temple, the tent is a place to which the godhead is summoned to make itself manifest. In many traditions, the tent's pole is linked with the symbolism of the pillar and column (as well as the tree), representing the connection between Heaven and earth. Bedouin tents symbolize the duality of male and female. They are usually divided into two sections, one for men, one for women, by a curtain known as a *ma'nad*. The men's area is called the *mag'ad* (sitting place) and is for the reception of most guests. The *maharama* (place of the women) is where the women cook and receive female visitors.

TRIBAL AFRICA

ABOVE A Tongan shaman from Zambia sits in his grass hut with various gourds, animal horns, and other symbolic items spread before him.

FETISHES

A fetish is a symbol of divine energy encapsulated into an object. Natural fetishes, such as pieces of wood, shells, pebbles and feathers, are believed to owe their magical properties to the spiritual forces that dwell in them. Carvings or statuettes can also become permeated with this power when activated through the rites and incantations of the *nganga*.

A land of deserts, savannah, high mountain ranges and dense, equatorial rainforests, Africa is a vast and diverse continent. It is home to many different social systems, where more than 1,000 languages are spoken and where myths and cosmologies are interlinked with moral codes and ways of seeing the world.

Although it is impossible to come up with a homogeneous view of African culture, it is fair to say that for thousands of years, the way of life for many Africans has changed less than in more industrialized parts of the world, and that traditionally people have made their living by herding, hunting or farming. Symbols in African religion, art and culture reflect this social and historical continuity, and in most African societies the spiritual world and natural world is reflected in everyday life.

SPIRITUAL BELIEFS

In many traditional African societies the spiritual world and the everyday world are one and the same, with all aspects of life permeated by a strong power or vital force. In some societies this is seen to emanate from a supreme creator spirit – the Masai of Kenya call him Ngai, while the Nupe in Nigeria say that their god Soko is in the sky, for instance. There is often a hierarchy of spirits, from the nature spirits of rivers, rocks, trees and animals, through ancestor spirits of the dead, to divinities who derive their power from the creator spirit. The Lugbara of Uganda have a cult centred on the spirits of the dead, in which the living are considered to belong to the "outside" world while the dead belong "in the earth". If the ancestors are neglected, the dead punish their descendants by inflicting misfortune and sickness.

It is widely believed that spiritual power can be manipulated for good or bad. Positive mystical power is productive, can cure illnesses, and is protective, while negative power eats the health and souls of its victims and causes misfortune. A variety of specialists such as witch doctors, medicine men and women (known as *nganga* in most Bantu languages), diviners and rainmakers possess knowledge of this power and use it in the making of "medicines". Medicines may be used to encourage or prevent rain from falling, to aid hunting, for protection against malign spirits, for success in love affairs, or to find stolen property.

They may also be used for treating illnesses. Medicines can be made from almost any material, but natural materials such as trees, plants and animal skins or feathers are common, and are fashioned into amulets and charms with symbolism that varies according to the materials used and the purpose for which it was created.

MASQUERADE

Among traditional African societies, masks are used for many different social events and rituals, particularly those surrounding initiation ceremonies and rites of passage. Combined with a costume to hide the identity of the wearer, the role of the mask has many functions, both spiritual and temporal. Masks are worn to inform or educate, discipline or lend authority, to give the wearer access to special powers, or simply to entertain. The role of the mask is communicated through movement and dance – masquerade – where the complete costume becomes a powerful and energetic force that represents both the human and spiritual world. Masquerade is often performed by men who are members of secret societies: among the Dogon of Mali, for instance, the men's secret society or *Awa*, organizes all funeral events, with masked dancers in funeral processions. The masks have strong symbolic meaning, and the dancers represent figures of male and female powers and figures from the animal world, and the afterworld.

In traditional Yoruba society, women are considered to have two distinct sides to their nature, the power to create and nurture life, coupled with the potential for great destruction. Among the Yoruba, the Gelede masquerade, danced in either male or female pairs, is supposed to ensure that women's power is channelled for the benefit of the community. Gelede masks come in many different designs and are usually worn on top of the head, adding greatly to the wearer's height.

Whatever their purpose, all costumes and masks are highly stylized creations, their symbolism varying depending on the context. Among the Ogoni of

Nigeria, many masks are designed to look like animals, with the wearer assuming the spirit or character of the mask and performing athletic displays in imitation of the animal he represents. Many masks are highly elaborate constructions: the Sande female initiation society of the Mende of Sierra Leone have a wooden mask decorated with carvings that represent ancestors who preside over the initiates.

ADINKRA SYMBOLS

The art of adinkra – symbols hand-printed on cloth – is characterized by symbolic motifs, graphically rendered in stylized geometric shapes. The symbols relate to the history, philosophy and religious beliefs of the Ashanti people of Ghana and the Ivory Coast and are grouped into

THE UNIVERSAL CALABASH

A calabash is a gourd that has a hard rind, which makes it a useful container once the flesh has been scooped out. It can be used as a water pot or else filled with seeds, as a rattle. When cut in half horizontally, a round calabash is often used as a container for offerings or symbolic objects in temples, and is usually decorated with carvings or paintings of geometric patterns, as well as pictures of humans and animals. In Abomey, in Benin, the universe is likened to a round calabash, the line of the horizon being where the two halves of a divided calabash meet. The sun, moon and stars are said to move in the upper part of the calabash, while the Earth is flat, floating inside the sphere in the same way that a small calabash may float in a big one.

various categories, including creatures, plant life, celestial bodies, the human body and non-figurative shapes. Initially used for funerals, the cloth is now worn for many other occasions, providing the symbols are appropriate, and is itself seen as a symbol of the Ghanain culture.

ABOVE LEFT Akoben, the adinkra symbol for vigilance and wariness.

ABOVE RIGHT Gye Name, meaning "except for God", is the most popular adinkra symbol of Ghana.

BELOW The masks of the Dogon form a line, symbolizing connection between the sun and Earth through the conduit of the dancer's body.

BELOW Adinkra cloth was originally specially made for funerals. Its name translates as "saying goodbye to one another".

SOUTH AND SOUTH-EAST ASIA

ABOVE The Chinese emperor, dressed in symbolic yellow, in front of a dragon-motif screen.

ABOVE The Japanese Flag, showing the "sincere" red sun on a "pure" white background.

KOI CARP
The Japanese Koi carp found swimming in many Japanese water gardens are symbols of the patience, courage and strength required to achieve big goals in business and life.

The cultural, political and spiritual history of East Asia has been rich and dramatic, and it is a huge reserve of symbolism, stretching from the ancient traditions to modern times. Great civilizations had been established in India by 2500 BC and in China by 2000 BC. Japan viewed itself as the "third kingdom", equal to China and India, and by tradition was founded in the 7th century BC by the Emperor Jimmu, whose imperial dynasty continues unbroken to this day.

EMPERORS
Far Eastern emperors have long associated themselves with elemental and mythical sources of power. Nippon, the Japanese name for Japan, means "the land of the rising sun", and the imperial family emphasized its central role in the country – and its authority – through the use of solar symbolism. Japanese emperors, through their legendary ancestor Jimmu, traced their ancestry back in a direct line to the great sun goddess, Amaterasu,

the central deity of the Shinto pantheon. The imperial seal was the chrysanthemum, a symbol of the sun and the national flower of Japan. In modern Japan the emperor continues to occupy the chrysanthemum throne: the long unbroken dynasty symbolizes continuity with the past, and the emperor is constitutionally defined as the symbol of the state.

Emperors in China were the rulers of the Middle Kingdom (the everyday world) and the Four Directions, maintaining harmony between Heaven and Earth. They had nine insignia: the dragon, mountains, the pheasant, rice grains, the axe, flames, pondweed, the sacrificial bowl, and patterns symbolizing justice.

The dragon is symbolic of imperial power and the emperor's role in mediating between Heaven and earth. It appeared on the Chinese national flag during the Qing dynasty, and was embroidered on court robes. The Chinese believed themselves to be the direct descendants of the Yellow Emperor, who was said to have the head of a man and the body of a dragon. Yellow, symbolic of the Earth and therefore of farming, remained the imperial colour. From the Han dynasty (206 BC–AD 220) onwards, dragons were also depicted in other colours, each with different symbolism: the turquoise dragon became the symbol of the emperor, connected with the East and the rising sun.

In 1950 the Indian government adopted, as a national symbol, a sculpture from the reign of Emperor Ashoka (r.272–232 BC).

This pillar of carved stone depicts four lions, an elephant, a horse, a bull, and another lion, all separated by a lotus at the base with the inscription "truth alone triumphs". The sculpture is founded upon the wheel of law or dharmachakra, which symbolizes the teachings of the Buddha.

ARCHITECTURE
The Great Wall of China is a universal visual symbol for China. It snakes its way across the country's entire northern boundary and was completed by the Qin emperor Qin Shi Hang as a means of defence against barbarian tribes from the north. Thousands of slaves died during the building of the wall, which led to it becoming a symbol of tyrannical oppression.

During the Ming dynasty (1368–1644 BC) the wall was refortified in the grand style seen today, and it is considered one of the seven great wonders of the world. From various perspectives it can be seen as a symbol of power, division, closed attitudes and oppression.

In India near the city of Agra, the Taj Mahal is an enduring and profound symbol of love. Completed in 1652, this magnificent tomb was built by the Mogul emperor Shah Jahan, in memory of Mumtaz Mahal, his favourite wife, who had died in childbirth. Centrally sited among canals and tranquil gardens, the tomb is built of shimmering white marble, embellished with semi-precious stones. The four canals in the gardens symbolize the four rivers of Paradise described in the

Qur'an, while the gardens represent the final resting place for the souls of the dead.

The Taj Mahal was erected as a symbol of love, but perhaps also as a demonstration of Shah Jahan's greatness. It is said that he planned a second mausoleum for himself, built in black marble on the opposite side of the Jamuna river and connected to the first by a silver bridge, but he died before his plan could be carried out and was buried in the Taj Mahal.

RICE AND TEA

Throughout Asia, rice is a staple food, generally associated with abundance, prosperity and fecundity, a symbol of life. The Balinese, who eat rice at every meal, refer to it as *nasi*, meaning "nostril": in other words, eating rice is seen to be as important as breathing. In China, girls with poor appetites have been told that every grain of rice they do not eat will be a pockmark on their husband's face.

In Japan rice is seen as sacred, and the eating of rice as a sacred ritual. Offerings are made to the Shinto deity Inari, the bearer of rice. The Japanese believe that soaking rice prior to cooking releases life energy, which can bring peace to the soul. Sometimes rice grains are referred to as "little Buddhas" to encourage children to eat them.

In India, rice is considered an auspicious food. The new crop is celebrated as part of the festival of Pongal, when it is cooked in pots until they overflow. People decorate the ground in front of their homes with coloured rice

flour and make offerings to the gods. It is said that grains of rice should be like two brothers, close but not stuck together. At Hindu weddings the couple hold rice, oats and leaves, symbolizing health, wealth and happiness.

In China, tea is served to a guest as a symbol of respect and goodwill, and refusing a cup of tea is considered rude. The teacup is filled only seven-tenths full, the other three-tenths being filled with friendship and affection. According to legend, tea drinking began when the emperor Shen Nung rested one day in the shade of a tea plant, and several leaves tumbled into his cup of hot water. Upon drinking the golden liquid a wonderful sense of well-being came over him.

Green tea was taken from China to Japan by Zen Buddhist monks, who drank it to keep

RIGHT The fabulous Taj Mahal, an Indian emperor's passionate symbol of his eternal love for his princess, Mumtaz Mahal.

them awake while meditating. The Japanese elevated the drinking of tea to an art, in the form of a Japanese tea ceremony, or Chanoyu, which embodies elements of Zen philosophy. The Chaji tea ceremony consists of up to five hours of ritual movement.

THE LOTUS

Although it grows in the mud, the lotus maintains its beauty. As India's national flower it is a symbol of pure spirit rooted in mundane reality. The Buddhist mantra "Om mane padme" refers to enlightenment, the "jewel in the lotus".

LEFT The Great Wall of China is an example of how one thing can have diverse symbolic meanings, depending on one's cultural or political perspective. The wall is variously seen as a symbol of protection, power, and achievement, or of oppression, isolation and division.

OCEANIC TRADITIONS

ABOVE A mask from the Malay Archipelago (New Guinea) using elements that link the human world with the natural one.

TOP Polynesian canoes are intricately carved, symbolizing spiritual power and prestige.

The thousands of islands in the central and southern Pacific Ocean, including Australia, New Zealand, Polynesian Hawaii and the Malay Archipelago, together make up Oceania. There are three major cultural groupings: Polynesia, Melanesia and Micronesia. The indigenous people of Australia are another important cultural grouping from this area.

INDIGENOUS AUSTRALIANS

"Aborigine" is a Western term used to describe indigenous people who have been conquered or colonized by Europeans. The indigenous people of Australia have occupied the country for over 60,000 years, probably coming originally from the Malay Peninsula. Their spirituality is intimately linked with their relationship with the land through the "Dreamtime".

The Dreaming is a vital concept of creation. It refers to the creation of the earth, humans and animals, but at the same time it is eternally present on a mythical level. All life is believed to be imbued with the Dreaming. Dreamtime stories portray the Ancestors moving through the earth, shaping the land, and giving life to plants and animals. Through the Dreamtime the Aboriginal people and the earth are part of one another. The individual tries to live his or her life according to the law laid down by the Ancestors.

As the Spirit Ancestors journeyed through the land, they created dreaming tracks, often

called "songlines", as they sang the land into life. The aboriginal peoples believe that by singing specific songs, at key points on the land, they directly connect with the Dreaming.

Totem animals play an important part in aboriginal society. Clans have a totemic relationship with a specific animal, and it is taboo for them to eat the meat of that animal, as it would be like eating a close relation. The characteristics and qualities of the totem animal become accessible to the clan. Some Australian Aboriginals still adhere closely to the Dreaming of their totem. One man whose totem was the cockatiel was allowed to travel the world because the nature of the cockatiel was to fly over borders.

POLYNESIA

Encompassing much of the eastern area of the South Pacific, with the major islands of Hawaii and New Zealand, Polynesia was one of the very last areas in the world to have been populated, mostly in waves of migration.

Although the islands are widely separated, Polynesian societies have a thread of unity running through their belief systems and social structures. These are aristrocratic societies, led by chiefs. The nobility are thought to have spiritual power, known as "mana", which is brought out through ritual and art.

The Polynesian sculptor brings out the mana in his or her art by revealing the beauty and essential qualities in the wood or stone. Ornamental carvings appear on

spears, canoes, jewellery, house beams and on many other kinds of domestic and spiritual objects. Tiki Man is a male figure found throughout Polynesia, in wood sculptures, carved in stone, and in tattoo and clothing designs. He is believed by Polynesians to be their first ancestor or the original human, and symbolizes the phallus or procreative power.

Carvings made by the Maori of New Zealand, in bone, shell, jade and wood, depict important mythological themes and patterns in nature. The *koru* represents the fern frond, a symbol of new life and purity coming into the world. The twist is a vertical form in which two spirals interweave. This represents eternity and the eternal relationships of couples or cultures. *Hei-matau* is a stylized fish-hook, representing prosperity and abundance and a deep respect for the ocean. It is a symbol of power and authority and is said to give the wearer protection when travelling at sea.

The huge Easter Island statues are carved in stone, and probably represent guardian gods, facing inwards towards the island peoples. The oversized head in Polynesian sculptures highlights the sacred attributes of the head.

POLYNESIAN TATTOOS

There are two kinds of Polynesian tattoo. *Enata* are natural symbols that refer to the individual's life, origin and social rank. They also protect the wearer: a fisherman would have designs that would protect him against sharks, while a warrior's tattoos would defend him against attack. *Etua* are mystical symbols referring to past ancestors – a lineage of shamans, chiefs and divinities. These symbols showed mana, which was passed down the lineages.

MELANESIA AND MICRONESIA

There are many cultures and over a thousand languages in Melanesia and Micronesia. The Papuans were the first inhabitants of Melanesia, arriving at least 40,000 years ago. Traditional society is based upon agriculture, the domestication of pigs, hunting and trade.

Melanesian religious art usually displays brilliant colours and is made from a broad range of materials. Much religious artwork honours and placates the powerful influences of animal and nature spirits, as well as showing respect for the ancestors. It often consists of a network of human, animal and natural images. Effigies of the totem animal of a

BELOW The Rainbow Serpent appears in aboriginal paintings up to 6,000 years old.

clan, such as a fish, snake or crocodile, sometimes show the animal devouring a clan father. Although this looks sinister, it probably indicates the spiritual identification of the people with their totem animals. For the Latumul people of New Guinea, the saltwater crocodile is the creator of all things. It is said that Crocodile, who was the first human being, mated with a crack in the ground (the first woman) to engender life. The lower jaw of Crocodile became the earth and the upper jaw the sky. The people believe that, during initiation, boys are swallowed by Crocodile and regurgitated as men.

Respect for the ancestors is important for the Melanesians, as they are thought to influence the living relatives. Much symbolic art is aimed at maintaining a good relationship between the earthly and the spiritual realms. The wearing of masks is one important way of honouring and depicting the ancestors. The masks of north central New Guinea depict supernatural spirits and ancestors. Made from an array of shells, animal skins, seeds, flowers, wood and feathers, these masks are understood to be a dwelling-place for the spirit, and a great source of strength in business and in warfare.

In traditional Vanuatuan society the human–pig relationship is of intense importance, to the extent that when a pig is slaughtered it is sung to and caressed before and during its death. Pigs are believed to have souls and may be considered family members. The number of pigs owned relates to the leadership status of the owner, as does the length of their tusks. When pigs feed naturally the tusks wear down and, to avoid this owners feed them by hand. The pig is also a sexual symbol, embodying the relationship between men and women.

ABOVE The Easter Island statues are symbols of religious and political power, and are believed to be repositories for sacred spirits.

ABOVE The *koru*, a Maori fern spiral, represents the unfolding of new life.

BELOW The crocodile is an honoured totem animal in many Oceanic cultures.

RAINBOW SERPENT

The Rainbow Serpent is central to the beliefs of the people of Arnhem Land, but is found in aboriginal art throughout Australia. It is a large snake-like creature associated with the waterways of Australia. It represents the source of life and protects the people and the land, but if not respected it becomes destructive.

CENTRAL AND SOUTH AMERICA

ITZAMNA

The most revered god of the Maya pantheon was Itzamna, a benevolent sun god, lord of the east and west, of day and night, and founder of Mayapan, the Maya capital. He brought knowledge, culture and writing to his people, and at ceremonies in his honour, priests presented writings to his effigy. Itzamna was responsible for bringing maize and cocoa to humankind, establishing religious ceremonies and dividing out the land. He was usually represented as a kindly old man with sunken cheeks, toothless jaws and a large nose, often enthroned as a king, priest or scribe. Human sacrifices were regularly made to a gigantic statue of a crocodile, believed to represent him, at Chichén Itzá in the Yucatán peninsula.

ABOVE RIGHT A temple relief shows the Mayan Jaguar god conducting a blood-letting ritual with his wife, Lady Xoc.

ABOVE The jaguar is a central motif throughout Central and South America, frequently associated with deities.

BELOW The markings on the ancient giant Sun Stone are symbols linked to Aztec cosmology.

At the time of the Spanish conquest in 1519, great urban civilizations existed in Mesoamerica – controlled by the Maya and Aztecs – and the central Andes region – under Inca rule. The foundations of these civilizations were laid by earlier cultures such as the Olmec, Chavin, Nazca and Toltec, and shared many features: monumental architecture, ceremonial centres with pyramid and plaza complexes, complex calendrical computations and – for the Maya – hieroglyphic writing. The art and culture of

these civilizations was rich in symbolism, linked especially to the natural world.

THE JAGUAR

Once known as the people of the jaguar, the Olmec worshipped gods that were half-human and half-animal. The jaguar was their most favoured and feared deity. Admired for its strength, ferocity and hunting ability, the jaguar was one of the most powerful symbols in both Mesoamerica and South America, and its stylized form appears on artefacts throughout the region. Gods were often portrayed wearing the jaguar's skin as a sacred costume, and the cat was venerated as the divine protector of royalty by both Maya and Aztec rulers. The supreme Aztec god and patron deity of royalty, Tezcatlipoca (Lord of the Smoking Mirror), was said to possess an animal alter-ego in the form of a jaguar, which inhabited mountain summits and cave entrances. According to Maya mythology, copal resin, one of the most important and sacred incense-burning substances of the ancient American cultures, was a gift of three different jaguars, white, golden and dark, corresponding to the three different colours of the resin.

CALENDARS

A calendar is a symbolic representation of time. It is a way of pinpointing the regular recurrence of natural phenomena – such as the rising and setting of the sun – against which human events can be set. The Maya used two calendars of different lengths,

one sacred, one secular; dates were calculated on the two planes of existence concurrently. The two calendars were so complex that the same juxtaposition could not recur for 374,440 years.

The great Aztec calendar stone (also known as the Sun Stone) is the largest Aztec sculpture ever found. Measuring 4m (13ft) in diameter, its markings were more symbolic than practical and relate to Aztec cosmology. The Aztecs believed that the world had passed through four creations, which had been destroyed by jaguars, fire, wind and water. The sun, moon and human beings were created at the beginning of the fifth and current creation, which is predicted to be destroyed by earthquakes. The calendar stone was used to calculate such danger periods. At its centre is the face of the Earth Monster, surrounded by symbols of previous creations. Twenty glyphs representing the names of each day in the Aztec month occupy the innermost circular

ABOVE This Aztec carving of their ritual ballgame shows a decapitated player (right): the blood streaming from his neck is shown in the form of snakes, which were symbols of fertility.

band. Each day the sun god had to be fed with human hearts and blood to give him strength to survive the night and rise again.

HUMAN SACRIFICE

Religious rituals involving human sacrifice formed part of the Inca, Aztec and Maya traditions. Human sacrifice was a symbol of communion with the gods, particularly the sun, rain and Earth deities. For the Aztecs and Incas, these bloody acts took place in temples or on mountains, while the Maya sometimes sacrificed their victims in wells. The Aztecs usually sacrificed their captured enemies, and it is said that in one four-day period of great celebration, some 20,000 victims were killed. Men, women and children could all be chosen.

The Aztecs preferred to stretch out their victims over a sacrificial stone and pluck out the still-beating heart; this symbolized the most precious organ that could be offered to the gods and replicas

were sometimes made in jade.

Prized more highly than gold, jade was a symbol for life and agriculture. Ritual vessels thought to be for the blood or hearts of sacrificial victims were often decorated with skulls, a symbol for fame and glory, or else defeat, depending on the situation. Human skulls were sometimes made into masks and used in ritual performances.

THE BALL COURT

For the Mayas and Aztecs every aspect of life, including sports, revolved around religion. In particular, the Mesoamerican ball game *ulama* had a sacred symbolism. Only nobles could play the game, in which two teams of two or three players aimed to propel a small, solid rubber ball through rings in order to score points. The rings were variously decorated, sometimes with snakes and monkeys. The ball-court represented the world, and the ball itself stood for the moon and the sun. The game was fiercely competitive, as the losing team was often sacrificed; it represented the battle between darkness and light, or the death and rebirth of the sun. It was also

believed that the more the game was played, the better the harvest would be.

NAZCA LINES

More than 1,000 years ago perfectly depicted giant figures, including animals such as a hummingbird, a whale, a monkey and a spider, were carved into the coastal desert floor near Nazca in southern Peru. Some are so large that they can be appreciated only from the air. It seems likely that they had some kind of sacred significance, perhaps as offerings to the mountain and sky gods.

ABOVE Maya numbers, from top, left to right: 0, 1, 4, 5, 11 and 18. The Maya number system used 3 signs – a dot for 1, a bar for 5 and the shell for 0. Other numbers were made by combinations of these signs.

HUACAS

The Incas' sacred sites were known as huacas, often natural spots in the landscape, such as caves, springs and boulders. The term *huaca* was also applied to portable objects such as amulets and figurines. These symbolic objects were thought to offer protection and were regarded as sacred.

Native North Americans

ABOVE White sage is a sacred herb that symbolizes purification, and is often used in North American rituals.

MIDDLE The eagle stands for power and vision.

TOP The quadrated circle of the Medicine Wheel, symbol of the earth.

FAR RIGHT Many Native American peoples revered the bison as a symbol of power and good fortune.

BELOW The bear represents both power and healing to the Native Americans.

The indigenous peoples of North America probably came from Asia 12,000–25,000 years ago via the Bering Strait. Waves of migration from Alaska to the east and south led to a large number of different tribes or linguistic families populating seven major cultural areas: the Arctic, the North-west Coast, the Plains, the Plateau, the Eastern Woodlands, the North and the South-west. A commonly understood sign language was developed among these people, who were often on the move and sometimes at war. The arrival of Europeans, from the 15th century, led to huge population collapses from imported diseases to which the indigenous people had no immunity. Many wars also took place between the Native Americans and the expanding white community.

The Native Americans were shamanic societies who lived in a close spiritual relationship with the land. Their lifestyle was adapted to various ecosystems, sometimes sedentary and sometimes nomadic, with an emphasis on hunting, gathering, fishing or agriculture. Their history and relationship with nature inform the mythologies and symbol systems that appear in the art, music and rituals of these peoples.

THE MEDICINE WHEEL

Sometimes known as the Sacred Hoop, the Medicine Wheel is an important representation of Native American spirituality, but is also conceived as a living entity in which humans and nature are interrelated. The Medicine Wheel

is a circular model in which the individual or culture orientates itself with all aspects of nature on the journey through life.

The Native Americans believe that the Great Spirit created nature in the round. The sun and moon are round, circling around us and marking circular time. The sky is a circle and the horizon is the edge of Mother Earth, from where the four winds blow. Each year is a circle divided by seasons, and the life and death of an individual is also seen as a circle.

The wheel is a quadrated circle, with the four directions and the four sacred colours marked upon it. Each direction represents particular natural and animal powers and the qualities that go with them. The eagle is found flying in the east and is a symbol of vision, endurance and strength. The mouse and innocence may be found to the south, the bear and introspection to the west and the buffalo and wisdom to the north. In addition to these four are three more directions: Father Sky (above), providing rain and warmth for things to grow; Mother Earth (below) the source of life-sustaining plants and animals; and the sacred fire at the

centre, where the people are attached to the Great Spirit.

To the Native American, "medicine" means power, a vital energy force in all forms of nature. The individual is placed on the wheel at birth, with certain perceptions and medicine powers, and as they walk their path on the wheel they acquire medicine power or wisdom from new perceptions and aspects of nature.

ANIMAL MEDICINE

Bison medicine was often seen as a representation of the feminine principle of the nourishing and life-giving force of the earth. The bison was considered to be the chief over all animals of the earth. Bear medicine has male aspects of strength and power, as well as more feminine aspects associated with knowledge of healing using roots and herbs, and introspective qualities related to hibernation.

The eagle is the lord of all birds and holds the greatest power. Eagles, and birds in general, are thought to have a very similar spirit to humans, as they fly in circles, with circular nests, and are not bound to the earth like four-legged animals. The eagle embodies great vision and overview, and a tremendous power to overcome all enemies and to strike with impeccable intent. When worn, the eagle feather is a reminder that the Great Spirit is present: the eagle is associated with the sun and its feathers with the sun's rays.

TOTEM POLE

The Algonquin word *totem* means a person's personal guardian, usually an animal or plant by which the Native American is adopted through a rite of passage at adolescence.

The totem pole is carved, often out of cedar, and is both a family or clan emblem and a reminder of their ancestors. It is a symbol of dignity and accomplishment, the historical and spiritual rank of the people. Many of the symbolic meanings and stories associated with the images are known only to the people of the clan. For example, the stories of the Northwest Pacific Coast tribes tell of the transformation of animals into humans as wel as humans into animals. The salmon or whale people are said to live in great happiness in cities beneath the waves. Thunderbirds are said to dive from the sky, snatching huge whales for their dinner. Wolves, becoming tired of hunting on the land, become killer whales and hunt in the sea.

THE CORN GODDESS

Corn, or maize, originated from a wild grass called *teosinte*, which grew in southern Mexico 7,000 years ago. The Native Americans selectively cultivated corn, and once the Europeans arrived, corn

agriculture quickly spread to the rest of the world. As a staple food, corn has inspired many important myths. It is said to be one of three sisters, Corn Woman, Squash Woman and Bean Woman, goddesses of fertility.

The Iroquois corn goddess (Onatah) is the daughter of Mother Earth (Eithinoha). Onatah is caught by spirits from the underworld, and must be rescued by the sun so that the crops can grow. Similar stories relating to the seasons are found in many agricultural societies.

THE VISION QUEST

An individual seeking guidance or answers to questions may embark on a vision quest, a ritual practice through which helpful signs may be given, which can be interpreted as guidance from the spirits. Vision quests occur when an adolescent makes the transition to the path of adulthood. The seeker asks the shaman for help. A remote site in nature is found and marked out with a rectangle or circle, where the seeker waits for a vision. Sacred offerings such as tobacco (which blesses the earth) are placed within this area for the Great Spirit. Sometimes sage, the purification herb, is laid on the ground as a bed for the seeker. The seeker stays in the sacred area for one night or several, praying and awaiting signs from the world around. The Great Spirit might speak through any experience, even insignificant encounters with animals and birds or other forces in nature. Eventually thanks are given to the

RIGHT Eagle feathers on the headdresses of Native American chiefs symbolize the sun's rays.

Great Spirit for what has been given, and the seeker shares the experience with the shaman to gain understanding.

THE GIVE-AWAY

Potlatch is a Chinook word for a "give-away" ceremony in which prominent people give a feast and give away their possessions, redistributing them among the tribe. Sometimes at the end of the ceremony they burn down their house and become poor, until they build up their wealth again.

Giving is important to the Native American, who considers it a great honour on the part of the one who gives and for the one who receives. One should share one's wealth and never hold on to more than is needed. The turkey is thought of as the give-away or earth eagle. The turkey is a free-spirited bird of sacrifice, opening the channels to others.

ABOVE The totem pole is carved with figures and faces placed on top of each other. They represent ancestors or supernatural beings encountered by clan members, or who have given them special gifts.

Arctic Traditions

ABOVE For the Innuit the igloo is a symbol of home and family life. In Canada it is a registered trademark for the Inuit.

BELOW Some of the symbolic tools of the Inuit: the box top, *kepun* axe and the *cavik*, a curved knife.

Within the Arctic Circle, a large ocean is surrounded by land, with tundra at its fringe and animal, human and plant life throughout the area. The Arctic includes Siberia and other parts of northern Russia, Alaska in the United States, northern Canada, Greenland, Lappland in Finland, northern Norway and Sweden. It is peopled mainly by the Inuit of Alaska, Canada and Greenland, and the Finno-Ugrians of northern Scandinavia and Siberia, which include the Saami.

The ecology, climate and geology of the Arctic influence the signs and symbols of its peoples. The Arctic is known by the people who live there as the "land of the midnight sun": in the summer the sun never sets, and in the winter it never rises. The taiga and tundra are featureless landscapes with wide horizons, a good home for reindeer or caribou, and thus suit nomadic cultures that rely on reindeer for food. Seal hunting, whaling and saltwater fishing are also important to human survival.

INUIT SPIRITS

The name "Inuit" means "the real people": the Algonquin named them "Eskimos", meaning "raw flesh eaters". Inuit spirituality is concerned with conciliating the gods and nature spirits, to help humans survive in harsh conditions. Unseen forces in nature are called *innua*, and they can be found in the air, water, stones and animals. The *innua* can become totemic guardians of men, known as *torngak*.

Stone and bear spirits are considered particularly powerful. When a bear spirit becomes a man's *torngak*, he is symbolically eaten by the bear and reborn as a sorcerer or *angakok*.

The *innua* of animals are thought to be very sensitive to the craftsmanship of the weapons by which they are killed. If they were killed by a poorly made tool they would report this to the spirit world, and the animal spirit might not return to earth in another animal body. To avoid this the Inuit take great pride in their craftsmanship.

THE IGLOO

The word igloo means "dwelling", and the *igluvigaq* is the ice dwelling used by the Central Inuit in the winter. Constructed from upward spiralling blocks of ice, the igloo walls curve inwards, creating an ice dome with a hole for ventilation in the top.

The igloo is a symbolic extension of those who built it and their relationship with their surroundings. The igloo is built from within, and once the "keystone" has been placed at the top, the igloo and its builder become one. The igloo enables the Inuit to survive harsh conditions, and is built from the very elements of that extreme environment.

In Inuit mythology, Aningan is a moon god and a proficient hunter who has an igloo where he can rest in the sky, when not being chased through the sky by his brother the sun. He shares the igloo with Irdlirvirissong, his demon cousin, who sometimes comes out to dance in the sky making people laugh.

The igloo symbolizes a resting-place and psychic home for different facets of human nature. In 1958 the Canadian government registered the image of the igloo as a trademark to protect the work of Inuit artists and woodcarvers.

SYMBOLIC TOOLS

Two other important items in Inuit culture are the *inuksuk* and the *ulu*. A common symbol in northern Canada, the *inuksuk*, means the "likeness of a person" in Inuktitut. It is a signpost guiding the Inuit through the featureless tundra. Made from rock, *inuksuk* appear as human forms with their legs outstretched, and often serve the purpose of guiding caribou into places where they can easily be captured. The longer arm of an *inuksuk* points the hunter in the appropriate direction. If an *inuksuk* points towards a lake, it is an indication that fish can be found in the lake at the same distance the *inuksuk* stands from the edge of the lake.

The *ulu* is a woman's knife with a crescent-shaped blade, used for cutting out clothing, preparing skins, and in cooking. The *ulu* is a symbol of femininity and the woman's role in Inuit society.

THE COSMIC TENT OF THE SAAMI

Formerly known as Lapps, the Saami are part of the Finno-Ugric race, a large group of tribes speaking many different dialects of one parent language. The Saami were traditionally hunters and fishermen, who also farmed domesticated reindeer; since the reindeer have been dying out, they have become more nomadic.

As an essentially shamanic culture, the Saami conceive of a world with different levels of reality: the lower world, the middle world and the upper world. The world is imagined to have been constructed as a kind of cosmic tent, with the central pole of the World Tree reaching up from its roots in the lower world, through the middle world of everyday life, to the upper world constellation of the Great Bear at its top. The central pole is also described as a four-sided world pillar.

The sky is thought to have been fixed in place by the "north nail", the Pole Star, and prayers ensure it stays in place so that the sky does not fall down. The Saami are concerned that the Pole Star might one day move, leading to the destruction of the earth.

The traditional Saami dwelling is a conical compound tent or *kata*, a predecessor of the yurt, capable of withstanding very strong winds and snow. It is a symbolic map of the cosmos, with the hearth at the centre, the skin of the tent representing the sky, held up by wooden supports equivalent to the world pillar.

Within the *kata* there is a sacred area where the sacred drum is kept. The Saami also believe that when a member of the family dies the body should be taken out of the tent through the *boasso* (or kitchen) side, otherwise someone else will die.

REINDEER

The reindeer has central importance within Saami culture, and reindeer herding is a symbol of personal, group and cultural identity. Saami children are often given a "first tooth" reindeer and a "name day" reindeer, and more reindeer are given to them at their wedding, so that a new household is usually equipped with a small herd of reindeer with which a couple can start their new life together. The reindeer is also often associated with moon symbolism and with funerary ritual and passage.

ABOVE The reindeer is an all-encompassing, multi-faceted Saami symbol of life and death. It is believed to conduct the soul of a dead person to the upper world.

KALEVALA

Elias Lönnrot, a Finnish scholar, collected the mythic and magical songs passed down orally by generations of peasants, and published the *Kalevala*, the Finnish national epic, in 1835. Its poems and sagas offer important insights into the beliefs and traditions of the Saami peoples.

SACRED DRUM

The sacred drum is important to the Saami. Constructed from birch, with a drum head of reindeer skin, the drum is commonly painted in alder juice or blood with figures of people, the nature spirits and the four directions around a central symbol of the sun. A series of small rings moves as the drum is beaten, and where they eventually come to rest leads to shamanic predictions and divinations. The Saami use their drum as a guide in daily life, to find things that have been lost, and for healing purposes.

Symbols of Spirituality

Both signs and symbols play a vital role
in all the world's religions as objects on
which thoughts and prayers can be focused.
Spiritual symbols point a way through the
numinous world of religious belief, acting
as badges of faith, teaching tools and aids
on the journey towards an understanding
of complex philosophies.

RIGHT In many cultures thunder and lightening are symbols of divine
power, often as signs of the anger or vengeance of the gods. In the
Bible thunder is the angry voice of god, while in Africa thunder and
lightening are associated with earthly rulers.

SHAMANISM

ABOVE Seedpods are commonly used for making shamanic rattles.

BELOW A North American shaman, holding a drum and spear, "shape-shifts" into a wolf.

The ancient tradition of shamanism involves the individual entering altered states of consciousness to visit other levels of reality, from which teaching, healing or visions may come for his or her community. With its origins in the Palaeolithic period, shamanism may be found at the roots of many of the world's major religions, and at the fringes of many others.

The word *saman* comes from the Tungus of Siberia, and means "one who knows". Shamans are adepts of trance, an ecstatic and altered state in which they are thought to leave their bodies, ascending into the sky in "magical flight" or descending into the underworld, to meet with the ancestors and commune with nature spirits. Many of the symbols of shamanism represent transcendence or release from one way of being into another.

Traditional shamanism is now little practised, but a wave of interest has developed in the West, inspired by Jung's linkage of it with his ideas about the "collective unconscious", and a growing recognition of the importance of travelling between different worlds or states.

THE CALL OF A SHAMAN
Shamans may inherit their role, but more often they experience a spontaneous vocation in which they are called or elected by nature. The shamanic calling is itself a symbolic occurrence. Often an initiate is called by a near-death experience, such as being struck by lightning or surviving a life-threatening illness. Some have a lucid dream-like experience of dismemberment, whereby they metaphorically die and are then reborn.

Other shamans may be "called" by meeting a divine or semi-divine figure in a dream. Often these dream figures are the dead ancestors of the shaman who inform him that he is being elected. Some shamans have celestial husbands or wives by whom they are called to their shamanic path.

Facing your own death, or journeying into death, is powerfully symbolic of the shamanic ability to transcend the everyday self and to live impeccably in the face of the attacks and challenges of life. It is said that some shamanic warriors have become so centred that they can walk across a firing range without harm. Psychologically, the deathwalk is the ability to drop personal history and identity, so there is nothing to be attacked.

SHAMANIC FLIGHT
A shaman is said to be able to take flight in the form of an animal, or a spirit detached from the body. In this way shamans can move about the universe bridging Earth and the heavens, many symbols reflect this belief.

Palaeolithic cave paintings at Lascaux, in France, show the shaman in a bird mask, and Siberian shamanic priestesses still wear bird costumes. In rock art of the San (Bushmen) of southern Africa, the *ales*, or "trance buck" is an antelope-like creature, with its legs raised in flight. It probably symbolizes the shamanic ability to commune with the ancestors, since in San mythology the dead are transformed into elands. Similar flying animals occur in Siberian shamanic mythology (and may be the source of the flying reindeer of Santa Claus).

PARALLEL WORLDS
The basic shamanic cosmology consists of three levels or worlds – the upperworld, middle earth

and the underworld – but some traditions describe as many as seven or nine different worlds.

The role of the shaman is to make links or travel between these worlds, and many symbols refer to the connection between them. In Native American traditions the smoke rising through the smoke hole of a tipi refers to the passage of spirit between earth and sky.

The world tree is a shamanic symbol that occurs in many cosmologies – the Norse god Odin, who hangs himself on the world tree Yggdrasil, achieves knowledge through the altered state that results from his suffering. The ladder is a similar symbol, seen in the seven-notched birch trees of Siberian shamanism, but also in other traditions, such as in the Egyptian Book of the Dead and the Old Testament.

For many shamans there is a direct relationship between themselves and the natural world. A Romany shaman speaks of the earth as his grandmother, and the plants, animals, sun, moon and stars as his relatives, with whom he communicates for guidance. All of nature thus becomes a form of living symbolism.

Some psychologists see a direct connection between the parallel realities of the shaman and the relationship between dreaming and everyday reality. From this perspective signs and symbols from the unconscious, or in nature, are doorways calling us into another level of reality. A dream about a flying eagle, for example, may invite us to take a

RIGHT A Tungus shaman of Siberia wears the skin and antlers of his spirit ally, the reindeer, to deepen his relationship with the animal.

detached overview, with sharp-focused attention.

THE DRUM

Used to induce a shamanic trance, the drum has particular symbolic significance as a vehicle into altered states or otherworlds. The repetitive rhythm played upon the drum, and sometimes on rattles or other instruments, blocks out other sensory information, enabling the shaman to enter a different state of consciousness. The drumbeat relates to the primal sound sometimes thought of as the heartbeat of the earth.

For the shamans of the Altai of central Asia, the drum skin stands for the division between the upperworld and the lowerworld. In all shamanic cultures the drum is symbolic of the relationship between the upperworld, often associated with the male, and the underworld or womb, associated with the female.

THE SHAMAN'S ALLY

A shaman has an ally or teacher in the form of an ancestor, a dead shaman, or often an animal or nature spirit, who helps them reach altered states. Through this relationship the shaman finds their double or individuated self. They may imitate the actions and voice of an animal ally as a way of sharing their perceptions, gifts and intelligence. Saami shamans are said to become wolves, bears, reindeer or fish. The Tungus shaman of Siberia has a snake as a helping spirit and during the shamanic trance replicates its reptilian movements.

SHAMANIC JOURNEYS

The symbolic world of the shaman can be meaningful to people who suffer breakdowns or near-death experiences. The shaman can leave the present reality in order to find wisdom or knowledge in alternative realities. The helpful spirits of animals and ancestors may be seen as aspects of a person's unconscious, encountered on life's journey.

BELOW A shamanic drum with a stylized image of a running horse painted on its surface.

TAOISM

ABOVE The "all-powerful" seal of Lao-tzu, a Taoist magic diagram harnessing cosmic *chi*.

BELOW According to legend, Lao-tzu, saddened by people's inability to accept the "way" he proposed, departed from civilization and rode into the desert on a water buffalo. At the last gate of the kingdom he was persuaded to leave a record of his teachings, and wrote the *Tao Te Ching*.

Taoism is a religious and philosophical system, said to have been founded in China by the sage Lao-tzu (or "the old one") in the 6th century BC. Taoism was influential in China and Japan, and in modern times interest in it has also spread to the West.

According to tradition, Lao-tzu was the author of the *Tao Te Ching*, or "Book of the Way", a collection of aphorisms concerned with the nature of the world and the alignment of humanity to this nature. Its central principle is non-action – not passivity but an active responsiveness to the nature of life, an appreciation of life as it is, rather than striving to fulfil a succession of desires.

Both Taoism and Confucianism have been highly influential upon Chinese culture and history. Confucianism is an ethical approach to living and government based on fixed principles, rooted in the belief that civilization can build a better society, while Taoism is more concerned with living in accordance with the nature of things as they are.

THE TAO

Both a personal and a cosmological principle, the Tao (or the "way") describes the origins of the universe and creation. It refers to the source of nature's patterns and the ebb and flow of natural forces. At the same time, the Tao is a mystical path that can be followed by living in a state of simplicity, in accordance with nature's rhythms.

Whereas in the West the heart is seen as a source of courage or love, to the Chinese it is the source of sensation, the seat of the five senses. Discovering the Tao depends on "emptying" the heart of the ever-changing illusions of the senses, so that it is true and eternal. Lao-tzu is commonly quoted as stating that "the Tao which can be spoken is not the eternal Tao". This means that the Tao refers to that which precedes all manifest things (or "myriad things") in nature.

Whereas many religious systems view heaven as a state outside of the human earthly existence, Taoism, and much Chinese thinking, is more concerned with oneness, in which a person lives in and identifies with the Tao. Thus living according to the Tao means to be guided by the deepest path in nature, which lies between earthly and heavenly existence.

YIN AND YANG

For Lao-tzu there was no such thing as a fixed definition of good or evil, in that as soon as a state of "goodness" is described it immediately and inevitably invokes a balancing state of "non-goodness" as an opposing force. The yin/yang symbol is indicative of the balancing natural law or cycle of change, in which every movement contains or eventually turns into its opposite: strength leads to weakness, life to death, and male to female.

Yin, the female principle, is associated with coldness, darkness and the earth; yang, the male principle, with light, warmth and heaven. The symbol shows that life must be viewed as a whole and cannot truly exist in isolated parts. The dark and light parts of the symbol are directly opposed yet interlocking and mutually dependent; the two small spots in the symbol show that each opposing force contains the seed of the other. Together the two shapes form a perfect circle, symbolizing the wholeness of nature.

A contemporary example of this principle is evident in humankind's relationship with the ecology of the planet. Our ability to harness power, resources and information has grown enormously, but if we fail to recognize our dependence on the greater whole – the animals and forces of nature around us – our strengths will eventually bring about our demise. The yin/yang symbol shows how each force, when at its most powerful, gives rise to its opposite.

DIVINE FIGURES

Originally, Taoism had no static religious doctrines, nor was it involved in deity worship, but over time, as it became popular, it was mixed with older Chinese beliefs such as the theory of the five elements and the veneration of the ancestors. It became something more akin to a folk religion, and a whole pantheon of divinities was worshipped, including the mythical Jade Emperor. Lao-tzu himself was deified and became one of the most important Taoist gods.

The Taoist pantheon mirrors the imperial hierarchy in Heaven and Hell, and Taoist priests relate to these divinities through meditation and visualization. Sometimes for the general public, metaphysical or symbolic theatrical rituals have been devised to portray the meaning and workings of the divine hierarchy. Many Taoists pray to these divinities or make offerings at shrines devoted to them.

Lao-tzu is said to be one of the reincarnations of the Great Supreme Venerable Lord, or T'ai-shang Lao-chun. He is symbolic of one who has become one with

the Tao, thus succeeding in the creation of an immortal body that separates from the physical body at death.

Yu-huang, the Jade Emperor, also known as the Lord of Heaven, is said to be the supreme ruler of the heavens and of the underworld. For the Chinese, jade symbolizes nobility, perfection and immortality, and is considered the "stone of heaven". The Jade Emperor is the chief administrator of moral justice and also the protector of humanity. In Chinese tradition, the heavenly administration was regarded as a replica of the emperor's government on Earth, and the Jade Emperor was in direct communication with the emperor of China.

P'AN-KU AND THE FIVE SACRED MOUNTAINS

Another important Taoist figure is the mythical P'an-ku, who is said to be the first created being. Upon the creation of the universe, in which Chaos was divided into the forces of yin and yang, the interaction of these opposing principles led to the creation of P'an-ku, who thereupon picked

up a chisel and a mallet and began to carve the rest of creation, and in particular the space that lies between Heaven and Earth. P'an-ku lived for 18,000 years, growing every day, and when, on completion of his task he lay down and died, his body became the world, the extent of which was marked by the five sacred mountains of China. Symbolically linked to the five elements, these stood at the four cardinal points and in the centre of the empire, and were believed to support the heavens.

Lao-tzu advised his followers to "be still like a mountain and flow like a great river", and many have sought the Tao by retreating to live alone in the mountains. In Taoist belief, mountains are a medium of communication with the immortals and with nature. Like the image of the world tree, they link the worlds above and below. The sacred mountains are sites of pilgrimage. They have been worshipped as deities in their own right, monasteries cling to their slopes, and the emperor himself climbed annually to the summit of the holiest peak, Tai Shan, the mountain of the east, to offer a sacrifice.

ABOVE The Jade Emperor was revered as the divine head of the hierarchy of heaven and hell.

TOP The yin/yang symbol represents the endless interplay of opposing qualities in nature.

THE TAO AND THE MOON

According to some texts, the earliest Taoists were shamans who flew to the moon and there learned all the secrets of change. In contrast, the Taoist view of the sun was of something constant. These early Taoists were far more interested in what could be learned from the moon and its phases.

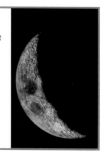

HINDUISM

ABOVE The four heads of Brahma represent the four directions.

TOP Ganesh, the elephant-headed god, symbolizes sacred wisdom and abundance.

With no single historical founder, no set of creeds or dogmas and no one source of authority, Hinduism encompasses a huge variety of beliefs and rituals, intricately woven into the land and culture of India. Of the world's major religions, Hinduism has the third largest number of followers (the majority of whom live in India and Nepal). Many Hindus, however, do not recognize the term Hinduism as a description of their religion, referring instead to *sanatana dharma* – the eternal religion or law. The complex Sanskrit word *dharma* refers to the natural unchanging laws that sustain the universe and keep it in balance, a similar concept to the Tao. It translates in daily life as an obligation to follow certain laws and to fulfil social and ethical responsibilities, so that for many Hindus there is no division between secular and religious life.

BRAHMAN

In Hindu thought, there is one ultimate Supreme Being – Brahman – who is infinite and eternal. Brahman is the source of life, the world soul, and is present in all things as the *atman*, the true self or the unchanging essence of the individual living being.

Just as all living beings represent tiny parts of the universe, so Brahman takes different forms, representing certain aspects of the divine. Consequently there are many gods and goddesses in the Hindu pantheon, including the elephant-headed Ganesh, god of good fortune and wisdom; Hanuman, the monkey god, representing loyalty, courage and devotion; and Lakshmi, the four-armed goddess of fortune.

THE TRIMURTI

The word *trimurti* means "having three forms" in Sanskrit, and is the term used to describe the supreme trinity of Hinduism: Brahma (the Creator), Vishnu (the Preserver) and Shiva (the Destroyer). Brahma the Creator (sometimes depicted with four heads facing in four directions) is the balancing force that links Vishnu, the agent of light, and Shiva, lord of darkness, together. Although Brahma is important, there are only two known temples dedicated exclusively to his worship, while both Shiva and Vishnu are worshipped extensively as principal deities.

LEFT Vishnu and his consort, Lakshmi, ride upon Garuda, the eagle who symbolizes the wisdom attained by an open mind.

VISHNU

Also called the Preserver, Vishnu maintains the harmony of the universe and is a manifestation of the sun as it crosses the heavens each day with three great strides, at dawn, noon and sunset. As preserver of the world, he is said to have assumed ten incarnations, referred to as "avatars" (literally "one who descends"); these include Rama, Krishna and the Buddha. As Lord of the Universe, Vishnu floats on the primeval waters, asleep on the serpent Ananta. His four main symbols are the *shanka* (or conch shell), used to dispel demons, the *gaddha* (or club) to represent power, the *chakra* (or discus) used against evil forces, and the *padma* (or lotus) symbolizing reincarnation. *Tulasi* (sweet basil) is sacred to Vishnu and is kept in temples dedicated to him, its leaves used in sacred ceremonies.

SHIVA

A deity of contrasting and often contradictory characteristics, Shiva represents not only destruction, but also regeneration, just as order arises out of chaos, and new life emerges after death. As Nataraja, he is lord of the universal dance of creation and destruction through which he maintains the balance of the cosmos. The dancing Shiva is usually depicted with four hands surrounded by a circle of flames, representing the sun disc and the creation and continuation of the cosmos. Shiva is also the supreme god of masculine virility, symbolized by the phallus-shaped linga (the counterpart of the female yoni), as well as an ascetic yogi, clad in ashes and animal skins. His third eye (the chakra in the middle of the forehead) can destroy with fire all those who look upon it, while also granting transcendent wisdom. Shiva is sometimes depicted riding the white bull, Nandi, symbol of power and virility, who often appears at shrines to the god.

SHAKTI

The concept of Shakti is another important aspect of the divine. Shakti is the feminine principle, the dynamic life-giving energy of the universe that activates creativity; without Shakti, the other gods remain passive and lacking in motivation. Shakti is often shown embracing Shiva and has two sides to her nature, one gentle and serene, the other fierce and formidable. The goddess Kali, usually shown with a black tongue, rolling eyes, pointed teeth and a garland of skulls, is a personification of the latter, while Parvati, consort of Shiva, represents the former.

THE SOUND OF OM

In Sanskrit calligraphy, the mystic syllable *om* is the symbolic representation of Brahman. It is described in the Upanishads (one of the sacred texts of Hinduism) as the sound that creates and sustains the cosmos, and it is thought that through its utterance, the whole universe (past, present and future) is encapsulated. The sound contains the three sounds of A, U and M, representing the three gods (Brahma, Vishnu and Shiva) who

control life. They also symbolize the three human states of dreaming, sleeping and waking, and the three capacities of desire, knowledge and action. Om is used as a mantra in meditation as well as in sacred ceremony.

DAILY WORSHIP

Puja, or daily worship, is usually carried out in the home and is the main form of Hindu worship, although worship led by a priest also occurs twice a day at the *mandir* (temple). At home, worship is held at a shrine, where the family's chosen deities are represented in the form of pictures or statues, known as *murtis.* At the mandir, a highly ritualized ceremony known as the *arti* takes place. This involves the lighting of five divas by the priest, who circles the lamps in front of the central deity, while the worshippers sing a devotional scriptural verse. At the end of the ceremony, a symbolic offering of food (such as fruit, nuts or sweets) is presented to the deity for blessing and then shared among the congregation.

FESTIVALS

The Hindu year contains many festivals to mark events in the lives of deities or to celebrate the changing seasons. They are lively, colourful affairs involving music, dance and drama and provide an opportunity for families and friends to come together. Held in honour of the goddess Lakshmi, Diwali, the festival of lights, is the most widely celebrated festival in India, symbolizing the triumph of good over evil. In some regions,

RIGHT Diwali (the festival of lights) involves the symbolic offering of light to represent the triumph of good over evil.

RIGHT Diwali (the festival of lights) involves the symbolic offering of light to represent the triumph of good over evil.

Diwali (in October or November) marks the new year; it augurs a fresh start, and is a time when debts are paid, and homes are cleaned, repainted and lit with an array of lights. The festival of Holi, in March, celebrates the grain harvest and is very high-spirited, with bonfires, tricks (such as showering people with coloured dyes) and dancing.

THE GANGES

In a land of heat and dust, the great rivers of India are an important source of life and energy and unsurprisingly are revered as holy. The most important is the Ganges, worshipped as the goddess Ganga, which flows across India from its source in the Himalayas, also held sacred. Pilgrimages are made to Varanasi (associated with Shiva) on the Ganges' banks to wash in the river's sacred waters. It is believed that Ganga offers liberation from *samsara,* the cycle of rebirth, and Varanasi is considered an auspicious site for cremation and for scattering the ashes of the deceased. Pilgrimages are also made to holy sites in the Himalayas, particularly to Mount Kailas, where it is said that Shiva sits in meditation.

ABOVE The Om symbol represents the sacred sound of creation.

BELOW Shiva, dancing in a circle of flames, is a cosmic symbol of life, death and rebirth.

THE COW

In Hinduism, the cow is held sacred, and slaughtering one is considered a terrible crime. Symbols of fertility and plenty, cows are central to Indian agriculture, their milk is an important food source, while oxen are used to pull the plough, allowing the planting of grain.

BUDDHISM

ABOVE When the Buddha cut off his hair he was using the act as a symbol of his decision to renounce the world.

BELOW A Buddha's footprint decorated with Buddhist symbols, including the reversed swastika, an ancient symbol that predates the German Nazis.

Some 2,500 years ago, Siddhartha Gautama, the founder of Buddhism, was born on the border between Nepal and northern India. The Buddha – or Awakened One – is the title he was given after he achieved spiritual self-realization, or "enlightenment", becoming the embodiment of perfect wisdom and compassion. Buddhism is not based on a belief in God, nor does it have a set creed, a central authority, or a universally accepted sacred scripture. Never demanding sole allegiance from its followers, Buddhism has coexisted with local religious traditions and has given us a rich tradition with a diversity of symbols and mythic thinking.

LIFE OF THE BUDDHA
Siddhartha Gautama's life story is fundamental to Buddhism, symbolizing many of its basic teachings, including the need for

great effort, complete detachment and boundless compassion. Raised as a prince, Gautama renounced his riches and abandoned his family in search of the cause of life's suffering. After many years as a wandering ascetic, he concluded that neither indulgence nor extreme austerity held the answer and sat down to meditate on the problem under a bodhi tree in the village of Bodhgaya, India. It was here that he became enlightened and experienced nirvana – a blissful state of perfect peace, knowledge and truth. Though no longer bound to the physical world, the Buddha decided, out of compassion, to spend the rest of his life teaching. He gave his first sermon to a small group of disciples at Sarnath, where he taught the Four Noble Truths and the Eightfold Path, teachings which explain the nature of suffering and how to end it. The path involves discipline of thought and action and endorses a way of life that seeks to harm no one. The monastic sangha (assembly) was inaugurated by the Buddha to preserve and spread his teaching.

THE BODHISATTVAS
While some forms of Buddhism focus upon personal salvation, there is also a way to Buddhahood referred to as "the path of the bodhisattva". A bodhisattva is a disciple of Buddhism (either male or female) who is capable of attaining nirvana – and hence freedom from samsara (the rebirth cycle) – but chooses to remain in the

physical world in order to help others. In Pali (a language derivative of Sanskrit), the word bodhisattva means "one who is the essence of truth and wisdom". Bodhisattvas are differentiated from the Buddha by their relaxed pose, often depicted seated or lying down to show their continuing relationship with humankind. Among the most important bodhisattvas are Maitreya (Mili in China), a benevolent figure of the future, an awaited messiah of Buddhism, usually shown seated in the Western style; and Avalokiteshvara (Guan-Yin in China), the embodiment of compassion and mercy.

BUDDHIST COSMOLOGY
Unlike the Western view of a cosmos that proceeds from beginning to end, Buddhist cosmology is cyclical. This not only applies to human life (the endless birth, death, rebirth cycle) but also to world systems. These will come into being, pass away and be succeeded by a new order. Some Buddhists also believe that there are countless world systems in existence simultaneously, each having its own Buddha, some of whom have names and can be interacted with. Thus buddha icons do not always represent the historical Buddha Gautama, (also referred to as Shakyamuni Buddha), but may depict buddhas in different incarnations. One such is Amitabha, the Buddha of Infinite Light and guardian of the West, who is often shown holding a lotus flower and accompanied by a peacock.

THE STUPA

One of the most important and easily recognizable symbols of Buddhism is the stupa. In ancient texts, the word stupa meant "summit", and originally stupas were burial mounds containing sacred relics of the Buddha, or else of his main disciples (some of whom also attained enlightenment). As well as being a symbol of the Buddha and his final release from samsara, the stupa is also a cosmic symbol. Although there are many architectural variations, typically it consists of a dome (*anda*), symbolizing both the "world egg" (an archetypal symbol of creation) and the womb, while the relics it houses represent the seeds of life. Usually the dome rests on a square pedestal, which is typically aligned with the four cardinal points, signifying the dome of Heaven resting upon the earth. Stupas later developed into places of worship, and have sometimes been built to commemorate important events.

PRAYER WHEEL

A rotating drum inscribed with or containing prayers is known as a prayer wheel. One clockwise revolution of the wheel is said to be the equivalent of a spoken prayer. Large prayer wheels are found outside Buddhist shrines, and are rotated by pilgrims as they walk around the shrine.

BUDDHA'S FOOTPRINT

In Buddhism (and also Hinduism) footprints can represent the presence of a holy person or deity, encapsulating all their qualities and attributes. Many Buddhist temples contain carvings of copies of the Buddha's footprint, often with auspicious Buddhist symbols such as the eight-spoked wheel, symbolizing the Buddha's law. The Buddha's footprints are also decorated with symbols such as the fish, swastika, diamond mace, conch shell, flower vase and crown. It is thought that if devotees follow in the Buddha's footsteps, they too may attain enlightenment or Buddhahood.

TIBETAN BUDDHISM

Buddhism has tended to adapt itself to the different countries and cultures to which it has spread. Sometimes referred to as the Vajrayana (Diamond or Thunderbolt vehicle), Tibetan Buddhism is characterized by a pantheon of Buddhas and bodhisattvas, and many colourful rituals, artefacts and works of art. The importance of living teachers is stressed; some (known as lamas) are believed to be

reincarnations of holy teachers from earlier times, living on earth as bodhisattvas. Ritual practices involve making mandalas (abstract, wheel-like designs), chanting mantras and performing mudras (symbolic hand gestures). Statues and mandalas are used to focus the mind in meditation.

ZEN BUDDHISM

Space and simplicity characterize Zen Buddhism. Developed in China, Korea and Japan, the Zen tradition has influenced Sino-Japanese art forms, such as calligraphy, painting and poetry, as well as the arrangement of flowers and gardens, the tea ceremony, and even martial arts, all of which share order, simplicity and set procedures.

ABOVE A golden Dharma-chakra, an 8-spoked wheel that symbolizes the teachings of the Buddha, stands between two statues of deer, representing the Buddha's first sermon at Deer Park, Sarnath. Jokhang Temple, Lhasa, Tibet.

ABOVE The many-layered symbol for the stupa.

THE ELEPHANT AND THE BUDDHA

The story of the Buddha's birth is surrounded by portents of his greatness. While pregnant, his mother dreamed of giving birth to a white bull-elephant with six tusks. The arrival of a chosen one had long been predicted, and interpreters took this dream as an announcement of his impending arrival. In Indian culture, the white elephant is the mount of Indra, king of the gods, and elephants are called "the removers of obstacles", an attribute given to the Hindu elephant-headed god, Ganesh. In Buddhism the elephant is sometimes used as a symbol of the Buddha, representing his serenity and power.

JUDAISM

ABOVE The eastern wall of every synagogue contains the Torah scrolls, which are read from a raised platform to signify respect. A lamp burns perpetually as a symbol of the Jewish people's covenant with God.

ABOVE The Ark of the Covenant is a symbol of the Exodus.

The world's oldest monotheistic religion, Judaism has a continuity of tradition covering some 4,000 years. The name "Judaism" is derived from the tribe of Judah, one of the twelve tribes of Israel, but it is the life of Abraham – known as the father of the Jewish people – and his relationship with God that is fundamental to Judaism. The Jewish scriptures tell how God made a covenant, or agreement, with Abraham: that his descendants would be God's chosen people, in return for which the people should keep God's laws. These laws were given

to Moses on Mount Sinai as he led the Jewish people out of captivity in Egypt (the Exodus) to Canaan (Israel), the land God had promised to Abraham.

THE PROMISED LAND

Judaism's history is rooted in Israel, the promised land. More than just a place, it is one of Judaism's most important symbols, part of the Jewish people's ethnic identity. Jerusalem, city of David, Israel's greatest king, is particularly important. It was here that David's son, Solomon, built a temple, a symbol of communion between man and God. The temple was rebuilt many times until its final destruction by the Roman emperor Titus in AD 70. The Wailing (or Western) Wall is the last remnant of the temple and is a place of pilgrimage and prayer for Jews from all over the world.

THE TORAH

Study of the holy scriptures is one of the most important aspects of the Jewish faith. The first five books of the Hebrew Bible are known as the Pentateuch, or Torah, believed to contain all of God's teaching as revealed to Moses on Mount Sinai.

More than a repository of laws and stories, the Torah is seen as the inner, or spiritual, dimension of the world itself, the medium through which the individual may gain access to higher realms. Every synagogue has a set of parchment scrolls (the Sefer Torah) on which the Torah is handwritten in Hebrew by a specialist scribe; it can take a year to complete. Each scroll has a belt to hold it when rolled, a breastplate and a crown, together with a silver pointer used when reading, to avoid finger contact with the parchment. One of the most sacred symbols of Judaism, the Torah scrolls are kept in a special cupboard or alcove (known as the Holy Ark, after the Ark of the Covenant) in the wall that faces Jerusalem.

THE SYNAGOGUE

After the destruction of the temple, the Jews were scattered throughout the Roman Empire, and the synagogue became the centre of Jewish community life. The synagogue has three main functions: it is a house of

BELOW The *shofar* is a ram's horn trumpet used in Jewish rituals. It recalls the story of Abraham and Isaac and is a sign of God's grace.

JEWISH MYSTICISM

The Torah is said to comprise four levels of meaning: the literal, the allegorical, the homiletical (teaching or preaching) and the secret or mystical. Mystical interpretations view the Torah as a means of understanding the nature of God. The Kabbalah, the most influential strand of Jewish mysticism, conceives of God's attributes as a series of ten spheres (or sephiroth), through which the individual must pass in order to reach the divine source. All aspects of human life are ultimately expressions of the sephiroth, which constitutes the deepest reality, our contact with God. The Kabbalah's central text is the Zohar (Book of Splendour), which was first circulated in Spain in the 13th century. Symbols associated with the Kabbalah include the Star of David and the Tetragrammaton.

assembly where the Jewish community can meet for any purpose; a house of study, where the scriptures are studied and children learn Hebrew and study the Torah; and a house of prayer, where services are held on the Sabbath (Shabbat). Men and women occupy separate areas, and in obedience to the Second Commandment, there are not usually any images of people or animals. Every synagogue also has a perpetually burning lamp before the Ark – a symbol of God's eternal light, illuminating the darkness of ignorance.

TETRAGRAMMATON

According to tradition, God's name was revealed to Moses, but was so sacred that it could never be spoken aloud. The tetragrammaton comprises the four letters, Y, H, W, H, which spell the true name of God in Hebrew, referred to as "the name" (*ha shem*), or Adonai ("My Lord"). When vowels are added, the letters spell the name Yahweh, which some Christians translate as Jehovah.

The tetragrammaton was engraved on the rod of Aaron and the ring of Solomon, both emblems of authority. The rod was also believed to have miracle-working properties (like the wand, common to many traditions), and Solomon's ring was said to give him powers of divination. In Kabbalism, the tetragrammaton was believed to signify life and to possess magical and healing powers. It is often written on amulets and on plaques displayed in the

synagogue, as well as in Jewish homes, a constant reminder of God's omnipresence.

LAWS AND CUSTOMS

It is said that the law was given to Moses at Mount Sinai on two stones, known as the Tablets of the Decalogue (the Ten Commandments), engraved by the finger of God. At the heart of Jewish belief is the Shema, the first commandment – love of God. The words of the Shema are written on tiny scrolls and placed in small boxes (tefillin), with straps or tapes attached to them. During weekday prayers, Orthodox Jewish males wear the tefillin bound to their foreheads, left arm and hands. Shema scrolls are also put into small boxes called "mezuzah", which are nailed to the doorways of the home (usually outside every room, except the bathroom and toilet), harking back to the time when the words of the Shema were carved into doorposts.

Typically, Orthodox Jewish men wear a small cap (yarmulke) to show their submission to God. The tallit is a fringed garment – usually a cloak or shawl – worn by male Jews. This refers to a passage from Numbers (15:38–39), which instructs that tassels with a blue cord should be attached to undergarments as a reminder of the commandments of God. Orthodox Jewish women are required to cover their hair in the presence of men other than their husband, as a sign that he alone may enjoy their sexuality; most achieve this by wearing a wig in public.

FESTIVALS

Jewish history and teaching is embodied in its festivals, in which traditions are passed on by means of stories, actions, symbolic food, and singing. There are five major festivals, or Days of Awe, laid down in the Torah: Rosh Hashanah (Jewish New Year), Yom Kippur (Day of Atonement), Pesach (Passover), Shavuot (Pentecost) and Sukkoth (the Feast of the Tabernacles), with many symbols connected to each.

Laws governing the consumption of food are a central part of the Jewish faith. During Pesach only unleavened bread (matzah) is eaten, as a reminder of the Exodus, when the Israelites had to leave Egypt in a hurry, with no time to bake ordinary bread. Bitter herbs symbolize slavery in Egypt, and a lamb bone symbolizes the Pesach offerings that would have been brought to the temple in Jerusalem.

The *shofar*, a ram's horn trumpet, is blown during Rosh Hashanah, a call for people to repent and start the new year afresh. This horn is a reminder of God's grace when he allowed Abraham to sacrifice a ram instead of Isaac. There are three main sounds blown on the *shofar*, and during Rosh Hashanah, they are repeated 100 times.

BELOW The Tetragrammaton spells the true name of God in Hebrew, which is never spoken aloud.

STAR OF DAVID

One of the most widely recognized signs of Judaism, today the Star of David is a symbol of the State of Israel, appearing since 1948 on its national flag. A six-pointed star formed from two interlocking triangles, it is said to derive from the hexagrammic shield that David carried against Goliath. The white of the upper triangle and the black of the lower triangle symbolize the union of opposites.

CHRISTIANITY

TRIQUETA

This geometrical shape is often used to express the Trinity. Comprising three interlocking arcs, the whole symbol signifies eternity, while the triangle-like shape at the centre represents the Trinity and its intangibility.

ABOVE The labarurm, or Chi-Rho cross

ABOVE Jesus crucified on the cross is a central Christian motif.

ABOVE One of the oldest secret symbols for Christ.

Together with Islam, Christianity is the most widespread of the world's religions. Emerging out of Judaism, it has many different traditions, but its central tenet is that the Jewish-born Jesus of Nazareth is the Son of God, the long-awaited Messiah whose coming was foretold by the Old Testament prophets. The life of Jesus, from his humble birth to the Virgin Mary to his crucifixion, death and resurrection, form the basis of Christian theology as told in the Gospels (meaning "good news") of the New Testament.

SYMBOLS OF CHRIST

Christianity takes its name from the Greek translation of the Hebrew "Messiah" (the Anointed One). Christ is the title Jesus was given by his followers and is symbolized in many ways.

The fish is one of the earliest Christian symbols, found on graves in the Roman catacombs – an ancient, secret meeting place when the Christians were persecuted by the Romans for their faith. It is based on an acrostic: the initial letters of the Greek words for Jesus Christ, Son of God and Saviour spell out ichthus, the Greek word for fish. Christ also referred to his apostles as "fishers of men", while the early Christian fathers called the faithful pisculi (fish).

Another of the earliest symbols for Christ is the labarurm, a monogram composed of the first Greek letters of Christ's name, X (chi) and P (rho). Also known as the Chi-Rho cross, the letters are usually inscribed one over the other, sometimes enclosed within a circle, becoming both a cosmic and a solar symbol. It is said that the Roman emperor Constantine I had a vision of the Chi-Rho cross promising victory to his army, after which he converted to Christianity. Byzantium, the capital of the Eastern Roman Empire, was renamed Constantinople (Istanbul) and became the centre of the Eastern Orthodox Christian Church.

Other symbols associated with Christ are objects linked to the Passion (or crucifixion). These include the cross on which he died, a crown of thorns, a scourge or whip, the hammer and nails used to fix him to the cross, a spear that the Roman soldiers used to pierce his side, and the ladder by which he was lowered from the cross. From the 14th century, these objects became the

BELOW Jesus the Good Shepherd carries a lamb back to the fold, a symbol of Christ as Saviour.

ABOVE The crown of thorns is a Christian symbol of the crucifixion.

focus of intense devotion among some Christians, designed to arouse an emotional response to Jesus' suffering.

SHEEP AND SHEPHERDS

Jesus drew heavily on his native land and culture for symbols to use in his teachings. For instance, many people in the region would have kept sheep, and the comparison between Jesus as a shepherd and his followers as his flock is a key metaphor.

In John's Gospel, Jesus is referred to as the Good Shepherd who will lead those who have gone astray back to a proper relationship with God, while he is also referred to as "the lamb of God", symbolizing the sacrifice he made, dying in order that humanity's sins may be forgiven. In Christian iconography, Jesus is often shown with a lamb draped over his shoulders, symbolizing his ability to save lost souls. He also carries a shepherd's crook, or crozier, which has been adopted by bishops of the Church and has become a symbol of their pastoral authority over their congregation, as well as a reminder of Jesus.

THE DOVE

In Judaic and Christian cultures, the dove holding an olive branch symbolizes God's grace. As punishment for humanity's wickedness, God had sent a great flood, symbol of destruction and also purification and cleansing. The righteous Noah was warned, and built an ark in which his family and a pair of every animal were saved. After the rain stopped, Noah sent out a dove to search for dry land. It returned, carrying an olive branch from the Mount of Olives, a symbol of God's forgiveness. In Christian iconography the dove is used to represent the Holy Spirit, with seven doves signifying the Holy Spirit's seven gifts.

THE TRINITY

Although Christianity is monotheistic, Christians believe that God shows himself in three different and distinct ways – as Father, Son and Holy Spirit. This threefold nature of God is known as the Trinity. Although each aspect of the Trinity is whole in itself, each is also part of God and the one Godhead. In the 5th century, Saint Patrick used the shamrock, a plant with one stem and three leaves, to try to explain the concept: just as each leaf is distinct, so each is also an integral part of the plant. According to John the Baptist, the Trinity was present at the baptism of Jesus: the Son in the water, the Father speaking words of approval from the heavens, and the Holy Spirit descending to Earth in the form of a dove.

THE VIRGIN MARY

Also known as the Madonna (Italian for "my lady"), the Virgin Mary is honoured as the chosen mother for God's holy son, particularly by the Roman Catholic Church. Mary is represented by a great variety of symbols, including the Madonna lily and white rose, which represent her purity, and the red rose (the Passion of Christ), as well as the sun, moon and a halo

of twelve stars, which appear to be linked to the apocalyptic vision described in Revelation (12:1) of a woman "robed with the sun, beneath her feet the moon, and on her head a crown of twelve stars". Other symbols of her sanctity and virginity include an enclosed garden, a closed gate and a mirror. She is usually shown with a halo (a symbol in Christian iconography for divinity and majesty) and wearing a blue cloak, the cloak signifying protection and its colour linking her with the skies and the heavenly realm, as well as with the waters of baptism. The Virgin also became a symbol herself, worshipped as the Divine Mother.

THE CHURCH

Although we use the word "church" to describe a building where Christian worship takes place, strictly speaking it means "group of believers", or those who gather together in the name of Jesus. Traditionally churches are built in the shape of a cross, the universal symbol of Christianity, a reminder of Jesus' death.

THE EUCHARIST

Most churches hold a service known as the Eucharist, also known as Mass or Holy Communion, to commemorate the Last Supper. This is the meal that Jesus shared with his twelve disciples the night before his arrest. Like the Last Supper, the Eucharist involves sharing bread and wine, representations of the flesh and blood of Christ, to symbolize taking Christ's body, or essence, within.

ABOVE An image of the Virgin Mary, showing her with a halo in which there are twelve stars. This picture depicts the immaculate conception, and Mary stands on a crescent moon, a symbol of chastity. She also wears the blue robes that link her with heaven.

THE FOUR EVANGELISTS

The writers of the first four books of the New Testament – Matthew, Mark, Luke and John – are known collectively as the four Evangelists. Apocalyptic visions in the Book of Revelation, as well as those of the Old Testament prophets Daniel and Ezekiel, associate Matthew with an angel, Mark with a lion, Luke with an ox and John with an eagle. In the Western Hermetic tradition, they are linked respectively with the Zodiac signs of Aquarius, Leo, Taurus and Scorpio, the four points of the compass, the four directions and the four elements, as well as the Archangels Raphael, Michael, Gabriel and Uriel.

ISLAM

ABOVE A detail from the Qur'an, the words themselves of which are believed to signify the divine presence.

ABOVE The star and crescent moon symbol is an emblem of the Islamic world.

The name Islam is from an Arabic word meaning "to submit", with a Muslim being "one who submits" – that is, one who lives in the way intended by Allah (God). As Allah is One, there is no division between the sacred and the secular, with every aspect of life governed by Islamic moral principles. The central tenet of Islam is that it is the original religion, the faith revealed to all the prophets, including Adam, Abraham, Moses and Jesus, but culminating with Mohammed, the

last and most important of Allah's divine messengers. Mohammed (or "the Prophet") was born in Makkah, Arabia (now in Saudi Arabia), in the 6th century AD. He is believed to have restored the purity of the teachings of Allah, so bringing Allah's message of guidance to the world to completion and perfection.

FIVE PILLARS OF ISLAM

Islam is built on five main beliefs: belief in Allah, in the Qur'an, in the angels, in Mohammed and the prophets who went before him, and in the Last Day. Muslims also believe that faith alone is meaningless but must be backed up by action in everyday life. These actions are known as "the five pillars of Islam" (a pillar symbolizing support) and are faith, prayer, fasting, pilgrimage and charity.

THE QUR'AN

The sacred text of Islam is known as the Qur'an (derived from the Arab word for "recite"). Muslims believe that this is Allah's own Word, not that of any human being, as directly transmitted to Mohammed over a period of 23 years through the Angel Jibril (Gabriel) in a series of visions. As Mohammed received each portion of the text, he learned it by heart, with Allah teaching him how to recite it.

The actual words of the Qur'an are seen to signify the divine presence of Allah, and so must be written clearly and carefully in the original Arabic; translations are never used in worship. Qur'anic calligraphy has

developed as a devotional art, with passages from the Qur'an used to decorate buildings and artefacts – figurative representations are not encouraged in Islam as they are considered tantamount to idolatry. Copies of the Qur'an are always handled with great care, and are kept on a high shelf, wrapped in a clean cloth. A stand is used to hold the book open while reading, and before handling the book, Muslims always make sure that their hands are clean.

THE MOSQUE

Muslims worship Allah in the mosque, or masjid (place of prostration), oriented towards Mecca – with its direction indicated by a mihrab, or niche in the wall. As Islamic sacred art is non-figurative, mosques are decorated with arabesques and geometric patterns, as well as calligraphy from the Qur'an. The patterns reflect the fundamental harmony of the universe and the natural world, derived from the Islamic belief that Allah is One. Although styles of mosque architecture and decoration vary according to local custom and period, many mosques have a domed roof representing the heavenly sky, the universe and creation, usually crowned by a minaret. Other characteristic features include an enclosing courtyard, walkways, and fountains (or showers) for the ablutions required by Islam. Shoes are not worn in the mosque, as they are regarded as unclean. Because Allah is

THE MINARET

The word "minaret" is derived from the Arabic *manara*, meaning "giving off light", alluding perhaps to its symbolic function as a beacon of illumination to the surrounding community. A minaret is a slim tower with a balcony from which the muezzin (caller) calls the faithful to prayer, a constant reminder of Allah's presence. The minaret itself suggests mediation between the people assembled in the mosque below and the heavens above to which it points. The crescent moon, one of the symbols of Islam, is sometimes positioned at the top of the minaret.

THE HAND OF FATIMA

Fatima was the daughter of Mohammed and his beloved wife Aisha. Although she is not mentioned in the Qur'an, the Shiite Muslim tradition gives her similar attributes to the Virgin Mary, referring to her as the "Mistress of the Women of the Worlds", the "Virgin" and the "Pure and Holy", and says that she was created from the light of Allah's greatness, or from the food of paradise. In popular religion, the faithful rely on Fatima, who takes the part of the oppressed in the struggle against injustice begun by her father. Shiite women travel to shrines dedicated to Fatima, where they pray for her help with their problems. Amulets known as "the hand of Fatima" are sacred and are worn for protection. The five fingers of the hand also symbolize the five pillars of Islam.

ANGELS

In Islam, angels are creatures of light who praise Allah and carry out his instructions. Jibril, chief of the angels, was responsible for bringing Allah's guidance to all the prophets, including Mohammed. Angels pray for human beings, especially believers, and support the faithful. Muslims believe that everyone has two angels whose task is to record that person's deeds for the Last Day.

everywhere, Islam teaches that the whole world is a mosque, so that the mosque itself can be thought of as a world symbol. The mosque is also regarded as a centre for education, and some of the great mosques of history have had schools and libraries attached to them.

RITUALS AND CUSTOMS

Mohammed decreed that "Cleanliness is part of faith", so before *salah* (prayer), worshippers must wash. This ritual cleansing, or *wadu*, is a symbolic act, the water not only washing the physical body but also cleansing the soul from sin. If water is unavailable, dry ablution using dust or sand is permissible.

In communal worship, Muslims stand side by side, symbolizing the equality of all in Allah's eyes. Men and women are separate, however, and the Iman, who leads the prayers, is in front. Parts of the Qur'an are recited, followed by a series of formal actions that include bowing and prostrating, (signs of submission to Allah). Special mats are used for prayer, and they are always rolled, not folded, after use.

Fasting plays an important part in Islam, and involves abstaining from food, drink and sex during the daytime. Muslims believe that fasting increases their awareness that they are always in Allah's presence, and many Muslims fast regularly on certain days all the year round. It is, however, essential for the whole month of Ramadan, the ninth month of the (lunar) Muslim calendar, which commemorates the time when the first words of the Qur'an were revealed to Mohammed. The end of Ramadan is marked by the new moon, when Muslims break their fast with a family feast.

PILGRIMAGE

Every year, millions of Muslims make their pilgrimage (*hajj*) to Mecca, Islam's holy city, a place so sacred that non-Muslims are not allowed to enter. The pilgrims stay in a huge encampment, and before entering the city, they set aside their normal clothes and put on a simple white garment, a sign of equality with others and humility before Allah.

When in Mecca, they pay homage to Islam's most holy structure, the Ka'aba (cube), the central focus of Muslim worship throughout the world. Standing in the courtyard of the Great Mosque in Makkah, the Ka'aba is a simple cube-shaped stone building that, according to tradition, is the first ever house built for the worship of Allah, rebuilt by Abraham and his son Ishmael. The Ka'aba symbolizes Allah's presence and is covered by a black velvet cloth called the *kiswah*, which is replaced each year. The cloth is a sign of humility and respect, because to gaze on the Ka'aba directly would be akin to looking at Allah, which is forbidden. It is embroidered in gold with passages from the Qur'an, especially on the part over the door – leading to the sacred interior. Reciting prayers, the pilgrims circle the Ka'aba seven times (a mystical number). Walking anticlockwise, they begin at the corner where the sacred Black Stone is embedded in a silver frame. The stone is believed to be a meteorite, a symbol of divine grace and power fallen from Heaven.

BELOW The Ka'aba in the courtyard of the Great Mosque at Mecca is one of Islam's most sacred and profound symbols.

Symbols in Society

Modern Western theories about the meaning and use of symbols have been greatly influenced by psychology, the scientific study of the human mind. Symbolism in dreams has been a subject of fascination since ancient times, but in the 19th century pioneering psychologists began to explore its use as a psychoanalytic tool. The meaning of a symbol in dreaming and psychoanalysis is not intrinsic in the thing itself, but relies on its cultural and historical context and can change over time and space.

RIGHT The mushroom formation of a nuclear explosion has many of the symbolic attributes of fire, but its social significance might include association with fear, dread, uncertainty and powerlessness.

FREUD AND JUNG

Sigmund Freud (1856–1939), who is often referred to as the "father of psychoanalysis", differentiated between the conscious and unconscious mind. His seminal work, *The Interpretation of Dreams* (1900), postulates that symbols are a product of the unconscious, typically produced while in the dreaming state as a way of communicating with the conscious self, or ego. A one-time pupil of Freud's, Carl Gustav Jung (1875–1961) broke away from his mentor, developing his theory of the "collective unconscious", a mythical level of the unconscious whose symbolism is archetypal rather than personal.

EROS AND THANATOS

Freud identified two coinciding and conflicting instinctual drives: *eros* and *thanatos*. Eros, or sexuality, is the drive of life, love and creativity; thanatos, or death, is the drive of aggression and destruction. The struggle between them is central to human life, with neuroses occurring when instinctual urges are denied (because they are painful or anti-social) and repressed in the unconscious mind. As products of the unconscious, symbols are a way of finding out more about these repressions.

SEXUAL SYMBOLISM

Put simply, anything that is erect or can penetrate, or resembles a phallus in any way, is a symbol of male sexuality. Freud remarks: "All elongated objects, such as sticks, tree trunks and umbrellas (the opening of these last being

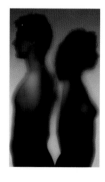

comparable to an erection), may stand for the male organ." Other examples could include mountains, tall buildings, trains, pens or bananas. Conversely, anything that can be entered, that is concealed, or resembles the vulva and/or vagina in any way is a symbol of female sexuality: for instance, valleys, caves, doorways, boxes, drawers, cupboards, fruit such as figs, or flowers such as roses. Female breasts are suggested by curving or round shapes, for instance domed buildings, rolling hills or any round fruit such as gourds or melons. However, Freud himself recognized that such things are not inevitably sexual symbols, and is reputed to have said: "Sometimes a cigar is just a cigar."

ANIMA AND ANIMUS

For Jung, male and female sexuality were expressions of deeper creative forces, referred to by him as the "animus" and "anima". The animus represents the male, or rational, side of the psyche and the anima the female, intuitive, side; the way they are symbolized varies. If one or the other is repressed, it can become destructive: a "negative animus" could lead to a rigid, controlled or controlling personality. It could also be experienced symbolically in dreams as a threatening male figure, or in waking life as fear of a male authority figure.

COMPENSATION

Jung saw the psyche as self-adjusting: trying to compensate for areas that are out of balance to reconcile its opposing parts.

When these are reconciled we are psychologically balanced and achieve a state of wholeness. He believed symbols could be used to explore the boundaries between oppositions, and in his clinical work he analyzed the symbols in his patients' dreams, seeing them as clues to their state of mind and indicators of their rate of progress.

THE LIFE PROCESS

Organic growth is fundamental to Jung's thinking, with the human organism designed to develop to psychological as well as physical maturity. Jung referred to this as "the process of individuation", with the symbols arising from the unconscious providing clues to the individual's current stage of mental and emotional development. This process is not something that can be brought about by conscious willpower, but just as a seed grows into a plant, is something that happens

SYMBOLIC STRUCTURES

Freud thought of the mind as having three conflicting internal tendencies: the *id* is the unconscious, seat of instinct and desire, the *ego* is the conscious self and the *superego* is an internalized self-critic. To avoid censorship by the super-ego, the id uses symbolic imagery to communicate with the ego. For Jung, the mind also has three main parts: the conscious mind; the personal unconscious, a storehouse of individual "memories"; and the collective unconscious.

ABOVE Carl Jung developed the theory of the collective unconscious, a layer of the mind that uses symbols to express universal human themes.

involuntarily, according to a predetermined pattern. Jung also believed that there was an organizing intelligence in each person's psychic system, the inventor and source of symbols. He referred to this as the Self, and saw it as both the nucleus and the totality of the psyche. Other

BELOW An atomic explosion symbolizes Freud's concept of thanatos, or the death wish.

cultures have also expressed an awareness of an inner centre: for instance, the Greeks referred to it as a *daimon*.

SIGNS AND SYMBOLS

Jung differentiated between signs and symbols, saying that a sign was always linked to the conscious thought behind it, and by implication was always less than the concept it represented. Symbols, on the other hand, always stood for more than their obvious and immediate meaning, hinting at something not yet known. He thought they were produced spontaneously in the unconscious, and were not something that could be created by conscious intent. He believed they occurred not only in dreams, but in all kinds of psychic manifestations, saying that thoughts and feelings, acts and situations can all be symbolic. He went so far as to say that even inanimate objects can appear to

"cooperate" with the unconscious in the arrangement of symbolic patterns, citing examples of well-authenticated stories of clocks stopping, pictures falling, or mirrors shattering at the moment of their owner's death.

ABOVE LEFT From a Freudian perspective, the soft rolling contours of a hilly landscape can symbolize the curvy shape of the female form.

A MULTI-STOREYED HOUSE

Jung frequently used the symbols generated by his own dreams to further his understanding of the psyche. For instance, he referred to his dream of exploring a house with several floors to describe the layers of the mind.

The dream began in a first-floor (US second-floor) room, a pleasant sitting room from the 18th century; the surroundings felt comfortable and reasonably familiar. On the ground (US first) floor, the rooms became darker and the furnishings much older, dating back to the 16th century or before. Becoming curious about what was in the rest of the house, he came upon a heavy door. Opening it, he went down to the cellar and found himself in a beautifully vaulted room that looked very ancient. Feeling very excited, he saw an iron ring on a stone slab and pulled it. Beneath the slab was a flight of stairs leading down to a cave, which seemed like a prehistoric tomb, containing skulls, bones and shards of pottery.

Jung thought the first floor related to his conscious self, the ground floor to the personal unconscious, the cellar to the collective unconscious, and the cave to the most primitive layer of the unconscious, bordering on the "animal soul".

ARCHETYPAL SYMBOLS

ABOVE Batman's heroism arises from his ability to integrate his "bat" or Shadow nature with his human nature.

The belief that there are patterns or tendencies organizing nature and human experience has been commonly held throughout human history and across world cultures. The pagan notion of *wyrd* as a preordained web of fate, the Aboriginal Dreaming, and every other mythological system, pantheon of gods or single deity presupposes the idea of an unseen influence behind everyday life. Carl Jung took this principle and developed a psychological theory of deep organizing patterns, or archetypes, shedding light on the shared source of symbolism throughout the world.

BELOW Sir Galahad, from Arthurian legend, represents the ability to be true to our inner nature, thus fulfilling the Holy Grail quest.

THE COLLECTIVE UNCONSCIOUS

Contrary to Freud, Jung believed that the symbols produced by the unconscious did not relate to personal material only. He noted a recurrence of certain symbolic imagery, and a similarity between many of the images he found and the symbols that appear in myth, religion and art, and esoteric traditions such as alchemy. Jung argued that symbolism plays an important role in the psychic processes that influence human life, containing information about human emotions and expressing profound spiritual truths.

JUNG'S ARCHETYPES

An archetype is a basic underlying pattern that gives an event symbolic meaning. Archetypes are not exactly motifs or symbols themselves, but are rather the deep-rooted tendencies or trends that influence symbol formation. Jung understood archetypal images to be grounded in the biology of the body and its organs, connecting us to our evolutionary history and our animal natures. He gave them names such as Anima, Animus, Self, Eros, Mother and Shadow.

Jung considered archetypes, operating at the level of the collective unconscious, to be common to all humanity, beyond the diversities of race, place or history, though the symbolism that arises from archetypal patterns varies: the anima and animus, for example, may appear as fairies and elves or gods and goddesses that are specific to each tradition or mythology.

Archetypes help us to understand common human experiences, such as birth, death, change or transformation, wholeness, growth and development, achievement or failure, wisdom and love.

THE SELF

Jung defined the wholeness for which all humans strive as the Self; it is often symbolized by the circle or the square. The Self is the goal of the individuation process, through which we become our true selves.

The quest for the Holy Grail, in Arthurian legend, can be seen as representing the Self: Sir Galahad finds the Grail and ascends to heaven, or fulfilment of his true nature. The symbol of the car or chariot commonly represents the journey to the Self, demonstrating where a person is on their life path in relation to their wholeness. A house can represent the structure of the Self, and other symbols of the Self include the hero and the mountain.

THE SHADOW

Aspects of a person's nature that are unconscious or not integrated, and which they regard as inferior or bad, are represented by the archetype described by Jung as the Shadow. They include unacceptable desires, undeveloped feelings or ideas, and animal instincts. Lived unconsciously, the Shadow appears as bad or evil figures in dreams or myths. In a dream, the Shadow might appear as a burglar of the same sex as the dreamer.

In cultures with restrictive

social codes, the Shadow compensates through becoming more prominent. Vampires are an image of the Shadow. Having a human appearance, they live in the darkness, with hidden desires, feeding on the blood of the living, and drawing power from what we call "normality".

THE MOTHER

Nurturing and protection are embodied in the Mother archetype. She gives life energy to her children, friends and community, and is also associated with reproduction and abundant growth in nature. The negative mother is domineering, interfering, jealous, and may take or destroy life. Some Jungians argue that a woman who is strongly connected with the Mother archetype must learn to nurture herself and her own creative life-force, in order to avoid becoming destructive.

The Mother archetype is found in goddesses of the earth and sky and other Great Mother figures. The Egyptian sky goddess, Nut, is a figure of overarching maternal protection. The Greek earth goddess Demeter (Roman Ceres) is associated with both motherhood and the harvest, and her principal symbols are barley and corn, crops essential to life. The maternal aspect of Mary is found in her manifestation as Queen of Earth.

The destructive aspect of the Mother archetype is more obvious in the Hindu goddess Kali, who is a destroyer but also a mother goddess of creation and protection. Witches in dreams

and fairy tales can also represent the negative aspect of the archetypal Mother. A witch may personify a jealous attitude that resists another person changing or developing for the better. She casts spells on people to hypnotize them, send them to sleep or trap them in a certain place, thus maintaining control. We may dream of witches at a time of transition, when it is hard to leave a certain way of life or belief system.

THE TRICKSTER

Wisdom within foolishness is represented by the archetype of the Trickster. He does not conform to the laws of the everyday world, and challenges authority. Clown figures are common to most cultures throughout the world. In Shakespearean drama, the fool, or court jester, is a recurring character, whose riddles and humour counterbalance the rigid authority of the ruler, indirectly offering him wisdom.

In Nigerian mythology, Edshu was a trickster god who took great delight in provoking arguments among members of a community. He would wear a hat that was red on one side and blue on the other, so that the people would argue about what colour hat he had on. Thus, while appearing to have a destructive effect, through his mischief he helped people to see that there was more than one way of looking at things.

TIMESPIRITS

The contemporary therapist Dr Arnold Mindell has used the word "timespirit" to describe the concept of archetypal roles and relationships that are not static but evolving. It presupposes that we live in a kind of field, like a magnetic field, which both organizes our experience and is influenced by our actions.

Mindell envisages an archetypal or mythical stream flowing through the world, whose flow and direction changes over time. Particular roles that are relevant to a culture, region and history arise, make themselves known within everyday life, then fall away. We are said to be immersed in this stream, and at one time or another we are carried by particular roles or spirits, which touch us personally but are also part of the greater stream.

The concept formalized in such theories, of dreamlike or mythical patterns underlying everyday life experience, suggests that symbolic processes are calling on us to be lived consciously and with awareness. One way of understanding this is that behind every human conflict there are mythical stories trying to unfold.

DREAM SYMBOLISM

According to Jung, the totality of a person's dream life represents their potential for individuation. As we respond to our personal world of symbolism, we travel along a path that leads to self-realization, or the Self, Jung's archetype of wholeness.

THE LIFE-MYTH

The Self has parallels in the inner *daimon* of the Greeks, the *genius* of the Romans and the ancient Egyptians' Ka (the spirit or life-force that was created with an individual, and reunited with them at death); in more primitive cultures the idea of a guiding or accompanying spirit is seen in the totemic animals and plants that protect members of a clan. The Naskapi Indians, from the Labrador peninsula, believe their soul is an inner companion called Mista'peo (or "Great Man"), who resides in their heart and after death is thought to reincarnate in another being. They find their way in life by following guidance given to them in dreams.

Childhood dreams are said to contain patterns that are symbolic of our life-myth or path. They commonly portray the everyday personality being threatened and overwhelmed by a powerful mythical figure such as a witch, a Yeti, or a wave, representing aspects of our wholeness that will be met during the course of our lives. For example, a girl may suffer frightening dreams in which she is pursued by a witch, but encouraging her to play at being a witch herself may help her conquer her fears by finding new feminine powers of her own.

The life-myth is the fundamental pattern, or mythic potential, that informs and organizes a person's life path. Dr Arnold Mindell refers to this mythic potential as the "Big You", which underpins the twists and turns of our lives. Every difficulty in life, such as a relationship break-up, chronic physical symptoms, addiction or the loss of a role or identity, would therefore be connected to the life myth. The challenge to the everyday self, or "Little You", is to take the heroic challenge and wrestle with the Big You until it becomes an ally and will give up its secrets.

AMPLIFICATION TECHNIQUES

A great deal of focus has been given to the interpretation of signs and symbols according to our rational understanding and knowledge of their meaning. But, approached more holistically, it becomes evident that a deeper understanding of the signs and symbols of the psyche will involve not only our minds but also the wisdom of our bodies and nature. Amplification refers to focusing on symbolic content, whether in dreams, the imagination, in our bodies or in nature, and strengthening the experience so that it can unfold, allowing its wisdom to flower.

JUNG'S ACTIVE IMAGINATION

Active imagination is a psychological tool that can help towards achieving wholeness or individuation. It involves direct contact or confrontation with the unconscious, without the need for tests and interpretations.

When a patient is in analysis, the first stage involves some degree of "symbol transference", in which the patient unconsciously transfers symbolic content on to the therapist, who holds these projections until the patient is ready to integrate them. For example, the therapist may represent a negative or positive mother, father or authority figure for the patient; through the therapeutic relationship, the patient can learn to integrate the qualities that have been projected.

Jung once said that stepping into dreams and using active imagination is the essential second half of analysis, and that without active imagination one could never become truly independent of a psychotherapist.

The basic approach of active imagination is to sit down alone as free as possible from disturbance, concentrating on whatever comes from the unconscious. Often an image or sound will arise in this situation, which must then be prevented from sinking back into the unconscious: this may be achieved by representing it in drawing or painting, writing it down, or possibly expressing it in movement or dance.

A more indirect approach to active imagination is to write stories about another person; this process inevitably brings the storyteller's unconscious into play. Jung also spoke of having conversations with the personified voices of the unconscious, as a later stage of active imagination. At a time when he was in a particularly low point in his life, and was feeling depressed, Jung said he had long and deep conversations with a wise inner figure called Philemon, from whom he felt he had received great insights.

Jung viewed active imagination in many respects as replacing the importance of dreaming, in that it was a direct contact with, and

amplification and expression of, the archetypes. In his latter years, Jung spent a great deal of time engaged in active imagination, playing in the sand and carving stone sculptures at his home in Bōllingen, Switzerland.

PROCESS AMPLIFICATION

Inspired by Jung's approaches to amplification, Dr Arnold Mindell developed a more explicit approach to amplifying dreamlike information as it occurs in different channels of perception.

As individuals we have preferred, or "occupied", channels of perception (or senses), and less preferred, or "unoccupied", channels. Some people think and perceive physical sensations primarily in pictures, while others interpret the world in words. If a person tends to perceive the world through vision or through sound and words, then they have occupied visual or auditory channels. A person who naturally favours "feeling" or movement is said to occupy the proprioceptive or kinaesthetic channels of perception. In each case other

channels will be relatively unoccupied. The information that does occupy these channels tends to disturb us, and yet at the same time it can have meaningful symbolic content, pointing to less-known aspects of ourselves.

THE SENOI TEMIARS

For some cultures, the amplification of dream symbols is second nature. The Senoi Temiars of northern Malaysia place great value upon dream-life, and the exploration and expression of this dream-life is used to further the social life and projects of the community. They use a playful form of trance dance and community singing in order to connect with and amplify dream material.

The Senoi Temiars also encourage the telling of dreams at breakfast time, and if a child is fearful of a dream, for example a dream in which they are falling, the parents will help the child to learn to dream lucidly, so that they can control the course of the dream – they can then change the uncontrolled falling into controlled flight.

ABOVE The dreams of young adults and children, whether benign or malign, are believed to contain patterns that symbolize our life path.

THE JEWEL IN THE WOUND

Rose-Emily Rothenberg used active imagination to work with a serious skin disorder that she had had from childhood. She described how she remodelled herself through creative play. Initially she viewed the scars on her body as an inferior part of her, which she wished to have removed, however, over time she began to relate to the scars as "stars" or jewels, guides to parts of her that she felt were out of control and in pain.

MEANING AND CONNECTION

ABOVE Street signs use a "visual shorthand" of pictures, letters and numbers to convey practical information.

TOP For motorists throughout the world, a red traffic light is the universal symbol for "stop".

RIGHT There are many different words for "cat", each suggesting a slightly different meaning.

In the 20th century, theories began to be developed about the meaning and origins of signs and symbols in human society. The American philosopher Charles Sanders Pierce (1839–1914) and the Swiss linguist Ferdinand De Saussure (1857–1913) were the founding fathers of semiotics, the philosophical study of signs and sign systerms, and the way in which meaning is produced and exchanged within a culture.

SEMIOTICS

Pierce referred to three types of signs: "iconic" signs, or those that clearly represent the objects they depict (for instance, a road sign showing the silhouette of a car and a motorcycle); "indexical" signs, which represent concepts that we have learned to associate with a particular sign (for instance, smoke is an index of "fire"); and "symbolic" signs, whose meanings are determined by convention and do not resemble the original object to which they refer (for instance, the international symbol for nuclear waste – three black triangles in a circle on a yellow background – or a red traffic light to indicate "stop"). Pierce noted that as people view the world through the filter of personal and cultural experience, the same symbol can hold different meanings for different people.

Pierce's contemporary, De Saussure, applied this theory more specifically to language, which is itself a system of signs that endeavours to communicate information and meaning. De Saussure identified two parts of a sign: the "signifier" (the actual sign itself) and the "signified" (the conceptual meaning ascribed to it, which is arrived at by cultural convention). For instance, the letter formation c-a-t (the signifier) in the English language describes a furry animal with four legs, a tail and whiskers, that purrs and miaows (the signified). The signifier is a symbolic sign: the same letter formation could just as easily be used to represent anything else, while to a non-English speaker, it may mean nothing at all.

CULTURAL CONVENTIONS

While this may seem obvious, for De Saussure the implications were profound, extending far beyond the reaches of simple word formations. He argued that the signs we use may appear to be arbitrary, but in fact embody cultural ideologies and values that we then come to think of as "norms". This view shifted the emphasis away from the notion that there is some kind of objective reality "out there" to the idea that "reality" is always encoded, that the way we perceive and make sense of the world is through the codes of our own culture.

De Saussure also pointed out that meanings operate within a paradigm; we choose signs from a whole range of alternatives. To use the earlier example again, there are several alternative signifiers – puss, pussy, moggy, puss-cat, kitty – that we could use instead of "cat", each one of which confers a slightly different nuance of meaning. Semioticians such as De Saussure have argued that we live among and relate not to physical objects and events, but to systems of signs with meanings. These meanings are not "natural" or inevitable but are embedded in our social structure and value systems.

STRUCTURALISM

De Saussure had examined language as a structure, arguing that this method could equally be applied to any system of making meaning: a set of signals or codes, such as the rules of a game; a tribal or community ritual (a wedding, a rain dance, a funeral); "fashion" (in clothes, food and possessions); and the visual arts, literature, advertising and cinema.

De Saussure's work had far-reaching implications, within not only linguistics, but also the study of all communication. It influenced sociology and was taken up by the leading proponents of the Structuralist movement, the anthropologist Claude Lévi-Strauss (b.1908) and the philosopher Roland Barthes (1915–80).

De Saussure had asserted that a signifying system is any structure

ABOVE Structuralism examines how our perceptions are formed by sets of signals, this image rocker signal either beauty or danger.

or system or organization that creates meaning out of cultural signs. As an anthropologist, Lévi-Strauss applied these ideas to kinship systems, cultural organizations and myth, while Roland Barthes explored contemporary Western cultural "signs", particularly in the realms of food, advertising and clothing.

KINSHIP SYSTEMS

Lévi-Strauss came to the conclusion that regardless of content, all systems of cultural organization share the same fundamental structures. One of these is kinship: every society has had some system for deciding who can marry whom, who can inherit what and from whom, and how these relationships are named. A kinship system is a structure that contains units (men, women and children) who are labelled (fathers, mothers, children), with rules for connecting them; this can be represented visually as a genealogical chart.

Kinship systems structure how

goods, people and ideas are "exchanged" within a culture; for example, family groups may "give" women to another family in exchange for something of value (a dowry). Lévi-Strauss insisted that relationships within the structure occur in pairs, which are either similar or opposite. In his book *The Raw and the Cooked* (1964), Lévi-Strauss argues that binary pairs, particularly opposites, form the basic structure of human culture (man and woman, for instance) and ways of thought (good and evil). He notes that in every pair, one is favoured – the "cooked" (culture and civilization) is better than the "raw" (natural and "primitive"), good is preferred to evil, light to dark, and male (in many cultures) to female.

ABOVE A wedding, like any other social ritual, has its own set of rules or signals that are similar to the rules or signals of a language.

Like Jung, Lévi-Strauss was also interested in explaining why myths from different cultures seemed so similar. Rather than looking at their content, however, Lévi-Strauss applied a structural analysis, arguing that structure is what they share. He argued that like language, a myth is made of units that are put together according to certain rules or conventions (such as repetition, for example or the telling of the story in layer after layer). He went on to say that these units form relationships with each other, based on binary pairs or opposites, which provide the basis of the structure.

BELOW Fast food is a hallmark of modern society, while fresh fruit and vegetables symbolize natural goodness and are associated with health.

MYTHOLOGIES

Between 1954 and 1956, Roland Barthes produced a series of 54 articles on a variety of subjects for a French left-wing magazine. Collectively entitled "Mythologies", they provide insights into Barthes' ideas about the construction of meaning, especially in popular culture – films, advertising, newspapers and magazines, photography, cars, children's toys and popular pastimes. Barthes was fascinated by the meaning of things that surround us in everyday life and wanted to challenge their seeming "innocence" and "naturalness". For instance, a sports car and an unpretentious family vehicle share the same functional utility – they are both means of transport – but they connote different things about their owners. It was these secondary signals that Barthes explored, concerned to analyse what he referred to as the "myths" that circulate in contemporary society and that construct the world and our place in it.

ROLES AND RELATIONSHIPS

ABOVE Cigarette smoking by western women in the early 20th century was associated with women's growing independence and equality.

BELOW The symbolism of the veil has varied in different times and places according to social, religious and political conditions.

Social-role theory of the 1960s showed that in any community various roles tend to arise. The successful functioning of the community relies upon the interactions of all these roles, and each one is defined in terms of its relation to all the other roles. Each role is a living symbol of the cultural values of the community.

As societies have become more complex, so too have the role structures within them. In modern societies it is increasingly that an individual will occupy true multiple roles, over time and

even simultaneously. A great deal of symbolism is used in defining human roles and role changes, making use of such pointers as uniform, social behaviour or symbolic rites and rituals marking role transition.

Early role theory described roles as social constructs determined by social expectations and the values that needed to be fulfilled within a community. Culturally defined gender roles, particularly, were seen to govern family and occupational activities. More recent theories suggest that roles are also determined by field patterns in nature; they recognize "ghost roles", which, though not explicit, represent undercurrents of feeling in a community.

AGE AND GENDER

In societies where survival is not a given, roles tend to be fewer in number and clearly delineated by gender and age. In more complex societies there is more variation of roles, and more specialization. Complex societies tend to have a greater need of symbols such as uniforms, conventions or rules of conduct to frame the roles.

In the Native American Comanche society, a hunting and warrior people, a boy was expected to be aggressive and to seize what was his. But as he grew older his role changed towards eldership, and he was expected to settle disputes and avoid making enemies unnecessarily. His role became one of wisdom, gentleness and endurance.

In patriarchal societies throughout the world, women and children have held less

privileged roles than men, with consequential fights for the rights of both women and children. The 19th-century American reformer Elizabeth Cady Stanton wore Turkish trousers instead of a restricting crinoline; they were taken up by, and named after, Amelia Bloomer, who promoted them as a symbol of the women's rights movement.

The emancipation of women in Iran has been a complex process in which clothing has also been a central symbol. Women came to the fore during the anti-Shah movement, during which their black veils became revolutionary symbols. Upon establishing an Islamic republic, the veil once again became a part of the state's definition of women. Modern Islamist feminists are now trying to differentiate between patriarchal tradition and the values of Islam, with the veil now a complex symbol, often meaning different things to different people, affected by religion, culture or gender.

Many North American tribes honoured the role of the *berdache*, a man or woman whose gender identity differed from his or her sex. Berdaches symbolized spiritual power, were natural "go-betweens" in gender disputes, and were consulted by tribal elders, as they were thought to be connected to the Great Spirit.

RANK AND PRIVILEGE

All societies have systems of rank and associated privileges that are related to the predominant values and beliefs of the culture. Among the Iban of Borneo, for example,

BOTTOM RIGHT A common theme in the discrimination against gypsies is that their differences make them inferior to settled societies.

RIGHT Michael Jordan has been an important role model for young black men, particularly in the United States of America.

the witch doctor works with the extremes of society, with life and death and the healing of the sick, interacting directly with the spirit world. His role gives him a high rank in the tribe, represented by his elegant feathered headdresses, jewellery and masks.

Sometimes ranking systems are in place for the good of the whole society, and at other times they represent biases within the society, in favour of some people and opposing others. Gypsies have suffered discrimination worldwide, and studies show how they have been subtly ranked as "other" and therefore inferior, by associating them with animals. In India, the Hindu caste system rigidly defines the roles and interactions in traditional society, prohibiting marriage, socialization or even physical contact between members of different castes.

ROLE PLAY AND ROLE MODELS

People need positive role models in order to find the path of their own development. Through role play and role modelling children are able to learn about the roles they are growing into by playing them out in games.

Social learning theory teaches that a major part of child development occurs through role models. The child observes that a role model, often of the same sex, is successful or rewarded in society for their behaviour. The child then adopts the characteristics of the model, and finally identifies more fully with the characteristics of the role, which become his or her own.

Public figures often serve as role models, usually for other people of the same sex, gender, race or physical ability. The outstanding basketball player Michael Jordan, for example, serves as a powerful role model to black boys in America. Celebrities may become legends or icons when they come to symbolize or model specific values for other people's lives. The role model symbolizes what a young person (or an adult) might aspire to. But while many role models are famous people, some of the most important role models may be found within our personal circle: they may be parents, older siblings or other family members, teachers or friends.

CHANGING ROLES

Roles and their symbolism change within the bounds of a culture as its values shift. In Western society, it has been traditional for a woman getting married to wear engagement and wedding rings, and adopt her husband's surname to indicate her changed role. In recent decades, however, these customs have ceased to be universal, and new symbols of marriage are emerging. Women no longer automatically change their surname and couples now wear matching rings as symbols of mutual and equal commitment.

Roles may change gradually, mirroring cultural trends, or their overturning may define an abrupt or violent change, such as the deposition of a monarch during a revolution, or the transformation of intellectuals into farm labourers during China's Cultural Revolution in the 1970s.

TABOOS

ABOVE In this 8th-century banner of the Buddha preaching, he is insulated from touching the ground, as if his spiritual energy would be drained away by contact with the earth.

BELOW Lot's daughters, believing that all other men had been destroyed, felt forced to disregard the taboo of incest and trick their father into having sex with them by getting him drunk.

The word "taboo" comes from the Polynesian *tabu*, which is a system of prohibiting actions or the use of objects because they are considered either sacred or dangerous, unclean or accursed. Taboos may emerge from a moral consciousness and motivate individual and collective moral conscience, but they may also be used to maintain social hierarchies and order.

In animist and nature-based societies, the origin of taboos probably relates to the likes and dislikes of the various levels of spirits in relation to one another. In later cultures, taboos relate more to the people's attempts to appease their gods and goddesses. Within contemporary society, the word taboo has less spiritual significance, and more generally refers to things that are not allowed or not done within society for various social reasons.

PROTECTING DIVINITY

In many cultures, royalty has been seen as divine, and royal individuals have been protected from mundane reality by never being required to touch the ground. They would be carried on the backs or shoulders of others, on an animal or in a carriage, or would walk on carpets specially laid for them.

Montezuma, the Aztec emperor of Mexico, was always carried by his noblemen and never once set foot on the ground. Early kings and queens of Uganda never set foot outside the beautiful enclosures within which they lived. The king of Persia walked on carpets upon which only he could tread. Even today there is a worldwide custom of rolling out a red carpet for royalty on ceremonial occasions.

INCEST TABOOS

Incest – having sexual relations with someone who is a close relation – is a form of taboo that is found worldwide, probably because of the genetic defects it often leads to. Native American and Chinese cultures extend the idea of incest to having relations with people with the same family name. However, gods and royalty are often exempt in order to keep the royal or divine blood pure. While Freud interpreted incest

literally, and sexuality as a potentially dangerous force requiring taboo to avoid its dangers, Jung viewed incest as a symbolic image referring to the attempt of the individual to return to the mother's womb to be reborn.

Incest is a common mythological theme among gods, goddesses and royalty, and particularly in societies that are focused on maintaining their supremacy. When rulers are seen as divine, marrying someone outside the family would sully the pure royal blood. The Egyptian goddess Isis married her brother Osiris. Queen Cleopatra herself was the result of seven generations of brother–sister marriages. In the Old Testament Lot's daughters have sex with their father because there is no other male available to impregnate them. Inca rulers were allowed to marry their sisters.

GENDER TABOOS

In the traditional Kung Bushman society of the Kalahari, where living conditions are very harsh, social roles are strongly divided according to gender. The men hunt, and make weapons and fire, and the woman build a shelter for the family, prepare food, keep the fire and keep the house in order. The separation of their roles is emphasized by assigning different sides of the fire for where men and women should sit. If a woman sits in a man's place, it is thought she will succumb to a mysterious illness, and if the man sits on the woman's side of the fire, his hunting powers might be

lessened. It is also thought that if women touch a man's weapons, his power will lessen.

TABOO FOOD AND ANIMALS

In many cultures it has been believed that spirits could enter or possess inanimate objects, which then become objects of worship, or fetishes. When edible fruits or plants became fetishes they became taboo as food. As an example, the Levantine peoples never ate apples because they believed them to be inhabited by a nature spirit. Animals that were capable of eating human flesh would become a fetish; thus the dog became a taboo animal for the Parsees. Eating apes and monkeys is taboo in many societies because their appearance is similar to that of humans. Both the Phoenicians and the Jews considered the serpent a channel for evil spirits.

In ancient Egypt, animals were worshipped and cared for as vessels of good or evil powers. Their gods were considered incarnate in particular species, which were then protected by taboo. Like Jews and Moslems, they considered the pig an unclean animal, possibly because of its habit of scavenging. It was thought that if a pig was touched in passing, the person should immediately plunge themself in water for purification. Egyptian swineherds were considered of low caste and were not allowed to enter temples.

The cow is considered sacred in Hindu India, where it is a living symbol of motherhood due to its ability to produce milk. The feeding of the cow is therefore an act of worship. The majority of Hindus are vegetarian, and it is particularly taboo to kill or eat cows. As a result they may commonly be seen wandering the streets undisturbed. Even the urine from a cow is seen as sacred, and is sometimes used in purification rituals for people who have transgressed a taboo.

In societies where animals take on the role of totems, there are taboos against people eating or killing animals to whose totem clans they belong. In identifying with the animal, a person becomes a relative or guardian of the animal. However, another member of the community with a different animal familiar may freely hunt and eat the animal. The Euahlayi people of New South Wales and southern Queensland believe that a child who eats their own animal familiar by accident will become sick: in the case of taboo plains bustard or turkey eggs, this could result in the loss of sight, while eating taboo kangaroo flesh could cause their skin to break out in sores and their limbs to wither. However, while it is taboo for the Euahlayi to eat their animal familiar, it is acceptable to eat the totem animal of their clan.

MENSTRUATION TABOOS

Within patriarchal societies, menstruation has commonly been taboo, both in the ancient and the modern world. However, in matriarchal societies, which revered the female body, menstruation was considered a powerful and healing process. It has also been associated with great feminine powers. The menstrual cycle and the cycles of the moon were measured in pre-patriarchal times on wooden sticks that historians have called "calendar sticks". One possible origin of the menstruation taboo may be the fear that women could control the tides and seasonal changes through the monthly cycles of their bodies.

The Jews of the ancient world believed that menstrual blood had poisonous qualities. The Old Testament includes a prohibition against contact with it: Leviticus records that Moses received word from God that a man who sleeps with a menstruating woman should be cut off from his people, and that menstruating women are unclean for seven days.

Freud related the menstrual taboo to a negative view of women, whereas Bruno Bettelheim suggested that both the ability to bear children and to menstruate evoked intense envy in men, who created taboos in an attempt to make the sexes more equal. Feminists have called this "womb envy", partly as a protest against Freud's theory that women suffer "penis envy".

ABOVE For Hindus it is taboo to kill or eat a cow.

TOP The apple, a Judaeo-Christian forbidden fruit.

GROUP IDENTITY

ABOVE Every detail of a flag is symbolic – its colour, pattern and design, and motifs.

FLEUR-DE-LYS

Most commonly associated with French royalty and the right to rule France, the fleur-de-lys (lily flower) has three petals, standing for both the Holy Trinity and the triple majesty of God, creation and royalty.

Symbolism has always been used to denote identity and to confirm adherence to social groups or "families", the basic units of society. Whether based on shared beliefs or common interests and activities, all organized groups – whether at a local, regional, national or international level – have their own symbols of identity. These may be in the shapes of totems, banners, flags or standards, or expressed through dress codes or through the observance of certain ritualized forms of behaviour. One of the important features of such symbolism is its visibility: it is designed to provide an instantly recognizable sign of group identity, a way of codifying and structuring social relations, of creating a distinction between who's "in" and who's "out", and to stir an emotional response, such as fear, respect, humility or pride, in all who see it.

LEADERSHIP

When people started to form large groups to live and hunt together, a leader was appointed to rule them and settle disputes. As a mark of office, a leader might wear a ceremonial headdress and hold a long decorated staff, rod or spear, topped with an emblem. The staff was also used as a visible sign to rally around or to point out the direction of a march or attack. These early "flags" are known as vexilloids, and originally were made of wood, feathers and other animal pieces (bones, horns, skins). Aztec vexilloids, for instance, made extensive use of green quetzal feathers, and were decorated with precious metals such as gold, silver and copper, and precious stones. Today tribes in New Guinea use vexilloids that consist mostly of wood and dried grass, with emblems of painted wood, feathers and bits of cloth.

FLAGS

In China the invention of silk fabric led to the creation of banners, which were easier to carry and more visible from a distance than vexilloids. From China, the use of fabric flags spread to Europe, where they were first used as military and ceremonial signs, but later as a way of identifying rulers, their domains and nationality at sea. The 17th century saw the introduction of standardized regimental colours, war ensigns, jacks (the square flags hoisted up the "jackstaff" on a ship) and the house flags of the trading companies (a precursor of the modern logo). The first national flags on land appeared in the last quarter of the 18th century. During the 19th and 20th centuries, a host of other flags also appeared: of government agencies and officials; provincial flags; rank flags in all branches of the armed forces; and flags of schools, universities, scientific institutions, organizations, political parties, trades unions and guerrilla movements. There are also flags of ethnic groups, business corporations and sporting clubs.

All the elements of a flag are symbolic – its colours, motifs and overall design – and there are many customs surrounding flag etiquette. For instance, in a military parade, flags are saluted when being hoisted, lowered or passed; flying a flag at half-mast is a sign of mourning; a pall flag laid over a coffin, used mainly at government and military funerals, is a symbol of national respect for the deceased; desecrating a flag is a punishable offence in most countries of the world.

TRIBE AND NATION

In traditional societies, clans and tribes have used a variety of symbolic devices to distinguish one group from another. For instance, among many Native

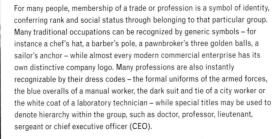

OCCUPATIONS AND PROFESSIONS

For many people, membership of a trade or profession is a symbol of identity, conferring rank and social status through belonging to that particular group. Many traditional occupations can be recognized by generic symbols – for instance a chef's hat, a barber's pole, a pawnbroker's three golden balls, a sailor's anchor – while almost every modern commercial enterprise has its own distinctive company logo. Many professions are also instantly recognizable by their dress codes – the formal uniforms of the armed forces, the blue overalls of a manual worker, the dark suit and tie of a city worker or the white coat of a laboratory technician – while special titles may be used to denote hierarchy within the group, such as doctor, professor, lieutenant, sergeant or chief executive officer (CEO).

ABORIGINAL FLAG

The flag of the Australian Aboriginals, officially adopted in 1995, is divided horizontally in two equal parts, a band of black on top and a band of red underneath, with a yellow disc at the centre. The black band represents the Aborigines, whose ancestors have lived in Australia for more than 40,000 years; the red band stands for the earth and the blood spilled by the aboriginal people in defence of their land; while the yellow disc at the horizon line symbolizes the life-giving sun.

Americans totems (natural objects, such as animals) are used to represent particular lodges and tribes, as well as individuals, while each clan of the Scottish Highlanders has its own tartan (a type of checked fabric) design. In medieval heraldry, most European rulers adopted coats of arms and armorial banners bearing one of the two most important heraldic figures: the lion (king of beasts) or the eagle (king of Heaven). The fleur-de-lys, another frequent heraldic motif, was particularly associated with the French court; it was later adopted by the international Boy Scout movement. Today many nations continue to be associated with a particular emblem: for instance, the USA with the bald-headed eagle, Canada with the maple leaf and England with the Tudor Rose.

There are also many nations without statehood (for instance in the USA there are more than 550 federally recognized nations and tribes) who have their own emblem of identity. For instance, eleven Sioux tribes living in South Dakota share a common white flag. The flag's central compass emblem symbolizes the Native American Medicine Wheel (and the four directions, the four seasons and the four elements) and is surrounded by eleven tepees, representing the number of tribes. There are also many groups within mainstream society who have chosen a symbol to identify themselves. For instance, in the West, the colour pink has been adopted by gay people, black by some racial and political groups, and green by the environmental movement.

POLITICS AND REBELLION

Political groups, rebellions and revolutions have always been associated with particular symbols. At the end of the 15th century, German peasants rebelled under a white pennant with the emblem of a golden peasant shoe, the Bundschuh, which in contrast to the boots worn by the nobility was a symbol of peasantry. Communism and fascism, two of the most influential political movements of the 20th century, also both made use of symbols. The symbol of communism was the hammer and sickle, representing the alliance between industrial and agricultural workers; for most of the 20th century, the hammer and sickle was the emblem of the Russian flag and the world's first communist state.

Fascism is a nationalist movement led by a dictator. It is named after the "fasces" symbol that was worn as a badge by the Italian dictator Benito Mussolini (1883–1945). The fasces comprised a bundle of birch or elm rods, bound by a red cord, sometimes wrapped around an axe, a symbol of justice, scourging and decapitation. It dates back to ancient Rome, when it was carried by lictors, officials who had the power to pronounce sentence. Hitler, however, used a different symbol for his fascist Nazi party: the swastika.

THE SWASTIKA

Hitler adopted the swastika, an ancient solar symbol with many profound meanings, as the sign for the Nazi party. The distinctive black sign in a white circle against a red background became the German national flag in 1935, and the emblem was used in many different places – including on children's toys – to promote Nazi propaganda and instil allegiance to Hitler. Today, some neo-Nazi groups continue to use the swastika or a three-legged variation as an emblem of identity.

ABOVE The hammer and sickle is a communist symbol, standing for the union of industrial and agricultural workers.

TOP The word fascism is derived from "fasces", the bundle of rods carried by Roman officials.

ABOVE The mermaid embodies a deep connection between woman and the sea.

BELOW Noah's Ark, a symbol of man's faith and hope when faced with life-destroying disaster.

From the earliest times, human beings have used stories to describe things they could not explain otherwise. Such stories attempt to answer some of the most fundamental questions about human existence – about why we are here and where we are going, about the nature of the world around us and how we fit into it.

Every culture has formulated its own poetic visions and sacred narratives – the metaphorical understandings that we refer to as myths. The word "myth" is derived from the Greek *mythos*, meaning word or story, but it has come to stand for a narrative that helps to explain the origin and character of a culture in symbolic terms. The meaning and content of such stories will vary across time and place, and from person to person, but one of the functions of myth is to celebrate the ambiguities and contradictions at the heart of human existence.

THE STORYTELLER

Long before myths were written down, they were transmitted by word of mouth. In order to survive the passage of time, they had to be presented as good, memorable stories, appealing to one generation after another, possibly evolving to adapt to new social needs. Storytelling could take place almost anywhere – in the home, in the marketplace or at the royal court – and traditionally the art of storytelling was highly valued, since it was the means by which a culture's social codes and values, its

ancestral lineage and history, and its connection to the divine were kept alive. The storyteller played a vital role in the community, sometimes as an official of a royal or noble court, sometimes as a wandering minstrel who travelled from place to place, delivering stories that were entertaining and instructive. Many religious figures, including Jesus and Mohammed, used storytelling as a vehicle for their teachings.

STORYTELLING RITUALS

The style or protocol of storytelling varies from culture to culture. In many traditional African societies, the audience feels free to interrupt, make criticisms or suggest improved versions to the storyteller. Throughout Africa, a common storytelling form is the "call and response", whereby a "caller" raises a "song" and the chorus in the community participate and respond to the call.

When the San people of the Kalahari tell stories about particular animals, they mimic the formation of the animals' mouths, pronouncing their words as the animals might, as a way of keeping in touch with and honouring the spirit of the animal. Smoking a pipe and passing it from person to person is often a part of storytelling rituals among Native American peoples, such as the Algonquin. According to the Algonquin, "if we cease sharing our stories, our knowledge becomes lost". In many parts of the world today, people are rediscovering the

THE VALKYRIE

In Norse myth, the Valkyries were supernatural women, death angels who hovered over the battlefields granting victory or defeat to warriors. After death, they took the spirits of the valiant slain to Odin's realm of Valhalla.

power of storytelling to make sense of their lives and to keep the connection with their cultural and ancestral lineage alive.

MYTHIC THEMES

Questions about life and death are explored through myth, and stories of the origins and the end of the world can be found in all cultures. Creation myths refer to a primal chaos, symbolized in many cultures as a watery, dark and mysterious place. Myths also anticipate the destruction of the world in a catastrophic event – such as the Norse cataclysm Ragnarok – while many refer to an earlier time when the world was nearly destroyed by a deluge. The Biblical story of Noah is the best-known example; in a similar Mesopotamian tale, Utnapishtim, a wise man who alone survived the flood, was made an immortal.

Typically, myths are tales of divine and semi-divine beings – gods and goddesses, heroes and heroines – archetypal figures who act out the struggle between good and evil, exploring moral conflicts and powerful human emotions such as desire and greed, jealousy and lust, ambition, love and hate. Notions of an underworld and an afterlife, as well as a magical otherworldly realm, are common, and animals with extraordinary powers helping humankind feature in many myths.

ANIMALS IN MYTH

Mythologies from around the world feature animals in one form or another, and they have often been deified. In ancient Egypt, shrines were set up for the worship of sacred beasts such as the Ram of Mendes and the Bull of Apis, while at one time, cobras and vultures were the prime deities of Lower and Upper Egypt respectively. In Africa, particular tribes and chiefs trace their ancestry back to an animal god. For instance, Haile Selassie (the "Lion of Judah"), founding father of the Rastafarian religion and one-time emperor of Ethiopia, traced his lineage back to the powerful god Simba the lion, while some Zulu chiefs claim descent from the python.

Creatures that are half-human and half-animal also appear in many cultures, such as Garuda, the eagle with the body of a man in Hindu mythology, or the centaurs and mermaids of classical myth. The hybrid man-horse centaur has been used to symbolize man trapped by his own sensual impulses, especially lust and violence.

In the stories of many other cultures, animals and humans enjoy a more symbiotic relationship: in Native American myths, animals are often addressed as "brother", while in the Arctic regions, there is a spiritual relationship between humans and the animals that are vital for the community's survival.

Animals sometimes appear as trickster figures in traditional stories; Coyote is the trickster god of the Native Americans and can change his form at will, while African stories feature Hare (Brer Rabbit in America) and Anansi, the spider. Such characters break the rules of nature, or the gods, though usually with positive results, and perhaps represent the irrepressibility and inventiveness of the human spirit.

MODELS OF SOCIETY

Mythology often reinforces and justifies relations of power and leadership. Typically this is explored through a pantheon with a hierarchical structure: a supreme god and/or goddess at the head (often associated with the heavens and the earth) followed by a host of greater and lesser deities. This structure follows that adopted by the human society. In China, for instance, Heaven was visualized as a bureaucracy, maintaining law and order in the same way as the imperial administration. In Japan, the tale of Izanagi and Izanami

ABOVE Odysseus's epic journey symbolizes individual endeavour, but also stands as a metaphor for the cycle of life.

ABOVE Centaurs are used to symbolize lust: the trap of animal sexual impulse.

ABOVE The cobra has a protective aspect in myth and sacred tradition.

ABOVE In some Native American traditions, the coyote is associated with evil, winter and death.

LEFT In Greek myth, a siren is a demonic figure, part woman part fish, which uses its song to enchant sailors and lure them to their death.

bad luck) – while rivalry between the gods is evident in Norse myth. In all these stories the gods exhibit character traits and behaviour that are entirely representative of human nature.

Veneration of the ancestors is an important part of the structure of many traditional societies, and thus features prominently in their mythologies; in Australian Aboriginal mythology, for example, it is the ancestors of the Dreamtime who are said to have shaped the landscape and determined the entire nature of the animal and human world.

HEROIC FIGURES

The exploits and journeys of heroic figures are frequently the subject of myth. Many owe their superhuman powers to some divine connection: Kintaro, the warrior hero of Japanese myth, was the son of a mountain spirit; Rama, in the Hindu epic the Ramayana, was an incarnation of the god Vishnu, while Heracles,

perhaps the greatest of the Greek heroes, was the son of Zeus. Through their actions and their personal qualities – such as bravery, persistence, patience and unconditional love – the heroes and heroines of myth offer a pattern on which people can model themselves.

Some myths show how humans can aspire to the divine: in China, Taoist myths of the Eight Immortals describe how, through their piety and devotion, the Immortals manage to earn everlasting life in Heaven; while Heracles, through his famous twelve labours (tasks given him as punishment for an early crime), became the only Greek hero to achieve immortality.

The medieval Celtic myth of King Arthur and his Knights of the Round Table was centred on the quest for the Holy Grail, said

BELOW The exploits of the divine hero, Rama and his wife Sita (an incarnation of Lakshmi) are told in the Ramayana.

CELTIC BARD

Responsibility for passing on Celtic tribal history, legend and folklore lay with the bard. The earliest bards on record include Aneirin and Taliesin from the 6th century AD. Stories were presented in the form of poems and songs as well as narratives, and the bard's skill was highly valued, in particular a quality called *hwyl* in Welsh – the passion that could inspire an audience. Today the Celtic bardic tradition is continued at Welsh cultural festivals called *eisteddfodau*.

(the first man and woman) served to justify women's alleged inferiority to men, although there are hints that originally Japan may have been organized on a matriarchal lineage, with the imperial family claiming descent from the sun goddess Amaterasu right up until the end of World War II in 1945.

The relationship of deities to one another is explained in human terms of kinship, love and hatred, competition and influence, with each deity responsible for a particular area of human life – fertility, childbirth, love and relationship, war and conflict, the arts, wealth and prosperity. Many stories of Greco-Roman myth concern the interactions of the gods – with humans often used as pawns in their power games (explaining the apparent randomness of good and to be the chalice used by Christ at the Last Supper, or used to catch his blood at the Crucifixion (though it also had pre-Christian roots, in the Celtic theme of the magic cauldron). The Grail became a symbol of immortality and perfection, attainable only through great virtue.

Many heroic figures are also "culture heroes", the discoverers of secrets of nature or of the ideas and inventions on which a civilization depends. Examples include the Greek Prometheus, who stole fire from the gods and gave it to humans, and the Polynesian Maui, who "fished up" land from the ocean and stole fire from the underworld.

DANGEROUS WOMEN

Women in myth are often bad, dangerous or demonic, either because of their curiosity and disobedience or because of their beauty or magic powers. In Greek myth, Pandora disobeys the gods and opens a box that unleashes sickness and evil into the world, just as in the Judaeo-Christian tradition, Eve disobeys God and is held responsible for humans' expulsion from paradise. The Sirens of Greek myth, sea monsters with an insatiable appetite for blood, lured sailors to their death by shape-changing into beautiful maidens, while in China, demon spirits associated with violent death were also apt to disguise themselves as beautiful girls. In India, it was said that the true character of a rakshasi (female demon) could be recognized by the way her feet pointed backwards.

RIGHT As punishment for giving the divine energy of fire to humans, Zeus bound Prometheus to a rock for eternity.

MODERN MYTH-MAKING

The myths of the ancient storytellers continue to resonate in modern times because they symbolize aspects of human nature and interaction that remain relevant to us, and they are constantly being reworked and adapted in art, literature and popular culture.

Although the tradition of storytelling as a formal way of preserving group culture and myth has largely died out in the West, many people still use photograph albums and scrapbooks to record important life events through pictures and words. Psychologists now recognize this as therapeutic for people who have lost direct access to their past through their families, such as adopted children or survivors of traumatic events.

THE HERO GILGAMESH

The epic of Gilgamesh is one of the earliest known hero myths and contains many archetypal motifs. Gilgamesh, King of Uruk in Mesopotamia, was part-human, part-god. He was becoming so arrogant that the gods created the warrior Enkidu to challenge him. After fighting, the two men became close friends and together defeated the monster Humbaba. Impressed by his courage and manly beauty, the goddess Inanna desired Gilgamesh as her lover. When he spurned her, she exacted her revenge by sending the Bull of Heaven to terrorize Uruk, but together Enkidu and Gilgamesh struck it dead. The gods demanded that one of the heroes must pay with his life for the slaughter of the bull, and Enkidu died. Distraught, Gilgamesh set out on a journey to try to learn why men must die. He travelled to the underworld and was carried over the bitter waters of death by Urshanabi, ferryman of the gods. In the underworld he met Utnapishtim, the immortal ancestor of humankind and the only man to have survived the great flood, who told him that like sleep, death comes to us all and is not to be feared. On his way home, Gilgamesh found a plant that could restore youth, but as he stopped to drink at a pool, a snake ate the plant. This is why snakes shed their skins and become young again, while men age and die. Gilgamesh returned home sadly to tell his story to his people, forced to resign himself to acceptance of his fate. His story encapsulates the timeless themes of human ambition, attachment and loss, the restless questioning of existence and its purpose, and the inevitability of death.

ART

ABOVE Masks are a feature of tribal art, linked with ritual practices and carrying many layers of symbolic meaning.

ABOVE TOP The Venus of Willendorf, prehistoric Mother goddess.

RIGHT Chinese art contains many symbolic items, much of it linking landscape to the human body or offering spiritual or moral messages.

Since the earliest times, many of humanity's most profound and enduring symbols have been recorded through art. Whether the cave paintings, sculptures and artefacts of tribal art, the highly elaborate creations of the European Renaissance, or movements such as Surrealism, symbols in art have been used in a variety of different ways to express the beliefs and preoccupations of the day. For whether consciously executed or not, it has always been the role of the artist to act as instrument and spokesperson for the spirit of their age, giving form to the nature and values of the time.

TRIBAL ART

The carvings, paintings and compositions of the indigenous peoples of Africa, America, Australia and Oceania have little in common except that they all evolved – like nearly all major artistic forms – in intimate association with religion and magic. Seldom decorative in intention, they are expressions of humanity's common endeavour to live in harmony with, or to control, natural and supernatural forces. Take for instance Easter Island's monolithic heads and half-length figures, sculptures up to 18m (60ft) high that were carved over a long time period (AD 900–1500). These are thought to symbolize the power that throughout Polynesia, ruling chiefs were believed to inherit from the gods and retain after death, when they themselves were deified. Carved and painted wooden masks are a feature of

both African and North American cultures. Some have life-like human faces, others incorporate animal forms, many are mainly animal. Often these are linked with shamanic practices, designed to transform the wearer and connect them to the magic power of the spirit-world, and are used in ritual and ceremony.

Australian Aboriginal art has remained visible at sacred sites over the millennia and has a continuity of tradition, using the surface of the earth, rocks, caves and tree bark as well as the human body to express a world view in which there is no distinction between the secular and the sacred, the natural and the supernatural, past and present, or even the visible and the invisible.

RELIGIOUS SYMBOLISM

The intimate relationship between religion and symbolism is expressed in the art and artefacts of all civilizations. In prehistory, the iconic Venus of Willendorf, a limestone statuette of a

full-breasted nude (c. 24,000–22,000 BC), is believed to be at once a fertility symbol and an archetype of the Great Mother. Other figurines from this period, having similarly exaggerated sexual characteristics, have led to speculation that these early European hunter societies had a matriarchal sacred tradition, venerating the Mother archetype of the Great Goddess.

Thousands of years later in ancient Egypt, funerary art reveals preoccupations with the afterlife, while in medieval Europe, narrative paintings with a multi-layered symbolism were used to instruct the illiterate masses in the Christian Scriptures and to spell out people's relationship with God and the cosmos. Islamic art is non-figurative – representation of living creatures is forbidden, since this would mean representing an aspect of Allah, which is beyond human capability. The art is therefore characterized by repeating geometric patterns and designs. Its only specifically religious

RIGHT The works of Max Ernst, like those of his fellow surrealists, is full of Freudian sexual symbolism.

RIGHT The works of Max Ernst, like those of his fellow surrealists, is full of Freudian sexual symbolism.

elements are its Qur'anic inscriptions, a reminder to the faithful that Allah is ever present and supersedes anything created by humans. Conversely, in both Buddhism and Hinduism, an emphasis is placed upon the visual power of symbols to elevate consciousness, and figurative symbolism appears in both traditions. Though the Buddha said he did not want to be worshipped, and early Buddhist art confined itself to representations of his footprint (to symbolize his presence) and of the wheel as a symbol of his teachings, people's desire for an image of the Buddha himself soon took over. One of the most impressive examples (dating from the 5th century AD) is a colossal carving, nearly 14m (45ft) high, cut into the cliff-face at the Longmen cave at Yungang, China, the site of a rock-cut temple.

CHINESE TRADITIONS

Highly stylized forms of symbolic expression are characteristic of Chinese art, which has always sought to inspire and educate the viewer, providing insights into the relationship between humans and the divine. Spiritual and moral messages were conveyed through certain set themes, particularly landscapes and the natural world. For instance, every part of the landscape was believed to symbolize an aspect of being human: water was blood, trees and grass were hair, clouds and mists were clothing, and a solitary wandering scholar was the soul. Bamboo, which can be bent without breaking, represented the

spirit of the scholar, while jade stood for purity. Japanese art also draws on nature for its symbolism: cherry blossom is a frequent motif, a herald of spring and token of good luck, and because of its transience a symbol of mortality.

THE RENAISSANCE

Beginning in 14th-century Italy, the Renaissance (French: "rebirth") represented a renewed interest in the art, architecture and literature of ancient Greece and Rome. Many artists looked to nature, the human body and Greco-Roman mythology for inspiration. For instance, the painting *Primavera* ("Spring") by Sandro Botticelli (1445–1510) recounts the story of the nymph Chloris, pursued by Zephyr, god of the wind, who transforms her into Flora, goddess of spring. At the centre of the painting is the goddess Venus, symbol of the season's fertility, while spring itself is also a metaphor for the Renaissance period, the return of an appreciation for the arts, science and learning.

Biblical themes were also invested with classical symbolism; for instance, in his painting *The Last Judgement*, Michelangelo (1475–1564) glorifies Christ as resplendent Apollo, the Greek sun-god, rather than portraying him as a crucified and suffering saviour. Raphael (1483–1520), who was commissioned to decorate the Vatican, combines the more traditional symbolism of God as a grey-bearded patriarch with mythical satyrs and nymphs in his Loggia.

SURREALISM

Beginning as a literary movement, Surrealism was strongly influenced by Freud's ideas about sexuality, free association, dreams and the subconscious. Sexual symbolism – phallic noses, pubic hair in unexpected places – pervades Surrealist imagery, as painters such as Max Ernst (1891 –1976), René Magritte (1898– 1967) and Salvador Dali (1904–89) tried to represent and liberate the workings of the irrational, subconscious mind, challenging the conventions of artistic Realism and polite society. Magritte intentionally mislabelled his paintings, Ernst created strange landscapes inhabited by extraordinary animals and organic forms, while Dali built up a new language of symbolic imagery of melting watches, spindle-legged creatures, flowers hatching out of eggs and other bizarre images.

POP ART

Emerging in Britain and the United States during the mid-20th century, pop art used the imagery of commercial art and other mass media sources. With a background in commercial art, Andy Warhol (1928–97) represented pop art at its most extreme and subversive, praising mechanical repetition and making a cult of the banal and superficial. His poster style paintings, which repeat the same image over and over again, can be viewed as powerful symbols of our modern consumer society.

ADVERTISING

ABOVE Steve McQueen in *Bullitt* with his 1968 Ford Mustang. Both the man and the car became icons representing rebellious male power.

BELOW Sexual imagery has long been used to sell products. Images of women as sex symbols may be targeted at both men and women, as epitomized in this advertisement for a bra.

Using the powers of persuasion to promote a product is an ancient practice. The symbolism used to persuade or influence people must appeal to the central concerns and beliefs of the consumer. In the modern advertising industry, successful advertisers relate to what people consciously or unconsciously respond to or want to be associated with, and design and package products to ride trends in cultural and personal taste.

While the intrinsic quality of the product and the good reputation of its manufacturer were central factors in early marketing, large-scale mass-production and international trade have distanced the consumer from the product and the producer, and advertising has stepped in to fill the gap, becoming a role and an industry in its own right. Most modern advertising is aimed at promoting an entire brand rather than an individual product, creating a sense of allegiance in its customers by matching its image to them through symbolism.

PSYCHOLOGY IN ADVERTISING

Freudian psychology influenced 20th-century advertising with its ideas about unconscious desires. Advertisers began to use "subliminal persuasion" and "symbolic association" to such a degree that the image or brand name became more important than the product. The car is no longer merely a form of transport: while it is designed to be streamlined and functional, it is also enhanced with feminine curves or phallic frontage to appeal to its potential male buyers. It is advertised as a symbol of status and lifestyle.

In the 1920s Freud's nephew, Edward Bernays, used his uncle's ideas for the manipulation of American public opinion, and is often called "the father of public relations". He showed corporations how they could match people's unconscious desires to their products and turned consumer items into lifestyle symbols: for instance, in a famous stunt of 1929 for the American Tobacco Company, he hired models to parade through the streets of New York, smoking, under the banner of "the torch of freedom". By linking smoking with the drive towards women's liberation, he effectively broke the taboo against American women smoking in public.

SEX IN ADVERTISING

The saying that "sex sells" is equally true of any other imagery that appeals to human emotions, such as the use of people's instinctive response to babies to sell a product. But sexuality is probably the most commonly used "attractor", and is widely used in marketing, both subtly and blatantly. Most advertising uses conventional sex symbols, depicting women as objects of lust and men as dominant.

Both the film and advertising industries continually explore and push the limits of sexual explicitness. Sexual imagery generates the greatest impact, inducing excitement and outrage, when it tugs on the morals and taboos of a given culture.

ADVERTISING AND CINEMATIC INTERFACE

The worlds of advertising and film use symbolism to evoke powerful emotions appealing to the popular culture of the time. These two industries borrow strongly from one another in their use of symbolism and genre: films are used to sell fashion items through product placement, and movie icons are used in advertisements, so that sometimes there seems little difference between the two.

A good example of the interplay of film and advertising is the 1968 film *Bullitt*, which some say starred both Steve McQueen and the 1968 Ford Mustang, both symbols of urban rebellion, toughness and male power. In the 2000s the original footage was cleverly remixed for an advertisement for Ford, creating the illusion of McQueen driving the latest model of the Ford Puma. Thirty years on, the actor's iconic image still had the power to sell a car.

THE CAR – A SYMBOL OF THE INDUSTRIAL AGE

Himself an icon of the industrial age, Henry Ford used mass-production methods to make cars that would not be restricted to a wealthy elite. General Motors overtook the success of Ford when their cars became symbols of the "Roaring Twenties", and were designed and sold as representing the new-found liberation, sexual freedom and self-expression of the "Jazz Age".

During the 1930s depression in the United States, closed cars or sedans conveyed a sober and puritanical image. But this period was soon followed by an explosion of car sales and competition, with the post-war car being sold as a symbol of the "American dream". Advertising now portrayed cars as dream-mobiles, inviting potential owners to fulfil their desires for sex, speed, power, wealth and status.

To this day, cars occupy what Arnold Mindell might call the timespirit of progressiveness and success. Modern car designs and advertising are beginning to play with less gender-stereotyped symbolism, in which androgyny, and the blurring of sexual roles, are explored. Where previously advertising for cars was directed only at men, it is now aimed at both men and women.

CORPORATE IMAGE

A company or business image is considered of great importance in modern marketing. Corporate identity is often expressed symbolically through logos and corporate style, relating to the "raison d'être" of the organization and to the impression it wishes to give to the outside world. Many apparently modern logos in fact have their roots in ancient symbolism. Tripartite symbols, for instance, which represent harmony and perfection, are used by companies such as Mitsubishi and Mercedes Benz. The ancient solar cross (an equal-armed cross within a circle) appears on the badges of Fiat and BMW. The golden arches of McDonald's can be interpreted as a giant M, but also match the ancient alchemical sign for fire.

Branding aims to identify the product with producers who can be trusted. Studies of corporate personality have shown the effectiveness of bright bands of colour when used as a part of the brand's image. One such colourful logo is that of Esso/Exxon, which also uses a tiger as a kind of company mascot – its famous slogan, "Put a Tiger In Your Tank", invited the consumer to identify with the power and beauty of the animal.

Company and brand names have significant impact on consumers faced with a market saturated with competing products. Each year the Chairman of the Board of Sony reinforces to staff the idea that the four letters S, O, N and Y are the company's most valuable asset, and that their actions must increase their value.

INTERNATIONAL ADVERTISING

The expansion of global markets has led to new challenges for international advertising, most of which relate to the meaning and values being communicated. One problem is the predominance of Western values and ideals depicted in adverts, which can both influence and offend other cultures. Countries with different moral or religious views often find the images of Western advertising sexually explicit, or disapprove of the roles played by women, and so the advertising may be experienced as subversive.

ABOVE Fiat's logo makes use of the ancient symbol of the sun cross.

TOP The tripartite Mitsubishi logo.

RIGHT The logo of McDonalds is an adaptation of the alchemical sign for fire, shown beneath.

BELOW In the 1920s car manufacturers presented their products as symbols of wealth, liberation and self-expression.

SYMBOLISM AND SCIENCE

THE CLOCK

Since it is closely related to modern concepts of control, productivity and autonomy, the clock is an important functional symbol of the machine age. In the 17th and 18th centuries clocks became sufficiently accurate to measure minutes and seconds, and during this period people shifted away from being guided by the symbolism and rhythms of nature, instead becoming ruled by the clock. The Jungian therapist Marie-Louise von Franz (1915–89) described the clock in post-Cartesian times as coming to symbolize a soulless universe.

BELOW The Copernican view of the universe.

Signs, symbols and symbolism play an important part in scientific research and the development of scientific theories. Scientific concepts are rooted in contemporary or emerging beliefs about nature, "symbolic models" or "paradigms" (patterns) that underlie and inform the development of understanding. Scientific dilemmas are often resolved through creative or irrational processes, even by the symbolism of dreams experienced by the scientific researcher. As science has evolved, so has its language – a shorthand of signs, symbols and formulae that enables scientists to formulate and communicate knowledge.

SCIENTIFIC PARADIGMS AND SYMBOLISM

New scientific eras come about through "paradigm shifts", characterized by a radical shift in the symbolic worldview that eventually shakes up and fundamentally reorganizes the technologies and social and economic structures of the day. When the pioneering chemist Antoine Laurent Lavoisier (1743–94) showed water to be a compound substance made up of different elements he was severely criticized, in particular by the pharmacist Antoine Baumé, for undermining scientific theories based upon the fundamental elements of fire, water, air and earth. Each change in scientific understanding is accompanied by doubts and resistance, and new paradigms inevitably involve radical shifts in the scientific foundations and belief systems of a civilization.

THE SCIENTIFIC REVOLUTION

In the medieval universe, Heaven and earth were seen as two separate realms. Heaven centred on God and was governed by eternal law, while earth and humanity were governed by natural law. Though Heaven was hierarchically superior, earth was considered to be the centre of the universe.

This worldview was overturned by the scientific revolution of the 16th century, which, challenged by the astronomy of Copernicus and observations made with Galileo's telescope, supported the view of a much larger universe centred on the sun, seriously challenging statements made in the Old Testament. The Catholic Church fought back but a new worldview emerged that symbolically removed both humanity and the earth from the centre of things.

THE MACHINE

The French philosopher René Descartes (1596–1650) was a key figure in the transition from medieval to modern scientific thought, proposing an analytic method of searching for scientific truth and accepting only things that are beyond doubt. In the Cartesian era, scientific enquiry favoured mechanistic values of quantity and function over the qualitative values of spirit, aesthetics, feelings, the senses and nature itself, and the machine became a central metaphor.

The steam engine, developed during the 17th and 18th centuries, paved the way for the invention of industrial processes, leading to mass production. The machine became a symbol of power, organization and human control over nature.

THE QUANTUM ERA

During the 20th century a radically new scientific perspective began to emerge, introducing a worldview of tendencies and interdependence: both observer and observed exist in a quantum entanglement, whereby the very act of observation affects the thing being observed. The physicist Werner Heisenberg (1901–76) stated that when we attempt to look objectively at nature and the universe we really encounter ourselves, suggesting that science has an inner and archetypal origin. To explore the relationship between archetypal symbolism and scientific concepts the scientist Wolfgang Pauli (1900–58) examined the deep

archetypal dreams he was experiencing, and he hypothesized a psychophysical unity, which Jung called the *unus mundus,* or "world soul".

DREAMS, SYMBOLISM AND SCIENTIFIC DISCOVERY

What is the connection between symbolism and scientific models? Science itself is not simply a rational process, as there are many examples of scientific discoveries being made through dreams and other irrational processes – such as the Newtonian legend that an apple falling upon Sir Isaac Newton's head led him to an understanding of the force of gravity. It seems that the unconscious can produce symbols that may inform the next step in scientific exploration.

The most famous example is the discovery of the benzene ring in 1865 by the German chemist Friedrich August Kekulé. The properties of benzene could not be explained in terms of linear molecular structures. One evening, dozing in front of the fire, Kekulé dreamed of long rows of atoms "winding and turning like serpents" until one of these serpents caught hold of its tail. On awakening he hypothesized the ring-like structure of benzene, leading to a prolific new period in the development of organic chemistry. At a convention in 1890 Kekulé advised his fellow scientists to "learn to dream" in order to seek the truth.

Also in the mid-19th century, a Russian chemist, Dmitri Mendeleev, dreamed the periodic table of the elements with remarkable accuracy, even predicting the existence of three previously "non-existent" elements, all of which were discovered within 15 years. In the early 20th century, the Danish physicist Niels Bohr, studying the structure of the atom, saw in a dream a nucleus with electrons spinning around it, and for his subsequent work received the Nobel Prize for Physics in 1922. Albert Einstein credited the source of his theory of relativity to a dream he had while at school, in which he rode upon a sled that accelerated to an incredible degree, transforming the stars around him into dazzling light as he approached the speed of light.

SCIENTIFIC SIGNS

In order to communicate, formulate and develop scientific knowledge, a shorthand language of scientific symbols and signs has evolved. The sciences of astronomy, botany, biology, chemistry, nuclear chemistry, physics, geology, mathematics and meteorology have each developed their own shorthand.

The earliest chemical symbols were used by the ancient Greeks, and adopted by Plato, to represent the properties of the four elements: earth, air, fire and water. The alchemists introduced a symbolic language – drawn from astronomy, astrology, cosmology and metallurgy – to depict various elements, including the seven metals. Copper was associated with the element earth. Gold, representing the perfection of matter, was symbolized by the sun. Mercury (or quicksilver), a liquid metal that transcended earth and Heaven, and life and death, was linked with the astrological planet of the same name, or the serpent. Silver was associated with the moon and tin with the planet Jupiter. Iron was represented by the symbol for the planet Mars and lead by that for the planet Saturn.

American astronomers use the symbol of a dashed circle to represent a group of galaxies, while a circle leaning to the right depicts a single galaxy.

MATHEMATICAL SIGNS

In mathematics two parallel lines together mean the same as or equal to (in the same dimension), while a group of three parallel lines shows an equivalence or similarity in identity where there is no real difference. Interestingly this same symbol in meteorology refers to mist, an atmospheric pattern in which everything looks milky-white and loses its identity.

The plus sign (which may have originated as an abbreviated form of the Latin word *et*, meaning "and") came into common use in the 16th century to denote addition. Signs for multiplication and division were introduced in the 17th century.

RIGHT, FROM TOP TO BOTTOM The alchemical signs for copper, gold, silver, mercury, tin, iron and lead.

PART TWO

SYMBOLS WE LIVE BY

EVERYDAY LIVING

The signs and symbols that permeate our culture are often dependent on our historical and social circumstances, but there are others that transcend culture, and are far more universal. This chapter follows the common threads that are formed by the signs we find in our everyday lives.

RIGHT A pathway or road has universal symbolism of the journey of life, it can also symbolize direction, opportunity or hardship.

Universal Themes

ABOVE The life-force and energy of nature permeates the "story" of life, in its rising and falling, birth and death.

ABOVE The swastika is an ancient nature symbol with multiple meanings, an example of how a symbol's meaning can shift and adapt. When it is facing anticlockwise it implies being against the currents of nature.

Over time, different cultures have evolved unique symbolic languages in an attempt to express their most powerful ideas, and emotional and spiritual responses to life. Symbolism displays cultural characteristics relating to the historical trends and geographical regions from which it emerges, and evolves in accordance with each culture's underlying core values and individual belief systems.

In spite of cultural differences, however, common themes also seem to underlie the world's rich diversity of symbolic expression. They may be thought of as a "living stream of dreaming" running like an invisible current through the everyday world.

ENERGETIC LIFE FORCE

Since the earliest times, people have described states and fields of energy that permeate and animate the universe. In many cultures, the universe, the Earth, and our

bodies are thought to channel subtle energy, or "life force". In India this is called *prana*, in China and Japan it is *chi* or *ki*, in Polynesia it is *mana*, in the Western tradition it is etheric. In alchemy, the life force equates with the philosopher's stone, the *quinta essentia* ("fifth essence") or the "world soul".

Modern science understands that the material world, although it appears dense and solid, is fundamentally made up of energy, with atoms, protons, neutrons, electrons and particles vibrating together at different frequencies. The universe can be conceived of as held together by invisible energetic "glue". The psychologist Carl Gustav Jung saw this force in what he called the "collective unconscious", a giant reservoir of archetypal energy patterns that we tap into and express symbolically – whether in dreams, art, sacred tradition or science. This may help to explain our enduring

fascination with symbols, why they appear in every conceivable form and why they have no single, correct definition.

MICROCOSM AND MACROCOSM

Attempts to explain the origins of life and the subsequent relationship between living creatures and the cosmos are two of humankind's most fundamental concerns. They lie at the root of philosophy, religion and science, and a great variety of belief systems and hypotheses have been formulated to provide explanations. A dominant theme is the idea that microcosm and macrocosm exist in parallel, so that the lives of individuals are intimately bound with the cosmos, "as above, so below". This concept existed in the ancient cultures of western Asia and has informed astrology, alchemy, divinatory systems, myth and sacred tradition throughout the world. In particular it dominated the mystical-symbolic thinking of medieval Europe, leading to ideas such as "cosmic man" – a human who embodied all the elements of the universe.

POLARITY AND WHOLENESS

Within a multitude of belief systems, another theme can be picked out: the symbolism of opposition. At almost every level, existence seems to be composed of binary pairs or opposites, such as sky/earth, man/woman, day/night. In terms of the earth's magnetic energy field, this opposition is expressed as the

polarity between positive and negative, attraction and repulsion or ebb and flow. Humans define abstract concepts in a similar fashion, seeing the world in terms of good or bad, success or failure, rich or poor, beautiful or ugly. Some traditions have created from this a moral universe in which one side of the polarity is favoured over the other, with far-reaching political and social implications. For instance, much of civilization has been built on patriarchal values with women's position seen as inferior.

Some traditions, however, while recognizing the pattern of opposites in nature, have seen the value of embracing the whole as an organic unity. This is the meaning of the Chinese yin/yang symbol or the alchemical figure of the androgyne, in which male and female were conjoined in a single body. A similar idea exists in different branches of psychology. In psychoanalytic theory, neurosis occurs when parts of the personality that are considered "bad" or unacceptable are "split off" and rejected. As a model for mental health, all aspects of the psyche need awareness, as they symbolize aspects of our fundamental wholeness.

Symbolism can be used to control and influence human lives, or to help us align ourselves with our deepest nature. Indigenous and aboriginal peoples recognize the importance of a sustainable relationship with nature, reflected in their symbolic world, which is also a living reality. They participate in the whole "web of life", honouring the Earth, sky, sun, moon, ancestors, nature spirits, fairies, animals and plants.

CHANGING SYMBOLISM

Although some symbols retain consistent meaning through cultures and ages, others rise and fall in significance, and their meaning evolves over time. An excellent example of this is how the symbolism of the goat has changed and developed through the centuries. In early Europe the male goat was a positive symbol of procreative power, the libido, fertility and the life force. The goat was particularly sacred to the Greek gods Dionysus and Pan. Pan, half man and half animal, with the horns of a goat, was the god of all things, in particular the procreative force.

In the Old Testament book of Leviticus, however, the goat became a "scapegoat" for the sins of humanity, and was sent into the wilderness, bearing this evil burden. From this point the animal increasingly came to symbolize sexual excess, with its rank smell associated with evil, until by the Middle Ages its characteristics had been attributed to the Devil. The personification of Pan, meanwhile, underwent a corresponding transformation into the goat-headed Satan. The goat has, however, maintained its positive associations in the Mediterranean, where it is viewed as a guardian, with the power to absorb malevolent influences.

DWELLINGS AS SYMBOLS

ABOVE A cave was a form of shelter, which has developed primordial symbolic significance, and can be associated with the womb.

ABOVE The house is a symbol of the self, and the way we depict it can symbolize aspects of our personality or attitudes.

BELOW Squareness in architecture may symbolize the human desire to impose ourselves on nature.

The physical structures within which we work and live possess both functional and symbolic qualities, and are usually an interweaving of both. Our homes and other buildings are indicators of rank and privilege, archetypal patterns, connection to spirits and ancestors, and our relationship with both community and nature. Homes very often have cosmological significance, mirroring a relationship to the centre while at the same time having a more personal significance for the families or individuals who live in them. The rich symbolism of the home becomes especially important when we examine the part it plays in both psychology and dream interpretation.

THE FIRST HOMES

Caves, trees and earth were important means of shelter for early humans and have provided both the inspiration and the materials for later dwellings. The dwellings of many primitive peoples are suggestive of natural arbours, with walls made from tree trunks and branches, and leaves as roofs. The trunk of the tree provides the structure while the canopy and leaves provide shelter from the elements. When the forest in which they lived was destroyed, the members of an African pygmy tribe became hugely disoriented upon leaving their vertical and horizonless world of the trees to live on the plain, demonstrating how "at home" and psychologically rooted we become in the environment, shelters and structures with which we are familiar.

The hallways and rooms in modern buildings are reminiscent of the networks of chambers in caves. The cave or cavern-like dwelling is like a womb within Mother Earth, and thus is symbolic of birth, rebirth, nurture and creativity. The home as symbolic of "mother" is a universal concept.

As early as 15,000 BC the nomadic hunters of Europe discovered the usefulness of turf and earth for building and insulation. From primitive mud huts, complex designs for earth lodges have developed throughout the world. Building with earth led to the use of clay bricks. The children's story of the three little pigs and the big bad wolf demonstrates how bricks represent security for our domestic (or pig) nature from the force of nature (or the wolf). The third pig stays safe as the wolf huffs and puffs but just can't blow down his brick house. However, while bricks can symbolize permanence and security, they are can also be used as symbols of the repression of nature through human strength and rigidity.

SYMBOLIC PLACEMENT AND ALIGNMENT

How a building or community is sited on the land is considered very important in many cultures. Houses were often built on local sacred sites, and the foundation stone of a house was similar to the omphalos, or "navel stone", of a temple – the central holy object that allowed communication with the gods. An old building tradition in Ireland involved the lighting of the "needfire" by rubbing together two of the first construction timbers in the shape of Brigit's cross. The needfire was the hearth around which the rest of the house would be focused.

Hunters and gatherers traditionally aligned their houses and communities by visualizing their territory as representing a cosmic creator or original ancestor in anthropomorphic form. The mud houses and towns of the Dogon people, who live on the Niger river at Timbuktu, are arranged according to cosmological and anthropomorphic principles. Their villages are built in pairs, signifying the relationship between Heaven and Earth. The Dogon believe that when they die they go to a paradise that is identical to their homes in life.

In China, where the art of feng shui is practised, the "bagua" is a template for buildings, with eight "guas" surrounding the centre. Each of its zones corresponds to

an area of life: prosperity, fame and reputation, relationship, family, health, creativity and children, knowledge and skills, work, and helpers. The dwelling needs to be designed in a proper relationship to the four directions, in such a way that chi flows freely through the different zones for the wellbeing of the inhabitants.

In India, *vasta purusa* is the spirit of the house, described as a tightly coiled male body. To ensure good fortune, the house must be aligned with his body in such a way that his head, heart and limbs are not disturbed.

The Mongol yurt is a microcosmic representation of the macrocosm, with the sacred hearth on the square earth, the circular roof as the sky, and the smoke-hole in the roof as the eye of Heaven through which comes the light of the sun. The yurt is divided into living quadrants, each relating to the roles of the family or community.

The book *A Pattern Language*, by Christopher Alexander, Sara Ishikawa and Murray Silverstein (1977), describes patterns common to many buildings and towns throughout the world. The authors spent years attempting to formulate a language of patterns that when lived in, are conducive to the well-being of individuals, families and community. They feel that many of these patterns are archetypal in nature, connecting humanity with the essential nature of things. An example is

the alcove, or smaller space within a room, which enables a family to be together while at the same time being involved in different activities; this is an archetypal pattern as relevant to the yurt-dweller as to those who live in a castle.

THE SYMBOLIC VALUE OF THE HOME

Psychologists often view the house as symbolic of a person's inner being, so that when a client draws a house, or describes a dream about a part of it, they are describing their psychic structure. The outside of the house can be seen as representing their outer personality, with the windows and doors showing their relationship to others and the world.

Attics and basements are places where the light of consciousness does not shine. They can symbolize spiritual elevation and the unconscious. In his autobiography, C.G. Jung described going to the basement of a building where he discovered a primitive part of himself. The foundations of a house can symbolize our relationship to the collective unconscious, our ancient beginnings and the non-human realms.

The kitchen, where things are cooked, is a place of alchemical transformation where nurturing takes place, so it may have associations with good or poor parenting. In the hearth or fireplace, glowing embers or

flickering flames are the source of life and dreaming, and may also refer to the spark of imagination or genius. Almost every culture has valued the hearth as the heart of the home, though in modern times it seems to have been replaced by the television set, which also glows and flickers with symbolic stories.

The significance of bedrooms depends upon their occupants. A child's room may represent a place of play or fantasy, while adult bedrooms may point towards sexuality and a person's relationship to sex.

As with all psychological interpretations there is never really any fixed meaning to any of these symbols. What is most important in determining the significance of aspects of the home is the individual's associations with those areas. For example, two people may visualize the front doors of their houses closed. If the first person has always lived in houses where the front door stood open and people were always welcome, whereas the second has lived in houses where the back door was the place of relationship, and the front door was always closed, these similar images need to be interpreted differently. Similar differences in interpreting the same symbols will occur in dream analysis, where the meaning of each home-based image will depend on the person who has dreamed it.

ABOVE Mongolian yurts are circular dwellings constructed from wood and felt, serving both as nomadic homes and symbols of the cosmos.

ABOVE LEFT The Dogon village is an earth-bound representation of what the Dogon people believe paradise to look like.

ABOVE Tree-houses symbolize a relationship between humans and nature, and offer spaces in which children can free their imagination.

BELOW In modern times the television has replaced the hearth as a source of focus and symbolism for the family.

THE GATEWAY

JANUS, GOD OF THE GATE

One of the most ancient gods of Rome, Janus was the warden of all gateways and master of initiation into the mysteries. Often carved on gateposts and doorways, his two faces meant that he could simultaneously see all who were coming and going, looking into both the past and the future. His attributes were the doorkeeper's keys and staff. He presided over beginnings, so that the first day of each month was sacred to him, as was the first month of the year. In the Gregorian calendar, January is named after him.

RIGHT The entrance to this cave in Bali is a monster's mouth with guardian statues protecting the threshold.

There are many symbols of transition, but the gateway or door is an archetypal motif that represents an entrance to another world (a room, a city, a palace, a temple, a social institution) or another state of being that may be either heavenly or hellish, a paradise or a prison. To pass through a gateway is to cross a threshold, to move from the known to the unknown. Gateways may be open but are often closed and guarded, so that the traveller needs a key or password, or must undergo a test, in order to pass through. Hence gateways are also a symbol of initiation: typically there may be a series of gates or worlds to be negotiated, each one leading to greater wisdom, before the ultimate state of bliss is reached.

HEAVEN AND HELL

There are many examples in religion of Heaven and Hell being entered through a gateway or door. In Judaism, for instance, it is believed that there is one gate to the Garden of Eden (a symbol of paradise), but 40,000 to Hell, showing how much more difficult it is to find and enter Heaven. For

Christians, Jesus is the entrance to salvation: "I am the door: by me if any man enter in, he shall be saved." (John 10:9). In Muslim tradition, different levels of paradise are reached through a series of gates, with 100 steps leading up to each level before the ultimate seventh heaven is attained. One teaching states that the key to these gates has three prongs: proclamation of Allah's oneness, obedience to Allah and abstinence from evildoing.

BIRTH AND DEATH

Doorways are often associated with death and also with rebirth. In ancient Egypt, the sun god Ra travelled through the underworld each night, passing through 12 gates representing the 12 hours of darkness before being reborn each morning. Ancient Egyptian coffins were sometimes painted with a small false door, symbolically allowing the *ha* (soul) to fly through. In ancient Rome the dead were often depicted in art as standing in front of half-open doors. The Hebrew word for "door" – *daleth* – also means "womb", the gateway of life.

GUARDIANS

Both good and evil influences can pass through a gateway, so guardians or protective deities may be assigned to oversee them. The gates of Chinese cities were set at the four compass points, watched over by fierce lions who attracted good but repelled evil influences, while the entrances to Babylonian and Assyrian palaces were guarded by gigantic winged lion-man sculptures called *lamassu*. In Asian temples, warrior figures called *dvarapala* performed the same function. Cerberus, the three-headed dog of Greek myth, guards the gates of Hades (the underworld of Greek legend), and his secondary function is to make sure that once admitted no one ever leaves.

In ancient Rome every section of a doorway was guarded by numina (minor deities); the god Forculus oversaw the door's panels, for instance, while the goddess Cardea looked after its hinges. The two-faced god Janus (see box) was the chief deity of

BELOW In myth and story, a small or hidden doorway can represent a secret entrance to a magical otherworld.

the gate. In China, it is the custom to paste images of the two Door Gods on the house door on New Year's eve, then lock it until midnight so that no evil spirits can enter, while in Japan *kadomatsu* – decorations made from the boughs of evergreen trees – are placed at the entrance to attract the gods and bring good luck. A similar tradition, linked to pagan customs, is practised in the West, where holly wreaths or bunches of mistletoe are put on front doors during the Christmas and New Year holiday: holly is associated with protection and good fortune, and mistletoe with magic and medicine – it was a symbol of immortality for the Celtic druids.

A cave mouth in Chalcatzingo, Mexico, has a monster's face carved around it, symbolizing the protection of the entrance as well as the transition from one world to another. In the Hindu tradition, a gateway also sometimes takes the form of a monster's mouth through which one must pass when travelling from life to death.

GATEWAYS OF VICTORY
Sometimes gateways are used as symbols of victory and power, both temporal and spiritual. For instance, the Ishtar Gate in ancient Babylonia (in modern Iraq) was built to glorify both the mother-goddess Ishtar and the great city of Babylon. It straddled the Processional Way, and provided an entrance to the city, which had walls so thick that two chariots could drive side by side along the top. In Beijing, the gates

of the Forbidden City represented the Chinese emperor's might, while the triumphal arches of ancient Rome embodied national and political power. More recently, Napoleon (1769–1821), who emulated Roman imperialism when he became emperor of France, began the construction of the Arc de Triomphe in Paris, in anticipation of a victory that never happened. Subsequently the arch became a war memorial dedicated to the soldiers killed in World War I (1914–18).

HIDDEN DOORWAYS
Gateways do not always have to be large and ornate to be significant. Sometimes small or hidden doorways provide access to other, often magical worlds. The entrance to Wonderland in Lewis Carroll's Alice stories (1832 –98) is first down a rabbit hole and then through a tiny door, which Alice cannot get through until she shrinks. In *The Lion, the Witch and the Wardrobe* by C. S. Lewis (1899–1963) the gateway to the magic land is through a wardrobe. Many enchanted gardens of European folklore are reached through tiny gates that are often obscured; for instance, in the tale of Sleeping Beauty the

entrance to the palace where the princess sleeps is overgrown by briars, which the hero-prince must cut through to reach her.

OPEN OR CLOSED DOORS
In Japan open archways known as *tori* mark the entrance to Shinto shrines. They represent a divine state of perpetual openness, and symbolize the point at which a visitor passes from the everyday world to the sacred. In Chinese tradition, an open door is thought of as active, or yang, and a closed door as passive, or yin. The opening and closing of a door represents the cosmic dance between yin and yang, where first one and then the other holds sway. In Taoism, the opening and closing of the Gates of Heaven are related to human respiration, so that holding the breath equates with shutting the doors, and breathing with opening them.

KEYS
In Japan, the key is a symbol of happiness because it opens up the door to the rice pantry, symbolic of the source of life. In the Christian tradition St Peter is often depicted with the keys to Heaven. The Church adopted keys as symbols of authority: the papal coat of arms shows two keys, one silver, one gold, previously emblems of the Roman god Janus.

SEXUAL SYMBOLISM
The vulva can also be likened to a gateway, as it is both the passageway into life at birth, and the entrance to the vagina during coitus. In Eastern traditions such as Taoism and Tantra, sexual union is itself a gateway of transcendence, through which it is possible to achieve an altered state of consciousness and experience the "bliss body". The mythical Yellow Emperor, Huang-tsi, one of the Eight Taoist Immortals, ascended to Heaven on the back of a dragon partly because of his skill in the art of loving, while early Chinese "bedchamber books" refer to the penis as the jade stalk and the vagina as the jade gateway, jade being the stone of Heaven and a symbol of perfection and immortality.

TRAVELLING AND JOURNEYS

ABOVE A winding road symbolizes the twists and turns of the pathway through life.

ABOVE In myth and story, shoes can possess magical properties, enabling the traveller to cross great distances speedily and safely.

BELOW The chariot is a solar symbol and as such is used as the vehicle of gods, kings and warriors in many traditions.

Journeys symbolize quests for personal advancement, either material or spiritual, or both. To travel is to tread the (potentially hazardous) path through life in which the ultimate destination is not death but spiritual enlightenment, mythically embodied as a promised land (such as the Isles of the Immortals in Chinese tales or religious sites of pilgrimage) or a precious object with special powers (such as the Holy Grail or the Golden Fleece). Sometimes journeys are subterranean, symbolizing entry into the underworld, and sometimes through the air, suggesting spiritual aspiration.

THE TRAVELLER
Boots or shoes are a symbol of the traveller. The might of the Roman army was built on walking power, symbolized by the soldier's boot. Many stories of Western folklore involve "seven-league boots" that magically enable the traveller to cover great distances at great speed without becoming tired, while Hermes the Greek god of travel wore winged sandals. In

many cultures charms and talismans are carried on a journey for luck and protection, and the traveller is wished "good speed" (or "God speed").

THE HORSE
The animal that is the most archetypal symbol of travel is probably the horse. In Celtic culture, white horses were sacred and drew the chariots of priests and kings. They were associated with the goddess Epona, one of the few Celtic deities to be worshipped by the Romans. In the 16th century, Europeans introduced the horse to North America (though it may have existed there previously and died out), and its arrival had a profound effect on many native tribes. For them, horses became associated with thunder because of the sound of their running hooves, and the horse became a symbol of wealth and power.

Horses feature in many myths of otherworldly transport, often pulling the chariots of the gods, and are endowed with mythical characteristics. Slepnir, the mount of the Norse god Odin, has eight legs, while in Greek myth Pegasus has wings and pulls the chariot that brings Zeus his thunder and lightning. Mohammed is said to have ascended to Heaven riding on the hybrid creature Borak (whose name means "lightning"), a winged horse with a human head and a peacock's tail.

THE CHARIOT
Chariots, or "triumphal cars", are the carriers of rulers and gods – in Renaissance art they are shown

carrying deities such as Venus, Jupiter and Mars. Chariots symbolize the power to lead and vanquish and are often associated with warfare: the Celtic battle leader, Boudicca, is usually depicted in her chariot, while the Achaemenids, the rulers of ancient Persia, are described as going into battle accompanied by the chariot of the supreme god, Ahura Mazda, drawn by eight white horses. The chariots of Indian deities, sometimes lotus-shaped, are drawn by different animals, such as horses for Agni and Surya, and geese for Brahma. The English word "juggernaut" is derived from the massive chariot of the Hindu god Jagganath.

TRAVEL BY WATER
Sailing ships, boats and canoes are all used to symbolize the journey through life. In ancient Egypt, sails symbolized wind and breath, representing the fickle "winds of fate" that can blow a traveller off course. In Egypt, and later in Rome, a new ship was sacrificed each year to ensure fair winds and calm seas: inscribed with holy words, laden with perfumes and baskets of flowers, it was launched into the sea for the winds to take it.

Voyages across water are frequently associated with death and transformation, and symbolic ships of the dead are common to many civilizations. In Indonesia, the dead are exposed in canoes, and in ritual practice the shaman uses a boat to "travel through the air" in search of his patient's soul. In ancient Egypt, the sun god Ra travelled through the underworld

ABOVE Boats can symbolize death, and in ancient Egypt were believed to carry the souls of the dead.

and across the sky in the "boat of a million years", while in China and Japan, paper boats are used as conveyances for spirits. Hindus use miniature flame-carrying boats symbolically to carry solar energy or prayers.

There are also many accounts of heroic journeys in ships such as the Argos, in which Jason searched for the Golden Fleece, or the Pridwen, taken by King Arthur and his men on their journey to the underworld. The sea represents the perils of the unknown, and apart from the danger of shipwreck the journey may bring encounters with mythical beasts such as sea monsters or demons.

For island peoples, boats are particularly important. For instance, Maori war canoes are said to bestow mana (prestige) on all those who own or sail in them, an idea similar to one held by the Vikings. Sea vessels are also symbolic containers and emblems of security: in Judaeo-Christian belief it is Noah's ark that preserves humanity against disaster by saving a breeding pair of every living creature.

MODERN TRANSPORT

Cars, buses, trains and aircraft have symbolic associations that are usually seen in psychological terms. Driving a car can be seen as a metaphor for an individual travelling through life in conscious control of their direction; issues of safety and danger, of conformity or rebellion (obeying or ignoring the rules of the road), of having a sense of direction or of being lost can all be highlighted. Unlike the car, the bus is a public vehicle and can suggest a person's relationship to society, so that difficulties in boarding or wanting to get off can be significant.

Trains operate according to fixed rules. Being late, missing or only just catching a train, travelling without a ticket or in a lower or higher-class carriage can all be interpreted in terms of a person's relationship to the world. Many psychologists believe that the departure platform is a symbol of the unconscious, the starting point of literal and metaphorical journeys, and luggage a symbol of what is being "carried" by the psyche, so that heavy bags can signify psychological burdens, while light bags may indicate inner freedom.

THE CROSSROADS

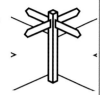

Traditionally a crossroads marks an important point of decision, and sacred monuments or shrines have been erected at such sites: for instance, votive stones left by travellers in the Peruvian Andes have built up into pyramids. The crossroads is a place of transition, a symbol of risk, opportunity, change, choice and transformation. Being the point where divergent pathways intersect, it is an important place of encounter, traditionally associated with otherworldly powers (both good and evil). In many places, crossroads are associated with ghosts, witches and troublesome spirits: in Europe, statues to Hecate, the Greek "dark" goddess, were erected at crossroad sites, while in Africa, the Bambara from Mali make offerings of tools, cotton and cloth to the Soba spirits who are thought to meddle in human affairs. Crossroads are also widely linked with divination: in Japan, people would go there at dusk, when the words of passers-by would reveal what fate might bring. This was linked to a belief that travellers might be deities bringing good fortune, and evolved into the custom of selling rice-crackers containing paper fortunes at crossroads.

The desire for flight is archetypal. Aircraft (and spacecraft) can symbolize spiritual aspiration, transcending human limitations by defying gravity, rising up to the purifying reaches of the sky and beyond. Aircraft can also be symbols of independence, freedom and speed. Running out of fuel, crashing or falling can suggest being brought "down to earth", a punishment perhaps for over-ambition, just as Icarus in Greek myth fell to his death after flying too close to the sun, which melted the wax of his wings.

ABOVE The horse is an archetypal motif. It symbolizes life-giving but dangerous forces, as well as power and strength.

BELOW A red car symbolizes male sexual potency and drive. It also suggests the thrill of speed and power.

THE GARDEN

ABOVE In the Hindu sacred tradition, as in many others, the garden is a symbol of paradise.

ABOVE Fountains are a symbol of life in many cultures, and are also an emblem of the feminine.

BELOW Pools and water features are often incorporated into gardens, with water used as a symbol of life in many cultures.

Almost universally, the garden is a symbol of earthly and heavenly paradise – the word "paradise" comes from *pairidaeza*, the old Persian word for a garden. Within the garden, the design and plants contribute to its symbolism. The first gardens were probably made in China around 4,000 years ago. From there they spread to the Mediterranean and Near East, and since then almost every culture that survives above a subsistence level has created gardens.

HEAVEN ON EARTH
Gardens are sacred symbols in many spiritual traditions. The Judaeo-Christian Garden of Eden is the ultimate Heaven on earth, created by God for man (Adam) and woman (Eve) to live in. Eden symbolizes the primordial state of divine innocence, when humans existed in harmony with God, nature and one another before they fell from grace after eating the forbidden fruit of the Tree of Life. The theme of Eden and the Fall is a favourite motif in

Western art and literature; representations include *The Garden of Earthly Delights* by the Dutch painter Hieronymus Bosch (c.1450–1516), and the epic poem *Paradise Lost* by John Milton (1608–74). In Islam, too, heavenly bliss is interpreted in the Qur'an as a garden, a home for the elect beyond the grave, and Allah is sometimes referred to as "the Gardener". In ancient Greece, the Elysian Fields, the place where the virtuous go after death, was also represented as a garden.

In China, the traditional lake-and-island garden was invented to attract the Eight Immortals – a group of Taoist saints alleged to live on the Mystic Isles – to Earth. The Emperor Wu Di's gardens of the 2nd century BC contained palaces and pavilions built on man-made mountains and connected by bridges to the islands that stood in the middle of a huge artificial lake.

PLEASURE GARDENS
In ancient Egypt, gardens were places of recreation. Pictures of gardens with pools and banks of flowers decorated tombs, suggesting the joys of the afterlife, as well as palace walls and floors. The Romans carried garden design to sophisticated heights, incorporating buildings, statues, stairways, colonnaded walkways, springs, grottoes, wells and fountains, and the garden became one of the symbols of civilization. This theme was developed during the European Renaissance, with the formal symmetrical designs of many gardens, such as the spectacular Italian gardens at Villa

Lante (Bagnaia) or Villa d'Este (Tivoli) symbolizing human power to tame nature.

In Mexico, the royal pleasure gardens of the Aztec emperor Montezuma combined the functions of a private garden with those of the botanical garden and zoo, preserving not only plants but also birds and animals, with some 600 keepers to tend them. Humans with unusual physical characteristics (such as dwarfs or albinos) were also housed there.

Gardens are widely associated with sensual pleasure, love and seduction. For instance, the classic Arabian erotic text on lovemaking is entitled *The Perfumed Garden*, while many of the great lovers of myth and legend (such as Rama and Sita in India) are frequently portrayed in a garden setting.

PARADISE GARDENS
In many cultures, the garden exists as a type of dream world, designed as an escape from the "real" world and intended to lift the senses from the mundane to the sublime. This is epitomized by the archetypal Persian garden, planted with fruit trees and sweetly scented plants and intersected by streams. In the hot desert land, both water (a symbol of life) and shade are important garden features.

The garden is enclosed and is usually entered by a magnificent gateway, a symbol of transition from one world to another. It is often designed around a large central pool, sometimes lined with blue tiles to create an impression of depth, with four

channels flowing from it; in large gardens, the grid pattern may be repeated, with fountains marking the intersections between the watercourses. As well as being cooling and refreshing, fountains symbolize the flow of life, while the intersections represent the connection between the everyday and the eternal. The geometric design is softened with vine fruits and flowers, particularly bunches of grapes and roses – in Persian, the words for flower and rose are the same.

In the Persian garden, moon-gazing was an important activity. Roses were planted to attract nightingales; the nocturnal habits of these birds linked them to the moon, while their song associated them with love and longing. Gazebos in the corners of the garden provided shelter for those viewing the night sky. The word "gazebo" is derived from a Persian word meaning "a platform for viewing the moon"; traditionally the structure would have a central hole in the roof through which the sky could be seen.

The gardens of Persia provided an oasis of inspiration for poetry, music and art. In his collection of poems and stories called the *Gulistan* ("The Rose Garden") the 13th-century poet Sa'di likened his thoughts to rose petals collected from the garden of his meditations. Persian garden

designs influenced some of the most famous gardens in the world, including the gardens of the Alhambra Palace in Spain, and the Mogul Taj Mahal in India.

THE ZEN GARDEN

In the East there is a saying that a sacred space is complete only when there is nothing more that can be taken away from it. The first Zen gardens in Japan were created by Buddhist monks as places of contemplation, designed to bring the mind to a point of stillness through simple but profound design. In a Zen garden nothing is left to chance and every element is significant. The aim is to create a harmony between the two cosmic forces of yin and yang, water and land. Traditionally, water is symbolized by gravel or sand, raked to form ripple patterns, while large stones

represent land. When plants are used, shrubs such as azaleas, cut-leaf maples, conifers and bamboos represent land, while moss represents water. Space is an integral part of the Zen garden, allowing the spirit of nature to move between yin and yang.

Unlike gardens in the West, which are designed to celebrate the changing seasons, Zen gardens are designed with permanence in mind, so they are more or less the same today as when they were first designed hundreds of years ago, and even the gravel is raked in the same patterns. This permanence symbolizes the transcendent spirit unbound by time or space.

BELOW In medieval times, the walled garden was a symbol of refuge. Here the Virgin Mary is shown surrounded by roses, symbols of her purity.

ABOVE The Court of the Lions at the Alhambra Palace in Granada is rich in symbolism, suggesting spiritual attainment and leadership.

WALLED GARDENS

In medieval Christian symbolism, the walled garden was the home of the soul and a place of refuge from the troubles of earthly life. Its enclosed, secret nature made it a symbol of the feminine principle and in particular of the Virgin Mary. The word "rosary", used to describe the string of beads used to count prayers to the Virgin, originally meant a garden of roses. Persian gardens were also surrounded by walls to separate them from the mundane world, and were filled with an abundance of perfumed flowers, upon which a range of symbolism is based; for instance, jasmine and rose are seen as the king and queen of flowers, while narcissus captures the scent of youth.

THE HOME

The traditional centre of domestic life is the hearth, an archetypal symbol, but many other common household objects enjoy a rich symbolic tradition: they include the broom and mirror, cooking pots, baskets and items of furniture. In the West some of these items – notably the hearth – are no longer in general use, but they retain their symbolic power.

THE HEARTH

As a source of light, heat and food, the hearth represents home and community, warmth, safety and family life. It has figured in the myths and religions of many civilizations. In Aztec tradition it was sacred to the androgynous Two-Lord Ometecuhtli, who was believed to live at the heart of the universe, while in both China and Japan the hearth gods attract abundance and good fortune to the household, with the Japanese god of the hearth residing in the hook on which the cooking pot is suspended over the fire.

THE BROOM

A humble piece of household equipment, the broom is also a symbol of sacred power and new beginnings. In some North African agricultural societies, the broom used to sweep the threshing floor is a cult object. In ancient Rome, houses were swept after funerals to clean away any bad spirits and symbolize a fresh start, and the Chinese observe a similar custom at the end of the year, sweeping the house to remove any bad luck in preparation for the next year.

THE CAULDRON

The freestanding cooking pot, or cauldron, is another powerful, cross-cultural and archetypal symbol. In Indo-European traditions, it is an instrument of mystical and magical power and transformation. In Celtic myth there are three types of cauldron: the Dagda's cauldron of plenty – an eternal source of food and knowledge; a cauldron of sacrificial death, in which the king of the old year was drowned while his palace was burned; and a cauldron of rebirth in which the dead could be revived.

In China, a three-legged cauldron had the power to bestow the ability of divination, the control of the seasonal cycle, and to grant immortality. The hero Yu the Great, founder of the Chinese Empire, cast nine sacred bronze cauldrons that were said to boil without fire and were filled by celestial powers. It was said that if the people of the Earth turned from virtue to vice, the cauldrons would disappear.

CONTAINING VESSELS

Aside from the cauldron, there are many other archetypal containers, including urns, vases, jars and bowls, as well as caskets, boxes, baskets and coffers, all of which have symbolic significance. In many cultures, rigid vessels are associated with death. The ancient Egyptians, when they mummified the dead, placed the heart and other internal organs in canopic jars – magical vessels that would protect the contents from evil influences. In Europe the dead are usually enclosed in a coffin before burial or cremation, and their ashes may be placed in an urn. In some South American countries, a broken vessel placed on a grave indicates the transition between life and death.

Urns and vases are also life symbols: the Mesopotamian goddess Ishtar is often depicted carrying an urn containing the waters of life. In the Kabbalah, the vase symbolizes spiritual treasure – a symbolism echoed in the Grail legends of medieval European literature, in which the Grail is the chalice or goblet said to contain the blood of Christ and with it the secret of immortality. In the Jewish Temple, golden bowls – a metaphor for vessels containing life – were used for ritual offerings.

Containers are also associated with the feminine principle. In the Americas, stories about baskets and basket-making are often related to women: for instance, in a Pawnee myth, Basket Woman is the mother of the moon and stars. The basket is a symbol of the womb and the attribute of many goddesses, including Diana of Ephesus, whose priestesses wore their hair dressed in a basket shape. Among the Shona of Zimbabwe, pottery bowls are sometimes shaped like a woman's body parts, and there is a saying that a husband must treat his wife with respect to prevent her from "turning the bowl upside down", or denying him access to her sexuality. Similarly, in the Japanese tea ceremony, the tea bowl represents the moon and yin, or the feminine essence.

MIRRORS

The Latin word for mirror is "speculum", and speculation – now an intellectual activity – originally meant using a mirror to scan the sky and stars. Mirrors – especially darkened mirrors – have also been used in divination, by gazing into them until visions were revealed: the Aztecs made polished black obsidian mirrors for this purpose, dedicated to the god Tezcatlipoca, or Smoking Mirror. In some Native American traditions, a blackened medicine bowl would be filled with water to create the same effect.

Sometimes mirrors are seen as reflecting the truth: in Greek myth, Medusa, whose gaze could turn others to stone, was turned to stone herself when presented with her reflection in Perseus' shield. The Chinese hang octagonal mirrors inscribed with the *Pa Gua* above the entry to a house, in the belief that by revealing the nature of evil influences the mirror will drive them away.

RIGHT The carpets of Arabia are associated with the home, and the colours and patterns used in their weaving are rich in symbolism. Every carpet has a mistake to illustrate the Islamic belief that only Allah can create perfection.

Mirrors are symbols of spiritual wisdom, knowledge and enlightenment: in Tibetan Buddhism, the Wisdom of the Great Mirror teaches that the world of shapes reflected in it is illusory, while for Taoists the mirror of the heart reflects Heaven and earth. Through its association with heavenly intelligence, the mirror is often a solar symbol: Japanese myth tells how the sun goddess Amaterasu was enticed from her cave by a sacred mirror to reflect her light upon the world. The mirror is also a female, lunar, symbol, and has associations with luck and superstition. In China, a mirror is a sign of harmony and happy marriage, with a broken mirror suggesting separation. In Western folklore, a broken mirror is said to bring seven years of bad luck to the person who broke it.

FURNITURE

In ancient Rome, emperors sat upon stools, while thrones were reserved for the gods. Today in parts of Africa stools are symbols of kingly office, while the golden stool of the Ashanti in Ghana is believed to enshrine the nation's soul. Because they elevate the sitter, chairs are associated with status and authority. In the Christian tradition, the Latin name for a bishop's chair was a "cathedrum" (from the Greek for chair, "kathedra"); churches presided over by bishops were therefore called cathedrals.

A table is a focal point, a meeting place where people gather together to eat or talk. For Jewish people, the family dining table assumes the role of an altar when it is sanctified by ritual and prayer during the Sabbath meal. The Round Table of the Arthurian legends represented a select community, an idea echoed in business today when board meetings are held around a table.

Both carpets and curtains have sacred and secular associations. In the Middle East, carpets are associated with the home and with the mosque, and are used to beautify and delineate domestic and holy spaces. Together with screens and veils, curtains provide concealment and define space. In the Temple in Jerusalem, a curtain was drawn over the Holy of Holies, the innermost sanctum that only the Jewish high priest could enter, while in certain Muslim societies, curtains are central to the practice of purdah, which involves concealing women from public view. To perpetuate their holy authority, the emperors of China always kept a veil between themselves and their visitors so that they could see their guests without being seen.

ABOVE The mirror has many complex meanings, associated with both the sun and moon.

ABOVE Curtains symbolize separation between different realms, either opening them up or concealing them.

STATUS AND WEALTH

ABOVE Beaded jewellery is a mark of status among many African peoples.

ANOINTING WITH OIL

In many cultures oil is thought to bear special powers. Olive oil in particular is a symbol of both spiritual power and prosperity. In the Judaeo-Christian tradition, kings and priests were ritually anointed with oil as a sign of divine blessing and God-given authority, power and glory. The Greek word "christos" and the Hebrew "messiah" mean "the anointed". They are used for Jesus as symbols of his royal, prophetic and priestly authority.

Symbols can be used to communicate power and authority – both temporal and spiritual. Every culture has developed symbols of power and rank that accord with its social values, beliefs and customs. Many are associated with royalty and office or with wealth and possessions. Traditionally, valuable commodities have been used to signify wealth and rank. What the specific items are may depend on cultural values – the wealth of nomadic peoples, for instance, may be measured in terms of camels or sheep.

PRECIOUS COMMODITY
Some of humankind's most precious commodities – such as gold, silver and gemstones – are valued both for their beauty and their rarity. A symbol of purity and incorruptibility, gold is associated with divinity, royalty, the sun and the highest aspirations of the spirit. The golden apples of the Nordic heaven, Asgard, like those of the Hesperides in Greek mythology, prevent the gods from growing old, while images of the Buddha are often gilded as a sign of enlightenment and perfection. As a traditional symbol of wealth, gold features in the regalia of monarchy and high office, and it is also used to symbolize human achievement – as in a gold medal or, figuratively, in the notion of a "golden age".

Like gold, silver is also related to immortality; the ancient Egyptians, for instance, believed their gods had golden flesh and silver bones. Silver is associated

with the moon, the element of water, female energies and purity; it is also symbolic of wealth, used in currency and given in tribute.

In ancient Mesoamerica jade was valued more highly than gold or silver; it was a symbol of purity and life and the preserve of royalty. Animals and plants have also yielded precious substances – pearls and ivory, musk and ambergris, spices, resins and oils. Liquid chocolate was used by the Maya as currency, while pepper was such a valuable spice that, in the 5th century, Attila the Hun is reputed to have demanded 1350kg (3000lb) of peppercorns as ransom for the city of Rome.

ABOVE A lavish portrait of Russian Empress, Catherine the Great, is full of the symbols of kingship, including crown, sceptre and orb.

MONEY
As production of goods and services became more diverse and specialized, trade by simple barter ceased to be practical. Universally recognized tokens, which gradually developed into money, solved the problem: as long as everyone accepted the symbolic value of the tokens they could be exchanged for anything. Items such as shells and beads were used by some societies, but metal, when it was available, was more versatile and was most commonly

used. Originally coins represented the intrinsic worth of the metal from which they were made, but the value of modern coinage, and of banknotes, is purely symbolic.

Designs impressed on the faces of coins usually signified the authority of the ruling body (typically the ruler's head). They also bore iconographic signs of the culture – such as horses, boars and trees on many Gaulish coins – a tradition that continues to this day. Chinese cash had a square hole in the centre symbolizing Earth surrounded by the circle of Heaven, with a superscription of the emperor, son of Heaven and Earth.

REGALIA OF OFFICE

One way of distinguishing rank is through ceremonial dress and accessories. The head is often seen as the "seat of the soul" and the noblest part of the body, and elaborate headdresses are almost universally used to indicate high status – the leader being the "head" of the group. They range from the elaborate feathered headdress of a Native American chief to the richly jewelled crown of a monarch. Many leaders carry a golden globe, or orb (a piece of regalia first used by Roman emperors to show their dominion over the world), and a sceptre similar to a staff. In Japan, one of the items of imperial regalia is a bronze mirror, associated with the goddess Amaterasu and passed down to the imperial family, who claim descent from her.

The principal item of clothing forming part of the regalia is typically a robe or cape. The Chinese emperor's robe had a round collar with a square hem, identifying its wearer as the intermediary between Heaven and Earth. The robe of a shaman bears a wealth of symbolism: in ancient Uralo-Altaic cultures, for example, it was decorated with a three-branched emblem known as the mark of the bustard, which symbolized the communication between the worlds of death and rebirth. Today in the West, white ermine, symbolic of moral purity and justice, is still used to decorate the robes of state, judicial, ecclesiastical and academic dignitaries.

The trappings of power help to maintain the mystique of those who occupy a "seat of office" that sets them apart from the lowly rank and file. This "chair" takes many different guises: the chairperson is the head of an organization, while in academia, the holder of a chair in a particular subject is at the very top of that discipline. A throne is a special chair that symbolizes the authority of a god or sovereign. It is often positioned on a raised platform to signify the ruler's elevated status, and is usually richly embellished. In the Bible, King Solomon's throne is described as being of ivory, overlaid with gold, standing at the top of six steps, flanked by a pair of golden lions. The intricately decorated beadwork thrones of the Bamum kingdom in Cameroon incorporate the figures of men and women to illustrate the monarch's wealth in people, while the beads themselves, the preserve of royalty, symbolize his material wealth.

SEALS

An ancient symbol of identity and authority is the seal, a small object carved with a unique design, which could be pressed into a soft clay tablet or into melted wax. It was used like a signature to guarantee the authenticity of a document such as a royal decree, and it could also ensure the security of a document in transit: when stamped into sealing wax securing folded or rolled paper, the seal could not be broken undetected. To this day seals are still used on legal documents, such as wills. Seals were sometimes worn in the form of rings, and inscribed with the names of deities or passages from holy texts, leading to their use as talismans.

ABOVE A sceptre or staff is a symbol of authority and rulership.

TOP A throne is the seat of power and authority in both the temporal and spiritual realm.

BELOW Traditionally, seals were symbols of authority and identity.

ALPHABETS AND WRITING

ABOVE The runic alphabet was used for a written, not spoken, language that was associated with magic, religion and prophecy.

In almost every culture, alphabets and letters are laden with symbolic meaning. In ancient times, they were particularly associated with magic, divination and sacred knowledge. Knowing how to read and write was a mark of privilege and a source of power – something that still holds true today, when almost half the world's adult population cannot, or can only just, write. Written language also made possible the dissemination of knowledge and information, first through written documents and centuries later through printed books.

ABOVE The Roman letter A stands for first grade or top class. It also symbolizes beginnings.

WRITING

Communication through writing relies on an agreed repertoire of formal signs or symbols that can be used in different combinations to reproduce the ideas the writer wants to express. It seems likely that the earliest writing systems – the cuneiform pictographs of ancient Mesopotamia, Egyptian hieroglyphs and Chinese ideograms – developed from the signs and paintings of pre-history.

When alphabets were developed (some time around 1000 BC) the number of different characters needed was drastically reduced: the Roman alphabet, which we still use today, contains 26 letters, while 1,000 basic signs are needed for writing Chinese.

BELOW More than merely a writing system for the communication of information, Chinese script has been elevated into a poetic art form.

ABOVE The pictorial cuneiform script could be used to infinite purpose. This inscription, dating back to the 13th century BC, is a contract for the sale of children.

EARLY INSCRIPTIONS

The population of Mesopotamia consisted largely of shepherds and farmers, and one of the first uses of writing seems to have been for agricultural accounts: the earliest known Sumerian clay tablets list sacks of grain and herds of cattle. Cuneiform script was based on pictograms, so that, for instance, the outline of the head of a cow stood for the animal, but ideas as well as objects could be represented: a bird and an egg side by side meant "fertility".

The characters used by the ancient Egyptians are known as hieroglyphs, from two Greek words meaning "holy engravings". Hieroglyphs were created from stylized drawings – of human heads, birds, animals, plants and flowers, as well as some man-made objects – and were written in different directions, depending

ABOVE The first letter-based alphabet, reading from right to left, was probably the Phoenician one, from which Hebrew, Aramaic and Arabic scripts developed.

on the text and where it was used. Like the Egyptians, the Chinese attributed a legendary origin to writing: according to one story the Emperor Huang-Tsi discovered it after studying the heavenly bodies and objects in nature, particularly bird and animal footprints. While hieroglyphs and cuneiform script were eventually supplanted by Arabic script, the system of writing invented by the Chinese remains essentially unchanged: the pictograms for words such as sun, tree, mountain, field and door have changed very little in 3,000 years.

ALPHABETS

The Phoenician alphabet is generally considered to have been the first, comprising 22 consonant characters and written from right to left. From

ABOVE In the ancient world, scribes formed an elite, high-status, social class, sometimes holding more state power and knowledge than the sovereign himself.

Phoenician, scripts such as Aramaic, Hebrew and Arabic developed, all of which are read from right to left, as well as some lesser-known writing systems, some of which have survived. These include Tifnagh, the script used by the Tuareg people of northern Africa, which is distinctive because of its highly geometric form. It is also very unusual as its use is confined to women, Tuareg society being matriarchal: a good example of the connection between literacy and social power. Other alphabets include Greek, Roman (which

forms the basis of the English alphabet), Sanskrit and Cyrillic.

Individual letters of an alphabet may possess symbolic value. Scholars have noted that in many ancient alphabets most letters depicted an animal, a human gesture or a physical object, while some alphabets, for example Hebrew and runic, are a sequence of specific words rather than letters. The Hebrew alphabet begins, aleph (ox), beth (house), gimel (camel), and not A, B, G.

EUROPEAN TRADITIONS
Runes are the oldest scripted signs of the ancient Germans. The word *runa* means "secret" in Middle High German, and was borrowed by Finnish as *runo*, meaning "song". Allegedly created

by the Norse god Odin, the 24 letters of the runic alphabet incorporate fertility symbols from prehistoric rock carvings and represent letters, words and symbolic concepts. For instance, the rune Ansuz (the equivalent of A) was concerned with messages and signals and was associated with the mouth as a source of divine speech, as well as the mouths of rivers, and the Norse trickster god Loki. The runic alphabet was linked to religious beliefs and magical practices, and was never used to represent a spoken language. Norse expeditions carried the runes to other places – Anglo-Saxon England, Iceland, Russia and possibly even North America.

Distantly related to the runes, the letters of the Celtic Irish or Ogham "tree" alphabet consist of 25 symbols, each made up of a series of horizontal or diagonal notches or lines. Originally cut into wood or stone, each glyph is named after a tree. One variation of the Ogham alphabet is named after its first three letters: beith (birch), luis (rowan) and nion (ash). The Ogham symbols were believed to come under the aegis of Ogma, the god of speech. Like runes, the Ogham alphabet was primarily a method of inscription and augury used by druids, seers and poets, rather than a system of ordinary writing.

ABOVE The letter Z comes at the end of the Roman alphabet and symbolizes endings.

BELOW A portrait of a scribe named Mery, head of the royal archives at Saqqarah, mid-4th dynasty (c.2575–2450 BC), on the door of his tomb. The fact that Mery had his own richly decorated tomb shows his high status in ancient Egyptian society. The relief shows Mery at work, making an inscription on a writing tablet, his stylus tucked behind his ear.

THE LETTER X

Many different symbolic associations are ascribed to the letter X. In countries where the Roman alphabet was used, illiterate people used it instead of their signature on legal documents such as birth certificates. After they had made their mark, it was customary to kiss it as a sign of their sincerity, which is why we use X to represent a kiss. In Roman numerals, X is the number 10, while in mathematics it denotes multiplication, or in algebra, a variable in a function. The latter, indicating an unknown quantity, has led to expressions such as "Mr X", where X expresses the idea of anonymity. The use of X to guarantee anonymity also occurs when voting. In contrast to a tick, indicating "correct", X is used to mark an error. On road and other signs it is a warning that something is forbidden or has been cancelled, and the use of crossed lines to pinpoint a position on a map has led to the expression "X marks the spot".

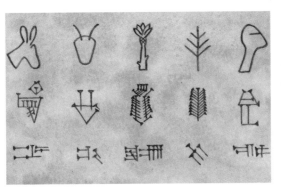

RIGHT These ancient Mesopotamian pictographs show the development of writing. The top row shows a simple drawing (donkey, ox, date palm, barley, head), while the next two rows show how the picture developed into cuneiform script.

high status in other Eastern countries, such as Japan, and in Islam, where inscriptions of texts from the Qur'an were used instead of religious imagery.

RELIGIOUS TRADITIONS

Almost universally, writing has been linked with sacred tradition. In ancient Egypt it was thought that writing was the gift of the god Thoth to humanity, while in India, Sarasvati, the goddess of speech, is also called the alphabet goddess; her consort Brahma, the creator god, is sometimes shown wearing a garland of 50 letters. According to the Biblical account, the Ten Commandments were presented to Moses inscribed on tablets of stone (which Moses symbolically broke when the precepts were not followed), together with the Torah, the primary document of Judaism.

For Kabbalists, the letters of the Hebrew alphabet are linked with numbers and thought to possess powers of creation, while in Islamic mystical traditions there is also a highly refined science of letters based upon their symbolic qualities. In Sufism, the letters of the Arabic alphabet can be classified according to the four elements (fire, air, earth and water), each of which, as a material representation of the divine word, bears a specific meaning. Some traditions have viewed vowels and consonants in terms of "spirit" and "matter" respectively. In antiquity, the seven Greek vowels were thought to symbolize the seven spheres of Heaven and the seven sets of stars moving within them.

BOOKS

The book is an important symbol in many traditions, variously linked with religion, wisdom, scholarship and divination. Judaism, Christianity and Islam are all "religions of the book", based on the holy texts or scriptures (meaning "writing") that have God-given status. Codes of conduct have evolved concerning the handling of holy texts: Moslems observe rituals of cleanliness before studying the Qur'an, and it is never put on the floor; in synagogues, books or scrolls that are too worn out to read, or pieces of paper bearing holy words, are not discarded but kept in a special box that is ceremonially buried when it is full.

In China, books were associated with Taoist sages and were symbols of great learning. In the ancient world, the Sibylline Books were believed to contain prophecies of Rome's destiny and were consulted by the Roman senate in times of emergency, while in medieval Europe books were thought to have divinatory powers, so that if a book was opened at random and a grain of wheat dropped on to a page, the text on which the grain landed would point to a future course of events or answer a question. Words from books have even been eaten as auspicious talismans, a way of ingesting the wisdom and power of the written word.

WRITING MATERIALS

Many different materials have been used for writing on, including papyrus (ancient Egypt), tablets of baked clay (Mesopotamia), marble (Greece), deerskin (Mexico), bamboo (Polynesia), silk (China) and wood (Scandinavia). Each material has called for the use of suitable writing implements, of which the most widely used are the pen and the brush.

In Islamic traditions, the pen (qalam) is highly symbolic. An agent of divine revelation, it was made of light and created by Allah to write upon the "book" or tablet. In Classical mythology, the stylus pen and tablet are attributes of Calliope, the Muse of Epic Poetry, and in Christian iconography the four Evangelists are sometimes associated with a quill pen.

In China, the writing brush, together with its accompanying ink and inkstone, are important symbols. With paper, they make up the "Four Treasures of the Study", symbols of the scholarly class that ruled China from the 2nd century BC, and they were used in calligraphy, in which writing was transformed into an art form practised by the elite. Calligraphy was also accorded

SECRET CODES

Writing has always been linked with magic and the occult (meaning "hidden") and has been used in symbols purposefully created to conceal information from all but initiates or the learned, especially in esoteric traditions whose ideas go against mainstream thought. For instance, Hebrew letters, Latin words and Kabbalistic signs have sometimes been used in five-pointed magical seals called pentacles, impressed on virgin parchment or engraved on precious metals. These symbolize occult powers and have been used in spells and magic.

The Western occult or "hermetic" tradition traces its origins to the Hermetica, writings of the 1st–3rd centuries AD that allegedly contain the teachings of Hermes Trismegistus (the Greek name for the Egyptian deity Thoth, god of wisdom and

writing). They enshrine a number of concepts central to many esoteric and occult traditions – for instance, the duality of matter and spirit, and the idea that salvation can be achieved through self-knowledge rather than through faith or belief. During the Middle Ages, magical "recipe books" called "grimoires" set out a system in which self-knowledge could be attained using the power of symbols to invoke spirits that the magician then had to confront and overcome. Today psychologists might interpret these as facets of the magician's own personality. Many magical symbols (known as "sigils") were devised during the 15th and 16th centuries, such as those created by Dr John Dee, astrologer to the English court of Elizabeth I. Some of Dee's sigils bear a resemblance to letters, such as an inverted L or Y or a back-to-front Z.

ALPHA AND OMEGA

The first and last letters of the Greek alphabet symbolize that which is all-encompassing, the two poles of the universe between which is contained the totality of knowledge, being, time and space. In the Christian tradition, they are ascribed to Jesus Christ, who, in the Book of Revelation declares: "I am alpha and omega, the beginning and the ending... which is, and which was, and which is to come" (1:8). In modern parlance, the phrase "from A to Z" means "completely, thoroughly and in detail".

ABOVE Today runes are popular as a divination device, with each symbol inscribed on a stone and then "picked".

FAR LEFT This frontispiece to John Dee's *Little Book of Love* shows Venus with magic sigils on her scroll and trumpet.

LEFT The printing press revolutionized the production of books, making the written word more widely available.

BODY LANGUAGE

ABOVE This Indian gesture, known as namaste, symbolizes the reconciliation of the duality in nature. It is also used as a greeting in China.

ABOVE The CND sign was devised using the semaphore signals for the letters N and D.

RIGHT The V for victory sign, two fingers raised in a "V" shape, palms outwards, was first used by Winston Churchill, Britain's prime minister, during the First World War. It is now used as a sign for triumph over adversity all over the world.

The body is a channel of communication, whether the information it conveys is conscious or unconscious, intended or unintentional. Its language is organized both by culturally constructed meaning and symbolism and by the symbolism of the unconscious, or the realm of dreaming. The body is a great source of symbolic expression, communicating both to ourselves, in the form of "body wisdom", and to others. Expressions such as "You are a pain in the neck", "I will hold you in my heart", "I feel it in my bones" and many more, suggest that our bodies can be channels of meaningful and symbolic information.

GESTURE AND GESTICULATION

The intended language of the body appears in gesture and gesticulation. In early humans, the use of both tools and symbols became possible when moving on two limbs freed the hands so that humans were able to physically and mentally "grasp" or apprehend the world.

Gestures play a part in creating and communicating meaning. In India and China, placing the hands together in a praying position at chest height is the "namaste" gesture, which can be interpreted as "The god in me greets the god in you" and also symbolizes the reconciliation of the duality of nature. Some gestures – such as a deferential stoop or bow, smiling or shrugging – appear truly universal, yet even the

commonest signs can have different meanings in different cultures. Though nodding the head signifies assent in most parts of the world, in India it is communicated by shaking the head from side to side.

Raising the thumb stands for "OK" in the USA, but is obscene or very impolite in Brazil, Russia and Greece. In Colombia, this sign placed over the nose implies that someone is a homosexual. Gestures implying a man finds a woman pretty vary widely: they include raising the eyebrows in America and Britain, grasping the beard in the Arab world, rotating a finger in the cheek in Italy and kissing the fingertips in France.

Sticking out ones tongue at someone can be seen as cheeky, provocative or insulting in many cultures. In Tibet, however, it is used as a polite greeting. In New Zealand, the Maori use it as a ceremonial warning. When visitors arrive a Maori warrior approaches them in a warlike manner, with bulging eyes and extended tongue, meaning, "We are willing to attack if you do not

come in friendship." If the visitors react passively they are then welcomed warmly.

The v-sign, popularized by Britain's wartime leader Winston Churchill, is now used throughout the world as a sign for victory, or triumph over adversity. If the sign is reversed, with the palm facing inwards, however, it is seen as rude and offensive.

Gesticulations are bodily gestures that accompany and enhance verbal communication. They are used everywhere but are particularly prominent in Italy, where every conversation is seasoned with such a wide array of hand signals that it is possible to understand its thrust from the other side of a piazza. As an example, a hand drawn away from the chin as if growing a beard means, "You are boring."

SIGN LANGUAGE

Formal body language systems may involve gestures that depict objects and ideas iconically, or communicate by spelling out words. The Native Americans of the Plains used a complex, mainly

MUDRAS

The mudras are symbolic and meaningful hand gestures of the Buddha, portrayed in Buddhist statues since the 5th century AD. *Dhyana* mudra indicates balance and meditation. *Ksepana* mudra means the sprinkling of the nectar of immortality. *Varada* mudra signifies charity and the fulfilment of all wishes. *Uttarabodhi* mudra represents supreme enlightenment.

iconic, system of signing for communication between tribes without a common language. In 1755 the Abbé Charles Michel de l'Epée developed a system of signing for the deaf, which has been the foundation for many modern sign languages.

The semaphore signalling system, originally developed for maritime purposes, uses arm positions and flags to communicate letters of the alphabet. Semaphore is the source of the campaign for nuclear disarmament (CND) symbol, which combines the signals for the letters "N" and "D": two arms in a downwards facing "V" shape for "N", and one arm pointing straight up and the other straight down for "D".

RIGHT Charles Michel de l'Epée, the French educationalist who invented a system of signing for the deaf, teaches a group of students.

DOUBLE SIGNALS

When we communicate two or more different things at the same time, we are double-signalling. Body language may disturb the intended communication, as when we say to someone, "It's nice to meet you", but simultaneously turn away, so that our body conveys the message "I am not interested in meeting you", or "My focus is elsewhere."

NON-VERBAL COMMUNICATION

Communication theory understands communication as the exchange of discrete pieces of information through signals. We communicate linguistically through words and language, but also "non-verbally" through our tone of voice, posture, movement or positioning of our body, the direction of our gaze, and touch.

Our interpretations of other people's non-verbal signals may be very accurate, or they may fall wide of the mark due to our own preconceptions, projections or cultural variations. For example, the behaviour of the eyes can communicate relative social ranking, dominance, submission or respect. They can also signal aggression, love and sexual interest or disinterest. For black Americans, lack of eye contact shows respect, but this may be misinterpreted by white Americans, who expect a direct gaze. Maintaining eye contact in conversation is respectful or can indicate trustworthiness for Arabs, Latin Americans and southern Europeans, while for East Asians and Indians

"peripheral gaze" or no eye contact is more acceptable. In Greece, it is common for people to stare at others in public, and Greeks can feel invisible or ignored in a country such as Britain, where it is rude to stare.

PERSONAL SPACE

Customs, conventions and body language exist in order to define personal or community space. Each community has different symbolic rituals and methods of engaging with visitors and enemies at the edge of their defined territory. Every individual has different needs for personal space, and these change according to time and circumstance. For example, monarchs and political leaders commonly command a wide berth in public life, unless they are making significant gestures such as the symbolic embrace and handshakes of two leaders, or conferring an honour on one of their subjects. In a different situation, with friends or family, the same individual will reduce their personal space to allow greater intimacy.

ABOVE Eye contact is an important part of non-verbal communication.

BELOW The handshake is valuable both for guarding personal space and also for breaking through spatial barriers.

BODY ART

ABOVE Painting the body with henna is an ancient art originating in Mesopotamia, and still practised in parts of India, as at this Hindu wedding, and the Middle East. It is the henna itself that symbolizes love, happiness and protection.

BELOW In this earliest known painting from South America, dated 1599, an Ecuadorian from Quito wears European dress but has the body piercings and jewellery of his own tribal tradition.

DON P. Z. ZA S.

Though fashions and customs vary, people of all cultures use the body to express their identity and to mark rites of passage. They alter and adorn it in both permanent and temporary ways, from tattoos, decorative scarring and piercings, to jewellery, hairstyles, make-up and clothes. Body art is used to symbolize social and cultural allegiance and difference, to denote rank or power, to accentuate beauty, and to make a statement about gender and sexual availability. It also plays an important part in ritual and ceremony.

DRESS AND TABOO

Aside from their practical use as protection from the elements, clothes have a moral significance in many cultures. In Victorian Britain it was considered risqué for a woman to show her ankle, while one of the symbols of the "sexual revolution" of the 1960s was the mini-skirt. In cultures that do not view nakedness as something to hide, clothing signifies an embellishment of the human form.

Dress can show adherence to a specific body of belief or part of society. Teenagers in the West choose clothes that conform to a recognizable style to indicate their social allegiance. In many religious traditions, the robes of monks or nuns symbolize their non-attachment to the material world and a lack of concern with individual characteristics, focusing instead on their relationship with the divine.

BODY PAINTING

In many parts of the world women dye their skin with henna. In parts of India this practice, known as *mehndi*, has been a tradition for more than 5,000 years. The drawing of intricate patterns over the hands and forearms or feet forms part of the wedding ceremony, and it is thought that the deeper the colour on the skin, the longer the love will last between a couple. In Morocco, henna symbolically blesses the wearer and is said to protect from evil and promote fertility and good fortune. In Sudan, the wearing of henna is an expression of happiness and of a wife's love for her husband, while not wearing it is thought to represent grief or lack of love.

Make-up is used to accentuate desirable facial features but also as a disguise. Often it is a means of conforming to current fashions and ideas about what constitutes beauty, but today's Goths, for example, use white face make-up and black or purple lipstick as a way of challenging the dominant culture. In Japan, where white make-up represents a traditional ideal of beauty and is still the mask of the geisha, it was once customary for upper-class women to shave off their eyebrows and blacken their teeth as a sign that they had come of age.

BODY PIERCING

The piercing of the body as a symbolic act is common to many cultures. In South America, the Carafa Indians insert a thin cane into their lower lip to show that they are in the prime of life. Tongue piercing was practised in a ritual form by the Aztecs and Maya as well as by some Native American tribes such as the Tlingit and Kwakiutl. Among the Berber, Beja and Bedouin of the Middle East, nose rings are very common: the size of the ring denotes the wealth of the family, and when a man marries he gives his ring to his wife as a security if she is divorced or widowed. In India, it is common for women to wear nose studs on their left nostril; this is because in Ayurvedic medicine, the traditional healing system of India, it is believed to connect with the female reproductive organs via the body's subtle energy system, so the piercing is thought to ease menstrual pain and facilitate childbirth.

Body piercings are also governed by aesthetic standards. For instance, the women of the Makololo of Malawi wear plates called *pelele* in the upper lip to enhance their beauty. Body piercing is also associated with erotica: the Kama Sutra, the Indian text on the art of lovemaking, talks of *apadravya*, a vertical barbell inserted through the glans of the penis for increased arousal, while in 19th-century Europe the "bosom ring" was worn by women in high society to enlarge their nipples and keep them in a state of excitation. Today in the West, body piercing involving the lips, tongue, eyebrows, nose, navel, nipples and labia is enjoying a revival. Some people think this represents a need to connect to something more enduring than the ephemera of consumer society; it is also associated with asserting individual and group identity, rebellion against society's "norms" and sexual fetish.

SCARIFICATION

For many indigenous peoples the practice of scarification (deliberate scarring of the body) is highly symbolic. Among the Karo in Ethiopia a scarified line on a man's chest shows that he has killed an enemy from another tribe and is a mark of respect, while Karo women enhance their beauty and sensuality with deep cuts made into their chest and torso. In initiation ceremonies practised by the Barabaig of East Africa, pubescent boys' heads are shaved and their foreheads are cut with three incisions from ear to ear to mark their entry into manhood. In West Africa, young girls have scarification marks around the navel as a reminder of

their ancestral mother, while the Djuka people of Dutch Guiana in the West Indies mark faces, shoulders and arms with Kaffa designs handed down from their African ancestors.

TATTOOS

Mummified bodies found in many parts of the world, including Egypt, South America, Africa, Russia and Europe, suggest that tattooing is an ancient art linked to ritual and sacred ceremony. The body of a Bronze Age man preserved in ice in the Austrian Alps had a total of 57 tattoos, thought to be connected with healing. The Inuit and some Native Americans use them to protect against disease, and in the Sudan, Nubian girls have "welts" thought to strengthen their immune systems while pregnant.

The word tattoo is from the Samoan *ta tau*, which means "balanced" and "fitting". The *ta tau* is used as a sign of maturity, demonstrating a readiness for life. Male *ta tau* are applied in a particular order, starting at the small of the back, with the navel design (*pute*) always applied last. Female Samoans always have a diamond-shaped design (*malu*) on the backs of their knees. Any *ta tau* that remains unfinished is considered shameful as it indicates an uncompleted ceremony. In Maori culture, intricate tattoos known as *ta moko* signify achievements and social rank. Lines and spirals are worn on the face and buttocks of men, and on the chin, lips and shoulders of women. Those of high rank also have *ta moko* on

their faces, the left side relating to the father's line, and the right side to the mother's.

Tattoos may denote allegiance to tribes, clans or gangs. For instance, in America a winged skull tattoo is the emblem of the Hell's Angels motorcycle gang. A tattoo common among Hispanic gang members is the pachucho cross, placed on the hand between thumb and index finger; another consists of three dots in a pyramid shape, which means *mi vida loca* or my crazy life.

A tattoo establishes a symbolic link between its wearer and what it depicts, which acts as a totem. This means tattoos may have a protective function: Melanesian fisherman use a dolphin tattoo to avoid shark attack. Alternatively, tattoos can be symbols of aggression: in the West, designs include eagles with their talons drawn to attack, black panthers, scorpions, skulls, or images of death and demons. Tattoos can also symbolize love and allegiance, so another popular design in the West is a heart pierced by an arrow, inscribed with the beloved's name.

ABOVE The Kaffa designs on the shoulders of a young Djuka girl are made by cuts filled with ashes that are allowed to heal and then recut and refilled until the scars reach the right level.

BELOW Tattoos have become common in the youth culture of the West as an identity statement or to enhance eroticism and beauty.

PATTERNS AND GRAPHICS

Some of the most compelling symbols
rely only on pattern or colour, line or
geometric shape, and it is often these
most basic symbols that represent the
grandest concepts, such as eternity being
represented as a simple dot, or the spiral
conveying the very rhythm of breathing
and life itself.

RIGHT Geometric signs are always mirrored in nature, the
triangle is represented by mountains, while the straight line
represents the horizon, the division between heaven and earth.

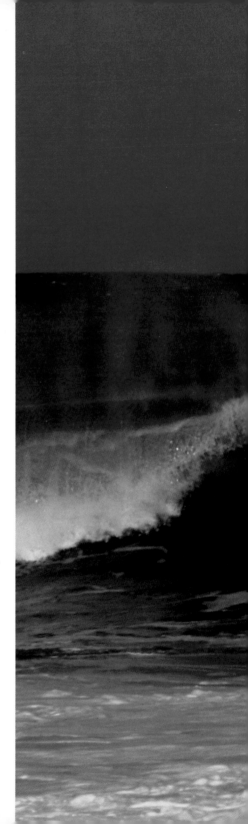

NUMBERS

ABOVE A six-pointed star is a symbol of balance and harmony. It is also an emblem of Judaism.

TOP Number one is the symbol of beginnings.

TOP RIGHT As a symbol of two twins represent doubled force, but also symbolize warring spirits.

The complex symbolism of numbers stretches back into antiquity. In many traditions, they are linked with cosmic principles that give order and structure to the universe, governing the movement of the moon and planets as well as plant, animal and human life. In ancient Greece, Pythagoras (c.569–475 BC), sometimes described as the first pure mathematician, is quoted as saying, "Numbers rule all things." Numerology is one of the oldest sciences of symbols. Cultures all over the world have used individual numbers symbolically: here are some of the main associations for one to ten.

1 Number one represents beginnings and the primal cause. It is a symbol of creation and the human species, and is depicted in the standing stone, the upright staff and the erect phallus. In monotheistic religions one is the number of God, while in Jungian psychology it is a unifying symbol. In the Native American Earth Count, one represents Grandfather Sun and fire, the spark of life. We use the

expression "number one" to refer to our own importance as an individual. In Pythagorean theory one represents the male principle.

2 Chinese numerology is based on the number two, for in Taoist belief the universe is made up of polarity, expressed in the complementary forces yin and yang. Two represents pairs and duality, separating creator and created, spirit and matter, man and woman, light and dark. Many cultures regard sets of two, such as twins, as especially lucky. In the Native American Earth Count, two represents Grandmother Earth, the body, Earth, death and introspection. For Pythagoreans it represents the female principle.

3 Number three expresses all aspects of creation, including birth, life and death; past, present and future; and mind, body and soul. To the Chinese it is a perfect number, expressing wholeness and fulfilment through the joining together of Heaven, Earth and

humanity. In Pythagorean theory it represents perfect harmony, the union of unity (one) and diversity (two). In Islam the number three represents the soul, and for Native Americans it is linked with water and the emotions. Among the Dogon it symbolizes the male principle. The symbolism of three is linked with the triangle.

4 The number four is related to the cardinal directions, the seasons, the elements and the phases of the moon. In Pythagorean theory, as the first square it represents perfection, and in the Native American Earth Count it symbolizes harmony. Its symbolism is connected with both the cross and the square, suggesting order, stability and solidity. In Islam it is related to matter, and in Christianity to the four Evangelists. It is a sacred number in the Hindu Vedas, which are themselves divided into four parts. The Japanese word for four, *shi*, sounds like the word for death, so it is replaced in conversation by *yo* or *yon*.

ZERO

The use of zero developed far later than our system for representing numbers, though Babylonion scribes sometimes left a blank space where it was intended to go. In ancient Egypt, there was no hieroglyph for nought. The Maya understood the concept of zero, and represented it as a spiral, suggesting the womb symbolism of the shell and foetal life. Zero represents the blank space of infinity, the void from which life arises and to which it returns. Zero is the symbol of complete potentiality.

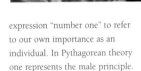

5 According to Pythagoras, five is the number of humanity, the human body with its four limbs and head fits inside a pentagram, or five-pointed star. In the Native American Earth Count, five denotes the human as a sacred being, bridging the gap between earth and sky, past and future and the material and spirit worlds. In China, it is the number of the harmonic union of yin (two) and yang (three), while in India and China it represents the elements – fire, air, earth, water and ether.

6 In China, six is the number of celestial power and longevity. In the Native American Earth Count it is associated with the ancestors. Expressed as a hexagon or six-pointed star, it signifies harmony and balance and is linked with the universal human, and in Pythagorean theory with justice. In Buddhism, there are several groupings of six, including the six realms of existence. Six is associated with sin in the New Testament Book of Revelation: as 666, it becomes the number of the beast of the Apocalypse.

7 Seven has widespread significance in magic and divine mystery. It is the number of the planets known in antiquity (Sun, Moon, Mercury, Venus, Mars, Jupiter and Saturn) and of the days of the week. There are seven branches to the shaman's cosmic tree, seven colours to a rainbow, and seven main chakras in the human body. In ancient Egypt, there were seven gods of light and seven of darkness, and seven was a symbol of eternal life. In

TWELVE

In Christian symbolism, twelve is a number of universal fulfilment, being the number of Christ's disciples, as well as the Tribes of Israel. There are also twelve gates to the Heavenly City of Jerusalem, and the "Tree of Life" bore twelve fruits. In many traditions, it relates to the space-time continuum (with the zodiac and the months of the year) and represents a completed cycle.

Judaism the New Year begins in the seventh month of the Jewish calendar. Muslims believe there are seven heavens, seven hells and seven earths, while for Christians it is the number of heavenly virtues as well as deadly sins.

8 Almost universally, eight is the number of cosmic balance. For Native Americans it is the number of all natural laws. In Buddhism it relates to the dharmachakra, or eight-spoked wheel of life, and the eight petals of the lotus, representing the eight paths to spiritual perfection. Taoists revere the Eight Immortals and Eight Precious Things, while the Hindu god Vishnu has eight arms corresponding to the eight guardians of space. Eight is also an important number in African belief: among the Dogon there are eight hero-creators and eight primal ancestors, and eight is associated with water and semen.

9 The number nine relates to the symbolism of the triple power of three – the three trimesters (three-month periods) of pregnancy or the three triads of the nine orders of angels. In China it is highly auspicious because it is the number of the celestial spheres. Among the Aztecs, a nine-storey temple echoed the nine heavens or stages through which the soul must pass. In the Native American

LEFT In antiquity, there were seven known planets, and the days of the week were named after them.

LEFT Through its association with pregnancy, the number nine is associated with gestation and the fulfilment of creation.

Earth Count, nine signifies the moon, change and movement.

10 In Pythagorean theory, ten represents divine power. In the Biblical tradition it is the number of God's commandments, and in Native American tradition it represents the intellect.

THIRTEEN

In the West the number 13 is generally considered unlucky. This superstition may derive from the 13 people (Christ and his 12 disciples) who were present at the fateful Last Supper. The Kabbalah lists 13 spirits of evil. In other cultures the number is considered sacred. In ancient Greece it represented Zeus, the 13th deity, and it is an important number in ancient Mexican astronomy, calendars and theology. In the Native American Earth Count 13 represents the Goddess.

DOTS AND LINES

ABOVE In the Hindu tradition, the dot, or *bindu,* is a sacred symbol and is often worn in the position of the third eye.

It may be hard to conceive that markings as basic as dots and lines could have any particular symbolic significance, yet these simple graphics are some of the earliest and possibly most profound symbols. As well as being important in their own right, they also form an integral part of many other symbol systems, including the visual arts, writing, mathematics, geometry and various forms of divination, as well as informing sacred traditions all over the world.

THE DOT

Like a star in the sky, the dot or point is the first emanation to appear from the infinite void, a pinprick of light from the world of spirit. It symbolizes the centre or source from which all life begins and to which it must one day return. It is emblematic of the bud or seed, symbolizing the start of a new life, of hope and promise for the future. It is the first sign of a presence and a source of power – the centre from which all else radiates and the essence that remains when all else is removed. It is the pupil at the centre of an eye and the navel in the middle of

the body – a visual reminder of the umbilical cord that connected the unborn child to life. As the full point at the end of a statement it can represent an ending, but also presupposes a new beginning with the start of the next sentence.

In Hindu teaching the dot is known as the *bindu* (from a Sanskrit word meaning "drop") and is a symbol of the absolute. It is represented in the yantra (a type of mandala) by the point at which the two triangles representing Shiva and Shakti (god and goddess of the universe) meet. The *bindu* is often seen painted or worn on the face at the "third eye" in the centre of the forehead. In Hindu and Buddhist traditions the *bindu* is the source of meditation and a symbol of spiritual integration or enlightenment; it is the centre at which all experience is compacted into total concentration before imploding back to its origin – the void or a transcendental state of consciousness. In Islamic mysticism it is a symbol of the creator and the eternal. Numerically it is related to the symbolism of zero.

HORIZONTAL AND VERTICAL LINES

As its name suggests, a horizontal line follows the direction of the horizon. It represents the division between earth and sky, the dividing line between human life and the realms of the gods, and

BELOW A zigzag pattern is one of the oldest known geometric shapes, thought to represent snakes or water.

RIGHT The horizon is the line that appears to divide the earth from the sky, or, figuratively, the human and spiritual realms.

— | ═   ‖   ≡   ⫴

ABOVE The straight line is one of the five basic elements in Western ideography. These are six of the most common variations. From left (1) to right (6): 1. The base; 2. Unity; 3. Equals sign; 4. Complete entities; 5. Similarity in one dimension; 6. The same as.

the base or ground we stand on. As an axis of direction, the horizontal line symbolizes movement on the earth plane: from left to right (west to east) or right to left (east to west), as well as movement in time. It is concerned with the temporal realm, with matter and substance, balance and stability. Traditionally it is linked with the female or receptive element, although in China it is a yang symbol, denoting active, masculine power. In mathematics, a short horizontal line is a minus sign.

If the horizontal line is associated with matter, then the vertical line embraces spirit and provides the link between the higher and lower worlds. It is associated with the male principle and describes the movement from above to below, from Heaven to Earth, from the nadir to the zenith and vice versa. Related symbols include the spine in the human body, the trunk of the World Tree, the staff, stave, sceptre or wand, and many different phallic symbols. It is also widely used in many alphabets: in the Roman alphabet it forms the letter "I", where it represents the authority of the self. In Greek it forms the letter "iota", which the ancient Greeks considered to be representative of destiny or fate. The vertical line is related numerically to the number one.

ZIGZAG LINES

One of the earliest carvings known is more than 300,000 years old. It appears on a bone fragment from Pech de l'Aze, in France, and shows a zigzag or meander pattern. A set of similar symbolic designs more than 40,000 years old was found in Bacho Kiro, in Bulgaria. It is thought that the zigzags represent either snakes or water: in ancient Egypt, the zigzag was the hieroglyph for water, while a horizontal parallel zigzag formation is used to represent the sign of Aquarius, the water carrier in Western astrology.

PARALLEL LINES

Running side by side and never meeting, parallel lines are symbolic of opposites as well as balance and equality. In early cuneiform script, parallel lines signified "friendship" while crossed lines meant "enmity".

Vertical parallel lines can be observed in pillars or columns, which in the architecture of the ancient and classical world were associated with both temporal and spiritual authority. Double pillars also appear in esoteric symbolism. For example, in the Tarot, the High Priestess is shown sitting between two columns, one black, one white, symbolizing the polarities of male and female, positive and negative, life and death, creation and destruction. This symbolism is echoed in esoteric Jewish lore with the two columns on the façade of Solomon's Temple in Jerusalem. The left-hand column, made of black stone, corresponded to the

moon, decay, the waning year and cursing and was called Jachin, meaning "it shall stand"; the right-hand column, made of white stone, was called Boaz, meaning "in strength" and corresponded to the sun, the waxing year and blessing.

ABOVE Buildings are constructed by combining horizontal and vertical lines or planes. The horizontal planes of floors and ceilings provide grounding and enclosure or protection, while the vertical planes represent stature, growth and aspiration.

DOTS AND LINES IN DIVINATION

The Chinese I Ching, one of the world's oldest divinatory texts, is based on a series of hexagrams composed of broken and unbroken horizontal lines. An unbroken line is yang and relates to the sun, daytime and the heavens, while a broken line is yin and relates to the moon, night and the earth. The patterns made by dots have also been used in divination, originally in the form of stones, nuts or seeds, which were thrown on to the earth and then interpreted. Dot patterns were later transferred to dice or dominoes, where they are used in gaming as well as prediction.

THE CROSS

ABOVE The ankh is the Egyptian version of the cross, and is one of its most ancient manifestations.

ABOVE The equilateral or Greek cross forms the ground plan of many early Greek churches, and is the motif of the Red Cross organization.

In Western culture, the cross has become almost inseparable from Christianity, yet it is actually one of the oldest and most all-encompassing symbols. Carved in stone or wood or worked in metal or bone, richly decorated or simply drawn, the cross has appeared all over the world. A stone disc with a carved cross, found in the Tata Cave, in Hungary, is estimated to be around 100,000 years old, while crosses carved on a mammoth statuette from Vogelherd, in Germany, date back more than 30,000 years. The cross is found in the ancient civilizations of China, Egypt and Central America, is a frequent motif in African art, and appears on Celtic pottery, jewels and coins. It is widely considered to be one of four basic symbols with the point, the circle and the square, to which it is also linked.

EMBRACING THE WHOLE

The cross creates a totality. Its intersection of two lines can be seen as the uniting of the male principle (the vertical) with the female (the horizontal). The two axes also stand for the dimensions of time and space, matter and spirit, body and soul, as well as the equinoxes and solstices.

Crossing horizontal and vertical lines are the basis of a "stick person", one of the most basic representations of the human figure, found in prehistoric rock art, and in children's drawings ever since. When aligned with the four cardinal points, the cross becomes a symbol of orientation to the terrestrial directions of north, south, east and west, which in turn informs the symbolism of the Native American Medicine Wheel. A cross within a circle also mediates between the square and the circle, emphasizing the connection between sky and earth. It has been suggested that the four arms of the cross represent the four phases of the moon, as well as the four elements, the four winds and the four seasons. Together with the square, the cross is closely linked to the symbolism of four, a number signifying wholeness and universality, although in China the number of the cross is five, the perfect number of the human being as microcosm. This is because the midpoint (where the two lines intersect) is also counted – emphasizing the centre or source to which everything is connected.

WORLD SYMBOL

In China the early symbolism of the cross was expressed in the ideogram meaning "Earth": an equilateral cross within a square. According to a traditional Chinese saying, God fashioned the Earth in the form of a cross. A similar view emerges in ancient Mexican mythic tradition, where the cross symbolizes the world in its

totality: The 1st-century Christian theologian, St Jerome, came to the same conclusion when he wrote, "What is it but the form of the world in its four directions?"

Although there are literally hundreds of different types of cross, several appear to be particularly significant.

THE GREEK OR EQUILATERAL CROSS

The equal-armed cross is one of the simplest. When enclosed in a circle it becomes the solar cross or sun-disc, a symbol similar to that adopted by the Assyrians to represent the sun god Shamash. In this form the circle emphasizes the cyclical nature of the seasons, while the four-armed cross represents the shadows cast by the rising and setting sun at the two solstices. This may explain why the cross appears in many examples of megalithic rock art. The Neolithic structure at Loughcrew, in Ireland, was made in the shape of a cross, with the central passage aligned to the equinoctial sunrise.

Centuries later, the Celts combined the cross and circle in a distinctive pattern that originally had links with fertility – the cross symbolizing the male generative power, and the circle, the female. In time the Celtic cross was used as a Christian symbol to represent the union of Heaven and Earth.

THE SWASTIKA

The Sanskrit *svastika* means "well being", and in India the swastika is a symbol of fertility and good fortune. It appears extensively throughout Asia, in both secular

---

THE CROSS AND HEALING

Because of its various spiritual and esoteric associations, the cross is connected with healing and miraculous powers. At one time, the cross was considered to offer protection against disorders such as epileptic fits, or to have the power to ward off supernatural phenomena such as vampires and devils. It is now associated with medicine and nursing through the Red Cross charity, which provides care for victims of war and famine.

LEFT In Central Australia the Aborigines use the form of a cross to control the composition of many sacred works of art.

and religious contexts. It is an ancient and widely used form of solar cross. Some of the earliest European examples appear on Bronze Age pottery found in Anatolia, in central Turkey, dating from about 3000 BC. It also appears on bronze articles among the Ashanti in Africa and was used by the Maya and Navajo.

Essentially the swastika is a spinning cross, with the angles at the end of each arm suggesting streaming light as it turns, just as the sun's rays light up the earth. Spinning anticlockwise it is said to represent the female principle, and clockwise, the male. The anticlockwise swastika appears in Buddhism, Taoism and in Native American cultures. In the modern Western world, however, the symbol tends to be associated with anti-Semitism because of its adoption by the German Nazi party in the 20th century.

THE T-CROSS

The Tau, or T-cross, is another very ancient cross symbol. It may have developed from the axe, a widespread and ancient symbol of the sun god, and appears to be phallocentric, its shape denoting testicles and penis. It forms the

LEFT In Central Australia the Aborigines use the form of a cross to control the composition of many sacred works of art.

basis of the Egyptian ankh, in which the upper arm is replaced by a loop. A symbol of immortality in ancient Egypt, the ankh was adopted by the Coptic Church as its unique form of the Christian cross. The handled cross also occurs in America, where it has been found engraved on monuments in the ruins of Palenque, in Mexico, as well as on pieces of pottery.

THE LATIN CROSS

There is disagreement about the type of cross that was used for the crucifixion of Christ. It was as late as the mid-2nd century that translators of the Gospels first used "crux" in descriptions of death by crucifixion. Many images show Christ hung either from a Y-shaped structure (*furca*) or a T-shaped cross, as well as the more familiar Latin cross, where the cross-bar is set approximately two-thirds of the way up. Over time, the Latin cross became the central symbol of Christianity. Some believe this coincided with the gradual tendency in the early Church to separate the spiritual and material realms in accordance with Christ's saying, "My kingdom is not of this world." This view has dominated ideas about spirituality in much of the Christian world, where earthly life (including nature), the world and the body have been seen as forces that have to be overcome, rather than parts of an organic whole.

For Christians, the crucifix is a seminal symbol, representing Christ's death, resurrection, the victory of spirit over matter and the redemption of humanity.

CROSS OF LORRAINE

A single vertical crossed by two horizontals (the upper shorter than the lower) is known as the double cross, or cross of Lorraine. When a third, smaller, horizontal bar is added, it becomes a triple cross, associated with the papacy. The cross of Lorraine is believed to represent the crucifixion, with the upper bar added for the inscription "INRI" (the Latin abbreviation for "Jesus of Nazareth, King of the Jews"), fixed above Christ by Pontius Pilate. The cross of Lorraine was the emblem of the medieval Dukes of Anjou, later the Dukes of Lorraine, and in World War II became the symbol of the Free French, in opposition to the swastika of the Nazis.

ABOVE The cross has become the most widely used version in depictions of the crucifixion of Christ, and as such has become perhaps the most widely recognised symbol of Christianity.

T

ABOVE For the early Christians the three directions of the Tau cross linked it with the Holy Trinity.

SPIRALS AND CIRCLES

ABOVE Because of their circular shape, rings can symbolize eternity, hence their use as love tokens.

TOP Like the Earth, the circle is a primordial symbol of perfection.

TOP RIGHT This triple spiral at a Stone Age burial site at Newgrange, in Ireland, is believed to symbolize the Celtic triple goddess.

BELOW Megalithic monuments were often arranged in a circle pattern that aligned with the sun's movement through the sky.

Both the spiral and the circle occur in nature as well as in art, myth and sacred tradition. The earliest known use of these shapes was in the Paleolithic age, when they were carved into bone or stone or painted on cave walls. Antler bone batons found in a cave at Isturitz, in France, dating back to c.25,000–20,000 BC, bear a relief forming a complex pattern of concentric arcs and spirals. A disc from the same period, found in Brno, in the Czech Republic, has a vertical line incised from the edge to the centre and is thought to be an abstract representation of a vulva, suggesting a link with the goddess worship characteristic of this period.

THE NATURAL WORLD

The sun, moon and planets all appear circular in shape, while spiral galaxies form some of the most breathtaking patterns in space. In the plant and animal kingdoms, spirals and circles appear in many guises, such as the concentric pattern of tree-rings, the centre of a flower, the shape of a bird's nest, the spiral of a snail or conch-shell, a coiled serpent or a twining plant stem.

Weather and water patterns also form spirals and circles in tornadoes, whirlpools, ripples on a pond and ocean waves. Nature itself circles and cycles through the changing seasons and the endless rhythm of night and day.

THE SPIRAL

Beginning with a single dot, the spiral develops from the initial seed and moves forwards in a clockwise or anticlockwise direction; thus it is connected with movement, energy and growth. Since the earliest times it has been a favourite ornamental motif linked with the symbolism of the moon and with cyclic development, involution and evolution, resurrection and renewal. It has also been linked to the erotic symbolism of the vulva, female sexuality and fertility, while many cultures believe the spiral represents the soul's journey after death. The motif is widely used in Oceanic art, where it is carved into door handles or canoe prows or tattooed on the body. To the Maori the spiral represents creation, and in Polynesia it is thought to be the key to immortality.

DOUBLE SPIRALS

Spirals often appear conjoined in twos and threes. The double spiral is said to symbolize duality and balance. It is also moving simultaneously in two directions – towards involution and evolution, contraction and expansion, or birth and death. This motif is seen in the wreathing of the twin serpents around the caduceus (the rod of

Hermes), or the double helix around the Brahman's staff. In Aztec mythology, the S-shaped counter-rotating double spiral is a symbol of thunder and of the phases of the moon. Spiral oculi (double twists resembling eyes) appear on entrances to sacred sites throughout Europe and are thought to be associated with the equinoxes, when day and night are of equal length.

TRIPLE SPIRALS

The triple spiral is often referred to as the spiral of life and was used consistently in Celtic art for nearly 3,000 years. One of the most famous examples appears in the "womb" chamber of the megalithic structure at Newgrange, Ireland (c.3200 BC), where a shaft of sunlight falls upon it once a year, at the winter solstice. It represents the Triple Goddess – maiden, mother and crone – who in turn is associated with the phases of the moon (waxing, full and waning) as well as the birth-death-rebirth cycle. It has been suggested that triple spirals might also be connected with the three trimesters of human gestation.

SACRED DANCES

Initiation rites and sacred dances often follow a spiral pattern that represents death and rebirth. Spiral formation dances can be a way of acknowledging and celebrating life's pattern of change and evolution. For instance, at New Year the Zuni (Pueblo) Indians chant "spiral" songs and dance spiral dances. One of the best-known forms of sacred spiral dance is that practised by the *mevlevi,* or "whirling dervishes" in Turkey, who spin round and round like a top. Exactly like the centre of the spinning top, the trunk of the whirling dancer symbolizes the still point in the midst of dynamic movement, the eye at the centre of the storm. Circle dances also symbolize life's pattern of change and flow.

A STAIRWAY TO HEAVEN

In ancient times it was thought that the heavens were reached by climbing a spiral path that ascended to a wheeling circle of stars. Souls ascended to Heaven along this pathway in the skies, which was mirrored on Earth as a spiral path up a sacred mountain, or the spiral staircase around a structure such as a ziggurat.

THE CIRCLE

With no beginning and no end, the circle has been used to signify eternity and wholeness, the heavens, the cosmos, the absolute and perfection. In Islam, the circle is seen as the perfect shape, and poets praise the circle formed by the lips as one of its most beautiful representations. In many cultures the circle represents the continuing cycle of the seasons and the sun's endless progression through the skies. It is often used as a symbol for the sun (itself a symbol of perfection) as well as for the full moon.

THE POWER OF THE WORLD

In Native North American traditions, the circle is perhaps the most important shape, related to the Sacred Hoop or Medicine Wheel: the Lakota Sioux shaman Black Elk (1863–1950) asserted that the power of the world works in circles, and that the circle contains all things.

In social and political life the circle is the preferred shape for an assembly of equals: the campfire circle, the council circle, the Round Table of the Arthurian legend. It is the easiest geometric shape to draw accurately, with stick and string, and may also represent the idea of a home or dwelling place, which in early societies was often constructed on a circular ground plan. In Australian Aboriginal art from the Western Desert, concentric circles were often used to represent sanctuaries or camping places, while lines between them were the paths and tracks of people or mythological beings. Here, the circles suggest places where ancestral power can surface from the Earth and return again.

POWER AND PROTECTION

Being a closed circuit and all-embracing, the circle is associated with protection, providing safety for all who put themselves within its boundary. The magic circle is used in occult traditions to guard against negative psychic forces, and the protective circle can also be worn – as a ring, necklace, bracelet, girdle or crown.

SPIRITUAL HIERARCHIES

Drawings of concentric circles have been used as a teaching device to symbolize different stages of spiritual development in Zen Buddhism, as well as in esoteric Christian schools such as Rosicrucianism. In Christian symbology, hierarchies of angels are sometimes shown arranged in circles around God and Christ, while in the Divine Comedy, the Italian poet Dante (1265–1321) describes Heaven, purgatory and Hell as being divided into different circles or levels.

ABOVE In ancient tradition the path to Heaven was seen as a spiral, reflecting nature's whirling patterns, an idea used by William Blake in his 18th-century painting of Jacob's ladder.

BELOW The spiral symbolizes movement, energy and connection with nature.

TRIANGLES AND SQUARES

ABOVE The triangle is often associated with sacred mountains.

PYTHAGOREAN TRIANGLE

The Pythagorean triangle was an important symbol to the Egyptians, who regarded the vertical and horizontal sides as the male and female forces respectively, and the hypotenuse as their "offspring". This triangle symbolizes construction and development.

BELOW The pyramids of Egypt were symbols of the creative power of the sun and the primal mound.

The triangle and the square are universally important motifs. They are connected to the symbolism of three and four and everything to which these numbers relate, and can only be separated from them in terms of their relationship with other geometrical figures. The triangle appears frequently in everyday life, for example on road signs or washing instructions, while, after the circle, the square is the most common geometric shape printed on textiles. Many buildings have a square plan and, in urban design, a central square is often a focus of activity, such as a town square.

THE TRIANGLE

An equilateral triangle has three sides of equal length. In Christianity it is a symbol of the Trinity, while in Islamic art it symbolizes human consciousness and the principle of harmony. The triangle features in many alphabets. It is the ancient Maya hieroglyph for the sunray, and in the Greek alphabet it represents the letter "delta", which for the ancient Greeks symbolized the four elements and hence was linked with completion and wholeness. Today the word "delta" is used in English to describe a triangular tract of land at the mouth of a river (such as the Nile Delta), which is often very fertile. The connection of the triangle with the four elements also appears in alchemy, where it is used in various formations to symbolize them.

UPWARD AND DOWNWARD TRIANGLES

The Maya likened the shape of the upward-pointing triangle to a shoot of maize as it breaks through the surface of the soil, linking it with fertility, and also the male principle (the erect phallus). For the ancient Hittites an upward-pointing triangle was a symbol of the king and of health. Among the Pueblo people of the south-western United States it represents a sacred mountain, while a downward-pointing triangle represents clouds.

The inverted triangle is also associated with female fertility, as it resembles an image of a woman's pubic region and her internal sex organs – the triangle formed by the two ovaries and the womb. The Sumerians used a downward-pointing triangle to represent woman, and it is also a

feminine symbol in China. In ancient Greece, Rome and India triangles were often used as decorative motifs in friezes. In all instances they seem to signify the same: pointing upwards, they stand for fire and the male sexual organs; pointing down they represent water and the female sexual organs. In more general terms, an upward-pointing triangle can symbolize reaching for the sky and so may be associated with aspirations, the attainment of goals, and new possibilities. It is also associated with arrowheads and the theme of spiritual quest. A downward-pointing triangle, on the other hand, is associated with receptivity, movement inwards rather than outwards, and consequently is often used as a meditation symbol.

CONJOINED TRIANGLES

The tips of triangles touching, one pointing up and one pointing down, can be used to denote sexual union, while intersecting triangles represent synthesis. Positioned with their bases meeting, two triangles can also represent the waxing and waning phases of the moon.

The six-pointed star combines two overlapping equilateral triangles and so relates to the symbolism of the triangle. It is an alchemical symbol for conjunction, relating to the union of the four elements. As the Star of David, it is the pre-eminent symbol of Judaism, while as the Seal of Solomon in Judaic mysticism it stands for the sacred number seven, represented by the six points plus the space at the centre, the place of transformation. In India, a six-pointed star is known as the Star of Lakshmi (the goddess of prosperity and abundance) and is often drawn in powder on doorways or village thresholds to keep away hostile spirits.

THE SQUARE

The ancient Greek philosopher Plato thought that, together with the circle, the square embodied beauty and perfection, while in ancient Egypt it represented achievement. It is one of the most common abstract symbols, representing Earth, material existence and the created universe. The square's shape suggests structure, order and stability, but also limitations – echoed in the expression of feeling "boxed in" to describe being trapped and constrained. It is often seen in relation and in contrast to the circle of the heavens, or of the limited in contrast to the unlimited, of matter as opposed to spirit, of static versus dynamic.

A quadrangular form has often been used for areas set apart for sacred or other reasons, such as altars, temples, castles or military camps. City squares traditionally lie at the heart of urban life. The Forum in ancient Rome was the market square at the heart of the capital, through which the Sacred Way ran up to the Capitoline Hill and the temple of Jupiter; the ancient Greek equivalent was the Agora, the commercial centre of Athens, surrounded by temples and public buildings.

MYSTICAL SYMBOLISM

The symbolism of the square is connected with its four corners, which suggest the foundations and sum of life: the four elements, the four seasons, the four stages of life (childhood, adolescence, adulthood, old age) and the four cardinal directions.

In ancient China, space was measured by the four yang or square directions; the earth god was represented by a square mound, and the capital city and imperial palace were both square, with the emperor at the centre. In Hinduism the square is the anchor that assures the order of the universe, while in Islam the human heart is symbolized as a square, as it is thought to be open to four possible sources of influence: divine, angelic, human or devilish. In contrast, the heart of a prophet is triangular as it is immune to the devil's attacks.

RELATED SHAPES

It is the number of sides of a geometric shape that gives it its symbolic significance. Other important shapes include the pentagon (with five sides) and hexagon (six), as well as three-dimensional shapes such as the cube and pyramid. In mystical Kabbalah, the pentagon relates to the fifth sephira on the tree of life, associated with justice, war and the planet Mars, while in Islamic mysticism, it is a symbol of the five elements (fire, water, earth, air and ether) and of the five senses. The hexagon is also associated with Islamic esoteric teachings, symbolizing the six directions of movement (up, down, forwards, backwards, left and right).

A cube is a six-sided solid figure representing the three-dimensional physical world. It also symbolizes the six directions of movement. In Islam it represents perfection: the Ka'ba in Mecca, said to be the centre of the world, is a black cube. In Freemasonry a cube of ashlar (smooth dressed stone) stands for the perfected human being.

With four triangular sides and a square base, the pyramid synthesizes the symbolism of both shapes, as well as the numbers three, four and five, connecting with the Pythagorean "tetrakis". The square base represents the earth plane, while the four upward-pointing triangles of the pyramid's sides meet to form a fifth point, suggesting the fifth element: ether. As the pyramid reaches up to the sky, its point represents the human soul striving to unite with the Cosmic One.

ABOVE Perhaps the most famous city square in history, Rome's vast Forum lay at the heart of the city's religious, commercial, ceremonial and public life.

ABOVE The cube's six sides make it a symbol of stability and truth.

THE TETRAKIS

The sum of the numbers 1+2+3+4=10. In Pythagorean theory, ten is a holy number representing divine power and the quintessence of perfection. It can be represented as a triangle of dots, four to each side and one in the centre, called the tetrakis.

COLOUR

ABOVE Red is the colour of sexual and romantic love, and symbolizes intense passion.

ORANGE

Midway between red and yellow, orange represents a point of balance between the libido and spirit: in India, it is the colour of the second chakra, associated with sexual energy and emotional relatedness. Through its association with the fruit, orange also symbolizes fertility and abundance.

Together with shape, colour is one of the fundamental building blocks of visual symbols. It is also closely associated with mental and emotional states, and can affect them profoundly. The seven colours seen in the rainbow correspond with the mystical number seven and other groups of seven, such as the number of notes on a musical scale or the number of chakras in the body.

COLOUR SHORTHAND

Different colours are often used as a shorthand to describe emotional states, gender or social and political status. In the West colours are traditionally used to distinguish between the sexes – pink for a girl and blue for a boy – and colours are chosen to differentiate sports teams from each other.

Colloquial English expressions that describe states of feeling in colour terms include "in the pink", "green with envy", "in a black mood", "feeling blue",

"seeing red" or "off colour". During the 20th century red was linked to the Communist party, while the green movement aims to put environmental issues on the political agenda. Similarly, colour is used to denote race, so that "black" and "white" carry social and political meanings depending on their context.

RED

As the colour of blood and fire, red is widely associated with life and warmth. In Paleolithic times, red ochre was mined and ground into powder. It seems to have been endowed with life-giving powers, and its presence in Neolithic graves may have been to help the dead in the afterlife. Thousands of years later, in Anglo-Saxon times, red was believed to protect against evil and objects, trees and even animals were painted red, while warriors covered their axes and spears in red paint to endow them with magic powers – a custom also practised by some Australian Aboriginals.

Red is linked with love and fertility. In ancient Rome, brides were wrapped in a fiery reddish-orange veil (the *flammeum*), a custom still observed in parts of Greece, Albania and Armenia, while in China, the wedding gown and veil are red. Red eggs are offered to the couple when a child is born. Red has been used to suggest passion and erotica in Indian and western tradition, or to suggest high energy and speed.

Red is associated with danger (the most serious crisis is described as a "red alert"), anger

and aggression (it is linked with Mars, the Roman god of war), or wickedness or evil. In ancient Egypt red was an accursed colour, associated with the destructive god Set, and "making red" was synonymous with killing someone. Evil doings were referred to as "red affairs" and scribes used special red ink when writing words of ill omen.

YELLOW

Closely related to the symbolism of gold, yellow is associated with the sun and its life-giving generative powers. In the Aztec pantheon, Huitzilopochtli, the victorious warrior god of the midday sun, was depicted in blue and yellow, while in Mexican cosmology, the earth's "new skin" (before the rain comes and turns it green) was golden yellow.

In China, yellow was associated with the centre of the universe, and one creation myth describes how the first humans were made out of yellow clay. It was the sacred colour of the emperor. Australian Aboriginals use yellow ochre to symbolize death.

Sometimes a distinction is made between different shades of yellow: in Islam, golden yellow symbolizes wisdom, whereas pale yellow indicates treachery. In Egypt and medieval Europe, yellow was the colour of envy; it also signified disgrace, and is still associated with cowardice.

GREEN

The colour of plant life, green can stand for awakenings, new beginnings and growth: in China and Japan it relates to spring. The

Celtic Green Man is an important vegetation and fertility god, and there are many instances of green being linked with superhuman powers. In ancient Egypt, cats with green eyes were feared, and in medieval Europe green was associated with the Devil and wearing it was considered unlucky. The "green ray" is an extremely rare manifestation of light that can be observed occasionally at sunrise and sunset, and in alchemy, the secret fire, or the living spirit, was envisaged as a translucent green stone. In Islam, green is the most important colour: Mohammed's green cloak represented paradise, renewal and spiritual refreshment.

BLUE

Whether celestial or oceanic, blue evokes wide, open spaces and is linked with infinity and primordial emptiness. The blue of the sky has been associated with the male principle, distance and the gods. In ancient Egypt, gods and kings were often depicted with blue beards and wigs, and the Hindu divinity Krishna is portrayed as blue. Still, deep water, on the other hand, also associates blue with the female principle. As a symbol of peace and purity, it is the colour of the Virgin Mary. Blue is associated with dreamlike states, contemplation, introspection and yearning. In parts of the Arab

world blue is thought to offer protection against the evil eye, and the old English custom of brides wearing "something blue" is meant to ensure fidelity.

PURPLE

Historically, in the West, purple dye was the most expensive to produce as it was made from *Murex* or *Purpura* molluscs, which were rare and also costly to process. Only the rich could afford purple garments, hence the colour's symbolic association with royalty and the priesthood. It was the preferred colour of the Byzantine and Roman emperors.

In China, purple was the colour of the North Star, the centre of Heaven and the site of the "purple palace" of the heavenly emperor. To identify the temporal emperor as the Son of Heaven, his imperial palace compound at Beijing was called the Purple Forbidden City. Buddhists regard purple as a sacred colour, and in Thailand it is worn by mourning widows.

BLACK AND WHITE

In some parts of the Arab world, black animals are regarded as unlucky: black dogs bring death in the family, and black hens are used in witchcraft. White, the colour of light, is considered lucky. However, black is also a symbol of power and authority: it became an emblem of the Caliphate in the 1st century AD.

Death and mourning are symbolized in the West by black and in the East by white. In Africa, white is the colour of the dead, but is also believed to have the power to drive death away and so is associated with healing.

In ancient Egypt, black was the colour of resurrection and eternal life, perhaps because new life was seen as emerging from the darkness. It is associated with the mother goddess and fertility, when it is sometimes linked to red, the colour of blood. In China, black represents the feminine principle (yin), with its opposite being yellow.

In the West, white symbolizes spiritual purity and innocence, and is the colour traditionally worn for baptism robes and wedding dresses.

ABOVE Berenice (c.273–21 BC), Queen of Cyrene and Egypt, wears a purple toga as a symbol of her imperial status.

TOP LEFT Blue symbolizes divinity and peace.

TOP MIDDLE In the West, white symbolizes innocence and purity,

GREY

Traditionally, grey is associated with old age and with the planet Saturn. Saturn, or Cronos, was lord of time in the Greco-Roman pantheon, and wisdom was one of his attributes. On the Kabbalastic tree of life, grey is also linked with wisdom.

MYTH AND THE COSMOS

A varied and enduring array of symbolism has been used to describe the origins of the universe. Creation mythology usually reflects a society's geography, culture and beliefs, and serves to align it with nature and the current preconditions of life. A number of general archetypal themes are interwoven with the creation mythologies of the world.

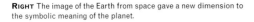
RIGHT The image of the Earth from space gave a new dimension to the symbolic meaning of the planet.

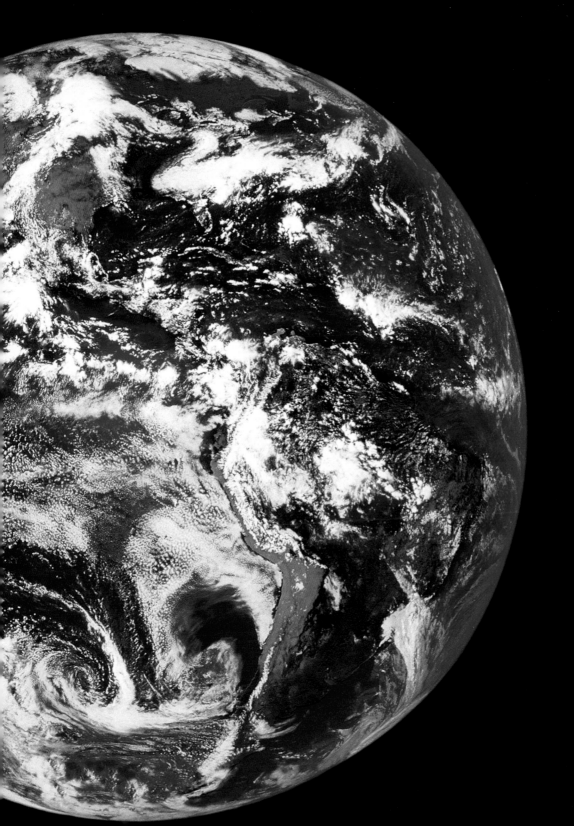

THE CREATIVE PROCESS

Creation may be described as one huge cosmic event, or a process in stages in which things become increasingly differentiated, sometimes leading to a natural hierarchy and at others to a sacred interrelationship between all aspects of nature. Whether the mythological creation of human beings coincides with the actual event of creation, or emerges slowly over time, the original man and the original woman are always seen as central symbols of primordial humanity.

THE CREATOR GODS

Creation is often actively brought about through the actions, dreams or reflections of divine beings. The Upanishads, Hindu scriptures of the 9th century BC, describe the Divine Self or Supreme Being who created the universe by reflecting

BELOW This painting of God creating the world is rich with Christian symbolism, including the globe, symbol of power and totality, held by Adam, the Greek letters alpha and omega on the front of God's book, represent God's role as the beginning and the end, and the animals and plants, symbolizing the abundance and variety of God's created world.

upon nothingness and finding only itself. This fundamental act of self-consciousness led to the first word: "This am I." In Samoan mythology, the supreme god Tangaroa created the world from nothingness by thinking of it.

Australian Aboriginal stories more than 150,000 years old attribute creation to Ancestors living in the mythical space and time known as the "Dreaming". These beings lived much like their human counterparts, travelling, hunting, loving and fighting, and shaping the landscape through their "walkabouts". In sleep the ancestors dreamed the events of the next day, dreaming up all living beings, the sun, moon and stars. Australian Aboriginals believe that every being shares a fundamental connection with the source of creation, reflecting their deep respect for nature.

The book of Genesis describes God bringing about all of creation single-handedly. He completed his work on the sixth day with the creation of humans, who were to "have dominion" over all life. Thus the Judaeo-Christian cosmology gives humanity a special place under God in the hierarchy of nature.

CREATION FROM CHAOS

The Greek term "chaos" refers to an initial dark, formless universe. From it sprang Eros, a fertility deity later associated with erotic love, but initially the creative urge behind life and nature. With Eros came Gaia, earth goddess, and Tartarus, god of the underworld. Gaia's son Uranus impregnated

her, giving rise to the Titans and the Cyclops and then to the seas, land and other natural features.

Since oceans encircle the world, in many creation myths the universe arises from a chaotic body of water. The creation of the Egyptian world from water is fitting in a land that depended on the periodic flooding of the Nile: from Nu, the original water, a hill of dry land emerged, followed by the first sunrise on the new horizon, then the rest of creation.

The Japanese gods Izanagi and Izanami disturbed the primordial waters with a spear, and the drips from it coalesced to form the island of Onokoro. The Arunta people of central Australia tell of a world covered with salt water that was gradually drawn back by the people in the north, revealing the first land. The myth of the Altaic shamans of Central Asia tells of a time before creation in which there was no earth, only endless water, over which flew a white gander, the god Kara-han.

CREATION FROM SEPARATION

The theme of separation explains the origins of life in terms of the splitting of a primordial state of unity. Usually this involves the rending apart of a male sky god and a female earth goddess, though in some cultures the male is associated with earth and the female with sky.

In Maori and other Polynesian myths the universe originally consisted of an eternal night or gloom. Eventually Rangi, the sky father, and Papa, the earth mother, coupled, creating the

land and many divine offspring. They lived in darkness until it was decided to split the parents apart. Tu Matauenga, the god of war, hacked at the sinews joining his parents, which bled with the sacred colour of red ochre. But it was only Tane Mahuta, god of the forest, who was able to separate them, drawing them apart to allow light and air in between sky and earth. In a similar Egyptian myth, the sky goddess Nut and the earth god Geb were separated by their offspring.

CREATION THROUGH DISMEMBERMENT

A common theme is of creation emerging from the death and dismemberment of a primordial being. Such myths may help people to reconcile themselves with the violent preconditions of life and the need for death in order to sustain life.

According to Norse creation mythology, Odin, Vili and Ve killed the giant Ymir, from whose body the world emerged. His flesh formed the land, the sea and rivers flowed from his blood, his bones became mountains and trees grew from his hair. Ymir's huge skull became the heavens.

Similarly, when the Chinese primordial being P'an-Ku died, his breath became the winds, his voice the thunder, his blood the water and his muscles the fertile land. His happy moods caused the sun to shine and his anger produced thunder and lightning. The Babylonian epic Enuma Elish, composed in the 12th century BC, tells of the god Marduk killing and cutting in two the body of Tiamat, the goddess of the ocean. The two halves became the sky and the earth.

Indonesian mythology tells of a time before creation in which there was no time, no birth or death, and no sex. Then a great cosmic dance occurred during which a single dancer was trampled and his body torn into pieces. Time began with this murder and brought about the separation of the sexes. From the buried body parts of the dancer grew plants. And so the first death produced the beginning of time, growth and procreation.

FIRST MAN AND WOMAN

The origin of humankind is symbolized worldwide in the images of the "first man" and the "first woman", representing the blueprint of humanity. But with humans comes the creation of evil or forces of torment with which they must contend.

In Sumerian mythology of the 3rd millennium BC, Enki, the fun-loving god of wisdom, with his mother/lover, the earth goddess Ninhursag, and twelve other goddesses, moulded the first humans out of clay from the bed of the river Euphrates. Having created perfect people, they had a contest to create people for whom the others could find no role, giving rise to human imperfection.

In the Biblical account, Adam (whose name means "made of clay") is created from the dust of the earth by Yahweh, the creator God, who breathes life into him. He is then given a female companion, Eve, who will be the mother of all humanity.

Although in both these myths the first humans are created from the substance of the earth, there are differences between them. Sumerian humans were created to be made slaves of the gods, Adam and Eve were created by one God and given dominion, and their task was to "subdue" nature.

FORBIDDEN FRUIT

The story of Adam and Eve living in the Garden of Eden represents them in a state of innocence in which there is no awareness of difference, sexuality, good or evil. By eating the fruit of the tree of the knowledge, the one thing God has forbidden, they gain a moral sense and are responsible for the corruption of human nature. It is often the apple that is portrayed as the forbidden fruit, but this probably dates from medieval rather than Biblical times, when artistic interpretations of The Fall were created. The pomegranate rather than the apple is often favoured by Hebrew scholars.

BELOW The first human beings, a man and a woman, feature in many world mythologies.

THE SUN

ABOVE Sunset symbolizes old age, endings and death in many cultures.

ABOVE The Eye of Horus was a symbol of royalty and immortality, and a talisman for protection.

MIDDLE The sun is an archetypal symbol, worshipped as a deity by many peoples.

TOP The lion is a solar symbol, a sign of power and leadership.

As our only source of light and heat the sun is crucial to life on earth and is one of the most important symbols in all world cultures. It is typically associated with power, manifesting both as a supreme deity and in emperors or kings. Its active energy is usually (though not always) regarded as male, and is associated with immediate, intuitive knowledge or cosmic intellect. The sun's counterpart in the heavens is the moon (often seen as female), and solar and lunar symbolism is contrasted by nearly all cultures. The solar principle is associated with animals, birds and plants (such as the lion, eagle and sunflower), with gold, and with colours such as yellow, orange and red. The sun is an important symbol in astrology, alchemy and psychology, where it represents the undivided self.

THE EYE OF THE WORLD

In many cultures the sun is likened to an all-seeing divine eye. It was the "eye" of the Greek god Zeus (and his Roman equivalent Jupiter), the Egyptian god Horus, the Hindu Varuna, the Norse Odin and the Islamic Allah. The Samoyed of the Arctic region regard the sun and moon as the two eyes of Num (the heavens), the sun being the good and the moon the evil eye. According to a myth of the Fulani of West Africa, when Gueno (the supreme deity) had finished the work of creation he took the sun out of his eye-socket and placed it in the heavens. He then became the one-eyed king, one eye being enough to see with, the other

providing light and heat. In many traditions the sun is poetically referred to as the "eye of the day".

SOLAR DEITIES

The link between the sun and divinity is archetypal, and many cultures have worshipped solar deities, including Shamash (Babylonian), Ra (Egyptian), Mithras (Persian) and Apollo (Greek and Roman). In Eastern traditions, the sun is the emblem of the Hindu god Vishnu and of the Buddha, whom some Chinese writers refer to as "Sun-Buddha" or "Golden Man". The Jewish High Priest wore a golden disc on his chest as a symbol of the divine sun, and Christ is sometimes compared to the spiritual sun at the heart of the world and called Sol Justitiae (Sun of Justice) or Sol Invictus (Invincible Sun), with the twelve disciples compared to the sun's rays.

Although the sun is usually regarded as male, in some cultures (African, Native American, Maori, Australian Aboriginal, Japanese and Germanic) the solar deity is female, because the female principle is seen as active through its life-giving powers. Japan's sun goddess, Amaterasu, retreats to a cave in protest at the neglect of his duties by her brother the storm god, and is enticed back out by other gods making much noise. In the cosmology of the Dogon of Mali, the sun is described as a white-hot earthenware pot (a symbol of the womb) surrounded by a spiral of red copper, representing the semen that will make it fertile.

TEMPORAL POWER

Many cultures and their rulers have claimed ancestry from the sun, including the Incas, the pharaohs of ancient Egypt, the Chinese and the Japanese. The Japanese imperial family are said to be direct descendants of the sun goddess Amaterasu, and the rising sun (represented by a red disc) is not only the Japanese national emblem but also the country's name (Nihon).

The rising sun is generally regarded as a symbol of hope and new beginnings, in contrast to a rayed sun, which signifies illumination. In China the sun was a symbol of the emperor who wore a sun design (a circle containing a three-legged crow) on his robes. Sun symbolism is a common motif on regalia. It appears on the thrones of the Kubu of southern Africa, while the Ashanti of West Africa use a gold sun disc to represent the king's soul. Modelling himself on the sun god Apollo, the French king Louis XIV (1638-1715) was known as the "Sun King", and court life revolved around him like planets around the sun, at his opulent palace at Versailles.

SUNRISE AND SUNSET

The disappearance of the sun each evening and its apparent rebirth the next morning make it a potent symbol of death, resurrection and immortality. This forms the basis of many myths and sacred rituals. In ancient Egypt the sun god Ra made a terrifying journey each night through the underworld, encountering his arch-enemy, the

monstrous snake Apophis, before rising again in the east; if Apophis were ever to defeat Ra, the sun would not rise and the earth would be plunged into darkness. In the Native American Cherokee tradition the sun is female, and when her daughter dies from a snake bite the sun covers her face in grief and the world becomes dark. To console her, the people dance and sing, whereupon she uncovers her face and the world becomes light. The Sun Dance of the Plains Indians is closely linked to this symbolism.

THE BLACK SUN

Some cultures refer to a black sun. The Aztecs showed it being carried on the back of the god of the underworld, while the Maya depicted it as a jaguar. As the antithesis of the midday sun at the height of its creative, life-affirming powers, the black sun is associated with death and destruction, foreshadowing the unleashing of disaster. Solar eclipses are therefore almost universally regarded as bad omens, heralding cataclysmic events that bring a cycle to an end: for instance, at the moment of Christ's crucifixion, the sun

ABOVE In many traditions, a solar eclipse was viewed with dismay and fear as a symbol of misfortune.

went dark. In alchemy, a black sun stands for unworked, primal matter yet to be refined; to the psychologist, it is an emblem of the elemental unconscious.

PSYCHOLOGICAL SYMBOLISM

The sun is often associated with the principle of authority, of which the father is the first embodiment. It is linked with individuality, will, ego and personality, at the highest level striving for psychic integration or enlightenment or at a lower level indulging in egomania, excessive pride and authoritarianism. The sun is also linked with creative energy, health and vitality, influencing both physical and psychological development. As the embodiment of male energy, it can be seen as a representation of the animus and may appear in dreams and myths as an emperor, king, god or hero figure.

SOLAR SYMBOLS

Symbols of the sun include a disc, a point within a circle (used in astronomy and astrology), a spoked wheel (a Celtic symbol) and a chariot – in many traditions (including Norse, ancient Egyptian and ancient Greek) the sun is viewed as a deity transported across the sky in a chariot. A rayed sun suggests illumination; a common graphic symbol is a circle with rays presented as alternating straight and wavy lines, suggesting the sun's power to generate light and heat. Traditionally there were seven rays, for the six directions of space and the seventh, cosmic, dimension. Sometimes the sun is depicted with a face – among the Native American Hopi, for instance, as well as in Western iconography. In Celtic myth, the sun was personified by Lug ("Light"), sometimes referred to as Grianainech ("Sun Face").

THE SUN AS DESTROYER

The sun's power causes drought. In ancient China, people would shoot arrows at it to hold it in check, while in Cambodia rain-making rituals involved the sacrifice of a "solar" animal.

ABOVE A halo of sunrays surrounds Amaterasu, sun goddess of Japan.

THE MOON

BLUE MOON

Two full moons within the same calendar month constitute a blue moon, a phenomenon that occurs every two or three years. Therefore "once in a blue moon" means hardly ever. In the Wiccan tradition an esbat (lunar festival) is celebrated in that year, on top of the usual 12, at which rituals and invocations are thought to have doubled power.

BELOW The stones of Stonehenge are believed to have served to astronomically measure the phases of the moon.

Being about 400,000 km/250,000 miles from the Earth, the moon exerts a powerful gravitational pull on both land and water. Its influence is most noticeable in the ocean tides, but many believe that plants and animals, including humans, are also affected. Next to the sun, the moon is the most obvious heavenly body, and its periodicity was of central importance in early concepts of time. The fact that its rhythms correspond almost exactly to the female menstrual cycle, and to the seasons and the annual cycle, led to obvious associations with the feminine and with earth or nature. The moon doesn't emit its own light, but reflects the light of the sun: the quality of this light has itself been a great source of religious and artistic inspiration.

THE MOON AND THE FEMININE

The symbolism attributed to the moon is predominantly (but not exclusively) associated with the feminine. The moon is connected to the imagination, intuition, psychic powers and dreaming, and is particularly associated with women, fertility and birth. Ancient civilizations performed fertility rituals and celebrated the moon at annual festivals dedicated to the goddess, to seek her help with conception. The time of ovulation for women was thought to occur during a full moon, and it was believed that during her time of menstruation a woman's powers of perception were heightened.

Moon goddesses are found in many ancient cultures. The moon is revered as a many-breasted mother of all, creator of all life on earth. The Greek goddess Artemis (the Roman Diana) is depicted with many breasts and with animals and plants springing from her head, limbs and chest. The Chinese moon goddess gave birth to all things after a flood; similarly, moon goddesses of Western Asia and Europe were the source of all living creatures. Inca beliefs about the moon changed over time: at first a goddess with no connection to the sun, she later became the sun's wife and the goddess of marriage. Her children were the stars. Finally she was thought to be her brother the sun's incestuous bride.

INNER WISDOM

The moon is a great reflector and embodies the qualities of receptiveness that are necessary for the intuitive process and to experience feelings. This receptiveness is another aspect of moon deities.

The moon is often associated with wisdom. The Greek and Egyptian goddess Sophia, or Lady Wisdom, is a moon goddess and the personification of divine knowledge. Shing Moo, a Chinese moon goddess, is called the goddess of perfect intelligence, and the Virgin Mary, sometimes called the Moon of the Church, is said to have perfect wisdom.

THE MOON AND THE MIND

As the moon pulls on the tides it can also be understood to pull on our emotions, which are often associated with water. Although the moon is sometimes linked with the acquisition of knowledge, it is more often associated with feeling, irrationality, and the unconscious or hidden. To be "under the influence of the moon" is to lose your reason, to be taken with moods and feelings, overwhelmed by the unconscious, which in its most extreme form manifests as madness or lunacy. (Despite all the folklore relating the two, there is very little reliable scientific evidence of a connection between the moon and madness.)

In early Japanese mythology the light from Tsukuyomi, Shinto god of the moon, could induce hallucinations and delusions. Hecate, the Greek goddess of the dark moon, bestowed visions but could also strike people down with madness. The same is true for most of the moon deities, with a thin line dividing inspiration and lunacy. There are stories of frenzied demons that are strongly influenced by the moon. The

Slavs tell of werewolves – people who are transformed into wolves by the light of the full moon. They are a great threat to people and are invulnerable to all weapons except for those made from silver, a moon metal.

PHASES OF THE MOON

The moon reflects the rhythms of life, undergoing an endless process of death and rebirth in its 28-day cycle; it therefore often represents transition and renewal and has come to symbolize cyclical time. The moon actually has 28 phases in its daily rising and setting, during which it passes through the entire zodiac. However it is more common to refer to four phases or quarters of the moon: waxing, full, waning, and the new or dark moon.

The waxing of the moon is associated with rising energy – mirroring pregnancy – and is often thought to be a good time to embark on new projects. The moon is at its strongest when it is full: it represents the fullness of female energy and echoes the symbolism of the circle, signifying wholeness. The waning moon is the time of decreasing, for letting go of things. The new moon is associated with restfulness and the beginning of the ascent from the underworld or death.

THE CRESCENT

As an emblem, the crescent moon is pre-eminently associated with female deities. The virgin goddess Artemis (or the Roman equivalent Diana) is usually depicted either holding a crescent or wearing one on her head. The upturned crescent is an attribute of the Egyptian goddess Isis, and in Christian iconography the Virgin Mary, inheriting some of the symbolism of Isis, is also sometimes shown on an upturned crescent. It is an attribute of the High Priestess of the Tarot, who is associated with mystery, intuition and the powers of the unconscious. In Hinduism the crescent moon is the emblem of Shiva, the god of transformation.

The crescent moon is a very important symbol in the Islamic world, symbolizing openness and concentration. Generally accompanied by a star, it is a symbol of paradise and of resurrection, frequently carved or painted on minarets and tombs. In the Arabic alphabet, the letter "n", shaped like a crescent with a dot above it, is the letter of resurrection, and prayers for the dead are written to rhyme with it; the letter is pronounced "nun", which is also the Arabic word for fish, and the fish is a symbol of eternal life in the Qu'ran.

ABOVE Since medieval times the Virgin Mary was associated with the crescent moon, in her role as reflector of the light of Christ.

LUNAR MYTHS

In Nordic myth, Mani the moon and Sol the sun were created by the gods and put in chariots to cross the sky. Mani's chariot often came close to the earth so that his light could have greater influence on those below. On one occasion he snatched two children who were fetching water, Hiuki and Bil, to be his companions, and they became the waxing and waning moon. Mani was often chased by the wolf Hati – when he caught him the atmosphere would become ghostly, and when he managed to drag him to the ground there was an eclipse.

TOP The new moon symbolizes the resting point of the cycle of life.

ABOVE A waning moon represents 'letting go' and 'decrease'.

MAN ON THE MOON

On 20 July 1969, Neil Armstrong symbolically made first physical contact with the moon, with the words: "One small step for man, one giant step for mankind."

THE STARS

ABOVE Stars are connected with spiritual illumination and divine presence.

RIGHT In the Christian tradition, it was a star that guided the Magi to the newborn baby Jesus, to whom they gave their gifts of gold, myrrh and frankincense.

ABOVE A five-pointed star was the emblem of the Assyrian goddess Ishtar (later Isis, Venus). It became a widespread symbol for spiritual and military ascendancy.

As pinpoints of light that illuminate the darkness, the stars have almost always been seen as heavenly symbols, signifiers of divine presence. They are archetypal symbols, appearing in sacred and secular traditions all over the world. According to the Yakut shamans of Siberia, stars were the windows of the universe. Their fleeting opening and closing gave or denied access to the upper world. In early societies, sky-watching was an important part of life, and astrology and astronomy were one. Celestial phenomena were of great practical significance, marking seasonal changes and providing a calendar for hunting and planting. As people noticed that certain occurrences in the heavens coincided with events on Earth, the parallels became fused into omens – a blood-red moon, for instance, was taken to indicate natural disaster or war.

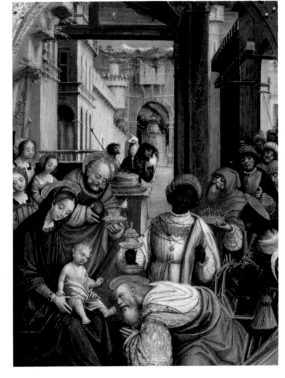

STAR MYTHS

Many stories are told about the symbolism of stars. According to the Kalevala, the national epic of Finland, the stars were made from shell fragments flung out when the World Egg cracked. Among

the Aztecs the Milky Way was called *mixcoatl* ("cloud-serpent"), and gave its name to Mixcoatl, the god of the Pole Star and of the hunt, who was thought to dwell in the stars. In the hieroglyphics of the Maya, stars are often depicted with rays of light shooting out from them. According to folk-belief in Guatemala and Peru, stars represent the souls of the righteous dead, while among the Inca the cosmic symbolism of stars extends to include not only humans but also animals and birds: they believed that in the heavens there was a double of every creature on Earth,

responsible for their birth and increase. In the Christian tradition, the birth of Christ was heralded by the appearance of the Star of Bethlehem. Today, stars are associated with dreams and wishes and the belief that if you make a wish when you see a shooting star it will come true.

THE MORNING STAR

Because the orbit of Venus lies within that of Earth it always appears fairly near the sun in the sky, and depending on its cycle it is seen near either the rising or the setting sun. It is therefore called both the Morning and the Evening Star. In Babylonian and

SHOOTING STARS

Generally regarded as a sign of divinity, shooting stars have been interpreted as sparks of heavenly fire or seeds of the godhead. They are said to perform a similar function to angels, acting as messengers between Heaven and earth and reminding human beings of their connection with spirit.

RIGHT In Native American
traditions stars are seen as the
campfires of the ancestors.

Assyrian mythology, Ishtar, the
goddess of love associated with
Venus, descended to the
underworld in search of her lover
then returned to life, just as the
Evening Star disappeaed from
view for a period, before
reappearing as the Morning Star
to herald the rising sun.

Among the Plains Indians the
Morning Star is a symbol of the
life principle – because it heralds
the dawn and the rebirth of
daylight – while the Cora Indians
of the south-western United
States give it equal importance
with the sun and moon, with
which it forms a heavenly trinity
in their mythology. In the
Mexican tradition, however, the
Morning Star was thought to
unleash disease, and doors and
windows were closed at daybreak
to protect against its dangerous
light; in Mexican folk art it is
often depicted with a bow and
arrow and wearing a skull-mask.
In the Christian tradition, one
name for the devil is Lucifer,
which means Morning Star.

THE POLE STAR

The Pole Star symbolizes the fixed
and eternal point at the centre,
around which the cosmos
revolves. In many parts of Europe
and Asia it is variously referred to
as a pivot, hub, navel, life-centre
or gate of Heaven. In the Turkic
tradition it is described as the
"tent-pole" of the heavens; the
Mongols refer to it as a golden
pillar, and the Saami of northern
Scandinavia call it the Pillar of the
World. In most northern Asiatic
traditions it is placed over the
summit of the World Mountain,

pinpointing the residence of the
almighty god in the skies;
consequently in these regions
altars are usually set at the
northern end of a temple.

The symbolism of the Pole Star
as the apex of the heavens mirrors
human hierarchies. In China, for
example, the heavens, with the
rest of the stars fixed according to
their relationship with the Pole
Star, are seen in terms of the
structure of society, in which the
emperor and ruling classes were
the pivotal point around which
everyone else revolved, each in
their correct place. In India, the
Pole Star is invoked in Vedic
marriage ceremonies, representing
the bridegroom as the pivotal
point of the relationship.

STAR SYMBOLS

A five-pointed star is known as a
pentagram and is an ancient
magical sign. It is a shape that
appears in art and classical
architecture, as well as in nature
(in starfish and certain flowers).
The lines joining its five points
divide each other in the ratio
known as the Golden Mean or
Divine Proportion, making it a
symbol of wholeness and
perfection. When drawn pointing
upwards the pentagram is said to

be a symbol of the cosmic
human, and in Christian tradition
it is a symbol of Christ as "Alpha
and Omega", beginning and end.

The followers of Pythagoras
used the pentagram as an
identifying sign, and it also
appears frequently as an emblem
in the regalia of Freemasonry, a
society that traces its history back
to the Pythagoreans.

In medieval Europe the
pentagram was used as a talisman
against evil to ward off demonic
powers. When inverted, however,
with two points uppermost, the
pentagram was associated with
the devil, the points being seen as
signifying his horns.

ABOVE Two versions of
the eight-pointed Star of
Ishtar, used throughout
the Near East for many
centuries before the birth
of Christ. The top star is a
Babylonian version, the
bottom is Phoenician.

THE PENTACLE

In the Western occult tradition
upright five-pointed stars were
engraved on discs of precious
metals such as silver or gold to
create a magic seal known as a
pentacle. Hebrew letters, Latin
words and Kabbalistic signs were sometimes inscribed within
the star shape. The seal symbolized the power of the occult, and
was believed to be able to cause earthquakes, inspire love,
cause misfortune and cast spells, as well as offer protection
against evil. The sign of the pentacle appears on the walls of
ancient temples, carved into the stones of churches and as a
pattern in stained-glass windows. When an apple is cut in half
across the core, the shape of the pentacle is revealed: the
European Roma call this the Star of Knowledge.

THE ZODIAC

ABOVE Aries resembles the head of a ram but also the fountain of life.

ABOVE Taurus resembles the head and the horns of an ox.

ABOVE Gemini symbolizes duality.

ABOVE Cancer suggests crab claws, and may represent a change in direction.

ABOVE Leo represents the lion's mane, or creative energy similar to the snake's.

ABOVE Virgo could be celestial wings, a woman holding a wheatsheaf or a snake.

Both a symbol in its own right and a collection of symbols, the zodiac is a belt of stars on either side of the "ecliptic", the apparent path across the sky of the sun, moon and planets. It is divided into 12 constellations or signs. "Zodiac" is derived from the Greek and means circle of living things. It is a concept that originated at a time when people thought that each heavenly body was inhabited by an astral spirit, and stems from a world-view that sees creation as a vast web of interconnected forces, reflecting or even influencing life and events on Earth. The constellations became associated with various life forms and objects, acquiring mystical significance in explaining human destiny and the complexities that make up human character. The signs are divided among the four elements, and each is given one of three "qualities": cardinal (creating or initiating), fixed (maintaining) and mutable (changing). Each sign is "ruled" by a celestial body.

ARIES, RAM
(21 MARCH–20 APRIL)

The astrological year begins at the spring equinox (in the Northern Hemisphere) when the sun enters Aries the ram. The ram is often shown running forwards but looking backwards. The sign is headstrong, enthusiastic, independent, ambitious and easily bored. Mars is the ruler of Aries; anatomically it relates to the head and face, its element is fire, its quality cardinal and its gemstone is the diamond.

TAURUS, BULL
(21 APRIL–21 MAY)

An ancient symbol of virility and fertility. Taureans are loyal, practical, calm, generous, understanding and patient. They enjoy sensuous pleasures, but can become stubborn and rigid. The ruler of Taurus is Venus; anatomically it relates to the throat and neck, its element is earth, its quality fixed and its gemstone emerald. A festival celebrating the Buddha's birth occurs on the first full moon after the sun enters Taurus.

GEMINI, TWINS
(22 MAY–21 JUNE)

As twins, Gemini signifies opposites and duality. Some traditions depict the sign as a man and woman, or as a pair of lovers. Gemini is associated with human contact, communication and the intellect. Its element is air, its quality mutable and its ruler Mercury. Anatomically it relates to the lungs, arms and shoulders, and its gemstone is agate. In India, the constellation is linked with Aditi, the Vedic mother-goddess.

CANCER, CRAB
(22 JUNE–23 JULY)

Cancerians are sensitive, moody, imaginative, romantic, protective and nurturing but can become possessive and overly emotional. Cancer is associated with the mother archetype; its ruler is the moon, its element water and its

RIGHT The zodiac circle is a symbol system representing cycles, stages of development, and aspects of the male and the female.

quality cardinal. Anatomically it relates to the chest and stomach and its gemstone is moonstone.

LEO, THE LION
(24 JULY–23 AUG)

When the sun enters Leo its power (in the Northern Hemisphere) is at its zenith and the sign is associated with warmth, generosity, creativity, courage and leadership, although it can also be egotistical, proud and autocratic. Its ruler is the sun, its element fire and its quality fixed. Anatomically Leo is related to the heart, and its gemstone is ruby.

VIRGO, VIRGIN
(24 AUG 23 SEPT)

Virgo, the virgin (in the sense of "independent woman"), comes at harvest. It has been associated with most major Western female goddesses, including Isis, Demeter and the Virgin Mary.

Virgoans are practical, discriminating, analytical and precise, but can be pedantic and critical. Ruled by Mercury, Virgo is related to the intestine, spleen and solar plexus. Its element is earth, its quality mutable and its gemstone carnelian.

LIBRA, SCALES
(24 SEPT–23 OCT)
When the sun enters Libra it is at the mid-point of the astronomical year when days and nights are of equal length. Librans are artistic, refined and good peacemakers, but can be indecisive. The ruling planet of Libra is Venus, its element is air, and its quality is cardinal; its gemstone is sapphire and anatomically it is related to the spine, kidneys and liver.

SCORPIO, SCORPION
(24 OCT–22 NOV)
The venomous scorpion is ruled by Mars and Pluto. It is associated in many cultures with decay and death. Scorpios are determined, forceful and inquisitive, with intense sexual energy and passion, although inclined to jealousy. Anatomically, Scorpio governs the kidneys and genitals, its gemstone is opal, its element water and its quality fixed. An eagle, phoenix or snake sometimes represents the sign.

SAGITTARIUS, ARCHER
(23 NOV–21 DEC)
The ninth sign, Sagittarius, represents the perfect human, a combination of animal and spiritual power and divine potential. It is usually shown as a centaur bearing a bow and arrow;

ABOVE The zodiac represents a perfect cycle, and its symbolism is therefore related to the wheel and to the circle.

its glyph represents the latter, a symbol of humanity aiming for the stars. Sagittarius is a symbol of higher wisdom, the spiritual seeker, philosophy, learning and travel, but Sagittarians can also be unrealistic and unreliable. Its ruling planet is Jupiter, its element fire, its quality mutable and its gemstone topaz. Anatomically, Sagittarius governs the liver, thighs and pelvic region.

CAPRICORN, GOAT
(22 DEC–20 JAN)
Capricorn, the goat, is ruled by Saturn, and heralds the depth of winter. Its element is earth, its quality cardinal, its gemstone garnet; anatomically it rules the knees, teeth and bones. Capricorn represents order, structure and stability, as well as ambition and hard work. Its name is linked to Capricornus, the mythological goatfish, and its glyph reflects the shape of both fish and horns.

AQUARIUS, WATER
CARRIER (21 JAN–19
FEBRUARY)
The water carrier's glyph represents water and communication. Saturn and Uranus govern Aquarius, which is

usually linked with humanitarian ideals, freedom, eccentricity and original thinking. Anatomically it is related to the lower legs, and blood. Its element is air, its quality fixed and its gemstone is the amethyst.

PISCES, FISH
(20 FEB–20 MARCH)
The 12th sign is Pisces, symbolized by a pair of conjoined fish swimming in opposite directions, with its glyph representing this contradictory aspect. Pisceans often feel tugged in two directions and are typically dreamy, intuitive, artistic and impressionable, their psychic sensitivities making it difficult for them to live in the everyday world. Jupiter and Neptune, god of the sea, rule Pisces, its element is water and its quality mutable. Anatomically it governs the lymphatic system and feet and its gemstone is bloodstone. As the last sign of the zodiac, Pisces represents dissolution, the return to the watery abyss before the creative cycle begins afresh.

ABOVE Libra depicts a pair of scales and also a sunset.

ABOVE Scorpio is based on the Hebrew letter *mem*, and the arrow represents the sting in the scorpion's tail.

ABOVE Sagittarius signifies projection.

ABOVE Capricorn links the goat's horns with the fish's tail.

BELOW Aquarius's glyph represents water, and conveys the idea of passive dualism.

ABOVE Pices is two fish swimming away.

GODS AND GODDESSES

ABOVE Zeus sits in victorious judgement with the rest of the Olympians, and banishes the last of the Titans to Tarterus. As a supreme god, Zeus symbolized male power and authority for both divine and human worlds.

Every culture has created its own mythology, theology and sacred rituals in its quest to come to terms with the mysteries of the universe. Although these are rooted in and specific to the culture in which they arise, there are nevertheless many striking similarities in the various deities of the world, making them powerful archetypal symbols that explore some of the most profound ideas of humankind.

SUPREME GODS

The idea of a supreme creator god is universal, symbolizing the primeval force from which all life begins. In many traditions, the deity is self-created and appears magically: for instance, in ancient Egypt, Atum (whose name means "the all") arose as a mound or hill from the chaos of the watery abyss, while the Zulu Unkulunkulu created himself from the vast swamp of coloured reeds that existed at the beginning of the world.

The supreme god frequently symbolizes male power and authority and is linked with the archetypes of father, king and warrior leader. He is seen as omnipotent and omnipresent, exercising authority over nature, animals and human beings. Odin, the warrior god of the Norse pantheon, was known as the "all-father". The Celtic Dagda, whose name means "all-powerful god", controlled the weather and the crops and offered his people protection and benediction. Both Odin and Dagda were renowned for their wisdom, another feature of supreme gods. At times the supreme god embodies righteous fury at human misdemeanours: the thunderbolt, which the god brandished when he was enraged, was an attribute of both Zeus, the ancient Greek ruler of Heaven and Earth, and the Inca creator god Viracocha ("lord of the world"). Other examples of supreme gods include Quetzalcoatl (Aztec), Vishnu (India) and Tangaroa (Polynesia).

Not all supreme deities are male, however. The Chinese goddess Nu Gua, whose lower body was that of a snake or fish, made all living things as she transformed herself into a multitude of shapes, while in the Native American Navajo tradition, Spider Woman (or Changing Woman) brought creation into existence by weaving patterns of fate just as a spider spins its web. The Japanese creator deities, Izanagi and Izanami, were twins, a brother and sister who created the land by stirring the waters of the primeval ocean with a spear.

THE GREAT GODDESS

The concept of an all-powerful goddess is very ancient. Worshipped as the great goddess or the mother goddess, she is typically identified with nature or the earth. In South America, the fertile earth goddess was Pachamama (her cult was adapted to the Virgin Mary in the colonial period), and among the Maori was Papatuanuku (or Papa), the goddess of earth and rock and mother of the people.

The goddess is not only the creator whose limitless fertility and generous abundance generates, feeds and sustains life, but is also the destroyer, who demands tribute as part of nature's regenerative cycle of birth, growth, death and rebirth. She is often associated with the moon, reflecting her cyclical

QUETZALCOATL

One of the major deities of the Aztec pantheon, Quetzalcoatl created humans by sprinkling bones from the dead of the previous creation with his blood. He was also lord of knowledge, god of the wind and the zodiac, vegetation and the arts. He was a compassionate deity who taught peace and was a force for good. His emblems were a turquoise-encrusted snake and a cloak.

nature and her light and dark attributes. In some early societies she was represented by a cone or pillar of stone, sometimes white and sometimes black, corresponding to her bright and dark aspects. In Chaldea, in Babylonia (modern Iraq), the goddess was worshipped in the form of a sacred black stone, which some scholars believe is the same holy stone that has become central to the Islamic faith, the Ka'ba in Mecca.

Representations of the Great Goddess include Selene (Greco-Roman), Isis (ancient Egyptian) and Ishtar (Babylonian). In India the Great Goddess is known variously as Shakti – the ultimate creative force – Devi or Maha-Devi ("great Devi") and is regarded as a personification of the feminine principle and the mother of all things. In her dark aspect she takes on ferocious forms, including Durga, the warrior goddess, and Kali, the goddess of death. Durga is usually depicted riding a tiger and carrying weapons in each of her ten hands, with which she slays her enemies, while Kali is shown with a garland of skulls, brandishing a sword in one hand and a severed head in the other.

THE TRIPLE GODDESS

In many traditions the goddess is split into separate entities, typically three – maiden, mother and crone – corresponding to the waxing, full and waning phases of the moon. In the Greco-Roman pantheon, Artemis (Roman Diana), Demeter (Ceres) and Hecate represent the three aspects of the Triple Goddess. Sister to Apollo, who is associated with the sun, the virgin hunter goddess Artemis is often shown carrying a silver bow and arrow, which she uses to protect but also to kill. Demeter is the goddess of the fruits of the earth, and her attributes are the wheatsheaf, sickle and cornucopia (horn of plenty). Hecate, goddess of night, darkness and death, is sometimes portrayed with three bodies or faces to symbolize her links with the moon. She is linked with places of transition as guardian of the gates of Hades, and goddess of the crossroads. Hecate is associated with magic and witchcraft in occult traditions.

LESSER DEITIES

There are gods and goddesses connected with practically every dimension of life – both in the natural world and in human society. Nature gods include deities of the skies, oceans and vegetation. For instance, Uranus (ancient Greek) and Rangi (Maori) are sky gods, Poseidon or Neptune (Greco-Roman) and Susanowo (Japanese) rule the oceans, while Tammuz (Sumerian) and the Green Man (Celtic) are fertility gods connected with nature and the renewal of life in the spring.

Although the Earth and the moon are typically associated with female deities, in some traditions they are male gods. Among the Inuit people, Igaluk, the spirit of the moon and a powerful and skilful hunter, is male, while in ancient Egypt the Earth was personified by Geb,

THE GODDESS ISIS

Isis was one of the most important deities of the ancient world. Her name means "seat" or "throne", and sometimes she is depicted wearing a throne on her headdress. She is also shown wearing a headdress of a pair of cow horns with a sun disc between them, linking her to Hathor, goddess of love and fertility. Isis was associated with magic motherhood, and nature. For the Greeks she offered protection to sailors, while in ancient Rome roses were her attribute.

who is usually depicted with a green body, to represent the earth's vegetation, and an erect phallus, showing his desire to reach Nut, goddess of the sky.

There are also deities of agriculture and fishing, mountains and forests, volcanoes and earthquakes, rivers and fish, the weather and wild beasts. Examples of these nature gods include the Hindu goddess Parvati, the consort of Shiva, whose name means "mountain daughter"; Pele, the Hawaiian god of volcanic fire; Chac, the Maya rain god; Thor, the Norse god of thunder; Sedna, the Inuit goddess of sea creatures; and the Native North American Selu, or Corn Woman, who brings the gift of knowledge of the cultivation of corn to her people.

In Africa, earth and water are invariably goddesses: among the Yoruba of West Africa, Ile is the mother goddess of the Earth and Yemoja is the goddess of water. Yemoja's messengers are the hippopotamus and crocodile, and her daughter is Aje, goddess of the river Niger.

BELOW The Hindu mother goddess Mahadevi is depicted here in her benign aspect, as Parvati (consort of Shiva), while the weapon-bearing arms symbolize Durga, the warrior goddess.

ABOVE According to legend, Venus, goddess of love, was born from the sea. She is shown here with the abundant, long hair that symbolizes her maidenhood.

BELOW Lakshmi, the Hindu goddess of fortune, is associated with the elephant (a sign of royalty) and the lotus flower, a symbol of purity.

GODS AND HUMANITY

Many cultures honour deities connected with society and human values. There are gods of love and courtship such as the Greek Eros (Roman Cupid) and the Aztec Xochiquetzal, and goddesses of marriage and motherhood such as the Hindu Lakshmi and the Chinese Kuan-Yin, the goddess of mercy. The Domovoy of Russia and the Lares and Penates of ancient Rome are household spirits that safeguard the home and family. Deities of the arts and crafts include Benten,

the Japanese goddess of music; Wen Chang, the Chinese god of literature; Tane-Mahuta, the Maori god of woodcrafts and carving; and Hephaestus/Vulcan, the Greco-Roman blacksmith god. Abstract concepts such as wisdom, justice, truth and knowledge are also deified by figures such as Athena/Minerva, the Greco-Roman goddess of wisdom and warfare; Maat, the ancient Egyptian goddess of truth and justice; and Brigid, the Celtic goddess of learning.

GODS OF LOVE

The need for love and relationship is fundamental to humankind. It is a force for integration and the resolution of conflict; through trust and surrender to the love partner, opposites may be synthesized, leading to union and wholeness for each individual. When depraved, however, it becomes a principle of division and death. Love can take many different forms – from sexual love and passion at one end of the scale to spiritual love at the other – and in its many guises is represented by a multitude of gods and

goddesses. These include Kama, the Indian god of love; Aphrodite/Venus, the goddess of love in the Greco-Roman tradition, who was allegedly born from the foam of the sea; Iarilo, the Slavic god of love and regeneration; Freya, the Norse goddess of fertility, sensuality and erotic love; and Bastet, the ancient Egyptian goddess associated with pleasure and sexual love. Bastet loved music and dancing, and her sacred symbol was a sistrum or rattle. The spectacular annual festival held in her name attracted large crowds, and more wine was consumed then than during the whole of the rest of the year.

GODS OF WAR

Though war predominantly symbolizes aggression, destructive power and the triumph of brute force, warrior values such as courage and honour are upheld in many societies and sacred traditions. Even in Buddhism, a religion well known for its pacifism, the Buddha is referred to as a "warrior in shining armour". War can also be seen in symbolic terms as an internal struggle, a transitional stage in a move from darkness to light, bondage to freedom. Examples of gods and goddesses of war include the Ahayuta Achi, the powerful twin gods of war of the North American Zuni Pueblo people, and the Morrigan, the war goddess of the Celts.

The Ahayuta Achi were children of the sun and displayed great courage when they stole rain-making implements from a ferocious warrior group. They were brave fighters and fiercely protective of the Zuni people, slaying monsters and wrongdoers on their behalf. They were also responsible for providing tools and knowledge of hunting to the people. The Morrigan, sometimes referred to as the Queen of Demons, often appeared as a triple goddess, her three aspects representing war, slaughter and death. Skilful in magic and prophecy, she appeared on the battlefield as crows or ravens (her symbols), feasting on the dead. She used her shape-shifting abilities to seduce men to satisfy her sexual appetite and engaged in a spectacular sexual tryst with Dagda, the Celtic supreme god.

Sometimes war gods are also associated with peace. The

THE MIMI TRICKSTER DEITIES

According to an Aboriginal myth from Arnhem Land, in the Northern Territory of Australia, the Mimi are said to inhabit gaps and cracks in the region's escarpments. They are sometimes depicted in bark paintings as slender, ghostly figures, and it is said they can be heard at night when they sing and beat on the rocks. The Mimi have a dual nature: on the one hand they are generous and helpful, teaching humans how to hunt, yet if disturbed they can wreak havoc, bringing illness and misfortune. Consequently bush hunters call out to warn the Mimi of their presence and avoid harming any wallaby that seems to be tame, as it might be a pet of the Mimi, who will inflict death on anyone who injures it.

Japanese deity Hachiman, though primarily a Shinto deity, is also acknowledged in Buddhism, where he is called Daibosatsu ("great bodhisattva"). His attributes are a staff and a dove, the latter symbolizing the peace that follows his actions. His function is to protect warriors and the community at large. Another protective peace-keeping god is the Chinese Guan-Di, a god of war, loyalty and justice.

TRICKSTER GODS

The trickster god is a rebellious, amoral and anarchic figure, an anti-hero who enjoys disrupting and upsetting the status quo – whether this be among gods or mortals. He is often of mixed nature with animal, human and divine characteristics. His mischief-making is viewed with ambivalence – sometimes he appears as a malevolent saboteur,

and sometimes his actions help humankind. The Norse Loki, for instance, was both a friend of the gods and a thief who stole their treasures, while the Native North American Coyote is both a hero and villain. Among the Navajo, Coyote is a co-creator with First Man and First Woman and comes up from the underworld bearing plant seeds, which he distributes to the different tribes; yet the Apache hold him responsible for the arrival of the Europeans, and the Maidu of California for bringing sickness, sorrow and death to humankind. Other examples of trickster gods include Eshu, of the West African Yoruba; the Polynesian Maui, bringer of fire to humanity; and the Australian Aboriginal Mimi.

FREYA

Norse goddess of fertility, sensuality and erotic love, Freya protected not only women in marriage and childbirth but also warriors and kings. She was an expert in magic and had the ability to shape-shift, wearing a cloak of feathers and transforming into a falcon to fly through the underworld.

BELOW This ancient carving shows a curly haired Loki, the Norse trickster god.

THE GOD TANE-MAHUTA

In the Maori tradition, Tane-Mahuta was the son of Rangi, the sky god, and Papa, the earth goddess. He was responsible for creating the realm of light by pushing his parents apart with his feet, thus separating earth and sky. Because his parents were naked, he created trees and plants to cover his mother and spangled his father with stars. Tane became lord of the forest and all the creatures that lived in it (including humans) and of all things made from trees. Consequently, he became the god of all those that work with wood. Canoe builders rest their axes in his temple and pray to him the night before they chop down a tree to make a canoe.

Heaven and Hell

ABOVE The Bible says that souls will be judged on Judgement Day between the saved who will go to Heaven, and the damned, who will go to Hell.

NINE HELLS

In Aztec mythology there were nine hells through which the souls of the dead were conducted by a dog, which was sacrificed as part of the funerary ritual. Their souls were literally returning to the land from which they originated. After passing the eighth hell, the soul was plunged into the ninth, the eternal house of the dead.

The division of the above and the below is a common mythical theme, symbolizing a fundamental duality in the universe. Different values and meanings have been ascribed to the two polarities, with the above associated predominantly with the abode of the immortals, a place of bliss, while the below is the abode of devils and divinities, where the souls of the dead are tormented. By way of contrast, in animist or shamanic traditions the above and below are seen as interdependent; a perspective that honours both life and death, and values the natural cycles of life.

In different cultures, and different times, Heaven and Hell have been understood both as literal places and as metaphors of various kinds.

SUMERIA

The earliest description of the underworld is in Sumerian mythology of around 2700 BC, when the goddess Inanna descends to the underworld and undergoes a symbolic transformation. She leaves the "great above" for the "great below" to face her twin sister Ereshkigal, the ruling goddess of the underworld. As Inanna descends she can pass through the seven gates of invisibility only by stripping away her life and fertility in the form of her sparkling clothes and jewels, until she arrives naked before Ereshkigal. She becomes a corpse, but the trickster god Enki finds a way for her to return to earth if she can find a substitute soul. Discovering that her lover

Dumuzi has not mourned for her, Inanna banishes him to the underworld in her place, while she returns to life for six months of each year.

Inanna is the goddess of fertility, and this story symbolizes the seasonal fertility cycle, in which plant life grows, matures and dies, and then is renewed. The story also represents the psychological journey in which a person faces their whole self by sacrificing their ego.

ANCIENT EGYPT

The Pyramid Texts are long columns of hieroglyphs inscribed on the walls of burial chambers. It is thought that they were written to aid the ascension of the pharaoh to the heavens in order to live eternally by the side of his father, Ra, the supreme god.

The first ruler of the Egyptian underworld was Anubis, depicted as a man with the head of a jackal. As the god of putrefaction and embalming, Anubis oversaw the judgement of the dead and protected them in the afterlife. Eventually Osiris, originally a god of vegetation, took over the role of judge of the dead. To reach the underworld, he himself died and was embalmed by Anubis: his mummification symbolized for the Egyptians a new and longstanding belief in the afterlife.

GREECE AND ROME

The ancient Greek underworld was called after its ruler, the god Hades, whose name means "unseen one". The Romans knew him as Pluto, the "rich one", and depicted him holding a horn of plenty, reflecting his command of the earth's resources.

Greek heroes, wise men and initiates went to a light and happy place in the underworld called the Elysian Fields, which Homer described as located at the most western point of the earth. Centuries later, the Roman poet Virgil (70–19 BC) portrayed the Elysian Fields as a place of perpetual spring, with its own solar system. The deepest part of Hades was Tartarus, the prison of the Titans and those condemned to eternal punishment.

JUDAISM

In Judaism there is no clear concept of a hell. Gehenna, which is described as a challenging and unpleasant place, can be understood to be a place in which the soul is purified or spiritually transformed in order that it can finally ascend to Gan Eden, or Heaven. Gehenna was originally the name of a rubbish tip just outside of the walls of Jerusalem, where fires were continually kept alight by adding brimstone to burn up the refuse. The bodies of criminals who had been executed were dumped there.

CHRISTIANITY

In the Christian tradition Heaven is a place associated with light, while Hell is dark, lacking the light of God's presence due to the sins of humanity. The early Christians believed Heaven to be a physical place above the clouds, but this notion was challenged by new ideas about the nature of the universe. Modern Christians do not see it as a physical place, but

may still believe in its physical existence in another dimension.

The original biblical depiction of Hell is of an underground cavern to which the souls of the dead, both good and bad, went for eternity. Later books of the Bible describe it as a place of annihilation or eternal punishment, and a more modern Christian image of Hell is of a state of great suffering.

ISLAM

The Qur'an describes Heaven and Hell in vivid detail. Heaven is seen as a paradise and Hell as a place of fiery torment, though there are divergent beliefs among Muslims as to whether these descriptions are to be considered literally or metaphorically. In Islamic belief, each person is judged according to whether they have lived life to their best abilities in accordance with the truth. Infidels who reject the truth of Islam are given no mercy, and will fall down into Jahannam, or Hell, while the good will live in Heaven.

BUDDHISM

In Buddhism there are six realms of existence, representing states of mind, which people continually pass through in cyclical reincarnations, until they attain liberation from the physical state. The deva, or heavenly realm, is a place of pleasant things, but it is also an impermanent state. The realm of humans is a place that can be both happy and sad. The realm of the asuras (jealous gods or demons) is a place of fighting. The world of the hungry-ghosts is

a place of dissatisfaction and discontent, where there is always hunger. The animal realm is a place in which there is no faculty of reason. Finally, the realm of Hell is a place of great suffering and pain. Someone who has become free from attachment and has seen into their true nature ultimately achieves the state of Buddhahood.

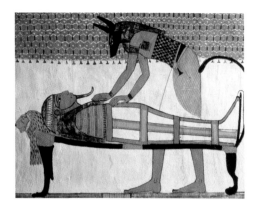

ABOVE The jackal-headed Anubis, first Egyptian ruler of the underworld, embalming a body on a lion-shaped couch.

BELOW Paradise (from the Old Persian word *pairidaeza*) is an enclosed or walled garden of pleasure where the righteous may live in the presence of God.

DEMONS AND ANGELS

BELOW RIGHT When illustrating John Milton's epic poem, *Paradise Lost*, William Blake said that, without realizing it, Milton had taken Satan's part and portrayed the Devil as having heroic status.

BELOW A more traditional image of the devil shows him as more beast than man.

Both angels and demons are beings with divine powers, existing somewhere between the gods and human beings. Angelic and demonic entities are predominantly characterized by qualities of light and shadow, and can also be associated with the light and shadow within the human unconscious. Jung noted that some religions split off the demonic aspect, focusing only upon the light, and pointed out that "divinity" is also symbolized within the realms of the shadow.

DEMONS

In Greek mythology, daimones were divine beings that carried out the will of the gods on human beings, in the forms of fate and destiny. A daimon was given to each person before birth, carrying their destiny as a set of images or patterns that must be lived out on earth. Destiny can be delayed and

avoided, but the daimon is irresistible and never goes away, demanding to be lived or else turning to possess the person, thus becoming their inner demon. With their ability to perceive someone's fate, daimones were thought to present flashes of intuition beyond rational thought, acting as inner guides.

The daimon is an individual's life calling, the equivalent of the Roman genius, the free-soul, animal-soul or breath-soul of the Inuit, the *nagual* of the Navajo, and the owl of the Kwakiutl of north-west Canada. In some cultures daimones are conceived of as particular animal species. They are often associated with fire, and a genius was described as a fiery nimbus or halo. For Jung, the term "daimonic" described a conscious relationship with the archetypal figures of the human psyche.

The origin of the concept of angels, and of angels and demons as embodiments of good and evil, lies in the interaction between Persian Zoroastrianism and Judaism. Zoroastrians describe the battle between two deities: Ahura Mazda, the "wise lord" and god of light, and Ahriman or Angra Mainyu, the "evil spirit" and god of darkness, in the midst of whose fiery battle the souls of humans are judged. Judaism, as a monotheistic religion, conceives of only one God. Thus the equivalent of the god of darkness, Satan, was symbolically cast out of Heaven.

Christianity inherited the idea of demons as angels who fell from Heaven when Satan rebelled

against God. Early Christians saw demons as vapour-like beings with no physical bodies, leading to great debate about whether or not they were divinities. In the 12th century, the Church conceded that demons, like angels, had spiritual bodies over which they were clothed with material bodies.

As pagan and polytheistic religions were increasingly taken over by monotheistic religions, daimones began to be portrayed as demons, and the hearing of inner voices came to suggest madness or the influence of the devil rather than divine guidance. The fallen angels, or demons, took on physical and mental deformities, and were portrayed with black hair, and human-like skin tinged with red, black or white. While angels had celestial wings and predominantly human characteristics, demons – in line

RIGHT A heavenly host of angels
preparing for battle. Many religions
tell of the battle between the
angelic forces of good and the
demonic forces of evil.

with the Judaeo-Christian attitude
of superiority over animals and
nature – embodied aberrant
qualities of the animal kingdom,
with bat wings, claws, horns and
tails, associating their evil with
pagan nature divinities.

THE DEVIL

Ahriman, the evil Zoroastrian
deity, is himself a creator. In
Christianity, however, the Devil is
a being created by God. The
name is derived from the Greek
diabolos, meaning "slanderer", but
the Devil is known by many other
names, including Satan, Lucifer,
Mephistopheles and Beelzebub,
and titles such as The Antichrist
or The Prince of Darkness. The
name Satan comes from the
Hebrew for "adversary" or
"obstacle", as he is the adversary
of God. Satan rebelled against
God, and was exiled to Hell. In
the Qur'an the Devil is known as
Iblis or Shaitan.

During the early Middle Ages,
Lucifer was seen as wicked but
not frightening. As Christian
imagery evolved, he was
portrayed as a new, terror-
provoking image of a beast with
horns, cloven goats' hooves,
wings and a spiked tail.

ANGELS

In one form or another, angels
appear in most of the major
religions as intermediaries
between God and humans. They
are invisible or semi-visible beings
who act as guides to the soul,
helping it to grow and evolve.
They are also believed to organize
the universe at its very
foundations, keeping the planets
on course, and controlling the
growth of life on earth.

Early Christian images of angels
were very similar to Greek and
Mesopotamian deities. They had
wings, reflecting their celestial
quality. Angels are also central to
Islam, and it is believed that the
angel Gabriel dictated the Qur'an
to the Prophet Mohammed.

ANGELIC HIERARCHY

Medieval theologians described a
heavenly hierarchy of angels. In
the first sphere are the heavenly
counsellors: seraphim, cherubim
and thrones. In the second sphere
are the angels who work as
heavenly governors: dominions,
virtues and powers. And the
lowest orders of angels, most
familiar to humans, are the
heavenly messengers, found in
the third sphere: principalities,
archangels and angels.

The seraphim, whose name
means "to burn" in Hebrew, are
angels who literally burn with
passion for the creator, wrapping
their wings around God and
never revealing his presence. They
continually sing his praises and
regulate the heavens with the
music of the spheres. The
cherubim, whose name may come
from an Assyrian word meaning
"to be near", are the guardians of
the light that shines down from
the heavens and touches the lives
of humans. After the Fall, God is

said to have placed the cherubim
east of the Garden of Eden,
between it and the human realm,
to protect the Tree of Life with
flaming swords.

Called in ancient texts the
"lords of the flame" because they
are formed of pure light or energy,
the archangels are the agents
through which the creative will of
God is executed. They bring
loving guidance, protection and
divine messages to humankind.
The names of the archangels are
Uriel, Tzadkiel, Khamel, Raphael,
Haniel, Michael and Gabriel.

FAIRIES AND NATURE SPIRITS

ABOVE A Hamadryad, or wood nymph, reveals herself to a woodcutter as the guardian spirit of the tree.

BELOW Fairies are often described dancing in a ring of enchantment.

The idea of a parallel universe occupied by sentient beings is at odds with the contemporary Western view of nature, and thus fairies and nature spirits have become relegated to the realms of the storybook. In popular belief, fairies have been on the decline since the 17th century due to urbanization and the supremacy of science, but there are still people who believe that the natural world is imbued with spiritual consciousness. Depending upon our perspective, fairies and nature spirits may either symbolize human aspects projected on to nature or be seen as independent beings with their own qualities and consciousness, living within their own reality.

Belief in nature spirits or fairies is most common where spirit is believed to animate nature. In Ireland, where there is still a connection to Celtic roots, and in Iceland, which is surrounded by wild nature, respect for the fairy peoples still thrives.

The Old French word "faerie" or "feyerie" originally referred to a state of enchantment, glamour or influence. Essentially amoral by nature, fairies or nature spirits often represent forces of fate that influence the human world for either malevolent or benign purposes. The fairy kingdom is often described as mirroring the human hierarchical structure, with the king and queen at the top, and also provides a picture of the structure of nature itself.

CHILDREN AND FAIRIES

Fairies are often connected with children, who are said to be more able to see them, and sometimes resemble them. Fairies are sometimes called "little people". In South America winged nature spirits, known as *jimaninos* and *jimaninas*, resemble well-fed children; they are said to be visible on the Mexican Days of the Dead. The tiny *abatwa*, from Africa, are said to live in anthills and are visible only to pregnant women and children.

A Christianized Icelandic legend tells that fairies were originally children of Eve. She was washing them when God called her, and she hid those who were not clean. God punished her for her deception, saying that what was hidden from God should be hidden from humans, and made the children invisible. This connects the separation of the fairy realm to a patriarchal culture in which women, children and nature have been devalued.

FALLEN ANGELS

Another Christianized view of fairies, this time Celtic, is that they were angels driven out of Heaven with Lucifer. As they fell to earth they became nature spirits of the earth, air, water, fire and plants. The *sidhe* of Scotland and Ireland are such spirits, known for their beauty and musical abilities. They are as tall as humans and live in underground fairy palaces.

The Tuatha de Danaan of Ireland are the fairy people of the mother goddess Dana. Legend has it that they built the Irish megaliths as gateways to the fairy world, and were the original guardians of the treasures of the Holy Grail. Finvarra, the king of the fairies, was obsessed by mortal women and enticed them to fairyland with his enchanting music. When someone is entranced by the music of a *sidhe*, they enter a trance – possibly the origin of the phrase "away with the fairies".

TREE SPIRITS

In the classical world, hamadryads (wood nymphs) were female spirits who lived within trees as their guardians, and who died if a tree was cut down. "Dryad" is a more general name for tree fairies found in enchanted groves. Often depicted as wisps of light, dryads are playful creatures, who may help, hinder or tease

humans, and become particularly active during the full moon.

In Japanese folklore Uku-No-Chi is a deity who lives in the trunks of trees, and Hamori is the protector of leaves. The elder mothers are Scandinavian tree fairies who live within elder trees, which are believed to possess a most potent magical power. The beautiful Swedish wood nymph Skogsra is the guardian of the woods and wild animals. Ghillie Dhu is a solitary tree fairy who lives in birch trees in Scotland.

THE ELEMENTALS
Elementals are spirits of the four elements, earth, water, air and fire, which, along with the moon, stars and sun, were the sources of all creation in ancient Greek mythology. The Swiss alchemist and philosopher Paracelsus (1493–1541) named them as gnomes (earth), salamanders (fire), sylphs (air) and undines (water) who inhabit a kingdom situated between the spiritual and material planes. They are said to govern natural and magical energies that influence human thoughts and desires.

Gnomes are spirits of the earth, appearing in the mythology and folklore of northern Europe. Depicted as dwarf-like beings who live underground, these elementals are associated with earth magic, herbal healing, protection, fertility and prosperity.

The Green Man is the archetypal earth spirit of green nature, commonly depicted entirely covered with green oak leaves. He appears as a symbol across most of Europe, where he is associated with spring fertility festivals and the power to make rain. Stone and wood carvings of the Green Man were used to protect people against evil.

The elemental water spirits Paracelsus called undines inhabit caves beneath the ocean, lake shores, bogs, marshland and river banks. They possess the qualities of sunlit water, shimmering rhythmically. Nixies are water sprites of rivers, springs, lakes and marshes that often appear as beautiful maidens. They love music and dance and possess powers of prophecy. While they can bestow gifts upon humans, they can also be harmful, sometimes drowning people.

The water element is associated with the chalice, which symbolizes intuition and the emotions in the Western magical tradition, and with healing in such matters as love, sex, relationships and children. Water spirits can be consulted through "scrying", a form of divination that involves gazing into water in search of symbolic images.

The sylphs are ageless, winged elemental beings of the air, who live on mountaintops. They are commonly associated with logic, communication, learning and travel. Sylphs are invoked through the burning of incense or aromatic oils, and are connected to the ritual knife or sword, a magical tool of command.

Salamanders are elemental spirits of fire, originating from the fire lizard of the Middle Eastern deserts. Salamanders live in molten lakes, volcanoes and forest fires. They have flickering tongues

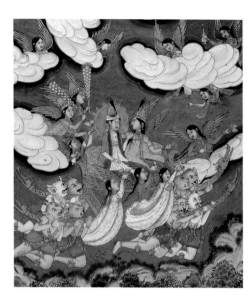

ABOVE This illustration from the One Thousand and One Arabian Nights shows djinn carrying their princess and her lover.

and change shape like fire itself. They are commonly associated with power, light, inspiration, purification and creativity.

In the Islamic tradition fire spirits are called "djinn". They inhabit the mountains that encircle the world and are known for their immense powers and their ability to shape-shift, sometimes appearing as gigantic men. The djinni (or genie) of Aladdin's lamp is such a spirit.

BIRTH FAIRIES
Birth fairies are said to be present when a baby is born, and bestow gifts or talents that will send the person on a particular life path. In the fairytale *Sleeping Beauty*, the 13th fairy bestows a curse instead of a blessing.

EARTH LIGHTS
Will-o'-the-wisps or Jack-o'-Lanterns were earth lights that floated in groups, thought to be fairies guarding lost treasure, with the intention of leading travellers astray. The light was actually that of burning marsh gas.

FANTASTIC CREATURES

ABOVE Giants appear in the mythologies of many cultures and are often viewed with terror, but in some creation myths they are symbols of the formation of the world.

ABOVE The flame-breathing chimera of classical myth had a lion's head, a goat's body and the tail of a serpent.

It seems likely that in early cultures, imagination and reality were not separated in the way that is habitual to the modern mind. Instead they represented two equally valid dimensions of existence, an inner and an outer world, each with its own wisdom. Fantastic creatures are inventions of the human imagination and occur in many traditions. They are attempts to explain the inexplicable, to catch hold of a dimension of experience that resists objective analysis and to explore important human issues through their symbolism.

ELEMENTAL BEASTS

Fantastic creatures usually inhabit a dimension that spans both the everyday world and other, magical worlds, acting as helpful messengers or teachers, or else as monstrous obstacles that must be overcome to reach a goal. Often they are hybrids – part-animal, part-human, or a combination of different animals, bringing together the symbolic properties represented by each to create something new. They are generally endowed with supernatural powers and linked to one of the four elements – earth, air, fire and water – although some are associated with more than one element: for instance, a mermaid is a fish with a human torso, linking her with both water and earth. As creatures of light or darkness, they also symbolize the struggle between good and evil and the spiritual journey of the soul as fears are confronted and transformed.

GIANTS

Named after the ancient Greek *gigantes*, who fought the Olympian gods and lost, giants are humanoid beings of enormous size. They are relics of a former age, existing at the beginning of the world or even, in some traditions, creating it, and may embody forces of nature. In China, trees and rivers appeared from the body of the giant P'an-Ku, and in Japan, natural features such as mountains and lakes were created by giants called *kyojin*. In the Norse tradition, the world was created from the body of the frost-giant Ymir, who was killed by Odin and his brother gods. Ymir's bones became mountains, his skull the dome of the heavens and his blood the seas that drowned all the other frost-giants except Bergelmir and his wife, who later bore a race forever opposed to the Norse gods.

Giants are usually the cruel enemies of gods and humans, as is the one-eyed Cyclops of the Greco-Roman tradition, although humans may outwit them – as in the Old Testament contest between David and Goliath. Sometimes giants use their superhuman powers to help people: the Dehotgohsgayeh of the Native American Iroquois offers protection against evil.

THE WILD MAN

Many traditions have stories of a wild man who is closely allied to nature. The Tibetan Yeti is a

---

CHIRON THE CENTAUR

Some mythical beasts have a positive symbolism. In Greek myth, the centaur Chiron was exceptionally gentle and wise. He was taught by Apollo and Artemis, and in turn mentored several heroes, including Achilles. Wounded by Heracles, he gave up his immortality rather than continuing to live in agonizing pain. He is an example of the "wounded healer" – embodying the idea that suffering is part of the human condition and that experience of it can be used to help others.

fearsome, gigantic creature made of snow and ice and in the Native American tradition, Big Foot or Sasquatch (derived from a Salish word meaning "wild man of the woods") is respected as a supernatural spiritual being. In European folklore the wild man who lives in the forest is typically hairy, with large teeth and sometimes with horns. During the Middle Ages he was known as the "woodwose" and, like the Celtic Green Man, represents the forces of nature.

The wild man has links with the Greco-Roman satyr – a creature of the woods and mountains that had the upper body of a man and the horns and hindquarters of a goat. Libidinous and mischievous, but generally benign, satyrs represented the carnal instincts of men; the fertility god Pan was the chief satyr. Later, in the Christian tradition, the satyr was identified with Satan.

TAMING THE BEAST

Mythical creatures often symbolize the tension between instinct and reason, nature and civilization that is part of human life. It seems that the more civilized humans become, the more fearful and suspicious they grow of their "animal" nature, which is seen as an out-of-control beast that must be tamed. This is symbolized, in Greco-Roman mythology, by the conflict between the centaurs and the Lapiths of Thessaly. The lascivious centaur had a human head and torso on a horse's body, and represented the wild, lawless and

instinctive side of human nature. At the marriage feast of the Lapith king, the centaurs tried to abduct the bride, raped the female guests and attacked their hosts with tree trunks and stones. In the ensuring battle, the Lapiths defeated the centaurs, symbolizing the victory of intellect and reason over instinct and animal passion – which in this story led to barbarous chaos.

The dark, bestial side of humanity is also represented in Greco-Roman myth by the minotaur, a man with a bull's head and tail. Imprisoned by King Minos of Crete in the labyrinth below his palace, each year it devoured seven virgins and seven boys sent in tribute from Athens. Theseus, who was part of this tribute, killed the monster and used a thread given to him by Minos's daughter Adriadne (a symbol of divine guidance) to guide him out of the labyrinth.

Classical myth provides many examples of terrifying creatures that are eventually confronted and killed by a hero. The hydra was a swamp-creature with the body of a snake and anywhere between seven and 100 heads. If one of its heads was chopped off, two grew to replace it. Eventually the hero Heracles killed the hydra by cauterizing each neck stump as he severed its heads.

Another fearful monster was the chimera, a fire-breathing creature with a lion's head, a goat's body and the tail of a dragon or snake; it was sometimes depicted with a head coming from each part. It was the offspring of the monsters Typhon

and Echidna and was a symbol of elemental chaos and natural disasters (especially storms and volcanic eruptions). The Greek hero Bellerophon killed the monster, swooping down on it astride the winged horse Pegasus and thrusting a lump of lead between its jaws. The beast's breath melted the lead, and it choked to death.

ABOVE The beautiful white, winged horse Pegasus and the courageous hero Bellerophon symbolize the triumph of good over evil, as together they kill the monstrous chimera.

THE BASILISK

Also known as the cockatrice, the desert-dwelling basilisk has the wings, triple crest and claws of a cock on the body of a snake. A guardian of treasure, a basilisk's poisonous breath was deadly and its glance could kill – the only way to overcome it was to force it to look at its own reflection in a mirror. It was said to have emerged from a yolkless egg laid in dung by a cock, and hatched by a toad or serpent. In the Christian tradition, the basilisk became a symbol of the Antichrist and during the Middle Ages was associated with sins such as lust, treachery and disease (especially syphilis).

RIGHT The harpies or "snatchers" of Greek myth were terrifying hags with bird's wings and talons who were symbols of death.

LEVIATHAN

Possibly based on the crocodile, the Leviathan of Mesopotamian folklore is a primordial sea monster, referred to in the Old Testament as the "crooked serpent". In Judaism it was considered the counterpart of the Behemoth, the primordial land monster (associated with the hippo) by whom it will be eventually destroyed. Its eyes lit up the dark seas, and its foul breath caused the waters to boil. In Christianity, the Leviathan represents worldly power, while its gaping jaws symbolize the gateway to Hell.

THE GORGONS

In Greek myth, the gorgons were three terrifying sisters – Medusa, Euryale and Stheno – who had scaly skin, fangs and snakes instead of hair. Like the basilisk, their power was in their eyes: they could turn humans to stone by looking at them.

RIGHT Here the Hindu god Vishnu is shown flying Garuda, a giant bird of power and a solar symbol.

FEMALE HYBRIDS

There are many examples of female hybrids, all dangerous and destructive in some way. They represent male fears of the feminine principle, or anima, which is connected with instinct and irrationality. In classical myth, Scylla was a monstrous, six-headed creature with three rows of teeth in each mouth. She was named after the rock of Scylla where she lived, opposite the whirlpool Charybdis in the Medina Straits. She used her long necks to reach out and snatch sailors steering a course between the two obstacles.

The sirens were winged beasts with the heads and breasts of women and the bodies of snakes or birds. Similar to mermaids, they were known for the power of their singing, which they used to lure sailors to their death. Europeans once believed Amazonian manatees to be sirens.

In Greek legend the harpies were fierce and filthy flying hags, who could cause storms on land and whirlpools at sea; they were sent by the gods to inflict punishment on mortals. They symbolized sudden and early death and were also messengers of the underworld, to which they transported the souls of the dead. In common parlance, a "harpy" is a grasping or cruel woman.

MERPEOPLE

Mermaids and mermen appear in many mythologies. The Chaldean sea-god Ea was a man-goatfish, while the Philistine god Dagon, an ancient corn god, had a fish-like lower half. In Greek myth, merpeople inhabit Poseidon's underwater kingdom. Poseidon's son Triton, half man and half dolphin, directed the waters by sounding a horn or conch shell (heard by humans as the roar of the ocean) and was a positive symbol of power and control.

In European folklore, mermaids represented elusive feminine beauty as well as fickleness and vanity (symbolized by the mirror). They had magical and prophetic powers and loved music, they were often depicted holding a comb, which they used to control storms at sea. Usually dangerous to humans (especially men), mermaids such as the German Lorelei could lure mortals to death by drowning.

DIVINE CREATURES

As well as dangerous monsters, many fantastic creatures represent higher consciousness and offer protection. Pegasus, the winged horse of Greek myth, symbolizes the power for transforming evil into good. In China and Japan, lion-dogs are often placed outside temples and palaces to protect against evil forces and to signify the entrance to a holy or special place. In the Buddhist tradition, these creatures defend the Buddhist teachings, and male lion-dogs are sometimes depicted resting a paw on a globe, which signifies the *cintamani*, or Sacred Jewel, of Buddhism.

Popular among the Persians, Babylonians and Assyrians, the griffin has the head, wings and talons of an eagle (symbolizing vigilance and sharp-sightedness) and the body of a lion (symbol of strength). In ancient Greece it was sacred to Apollo (the sun god), Athene (the goddess of wisdom) and Nemesis (the goddess of vengeance). In medieval Europe the griffin represented strength, protection and solar power, and so became a symbol of Christ and the resurrection.

BIRDS OF POWER

Many traditions have examples of birds of power. In Hindu and Buddhist mythology, Garuda is the king of the birds and a symbol of spiritual power and victory. Half eagle and half man, Garuda is the emblem of the Hindu god Vishnu the preserver, who rides on his back. Garuda emerged fully formed from the cosmic egg and lives in the wish-fulfilling tree of life. He is the bitter enemy of the Naga – a legendary race of multi-headed serpents that inhabit the underworld and are symbols of water and fertility.

In the Native American tradition, the thunderbird is a powerful nature spirit. It is unimaginably vast (typically portrayed as an eagle) with lightning flashing from its eyes or beak and thunderclaps sounding when it beats its colossal wings. The Nootka of Vancouver Island believe it rules the heavenly realm, while tribes around the Great Lakes believe it is in continuous battle with the underwater panther, their battles causing storms that are dangerous to people in canoes.

THE PHOENIX

A mythical bird associated with fire and sun worship, the phoenix is one of the most important symbols of transformation, resurrection and immortality. It is often associated with the eagle and has fiery red or golden wings, suggesting the rising sun. In ancient Egypt it was known as the Bennu bird, and was said to return once every 1,400 years to

THE UNICORN

Usually white, with a single horn growing from its forehead, the unicorn is generally a symbol of purity. It has the body of a horse, the tail of a lion and the legs of an antelope, although it is sometimes depicted as a stag or goat. Unicorns were wild creatures that only virgins could capture, and so were associated with femininity and chastity. In Greek myth the unicorn was sacred to Artemis and Diana and was linked with the moon, while in Judaism the horn signifies unity of spirit. In the Christian tradition, the unicorn sometimes represented the Virgin Mary and also Christ – its horn was a symbol of the one gospel. In heraldry, its association with the moon makes it the counterpart of the sun-symbol lion. The unicorn also exists in China as the *qilin* (Japanese *kirin*), where it is depicted with a deer's body and white or yellow fur. This creature was so gentle that it would step on no living thing. Its appearance heralded times of peace and prosperity and it came to symbolize the wise rule of an emperor.

sit on the sacred *ben ben* stone at Heliopolis ("city of the sun"). In its most celebrated myth, the phoenix cremates itself on a wooden pyre set alight by the sun's rays, only to rise again from the ashes as a young bird. In Jewish tradition, the phoenix shrivels after 1,000 years, turning into an egg from which it re-emerges rejuvenated. In Persian mythology, it is called Simurg and is a symbol of divinity and of the mystical journey of the soul towards the light.

In China the phoenix is known as the Feng-huang; in its feng aspect it is a male, solar symbol, while as huang it is female and lunar, making it an embodiment of the union of yin and yang. It is depicted as a composite bird of colourful plumage, with the sun-like head of a cock and a swallow's back that suggests the crescent moon. Its wings signify the wind, its tails plant life and its feet the earth. Human qualities are also associated with the body parts of the phoenix, so that its breast signifies humanity and its head virtue. It is regarded as the emperor of birds and is one of the four sacred creatures (together

with the dragon, unicorn and tortoise) that bring peace and prosperity, its appearance heralding an auspicious emperor or prophet. Also known as the "scarlet bird", the phoenix is associated with summer, the south and red; it is also a Chinese bridal emblem, signifying unity through marriage.

In Japan the phoenix is called the Ho-O and is a popular symbol in Pure Land Buddhism, which emphasizes the reincarnation of the spirit. It is a popular motif on Shinto shrines (mikoshi) and, like the dragon, is a symbol of imperial authority.

ABOVE The phoenix is an archetypal symbol of transformation and immortality. As a solar symbol it is linked with death and rebirth in many cultures.

BELOW The griffin has the head, beak and wings of an eagle, the body of a lion and occasionally the tail of a serpent or scorpion. In Christian symbolism it is often used to personify Satan.

THE DRAGON

RIGHT Here, Saint George is depicted overpowering the dragon in a symbolic act of freedom from oppression.

ABOVE The Eastern dragon is a benevolent sacred or magical being with a serpentine body a lion-like head, and bird-like talons.

BELOW The western dragon, fire-breathing and often green in colour, represents a force to be reckoned with. It has none of the benign and auspicious symbolism of the Eastern dragon.

Dragons appear throughout the world as symbols of great power, with central significance to the cultures in which their legends are told. Their name derives from the Greek *drakon*, meaning "serpent". Dragon myths frequently deal with themes of chaos and disaster, fertility, rebirth and the cycles of the cosmos. Many ancient cultures have dragons or serpents with cosmological significance, such as the Greek Ouroboros, a serpent swallowing its own tail, which represents the destruction and eternal renewal of the universe.

Eastern dragons are more commonly symbolic of positive qualities, such as wisdom and strength, whereas in the West the dragon often embodies negative forces, or obstacles to be overcome by a hero on a quest. As a composite beast, the dragon combines different strengths and qualities of the animal kingdom.

CREATIVE AND DESTRUCTIVE DRAGONS

The earliest surviving dragon legend is that of Zu (or Asag), the Sumerian dragon who stole from the great god Enlin the Tablets of Law that maintained the order of the universe. Zu was killed by Ninurta the sun god, who thus prevented the universe from descending into chaos.

The Babylonian creation myth tells of a great beginning in which nothing existed except the two elemental forces: Apsu, the male spirit of fresh water and the abyss, and Tiamat, the female spirit of salt water and chaos. Tiamat was a dragon, with the

head of a lion, a scaly body, feathery wings, the legs of an eagle and a forked tongue. When she was killed by the god Marduk, her severed body became the sky and the earth, and Marduk created humans from her blood.

In the Bible the dragon is interchangeable with the serpent as a symbol of political opposition to God and his people. Representing the issue of evil, the essence of the devil and mankind's enemy, the dragon does not exist in the natural world, but remains a metaphor for evil in its many forms. Similarly in Persian myth the *azhi*, or dragon, had no regard for humanity, was in opposition to good and despised by the gods. Scandinavian myths tell of a

dragon that lurks in the pit Hvergelmir, gnawing at the roots of Yggdrasil, the World Tree that supports the universe, in a continual attempt to destroy it.

THE WESTERN DRAGON

In Western legend, battles with dragons often represent the fight between good and evil. Western dragons also represent greed, as they often guard hoards of treasure. In psychological terms, a fight with a dragon may represent an inner battle with a covetous nature or a resistance to development. The dragon can represent a huge psychological barrier to gaining access to the riches of the self.

A common mythical theme is that of the hero who leaves his familiar surroundings and meets

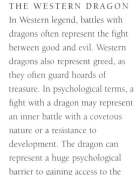

RIGHT Two dragons on a wall in China reflect how Eastern dragons are thought to be able to resolve the conflict of the opposites.

147

THE DRAGON

the monster or dragon at the edge of the known world. He faces the power of the dark forces and by killing the dragon is able to reconnect to life and the personal powers he has gained. The legend of St George tells of his fight with a mighty dragon that was wreaking havoc in Cappodocia (modern Turkey). The people had offered up a virgin princess in an effort to rid the area of the monster. George charged the dragon, killing it with his lance, saved the princess and freed the people from their oppressor. His example of bravery in defence of the weak chimed strongly with Christian values, and in the 14th century he was adopted as patron saint of England.

The red dragon is the emblem of the Welsh. The Mabinogion, a 12th-century collection of Welsh legends, includes the tale of the struggle between this red dragon and a white dragon, symbolizing the invading forces of the Saxons. The dragons were buried in a coffin of stone, representing the harnessing of the two powers: their containment was believed to protect Britain against invasion, and the story symbolizes the fusion of the fates of the Celts and the Saxons.

THE EASTERN DRAGON

Everything to do with dragons in the Far East is blessed. The year of the dragon, which occurs each twelve years in the Chinese calendar, is very auspicious and those born in it are destined to enjoy a long, healthy life and great wealth. Chinese people call themselves Lung Tik Chuan Ren,

"Descendants of the Dragon". The Chinese dragon, Lung, is a divine generative creature, the symbol of the emperor and imperial law and a key influence in Chinese culture. Lung symbolizes greatness, power, goodness and great blessings, and will overcome any obstacle to achieve success. He is intelligent, bold, noble, persevering and full of energy. The Taoist Chuang Tzu (399–295 BC) taught of the mysterious powers of the dragon to resolve the conflicts of opposites, making him a symbol of unity.

Dragons in the East are angelic in quality, beautiful, benevolent and wise. Temples are built for them, usually near the sea or rivers, as dragons live in and rule the waters. They create heavy clouds full of fertilizing rain, and are also associated with lightning and thunder, uniting the rain of Heaven with the Earth.

The royal family of Japan trace their ancestry back 125 generations to the daughter of a dragon king of the sea known as Princess Fruitful Jewel, and the emperors were believed to have the ability to transform themselves into dragons. Whether through ancestral lineage, or though a present relationship with a dragon figure, the dragon's qualities of power and wisdom are made accessible to the people.

DRAGONS OF THE AMERICAS

There are many different mythical creatures in the legends of the indigenous Native Americans. Some dragons of the Americas are benevolent figures with great

skills and wisdom to teach the people, while others are forces of destruction.

The Piasa, or "bird that eats men", of the Illini Indians resembled a dragon, being a large winged animal that ate flesh and lived in a cave by a river. It was greatly feared and attacked victims who came too close. The Piasa was eventually tricked from its cave by a chief called Quatonga, who killed it with poisoned arrows. The Chippewa and the Quillayute tell of a great thunderbird who created thunderclaps and winds with his wings, and whose eyes sparked lightning. His favourite food was the whale, who was forced to escape many times, eventually retreating to the ocean depths.

BELOW Quetzalcoatl (left), god of learning battling Cuauhtli, the eagle-god of renewal.

CONNECTING WITH SPIRIT

Every human society has developed its own
understanding of human life and its
relationship with the cosmos, and with this
has evolved some sort of spiritual practice,
moral code or belief system to make a
connection. Symbols such as the maze
or mandalas are seen as pathways to
enlightenment, and sacred objects act
as carriers of the soul.

RIGHT In many cultures, mountains are still viewed with awe and
respect as either a residence of gods, or a meeting place
between the human and the divine.

SACRED OBJECTS

ABOVE Many sacred traditions use strings of beads as an aid to prayer or meditation.

BELOW A Buddhist prayer wheel is a rotating drum containing scriptures. Setting the wheel in motion is a symbolic act.

Every sacred tradition has its own ways of connecting with spirit and uses a variety of symbolic objects in its rituals and ceremonies. These are usually regarded as objects of power and are sometimes so sacred that they are unseen and untouchable.

PRAYER STRINGS

Common in many religions, the prayer string has beads or knots along its length and is a device to aid prayer or meditation. The number of beads usually has symbolic significance, and the string or chain is also symbolic: on one level it represents the connection between humans and the divine, but on another level a prayer string signifies the bondage of the human soul.

For Muslims, 99 beads symbolize the 99 names of Allah (the 100th being known only to Allah himself). Prayer strings are known as *misbaha* or *subha* and,

as well as being used for the recitation of Allah's names and attributes, are a mnemonic device to aid the repetition of prayers. Hindus and Buddhists use a prayer string known as a *mala* when saying mantras, or sacred chants, in prayer and meditation. The 108 beads of a Buddhist string mirror the various stages of the world's development. A Catholic rosary usually has 165 beads, divided into 15 sets consisting of ten small beads and one large. They are counted by saying prayers: each small bead represents a Hail Mary and each large one the Lord's Prayer.

SACRED STICKS

Some cultures use sticks to connect with the divine. In the Native American tradition, special sticks for carrying prayers are made of painted wood and decorated with feathers, thread and other items. They are sometimes placed around the borders of a ceremonial site, or put into bundles and placed inside it. Maori priests use a god-stick to summon and hold the essence of a god or spirit. The stick, like a carved peg, is held by the priest or thrust into the earth. When people want to make a request, sacred strings are attached to the god-stick and pulled to grab the attention of the spirit residing in it.

PRAYER WHEELS, FLAGS AND STONES

Widely used in Tibetan Buddhism, the prayer wheel, or *khorlo,* is a rotating drum that is

inscribed with and usually contains prayers, a passage from a holy book or a complete paper scroll. As the vehicle for a sacred force, setting the wheel in motion establishes contact between the person at prayer and the heavenly beings. It is rotated clockwise as prayers are recited. Large prayer wheels placed outside Buddhist shrines are rotated by pilgrims as they walk around the holy site.

Stones and flags are also used to carry prayers, and inscribed stones are a common sight along the pilgrimage routes of Tibet. Prayer flags originated in China and India, but have become a colourful feature of the Tibetan landscape. People write their troubles on pieces of cloth and pin them to trees or suspend them on lines for the wind to blow the worries away.

As part of the natural landscape, stones are widely regarded as sacred objects and are often connected with myth and folklore: in China and Japan beautiful river stones were thought to hatch into dragons, and special stones were used to invoke rain and to bring a woman sons. In Nepal and Tibet *mani* stones, with prayers carved on to them, are put in temples and houses and alongside trails and passes, and probably number in their thousands.

In West Africa, the priests of the Yoruba god of thunder carry sacred stones that are thought to have been created by lightning. In the Celtic tradition, round stones with a central hole (known as "holey", or holy, stones) were

RIGHT A *mani* stone tablet, in Tibet, inscribed with "All hail the jewel in the lotus", referring to the pristine consciousness.

used for healing and fertility rituals – it was thought that the hole would trap bad spirits.

MEDICINE BUNDLE

Native Americans use a special pouch to contain sacred objects such as stones, herbs and amulets. Known as a medicine bundle, it may be for personal use, or used by a shaman. Sometimes the bundle is a collective representation of the spiritual power and cohesiveness of the tribe. During the ceremonies of the Crow tribe the medicine bundle would be opened and the women would dance with the weasel skins to obtain supernatural powers that ensured the fertility of the sacred tobacco, and so the growth of the Crow tribe as a whole.

AMULETS AND TALISMANS

An amulet is a small object or piece of jewellery that is believed to possess magical or divine power; an object inscribed with a charm is known as a talisman. Both are thought to connect humans with the otherworldly powers they represent.

In ancient Egypt, mummies were covered in amulets made of gold, bronze or stone to ensure the immortality of the dead; the scarab beetle, the eye of Horus, the girdle of Isis and the ankh (the symbol of life) all featured on amulets used for protection or to gain qualities such as vitality or knowledge. A popular Hindu amulet is the *vishnupada*, the image of Vishnu's footprint. In the

Native American tradition, animal amulets such as bears' claws are thought to embody the spirit of the animal. In China, talismans are sometimes written in invisible ink or "ghost script", so that only the spirits can see them. In Japan, talismans known as *gofu*, designed to bring good fortune, are sold or given at Shinto shrines: they are usually pieces of paper bearing the name of the deity. In Islamic tradition, a common talisman is the *tawiz*, a plaque bearing an inscription from the Qur'an.

CANDELABRA

Candlesticks and candelabra are sacred objects in many traditions. They illuminated Greek and Roman temples, appearing in classical art to represent piety and sacred ritual, and are used on Christian altars and in Buddhist ritual. In Mexico, "tree of life" candelabra combine pre-Christian symbolism with images of Adam and Eve and the serpent of knowledge, while death may appear as a skeleton in the "branches". The menorah is a seven-branched candelabrum that symbolizes the Jewish faith.

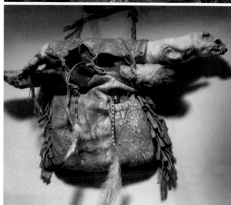

ABOVE A Native American medicine bundle is a pouch containing sacred objects of power. This bundle contains tobacco.

THE MENORAH

The seven-branched menorah is one on the most important symbols in the Jewish faith. It dates back to the Exodus of the Jews from Egypt. According to tradition it created itself from gold cast into the fire by Moses. Its seven branches symbolize the planets, the days of the week and the seven levels of Heaven.

ALTARS AND SACRED PLACES

ABOVE Salt can be used as an offering as a symbol of the earth, and also as a symbol of its life-preserving qualities.

TOP Burning incense is an ancient ritual act of consecration, the smoke often symbolizing the soul's journey heavenwards.

The word "altar" comes from the Latin *altus*, meaning "high", and describes a raised area that forms the focus of sacred ritual and worship. It is usually erected within a building or area dedicated to a deity, although some altars are not fixed but set up for particular ceremonies and then dismantled. Shrines also provide a focus for sacred activity, and vary from a small niche containing some kind of holy object (such as a statue) to a place of pilgrimage. All sacred sites, whether natural or constructed, symbolize ways of connecting with spirit and are places of meaning and power.

ALTAR SYMBOLISM

The altar reproduces on a small scale the entire sacred tradition it represents, and can even be seen as a microcosm of the universe. It has sometimes been thought of as the spiritual centre of the world, so its symbolic meaning is related to the world tree or the cosmic mountain. An altar may also symbolize the time and place where a person became holy or performed a holy act. Like the hearth at the centre of the home, the altar is the focal point of sacred activity: in the Christian tradition, transitional ceremonies

or celebrations such as weddings and funerals take place before it.

Traditionally altars were a place of sacrifice. The earliest altars were open to the sky, so that the smoke of burnt offerings rose up towards the gods; it was only later that they were enclosed in purpose-built temples in honour of specific deities, but the association with fire remains. In the Philippines, palm leaf prayer books are used as offerings, burnt on stone altars (*batong buhay*), while candles and incense are placed on altars in many traditions, symbols of the illuminating and otherworldly qualities of fire and smoke. Native Americans often use tobacco (which they believe to be a sacred herb), and sometimes salt, as an altar offering.

SHRINES

In many cultures shrines are an everyday part of life, appearing at the roadside, in the home, in shops and offices, as well as in holy buildings. In many Christian countries it is common to see roadside shrines dedicated to the Virgin Mary or to specific saints, while in India, China and Japan household shrines are dedicated to various deities to gain their blessings for the home. In a similar way, the lares and penates, the household gods of ancient Rome, were honoured with daily prayers and offerings.

A shrine may commemorate the dead: in China, ancestor deities appear on household shrines. A Christian grave, with its tombstone and offerings of flowers, is also a type of shrine.

THE SACRED IN NATURE

In traditional societies in which people are closely connected with nature, holy sites tend to be places in the landscape. Practically every feature of the natural landscape has been associated with some kind of sacred tradition. There are holy mountains, rivers and lakes, caves, canyons and craters, as well as trees and forests. Mount Fuji, a dormant volcano and Japan's largest mountain, is revered by both Buddhists and Shintoists and is the site of many temples and shrines – even at the bottom of its crater. The Nile was sacred in ancient Egypt and remains so today among traditional African peoples, while Lake Titicaca, the largest freshwater lake in South America, was sacred to the Incas, who believed the god Viracocha rose from it to create the sun, moon and stars.

For Australian Aboriginals, Uluru – possibly the world's most famous monolith – is the sacred site of the Dreamtime. The gigantic Serpent Mound of Ohio is a sacred effigy built by Native Americans; it is in the shape of a snake and is possibly connected with worship of the earth as a divine mother.

In Europe, the site of Chartres Cathedral was once a sacred forest, as was the site of the Temple of Apollo, at Delphi, in Greece, and groves of oak trees were sacred to the Druids. The Ajanta Caves, in India, are rock temples carved into almost vertical cliffs above a wooded ravine with cascading waterfalls; the caves contain five Buddhist temples and 24 monasteries. A meteor crater near Flagstaff, Arizona, which is deep enough to hold a 50-storey building, is regarded as a sacred site by the Navajo, who believe it was made by a flaming serpent god. Chaco Canyon in New Mexico was the dwelling place of the Anasazi, or "ancient ones", ancestors of the Hopi and Zuni peoples. It contains circular chambers known as *kivas*.

SACRED BUILDINGS

As societies became more complex, people began to construct sacred buildings and towns and cities grew up around them. Varanasi, on the banks of the holy river Ganges, is India's most holy city, with 6km/4 miles of riverside temples and palaces. In the central highlands of Java, Borobudur (which means "temple of the countless Buddhas") is the largest Buddhist shrine in the world. The way up to the summit was designed as a clockwise path of pilgrimage, with each tier representing a progressively higher level of spiritual experience.

There are many examples of the sacred sites of one culture being adopted by another. Ephesus in Turkey was once renowned as a centre of magic and the occult arts, and its temple to Artemis, the moon goddess, was alleged to be the greatest of the seven wonders of the ancient world. After Christians destroyed the temple the site became associated with the Virgin Mary; it has been a shrine for many centuries.

The great golden-roofed Potala Palace in Lhasa is the holy residence of the (currently exiled) Dalai Lama, and is a place of pilgrimage for Tibetan Buddhists.

Its name, meaning "Pure Land", comes from the mythical Mount Potala, in India, a place roughly equivalent to paradise and the home of the Bodhisattva Avalokiteshvara, of whom the Dalai Lama is the incarnation. The palace houses the tombs of earlier Dalai Lamas, one of the most splendid of which has a massive golden stupa and a beautiful mandala encrusted with more than 20,000 pearls.

ABOVE The magnificent Potala Palace in Lhasa, Tibet, is a place of pilgrimage for Tibetan Buddhists and stands at one of the highest points of the world.

ABOVE LEFT This gigantic meteor crater at Flagstaff (Arizona) is a sacred site for the Navajo.

ALCHEMICAL TRANSMUTATION

ABOVE Alchemists at work, in a 14th-century manuscript. The transformation processes they used in their scientific practices (here, distillation) have since become symbols of psychological and spiritual progress.

ABOVE The alchemy symbols for Mercury (top) and Sulphur (above).

Alchemy is a philosophy and practice that spans both science and mysticism. It has influenced the development of modern chemistry and even modern depth psychology. The alchemist sees direct relationships between matter and spirit and between organic and inorganic nature.

First conceived as a process similar to fermentation, in which common metals might be transmuted into gold or silver, the alchemical process became an analogy for psychological and spiritual transformation. The earliest references to alchemy are to be found in the records of ancient Egypt. The art was developed in ancient Greece and the Arab world, returning to Christian Europe via Moorish Spain during the 12th century. But alchemy – particularly the theoretical connection between

gold and longevity – was also known in ancient China and India. The process is described using a wealth of symbolism derived from astrology, astronomy, mythology and early science.

HERMETIC WISDOM

The philosophy behind alchemy is directly linked with the teachings of Hermes Trismegistus ("Hermes the Thrice-greatest"), who was described as a great teacher and imparter of wisdom. He appears to be a syncretization of the Greek god Hermes, who conducted souls to the underworld and carried the messages of the gods, with the Egyptian deity Thoth, patron of learning and magic. Hermes was represented wearing a winged cap and sandals and carrying the caduceus, a winged staff entwined with two snakes. His attributes symbolized the linking of the underworld with material reality and the transpersonal experience of "winged flight": he was essentially a mediator or guide between the worlds. Hermes Trismegistus was said to be the author of thousands of texts on science, philosophy, the occult and many other subjects that encapsulated all the wisdom of the ancient world.

Hermetic philosophy centres on the interrelationship of the microcosmic and macrocosmic worlds, contained within the idea "as above, so below", and that all things come from "the One". Applied to alchemy, this means that the human microcosm, where body, soul and spirit meet, is directly related to the elements,

the stars, planets, moon and sun, all of which are understood to be mirrored within each person as the "cosmic soul".

THE SYMBOLIC MAP

C.G. Jung considered alchemy to be a useful symbolic map for inner experiences. He related the different phases of the alchemical process to the stages a person goes through when receiving analytical therapy. Jung commonly used the term *unus mundus*, which he borrowed from the medieval alchemists. It is a description of a "one world" experience, in which the individual's body, soul and spirit are consciously reunited with the cosmic soul.

ALCHEMICAL TRANSFORMATION

The alchemical process, also known as the *opus magnum* or "great work", is essentially a process of change or transmutation, which may be physical, psychological or spiritual. The goal of alchemy is the transformation of a basic substance into a higher substance. This can be understood as changing base metals into gold, or as transforming the most basic of human awareness and experience into deep insight.

The result of the alchemist's dedication to the process was expressed as the *lapis philosophorum* or "philosopher's stone", an "inner treasure" or state of perfect harmony symbolized by the correct mixing of sulphur and mercury (which the alchemists believed were the principal

RIGHT Every tool, ingredient and scientific process in alchemy has its own sign or symbol.

RIGHT Every tool, ingredient and scientific process in alchemy has its own sign or symbol.

materials of all metals). Alchemy is also associated with the process of prolonging life and striving for immortality by creating an "elixir of life" or "drinkable gold".

STAGES OF THE WORK

The *prima materia* is the raw material of the alchemical process, the prime matter that precedes the division into the four elements – water, air, earth and fire. In this raw state all the oppositions of life are present. The *prima materia* corresponds with the psychological state of minimum awareness.

The basic raw material is contained in an athanor, or oven, consisting of an egg-shaped glass vessel heated over a fire. The oven symbolizes the human, in which body, soul and cosmos are linked. It can also represent a ritualized space in which any transformative process is contained. The fire represents the generative force behind the process of transformation. Air from the alchemist's bellows is required to kindle the flames and amplify the process. The warmth within the vessel corresponds to a natural vital energy that is said to be within all things.

The *nigredo*, or "blackening", phase is the stage in which the raw material melts into a black liquid. This symbolizes the early awakening of awareness, and is also associated with the archetype of the wounded healer and the beginning of healing power. The *nigredo* can represent depression, through which a person begins to examine their life and face feelings of guilt, worthlessness

and powerlessness. As the elixir continues to be heated the next phase is the *albedo*, or "whitening", during which the molten metals begin to recombine in a purer form. In psychological terms this represents something like daybreak, during which depression shifts and life begins to return. The final phase of the great work is called the *rubedo*, or "reddening", and is analogous to sunrise. This is a point of great intensity in the work, in which the opposites begin to unite in the *coniunctio oppositorum*, or "sacred marriage", resulting in the the philosopher's stone.

SACRED MARRIAGE

The main symbol of alchemy is the uniting of the king and queen within the fire of love. The union is symbolized by the marriage of sulphur (masculine) and mercury (feminine) or of the sun (spirit) and moon (soul). Alchemy presupposes that humans are in a state of chaos and discord, having lost their connection with "Eden", the primordial state of contentedness. The image of the sacred marriage refers to the renewal of this integral nature through the coming together of the central forces within us.

The marriage of the king and queen also corresponds with a surrendering to our androgynous nature, represented by the half-male, half-female figure of the hermaphrodite. A hermaphrodite symbolizes the attainment of intuitive insight, as opposed to the one-sided power of rational knowledge and discourse. The term hermaphrodite is a

combination of the names of two gods; Hermes, the god of the intellect and communication and Aphrodite, the goddess of sensuality and love. This androgynous unity represents a primordial state of humanity, before the fall into the world of opposites. It is embodied in the philosopher's stone, a kind of spiritual solidity.

BELOW The science of alchemy has a wealth of symbolism of its own, with every element and process given its own graphic sign, but it also has great thematic symbolism, rooted in the way the alchemists looked at the world and explored its possibilities for change.

LABYRINTHS AND MAZES

ABOVE The classic shape of the maze.

ABOVE The labrys, an axe whose double curved blades link it with the moon, and with the root of the word "labyrinth".

BELOW RIGHT This modern picture portrays modern cosmopolitan life as a maze (looking also like computer chip circuitry).

BELOW This classical Italian maze design is an example of a unicursal (one-path) maze.

The labyrinth is a symbol for life that has been interpreted in different ways to represent the central spiritual and psychological concerns of each culture that makes use of it. As a "walk-through" symbol, it is a creative or ritual space that reflects our sense of unknowingness and disorientation as we move through the challenges and obstacles of life. The labyrinth charts the connection between everyday life and the underworld, our conscious self and the unconscious or collective unconscious, and our waking consciousness and the dreaming process. This ancient symbol represents both the womb and the tomb, and the thread that helps us find a way through it represents the awareness needed to get through life.

The ancient root of "labyrinth" is "la", meaning "stone", referring to something firm and on the ground. The labrys is a double-headed axe from Crete, whose two curved blades symbolize the waxing and waning moon, in the centre of each blade is an image of the four-pointed cross. It is often shown held by a goddess who is guarding the entrance to the labyrinth or the underworld. The word "maze" is derived from the Old English *amasian* meaning "to confuse".

LABYRINTH FORMS
A labyrinth is "unicursal": it has only one path that twists and turns but eventually leads to the centre. A "multicursal" maze can have many pathways, and therefore dead ends. The first will disorientate, but the second can both disorientate and render you completely lost.

The simplest form of labyrinth is the "three-circuit" design, but the archetypal pattern is the classical, "Cretan" or "seven-circuit", labyrinth. It has only one entrance and one route to the centre. It may be either square or circular, and is found in Europe, North Africa, India, Indonesia, and North and South America. Almost every ancient labyrinth follows this design. Classical labyrinths with 11 or 15 circuits have been found, such as the 11-circuit labyrinth made from boulders at Visby, Sweden.

MEDIEVAL DESIGNS
The Romans elaborated the genre with meandering, spiralling and serpentine patterns, working them as mosaics on walls and floors. It was later adopted by the Church: the oldest known example dates from the 4th century and is in the pavement of the Basilica of Reparatus at Orleansville, Algeria. Church labyrinths became more common in the 9th century, and designs large enough to be walked as pilgrimage or penance were laid out in the naves of French cathedrals: the most famous was constructed at Chartres around 1230. A six-petalled flower at its centre represents the flowering and healing union of the masculine (Christ) and feminine (Mary) energies.

In the late Middle Ages a new form developed in the gardens and palaces of Europe. These mazes, constructed in topiary, included many wrong turns and dead-ends. The "simply connected" maze, although complex, has one continuous wall and it is possible to navigate by keeping one hand on the wall at all times. By the 19th century "multiple connected" mazes were formed with islands in them, which could not be solved by the "hand on the wall" method.

THE SACRED JOURNEY TO THE UNDERWORLD
Early labyrinths were maps to aid the passage of the soul to the underworld after death. Ancient labyrinth dances and rituals depicted the movement between life and death, through the

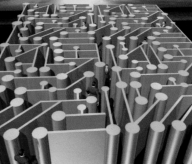

gateway of the tomb and into mother earth. The earliest recorded labyrinth was described by Herodotus in the 5th century BC, built by twelve Egyptian kings as their memorial beside a vast man-made lake. A pyramid rose from one wall of the labyrinth, which had an upper and an underground level. It enshrined the bodies of the twelve kings, and tombs of sacred crocodiles.

THE HEROIC JOURNEY

The most famous labyrinth is that of King Minos at Knossos in Crete, which is associated with the myth of Theseus and the bull-headed monster called the Minotaur. Theseus, King Aegeus of Athen's son, vowed to kill the creature to bring an end to Athen's enforced tribute to King Minos. Minos's daughter Ariadne fell in love with Theseus and gave him a ball of golden thread, the end of which she held as he descended into the labyrinth. Theseus met the Minotaur at the centre of the maze, killed him and returned to Ariadne by following the thread.

This myth has several important symbolic features: the "penetration" of the labyrinth, the experience of disorientation, the meeting and killing of an inner monster, and the resolution of the maze symbolized by the thread, which represents the cord of life joining the two worlds, upper and lower, with awareness. The relationship between male and female principles is another theme. The myth of Theseus and Ariadne describes a golden thread between man and woman. At the

Rad labyrinth in Hanover, Germany, and at the 300-year-old turf labyrinth at Saffron Waldon, in England, a ritual was enacted in which a girl stood in the centre and two young men raced to claim her.

PATHS TO SALVATION

The adoption of the labyrinth by Christians led to a change in symbolic meaning. The centre no longer meant an encounter with death or a monster but represented salvation, with the labyrinth as the path through the entanglements of sinful human nature. A symbolic pilgrimage or penitential journey through the labyrinth might be prescribed for sinners too frail to undertake a longer pilgrimage, and medieval monks might walk church labyrinths in contemplation.

FERTILIZATION AND BIRTH

The entrance to the labyrinth may represent the vulva, and the centre the ovum or the womb, suggesting a fertilizing journey of new hope, life and the potential for rebirth. This theme is connected to the journey into the earth mother and the underworld, thus linking the themes of life, death, fertility and birth.

A fivefold labyrinth with nine circuits is used as a motif on baskets woven by the Pima people of Arizona and also forms the great seal of the Piman tribal council. This design unusually features an entrance at the top, and is thought to depict a heroic journey into the womb.

The Chakravyuha labyrinth is an evolution of the classical form, and is found in India. It is based upon a threefold centre rather than the usual cross, displaying a spiral at its centre, and is thought to symbolize birth, mapping the way for the unborn child through the labyrinthine uterus. In the Indian epic the Mahabharatha, the Chakravyuha is an inescapable circular formation of standing warriors devised by the magician Drona.

Hopi labyrinths from the 12th century found in Arizona come in two forms. The Tapu'at form suggests a baby curled in the womb, or newly born nestling in its mother's arms; the entrance and exit paths suggest the umbilical cord and the birth canal. The second form is more rounded and symbolizes the sun father, who gives life. It represents the journey through life, and may also depict the boundaries of the Hopi territories.

ABOVE Theseus holds the thread, by which he maintained his link with the everyday world, given to him by Ariadne. This myth depicts Theseus as the symbolic hero-saviour, who overcomes the brutish aspects of his own nature as well as that of the Minotaur. The labyrinth, therefore, becomes a symbol of initiation and rebirth.

MULTIPLE DIMENSIONS

Adding a third dimension brings new levels of complexity to maze design, making it possible to move between levels by bridges or stairways. It is theoretically possible to keep adding dimensions to mazes, but this moves them out of the realm of the everyday world. Computer game designers use multi-dimensional mazes and labyrinths to create a "hero's journey" in the player's own home.

MANDALAS AND YANTRAS

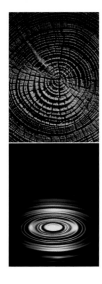

ABOVE The ripples created when a stone is dropped in water form a type of mandala.

TOP Mandala patterns occur in nature, as the concentric circles on this tree trunk show.

BELOW Mandalas are meditation devices in spiritual traditions such as Buddhism. This one from Tibet is used in the Vajrayana Diamond or Thunderbolt vehicle.

The Sanskrit words "mandala" and "yantra" mean "circle" and "instrument" respectively, and describe schematic images designed to both represent and assist spiritual experience. Although rooted in the sacred traditions of the East, many aspects of their symbolism seem to be archetypal, and they appear in different guises all over the world. Mandala-like patterns occur in nature as well as in traditions as diverse as those of the Maya, Native Americans, Celts and Christians. They also feature in dreams and in spontaneous doodles and drawings, leading Jung to suggest that they are an attempt to preserve psychic order and a symbol of the individuation process.

THE TEACHINGS OF THE MANDALA

Just as a rainbow is created only when water droplets, light and the observer's sight come together, so the visual effects of a mandala are such that nothing exists except as an encounter between various fields and patterns of energy. The order of the cosmos is depicted through the balanced arrangement of geometric shapes (predominantly the circle, square and triangle), colour, and symbols such as deities or spiritual beings. Within an outer circle or square, concentric elements of the design radiate from and to the sacred space at the centre, symbolizing the divine presence. In Hinduism, this space is the *shunya* ("absolute void") and the *bindu* ("cosmic seed"), the creativity and spiritual fulfilment that emerge from

nothingness, the space from which all things are born and to which everything returns. Although the symbols used on the mandala are culture-specific, its overriding purpose is to bring the mind to a place of stillness and emptiness, disentangling it from the illusions of permanence in the everyday world in order to experience transcendence.

The traditional Hindu mandala is a square subdivided into smaller squares. As well as an image for contemplation, it is also a template for the ground plan of Hindu temples: the central square is the Place of Brahma and contains the womb-chamber, the holy area of the temple where the altar is situated.

Tibetan Buddhists create mandalas on rolled cloths called *thang-ka*. These are usually rectangular paintings showing the teachings of the Buddha, the wheel of life, the cosmic tree, saints and other spiritual guides in richly coloured images. Circular mandalas called *kyil-khor* are also used for meditation. Each symbol is considered in turn, moving from the edge inwards. Meditating Buddhas, protective and destructive creatures, clouds, mountains, flames and thunderbolts are all common icons on Tibetan mandalas, symbolizing the obstacles that must be faced before the centre can be reached.

MANDALAS IN NATURE

Many mandala-like patterns occur in nature, such as the concentric circles of a tree trunk, ripples on the surface of a pond, a spider's

web, a snowflake or a sunflower. Even natural formations in the landscape have been compared with mandalas. Mount Kailas, one of the tallest peaks in the Himalayas, has four distinct facades facing north, south, east and west, and is compared to an enormous diamond. Buddhists regard it as a mandala, a sacred circle from which four holy rivers (the Indus, Sutlej, Bramaputra and Ganges) flow like the spokes of an eternal wheel.

At the levels of both the macrocosm and microcosm, mandalas seem to be a universal pattern of life: the earth rotates around the Milky Way, while in the cells of every living creature electrons spin around a central nucleus. Even the human eye is a type of mandala.

SAND MANDALAS

Mandalas are not always painted. In Tibetan Buddhism, the *kalachakra*, or "wheel of time", a flat representation of all the cycles of the universe, is created in coloured sand as a symbolic ritual. It begins with a ceremony to call on the goddess of creation and consecrate the site. The mandala is then created from the centre outwards, symbolizing the growth of life from a single egg into the universe. One monk works at each of the four directions, pouring sand from a metal rod called a *chak-pur*. Once the mandala is finished, its role is complete, and a final ceremony is performed to release its healing powers into the world. The sands are swept up from the outside to the centre of the circle and placed

159

Stone circles, burial
mounds, labyrinths
and mazes have all
been likened to
mandalas, as have
the Native American
medicine wheel and
dream-catcher, the
latter a mandala of
the dream world. The
pre-Christian Celtic
cross, symbolizing
the four seasons and
the four directions,
was positioned over a
circle symbolizing the
earth. The Christian
tradition has its own
versions of mandala
formations, such as
the rose windows that
adorn cathedrals and
churches.

in an urn. This is carried in a
ceremonial procession to a nearby
river where it is emptied, carrying
the healing sands out into the
ocean to bring peace and
harmony to the whole planet.

The Navajo also use sand
paintings in healing rituals. The
medicine man or woman
performs a ceremony centred on a
mandala sand painting called the
iikaah ("the place where the
spirits come and go") – a doorway
through which helpful spirits will
pass as they are called upon in
the ritual. The ceremony begins at
dawn and takes place in the
hogan, a sacred lodge that has
been blessed for the ceremony.
The mandala is created using
string and other markers, as the
positions of the spirit figures must
be precise to create a place of
harmony. The base of the painting
is built from sand, corn and
pollen or crushed petals, then
charcoal and ground stone are
carefully poured to create
outlines. The figures are solid
shapes, with the image of their
bodies, both back and front,
poured into place to bring their
complete presence into the circle.

At dusk, the person in need of
healing comes to the hogan and
sits in the centre of the mandala,
with the images of the spirits in
direct contact with his body to
draw away the illness so that it
falls into the mandala. The sand is
then ritually disposed of.

YANTRAS

A variation of the mandala, the
yantra is used in both Hinduism
and Buddhism. It is a complex
geometric figure that visually
expresses a mantra or prayer.
Sometimes the mantra is written
to "fix" it, but predominantly
geometric symbols are used in a
mystical representation of creation
and the interaction of cosmic
forces. The powers inherent in the
yantra are brought to life through
ritual acts, such as smearing it
with perfume and chanting the
mantra over it.

The *shri-yantra*, considered one
of the most potent yantra designs,
is used in Hindu tantric ritual. It
consists of a square, concentric
circles and nine intersecting
triangles. The external square
functions like a city wall, with
gateways to the four points of the

compass. It represents the
physical world and protects and
encloses the interior. The
concentric circles represent
spiritual expansion and cosmic
unity, while the triangles
represent the joining of the linga
(phallus), represented by the
upward-pointing triangle) with
the yoni (womb), represented by
the downward-pointing triangle,
or the sexual play of the divine
couple, Shiva and Shakti.

The *shri-yantra* can be engraved
only on eight surfaces: gold,
silver, copper, crystal, birch,
bone, hide (including paper) and
a special "Vishnu" stone named
after the preserver deity. Only
these materials, in combination
with the correct colours – red, to
symbolize the female, or white,
symbolizing the male – will create
the necessary balance and
harmony of energies.

BELOW Yantras use
abstract geometric
shapes in their design,
typically triangles,
squares and circles.

ORACLES AND DIVINATION

ABOVE Tarot cards and a crystal ball are two methods of divination still used today.

RIGHT In a medieval illuminated manuscript classical Greek astronomers inspect the the stars from Mount Athos. They believed that reading these patterns would help them predict likely future events.

Speaking in a symbolic language, oracles and divination are a way of communing with the unseen influences beyond the reach of the everyday world. From a psychological perspective, they can be seen as a way of tapping into the deeper layers of the unconscious mind.

Above the entrance of perhaps the most enduringly famous oracle in the ancient world, the Greek oracle at Delphi, was carved the inscription, "Know thyself." Divination is not a method of predicting the future – this would imply that life is a fixed programme – but is best understood as something fluid, a process that involves an ongoing dialogue with the spiritual or mythical dimension. Through this relationship it is possible to read certain signs that would otherwise remain hidden, thereby increasing self-awareness.

ORACULAR DEVICES

Divination uses chance to create a doorway for the spirit to express itself through symbolic patterning. This can be anything from random patterns in tea-leaves, bones or sticks, cloud formations, weather patterns, the formations of the stars and the communications of plants and animals to sophisticated symbol systems such as the Tarot or the I Ching. To read these patterns and elicit meaning involves an intuitive leap of faith, as oracles will not be understood by the rational mind, which tends to reject or overlook the significance of information that comes through by chance.

THE I CHING

Paradoxically, the only certainty in life is change. In all change, however, there are patterns, and it is this predictability that the shamans of ancient China referred to when they were called upon to give advice on forthcoming events. Originally, the answer to a question was divined from the patterns on animal bones or tortoise shells. This developed into the I Ching, or "book of changes", which became much more than an oracular device: for the ancients it symbolized the workings of the whole universe.

The basis of the I Ching is the trigram, an arrangement of three lines that are either solid or broken. The solid line represents yang energy, and the broken line yin energy, yin and yang being the two opposing principles that

underlie the whole of creation. Eight arrangements are possible, and the trigrams symbolize eight stages in the cycle of growth and decline, or ebb and flow, observable in all areas of life. Each has a name taken from nature: Heaven, earth, thunder, water, mountain, wind/wood, fire and lake. Trigrams once decorated the clothing of temporal and spiritual leaders and can be used as amulets. Combined in pairs, the trigrams make up the 64 hexagrams of the I Ching, with names such as "the creative", "decrease", "the receptive", "family", from which interpretations of human situations are made. These are further amplified by "changing lines", which increase the possible number of permutations to more than 10,000.

THE TAROT

The exact origins and purpose of the Tarot are unknown, but it was in use for gaming and divination in Italy, France and Germany by the late 14th century, though medieval churchmen denounced it as "the Devil's picture book". The Tarot is a card-deck illustrated with highly symbolic imagery. It may have been a way of disguising spiritual teachings that ran counter to the prevailing doctrines of the Church, but also seems likely to have formed part of a memory system. During the Renaissance, *ars memorativa* (pictorial memory systems) became linked with magical talismans or amulets for invoking a particular power.

The Tarot divides into two parts: the 22 cards of the Major Arcana and the 56 cards of the Minor Arcana. "Arcane" means mysterious or secret, and the Tarot is sometimes known as the Book of Secrets. The Major Arcana deals with archetypal themes that reflect turning points in life, symbolized by cards such as the Fool, the High Priestess, the Lovers, the Hanged Man and the World. The Minor Arcana is sub-divided into four suits, which are related to the four elements as well as everyday concerns: wands (fire and ambition), swords (air and ideas), cups (water and emotions) and pentacles (earth and material resources).

AUGURY

Today the term "augury" refers to all forms of divination. Originally, however, it meant interpreting oracular messages from birds,

often viewed as messengers to humans. Augury is one of the oldest forms of divination. Accounts from China, India, Persia and many other regions show that people paid careful attention to birds for divinatory purposes – their songs, movement, flight patterns, behaviour, even their eggs, as well as the particular species. For example, the Kakajarita, a 9th-century Tibetan text, gives detailed instructions for divining the meaning of crow cries.

Augury does not, however, require an organized system of signs. Originally it must have depended on an intimate rapport between birds and humans, with people entering into a mystical experience of bird-consciousness. The Roman state always referred to the augur before making an important decision, while by tradition, the site of the Aztec city Tenochtitlan was chosen when an eagle was seen on a cactus with a snake in its mouth, seen as an auspicious sign from the gods. The Bununs of Taiwan rely upon the chirping and the flight patterns of birds as hunting omens: a chirp on the left side is seen as a bad omen, and they invariably return home.

THE CLEDON TRADITION

Oracles can work in many different ways. In the classical world, words heard at random or out of context that struck a chord with the listener were regarded as oracular messages. Known as *cledon*, these symbolic fragments of speech that seemed to answer a

question or give advice were usually uttered unwittingly by strangers, children or passers-by. As with any other oracle, the success of the method depends as much upon the recipient's openness to the message and ability to comprehend it as on the oracle itself, divining being an interactive process.

THE DODONA OAK

One of the most revered oracles of antiquity was a great oak tree growing at Dodona, in north-west Greece. For centuries, pilgrims travelled to seek the tree's guidance. In the earliest stories about Dodona, oracles were delivered by the oak itself, but by the time of Homer, around 800 BC, a group of interpreters called the *selloi* – who, according to the Iliad, were "of unwashed feet and slept on the ground" – had established themselves at the site. Pieces of wood taken from the tree were said to have the same oracular power.

THE RAVEN

Often presaging death, the raven is usually seen as a bird of ill omen, but it may also augur well. In Genesis it was sent off by Noah to determine the extent of the flood, but never returned. The raven also appears in the flood stories of the Algonquin Indians. In Scandanavia ravens are thought to be the ghosts of murdered people, while according to a Chinese tradition, the soul of the sun takes the form of a crow or raven.

THE CYCLE
OF LIFE

How humans see their bodies, their physical
position in the world, and their own lifespan,
gives rise to the rich symbolism that surrounds
birth and death, love and relationships, ritual
and creativity. Iconic symbols such as the heart
and the wheel are central, but so are thematic
symbols such as marriage and sunrise.

RIGHT The cycle of birth, death and renewal is often symbolized
in the annual agricultural cycle of sowing and harvesting. Wheat
and other staple crops are linked with fertility and the life force.

THE HUMAN BODY

ABOVE The human body is a rich source of symbolic meaning. The female form can represent different aspects of woman, such as fertility and female sexuality.

ABOVE The head is associated with humans' thinking capacity. It can also be used to describe a person in charge.

Many ancient traditions saw the human body as a microcosm (literally a "little world"), containing in miniature all of the various stages of creation. The Chinese regarded the body as both yin and yang, and thus a symbol of perfect balance and wholeness. In some traditions the body is regarded as a "temple of the soul", which mediates between Heaven and earth, assisting each person to realize their divine purpose and unique potential. Other traditions have viewed it as an enemy that has to be overcome, the repository of the base instincts and passions that threaten to lower humanity to the level of the animal world. In addition to the symbolism of the body as a whole, practically every individual part has its own symbolic associations.

THE HEAD
Almost universally, the head is considered to be the seat of learning, the instrument of reason and of the spiritual and social capacities that raise humans above animals. Symbols of authority such as crowns are

worn on the head, while bowing the head denotes submission to a higher being. In many African tribal cultures an elongated head is a sign of good character, wisdom and leadership, and elaborate hairstyles and headdresses are designed to accentuate this quality.

The head is sacred in Maori tradition, and the Celtic cult of the sacred head is illustrated by numerous myths. In many traditions, beheading an enemy is thought to humiliate the individual. The Hindu goddess Durga is often shown holding her own decapitated head, while Christian iconography has many instances of saints carrying their own heads, signifying the power of the spirit to conquer death.

THE HAIR
The hair often represents virility and strength, as in the Old Testament story of Samson, who lost his strength when Delilah cut his hair. The Khalsa community of Sikhs let their hair and beards grow because they believe it is a symbol of God's love. In China a shaved scalp was on a par with emasculation and could debar a person from public office. A shaved head can also indicate sacrifice or submission: monks and nuns in both Buddhist and Christian traditions may cut off their hair as they enter religious life. For the Gauls and other Celtic peoples' long hair was a symbol of royal power, or of liberty and independence.

Long loose hair in women once indicated youth and virginity, while braided or bound hair

could symbolize either a married woman or, conversely, a courtesan. In Christian art the redeemed and sanctified St Mary of Magdelene is often shown with very long, loose hair as a symbol of her chastity, love and humility.

Haircuts and hairstyles are frequently signifiers of social or religious difference, as with Rastafarian dreadlocks or the long ringlets of Hassidic Jews. In Hindu and Buddhist traditions, the topknot is believed to cover the area where the divine spirit enters the body at birth and leaves at death; it is associated with holy people. Body hair is associated with virility or animal tendencies: in Christian art it is used as a symbol of the devil.

THE EYES
As may be expected, the symbolism of the eye is connected with perception and vision, the ability to see beyond the purely physical to the realms of soul and spirit; consequently blindness is often used as a metaphor for the inability to see spiritual and moral truth. However, blindness can also be associated with wisdom and spiritual gifts.

In some traditions, including Hindu, Taoist and Shinto, the eyes are identified with the sun and moon, with the right eye corresponding to the active and the future (the sun) and the left to the passive and the past (the moon). To unify perception, some cultures believe in the existence of an invisible "third eye" in the middle of the forehead. Both the Hindu god Shiva and the Buddha are depicted with a third eye, the

ABOVE An unlidded eye within a triangle is a Masonic symbol, shown here on a society apron. It symbolizes spiritual awareness.

vehicle of perception that is directed inwards in meditation.

In ancient Greece the eye symbol had magical powers, and eyes painted on the prows of warships had the power to guide them. In ancient Egypt the wadjet, or eye of Horus, had a healing and protective function. One of the symbols of Freemasonry is a single, unlidded eye (a symbol of divine knowledge) enclosed within a triangle – an image that appears on the back of the US dollar bill. The phrase "eyes wide open" signifies a state of awareness.

THE MOUTH
As the organ of speech and breath, the mouth embodies the power of spirit and the inspiration of the soul, an elevated state of consciousness and the ability to reason and communicate. Through its association with eating the mouth is also linked with destruction, as

with the mouth of a monster: in Christian iconography the entrance to hell is a fanged demon's mouth. Medieval artists depicted small demons flying from a person's mouth to signify evil words or lies.

INSIDE THE MOUTH
The tongue and teeth have their own symbolism. In African sculptures, teeth can indicate a creature's terrifying power to consume, although they can also be associated with strength and growing wisdom. In Persian and European love poetry, teeth are frequently compared to pearls.

The tongue is sometimes compared with flames and in the Christian tradition tongues of fire symbolize the Holy Spirit. It symbolizes speech but is also associated with ferocity: rolling tongues were depicted on ancient Chinese tombs to frighten away evil spirits. In Tibet, sticking out the tongue is seen as a friendly greeting, while in Maori culture it is a defiant, provocative (and also protective) gesture of greeting.

RIGHT The heart is not a symbol only for love but is also associated with moral courage and truth.

THE HEART
In the West the heart has been linked with love, especially romantic love, since the Middle Ages. In the ancient world, however, it was a symbol of the centre and was often thought of as the place where the soul resided. Similarly, in China the heart was thought to be where the *shen*, or spirit, resides, and was also considered to be the source of intelligence.

BELOW Mary of Magdelene is often portrayed with long, loose hair as a symbol of her chastity, and an allusion to the time she washed the feet of Jesus.

as their servant, a gesture that was later imitated by English kings who washed the feet of the poor to show their humility. In the Fon Republic of Benin, the god of war is usually shown with large feet, symbolizing his ability to stamp out his enemies.

BREATH AND BLOOD

Both breath and blood are associated with the life force and divine power. Native Americans use the breath to pass power between people, and it had magical properties for the Celts: the Druid Mog Ruith was able to turn his enemies to stone by breathing on them.

Many cultures consider blood to be sacred because it embodies the soul: in West African voodoo, sacred statues are smeared with chicken's blood to bring them to life, and a similar practice was performed by the Norse, who smeared their sacred runes with ox blood to activate them. Blood has been used to seal oaths, and 14th-century Japanese warriors stamped their fingerprints in blood to assure a contract. Christians ritually ingest the blood of Christ, in the form of wine, at the Eucharist ceremony.

However, in some traditions blood also has the power to contaminate. In the Shinto religion, the word for blood (chi) is taboo, while neither Jews nor Muslims are permitted to eat meat that contains any residue of blood. Jews regard menstrual blood as unclean, though it has also been linked with fertility, as in ancient Egypt.

THE NAVEL

As well as being a visual reminder of the body's connection to life through the umbilical cord, the navel is often used as a symbol of the centre of the world from which creation emanated. Muslims describe Mohammed's birthplace as the "navel of the world", and in ancient Greece Delphi was the site of the sacred *omphalos,* or "navel stone", a cylindrical stone with a rounded top that symbolized the connection between the three worlds (Heaven, earth and the underworld).

The pole star is sometimes referred to as the navel star, around which the heavens seem to rotate. In West Africa, the navel is viewed as an ancestral matriarchal symbol that relates to fertility; scarification marks are ritually made around a girl's navel at puberty.

BELOW The symbolism of the navel is connected with the centre of the world, life and creation.

HANDS AND FEET

Traditionally the hand is a symbol of active divine power. Handprints frequently appear in Australian Aboriginal cave art, representing the artist's spiritual imprint and signature. In Hinduism and Buddhism, the hand is a guardian and fragment of the universal soul, and in India handprints on walls, doors or other objects signify protection. In Christian iconography, a hand represents God's blessing and intervention, and the "laying on of hands" is used in churches in healing and ordination rituals.

The foot is the part of the body that most closely relates to the earth. It is associated with both stability and movement. Bare feet traditionally indicate humility, and have also been a sign of mourning. When Christ washed the feet of his disciples, he was using the act to symbolize his role

SEXUAL ORGANS

The sexual and reproductive organs of both men and women carry a profound symbolism. As well as being linked with fertility, the womb is associated with protection and mysterious hidden powers. Vessels of transformation, such as the crucible and cauldron, are linked with womb symbolism, as are natural features in the landscape, such as caves. The womb is often linked with the mother goddess: Delphi in ancient Greece, the site of the oracle and sacred to the great mother of earth, sea and sky, was named from the Greek word *delphos*, meaning "womb".

The vulva is also usually associated with mother goddesses. In Hinduism it is symbolized by the yoni, represented as a vulva-shaped shallow basin and the graphic symbol of the triangle. The Bambara of Mali refer to it as "lovely big mother" and regard it as a gateway to hidden treasure and knowledge. The vulva symbolizes the dark, devouring aspect of the goddess, the jealous, possessive, over-protective mother who won't let go of her children, or the woman her lover. The concept of the vagina dentata ("toothed vagina") may be associated with this aspect and may also represent a man's castration anxieties – that once he enters a woman's body he will be unable to escape – and the fear of surrender to his instincts.

The phallus is a symbol of the masculine, active principle, the power of procreation and a channel for the life force. It is worshipped in many cultures as

the source of life. In Hinduism it is associated with the god Shiva and is symbolized by the linga, an upright stone that typically appears conjoined with the yoni, symbolizing the union of spirit and matter, of the male and female principles. Phallic objects were worshipped in ancient China, and the Japanese god of marriage is portrayed in a phallic shape. Fertility gods such as the Roman Priapus are often depicted with an erect phallus, and satyrs were shown with gigantic erections as symbols of their libidinous nature. In Kabbalistic thought, the phallus was responsible for maintaining equilibrium; through its hardening or softening in the presence or absence of energy it is a balancing agent whose role is to sustain the world.

THE ENERGY BODY

Many traditions believe in an animating force that runs through every living thing, including the human body. Known by various names (such as chi in China and prana in India), the life force runs along a web of energy pathways known as meridians (China) or *nadis* (India). Esoteric and healing systems, such as yoga, reflexology and accupuncture, are based on this system, associating physical and emotional distress with imbalances in the body's energy

field. In Hindu and Buddhist thought, subtle energy enters and leaves the body through chakras, or energy centres, which are gateways between the physical and the immaterial realm. The principal chakras are arranged along a central meridian running from the base of the spine to the crown of the head.

BELOW Hindu linga stones are shown nestling in round-shaped yoni carvings. The linga and yoni symbolize the male and female reproductive organs and the masculine and feminine principles.

BIRTH AND DEATH

Both birth and death are feared and welcomed in every culture, each representing both beginning and ending. Birth is the beginning of life, but may also be considered the ending of a previous life or soul journey, and the end of gestation. Death is an ending, but for some it is also the beginning of a significant new journey to the underworld, Heaven, or the next incarnation. Both are events of mysterious beauty, awe and terror, sources of inspiration and superstition for a huge body of symbolism informing religion, culture and science.

BIRTH AND DEATH FORETOLD

A great deal of symbolism surrounds the foretelling of birth or death, perhaps because these events are so mysterious, unpredictable and life-shaking. Astrology predicts likely times for births and deaths, and unusual heavenly signs have often been interpreted as pointing to the comings and goings of important people. In ancient times the sighting of a new star was the sign of a newborn king; thus the birth of Christ was predicted on this basis, possibly when Jupiter (known to the Jews as the "king's star") aligned with Saturn,

creating the "star of David".

Many signs and symbols in nature are taken as omens of birth or death. Perhaps because it is a symbol of transformation, the butterfly is variously taken to portend either. In the Orkney Islands a rainbow presages a birth, and an old English folk rhyme associates the sighting of magpies with birth: three for a girl and four for a boy. In Europe the death's head sphinx moth was commonly taken to predict death because of the outline of a skull on its back. The Samoans believed that if they captured a butterfly they would be struck down dead. The Celts believed that seeing a butterfly flying at night signified death, and in Christian art a chrysalis is a symbol of death.

The ancient Romans hated owls as they saw them as portents of death. Many carrion-eating birds, particularly ravens, are thought to be able to smell death before it occurs, and they are therefore a bad omen, but in African and Native American cultures the raven is also a helpful guide to the dead on their journey. The howling of a dog or the sighting of a ghostly black dog may both warn of death. Dogs also appear in shamanic lore as guardians and guides to the underworld.

BIRTH SYMBOLISM

Many cultures consider giving birth a powerful and natural initiation, and give great importance to the various stages for both mother and child. The birth process mirrors the process of initiation. Traditionally the

mother is removed from society – leaving her usual roles behind – to a sacred place for birth, and undergoes rites of purification and cleansing. Labour has strong associations with the "threshold" phase of initiation, in which there is often great pain and mystery, and in many cultures post-partum blood is considered powerful and unclean, possibly because it represents a strong link with the world of the spirits. During childbirth the gods and spirits are often deemed to have great influence. The Anglo-Saxons prayed to the goddess Freya during birth. Celtic cultures sometimes hid the birth from supernatural creatures that might otherwise have created mischief.

THE PLACENTA

The placenta is revered in many parts of the world, symbolizing life, spirit and individuality. It is often buried in the ancestral territory to provide a sacred link between the child and the land: the Maoris call the placenta *whenua*, which also means "land". The Aymara and Quecha people of Bolivia consider the placenta to have a spirit. It is washed and buried secretly by the husband, otherwise, they believe, the mother or baby may become ill. The Ibo of Nigeria and Ghana give the placenta a proper burial as they believe it to be the dead twin of the newborn, and the Hmong of South-east Asia consider it to be a "jacket" – the first clothing of the child. They bury it in the belief that after death the soul will travel back to find its clothing.

THE MIDWIFE

Traditionally, midwives had a similar status to shamans or priests. In modern society the midwife may no longer have such high status, but midwives protect and support the mother and child. In British Columbia, the word for midwife among the Nuu-chah-nulth people means "she can do everything" and for the Coast Salish people it means "to watch, to care". The Greek goddess Hecate was the divine midwife.

SECOND BIRTH

Water has always been symbolically important for birth rites. Christian baptism, which may involve total immersion of the child or adult in blessed water, symbolizes a "second birth", representing the death and rebirth of Christ, and the cleansing of sin. The ritual is thought to have originated in India, where priests still practise a similar rite today. An ancient Irish tradition was the immersion of the child in milk, based on the belief that its spirit was formed through being breastfed. The Catholic Church banned the practice in 1172.

DEATH SYMBOLISM

Death has many emblems, most of them alarming, although the symbolism of hope and that of fear sometimes appear simultaneously. In art the most familiar depiction of death is the Grim Reaper, a skeleton robed in black and carrying a scythe, trident, sword or bow and arrows, and sometimes the hour glass that he uses to measure a life's span. Other symbols of death include the skull, or a tomb or gravestone and the plants poppy, asphodel and cypress. Death ships or barges symbolize a journey to the afterworld, particularly for the ancient Egyptians.

BURIAL AND CREMATION RITES

Funerary rites vary tremendously according to cultural attitudes and beliefs, and the combination of fear and celebration with which people approach death. The practice of burial is known to date back as far as 80,000 years, and is common in societies where doctrines of bodily resurrection are popular. At sites such as the Shanidar Cave in Iraq, Teshiq-Tash in Iran and the Grotte des Enfants in France, bodies have been found buried with tools and jewellery, and often decorated with red ochre, to symbolize the blood of the earth.

Australian Aboriginal death rites are complex and vary by clan and region. Essentially death is understood as a transformative event involving the parting of dual aspects of soul from the body. The spiritual being is thought to reintegrate with the ancestors in the Dreaming, in a sense returning home. After death the community sing songs containing symbols of death, such as a worm-eaten mangrove tree representing the dead body, or the tide marks of a "king tide", referring to a cleansing process and removal of the physical being. The coffin is a talisman painted to ask the spirits to help the deceased on his journey.

To ancient Indo-Iranian peoples and across Europe, from the Bronze Age onwards, cremation symbolized purification, sublimation and ascension. The fire itself signified the freeing of the soul, while the smoke symbolized its ascension. Roman funerals involved a procession to the tomb or pyre, with important relatives wearing masks of the deceased ancestor. Nine days later a feast was given, and the ashes were placed in a tomb.

ABOVE The black skeletal image of Death was a common medieval image.

ABOVE LEFT The first baptism, of Christ by John the Baptist. is used to symbolize divine grace and rebirth.

BELOW The gravestone, the Grim Reaper, and the hourglass symbolize the negative view of death.

Sex and Fertility

ABOVE Water is a prime symbol of fertility, especially when in the form of rain.

TOP Sex and fertility have many symbolic associations, from the everyday to the sacred.

TOP RIGHT In this depiction of Love fighting Chastity, the symbols of chastity – her girdle and the arrow-deflecting shield – are in evidence.

ABOVE Grain is a symbol of the earth's fertility and is also used to symbolize human fertility.

Human beings are first and foremost sexual creatures, and to ensure the continuation of the species nature has ensured that sex is a pleasurable, health-promoting activity. Many traditions recognize a connection between sex and spirit, seeing sex as a vehicle for both bliss and transcendence.

FERTILITY RITES

In many traditions there is a connection between the fertility of the land and sexual symbolism. The Mongols and early Chinese saw rain as "seeds" sent from the sky to fertilize the earth; similar beliefs persist in parts of Africa and Australia, where women may lie down in the rain to help them get pregnant. In the myths of hunting societies, knowledge and power, and even human life itself, come from animals, and it is not uncommon for these gifts to have been obtained by sexual means. For instance, the survival of the Mandan of the North American plains depended on the bison. Human society was thought to descend from a sexual transfer of power between a bison and a woman, and the people's sacred buffalo dance mirrors this primordial act. In a ritual dance of the Blackfoot, a man decks himself with feathers and imitates the mating display of a prairie cock to ensure a good harvest.

Fertility and the attraction between male and female have been regarded as gifts of the goddess, associated with the Earth's seasonal cycles. In ancient Babylon, the king and the high priestess would perform ritual

intercourse as a fertility rite, symbolizing the mystical marriage of Tammuz, son and lover of the goddess Ishtar. The myth of Tammuz and Ishtar concerns the goddess's journey to the underworld to seek the release of her dead lover. While she is away, the earth is barren, but on her return, fertility returns to the land. This archetypal myth is echoed in the ancient Egyptian account of Isis and Osiris, or the ancient Greek story of Demeter and Persephone.

FERTILITY SYMBOLS

The bow, as a symbol of stored energy, is associated with dynamic sexual tension, and is an attribute of the god Apollo, a symbol of the sun's fertilizing power. Paintings of gods of love with bows often symbolize the tension of desire.

As the sacred tree of life, the fig tree also has sexual symbolism. For the Greeks the fig was an attribute of Priapus and Dionysus. In Egypt and in India it is linked

with procreative power, in particular that of Shiva and Vishnu. Graphic links between the fig leaf and the male genitals may have begun because of the milky juice that can be extracted from larger varieties. It was fig leaves that Adam and Eve used to hide themselves behind when they had eaten fruit from the tree of knowledge. The fruit of the fig is linked with female genitalia, but the fruit most commonly linked with sex and fertility is the apple, which appears almost everywhere in Europe as an emblem of love, marriage and fertility. The fish is a phallic symbol of sexual happiness and fecundity, linked with their prolific spawn, the fertility symbolism of water and analogies of the fish with the penis.

Corn dollies are traditional pagan fertility talismans made at harvest time. Sometimes they are decked with red ribbons, symbolizing blood and vitality, and set over the hearth until spring. The advent of spring is celebrated by a ritual dance around the maypole. The pole, decorated with ribbons, is both a phallic symbol and a representation of the world axis, or cosmic tree.

INFERTILITY

Just as crops are signs of the earth's abundance, so children are the "fruits" of a couple's sexual union. Traditionally the inability to have children was attributed to a woman's "barrenness", and divine assistance was often invoked. This involved petitioning fertility goddesses such as the Sumerian Inanna or the Greek Artemis, or ithyphallic (perpetually aroused) gods such as Legba, a deity of the Fon of West Africa. Phallic emblems are also common fertility charms.

ABSTINENCE, RESTRAINT, CHASTITY

While some cultures believe that expending sexual energy can inspire similar activity in nature, others think it may interfere with the earth's fertility: the Akan of Ghana believe that if a couple have sex outside they will be struck by madness and the earth goddess will make the ground where they lie infertile. Another belief is that by abstaining from sexual activity, a store of energy will be built up that will help the earth replenish its resources.

Chastity is often personified as the foe of erotic love, often a woman carrying a shield as a defence against the arrows of love or desire. Another common personification of chastity is the

unicorn, while other symbols include the colours blue and white, bees, chestnuts, doves, girdles, hawthorns, irises and lilies. Ermine was associated with chastity because its white winter coat linked it to purity.

TANTRA

Sometimes referred to as "the technique of ecstasy", tantra is a Sanskrit word meaning "web" or "weaving". Although the philosophy has many different schools, a common theme is that the everyday world (samsara) contains seeds of that which is eternal and unchanging (nirvana or enlightenment); similarly, the body-mind is a mirror of the universe. Hence enlightenment may be achieved through conscious participation in everyday life rather than through denial, and the body is a vehicle for transcendence.

A common tantric theme is the idea of cosmic sexuality. Through the desire and interplay of the primal couple, Shiva and Shakti, an all-encompassing creation arises; the couple are sometimes depicted in Hindu iconography as the hermaphrodite Ardhanarishvara. Through ritualized sexual intercourse, the divine fusion of the male and female principle is re-enacted, with each partner aiming to activate the energy of the opposite sex to achieve energetic and psychic wholeness. Sexual energy is symbolized by a coiled serpent (or kundalini), which lies dormant at the first chakra, at the base of the spine. Through sexual practice it is awakened and

CORNUCOPIA

The cornucopia or horn of plenty, is a classical symbol of inexhaustible fecundity. Perpetually filled with abundant flowers and fruit, its phallic, hollow shape represents the fertile union of male and female. Zeus/Jupiter was said to have created the cornucopia from the broken horn of Amalthea, the nanny goat who had suckled him, so that it represented divine and unasked-for bounty. Over time, it came to mean generosity, prosperity and good fortune, as well as the harvest season.

refined into increasingly subtle levels until it finally merges with cosmic energy and a state of blissful euphoria occurs.

Tantrikas (followers of tantra) were often found living in graveyards, a symbolic reminder of the impermanence of the world and the desire for sublimation that transcends death. The teachings of tantra were often considered shocking and a threat to the social order, as its practice was specifically designed to break caste barriers and taboos.

BELOW Ardhanarishvara, the Hindu hermaphrodite figure of Shiva and Parvati conjoined, symbolizes the reconciliation of opposites, and the achivement of union.

LOVE AND KINSHIP

ABOVE An allegorical painting of a happy marriage, in which the love and fertility symbols of the cornucopia, the laurel wreath, an olive branch, Venus, girdles and chains are all used.

The bonds that draw us together may be sexual attraction, a sense of common purpose or meaning, a marriage commitment or family and community. Since love does not always accommodate itself to social forms and conventions, the symbolic systems and rituals of love and kinship are diverse and changeable, as are the meanings associated with them.

Eros, who originated as a primeval creative force, became the Greek god of love and the son of Aphrodite, goddess of love. His Roman counterpart was Cupid (or Amor), the son of Venus, a cherubic winged boy shooting arrows of desire from his bow. His equivalent in Hindu mythology is Kama, who shoots sweet but painful arrows of desire into people and gods, suggesting the pain involved in love – his five arrows of flowers can make the heart glad, lead to great attraction, cause infatuation, weaken, or kill in a pleasurable way. In psychology the term "eros" refers to the libido and the urge for life, but to the Greeks it was a passionate and impersonal kind of love. Plato understood eros as desire that seeks a deep quality of beauty, an ideal of which the person before us is a reminder, hence the term "platonic love".

The Greek term "agape" refers to a kind of spiritual or selfless love, the love of God for humanity and of humanity for God, which also includes a love for fellow humans. Agape was not passionate but compassionate love. Agape feasts were rituals in which early Christians celebrated the Eucharist and the Jews celebrated Passover. Another Greek term, "philia", refers to a fondness and appreciation for the other, and is closer to what we understand as platonic love, meaning friendship and loyalty.

"Amor", derived from a name for the Roman god of love, described a new approach to love as a high spiritual experience: the courtly love celebrated by the troubadours, the poet-musicians of medieval Europe.

ROMANTIC LOVE

Courtly love was a personal and romantic form that involved two people falling in love with one another's virtues, rather than with an ideal. A knight was expected to show deep respect to the lady with whom he was in love, and had to be willing to suffer for his love. Much Renaissance literature refers to common motifs of love as a "torment" or "disease", with lovers becoming sick or unable to sleep and eat. Women took on an almost divine symbolism: their eyes became centrally important as channels of emotion, while their feet, ideally white and narrow, with a high arch, became a powerful sexual symbol.

LOVE SYMBOLS

Flowers frequently symbolize love. For Hindus it is the white flowering jasmine, in China the peony; to the Romans red roses were the flower of Venus, and have remained a strong love symbol in the West. In Iran wild olives and apples both symbolize love. A pair of mandarin ducks represents enduring and committed love to the Chinese, and doves and pigeons commonly represent lovers, either because they mate for life or because they coo while looking into each other's eyes. Lovebirds, colourful small parrots from Africa, also represent lovers because they sit close together in pairs.

ADINKRA LOVE SYMBOL

The people of Ghana weave symbolic designs into brocade called adinkra. The love symbol is called *osram ne nsoroma*, and it features a star "woman", above a moon "man"; it is used to symbolize a faithful, harmonious and fond love.

ABOVE Red roses are a well-used modern symbol of love, courtship and romance.

ABOVE The indestructable quality of the diamond makes it a symbol of enduring love.

ABOVE Heart-shaped items are used endlessly, and across cultures, as a symbol of romance.

ABOVE Rings symbolize eternity and are perhaps the ultimate love symbol.

Precious stones are significant emblems of love, first because they are "precious", and second because of their individual qualities. The diamond, because it is indestructible, represents enduring love. The red ruby symbolizes passion, sexual desire and power. Lace became a symbol of romance because a woman might drop her lace handkerchief so that the right man could pick it up for her. But the most enduring and cross-cultural of love symbols is the human heart: whole, bleeding, or pierced by arrows of love, the heart feels the passions and pain of love. It also represents warmth and openness to the "other".

Each culture uses its own symbol system to designate relationship status. Traditional Mennonites paint their door green if their daughter is eligible for marriage, and the Zulus of South Africa use beads of seven colours to depict a person's status: for example, a white bead (representing purity and spiritual love) next to a blue bead (representing faithfulness) is commonly used to show engagement, while blue, white and black beads show marriage.

The wedding ring dates back to Egyptian times, when brides were given circles of hemp or rush. The Anglo-Saxons used a ring as a token of the promise of love, and the gold wedding ring has become a symbol of eternal love and unity. The Egyptians and Romans believed that the vein in the third finger (*vena amoris*) was connected with the heart; so wearing a wedding ring on that finger symbolizes the linking of the couples' hearts. Christian priests would count the Holy Trinity from the thumb, and end up at the ring finger, using powerful unifying symbolism. The Irish wedding ring is the *claddagh*, with two hands holding a heart and crown to symbolize love, loyalty and friendship.

MARRIAGE AND KINSHIP
Kinship is a "family-like" relationship that is essential to the effective functioning of societies. Its structure and rules vary from culture to culture, but kinship systems are often built on the institution of marriage. Though this is usually the formalized bond between a man and a woman, other successful forms also exist, such as same sex marriage, polygamy and marriages of convenience. Marriage serves as a foundation for living, working and surviving together, for reproduction and sustaining a family.

For most traditional cultures, the predominant form is the arranged marriage, in which the parents or elders determine who will marry whom. In the Western world after the Middle Ages it became increasingly acceptable to marry as a consequence of falling in love. Marriage itself is a symbolic act in which the partners become two halves of a symbolic whole or "we". It is depicted in the symbolism of rings, "tying the knot", and the sharing of property and dowry.

LEFT One of the Hindu symbols of love is white flowering jasmine, given by lovers to each other as a sign of their commitment.

CELTIC CLANS

The word "clann" in Gaelic means family or children. A clan is another word for a descent group; if the clan's ancestor is considered to be an animal, it is a totemic clan. In Welsh medieval society, the number nine symbolized the whole, and therefore the ninth generation was considered to be the limit of the kin relationship. In Ireland kinship was recognized until the 16th or 17th generation.

IBHEQE

A Zulu token like a Valentine, called an *ibheqe*, is worn around the neck. The downward-pointing blue triangle inside a red band, inside a white, worn by a girl, means something like "Will you be my love?" A boy's request to a girl would be the same, but the triangle would be pointing upward as the symbol for "girl".

VALENTINE'S DAY

The origins of Valentine's Day probably lie in a pagan ritual in honour of Juno, Roman goddess of women and marriage. The feast of Lupercalia was celebrated on 15 February. On its eve, girls' names were written on paper and drawn like a lottery by young men, establishing their partnership for the period of the festival. Common Valentine symbols are pictures of Cupid, love arrows and bleeding hearts – all symbols of being love-struck.

RITES OF PASSAGE

ABOVE A Muslim woman hands out sceptres to three boys in white costumes preparing for their circumcisions at an Istanbul mosque. On the day of their circumcision, Muslim boys become a prince for the day.

THE BIRTHDAY

Much symbolism associated with birthdays has ancient origins. The birthday cake may have originated in moon-shaped cakes given as temple offerings to Artemis. The candles may suggest the glowing of the moon, while in Germany a large central candle represents the "light of life".

Formalized rituals symbolically mark the passage of an individual or group through major life transitions, such as birth, puberty, marriage and death. Others mark important societal transitions and the celebration of nature. All are powerful symbolic processes.

INITIATION RITUALS

Many cultures value initiation ceremonies as part of the movement through life transitions. They all involve recognizing the role or status a person is moving into, and throwing off the old one. Most initiation ceremonies are grounded in cultural stories and symbolism. The French anthropologist Arnold van Gennep (1873–1957) saw the rite of passage as an essential process in cultural rejuvenation and described the phases of initiation as separation, transition and incorporation.

Separation involves removing a person (or sacred object) from a previous situation or status. It may involve the removal of identity, such as the removal or changing of clothes, hair or teeth, or scarification and tattooing. Another important factor is the preparation of ritual space, by drawing a circle, erecting a building or travelling to a different location such as a cave or mountain. The church, the mosque, and the medicine wheel are all examples of ritual spaces that allow people to separate from their everyday reality to connect with the divine. The registry office, where people are legally married, is an example of a legal ritual space.

Transition, the "threshold" or "liminal phase", involves undergoing certain trials, tests, ordeals or ritual actions, which essentially involve a metaphorical death and rebirth. The previous identity is broken down, making the way for a new identity to come forth. Taking an oath is an example of this phase, as when a person becoming a citizen of the United States pledges allegiance to the national symbols of the American flag.

Incorporation means returning to the "body" of the community, or else reconstituting the person, with new roles, awareness and responsibilities. The ringing of bells after the coronation of a monarch symbolically celebrates their new role. After a major sports tournament, such as the Olympic Games or the World Cup, the successful teams often return to their homeland and parade the streets victoriously. Eating and feasting is common symbolism for the incorporation phase. The Christian holy sacrament involves symbolically incorporating or swallowing the body and blood of Christ in the form of bread and wine.

PUBERTY

The time of puberty marks the transition from childhood to adulthood, involving dramatic physical and emotional changes, as well as changes in roles and responsibilities. Ritual initiation at puberty varies from culture to culture, but fundamentally honours and marks this major life transition. In the Muslim tradition, boys of 10 to 12 who undergo circumcision are paraded as princes for the day, sometimes on a horse, and often showered with gifts. The Luiseño people of southern California proudly celebrate the onset of menstruation in their daughters, who are partially buried in warm sand, possibly to symbolize their strong connection with the earth.

A Jewish boy becomes bar mitzvah ("a son of the commandment") at the age of 13. On the first Saturday following his birthday he reads from the Torah in the synagogue and may lead part of the service. In preparation he must study Jewish history, ancient Hebrew and his spiritual roots, discussing his learning with the rabbi and his family in relation to his own life and oncoming adulthood.

BAPTISM

The Jewish and Christian practice of initiating people into the faith by dipping them in water represents the purification and cleansing of the spirit. Early

Christian writings describe a meal of milk and honey accompanying baptism, representing the entry of the Israelites into the promised land of Canaan. Roman Catholic baptism also involves the exorcism of the devil and anointing with olive oil, a symbol of the gifts of the Holy Spirit.

MARRIAGE

The meaning and symbolism of marriage reflects the underlying beliefs of the culture, but most are redolent with the ancient symbolism of a couple attaining a semi-divine state of wholeness necessary to create and protect new life. This idea of the union of the human and divine is echoed in the Christian tradition of calling its nuns "brides of Christ".

One of the most significant symbols of marriage still in use is the ring, a circular symbol of eternity, union and completeness. This is echoed in the Christian ceremony when the couple's hands are joined together by the priest, and in the Hindu ceremony when the bridegroom ties a ribbon around the neck of his bride. Other symbols of

marriage include bells, as a means of proclaiming good news, and peach blossom, which is believed by the Chinese to be linked with immortality, longevity, spring, youth and marriage and is also an emblem of virginity.

Symbols of fertility were once central to wedding ceremonies, and are echoed in modern times by the rice (or confetti made of rice paper) thrown over the couple. The wedding cake was once a symbol of fertility, food being a sexual symbol and its formal sharing during the feast a symbol of the two families coming together. Bridesmaids are symbols of sympathetic fertility magic, while the flowers they carry are further symbols of femininity and fruitfulness.

DEATH RITES

A person's death represents a considerable transition, for both the individual and the family and community around them. The deceased is ritually prepared to move on, possibly as part of a journey into another reality, and the mourning process employs a great deal of symbolic ritual to

**RIGHT** Weddings are a significant rite of passage in most cultures. However they are celebrated, the central theme is transition.

express and channel the emotions involved in losing a loved one.

The wearing of black is widely associated with death and mourning. In early times, bodies of the dead were stained with red ochre to symbolize blood and the connection with the earth. Another common symbol of mourning is the shaving or dishevelling of the hair. Cultural values are clearly mirrored in funeral rites. Even the expressing of emotion reflects cultural attitudes: in some cultures, such as Sikh, wailing is discouraged, whereas in others it is expected.

The deceased are often treated as if they are undergoing a journey: they are dressed in special clothes and accompanied by personal and religious objects or talismans. Burying the body may symbolize the person's return to Mother Earth or to the dead ancestors. Cremation represents the liberation of spirit and release from Earth. For the Hindus, the flames symbolize Brahma.

LEFT In a Hindu funeral the colour of mourning is white, and coffin, deceased and mourners are all dressed in it.

ABOVE A bell is one of the symbols of a wedding, and is often used as a motif on the invitations, orders or service and menus, and silver bell-shaped ornaments might be carried by the bride and bridesmaids.

TOP The Romans would break the cake over the bride's head, but in modern ceremonies the cutting of the cake symbolizes the first task in the couple's life.

CHILDHOOD AND GAMES

ABOVE Painting allows the child to mix the worlds of symbolism with the everyday world.

TOP Children use building blocks to explore creation and destruction.

BELOW Children love dressing-up as adults. Here a group of boys dress up as musicians at the Indian spring festival of Bahag Bihu.

In cultures dominated by logic, intellect and linear thinking, life becomes a problem to be solved rather than a mystery to be enjoyed. Yet creativity and play are essential to human development, and are natural activities that children engage in spontaneously. Through creativity and play we journey into archetypal or mythical realms, experiment with roles, relationships and social structures, and engage in a symbolic dialogue with the trends and movements of history.

CREATIVE SYMBOLISM

The word creativity comes from the Latin *creare*, meaning "to bring forth, produce, and cause to grow". It is the generative force at the root of symbolism. Jung described it as a process that connects us with archetypal themes, expressed in a language relevant to the present day. For instance, an archetypal theme such as the battle between good and evil is given creative

expression in modern society in the form of computer games. Jung believed that the creative impulse can compensate for the one-sidedness of the present, so that part of the artist's role is to comment on or challenge the prevailing norms. Both the artist and the child are inspired by a creative impulse, and then create a language or metaphor to express what has moved them.

THE CHILD

In many cultures, the child is a symbol of innocence and spontaneity. In the Hindu tradition, childhood is a heavenly state of innocence prior to any knowledge of good or evil.

In the Christian tradition, Jesus said that unless adults become like children they will not enter into the kingdom of Heaven, which also reflects the relationship between the child and paradise. In Taoist literature the child embodies the qualities of the holy sage – innocence and open-heartedness.

Though he was writing at the end of the 19th century, when children were largely undervalued and to be "seen and not heard", J.M. Barrie created Peter Pan as an archetypal pattern for the child within us. Peter teaches the other children to believe in their imaginations, their ability to fly and to travel to Neverland. Peter is an example of the eternal child, the childlike imagination, which lives in us all.

PLAY

In modern society, we tend to associate play with childhood and regard it as something that people stop doing once they have "grown up". However, in other parts of the world, play continues to be highly valued in adult life, often in the form of ritual enactments. In Burkina Faso and Mali, masquerades entirely created by children, independent of the adults, are considered highly important to the wellbeing of the whole community. Eastern coastal fishing villages in Korea enact communal shamanic rituals known as *kut* – a mixture of prayer, laughter and play thought to bring the gods down to the level of human beings, helping them to deal with the powerful emotions surrounding major crises and death. The kut are healing rituals that involve a playful and symbolic participation in theatrical representations of the pain, beauty and mystery of life.

In Hopi society "sacred clowns" help to balance society by mocking and making fun of excessive behaviour, so setting and balancing moral standards.

Play and playfulness involve a loosening of, or detachment from, our everyday identities, and an interest in entering into and experimenting with other roles and possibilities.

In their early years, children engage in "embodiment play", exploring with their senses, making sounds, rhythms, marks and movements, beginning to imitate and relate to toys and objects around them and creating stories. At this point they are developing the skill of interacting symbolically and beginning to understand and experiment with different roles and relationships, and objects can have meaning and significance attached to them. It is not uncommon for young children to become attached to a certain toy or blanket, a symbol of security, love or friendship.

FANTASY

For children the everyday world is interlaced with the world of fantasy and the imagination. Children love to role-play through dressing up as their favourite characters and creating dramatic stories around them. Through the medium of play, the child learns, grows and develops.

Many archetypal or mythical figures emerge in children's play. The ancient Chinese believed that the playful songs that children sang spontaneously were intimately linked with the divine, and even listened to them to guide them in matters of state. Through fantasy and play, children explore the great underlying themes and spirit of the times, stories of good and evil, love, magic and power. They explore the "evil" in terms of monsters, giants and witches, and play with the forces of good, magic and transformation through the roles of fairies, white witches and wizards. They experiment with rank and power by playing kings and queens, famous leaders and the rich and famous, and they explore heroic themes as superheroes, with action figures and toy soldiers.

TOYS AND GAMES

Games are models for archetypal forms of relationship and interaction, involving different combinations of chance, skill and creativity. In the game of chess, the movement of the kings, queens and pawns may be understood as metaphors for the shifts of power in war or conflict at various levels in the universe. Many games reflect the creative impulses of the universe, as in the throwing of dice and other games of chance, which probably originated from ancient divinatory practices in Mesopotamia, India and East Asia. Pick-up sticks, also known as "spillikins", which involves dropping a set of sticks in a heap and then trying to pick them up one at a time without disturbing the others, may have its origin in the Buddhist divinatory practice called Chien Tung, in which a person's fortune is foretold by shaking a box of sticks until one emerges.

The origin of the spinning top, or dreidel, is completely unknown, but it has been used as a toy or for gambling throughout the world. The dreidel is itself the symbol of the Jewish festival of Hanukkah, when rabbis allowed games of chance to be played and the four-sided dreidel came out for gambling. Its four sides represent "take nothing", "take everything", "take half" and "put in". Another symbolic quality of the spinning top relates not to how it falls down by chance, but rather to how it stays up as it spins, a beautiful symbol of life and the universe.

The universal game of tag, or chase, involves passing a symbolic quality from one person to another. One child is chosen to be "it", and chases the other children with the purpose of transferring the "it-ness" to another. The child who is tagged is then "it" and so the game goes on. The symbolic quality may represent authority, infectiousness, or any other differential. The appeal of the game lies in the challenge of the chase, and the excitement and tension engendered by coming near or in contact with the person who is "it".

ABOVE The Dreidel, a four-sided top, played with by Jewish children, is seen as a symbol of life and the universe.

BELOW The game of chase has many variations and is played endlessly by children all over the world.

THE WHEEL

ABOVE The traditionally shaped wheel, as in this representation of the Buddhist eight-spoked wheel, holds the symbolism of the sun and the cosmos. The wheel is also an enduring symbol of human endeavour and advancement.

The symbolism of the wheel relates to the passage of time, the world, and the unity that exists at the heart of diversity. It is associated with the zodiac and with life's ups and downs (as the wheel of fortune); as the Native American medicine wheel it provides a blueprint for living. As an archetypal motif, the wheel's significance relates to its shape – a circle containing spokes radiating from a central hub – and its mobility. It combines the symbolism of the circle with movement, representing the cosmos as an eternal round of creation and dissolution. In many cultures it appears as a sun symbol, with countless beliefs associating it with solar myths, although some have argued that it was pre-eminently a lunar symbol, signifying the continuous cycle of the moon.

SOLAR AND LUNAR SYMBOLISM

The wheel has both solar and lunar associations. The simplest form has four spokes, which may reflect the four directions and four seasons (as in the medicine wheel), as well as the four-stage lunar cycle: waxing, full, waning and dark. Arianrhod, the Welsh goddess of weaving and spinning, was connected with the moon; her name means "silver wheel".

Wheels with 12 spokes appear frequently in Indian literature and art, suggesting the movement of the sun through the zodiac, while the traditional Chinese wheel has 30 spokes, signifying the lunar cycle. In classical antiquity, the wheel was linked with the god Apollo (and so with the sun), as well as to thunderbolts and the lighting of fires.

The wheel as a solar symbol persists in European folklore. It was traditional to carry blazing wheels by torchlit procession to a hilltop at the summer solstice and roll the wheel down the hillside at the winter solstice.

SACRED TRADITION

The wheel, or chakra, is an important symbol in both Hindu and Buddhist traditions. In Hinduism, the wheel represents the unity of time and space and is a symbol of completion: a six-spoked wheel is one of the symbols of the preserver deity, Vishnu. In Buddhism, the eight-spoked dharmachakra is the wheel of the law or truth (dharma). It often appears on carvings representing the footprints of the Buddha and symbolizes the power of his teachings to roll over and stamp out lies. Like human fate, once the wheel is set in motion there is no power that can stop it or reverse its direction. The eight spokes represent the eightfold path of Buddhism, the hub the moral anchor of the Buddha's teachings, while at the motionless centre stands the *chakravarti* ("he who makes the wheel revolve"), the Buddha himself. His Celtic equivalent is Mag Ruith, the mythic druid who was an incarnation of the supreme god, the Dagda. Mag Ruith was the *magus rotarum*, or "wizard of the wheels", and it was with the help of wheels that he spoke his druidic oracles.

In the Old Testament, Ezekiel compares the throne of God to a chariot with four wheels, each wheel representing one of the Four Living Creatures and the seasons, while in Daniel's vision flaming wheels appear around God's head. On early Christian gravestones, the wheel is sometimes found as a symbol of God and of eternity.

THE CATHERINE WHEEL

As the emblem of St Catherine of Alexandria, the wheel is associated with torment. She was said to have been a Christian convert of the early 4th century, who was mystically married to Christ in a vision. The Roman emperor Maxentius desired to marry her, and when she refused him he ordered her to be tortured on a spiked wheel. The wheel miraculously broke when she touched it, but she was eventually martyred with a sword. She is usually depicted with the wheel, which subsequently gave its name to a spinning firework.

THE WHEEL OF LIFE

In Hindu philosophy, the symbolism of the wheel is used to refer to samsara, the continuous cycle of life, death and rebirth. In Chinese symbolism, the hub relates to Heaven and the rim to Earth, with humankind represented by the spokes that link the two. The Chinese noria (waterwheel), and the Taoist sage Chuang Tzu's potter's wheel both represent the ceaseless whirlpool of creation and the never-ending life–death cycle. The point of liberation is at the hub, pointing to the spiritual journey as a movement from the periphery to the centre, from activity to stillness, which is the purpose of meditation. In the Celtic tradition, the year is seen as a wheel, with the summer and winter solstices and the spring and autumn equinoxes marking four points of transition as the sun's power rises and decreases with the changing seasons.

WHEEL OF FORTUNE

Its turning nature means that the wheel has often been associated with chance and fortune, both fickle and fortuitous. It frequently appears as a motif in medieval European art and was an attribute of Fortuna, the Roman goddess of fate (Tyche was the Greek equivalent). Fortuna represents each moment's potential for luck or ill, with the turning of her wheel bringing happiness and success to some, and ruin and

RIGHT A blindfolded Fortuna, goddess of fate, rolls her wheel at random and without mercy over crowned kings.

misery to others, in a seemingly random way. She is often depicted as blind or blindfolded, because fate is morally blind. Her wheel teaches that what goes up must come down and vice versa – so that success and failure follow on each other's heels, just as life and death cycle and circle. In the Tarot, the Wheel of Fortune is the tenth card of the Major Arcana and represents an important turning point.

THE MEDICINE WHEEL

In many traditions, the wheel is a symbol of the world. This forms the basis of the Native American medicine wheel – a cross within a circle emanating from a central hub. The wheel is drawn on the ground, and the four spokes represent the four seasons, the four elements and the four directions. The seasons symbolize time, and the compass points, space. The fifth and sixth directions (above and below the wheel) represent father sky and mother earth. Each place on the wheel is associated with a particular colour, an animal totem and a quality, and the whole wheel represents the journey through life.

RIGHT The Native American symbol of the medicine wheel, a circle segmented by a cross, is reproduced here in stone.

Flora
and Fauna

The symbolism of trees, plants, flowers and animals has been central to symbolic conceptualization since prehistoric days. Animals have been particularly important, worshipped as gods or protective spirits, and, like fruit and vegetables, vital for life in the food they provide.

RIGHT The horse is a symbol of animal vitality, velocity and beauty. As the emblem of the god Poseidon, it is also associated with the power of wind, storm, fire, waves and running water.

TREES

ABOVE The banyan tree is sacred to the Hindu gods: watering its roots and placing offerings is thought to bring happiness and fertility.

ABOVE In ancient times sacred groves of trees were places of sanctuary and worship.

The tree is a central and archetypal symbol in most parts of the world. In the West, trees are deeply associated with time and historical continuity. Elsewhere they tend to have stronger associations with life, health and potency. Ancient peoples worshipped in sacred groves, with their trunks and canopies of branches, which were later echoed in the design of churches. The words "truth" and "trust" are derived from the Old English word for "tree".

THE WORLD TREE

The cosmic tree, symbolizing the ultimate reservoir for the forces of life continually regenerating the world, is central to many creation myths. It frequently represents the axis of the universe, connecting a number of realms: its branches hold up the heavens, its trunk stands in the earthly realm and its roots descend into the underworld. Other commonly associated symbols are reptiles crawling in the roots and birds in the branches symbolizing shamanic flight.

The world tree is usually represented by a species that is particularly important in a geographical region. Norse mythology tells of the ash tree Yggdrasil, which grew between Asgard, the realm of the gods, Midgard, the realm of humanity, and Hel, the underworld. The ancient Egyptians believed a holy sycamore grew at the threshold between life and death; in Mesopotamia the world axis passed through a palm tree. Hindus hold the banyan tree as sacred, while the Maya believed

in Yaxche, the sacred tree whose branches supported the heavens. The Chinese sacred tree was thought to grow from the centre of the world, emitting no echo and casting no shadow. The sakaki tree is venerated as the "heaven-tree" of Japanese mythology, and a branch is stuck in the ground as a sacred centre around which a wooden Shinto shrine is built.

Trees are also powerful symbols of the interconnectedness and ecology of life. The Native American elder Black Elk saw in a vision the "sacred hoop" of his people combining with many others to create a larger hoop, within which grew a mighty and holy tree of protection. The world tree of the Amazon region is the ceiba, or yuchan: the Huaorani creation myth tells of the giant ceiba tree Bobehuè, which contains all forms of life. It thus represents an entire ecosystem central to life on earth, which may be not far from the truth.

TREES AND THE ORIGINS OF HUMANITY

The world tree is commonly associated with the origins of humankind. The Yakut of Siberia believe in a tree with eight branches, which stands within the golden navel of the earth, growing into a primordial paradise where

ABOVE The European oak is a symbol of strength, stability, firmness and an enduring nature.

THE MAYPOLE

In Europe, on 1 May, the spring fertility ritual of the maypole dance symbolizes the marriage of the vegetation god to the May queen. The pole, representing the spirit of the tree (and with obvious phallic symbolism), was erected and decorated, and danced around with abandon.

the first man was born and suckled on the milk of the woman, who was herself part of the tree. The first man in ancient Indian mythology, Yama, drank with the gods beside a magnificent tree.

A common Indo-European mythical theme describes an apocalypse during which tempests, fire or floods devastate the earth, leaving as the only survivors the ancestors of humanity, who are made of wood.

TREE OF LIFE

In one of its aspects, the world tree is the tree of life or immortality. It is often associated with a nourishing and protective universe from which the elixir or bounties of life may be received – a state of grace from which humans may fall. The Egyptian sky goddess Nut was depicted emerging from a sycamore fig to offer the bread and water of eternity to the dead.

Seraphim wielding swords of fire guard the biblical tree of life. In Taoist tradition it is the divine peach that confers the gift of immortality, while the apples of the goddess Idun are the source of the powers of the Norse gods.

The Qur'an describes the prophet Mohammed coming across the tree of Tuba standing in the heart of paradise, glowing with emeralds, rubies and sapphires; milk, honey and wine sprang from its roots.

THE INVERTED TREE

The symbol of the inverted tree is found in the Jewish Kabbalah and in the Hindu yogic Bhagavad Gita. This tree of life has its roots in the heavens and its branches below, representing God in Heaven as the origin of all things. The inverted tree image can be related to the human nervous or chakral system, underlining the connection between the human microcosm and the macrocosm.

TREE DRESSING

The practice of tree dressing is found throughout the world. The Karan is a Hindu ritual in which a tree in the centre of a village is covered with butter, and decorated with vermillion, turmeric and garlands, after which women dance with marigolds in their hair. In Africa trees are revered as the centre of life and fertility, and are dressed as a way of connecting with the ancestral spirits. Evergreens are dressed at Christmas in Christian cultures as a symbol of life.

TREES OF DEATH

Evergreen trees are ancient symbols of death and the potential for eternal life, but the cypress tree symbolizes the finality of death because, once cut, it will never again sprout from its stump. Images of tree stumps or trunks are found in heraldic emblems representing death and rebirth.

In Britain, the yew tree is most closely associated with death. It was considered immortal by the Druids, and is commonly found in graveyards and at ancient sacred sites. Its roots were believed to soak up the spirits of the dead, releasing them to the winds from its branches.

THE MULBERRY

In China the mulberry tree represents the cycles of life. Its berries start white, representing youth, then turn red for the middle years, and finally ripen to black, suggesting wisdom, old age and death.

CHRISTMAS TREE

The modern variation of decorated trees at Christmas originated in 16th-century Germany, where fir trees were dressed with apples and coloured paper. The tradition has become a Christian ritual, perhaps referring to the tree of paradise, but its roots are older, an emblem of rebirth dating back to at least Roman times when the celebrants at the feast of Saturnalia used evergreens to celebrate the new year.

PLANTS, HERBS AND SPICES

ABOVE In European folklore, the mandrake was associated with death, insanity, witchcraft and magic. When picked it was said to utter a piercing human-like scream.

ABOVE Saffron, the stamen of a type of crocus, is a sacred herb in Buddhism. In Europe it is associated with royalty.

The symbolism of plants is closely related to their perceived magical properties and power to influence humans on many different levels – physical, mental, emotional and spiritual. In symbolic terms, they are associated with ideas of balance and cosmological order, which have often been reflected in sophisticated theories of the nature of health and disease.

THE DOCTRINE OF SIGNATURES

According to the "doctrine of signatures", everything in nature is marked with a pattern or sign that indicates its potential properties. The name evolved from the Signatura Rerum (The Signature of All Things) by Jakob Böhme (1575–1624), a German shoemaker whose philosophy was informed by a mystical vision in which he saw the relationship between God and humans. The doctrine was applied to the powers of plants for medical application. For example, the heart-shaped leaves of the purple foxglove were used as a heart medicine (digitalis), while the purple veins and yellow fleck of the eyebright flower, which suggest an unhealthy-looking eye, designated the plant as a remedy for eye ailments.

Because of its resemblance to the human form, the mandrake was credited with human and superhuman powers in European folklore. It was said to thrive around the gallows, fed by the faeces and urine falling from those hanged, and to scream when it was pulled up or disturbed: the sound led to deafness and insanity in those unfortunate enough to hear it. The mandrake was associated with witchcraft and used in love magic, and a mandrake root doll was said to have the power to

BELOW In European plant lore, rosemary is a symbol of remembrance, love and fidelity.

make its owner invisible. Medicinally, it was also used to treat arthritis, ulcers and inflammation, to induce menstruation, ease delivery in childbirth and aid conception. In the Jewish tradition the mandrake is associated with fertility and love – its Hebrew name means "love plant".

HERBS

A great variety of symbolic meanings are attached to common herbs. In ancient Greece, students wore sprigs of rosemary to improve memory and concentration, and the plant came to symbolize remembrance. It was also associated with love and fidelity and became a symbol of immortality in funeral rites. Sage was also associated with immortality and was thought by the ancient Greeks to promote wisdom. It takes its name from the Latin *salvare,* meaning "to save" and in European herbal medicine was thought of as a cure-all. Native Americans consider sage a healing and cleansing herb, especially the variety known as white sage; its

BELOW Sage is a sacred herb in Native American traditions, used for cleansing and purifying.

dry leaves are often formed into smudge bundles for burning, the smoke being ritually smudged, or wafted, to purify the atmosphere. In ancient Rome, peppermint was associated with clear thoughts and inspiration and was used as a brain tonic, while in the Arab world it was widely believed to stimulate virility and has been drunk as a refreshing tea for centuries, offered to guests as a symbol of hospitality.

In India, *tulsi*, or sweet basil, is sacred to Vishnu, and the funeral custom of laying a basil leaf on the chest of the dead was thought to open the gates of Heaven for the departed; in Tudor England departing guests were given a miniature pot of basil to help them on their journey. In the central Congo, basil leaves protect against evil spirits and bad luck, while in ancient Greece they were an antidote to the deadly venom of the basilisk, a fabulous creature whose glance was fatal. The plant takes its name from the Greek *basilikon*, meaning "royal".

SPICES

Many spices are similarly rich in symbolism. Black pepper, one of the earliest known spices, was widely regarded as an aphrodisiac in antiquity. Saffron is a species of crocus (*Crocus sativus*) whose stamens yield a deep yellow dye. Traditionally it was used to dye the robes of Buddhist monks, and the colour became associated with the Buddhist paradise and with wisdom. In Europe, saffron was linked with royalty and gold because of its costliness as well as its colour. In ancient China,

coriander seeds were believed to contain the power of immortality, and cardamom pods share a similar symbolism in India and the Middle East. In China and Japan, cloves represent sweetness and health, and in Japanese art they were one of the objects associated with the Seven Deities of Good Fortune.

TOBACCO

The tobacco plant is indigenous to North America, and the Native Americans are said to have been the first people to use it. They regard it as sacred, and it has widespread ritual and ceremonial use. The Machiguenga of Peru use the term *seripegari*, meaning "he who uses tobacco", to describe a shaman; roasted tobacco leaves (*seri*) are used in shamanic rituals. To many Pueblo people, tobacco was the gift of the hummingbird, who brought smoke to the shamans so that they could purify the Earth.

In Europe, smoking tobacco was originally associated with dissolute young men and soldiers, so that when women first began to smoke in public in the late 19th century it was regarded as shocking. Today the symbolic associations surrounding tobacco are ambiguous. On the one hand it has become synonymous with deadly illnesses such as cancer and heart disease, yet on the other it retains an element of sophistication and rebellion.

MISTLETOE

The Celts associated mistletoe (*Viscum album*) with magic and medicine. To the Druids it was a

CANNABIS

Rastafarians, who know it as ganja, regard cannabis as a holy herb mentioned in the Bible, where it performs a sacramental function, producing an altered state of consciousness through which it is possible to attain a glimpse of the divine. The cannabis leaf became a symbol of Rastafarianism, as well as representing a protest against the dominant social order, which had deemed its use illegal. In the Western world today, many teenagers see the cannabis leaf as a symbol of rebellion against adult authority and mainstream society.

GARLIC

An ancient Egyptian medical papyrus includes more than 200 prescriptions for garlic. It was used to treat headaches, physical debility and infections, and raw garlic was included in the diet of Egyptian workers to keep them strong. In ancient Greece and Rome garlic was a symbol of strength, and athletes chewed it to maximize their chances of winning races. In many traditions, garlic is believed to offer not only physical but also metaphysical protection, hence the popular belief in European folklore that garlic cloves can keep werewolves and vampires at bay, or in ancient China that it could ward off the evil eye.

symbol of immortality and the soul of their sacred tree, the oak, on which it grew. The Celts believed that mistletoe was created when a lightning bolt struck an oak tree, giving it magical properties, and ritual demanded that a white-robed Druid cut mistletoe after the winter solstice using a golden sickle (both a solar and a lunar symbol). The plant had to be caught in a white cloth, as it was believed that it should never touch the ground. Mistletoe was used to treat many different health conditions and was also a fertility symbol. The custom of kissing under the mistletoe at Christmas has its roots in the plant's ancient associations.

BELOW Mistletoe is a symbol of immortality and was associated with magic and medicine for the Celts.

FLOWERS

ABOVE Cultures all over the world have used bouquets of flowers at funerals as a way of honouring the dead.

BELOW The Hindu goddess Lakshmi sits on the lotus, symbol of enlightenment and elevation of the spirit. Hindu dieties are often pictured with this flower.

While the aesthetic beauty of flowers has inspired poets and artists through the ages, they also have a long tradition of use in healing and ritual – more than 100,000 years ago, the Neanderthals made flower offerings to their dead. To this day, flowers are given as tokens of love or thanks, to acknowledge achievement, honour the dead and to mark transitions of all kinds. They have become symbols of a wide range of human experiences and are woven into myth and sacred tradition.

In general, flowers represent the culmination of a growth cycle and a crowning achievement. Growing from the earth and receptive to the sun and rain, they are related to the power of the passive, feminine principle, manifesting beauty literally and physically as well as spiritually and metaphorically. In Hindu ritual, the flower corresponds to the element ether (or spirit); in the Taoist text The Secret of the Golden Flower it represents the attainment of a spiritual state.

SAY IT WITH FLOWERS

Many different cultures, including those of China, Egypt and India, have evolved their own "language of flowers". Contemporary audiences of the plays of William Shakespeare (1564–1616) would have been familiar with the hidden meanings contained in his floral references: for instance, thyme symbolized sweetness, oxslips meant comeliness, the violet meant "love in idleness", eglantine or honeysuckle meant "united in love", and pansies stood for thoughts. The Victorians developed this language into a popular art, instilling meaning in the colour, arrangement and presentation of flowers as well as the species.

IKEBANA

Practitioners of ikebana, the Japanese art of flower arranging, have developed a complex symbolism to reflect the precepts of Zen Buddhism. The Zen ideal of *wabi* (deliberate understatement), for instance, is reflected in the minimalist form of the arrangement. Traditional ikebana arrangements follow a ternary plan, with the upper spray representing Heaven, the central one humanity, and the lower one earth – a symbolic pattern of all that lives, with humans as the intermediaries between Heaven and earth. In the "flowing" style, the sprays hang down, suggesting the decline and flow into the abyss, while the "standing", or *rikka,* style reaches up, symbolizing loyalty – between husband and wife, to the emperor and to the divine. Rikka arrangements are asymmetrical and are intended to suggest an aspect of nature, such as the interplay of light and shade.

LOTUS

In the East, the lotus is the flower most commonly associated with the elevation of the spirit. Brahma, the Hindu creator god, was born from a golden lotus sprouting from Vishnu's navel (a symbol of the centre of the world). A thousand-petalled lotus is a symbol of spiritual enlightenment. The Sanskrit names for lotus are *padma* or *kamala*, which also describe the vagina, and lotus blossom also represents the vagina in China.

LILLIES

In the Christian tradition, the lily is associated with repentance: it is said to have grown from the tears of Eve as she left the Garden of Eden. It is the flower of the Virgin Mary: the white Madonna lily symbolizes purity and chastity; it also represents purity in alchemy. In Australia, the Gymea lily is linked with courage and steadfastness: in an Aboriginal dreaming story the young man Kai'mia rescued members of his tribe even though he was wounded, and lilies grew where his blood fell. In China and Japan, the day lily (*Hemerocallis*) was believed to have the power to dispel grief, and women wore them in their belts to forget the sorrow of a lost love.

ROSES

In classical antiquity it was said that the first rose was created by Chloris, the goddess of flowers (whose Roman equivalent is Flora), from the body of a beautiful nymph. It was sacred to Aphrodite/Venus, the goddess of love. In the Arab tradition, the first rose was brought to life by the rays of the rising sun in the Great Garden of Persia, spreading its seeds to all other lands, and was a symbol of fertility, beauty and purity. A nightingale sang when the first white roses bloomed, but was so overcome by their perfume that it dropped to Earth, its blood staining their petals red.

In Islam, the rose is sacred to Mohammed; for the mystic Sufi sect, the rose is associated with pleasure, but because of its thorns, it is also linked with pain.

In Christianity, red roses symbolize the blood of martyrs and life after death, while white roses are associated with the Virgin Mary. The Rosicrucian Brotherhood, a Christian sect founded in Europe in the 15th century, combined the symbol of a rose with the cross to form the emblem of their society.

TULIPS

In ancient Persia, the tulip was a symbol of perfect love, exalted in poetry as one of the blooms found in the gardens of paradise. During the Ottoman period, the Turkish word for tulip was spelled using the same letters that form the word "Allah", so the flower came to symbolize divinity, and the tulip became the emblem of the Ottoman rulers. Tulips were exported from Turkey to Europe in the mid-16th century, and were hybridized to produce rare and distinctive flowers. Their value rose to fantastic heights in The Netherlands during the 1630s, when they became symbols of wealth and beauty. The tulip is the symbol of The Netherlands.

CHRYSANTHEMUMS

In China and Japan, the chrysanthemum is linked with autumn and is a symbol of long life, good luck, happiness and wealth. Its radiating petals make it a sun symbol, leading to its use as the emblem of the Japanese imperial family and Japan's national flower. With the plum, orchid and bamboo, the chrysanthemum is one of a group called the Four Gentlemen, believed to represent the virtues of a Confucian in their simplicity, uprightness and hardiness. In the West the chrysanthemum is associated with autumn and is used in art to represent decadence and death.

POPPIES

Because it produces the narcotic opium, the poppy was associated with sleep and death in ancient

Greece, where it was dedicated to Hypnos and Morpheus, the gods of sleep and dreaming. It was also linked to the myth of Demeter and Persephone – the latter was picking poppies when Hades abducted her – in which it came to represent the annual death of nature. Since World War I, red poppies have commemorated fallen soldiers: the flowers grew on the battlefields of Flanders. In Britain red poppies mark Remembrance Sunday, the day when the sacrifice of soldiers in all wars is remembered.

SUNFLOWERS

The sunflower arrived in Europe from the Americas, where the Spanish called it *girasol*, or "turn to the sun" because of the way it turned to face the sun. In China the sunflower was linked with immortality, and eating its seeds was said to promote longevity.

BELOW In Japan, the art of ikebana has developed its own symbolic language and ritual and reflects the simplicity of Zen Buddhism.

RIGHT In the Western world, white roses are associated with purity and spirituality, and are a favourite flower at weddings.

FRUIT

ABOVE In this allegory of the Earth, the artist uses an abundance of fruit to symbolize wealth and prosperity, the cornucopia suggests plenty, and the beautiful, curvaceous young woman reinforces the symbolism of fertility.

ABOVE In addition to its role as the "fruit of knowledge", the apple has also been used as a symbol of love, marriage, youth, fertility and longevity.

Most of the symbolism of fruit appeals directly and powerfully to the senses. The eating of fruit easily conjures up associations with eroticism and sensuality, and this imagery has been much used in art. Fruit also suggests abundance and fertility: it spills out of the cornucopia in classical mythology, representing the generosity of the gods and a good harvest. The fruit of the tree of life is food for the immortals, and contains seeds for reproduction and growth.

APPLES
The apple is identified as the "fruit of knowledge", whether of good and evil, as in the Garden of Eden, or of life, wisdom and immortality, as in the Greek myth of the golden apples of the

Hesperides. The Celts saw the apple tree as the "otherworld" tree, the doorway to the fairy world. Celtic kings and heroes such as King Arthur took refuge on the legendary Isle of Avalon, the "apple orchard".

In China, apple blossom symbolizes feminine beauty, and apples are symbols of peace. But as the Chinese word for "apple" is very similar to the word for "illness" it is thought inauspicious to give an apple to an invalid.

New symbolism evolved around the apple in the early 19th century, when Johnny Appleseed pursued his dream of a land of blossoming trees where no one went hungry, by planting apple seeds throughout America. The great metropolis New York City is known as the "Big Apple".

FIGS
The fig tree and its many-seeded fruit are symbols of plenty and fertility often associated with feminine qualities. The Ruminal fig in the Palatine temple in Rome was said to be the tree beneath which Romulus and Remus were suckled by a wolf. Romans considered figs lucky or unlucky according to whether they were light or dark.

In the Book of Genesis, Adam and Eve used fig leaves to cover themselves when they became shamefully aware of their nakedness, and the forbidden fruit they ate may have been a fig rather than an apple. In Africa, the Kotoko people of Chad connect the fig with childbearing, and its milky sap is thought to increase lactation.

BANANAS
The banana plant's botanical name, *Musa sapientum*, means "fruit of the wise men" and was given by Linnaeus, a Swedish botanist, who had heard that Alexander the Great encountered sages in India who lived entirely on bananas. According to the Qur'an and in Islamic stories, the banana was the forbidden fruit in paradise. For the Buddha, the banana tree symbolized the transient nature and weakness of matter and mental constructions. In the Hindu tradition it is a symbol of fertility and prosperity, due to its tendency to fruit regularly, and thus bananas may be left in front of houses where a wedding is taking place.

CHERRIES
A cherry colour in the lips of a Chinese woman is considered a quality of great beauty, and the phrase "eating cherries" is a euphemism for sexual intercourse. In the West the cherry is associated with the hymen, and the phrase "losing one's cherry" refers to the loss of virginity. Cherry blossom is the national flower of Japan. Samurai warriors would meditate upon life and death beneath a cherry tree, as at the height of its flowering the blossom would gracefully fall to the ground and die, paralleling the Samurai's willingness to face death in his prime.

PLUMS
In the Far East the plum tree is a common symbol for the spring, and also for the end of winter: as it blossoms at the threshold

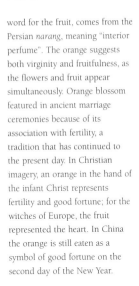
between the two seasons, it represents the renewal of youthfulness. It was also thought that the immortals fed from plum blossoms, so the tree was connected with immortality. In both the Japanese and Christian traditions it is a symbol of fidelity.

PEACHES

The peach tree originated in China, where it was considered the holy tree of life, producing an elixir of immortality. The Taoists associated peach blossom with virginity and with the female genitalia. ("Tao" is the Chinese word for "peach".) In early Europe the peach was called the "fruit of Venus" and was sacred to Hymen, the Roman god of marriage. In Christian imagery a peach in the hand of the infant Christ symbolizes salvation.

APRICOTS

In China the apricot is associated with a woman's beauty and sexuality. Red apricots symbolize a married woman who has taken a lover, and the eyes of a beautiful woman are often compared to the stones of apricots. It has also been used to symbolize female genitals.

POMEGRANATES

Growing in Mediterranean climates, by the end of the summer pomegranates swell to become red-orange spheres glistening inside with juicy red, jewel-like seeds. Their name means "apple of many seeds". It was one of the gifts of Allah in the Qur'an, and for the Israelites it represented the charm of their land and the wisdom of its

people. The pomegranate has often been associated with fertility – symbolizing the womb – but also with death. Pomegranates were left as food in Egyptian tombs to accompany the dead on their journey. In Greece, at weddings and on New Year, a pomegranate is broken on the ground as a symbol of fertility and abundance.

DATES

The date palm originated near the Persian Gulf, and has always grown prolifically in Iraq. To the Egyptians the fruit was a fertility symbol. The date palm is referred to as the "king of the oasis" and a "tree of life" by the Arabs, who state that the tree is at its best when its feet are in water and its head is in the fires of the heavens.

LICHEES AND MANGOES

The lichee is a small fruit from southern China with a rough reddish brown skin and a large shiny brown stone. Placing lichees under the bed of a married couple expresses the hope that they will be blessed with children.

Mangoes, with their succulent orange flesh, are native to eastern India, and Burma. In India they are considered sacred, representing fertility and good fortune. Legend has it that the Buddha was given a mango grove in which he could seek repose.

ORANGES

The orange tree's Latin name, *Fructus aurantia*, refers to the golden colour of the orange, whereas *naranja*, the Spanish

word for the fruit, comes from the Persian *narang*, meaning "interior perfume". The orange suggests both virginity and fruitfulness, as the flowers and fruit appear simultaneously. Orange blossom featured in ancient marriage ceremonies because of its association with fertility, a tradition that has continued to the present day. In Christian imagery, an orange in the hand of the infant Christ represents fertility and good fortune; for the witches of Europe, the fruit represented the heart. In China the orange is still eaten as a symbol of good fortune on the second day of the New Year.

GRAPES

Vines and grapes often appear in Roman art, suggesting wealth and pleasure, and are associated with Bacchus, the Roman equivalent of the Greek Dionysus, god of the vine, sexuality, fertility, and the liberation of passion and expression. Grapes from the Promised Land represented the possibility of new life for the Israelites. For Christians, wine is a symbol of the blood of Christ.

ANIMALS

ABOVE Cats were sacred to the ancient Egyptians and appeared throughout the culture in sculpture and in paintings.

ABOVE The wolf is at times associated with courage and victory, and at others with cruelty, cunning and greed.

TOP In China, the tiger (and also the leopard) is king of beasts and guards the gates of Heaven.

Throughout history, animals have played an important part in the symbolic language of many different cultures. They have been worshipped as gods and seen as sources of wisdom and power, as harbingers of good or bad fortune, as protective spirits and guides to other worlds, as well as symbolic representations of human characteristics. Animals have been used in ritual sacrifice and hunted to provide food, medicine, clothing and cosmetics, as well as to satisfy human vanity. Symbolically, they touch on all levels of the universe – Heaven, Earth and the underworld.

DOGS AND WOLVES

The dog is probably humankind's oldest domesticated animal, and signifies loyalty, protection and companionship. Dogs are widely connected with death and the spirit world: the Ainu people of Japan believed their dogs had the psychic power to detect ghosts; for the Incas, the howling of a dog could signal the death of a

relative; and in Greek myth, Cerberus the watchdog guarded the underworld. The Maya buried dogs with their masters so that they could guide them through the afterlife.

Along the north-west coast of America the wolf is a powerful spirit animal that can endow the shaman with supernatural abilities, and many shamanistic cultures speak of sorcerers obtaining their powers from a woman disguised as a wolf. In Christian tradition, the wolf is usually contrasted with the lamb, the latter symbolizing the faithful and the wolf the powers that threaten to destroy them. The colloquial expression "a wolf in sheep's clothing" refers to feigned innocence, while the American Plains tribes regard the prairie wolf, or coyote, as a trickster and figure of deceit. This idea also appears in European folklore in the story of Little Red Riding Hood, in which the wolf symbolizes a predatory male.

THE BIG CATS

Because of its mane, golden coat and regal bearing, the lion is an ancient solar symbol and the embodiment of earthly power. In ancient Egypt, the pharaoh was often depicted as a lion, and African kings used images of lions as personal symbols. In alchemy, the lion represented sexual passion, while a green lion was linked with the wild forces of nature. The lion was also associated with the mother goddess – it was one of the symbols of the Babylonian goddess Ishtar. In the classical

world, it was a guardian of the underworld and a symbol of divine protection. Both the Buddha and Christ have been associated with the lion, making it a symbol of spiritual zeal and enlightenment.

For the Chinese, the tiger, rather than the lion, is the king of beasts. A guardian spirit, initially of hunting and later of farming, it is the third sign of the Chinese zodiac. The white tiger is associated with the moon and, because it can see in the dark, it symbolizes illumination. In Hinduism, the tiger represents unbridled passion and loss of control – the deities Shiva and Durga ride tigers when destroying demons, demonstrating their ferocity and fearlessness.

Among the pre-Columbian civilizations of Central and South America, the jaguar was king of the jungle and was said to have given humans the gift of fire and hunting. The Maya considered it a creature of the underworld that knows the mysteries of the earth; by gazing into its eyes it was thought possible to see the future. Today, many Amazonian tribes continue to revere the jaguar as a *nagual* (spirit guardian) and a source of healing, associating it with fertility, water and rainfall; the Matses people believe that jaguars eat the souls of the dead.

DOMESTIC CATS

The ancient Egyptians venerated and mummified cats, and it was a capital offence to kill or injure one. Conversely, in Buddhism, cats and snakes were cursed because they did not weep when the Buddha died – although from a different perspective this may be perceived as a sign of spiritual wisdom. The early Jews reviled cats as unclean, while medieval Christians associated black cats with witchcraft.

RABBITS AND HARES
Both the rabbit and the hare have lunar associations and are fertility symbols in many cultures. Eostre, the hare-headed Saxon goddess of spring, brought dawn and new life. In China the hare represents reproductive power and longevity. The hare and rabbit both appear as trickster figures, most notably in the Brer Rabbit stories, traditional African stories taken to American plantations by slaves.

ELEPHANTS
Both Africa and India are often symbolized by the elephant. It is a symbol of strength, longevity, wisdom and good luck; ridden by rulers, it also represents power and authority. In the mythology of India and Tibet, the elephant holds up the world and symbolizes unchanging stability. Ganesh, the Hindu elephant-headed god, is the remover of obstacles. In Buddhism, the white elephant is sacred: the Buddha's mother dreamt of one at his conception. In Thailand, Laos and Cambodia it is said to grant rainfall and bounteous harvests.

BULLS AND COWS
Traditionally the bull is a symbol of virility, the cow of motherhood and fertility. Because its curved horns resemble the crescent moon, the cow is a celestial symbol of mother goddesses (such as the ancient Egyptian deities Isis and Hathor). In Norse mythology, the primordial cow – the Nourisher – licked the ice to create the first human. For the Hindus, the cow is a sacred animal and may not be killed; the animals wander the streets of India freely.

Unlike the cow, which has rarely been sacrificed, the bull's use as a ritual animal is widespread. In ancient Rome, a bull was sacrificed annually as its blood was believed to fertilize the earth and confer virility; echoes of such beliefs survive today in Spanish bullfighting. Because of its roar, the bull was the animal of thunder gods such as the Norse Thor. The Apis bull in ancient Egypt was a symbol of creation and was often shown carrying the sun disc of Ra between its horns, yet it was also sacred to Osiris, god of the underworld.

BISONS AND BUFFALO
Evidence from cave art (such as in Lascaux, France) reveals the central role played by bison in the physical and spiritual life of early hunter societies. Related to and at times synonymous with the bison, buffalo were also revered.

The Zulus believe the buffalo is able to possess the soul of a human, while the Dakota Sioux see it instead as a manifestation of the supreme creator, and it plays a central role in their vision-quest ceremonies.

BEARS
In many shamanic traditions, the bear is associated with medicine, healing and magical wisdom. In northern Europe, the bear is king of the animals and is associated with warriors: the feared Norse "berserkers" went into battle dressed only in bearskins. In Christian symbolism, the bear was regarded as cruel and vicious and a devilish image of carnality.

ABOVE A Mughal emperor is shown riding a white elephant, a symbol of royalty, power and wisdom in India.

MONKEYS
The baboon god Thoth of Egypt was credited with the invention of numbers and writing. The Maya believed that the monkey created art, numbers and writing.

THE HORSE
An ancient animal symbol, the horse is linked to sun and sky gods. It represents the elemental power of wind, storm, fire, waves and running water. Death is shown riding a black horse, while the white horse is a symbol of light, life and spiritual illumination. The Buddha is said to have left his earthly life on a white horse. Horses drew the sun chariot in classical, Iranian, Indian, Nordic and Babylonian myths.

BIRDS

ABOVE The Seal of the President of the United States of America, changed by President Truman in 1945 from the original 1880 version; the turning of the eagle's head from right to left (towards the olive branch, symbol of peace) was thought at the time to signify a move from war to peace.

BELOW In Greek myth the markings on a peacock's tail feathers were said to be the eyes of the slain giant Argos.

BELOW RIGHT In Western folklore, the stork is said to bring babies to their mothers, while in many parts of the world it is the bearer of good news.

Because they can fly, birds are often seen as mediators between Heaven and Earth, acting as messengers of higher or otherworldly powers. They are also widely regarded as embodiments of the spirit or soul, because flight symbolizes freedom from the physical restrictions of the earthbound world and is frequently used as a metaphor for mystical experience.

BIRDS OF PREY

Warriors and nobles have been associated with birds of prey, especially the eagle, hawk and falcon. Falcons, used for hunting by the aristocracy of China, Japan and Europe, have come to symbolize nobility; in China, the banners of high-ranking lords bore falcon-headed images. In ancient Egypt, the falcon was the king of birds, and the hieroglyph for falcon meant "god"; it was also the symbol for the sky god Horus. Native American tribes regard the hawk as a messenger of the ancestors, while in Polynesia the bird is connected with the powers of healing and prophecy. In China, the hawk denotes war, as well as being a solar symbol. For the early Christian Church, the hawk signified evil, but a tamed

hawk represented a converted pagan and a hooded hawk hope for illumination.

The eagle is widely associated with power and leadership and has been adopted in various guises by ambitious, expansionist civilizations (including ancient Rome and the USA) as a symbol of national identity and sovereignty. In China, the eagle symbolizes strength, while in Celtic folklore it is a symbol of longevity and rejuvenation. For Christians the eagle symbolizes the omnipotence and omniscience of God, as well as Christ and St John the apostle. In many Christian churches, the Bible is placed on an eagle-shaped lectern, symbolizing the power and inspiration of God's word.

RAVENS AND CROWS

Many cultures do not distinguish between the raven and the crow, and the birds share a similar symbolism. Both are widely seen as birds of ill omen, war, death and the supernatural. In the Judaeo-Christian tradition, the raven is the dark counterpart of

the dove; it was also believed to be the spirit familiar of witches. In the Greco-Roman tradition, crows were sacred to Athene/Minerva, goddess of war, but they were prevented from landing on the roofs of her temples as this foretold a death. The name of the ancient Welsh king Bran means "raven"; his head is said to be buried beneath the Tower of London, and ravens are kept there in line with the popular myth that if they should ever depart the English would fall.

Some Native American tribes believed that the raven brought light and fire to the world. The Inuit of Siberia and Alaska share a similar belief – that the bird came from the primeval darkness and stayed to teach the first humans how to survive. Consequently the raven represented the creator god, and it was said that killing one would bring misfortune and bad weather. The crow is a bird of prophecy in China.

DOVES

Today the dove is widely used as an emblem for world peace. In the Old Testament, it was the bird that returned to Noah's ark bearing an olive leaf, indicating reconciliation between God and humankind, while in Japan a dove bearing a sword announced the end of war. The dove is also a symbol of purity and the soul; in the Christian tradition, it represents the Holy Spirit; in Arthurian legend it is associated with the Grail. For Romans, the dove was sacred to Venus, and in China it was associated with fertility and longevity.

BIRD FEATHERS

The indigenous people of North, Central and South America use feathers as decoration in spectacular head-dresses. The Aztecs used green quetzal tail feathers for their rulers (a symbol of their supreme god, Quetzalcoatl), while for Native Americans, the feathers contain the power or "medicine" of the bird they come from, with eagle feathers being most prized.

PEACOCKS

Because of its grandeur, the peacock represents divinity, royalty, love and beauty. In Persia, it dwelt in the gardens of paradise, and the court revolved around the "peacock throne". In Hindu tradition, the bird is the cosmic mount of Kama, the god of love, and sacred to Sarasvati, goddess of wisdom and the arts. The peacock's distinctive tail markings have long been identified with eyes, and likened to the stars, as well as to solar symbols. In Buddhism it denotes compassionate watchfulness.

STORKS

In many cultures, the stork is the herald of good news. As a migratory bird, it is the emblem of the traveller, and in the land to which it migrates it represents the arrival of spring and hence new life. In ancient Greece the bird was sacred to Hera, goddess of marriage and protector of childbirth. The Western saying that the stork brings babies relates to the idea that the souls of unborn children live in marshes and ponds – the stork's natural habitat – and are discovered by the stork as it searches for fish.

SWANS AND GEESE

Both the goose and the swan are large, web-footed water birds that have otherworldly associations in many cultures. In Siberia, the swan symbolizes the shaman's immersion in the underworld, and according to the Tungu it was the guiding spirit of the first shaman. The migrating goose is also regarded as a spirit-helper, carrying the shaman on celestial adventures.

In Hinduism, the two birds are mythically interchangeable, so that the Hamsa – one bird made of two – can appear as either a goose or swan, and symbolizes perfect union and balance. Because swans often mate for life, they are associated with fidelity in Western traditions.

OWLS

With its night excursions, haunting call and intense eyes, the owl is widely associated with supernatural powers. It was the bird of death in ancient Egypt, India, China and Japan: in China, its hooting was thought to sound like the word for "dig dig", predicting that someone was about to die and a grave should be prepared. The owl's superb night vision may account for its traditional link with prophecy. Among the American Plains tribes owl feathers are worn as magic talismans, while for the Pawnee tribes of Nebraska, the owl is a nocturnal protector. In ancient Athens, the bird was sacred to Athene, goddess of wisdom; similarly, in alchemy, the owl is considered to be the wisest of the birds and also a symbol of the true alchemist.

MAGPIES

In Australian Aboriginal lore, magpies are associated with happiness and enthusiasm, while in China the bird's name means "bird of joy". When shown carrying a Chinese coin, they represent the desire for world peace. However, in European folklore, magpies are regarded as thieves and birds of ill omen.

ABOVE LEFT In the Greco-Roman tradition, the swan was sacred to Aphrodite/Venus; it also appears in the myth of Leda, who is seduced by Zeus when he takes the shape of a swan.

ABOVE In many traditions, the owl is associated with magic, the otherworld, wisdom and prophecy.

CRANES

In China and Japan, cranes are traditional symbols of longevity, wisdom and fidelity. In Western art they personify vigilance.

AQUATIC CREATURES

The symbolism of aquatic creatures relates partly to their habitat, partly to their appearance and behaviour and partly to the significance they have for human society. Water creatures have been variously revered as deities, feared as monsters and hunted for their flesh, oils, eggs, skin and bones. They play a significant role in myth, folklore and religion.

FISH

Many traditions use the fish as a symbol of spiritual wisdom. In Christianity it is a symbol of Christ, and in Hinduism, Vishnu appeared as the fish Matsya to save humankind from the flood and reveal the Vedas, or holy scriptures. Because of the vast number of eggs they lay, fish are also widely linked with life and fertility. In China they are symbols of good luck.

Particular species have been singled out for their symbolic properties. For example, in Japan, the carp symbolizes love, courage, dignity and good fortune, while the Celts associated the salmon with wisdom, prophecy and inspiration.

WHALES, SHARKS AND DOLPHINS

In Japan, the whale was one of the Seven Deities of Good Fortune and was worshipped as a god of fishing and food. In Maori tradition, it symbolizes plenty and abundance; the *pakake* figure – a stylized whale with large spirals for its jaws – is a popular motif.

In the Judaeo-Christian tradition, the Old Testament account of Jonah and the whale associated it with death and rebirth. It is sometimes claimed that the story relates to a man-eating shark rather than a whale, and the Hindu god Vishnu is at times portrayed as emerging from the mouth of a shark. They are symbols of the dangers of nature.

In ancient Greece dolphins were linked with Apollo and his gifts of wisdom and prophecy, and with the water-born goddess of love, Aphrodite, signifying a union of the masculine, solar world and the feminine, watery realm; the dolphin's Greek name, *delphis*, is related to *delphys*, "womb", after which the sacred site of Delphi is named. In many Native American cultures, the dolphin is both a divine messenger and a form of the Great Spirit, while the seafaring Nabataean Arabs believed that dolphins accompanied the souls of the dead to the underworld.

CROCODILES AND ALLIGATORS

Crocodilians inhabit two worlds – land and water – making them symbols of fundamental contradictions. Some African tribes revere crocodiles as intermediaries between the everyday and the spirit world and as oracles for water deities. In many parts of West Africa the crocodile's liver and entrails are credited with powerful magic and are sometimes used by shamans to cast destructive spells.

In ancient Egypt, crocodiles were sacred and were sometimes mummified. A cult centre existed at Crocodilopolis, where tame crocodiles were adorned with golden earrings and ritually fed in order to honour the crocodile god, Sobek. Sobek was linked both to the evil and destructive powers of Set, god of the underworld, who took crocodile form after the murder of his brother, Osiris, and also to Ra, the benevolent solar deity.

For the Aborigines of Australia's Northern Territory, large crocodiles embody the spirits of important people and are associated with wisdom, while the Madarrpa peoples of north-east Arnhem Land believe that Crocodile Man created fire. In China, the alligator or crocodile was the inventor of singing and the drum, and plays a part in the rhythm of the world. In early Christian belief, being eaten by a crocodile indicated that a person had gone to Hell.

FROGS AND TOADS

Traditionally both frogs and toads were lunar animals, and their radical growth stages were linked with the changing phases of the moon. Both creatures are also linked with fertility, the watery processes of birth and rainfall and with transformation and

ABOVE In the fairy story, the frog is changed into a prince when kissed by the princess, symbolizing transformation.

ABOVE The turtle is a sacred animal in many traditions. In Native American traditions it is a symbol of the earth.

SHELLS

Because it is a structure that shelters life, the symbolism of the shell is often connected with the womb, birth and creation. In Greco-Roman myth, Aphrodite/Venus emerged from a huge scallop shell, and in Hinduism, the conch shell symbolizes the origin of existence, its shape forming a multiple spiral evolving from one central point. Conch shells have been used as ceremonial horns by the Maya and Aztecs and are also one of the emblems of Buddhism. In Benin, cowrie shells were once used as currency and are associated with wealth, royalty and prestige. In Christian iconography, the Virgin Mary is sometimes compared to an oyster shell, and Christ to the pearl.

immortality – hence the theme of frogs changing into princes in Western folklore. To the Celts, the frog was lord of the earth and the curative powers of water, and for the Maya and Aztecs it was a water deity whose croaking predicted and made rain. In ancient Egypt, Heket the frog goddess was associated with magic and childbirth, and in China and Japan both frogs and toads were associated with magic. In Japan, the toad was associated with lunar eclipses and in China with wealth and longevity. Both frogs and toads were linked with magic and witchcraft in medieval Europe. In the Bible, frogs were one of the ten plagues of Egypt.

TURTLES

Because of the sturdiness and shape of its shell, the turtle (or tortoise) is a symbol of the world in many cultures. It is the oldest Native American symbol for the Earth or earth mother – while earthquakes and thunder are the cosmic turtle shaking its earthly shell. The Maya also envisaged the Earth as a huge turtle, as did the Chinese, who regarded the marks on the turtle's shell as a map of the constellations and used them in divination. Of

China's four sacred creatures, the turtle was the only real animal (the others being the dragon, the phoenix and the unicorn), and it was a symbol of longevity.

In Hindu myth, the turtle Chukwa is one of the ten incarnations of Vishnu. It is a symbol of meditation and spiritual wisdom. In Australian Aboriginal myth, the turtle was said to arise from the creative waters that were melted from the primeval mountain of ice by the sun goddess, while in Polynesia, the turtle embodies the power of the ocean deities. Among African tribes, turtles are often sacred to water gods.

SEALS AND WALRUSES

In some Inuit stories, these creatures figure as primordial ancestors, capable of assuming human form and teaching people to swim and hunt fish; they are also messengers, moving between the world of spirit (water) and matter (land). Inuit custom dictates that, when the animals are killed in a hunt, their bladders are thrown back into the sea, as it is believed they will then be reborn as living seals or walruses. The walrus is also known as the sea elephant.

CRABS

Because its movement is governed by the lunar tides (hunting as the tide comes in, retreating as the tide goes out), the crab is often associated with the moon. In Inca tradition, it was an aspect of the great mother, who devoured both time and the waning moon.

OCTOPUSES

In classical antiquity, the octopus was seen as a monster that would attack shipwrecked sailors by pulling them apart. Like the crab, it was associated with the moon and the summer solstice. The octopus was much used in the art of the Minoan and Mycenean civilizations in the Mediterranean, where it sometimes occurs in conjunction with the spiral or swastika. Its tentacles associate it with the unfolding of creation from the centre.

CORAL

According to an ancient Chinese belief, coral came from a tree growing at the bottom of the sea. In alchemy it was known as the tree of life, filled with a blood-like substance (because of its colour). In Buddhism, coral trees are said to grow in paradise.

BELOW Seals play a prominent role in the myth and custom of the Inuit, where they are often seen as primordial ancestral figures.

INSECTS

ABOVE This portrait of Napoleon makes use of the motif of the bee, embroidered not only on the emperor's robes but also on the podium on which he stands. It is a symbol of equals under one leader.

BELOW RIGHT The butterfly is a symbol of spiritual growth and transformation. In Latin America it is also used to describe a prostitute, flitting from one man to the next.

From a perspective that sees the universe as an interconnected web of being, every part of nature is significant, no matter how small or ordinary. Consequently even the tiniest insects are rich in symbolic associations, frequently associated with the gods, spirits and the otherworld. For instance, in the mythology of Central America, small flying insects were regarded as the souls of the dead revisiting earth, and a similar belief endures in Guatemala, where they are linked with the stars. As with other animals, the symbolic associations of insects are based on their behaviour and physical characteristics and are rooted in culture and time.

FLIES

The name of Beelzebub, the chief devil mentioned in the Bible, comes from a Hebrew word meaning "lord of the flies", pointing to the fairly common belief that flies are harbingers of disease and devilish misfortune; they were the third of the ten plagues of Egypt. However, in the ancient Egyptian New Kingdom (1550–1100 BC), flies were noted for their persistence and bravery and were adopted as warrior symbols: magic wands decorated with fly amulets have been discovered from this period. Among the Navajo, Dontso ("big fly") is a spiritual messenger associated with healing.

BEES

Because of their diligence, social organization and collaborative labour, bees are often used as models of human society. The beehive became a metaphor for the ordered and charitable life of Christian monastic communities. Bees have also long been valued for their honeycombs, a source not only of sugar but also of wax, used in the making of candles. Thus they are associated with both sweetness and light. In ancient Egypt they were a solar symbol, born from the tears of the sun god Ra.

As the hive is organized around the queen bee, the bee was a regal symbol: it was adopted by the medieval kings of France and revived by Napoleon as an emblem of equals under a single leader. In Chinese art, a bee or butterfly hovering around a flower (symbolizing a woman) suggested buzzing desire. In ancient Greece, honey was

> ### DRAGONFLIES
> In some Native American cultures, dragonflies symbolize dreams, change and enlightenment and are associated with shamanistic powers. To the Chinese, the dragonfly represents summer, and, because of its darting, unpredictable movement, is also a symbol of unreliability.

THE ANTHILL
In the cosmologies of many African peoples (notably the Dogon and Bambara of Mali) the anthill plays a significant role. It is linked with language and the art of weaving, the female sexual organs and creation: it is a traditional fertility custom for a woman to sit on an anthill. The traditional pattern of Dogon huts is based on the anthill design, and the belief that ants know the location of underground streams means that wells are often sunk near an anthill. In Tibetan Buddhism, the anthill is a symbol of an industrious life.

associated with eloquence, while in the Celtic world, mead (a fermented drink made from honey and water) was regarded as the drink of the gods.

BUTTERFLIES

Because of its metamorphic life cycle, the butterfly is an archetypal symbol of transformation, mystical rebirth and the transcendent soul. Some Australian Aboriginals regard butterflies as the returning spirits of the dead, while in Greek myth, Psyche (the soul) is often represented as a butterfly. The creature's grace and beauty make it an emblem of woman in Japan, where two butterflies dancing together symbolize marital happiness, and in China it is associated with the pleasures of life and high spirits. Someone who flits from one thing to another and is never satisfied may be described as a butterfly, while in Latin America, the Spanish word for butterfly (*mariposa*) can refer to a prostitute, moving from one man to the next. The Aztecs associated the butterfly with women who had died in childbirth, while for the Mexicans it was a symbol of the "black sun" passing through the underworld during its nightly journey.

SPIDERS

In Australian Aboriginal cultures the great spider is a solar hero, but in other traditions it is a female force, a personification of the Great Mother in both her creative and devouring aspects. Among the Amazonian Tukano people, for instance, the spider's web is likened to the placenta, while Ixchel, the Mayan goddess of midwifery, appears as a spider. In Japan, spider-women are thought to ensnare travellers, while in the West predatory women are sometimes likened to spiders, using their feminine wiles to lure men into their web. Among the Ashanti of West Africa spiders are associated with Anansi, the trickster god, who taught humans the art of weaving. In some Native American myths the spider is said to have taught humans the alphabet, tracing the shapes of the letters in its web.

Because of the web's strength and near invisibility, Native American warriors decorated themselves with web designs. For the Celts, the web is the invisible structure that holds the pattern of life in a grand design. For Hindus and Buddhists, the web stands for the illusions of the world, while in Christianity it represents Satan's snare. In European folklore, however, it is unlucky to kill a spider, which is linked with money and good fortune.

SCORPIONS

Because of its poisonous sting, permanently unsheathed and ready to strike, the scorpion is associated with death and destruction: in Africa, many people use a euphemism for the creature since even uttering its name would release evil into the world. The scorpion has many links with the underworld: the zodiac sign of Scorpio is ruled by Pluto, lord of the underworld, while the ancient Egyptian scorpion goddess Selket (a sorcerer-healer) was one of four goddesses who protected the dead Osiris. Through its association with the desert, the scorpion can represent drought and desolation. Some Amazonian peoples believe it was sent by a jealous god to punish men for having sex with women whom he himself desired. In one version of the Greco-Roman myth of Orion the hunter, he died when he was stung in the heel by a scorpion, and both were turned into constellations, placed on opposite sides of the sky.

WORMS

The symbolism of the worm links new life with corruption and death. According to Chinese myth, the human race has its origins in the worms that fed on the corpse of the primordial being, and a similar belief exists in Icelandic tradition, where the worms feeding on the frost giant Ymir (from whose body the earth was created) assume human form. The legendary Irish Celtic hero Cúchulainn was said to have been born from a worm. In psychological terms, worms may be associated with destructive processes that erode personality.

ABOVE The scorpion is widely linked with death and destruction. In parts of Africa, many people refuse to say its name in the belief that this would bring evil into the world.

SILKWORMS

In ancient Japan and China, silkworms represented purity and virtue, and the Japanese believed they were created by the union of the fire god and the earth goddess. The Chinese made ritual offerings of silkworms and mulberry leaves in the spring. Silk is traditionally associated with nobility, luxury and opulence.

CRICKETS AND LOCUSTS

In Japan, crickets are linked with the moon and in China they are symbols of death and resurrection. Finding a cricket in the home is thought to bring good luck in China and in some Mediterranean countries. Because of their ability to destroy crops, locusts are usually connected with voracity and destruction.

THE SNAKE OR SERPENT

ABOVE The goddess of the snakes is a Cretan Earth Mother, shown here holding the snakes of death and rebirth.

Of all animal symbols, the snake is probably the most significant and complex. From very early times, snakes seem to have been linked with eternity, as creators and destroyers of the universe, and associated with both healing and wisdom; they have also been demonized and aligned with temptation, immorality and Satan.

SNAKES AND THE FEMININE

The snake was often associated with deities, particularly mother goddesses and Mother Earth. The ancient Phoenician fertility goddess Tanith, who is linked with Eve and Lilith, was associated with snakes. In Egyptian mythology Buto was a

snake goddess, often depicted as a cobra. Her image on the Pharaoh's forehead protected him from his enemies. The matriarchal cult at Delphi was symbolically dissolved when the god Apollo killed the female serpent Python, and the Iliad tells of Calcas interpreting an eagle carrying a wounded snake in its talons as a sign that the patriarchal Greeks would overcome the matriarchal traditions of Asia.

FROM PRIMARY GOD TO EVIL SERPENT

In many parts of the world snakes, with other reptiles and fish, have been used to represent nature in its most primordial or fundamental aspects. Because the snake sheds its skin and then starts life anew, it embodies the cycle of death and resurrection. The serpent was a primary god, existing at the roots of life, and has a strong chthonic or underworld connection, arising from the depths of Mother Earth, and psychologically from the collective unconscious. He was the lord of the tree of life, where time and eternity meet. Sumerian seals from 3500 BC show the serpent with the tree and the goddess giving the fruit of life to a visiting male figure.

The Canaanite deity was a mother goddess who was strongly associated with the serpent and represented the mysteries of life. When the Hebrews introduced a male god into Canaan, the female deity and the snake were

NAGAS AND WISDOM

In Indian mythology, nagas (from the Sanskrit word for "snake") are divine water-serpents, benevolent and wise, portrayed with a human face and the hood of the cobra. Indian alchemy, *nagayuna*, aims to unify the body's energies in a journey of self-realization to preserve the elixir of life.

relegated and associated with evil. The snake in the story of the Garden of Eden has Satanic characteristics, tempting Eve into the sin of disobedience against God, whereas the Nassene Gnostics (*nass* means "snake") honoured the serpent in the form of the Sumerian god Enki, a liberating influence who helped to make Adam and Eve fully human by introducing them to the tree of knowledge.

For Jung, snakes symbolized that which is totally unconscious and instinctual, nevertheless possessing an almost supernatural and unique wisdom, which can come into conflict with conscious

LEFT Eve pictured with the devil-serpent, and the forbidden fruit that it uses to tempts her to sin.

attitudes. The snake can therefore symbolize both evil and wisdom, easily overriding human morality. To dream of a snake suggests that there is a large gulf between the conscious and unconscious, and that the unconscious is making itself known in a compulsive and reflexive way. A snake in our dreams might also suggest that we have strayed from the serpentine path of our individuation.

THE SNAKE AS CREATOR AND DESTROYER

Serpents appear as the source of life in many creation myths, though they can also be figures of destruction. The Sumerians and Akkadians of Mesopotamia described the mingling of the waters of Apsu and Tiamat, from which emerged Lakhmu and Lakhamu, two monstrous serpents who gave birth to Heaven and Earth. The Rainbow Serpent appears in Aboriginal rock art in Arnhem Land from between 6,000 and 8,000 years ago. This Dreamtime ancestor is a life-giving creature associated with fertility, abundance and rainfall, as well as often being the creator of human beings. Its destructive side involves punishing those who go against the natural law by swallowing them in great floods and regurgitating their bones.

Ancient Germanic mythology associates the serpent with death and the continual undermining of the roots of the world tree. Norse tradition foretold a deluge that would destroy the world when Jormangand, the Midgard serpent, was awoken.

HEALING AND DEATH

Serpents have long been associated with healing and mediation between life and death. In Greek mythology, Asklepios, the son of Apollo and the mortal Coronis, was able to metamorphose into a snake and could bring the dead back to life, thus angering Hades, god of the underworld. One tale tells that he became a serpent to end a plague in Rome, and the Romans came to worship him as the god of medicine and healing. The Asklepian healing process, called incubation, involved the patient spending the night in a sacred place. They would be visited by the god in a dream, and its message was interpreted by a priest, resulting in a remedy.

The Asklepian symbol of a tree snake wrapped around a staff represents healing and is today used as a medical symbol. It is often confused with the caduceus, or "winged staff", of Mercury, on which two snakes were twined. These snakes were involved in a fight in which Mercury intervened, revealing his nature as a psychopomp, or conductor of souls between worlds.

The serpent's association with healing, life and death is found in the pagan-Christian Slavonic story of Bogatyr Potok, who when his young bride died, had himself buried with her, fully armed and on horseback, in a deep tomb. At midnight many monstrous reptiles appeared, including a great fire-breathing serpent. Potok cut off its head and brought his wife back to life by anointing her body with it. The homeopathic principle that "like cures like" is essential to the poisonous/healing nature of the snake.

THE TUKANO ANACONDA

The Tukano people of the Amazon ascribe a complex and contextual symbolism to the anaconda. They believe that monstrous anacondas live in forest lagoons and deep pools beneath waterfalls. They also compare the motion of the Milky Way to the intertwining of two copulating anacondas, reflecting seasonal periods of insemination, germination and fertility. The anaconda is the path that twists through the forest like the river, and when travelling upstream it represents a journey of initiation.

ABOVE Two snakes entwined upon Mercury's "winged staff" represent the transformative power to change male to female and vice versa. The Asclepian staff with its single snake was the original medical symbol; however, possibly mistakenly, this caduceus is also used for this purpose.

BELOW The art of the Australian Aboriginals often depicts the snake, and its association with fertility and abundance.

THE LIVING PLANET

Inevitably, much cultural symbolism stems from the earth and how we live out our lives on our planet. Seasons and cycles, time, distance, the elements and the land itself have all given rise to humanity's most ancient signs and symbols, which remain constant despite the way science has increased our knowledge of the planet we live on.

RIGHT The awe-inspiring power of volcanoes means that they are symbols of sudden fury and volatility, and are regarded with particular fear and respect.

SEASONS AND TIME

RIGHT The 22,000-year-old stone carving known as the Venus of Laussel. The horn she holds is thought to be marked with a year of thirteen lunar cycles.

Humankind has always used symbolism and ritual to relate to the rhythms and cycles of life. Nature punctuates existence with life events – the moments of conception, birth and death – and life goes on in interdependent cycles. The phases of life have always preoccupied us, and have been given their own universal symbolic language.

CALENDARS AND TIME

Early calendars were based on the phases of the moon. Cave paintings at Lascaux, in France, show that they were counted around 17,000 years ago, and the carving of the Venus of Laussel, which is about 22,000 years old, shows her holding a horn with thirteen markings, representing a year of lunar cycles. The lunar calendar is associated with the menstrual cycle, and predominates in civilizations that worship The Goddess. Britain's Stonehenge is a symbolic monument aligned with the movements of both sun and moon. Lunisolar and solar calendars emerged with the shift from female to male values.

To this day Jews and Muslims continue to use lunar calendars.

The Chinese calendar, another example of a lunisolar calendar, is still used to establish the timing of holidays and festivals, and is important to Chinese farmers who still plant by the moon.

Whereas time was originally associated with rhythm, rebirth and renewal in nature, symbolized by the circle and the yoni, the influence of Judaeo-Christianity led to the foundation of linear time. In the 14th century, Europeans conceived the universe in terms of clockwork, and in the 17th century, Isaac Newton characterized time as being absolute and uniform.

Technological advances have enabled us to ignore or colonize "nature's time", growing crops out of season and literally extending daytime into the night. It is only in recent years, since Einstein's theories of relativity, that time, along with space, has again been thought to bend.

THE CELTIC WHEEL OF THE YEAR

In the Celtic tradition, a symbolic circle of time represents transitional points during the year: Samhain, winter solstice; Imbolc, spring equinox; Beltane, summer solstice; Lughnasada, autumn equinox. The wheel of the year describes the cycles of death, birth, youth, maturity and renewal of life, and each point is

THE TYRANNICAL CLOCK

In Charles Dickens's 1848 novel Dombey and Son the clock is a tyrannical figure that makes itself heard and felt everywhere. Mr Dombey, an emotionless character, does everything by the clock. It is used as a symbol of a mechanistic way of life, showing how time had come to dominate the consciousness of industrial society.

PLEIADES

The constellation of the Pleiades has many symbolic associations. The stars represented the mother goddess Net in ancient Egypt, and in China they were the blossom or flower stars. The Khoikhoi tribe of South Africa call them Khuseti, the rain-bearing stars. In Hindu tradition they are the flames of Agni, the god of fire.

marked by seasonal celebrations.
Samhain (31 October–1
November) is also the Festival of
the Dead, when the veil between
the living and the dead is thought
to be at its thinnest. The year
begins in the dying and decaying
part of the wheel, reflecting the
Celtic understanding of the
importance of ageing and death in
order for life to thrive. This time
is symbolized by the figure of the
old woman, who is also an elder.
Youth, beauty, growth and
productivity are symbolized later
in the Celtic year by the maiden
and the mother, the other two
aspects of the triple goddess.

SEASONAL SYMBOLISM

Early measurements of time were
based on the appearances and
disappearances, and the changing
paths of the sun and the moon.
The main phases of the day had
their own symbolism that still has
resonance today. Dawn was a
universal symbol of hope, joy and
youth, while noon was the hour
of revelation in Jewish and
Islamic tradition. Twilight was
often linked with the shadowy
and uncertain time of decline and
therefore with death.

Again inspired by the cycles of
the moon, and the rising and
setting of the sun, the four

seasons were universal symbols of
birth, growth, death and rebirth.
In Western art, spring is depicted
as a young woman, at times a
child, sometimes linked with
blossom, the lamb or kid and
with the Greek goddess
Aphrodite. Summer is again a
woman, this time in the full
beauty of maturity, crowned with
ears of corn and sometimes
carrying a sickle. Autumn is
associated with Dionysus and
with harvest, and also with the
hare. Winter is at times depicted
as an old man or woman; the
blacksmith god Hephaestus is
associated with this season, as is
the salamander and the duck.

HARVEST FESTIVALS

Festivals of thanksgiving at
harvest time are common to all
agrarian cultures. They are
thought of as times to appreciate
the forces of nature and the
ancestors, bringing the
community together to share
ideas and experiences, tell stories
and strengthen social bonds.

The harvest moon festival in
Korea, called Chusok, takes place
on the 15th day of the eighth
lunar month. The same day in
China and Vietnam is Chung
Ch'ui, considered the birthday of
the moon and celebrated with a

feast and special "moon cakes",
symbols of togetherness.

Pongal is the southern Indian
Hindu harvest festival, which
starts on 14 January. Its name
means "boiling over" – a reference
both to the bounties of nature
and to a sweet rice dish. The
festival lasts three days, and
offerings are made to the rain and
sun gods, who watered and
ripened the rice, and to the cattle,
which are essential to a
prosperous community.

The Sikh festival of Baisakhi is
a northern Indian harvest festival
that is celebrated on 13 April, the
first day of the Sikh solar year. At
Baisakhi dancers and drummers
re-enact agricultural activities,
such as ploughing, and the
sowing, harvesting, winnowing
and gathering of crops.

BELOW A procession of Sikhs at the
festival of Baisakhi, which
celebrates the beginning of the
corn harvest, and takes place on
the first day of the solar year.

GOD OF TIME

The Greeks
conceived of two
types of time:
Chronos (shown
above, the snake
around him
symbolizing eternity),
was the god of
absolute, linear and
quantifiable time,
whereas Kairos was
the god of timing,
opportunity and
chance.

THE EARTH

RIGHT The view of the planet Earth from space changed the way we view our world, and symbolizes the wholeness and inter-connectedness of life.

BELOW The Psalter Map, with Jerusalem in the middle, is the earliest surviving map symbolizing Christ's role as overseer of the world.

What the Earth means to us has changed markedly over time. Its symbolism is strongly linked to our collective state of mind or consciousness, and reflects changes in human values and our relationship with nature.

THE FLAT EARTH

Most early societies conceived of the Earth as flat, as a huge wheel or disc. The ancient Chinese described the Earth as a flat square on top of a truncated, four-sided pyramid, below the circular heavens. In India, the Rig Veda described the Earth and sky as two wheels at either end of an axle. Classical, Hindu, Buddhist and Jain texts agreed that the Earth was in fact a flat disc, though some Indian myths saw it as spherical.

The ancient Hebrews, Egyptians and Babylonians all had flat Earth cosmologies. According to the Hebrew book of Enoch, the angel Uriel guided Enoch to the ends of the Earth, where he saw huge beasts and birds, and beyond which he saw Heaven resting on the edge of the Earth. The Egyptians envisaged a rectangular Earth, with the sky goddess Nut stretching her body like an enclosing dome over the land. The Babylonians imagined a flat land surrounded by ocean, with the vault of the sky resting either on the ocean or on pillars. In the West, the earliest description of the Earth is in the Iliad, where Homer described the sky as a bowl-like hemisphere, covering a flat, circular Earth.

THE ROUND EARTH

Although most early people thought the Earth was flat, there were exceptions. Japan's indigenous people, the Ainu, thought of it as a ball floating in the ocean, but their word for Earth means "floating land", suggesting that this was the localized perception of an island people. In 375 BC Plato described the Earth as a globe, in the context of an Earth-centred universe, and Aristotle (384–322 BC) suggested it was a sphere based upon his observations of circular shadows cast on the moon during a lunar eclipse. In 200 BC, the Egyptian Eratosthenes calculated the Earth's diameter using trigonometry, by measuring the length of the shadow of a vertical tower in Alexandria, when the sun was directly above Aswan, 800km/500 miles away.

However, the paradigmatic shift from a flat to a round Earth took place over many hundreds of years. In 1492 Christopher Columbus, by sailing partly around the world, proved by experience what, until then, had been surmised through calculation: that the Earth was indeed a sphere. It seems likely that Galileo and Copernicus were greatly encouraged by Columbus's experience, and dramatic new theories concerning a universe centred on the sun, around which the spherical Earth and moon orbited, rapidly followed.

EARTH AS A DEITY

The Earth was worshipped in ancient times as the supreme mother goddess and was believed to be both alive and divine. Mother Earth was a figure of great compassion and the source of all life and fertility. Paleolithic images of the mother goddess, dating from around 22,000-18,000 BC, include the Venus of Laussel, a rock carving from the Dordogne in France, and the statuettes known as the Goddess of Lespugue, found in Haute-Garonne, France, and the Goddess of Willendorf, found in Austria. Each depicts a female form with pendulous breasts and a full, rounded womb.

In the West, the last Earth Goddess was Gaia, no longer the supreme mother but nevertheless a conscious and living deity. In Greek her name means "land" or "earth". She was a triple goddess, differentiated as the maiden, or Persephone, the mother, or Demeter, and the crone or Hecate. During the Classical period there was a shift in emphasis from Gaia to her great-grandson Zeus, reflecting the replacement of the image of the divine mother with a far more remote male god, which swept across Europe, the Middle East, North Africa and India, gaining particular prominence in the Judaeo-Christian God.

In Christian times Mary, the mother of Christ, embodies or echoes some of the qualities of the ancient mother goddesses, and acts as an intermediary between Heaven and Earth. Meanwhile, the male God exists in Heaven, outside the earthly sphere, symbolizing a separation between Earth and deity.

THE HIERARCHY OF HEAVEN AND EARTH

The Judaeo-Christian worldview stresses a hierarchical relationship between Heaven and Earth, placing humanity closer to God than other living creatures, with the responsibility to assume dominion over the Earth and nature. This has been interpreted

RIGHT The Virgin in her role as quasi-earth mother, interceding with God on behalf of humankind.

by many to justify an image of the Earth as a resource for human use. With the divine no longer synonymous with nature, the Earth could easily become an object of interest and exploitation. Francis Bacon (1561–1626) spoke of nature in feminine terms, and advocated its domination for human benefit. He suggested that nature should be "bound into service", "moulded" by the machine and made into a "slave" – simultaneously representing prevailing attitudes towards both women and nature.

THE LIVING EARTH

When in 1969 the scientist James Lovelock conceived his Gaia hypothesis, he described feeling like an astronaut looking at the Earth while standing on the moon, and that at times he has felt that the whole planet is partaking in something like a "sacred ceremony". His vision of the Earth as a complex and self-regulating closed system, which operates as if it were a living being – a pragmatic and scientific view – has aroused a great deal of speculation concerning its potential as a modern religious symbol. Using the name of the Greek Earth goddess Gaia may well have furthered the power of this scientific model and symbolic imagery. For many, Gaia has come to represent the idea of the "living Earth", despite the theory's stress that the Earth acts only "like" a living system. For Lovelock, Gaia is something that humans can reconnect to by maintaining a sense of wonder for nature.

To the Kono people of Sierra Leone, the Earth is indeed a living being: she is God's wife and is hugely productive and fertile. The emphasis of the Kono lifestyle, like that of many indigenous peoples, lies in maintaining the harmony of nature, through human relationships and community, and relationships with the land and unseen forces.

NEW SYMBOLISM

The image of Earth as seen from space offers a meaningful symbolism for contemporary humans. It is Earth as seen from the "heavens", and this changed view shows us that the separations we perceive between different cultures, and between us and nature, are immaterial when viewed from a distance. Earth seen from space offers the symbol of a renewed relationship between humankind and nature.

THE HOLLOW EARTH

Since the scientific revolution, scientists have hypothesized that the earth may be hollow. John Cleves Symmes (1779–1829) believed it consisted of four hollow concentric spheres, with spaces between each, which were possibly habitable on their inner and outer surfaces. He believed there were two enormous holes at the North and South poles and proposed an expedition to the inner spheres. "Symmes' hole" became a phrase of ridicule in the 1820s.

MAPS AND DIRECTION

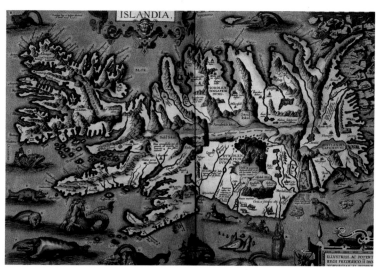

ABOVE A map of Islandia (Iceland), charted by Abraham Ortelius in the late 16th century, displays a wide array of sea monsters, polar bears, icebergs and the erupting volcano Mount Hekla.

BELOW A stone disk containing an Australian Aboriginal songline design. The Aborginals believe that the songlines draw together diverse groups into one common dreaming relationship with the land.

The symbolism of orientation and direction focuses on how people move through life and the world, what it means to be in a certain place at a certain time, and the relationship with places beyond our everyday experience.

MAPPING THE WORLD

How a map is drawn depends upon the worldview and beliefs of the cartographer, and what is considered central or peripheral, what is known, mysterious or threatening to the culture. The early *mappa mundi*, or world map, was a symbolic representation of the known world infused with the *imago mundi*, or the image of the world as an ordered cosmos. Early maps were as much cosmological and mythical as they were tools for practical orientation. The Beatus map, drawn by a Benedictine monk in AD 787, charts the world in a rectangle encircled by a world

sea. This form, called a "T-map" was common until the late Middle Ages. T-maps divide the world into three, the number of the Holy Trinity: Jerusalem usually lies at the intersection, with Eden either at the top or to the east, and the rest of the world divided into Asia, Africa and Europe. As the medieval worldview receded during the Renaissance, Jerusalem and Eden were no longer charted as central features and the edges of maps began to display unexplored regions, with strange hybrid creatures at the edges of the known world. The Carta Marina, by the Swedish Archbishop Olaus Magnus, first printed in Venice in 1539, showed the North Sea around Scandinavia filled with threatening sea creatures. It was the first map to chart the Nordic regions, which had previously been considered terra incognita (unknown lands).

CHARTING BY SONGLINE AND STORY

Australian Aboriginals believe that the topography of their land was created by the journeys, or "songlines", of the Ancestors. These songlines criss-cross Australia, and are sung by Aboriginals as they follow the sacred pathways.

In a hunting culture such as the Alaskan Nunamiut, a young man must learn the details of the hunting terrain before he can join the hunt. He builds up a symbolic map of the local topography by listening to the myths of spirits and heroes who populate the hunting grounds.

THE COMPASS

For some people the compass is a neutral symbol that unifies the people of the Earth, since we all share the directions north, south, east and west. However, it is also a symbol of exploration, orientation, expansion and even the conquering of nature. The phrase "moral compass" is now commonly used in the United States to refer to morally "straight" actions.

Practitioners of the geomantic art of feng shui (which means "wind and water") use a special circular magnetic compass known as the *luo pan* to locate houses and tombs where the energies are in harmonious balance for good fortune. Dragon lines, or dragon currents, which are thought to run through the land, consist of a negative yin current, symbolized by a white tiger, and a positive yang current, symbolized by the blue dragon. A yin countryside will have gently undulating feminine features, and a yang landscape will have sharp or mountainous male features.

ORIENTATION

Travellers and explorers on land and sea have, since ancient times, orientated themselves according to the positions of the stars in the night sky. Orientation is necessary both in everyday reality, to know where we are and where we are going, and for our personal and cultural sense of meaning and identity. Many cultures consider a place sacred to them to be the centre of the world, this might be represented by a holy mountain, world tree or sacred site; the people will "centre" themselves in relation to it in an act of renewal or balancing of nature and spirit.

Places of worship such as mosques, temples and churches, and graves and burial grounds, often align with the east-west axis, the directions of the rising and setting sun. Wherever they are in the world, Moslems face their sacred centre, Mecca, in daily prayer. Native Americans offer prayers to the four cosmic directions, often beginning with the east, where the sun rises.

THE HORIZON

An important orientation symbol, the horizon represents the furthest point the eye can see on the earthly plane. It is the place of vision, exploration and new discoveries. The sun on the horizon signals the dawn of a new day, world or era, and points to the potential for new beginnings and bright futures.

SACRED JOURNEYS

Myths and legend are filled with stories of journeys. Tales of migration, exploration, conquest, heroic quests and pilgrimage serve to focus or renew a people's identity, commune with the gods and spirits, and justify or honour their relationship with the land.

The Hebrew story of the Exodus describes how Moses led the Israelites out of servitude to a land promised to them by God. The Aztec migration of the 12th century was a journey of cultural renewal, in which the Mexica people were guided by the god Huitzilopochtli in their travels from the island of Aztlan to Tenochtitlan, their future capital.

A pilgrimage is a symbolic journey – representing spiritual reorientation, religious devotion, healing and renewal – through a sacred or meaningful landscape. A physical pilgrimage is a liminal act, meaning that at some point the pilgrim crosses a threshold, leaving their everyday life behind them and travelling towards a sacred destination.

In Islam the hajj is a pilgrimage to the holy city of Mecca. The ancient Greeks would travel to receive guidance from the oracle at Delphi, or healing from the shrine of Asklepios at Epidaurus. In 9th-century Europe many pilgrims journeyed to Santiago de Compostela in north-west Spain, at the outer edge of the known world, to visit the miracle-making relics of St James.

Hindus make a pilgrimage to Mount Kailas, the physical manifestation of the mystical Mount Meru, the centre of the world. The journey to Mount Sinai, where Moses received the tablets of the law, like many pilgrimages, reflects the spiritual, as well as physical, journey of Moses himself.

ABOVE The luo pan, or feng shui compass, was used as a source of guidance by ancient Chinese emperors and sages. The encircling symbols, such as 24 mountain stars, 64 hexagrams, 60 stems and branches and 12 mountain dragons, were used in helping to site and orient buildings, and for divination.

LEFT A Muslim prayer involves standing and then bowing or prostrating in the direction of Mecca.

BELOW The horizon often symbolizes our earthly limits, the end and the beginning of new possibilities and exploration.

THE LAND

THE PLOUGH

In ancient times ploughing was considered a spiritual act, as it made the land fruitful. The plough came also to represent the male active principle in relationship to the passive female principle of the Earth: ploughing thus symbolized the act of coitus.

Whether we think we own the land, or whether we borrow it or share it with the gods, it features prominently in world symbolism. From a perspective of ownership, the claiming of land is a symbolic act of power, wealth, nationhood or individual identity. The "discovery", conquest and colonization of other lands is often symbolized by setting foot on the soil, planting a national flag, or writing legal deeds conferring ownership.

For many indigenous peoples land is not owned by individuals but is understood as a living entity or divine gift, which warrants respect and relationship. The indigenous peoples of the Philippines, for example, consider the land as God's gift, and its ownership is assigned to their ancestors and the nature spirits. The land is held by them in trust and guardianship.

EARTHQUAKES

Understandably, the shock and turmoil of earthquakes have often been associated with the anger of the gods in reaction to the degeneracy of the people. The Japanese considered seismic activity to come from the storm god Susano-O, and the Greeks believed that the storm god Poseidon, also known as Enosicthon ("earth shaker"), was the cause of earthquakes. According to Plato, earthquakes and floods consumed the legendary civilization of Atlantis in a single day.

Earthquakes may be taken as omens predicting a huge change in religion or politics: the New Testament describes the quaking of the Earth at the time of Christ's death. Like other natural disasters, earthquakes frequently symbolize the vulnerable qualities of humanity in relation to the natural forces of the Earth.

THE SOIL

Fundamental to food production, soil is seen as "black gold" by agrarian societies. The Burmese consider it to be as valuable as metals such as gold, silver, iron, copper, lead and tin. Many creation myths tell of humans

LEFT In antiquity, earthquakes were seen as a sign of a deity's wrath, and early Christianity was no exception: here it is angelic trumpets that shake the Earth.

being shaped from clay, and we all share a dependence on the life-sustaining fertility of the soil.

Soil from a particular field or region may possess special qualities or essences. The Finno-Ugric people known as the Chuvash practise a ritual in which they "steal" a clod of earth from a productive field nearby to improve the fertility of their own land. Modern biodynamic growers make special preparations such as burying herbs in a cow horn during an astrologically significant time, then homoeopathically potentizing the mixture by stirring it in water and spreading it on the land. This is said to concentrate cosmic forces in the soil, so raising the vitality of the plants and those who eat them.

The fertility ritual of performing sexual intercourse in a field is common in pagan traditions. It is also found in a Greek myth about Demeter, goddess of the soil. She and the Cretan youth Iasion had sex in a thrice-ploughed field, as a result of which she bore a son, Ploutos ("wealth").

MOUNTAINS

A natural symbolic significance of mountains is that they are the part of Earth closest to the heavens, where humans may communicate with the gods. A high peak is frequently held sacred by the local culture as it is considered to be the world axis, linking Earth with Heaven. Moses climbed to the peak of Mount Sinai to receive the Ten Commandments, and Jesus made his ascent to Heaven from the

Mount of Olives. For Hindus, Jains and Tibetan Buddhists, the mythical Mount Meru is the centre of the universe, with its roots in the underworld and its peaks in the heavens. Its earthly manifestation is Mount Kailash in the Himalayas.

Sometimes mountains are literally thought to be the bodies of divinities. In Shinto tradition, Japan's Mount Fuji is a physical manifestation of the gods. The Navaho of North America believe particular mountains embody important male and female nature spirits. A male spirit stretches across the Chuska and Carrizo chains, with his head lying at Chuska Peak, while the female spirit spans the valley with her head on Navaho Mountain.

STONE AND ROCK

Rocks are symbols of eternity and immovability, and are often associated with divinity – many are thought to be inhabited by particular gods and spirits. Rocks store heat, cold and water, and crystals reflect and refract light – all qualities that lend themselves to symbolism – and astrology associates many precious stones with planetary influences.

The Sami of north-eastern Russia believe that certain stones are inhabited by the spirits that control the surrounding animal

life, and rituals are performed at these rocks to ensure good hunting. The Tungu people believe that the forest master, a fearsome woodland spirit, may take on the form of a rock, and thus they avoid rocks that have an animal or human shape. In Vietnam, stone is endowed with living qualities, and is thought to bleed when it is struck.

Unlike the symbol of the tree, which embodies the cycles of life, stone signifies the eternal and unchanging. The Greek omphalos, or navel stone, represented the birthplace of the cosmos. Ancient standing stones in northern France and the British Isles are thought to have been used by early agrarian societies to pin and harness the powerful energies of the earth, and were commonly aligned with cyclical movements of the cosmos. Stonehenge became the main

ritual centre in the south of England in around 2,100 BC and was probably used for sun worship. The phallic stones of Brittany have been associated with orgiastic rituals and were approached by women wishing to conceive a child, who would rub their bellies with dust and water from the stones' surface. Rocks with holes through them are also believed to have fertilizing qualities, and to pass through the hole can symbolize regeneration through the feminine principle. In parts of Africa, large stones are thought to hold ancestral souls.

ABOVE Tibetan Buddhist pilgrims circle the base of Mount Kailash, sacred mountain to both Buddhists and Hindus, and believed to be the home of the gods.

TOP LEFT Stonehenge is the most famous of England's stone circles, thought to have been built to link in with the movement of the planets.

THE DESERT

Symbolically, the desert may be understood in two different ways. It represents the primordial state before the emergence of life, but may also depict the superficiality of life, beneath which reality lies. The desert is barren and sterile, yet in Christian thought it may also symbolize the most divine grace when infused with the presence of God, and it was the chosen home of the earliest Christian monks, the "desert fathers".

WATER

ABOVE Waves in the ocean symbolize the movement of life from its most gentle to its most stormy aspects.

Like the other fundamental elements of life, water plays an important part in world symbolism and creation myth. It often represents the source of life, but also inevitably leads to death or the underworld. Water moves downward from above, always taking the easiest course, and for this reason it is a powerful shape-shifting symbol. Water is both dynamic and chaotic, moving in waves and spirals and never taking a straight path. Water's sacred powers are universal; as a psychological symbol it is linked with the unconscious, the soul, feelings and the flow of life.

POSEIDON

The Greek god Poseidon was the ruler of waters and earthquakes. He was a raging and stormy god who provoked intense fear and possessed powers to stir up life, using his trident to create surges of thunder, rolling waves and lightning. Poseidon had affairs with both goddesses and mortal women, who gave birth to monsters, heroes, and even the legendary ram with the golden fleece. His sacred animals were the horse, a symbol of gushing springs, and the bull, representing Poseidon's fertilizing power.

THE OCEAN

The vastness of the oceans of the world explains how a limitless body of water was often the precondition for creation in many mythologies. As bearers of all life, oceans have been endowed with maternal and life-giving qualities, nourishing those who live from her fruits. But seas are also unpredictable, representing sudden danger, lurking monsters, storms and the underworld.

For early Jewish writers the sea was a creation symbol. Conversely, the Dead Sea, which is saturated with salt, is lifeless and is described in Hebrew symbolism as a spiritual wilderness. The iniquitous cities of Sodom and Gomorrah are thought to have been on the southern shore of the Dead Sea.

RIVERS

A flowing river commonly represents time, history or the span of a human life. Its source can represent conception and birth, while its outlet into the sea often symbolizes death and the afterlife. Islamic, Jewish, Christian, Hindu and Buddhist traditions tell of four rivers of life that flow from paradise towards the four directions, symbolically dividing the earth into quarters. They are associated with enlightenment, spiritual power, nourishment and death.

The life-giving nature of rivers probably relates to the fertility of their banks, which led early civilizations to grow up around the Nile in Egypt, the Indus in India, and the Tigris and Euphrates in Mesopotamia. Rivers are also natural boundaries, and mythical rivers often separate the dead from the living, such as the sacred Styx that bounded Hades, and the Japanese Sanzunokawa.

The Yoruba of West Africa believe that the goddess Yemoja transformed into the river Ogun. In Russia, the Votjak throw offerings into the river to appease the water spirit after the festivities of Twelfth Night. The river Ganges is also revered as the goddess Ganga. Pilgrims take water from her *shakti*, or female

---

EL DORADO

The idea of a spring or fountain that can confer eternal youth occurs in various legends and myths. When the Spaniards landed in what is now Florida they were seeking a city called El Dorado (the gilded one) with a fountain from which flowed the elixir of life.

LEFT A painting that depicts Poseidon, or Neptune, creating the horse, one of his sacred animals, and a symbol of natural springs.

RIGHT This painting of a deluge powerfully illustrates the symbolism of floods as bringers of destruction, but also the possiblity of cleansing and regeneration.

source, in the Himalayas and pour it over a lingam (phallus) at a village called Ramesvaram, 3,200km/2,000 miles away, uniting the river goddess with Shiva, the male god of fertility.

SPRINGS, WELLS AND WATERFALLS

Water emerging from the ground has a special connection with the underworld and the source of life. Wells and springs are commonly associated with the womb of the earth and were thought to have powers to fulfil wishes, foretell the future and confer healing. In Europe, holy wells sprang up in sacred places where saints had been martyred, dragons had been defeated or the Virgin Mary had appeared. Those known as "granny wells" were believed to aid fertility and childbirth, and a closed well symbolized virginity.

Prophecies were often read in wells or pools by observing movements in the water surface, patterns made by floating leaves, or fish and eels swimming in their depths. At Glastonbury, in Somerset, England, the waters of the Chalice Well were said to be tinged red by the blood of Christ, which was carried to England in the Holy Grail.

Springs and wells commonly symbolize the source of life. The Zuñi people of New Mexico believe that the first humans emerged via springs from the underworld, and also tell of a plumed serpent living in the waters of their sacred springs. The Zuñi therefore avoid killing snakes to protect their water supply.

WHIRLPOOLS

The interaction of opposing currents in large bodies of water leads to vortices, which at their most powerful can suck a boat into the depths. In the Odyssey, the whirlpool that tries to suck Odysseus' boat into the sea is personified as the monster Charybdis, offspring of the gods Gaia and Poseidon. Odysseus survives only by clinging to the branch of an overhanging tree. In his poem The Wasteland, which explores the theme of loss, T.S. Eliot uses a whirlpool to symbolize death and annihilation.

FLOODS

All flood stories can be understood as symbolizing the chaos that arises when humanity is out of alignment with the spiritual laws of nature. The biblical stories of the flood that wiped out the human race probably originated in southern Mesopotamia (now Iraq), where the Tigris and Euphrates meet – a fertile area prone to severe floods, which may also have been the origin of the Garden of Eden. The biblical story of Noah

describes the Flood as God's punishment of human sinfulness. Noah, the virtuous man, builds an ark and survives the flood, eventually repopulating the world. In the Babylonian epic of Gilgamesh, Utnapishtim tells Gilgamesh of a seven-day flood, which he survived by building a ship for his family, servants and animals; it finally came to rest upon a mountaintop, whereupon the gods granted Utnapishtim and his wife immortality.

Flood stories are told in many other cultures. The Kimberley people of Western Australia have a place called Wullunggnari, where three stones represent a Dreamtime flood that devastated all, except for a boy and a girl, who grabbed the tail of a kangaroo that took them to higher ground. The two became the ancestors of all human beings.

A SIP OF WISDOM

The Norse God Odin sacrificed one of his eyes in exchange for sipping the water from the wisdom-giving fountain of the nature spirit Mimir.

ABOVE Whirlpools can represent the change from one state to another, for example life to death. Many animistic cultures believed that spirits dwelled within whirlpools.

WATER AND ISLAM

In the Islamic tradition water features centrally as the source and sustenance of life and for purification. Rain, rivers and fountains are symbolic of the benevolence and mercy of Allah, who is said to love those who purify themselves with water.

AIR AND SKY

ABOVE In mystical Islam, clouds are a symbol of the primordial, unknowable state of Allah before creation.

ABOVE RIGHT In many cultures, thunder and lightning are symbols of divine power.

The skies are the dwelling place of the gods, who control the elemental forces that impact on human life on earth, inspiring both fear and wonder. Hence clouds, wind and storm, thunder and lightning have all been seen as divine manifestations and imbued with symbolic associations. Air fills the space between earth and sky and in symbolic terms is linked with the wind, the breath and spirit. It is an invisible, animating force that links the individual with the cosmos, and very often is the medium by which the gods communicate with humankind. Air is usually related to the masculine archetype.

WEATHER VANE

The wind is a symbol of change – a new wind direction signals changing weather conditions. On churches, the traditional design for a weathervane is a cockerel perched on top of a cross indicating the four directions. The bird symbolizes watchfulness against evil, which could be "blown in" by the wind.

THE WIND

Typically, the wind is associated with the four compass directions. Each is represented by different deities or qualities, and is the harbinger of different weather conditions according to the local climate. Along the north-west coast of America, the native Tsimshian believe that the four great winds were the great chiefs of the four corners of the world; after deliberating how their powers should be balanced, the four seasons were established. For the ancient Greeks, the four winds were viewed as boisterous and rebellious gods imprisoned in the caverns of Aeolus, chief god of the winds; their names were Boreas (the north wind), Auster (the south wind), Eureus (the east and morning wind) and Zephyr (the west and evening wind).

Knowledge of air currents and their effects is central to the Chinese art of feng shui. The Chinese identify eight rather than four winds, corresponding to the eight trigrams that form the basis of the I Ching. According to one legend, the wind was the creation of the White Tiger of the West, while in another story the winds were let out of a sack. The Japanese god Fujin was also said to keep the wind in a sack. The Celts used their knowledge of the winds to predict the weather, while the supernatural "Druid's wind", created at will by the exhalations of a Druid, signified power over the elements and allied the breath with the wind as a vehicle for magic.

Among the Native American Apache, the whorls on the

fingertips are said to show the path of the wind entering the body at the time of creation, while the whorls on the soles of the feet show how the wind (or soul) will leave the body at death. The wind is widely thought to communicate with humans: among the Navajo, Wind's Child whispers to the heroes of their stories. Alternatively, the wind may "speak" through an instrument: examples include the bull roarer used by Australian Aboriginals and Native American shamans, and the Aeolian harp of the ancient Greeks. The wind's many "moods" are described in vocal terms such as "roaring", "sighing" or "whispering".

CLOUDS

Because of their cloaking character and their connection with the heavens, clouds are associated with the mysteries of the divine in many traditions. In the Judaeo-Christian tradition, clouds sometimes indicate the presence of God: in the Old Testament he appeared as a pillar of cloud to lead his people through the desert during the Exodus, and in Christian iconography he is sometimes represented as a hand emerging from a cloud, while Christ is said to have ascended to Heaven on a cloud. The Taoist immortals rose up to Heaven on clouds and, in Norse mythology, the Valkyries (female spirits and servants of Odin) rode on clouds.

As bringers of rain, clouds are connected with fertility and nature's abundance. In China, the word for cloud is a homonym for

RIGHT The Norse god of thunder, Thor, wields his mighty hammer, Mjölnir, in a fight against giants.

RIGHT The Norse god of thunder, Thor, wields his mighty hammer, Mjölnir, in a fight against giants.

WIND OF THE SOUL

In some traditions, it is thought that the vital energy of the cosmos is carried in the air, so that when people breathe, they are breathing in life force, known to the Chinese as chi and to Hindus as prana. The Inuit have a similar concept, known as sila, an all-pervasive, life-giving spirit that connects every living being with the rhythms of the universe. When a person is out of touch with sila, they are disconnected from their spirit.

"fortune", associating clouds with good luck. It is also said that wispy dawn clouds brought the five Chinese elements (fire, water, air, earth and metal) down from the five sacred mountaintops, and that clouds were formed from the union of yin and yang. In Taoism, they are symbols of the state that humans must pass through before reaching enlightenment – the mental fog that exists before clarity is attained. The colloquial expression "head in the clouds" suggests someone who is lost in fanciful ideas and out of touch with reality, while "living under a cloud" suggests a burden or disgrace. The Maori name for New Zealand – Aotearoa – means "Land of the Long White Cloud".

STORMS

Violent winds such as hurricanes, whirlwinds and tornadoes are symbols of elemental and divine power. Storm deities are figures of awesome power who embody the forces of disorder and turmoil; they include the Japanese Susano-O, the ancient Greek Poseidon

and the Maya storm god, Huracán, from whom we get the word "hurricane". As bringers of rain, they may also be associated with fertility, as with Baal, the ancient Canaanite storm god. The Maori say that blustery winds and storms are created by the wind god Tawiri-Matea to punish his disobedient brother Tane-Mahuta (god of mankind and the forests), who separated their parents, the earth and sky, to create light. In the West, storms have been seen as the work of the devil. In some Native American traditions, moths are associated with whirlwinds because of the swirly pattern of their cocoons and the whirring noise of their wings.

Storms are often associated with warrior gods and supreme male deities: Indra, the Hindu warrior god, was known as Vajiri ("wielder of thunderbolts") as thunder and lightning were his chief weapons, and a thunderbolt was the main weapon of the supreme Greek god, Zeus.

In the Bible, thunder is the voice of an angry God. The Celts interpreted it as a cosmic disturbance, a punishment from the gods who were invoking the wrath of the elements. In Africa, thunder and lightning are also associated with earthly rulers. The Yoruba of West Africa believe that Shango, the great god of thunder, was the greatest of their warrior-monarchs, while in Benin, thunderbolts are symbols of kingship, sometimes shown as brass pythons zigzagging down from the turrets of high buildings.

In Hinduism and Buddhism, a diamond-shaped thunderbolt

(vajra) symbolizes destructive and creative powers – destroying illusions and wrongdoing so that clarity and good can prevail. In Native American myth, the spirit of thunder and lightning is symbolized by the thunderbird, a fierce beast but also a protector of humanity; thunderstorms are believed to be the sound of its battles against underworld beings.

THUNDER HAMMERS

In many cultures the hammer or axe is a symbol of thunder and lightning. The symbol of Shango, the thunder god of the Yoruba, is a double-headed axe, representing the thunderbolts of stone that the god unleashes from the heavens. In Norse mythology, Mjölnir was the hammer of the thunder god Thor. Mjölnir created lightning when struck against stone and could turn into a thunderbolt when it was thrown. It was also a symbol of Thor's beneficence and was used in ceremonies to bless infants and brides.

BELOW This relief of the Canaanite god Baal shows his status as the god of storms by depicting him holding a thunderbolt, but Baal was also associated with fertility because of his rain-bringing qualities.

FIRE

The symbolism of fire is wide-ranging, though it repeatedly arises as a central motif for the life force. It can be an intimate and personal force of love, passion and warmth, or aggressively pent up in the form of hatefulness and revenge. But fire is also a universal symbol of divine power, wrath or truth, and also of the uncontrolled forces of nature wreaking destruction and bringing about renewal. In many world cosmologies fire is associated with both creation and apocalypse, shining in paradise and burning in Hell.

Fire has been harnessed by humans for protection, light and

warmth, and as a focus for stories, trance and dreaming. It is an essential element of transformation in cooking, initiation and funerary rites, and in driving the physical and spiritual processes of alchemy and science. The Chinese associate fire, rising upwards, with yang, or male, qualities. It is an active element associated with creativity and upward striving, and never rests until it has consumed that which fuels it.

Fire is often associated with strong emotions, conflict and war. Conflict can be the source of great emotional energy, and, like a fire, can lead to warmth, heat, motivation and light, but can also burn, damage and destroy. In the alchemical sense, the fire of conflict can truly lead to transformation, as long as it is neither given too much air, nor deprived of air or consciousness.

FIRE THEFT

The theft of fire is a symbolic theme pointing to its origins and its value to humanity. The act separates humans from animals in harnessing a force unavailable to

them. Australian Aboriginal myths tell of the secret of fire being stolen from the birds or animals. In Greek mythology, the cunning Prometheus stole fire for humankind from the supreme god Zeus. In revenge, Zeus ordered the creation of the first woman, Pandora, and presented her to Prometheus' brother. She brought with her a box containing great afflictions, which spread over the earth.

VOLCANOES

Every volcano in the world has a particular character or personality, from dormant giants erupting violently after long periods of time, to volatile fuming mountains that never quite simmer down. Whatever their character, volcanoes command both respect and fear. Psychologically they symbolize power, volatility and simmering or pent-up anger, followed by outbursts of violent aggression.

Vulcano was the name of a small island off Sicily, and also the chimney for the forge of Vulcan, the Roman blacksmith god. In his forge Vulcan beat out

THE PHOENIX

A mythical bird of Arabia, the phoenix was the size of an eagle with magnificent scarlet and gold feathers. At the end of its life it made a fire from its own nest and was consumed in flames, then reborn from the ashes. The ancient Egyptians viewed the phoenix as a symbol of immortality, while Christians related the myth to the resurrection and for Romans it represented Rome's undying nature. The Chinese saw the phoenix as a gentle creature, feeding on dewdrops and, through the union of the energies of yin and yang, embodying the qualities of virtue, grace, wealth and power.

FIREWORKS

It is thought that gunpowder was invented either in China or in India. The first firecrackers were made in the Chinese Han Dynasty (206 BC-AD 220) and was originally used to frighten away evil spirits. Later it was associated with prayers for happiness and prosperity. In America the early settlers celebrated holidays by firing black gunpowder. Nowadays, when many rites of passage have been lost, fireworks are used in dramatic displays marking important events such as New Year and American Independence Day.

MAYA FIRE CEREMONIES

The Maya believed that by creating a vortex of energy they could open a portal to the spirit worlds of the ancestors, through which they could pay respect and receive healing. They formed a sacred fire by drawing a circle of sugar on the ground, then placing on it resin, cedar, sage, rosemary, tobacco, lavender, flowers, and finally chocolate and honey, representing life's sweetness. The circle was set alight, with the belief that the offerings would be answered with blessings.

thunderbolts for Jupiter and weaponry for Mars, the god of war. Vesuvius in Italy is well known for entirely burying in ash the Roman towns of Pompeii and Stabiae in AD 79. The Roman poet Virgil (70 BC-AD 19) described its craters as seeping with the blood of giants, and wrote that a giant called Alyconeus lay beneath it. At the time of the eruptions, stories emerged of giants leaping through the smoke and ripping the mountainside to pieces.

In Hawaii, the islands have been formed by continuous volcanic activity, and legends tell of Pele, a most beautiful goddess of volcanoes, who is prone to periodic outbursts of anger. She caused earthquakes through the irate stamping of her feet and made volcanoes erupt by digging in the earth with her magic stick, the Pa'oa. Kilauea is the most active volcano on earth and is considered to be Pele's home.

Volcanoes are often associated with the wrath of the gods, but are also sources of light, power, and the tremendous fertility of volcanic ash. In British Columbia, the Tsimshian people believe that

the trickster Raven brought light to humanity from a volcano.

The Aztec goddess of the hearth, home and fertility was also the goddess of the volcano. She was a symbol of both pleasure and pain, and was the ruler of wealth and precious stones. The Taal volcano in the Philippines, which enchantingly floats in the Taal Lake, is one of the smallest volcanoes and yet is considered to be deadly. It is said to symbolize the fearless strength of the people of the Batangas province, which is hidden beneath their apparent calmness.

FIRE IN RELIGION

In many religious traditions, fire is associated with the truths and illusions organizing spiritual experience. Zoroastrians consider fire to be the source of all creation, and each household has a sacred fire, the lighting of which is associated with a blessing. Zoroastrian fire temples are places of community worship, attended by priests who feed the sacred fires with incense. These fires symbolize interaction with Ahura Mazda, the lord of wisdom.

Judaism considers fire to be a fundamental element that should accompany all offerings made to God, and perpetual fires were kept burning at the altar of the Temple. The image of the angel of the Lord appearing to Moses through a burning bush illustrates the Hebrew belief that fire signifies true communication from God. In Christianity, candles are a reminder of the presence of God, and also represent hope and life. Fire is a powerful symbol of renewal and baptism, burning away sinfulness to leave only God's truth.

Buddhism often uses fire to symbolize forces that remove a person from enlightenment, such as desire, greed, hatred and ignorance, and therefore the extinguishing of these fires symbolizes nirvana. But Buddhism also uses an inner flame to represent enlightenment.

THE GOMA

Japanese Yamabushi monks, adherents of Tendai Buddhism, have performed Goma fire cere-monies for 12 cen-turies, to appease the wrath of Fudo Myo-o, the lord of calamities such as war, earth-quakes and destruc-tive fire. The heart sutra is chanted to the beat of a drum, followed by the blow-ing of conch shell horns. The priest feeds a fire with oils, seeds and cedar to create the smoke that carries prayers to Fudo Myo-o.

BELOW Jews believed that God's appearance in fire marked it as a true divine communication.

THE RAINBOW

ABOVE The rainbow has variously been associated with healing and good fortune, dreams and imaginary worlds, fertility and childbirth, and even with transsexual experience.

Elusive, ethereal and transient, the rainbow appears symbolically in myth and folklore, sacred tradition, art and science, as well as in contemporary Western culture, with a range of meanings as diverse as its colours. In different traditions the rainbow has been venerated as god and goddess, feared as demon and pestilence, seen as a symbol of optimism and hope, of divine covenant and peace and as an omen of war and retribution. Its arching shape links it symbolically with the circle, the bridge and the bow, while in some traditions it is also associated with the serpent.

THE RAINBOW BRIDGE

The bridge is an archetypal symbol of transition, and in this guise the rainbow is the pathway between Heaven and Earth, or a link between different worlds. In the Japanese creation myth, the twin deities Izanagi and Izanami stand on the Floating Bridge of Heaven to create the land, and a belief of southern Gabon states that human ancestors arrived on Earth by walking down a rainbow. In Norse myth, Bifrost was the rainbow bridge that connected Asgard, the land of the gods, to Midgard, the earthly realm. Bifrost was said to be very strong and built with more skill than any other structure in the world. Heimdall, the guardian of Asgard, lived beside it to alert the gods to enemy invaders.

The Navajo believe that the rainbow is a bridge between the human and spirit worlds, while shamanic traditions across North America believe that supernatural journeys to the land of the dead involve crossing a rainbow bridge. Shamans of the Buryat, in Siberia, ascend to the spirit world via the rainbow, which they symbolize with a pair of red and blue ribbons tied to a ceremonial birch tree. Some rainbow bridges are manmade structures: the name was given to Chinese bridges of woven construction, spanning streams that were too wide or swift for conventional pier bridges – one built in the 13th century still bears traffic today. There are also rainbow bridges over the Niagara River and in Tokyo Bay.

DIVINE PRESENCE

The rainbow is often interpreted as a divine attribute and a sign of divine presence. Ishtar, the Babylonian goddess of love and war, wore an iridescent necklace, and the Inca believed that rainbows were the feather crown of Illapa, the god of thunder and rain. The bow – the archer's weapon – can betoken the god's wrath. Indra, the Hindu god of war, shot his thunderbolt from a rainbow, and in Cambodia and parts of India the rainbow is known as "Indra's Bow". Tiermes, the thunder god of the Lapps of Scandinavia, used the rainbow to fire arrows at evil spirits.

In contrast, in the Judaeo-Christian tradition the rainbow is a sign of peace and compassion, a symbol of God's promise after the Flood not to destroy humankind. Christ is sometimes shown enthroned on a rainbow at the Last Judgement, demonstrating

RIGHT The gods of the Vikings descend from Heaven to Earth using the rainbow bridge that the Norse legends named Bifrost.

his heavenly power and his mercy. In Tibet, where rainbows occur at transitional times of the year and indicate changing weather, they are associated with blessings from the bodhisattvas of Tibetan Buddhism.

There is a widespread belief among Central African Pygmies that the rainbow is an instrument of divine communication, and in some cultures it marks the location of a divinity or person of high birth: in Hawaiian folklore the noblewoman Hoamakeikekula was tracked by following a rainbow. The rainbow was associated with Iris, the golden-winged messenger of the Greek gods, who is often depicted holding a caduceus, the messenger's snake-entwined staff. The Maya made offerings of gold and silver to the patron deity of women, Ixchel, goddess of medicine, fertility and the rainbow, who controlled the rain.

RAINBOW LEGENDS

There are many legends and customs surrounding rainbows. The Sioux say that the rainbow is where all the bright flowers are stored before and after their brief blooming period on earth. In Irish folklore, the leprechaun is a mischievous sprite who keeps a pot of gold at the end of the rainbow; in Celtic tradition, rainbow coins were to be found there, buried in the earth but revealed after heavy storms.

However, rainbows are not always associated with beauty and

good fortune. Ancient Peruvians claimed that if a rainbow were to enter a person's body, it would cause illness; a cure was to unravel a ball of rainbow-coloured threads to undo the rainbow's ill effects. Ideas of rainbow-borne disease also appear throughout Africa, Asia and Australia: for the Senoi of Malaysia, walking underneath a rainbow causes fatal fever, and Australian Aboriginals associate it with leprosy. Pointing at rainbows is considered foolhardy in many parts of the world: Hungarian folk belief insists the pointing finger will wither, while the Sumu of

Honduras and Nicaragua hide their children in huts to stop them pointing or even looking at a rainbow. Getting jaundice, losing an eye, being struck by lightning or even disappearing are some of the dangers associated with rainbows.

ABOVE When Christ is pictured with a rainbow in Christian art it is usually a symbol of the merciful aspects of his heavenly powers.

THE RAINBOW BODY

Related to the chakra system, the rainbow body may be thought of as fields of energy surrounding the human body, each associated with different qualities.

Level	Colour	Body	Qualities
1st outermost circle or layer	red	physical (temporal)	the foundation upon which all other levels are constructed
2nd	orange	etheric (temporal)	early emotional environment and formative influences; the body's energy pattern
3rd	yellow	astral (transitional)	influences of culture and society, such as religious and educational institutions, and how these shape thought and action
4th	green	mental (transitional)	achieves purpose in life through relationship with others; interface between the temporal and eternal
5th	blue	causal (transpersonal)	attuned to soul; repository of the soul's memories, empowers its journey
6th	indigo	diamond (bliss body) (transpersonal)	thinking superseded by intuitively received knowing
7th innermost layer or core	violet	celestial (eternal)	enlightenment; the individual soul merges into the cosmos, union with the divine

PART THREE

ALL ABOUT
DREAMING

DREAMING THROUGH HISTORY

Since time immemorial, our dreams have been a source of awe and wonder. At various points in history, they have been seen as messages from the gods, and supernatural experiences involving visions of the future, as well as indications of the state of our physical and mental health. Dreams have been used to shed light on the past, gain understanding of the present, and even to predict the future. This has not only been true for individuals, but also for whole nations. Some dreams have even changed the course of history.

RIGHT Dreams have played an important role in some of the world's major religions, including Buddhism and Christianity.

SINCE THE DAWN OF TIME

HOW LONG IS IT SINCE WE BEGAN DREAMING? WE HAVE NO SURE WAY OF KNOWING, BUT STRETCHING BACK INTO THE
MISTS OF PREHISTORY, CAVE PAINTINGS IN FRANCE FROM THE NEANDERTHAL PERIOD SEEM TO INDICATE SOME SORT OF
DREAM DRAWINGS ABOVE THE HEADS OF THE HUNTERS. THOUSANDS OF YEARS LATER WHEN PEOPLE BEGAN TO DISCOVER
WAYS OF WRITING, THEY NOTED DOWN THEIR DREAMS. WE KNOW THAT DREAMING WAS AN IMPORTANT PART OF LIFE IN
THE ANCIENT CIVILIZATIONS OF SUMER, ASSYRIA, BABYLONIA AND EGYPT. DREAMS WERE ASSOCIATED WITH DIVINE OR
SUPERNATURAL POWERS, AND TEMPLES WERE DEDICATED TO THE GODS OF DREAMS.

THE FIRST DREAM RECORDS

Clay tablets dating back to around 3000 BC provide
some of the earliest surviving writings of the human
race. These tablets include the dream books of the
Assyrians and Babylonians, discovered at Ninevah in
the library of Ashurbanipal (c.669-626 BC), an
Assyrian king. Other similar tablets were discovered
during excavations of a pyramid-type temple at
E-zida, in Mesopotamia, on the top of which was a
shrine to Nabu, the Sumerian god of wisdom. The
tablets' cuneiform script reveals fragments of the
Babylonian epic of Gilgamesh, the legendary warrior
king of Sumer. They also tell us about Gilgamesh's
dreams and how his mother, the goddess Ninsun,
interprets them. Her interpretation is often credited
with being the first dream analysis, or at least the
first for which we have a written record.

THE DREAMS OF GILGAMESH

Night after night, the aggressively powerful warrior
king of Sumer, Gilgamesh, was troubled by bad
dreams. Disturbed, Gilgamesh takes the dreams to
his mother, who tells him that someone as powerful
as himself is about to enter his life. She predicted
that his struggles to gain supremacy over the
newcomer will fail, but that the two men will
become close companions and together achieve
great feats. Later on in the epic, Ninsun's
interpretation proves correct when Gilgamesh meets
Enkidu, a "wild man" (an embodiment of an
uncivilized, "primordial" human) who does indeed
become his friend and helps bring Gilgamesh back
down to earth. Further on in the tale, Gilgamesh is
warned in another dream of the death of Enkidu,
which also comes to pass.

ABOVE Gilgamesh, the
warrior king of the
Sumerians, is recorded
as being the first person
in history ever to seek an
interpretation for the
dreams that were
troubling him.
RIGHT Early cave
paintings have a strange,
almost dreamlike quality
about them; are they
portraying everyday life
or are they drawings of
dreams from the dawn of
time itself?

PORTENTOUS DREAMS

The primary interest in dreams at this time seems to have been in the salutary warnings they could provide about the future, although dreams were also used as a form of gambling, where the dream symbols were used to predict lucky wins. Furthermore the Assyrian and Babylonian dream books also reveal a concern with the dangerous aspect of dreams, allegedly sent by demons and spirits of the dead. To protect themselves from such harmful influences, people built temples to Mamu, the Babylonian goddess of dreams, and propitiatory rites were practised in her name. An Za Qa, the god of dreams, was recognized and worshipped by the Sumerians, Assyrians and Babylonians.

MYTHOLOGY OF DREAMS

Looking at the mythology of any ancient civilization has been likened to reading a dream. That is because these stories represent what are sometimes referred to as the "cultural pattern dreams" of that civilization. In other words, the gods and goddesses, the heroes and villains, and the shapes and symbols of the stories are the same ones that people would have dreamt of night after night. These characters represent what are known as "archetypal" images, presenting us with the themes and concerns that have always struck a chord deep within the heart and soul of humankind. Irrespective of time or place, these stories are able to teach or remind us of universal truths.

ABOVE In Babylon vast temples were built dedicated to Mamu, the Babylonian goddess of dreams; and dream interpretation was elevated to the status of a religion.

THE GODDESS ISHTAR

Throughout the ancient world, the Moon was worshipped in various forms. The Babylonian goddess Ishtar was known as Ashtarte in Canaan, Isis in ancient Egypt and Artemis in ancient Greece. Like the moon in its waxing aspect, the goddess is a symbol of fertility and all life emanates from her, yet like the waning or dark moon, she is also the destroyer, the one who disappears into the darkness. However, like the crescent moon, the goddess is reborn and appears once again in her beneficent aspect.

The story of Ishtar's descent into the underworld, where she is tortured and bleeds to death before being revived by the twins Plant and Water of Life, is a myth of regeneration, symbolizing the cyclical nature of life and the passage between worlds.

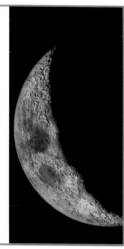

And the goddess Ishtar appeared to each man in a dream, saying: 'I will march before Ashurbanipal, the king whom I have created'.

BABYLONIAN LEGEND

ANCIENT EGYPT

Like the Babylonians, the Egyptians also regarded
dreams as warnings, although they believed they
came from the gods rather than from spirits or
demons. The Egyptians viewed dreams as a portal, a
gateway to another world which they passed
through every night. Here in this other world they
could travel in their astral or "dream body",
gathering knowledge of far distant places,
conversing with the gods and meeting with the
spirits of the dead. In general, dreams were regarded
as helpful, although they could also be malevolent.
In order to avert disaster the gods demanded
penance and sacrifices, although they would also
answer questions put to them by the dreamer in a
practice known as "dream incubation".

DREAM INCUBATION

The practice of dream incubation was widely
observed throughout the ancient world, although
our first record of it comes from ancient Egypt.
Throughout the land, a number of temples, known
as "serapeums", were dedicated to Serapis, the god
of dreams and dreaming. The most famous of these
was at Memphis, dating back to around 3000 BC.

Thebes was another important site. It was in such
temples that dream incubation was practised. This
was an intensely ritualistic procedure intended to
encourage an especially informative dream from the
gods. Dream incubation seems to have been very
popular and was used for a variety of purposes,
including seeking remedies for particular illnesses,
obtaining guidance on relationship and/or personal
issues and predicting what the future had in store.
The practice was often dedicated to Imhotep, the
god of healing.

INCUBATION RITUALS

Ritualistic preparations for dream incubation were
extremely complex and could last for several days.
Typically the incubant (the dreamer) would take part
in purification practices, such as fasting, bathing and
abstaining from sex, they would also make prayers
and offerings to the gods. Sometimes harmless
snakes were placed around the dreamer's bed at the
serapeum and the dreamer would then go to sleep
with his or her request in mind. Through their own
rituals, while the dreamer slept, the temple priests
often helped to "seed" the dreamer's request. At
times a "stand-in" dreamer was used in place of the

THE DREAM OF THOTMES IV

One very early prophetic dream dates back to around 1420 BC. It is recorded on a sheet of granite and held between the paws of the great sphinx at Giza where it can still be seen today (right).

While sleeping next to the sphinx, Thotmes dreamt that he would one day be ruler of Egypt and have a long and prosperous reign. However, for the dream to come true, the gods told Thotmes that he had to clear away the sand from the statue. At that time, the sphinx was neglected and beginning to disappear under the sand.

When Thotmes awoke he did as he had been instructed and then vowed to keep the sphinx clean and well cared for, for the rest of his life. Thotmes later went on to become one of Egypt's pharaohs.

person who was seeking help. The stand-in would be someone who was known to be a gifted dreamer. When the dreamer or the stand-in awoke, the dream would be related to the oracles or priests for their interpretation.

DREAM INTERPRETATIONS

Ancient Egyptian papyri reveal some of the conclusions the Egyptians reached about dream interpretation. One document, dating back to the 13th dynasty (1770 BC), concludes that if a woman dreams of kissing her husband, trouble lies ahead. This is an example of "opposites", in which it is thought that a dream means the reverse of what it appears to suggest.

One of the most famous dream records of the Egyptian era is the "Chester Beatty" papyrus, which was inscribed around 1350 BC. It came from Thebes and contains references to around 200 dreams, many of which date from an earlier period. Particularly interesting are the details of three modes of interpretation, which anticipate principles used by Freud centuries later, these are the detection of hidden associations, the use of opposites, and the use of visual or verbal puns.

DREAM PUNS

Puns in the world of dream interpretation are rather like games of free association, where one thing reminds us of another. Sometimes these "meanings" are catalogued and get handed down in dream dictionaries, where they appear as utter nonsense to later generations, whose cultural references and language are completely different. For instance, the Chester Beatty papyrus reveals that in ancient Egypt to dream about bare buttocks means the dreamer is about to lose his or her parents. This may seem absurd until we realize that the word used for "buttocks" closely resembled the word for "orphan".

DISPOSING OF BAD DREAMS

For dealing with a recurring bad dream, the ancient Egyptians had a curious ritual. On waking after another night of the same dream they would blow out their breath into a special receptacle – usually a wooden cup – which was then thrown into the fire. This symbolic act represented "burning" the dream, its negative power would be destroyed by the fire so that it could never return to haunt the dreamer.

THE CLASSICAL WORLD

ONEIROLOGY IS THE STUDY OF DREAMS. THIS WORD IS DERIVED FROM "ONEIROS", THE WORD FOR DREAMS IN THE ANCIENT
GREEK LANGUAGE. LIKE THEIR KNOWLEDGE IN SO MANY AREAS, THE ANCIENT GREEKS' UNDERSTANDING OF DREAMS WAS
ESPECIALLY SOPHISTICATED AND SEVERAL WELL-KNOWN THINKERS OF THE DAY DEBATED AND GAVE THEIR INSIGHTS ON THE
SUBJECT. THIS INFORMATION WAS LATER EXTENDED AND CLASSIFIED BY THE ROMANS TO GIVE US A WIDE BODY OF
KNOWLEDGE FROM THE CLASSICAL WORLD. BOTH CIVILIZATIONS USED DREAMS AS A FORM OF PREDICTION AND AS A WAY OF
GAINING INSIGHTS INTO THE MIND OF THE DREAMER.

GATES OF HORN AND IVORY

The earliest mention of dreams in Greek literature is
from Homer. We have little information about
Homer or his life, but many historians date his era
as some time in the 700s BC. We know that at this
time there was widespread belief in the divine origin
of dreams, which were regarded as messages to
humanity from Zeus, communicated by Hypnos, the
god of sleep and his son Morpheus, the god of
dreams. However, not all dreams were necessarily
reliable. Homer distinguishes between true and false
dreams, writing that true dreams come through a
"gate of horn", and false through an "ivory gate".
Such distinctions were not merely of theoretical
interest, as to act on a false dream as if it were true
could have disastrous consequences. Centuries later

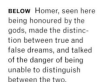

BELOW Homer, seen here
being honoured by the
gods, made the distinc-
tion between true and
false dreams, and talked
of the danger of being
unable to distinguish
between the two.

for instance the Persian leader Xerxes' dreams falsely
convinced him that an attack on Athens would end
victoriously. Acting on this advice Xerxes led his
army to destruction in 480 BC.

HOMER'S ODYSSEY

In his epic work *The Odyssey*, Homer enlarges on the
idea of true and false dreams through the character
of Penelope, who remarks that dreams are awkward
and confusing, for what is in them does not
necessarily come true. She says: "There are two gates
through which these insubstantial visions reach us;
one is of horn and the other of ivory. Those that
come through the ivory gate cheat us with empty
promises that never see fulfilment; while those that
issue from the gate of burnished horn inform the
dreamer what will really happen".

SIGNIFICANT AND NON-SIGNIFICANT DREAMS

Influenced perhaps by Homer's ideas, the ancient
Greeks also distinguished between two types of
dream: the significant and the non-significant.
Significant dreams were the ones which came from
the gods. These were the ones that people wanted to
have when they were about to undertake an
important project, such as a business venture, a
voyage or a new relationship. The non-significant
dreams were more personal to the dreamer. The
gods played no part in these and the way they are
reported makes them sound more like the sort of
dream we experience, for the most part, today.

DREAMS AND HEALING

The tradition of healing temples and dream
incubation is one that was continued by both the
Greeks and Romans, especially for acquiring
information to treat disease. In ancient Greece
famous sleep temples at Oropos and Epidaurus were

dedicated to Asklepios, the god of medicine, although it is believed that hundreds more temples existed throughout the ancient and classical world. The temples were situated in places of natural beauty, surrounded by fragrant plants and herbs, natural springs or shady forests. Another common feature was the serpent, and today the ruins at Epidaurus show us the pit where snakes were kept for healing and incubation purposes. This association of snakes with healing developed into the familiar symbol of the "caduceus", a healing staff entwined by two serpents. Today this symbol is widely used by many healing professions.

HIPPOCRATES

Known as the father of modern-day medicine, the Greek doctor, Hippocrates (460-377 BC), accepted that some dreams were of divine origin and could prophesy events. He endeavoured to put this capacity to scientific use by using the symbolism of dreams to diagnose the dreamer's state of health, associating the microcosm of the human body with the macrocosm of the universe. In his *Treatise on Dreams*, for instance, Hippocrates asserts that bright

stars in a dream indicate good health, whereas to dream of dim stars precedes illness. Dreaming of flowing rivers, he states, indicates problems with the urinary system, while dreaming of floods points to an excess of blood and the need to "bleed" the patient. Such dreams are referred to by Hippocrates as prodromal, from the Greek word *prodromos*, meaning "running before".

ABOVE Hippocrates, the Greek physician, believed dream interpretation was connected to physical sickness – if you dreamt of a specific sickness or disease it meant that you were suffering from it in real life.

THE DELPHIC ORACLE

The word "oracle" also means "answer" and oracle dreams were incubated at the famous site in Delphi (left), widely believed in ancient times to be the centre of the world. The site was situated on sulphurous hot springs and its entrance bore the inscription "know thyself". Hallucinogenic plants, such as henbane and jimsonweed, were burned to put the seer of the oracle into a trance, and make them ready to receive dreams and visions from the gods.

ABOVE Some Greek
philosophers would have
nothing to do with dream
interpretation, whereas
others were convinced
that dreams had mystical
importance. The two
groups debated the
issue endlessly.

THE PHILOSOPHERS

It would be wrong to assume that all Greeks
subscribed to the mystical significance of dreams.
Many famous thinkers challenged this notion and
their ideas have been highly influential in the way
dreams are regarded by Western society. Heraclitus
(450-375 BC) is generally regarded as the first
person on record to proffer a purely rational
explanation. Far from being a communication from
the gods, he asserted, someone's dream world is
entirely personal to them. It has nothing to do with
anything outside of the dreamer's mind and is
simply an ordinary experience, having less
significance than anything that happens while in
waking consciousness. However, perhaps more than
any other thinker, it is Aristotle (384-322 BC) who
comes closest to our modern way of looking at the
meaning of dreams.

ARISTOTLE'S CONTRIBUTION

From his observations of sleeping animals, Aristotle
concludes that it is not only humans who have
dreams. He uses this as evidence to counter any
theory that dreams have any divine or cosmic
pattern or that they have any particular significance.
He also notes that since all external sensations are
reduced or absent during sleep, subjective sensations
must be highlighted. He goes on to assert that
dream images can have an influence on subsequent
behaviour. In that sense dreams can be prophetic, as
our thoughts are influenced by what we have seen
during sleep. He also claims that the insights

THE EMPEROR'S DREAMS

After Calpurnia's prophetic dream about her
husband, Julius Caesar, Caesar's heir, the emperor
Augustus (above) (63 BC-AD 14), made a law
declaring that anyone having a dream about the
emperor's welfare should announce it in the
marketplace. According to another historical text,
Tranquillus' *Lives of the Caesars* Augustus set such
store by dreams that he made a fool of himself. He
went about Rome begging for alms because it had
been predicted that he would do so in a dream.

available from dreams are like objects reflected in
water: when the water of the mind is calm, the
images are easy to see, when the water is troubled,
the reflections become distorted. He says that the
more the mind can be calmed before sleep, the more
the dreamer can learn. Aristotle's theories were
outlined in three seminal works: *On Dreams, On
Sleep and Waking* and *On Prophecy in Sleep*.

DREAMS AND THE HUMAN PSYCHE

In his theories, Aristotle also links the hallucinations
of the mentally ill, the illusions of ordinary people
and the content of dreams and fantasies, concluding
that they may all share a common origin – an idea
which was later developed by the 20th-century
psychologist, Carl Jung. Plato (427-347 BC), another
of the Greek philosophers, also had ideas about
dreams which predate 20th-century psychology. He
describes the human psyche as possessing "a lawless,
wild beast nature which peers out in sleep". As we

no longer exercise rational control while sleeping, our lust and rage can enjoy free and full expression. Centuries later, such a view would be central to Sigmund Freud's ideas about defining human personality and behaviour.

PROPHETIC DREAMS IN ROME

Accounts of prophetic dreams have occurred throughout history with some of the most well-documented being those foretelling the death of the dreamer or someone close to him or her. The citizens of ancient Rome seemed particularly fascinated by the possibility of this phenomenon and there are several reported instances of such dreams. For instance, the Roman historian Plutarch (AD 45-125) tells us that Calpurnia, the wife of Julius Caesar (100-44 BC), dreamed of Caesar's assassination by Brutus the night before it happened. Similarly the day before Caligula was assassinated, in AD 41, he reputedly dreamed that he was standing beside the heavenly throne of Jupiter, when the god gave him a push with his big toe, causing the emperor to fall to the earth.

DREAM DICTIONARIES

While the Greeks may have brought elements of logic and reason to the world of dreams, it took the orderly Romans to catalogue and classify the information. One of the most outstanding contributions was Artemidorus' five-volume *Oneirocritica* (The Interpretation of Dreams). A Roman soothsayer of the 2nd century AD,

Artemidorus travelled extensively throughout the Roman Empire, researching into dreams and drawing on knowledge from earlier times. His work includes more than 3000 dream reports from his interviewees, and is today acknowledged as the first true dream dictionary ever written.

Artemidorus suggests that dreams are entirely individual and that the contents are relevant only to the dreamer. The dream symbols and imagery that are found in these personal dreams are both cultural and individual, and are influenced by such aspects as the dreamer's health, state of mind and occupation. Artemidorus notes two broad classes of dreams: insomnium are dreams about everyday things and somnium are those that concerned the future. His approach is thorough and systematic and some symbolism is identified. For instance, dreaming of ploughing the earth is regarded as a sexual symbol, while a dream of a mouth represents the dreamer's home. More than a century later, a second *Oneirocriticon* appeared, compiled by Astrampsychus. This one contains such axiomatic statements as "to wear a purple robe threatens a lengthy disease".

ABOVE The assassination of Julius Caesar by Brutus was said to have been foreseen in a dream by his wife, Calpurnia. This detail of the story has survived, and has continued to fascinate people, from ancient Rome to modern times.

She dreamt tonight she saw my statue,
Which like a fountain with an hundred spouts
Did run pure blood; and many lusty Romans
Came smiling, and did bathe their hands in it.

WILLIAM SHAKESPEARE, JULIUS CAESAR

India and the Far East

WHILE THE CIVILIZATIONS OF THE NEAR AND MIDDLE EAST ATTRIBUTED DREAMS TO A DIVINE AGENT, IN INDIA AND THE
FAR EAST THEY WERE REGARDED AS HAVING AN INNER SOURCE. IN CHINA DREAMS WERE THOUGHT TO EMANATE FROM THE
SOUL, WHILE IN INDIA AND TIBET THEY WERE ASSOCIATED WITH A STATE OF MIND. IN ALL THESE CIVILIZATIONS, DREAMS
WERE INEXTRICABLY LINKED WITH THE PHILOSOPHY, SPIRITUALITY AND MYTHOLOGY OF THEIR CULTURES. IN THE FAR EAST,
IN PARTICULAR, SURVIVING TEXTS REVEAL A SOPHISTICATED UNDERSTANDING OF DREAMS, AN UNDERSTANDING ECHOED IN
THE ORAL TRADITIONS OF MANY INDIGENOUS PEOPLES.

THE ATHARVA VEDA

According to legend, the 52 great Rishis (seers) of
ancient India travelled to the highest mountains of
the Himalayas seeking guidance to help humanity.
During their meditations they believed that they
discovered how the universe works. This knowledge
was eventually transcribed into the Vedas, the sacred
books of the Hindus, which scholars date between
1500–1000 BC. One of these texts, the *Atharva Veda*,
contains many references to dreams, providing
information about how they occur, what purpose
they serve and how to interpret them.

LUCKY AND UNLUCKY DREAMS

When trying to make sense of complex information,
a first response is often to classify it into opposites.
This holds as true for dreams as for anything else.
Where other ancient cultures distinguish between
good and bad, divine or demonic, and true or false
dreams, the Vedas focus on the distinction between
"lucky" and "unlucky" dreams, having particular

interest in a dream's predictive power. For instance,
the *Atharva Veda* comments that showing passivity
in a dream is a bad omen, whereas an aggressive
dream is favourable. However if the dreamer
receives any injury, this is considered an ill omen.
The omen is made worse if the injury, such as an
amputation of a limb, is something that could occur
in waking life. The effects of unlucky dreams can be
countered by performing purification rites, such as
burning incenses and ritual bathing.

TIMING AND PERSONALITY

For the first time, the personality type of the
dreamer is taken into account in dream
interpretation. For instance, a depressed person is
more likely to have depressing dreams, while a
hyperactive sort is more likely to have manic
dreams. The *Atharva Veda* also theorizes that a
person's dreams occur in cycles throughout the
night, with the most important dreams occurring
towards the end of the dreaming cycle or later on in

HINDU DEITIES

During the Vedic period a pantheon of Hindu deities
developed. A lot of these gods and goddesses have
strange, dream-like qualities to them. For instance,
Ganesh is the elephant-headed god of wisdom and
"remover of obstacles", and the god Shiva has four
arms, four faces and three eyes. Shiva wears the skin
of a tiger and has a snake entwined around his neck,
representing two powerful demons that he has
defeated. In his fight against a particularly powerful
demon, Shiva calls on the goddess Kali, the "dark side"
of his consort Devi, to help him. Kali (shown left) is
usually depicted wearing a girdle of severed arms and
a necklace of skulls. Her bloodthirsty tongue lolls from
her mouth and she carries a sword in her left hand.
Intoxicated by her murderous killings, she dances on
the bodies of her victims.

the night. In fact the later on in the night a dream occurs, states the Vedas, the more likely, as well as the more quickly, it is to come true.

THE TWO WORLDS

The Vedas also contains texts known as the Upanishads, philosophical works that expose spiritual truths. One of the most elaborate and important of these is known as *Brihadaranyaka*, sometimes described as a "cosmic meditation". This text declares that essentially there are two states, one in this world and one in the other. A third

intermediary state exists: the state of sleep and the land of dreams. It is while we are in the intermediary world that we have the capacity to perceive the real world and the next simultaneously. In this context, the dreaming state is considered to be more important than the waking state because it is then that we have access to realms of knowledge and experience denied to us when we are awake. To this end, techniques such as yoga and meditation were developed to help us "attain" or become more open to this other world, experienced as a place of heavenly bliss.

ABOVE The Hindus believe we can attain enlightenment during our dreams, only for it to evaporate when we wake.

THE FAR EAST

It was not only in India that dreams were linked with spirituality and states of mind. An important Chinese Taoist manuscript, known as the *Lie-tsu*, distinguishes between six different types of dreaming: ordinary dreams, day-residue dreams, dreams of waking, dreams of fear, joyful dreams and terror dreams. Taoism, and later, Buddhism, were hugely influential throughout the Far East. Both of these spiritual traditions assert that the worlds we see in our dreams are more or less identical to the worlds we will experience after death.

THE BARDO

The Book of the Dead is an ancient Tibetan Buddhist text. Written to help prepare the soul for death, it describes death as a dream-like condition. When the soul leaves the physical body it must pass through the "Bardo", which has three distinct illusory states.

RIGHT The Tibetan *Book of the Dead* is a very ancient manuscript written on wooden tablets. In it a dialogue with the dead, who are said to have entered the bardo, the dream state between the living and the dead, is carried out.

As we pass through each state we face a multitude of self-created thought forms which may be pleasant or fearful, according to our thoughts and expectations. By becoming aware at any time that what we are experiencing is an illusion, the soul is elevated to a higher plane and avoids the constant cycle of death and rebirth. Consequently, learning to remain conscious while sleeping, being aware that we are dreaming while still in the dream, is seen by Tibetan Buddhists as a vital part of the spiritual preparation for death. Today in the West this state or technique is referred to as "lucid dreaming".

P'O AND HUN

In ancient China, it was believed that we possess two types of soul. The material soul, or "p'o" motivates us in daily life and is implicit in our physical make-up. This soul dies when the body dies. Additionally, we possess an eternal soul, or "hun", which survives us at death, leaving the physical body and the material world for a different plane of existence.

Every night during sleep, the hun temporarily separates from the dreamer's resting body to travel the world of dreams. This concept is similar to the idea many Western esoteric traditions hold today of the dream body and astral travel. As the dreamer sleeps, the hun communicates with spirits, demons and ghosts, bringing back memories of its nightly travels to the dreamer.

THE CITY OF DREAMS

In ancient China, people believed in a divine City of Dreams. Known as Ch'eng Huang, the city was thought to hang halfway between heaven and earth and is the place we go to when asleep. To enter the celestial city the dreamer had to pass through the "moongate", which necessitated being pure in mind and body. Once safely inside the city, the dreamer could leave their body and astral travel anywhere in the world. In this context, it is interesting to note that the Chinese had a god of the South Pole, a geographical region they had not actually discovered. Did the Chinese know of its existence because they had travelled there in their dreams?

BEDROOM RITUALS

To pass through the moongate easily, rituals were practised before going to sleep. These included lighting incense and proceeding around the bedroom in an anti-clockwise direction, beginning in the east and moving through south, west and north before getting into bed. It was also important to make sure the bedroom was decorated in auspicious colours (typically red and gold), and to make sure that nothing hung over the bed which could interfere with the exit of the spirit body. Consequently it was thought inadvisable to sleep under such things as beams, canopies, mirrors or lights. Similarly great care had to be taken to ensure that the spirit body could safely return to the dreamer's physical body. Playing tricks on a sleeping person, such as altering their physical appearance in some way, or else waking someone up too abruptly was believed to be dangerous. The returning soul needed to be able to recognize the sleeping body and it also needed time to re-enter the body. If the soul could not return for some reason, the sleeper would die.

ABOVE The Chinese believe that every part of the natural landscape is ruled by mythical creatures who protect it. **ABOVE LEFT** The Chinese landscape has a dreamlike quality.

DREAMS AND ASTROLOGY

Written around AD 640, the earliest Chinese book of dream interpretations is the *Meng Shu*. It suggests that many factors should be taken into account before interpreting a dream. These include the time of year and astrological factors such as the position of the planets. It was also believed that external stimuli could be reflected in dreams. Sleeping on a belt, for instance, might produce dreams of a snake.

MU JEN DOLLS

In ancient China, great faith was placed in Mu Jen, the wooden man, or dream doll. For instance, if a child was suffering nightmares, the parents would "give" the dream to the Mu Jen doll, and he would then be sent away, taking the bad dream with him. Alternatively, if a dreamer wanted to make her wish come true, she would whisper it to the doll and then place him under her pillow as she slept. It was believed that during sleep the Mu Jen would come to life and be your "sacred warrior", capable of granting a person's wishes, protecting them from harm, and generally acting as a friend and helper.

EUROPEAN TRADITIONS

THE CUSTOM OF SLEEPING AT HOLY PLACES TO INCUBATE PARTICULAR DREAMS WAS NOT CONFINED TO THE ANCIENT AND CLASSICAL WORLD. THROUGHOUT EUROPE, THE PAGAN CELTS AND THE EARLY CHRISTIANS ALIKE PRACTISED THE SAME PROCEDURE, SLEEPING AT SHRINES TO ENCOURAGE VISIONS AND DREAMS OF HEALING POWER. FOR THE CELTS, THESE SACRED SPOTS WERE ASSOCIATED WITH NATURE SPIRITS, AND FOR THE CHRISTIANS WITH THE SAINTS AND MARTYRS OF THE EARLY CHURCH. AS THE INFLUENCE OF THE CHURCH BECAME MORE WIDESPREAD HOWEVER, DREAMS WERE REGARDED WITH INCREASED SUSPICION UNTIL, BY THE MIDDLE AGES, THEY WERE LARGELY SEEN AS THE DEVIL'S WORK.

CELTIC WISDOM

The Celts believed that all things possess an immortal soul, which exists through many lifetimes, learning from its experiences on the earthly plane in its journey towards perfection. To ascertain the will of the gods and help the soul along its way, many methods of prophecy and divination were used. The natural world was believed to be an infinite source of magic and spiritual wisdom, and symbolic significance was given to such things as the shape of clouds, a particular animal or plant species, as well as the portents of dreams. Dreams were interpreted by the druid, which literally means the "oak seer", or "one who sees with the aid of the oak". In fact, trees were especially important, and specific qualities were attributed to each species. Dreams were incubated in sacred groves, where the dreamer could ask the spirit of the trees for healing and assistance.

THE EARLY CHURCH

Traditional Celtic lore was frowned upon by Catholic doctrine, but theologians of the early Church also began to comment on their dreams. In his treatise *On the Making of Man* (380 AD), Gregory

BELOW RIGHT Dreams were part of the religious and artistic world of the Celts and artefacts from this era reflect this.
BELOW Dreams to early cultures were powerful messages from the gods, from nature, and from deep within. They were never to be ignored.

THE SALMON OF WISDOM

Stories about the source of all knowledge are practically universal. These symbolic tales have a rich, dream-like quality to them.

In the Irish Celtic tradition, the well of Nine Hazels is the dwelling place of the Salmon of Wisdom. The Salmon became wise when he imbibed the hazel nuts that fell into the well from the nine hazel trees. It is said that whoever catches and eats the salmon, will be imbued with its wisdom and filled with "imbas", or inspiration. Finn Eces, an elderly druid, captures the salmon and asks his young apprentice, Fionn mac Cumhail, to cook it for him. While it is cooking, some liquor from the fish splashes on to Fionn's thumb, and it is he and not Finn who gains the inspiration from the well.

of Nyssa asserts that dreams occur when the intellect and senses are at rest during sleep. The actual dream content is determined by the dreamer's memories of activities during waking life and his or her physical state. In other words, an individual's nature is revealed in his or her dreams. In Nyssa's view, dreams are most commonly motivated by the

passions, expressions of our "brute" nature which should be rigorously held in check by the intellect if we are to remain pure. Because the intellect is "off guard" during sleep, our passions can be given unbridled expression in our dreams. A little later, St Augustine (354-430 AD) noted that certain aspects of his mind were beyond his control, and he worried that God might hold him responsible for his dreams.

THE MIDDLE AGES

It was not long before the Christian Church associated human passions, especially sexual desires, with the devil or Satan. In their dreams, people were vulnerable to the temptations of the flesh: they could sin while asleep and not even know it, risking their souls to eternal damnation and the terrors of Hell. They therefore should practise great vigilance against the devil and all his works, as he was believed to intervene in human affairs in order to possess people's souls. A regime of devout prayer and austerity was recommended and any who continued to "sup with the devil" were branded as witches, facing persecution, torture and a terrible

death. Consequently the capacity to have vivid dreams was greatly feared and dream divination became linked with sorcery. It was at this point that dream divination in the West became anathema and consequently went underground, until its secular revival centuries later.

ABOVE Dreams are mysterious markers of landscapes that affect us very deeply – archetypes aren't just people but also symbolize aspects of ancient cultures.

TREE LORE

The Celts ascribed a symbolic meaning to trees. The oak, or "godhead" tree, held divine power and significance. Sleeping next to an oak tree could inspire prophetic dreams. Other important trees were the hazel, used as the druid's staff; holly, its red berries symbolizing the food of the gods; and ash, denoting health and immortal life.

THE DEVIL'S HELPERS

One of the dangers facing the dreamer was a nightly visitation from one of the devil's helpers. A succubus is a demon who assumes a female form and has sex with sleeping men. She then collects the semen, using it in magical rites to produce an "incubus", a male demon, satyr, faun or devil. Any man unfortunate, or some would say, wicked, enough to attract the attentions of a succubus was destined to follow the ways of the witch forever. By this means, Satan was said to "increase his horde, his progeny and to spread the diabolical craft of the witch".

ABOVE Today we are much more forgiving of people who suffer or enjoy sexual excitement while asleep but to the ancient Church such people were very wicked indeed, and were inevitably accused of Devilish practices.

Witches, it was claimed, had sexual intercourse with incubi in order that they could give birth to the children of demons.

NOCTURNAL INTERCOURSE

The word "incubus" means "to lie on", and it was believed that any heavy feeling in bed, such as a weight pressing down on your chest, especially if accompanied by nightmares, was a sure sign that an incubus (or succubus) had attempted to have nocturnal intercourse with you. Today we know that dreaming affects the body as well as the brain. For both men and women, the body regularly shows signs of sexual arousal (sometimes to the point of orgasm) during sleep, even when erotic dream content is absent. Given the religious fervour of the Middle Ages, it is not altogether surprising that the idea of a demon lover was believed to account for this phenomenon.

THE SHEPHERD AND THE SUCCUBUS

The 16th-century author, Nicolas Remy, reports that a young shepherd who was found guilty of witchcraft began his evil ways by being seduced by a succubus while attending his flocks. It was said that whenever he fell asleep in the warm afternoon sunshine, he would dream of his demon lover, who took the form of a dairymaid with whom he was in love. She would allow the shepherd to fulfil his sexual desires with her provided that "he acknowledged her as his Mistress and behaved to her as though she were God Himself". The shepherd claimed that "she so possessed me that from that time I have been subject to no will but hers".

FORERUNNERS OF THE MODERN AGE

Although St Augustine was concerned about his inability to control his dreams, it was hundreds of years later before the idea that something goes on inside us that we know nothing about was clearly formulated. Von Leibniz (1646-1716) compared the workings of the soul to the circulation of blood through the body: it is something that happens even though we are unaware of it. A little later, a German physicist, G.C. Lichtenberg (1742-99) made the first link between unconscious mental activity and dreaming.

At the beginning of the 19th century, signs of a renewed interest in dreams began to gather momentum. Robert Cross Smith from England became very successful as an astrologer, practising under the pseudonym of "Raphael". In 1830, he published *The Royal Book of Dreams*, which gave the reader interpretations of particular kinds of dream. However, it is through the work of a French doctor, Alfred Maury (1817-1892), that we begin to enter a new age of dream interpretation. From his study of more than 3000 dreams, Maury concludes that external stimuli are often responsible for what we dream about. Recent memories appearing in dreams, especially of the day before, are referred to as "day residues", and Maury discovered that stimuli such as noises and smells often register as we sleep and become included in our dreams.

ABOVE RIGHT Much of the accusations levelled against so called witches by the Church involved detailed, nightmarish descriptions of the devilish creatures the women were said to have under their control.
RIGHT The only way to redeem a witch or possessed person was to exorcise the malignant spirit and extract a confession from the accused.

MAURY'S DREAM

In one of his dreams, Maury dreamt he had been condemned to death by the guillotine. As the blade was falling, he woke up to find the top of the bed had fallen and hit him on the back of the neck at the exact time the guillotine would have struck him. This gave weight to Maury's theory that dreams happen so quickly that they are almost concurrent with the external stimulus that produces them.

THE DREAM DEMON OF MORAY FIRTH

Legend has it that in the 16th century, a demon lover lived near the banks of the Moray Firth River in Scotland. The lover seduces a young girl, but the lovers are caught when the girl's parents overhear sounds of lovemaking coming from her bedchamber. The parents call the priest and together break down the bedchamber door to find the girl fast asleep in the embrace of a "monster horrible beyond description". The priest recites from the gospels, whereupon the evil demon gives a terrible cry, setting fire to the furniture in the room and vanishing upwards, carrying the roof of the bedchamber with him.

INDIGENOUS PEOPLES

TRADITIONAL SOCIETIES ACROSS THE GLOBE HAVE DREAMING TRADITIONS THAT STRETCH BACK INTO THE MISTS OF TIME. IT SEEMS THAT DREAMS HAVE ALWAYS BEEN PART OF THE FABRIC OF LIFE FOR PEOPLES AS DIVERSE AS THE AUSTRALIAN ABORIGINES, THE INUIT FROM THE ARCTIC REGIONS AND THE PEOPLES OF AFRICA, AS WELL AS THE NATIVE AMERICAN INDIANS. EACH CULTURE HAS ITS OWN THEORY OF DREAMING AND PARTICULAR TECHNIQUES FOR INTERPRETING DREAMS. THEIR DREAMS AND SYMBOLS RELATE TO A PARTICULAR WAY OF LIFE, YET THEY ALL HAVE SOMETHING IN COMMON. THEIR DREAMS ARE RESPECTED AS COMING FROM A REVERED SOURCE AND ARE SEEN TO CONTAIN IMPORTANT INFORMATION.

ABOVE To the Aborigines of Australasia nothing is more sacred, more important, or more meaningful than the dreamtime, when the world was first created out of the seeds of the spirit ancestors.

THE DREAMTIME

Hundreds of thousands of years ago, the Aborigines travelled from Asia to the northern shores of Australia. Here they split into groups and moved around the land in search of water. They travelled great distances, and their legends say that as they did so they deposited the spirits of those yet to be born along the way, leaving marks on the landscape, on the rocks, mountains and other geographical features, to signpost the places they had been. According to legend, these ancestors were mythical figures, spirit beings who emerged from the earth, sea and sky and who took on various forms, particularly of animals. They were given symbolic names such as Red Kangaroo, the Blue Lizard or the Bell Bird Brothers. This era is known as the "dreamtime", when the ancestors created the landscape and set the pattern for the future. For centuries the Australian Aborigines have followed in the footsteps of their ancestors, tracing the paths trodden by these giant beings and marking their sacred sites with ritual, song and legend.

Those who lose dreaming are lost.

AUSTRALIAN ABORIGINAL PROVERB

The dreamtime is like a "cosmic dreaming energy" which can be set free if the ground is rubbed or stroked at the exact spot where the ancestor left the world at death and went into the ground. In ritual dances, these sacred sites on the landscape are struck and the power of the ancestors is brought back to life from the sleep of death. If no-one remembers or honours the dreamtime, the stories say, we shall remain trapped in the earth when we die and will cease to be.

THE DREAM IS LIFE

The dreamtime of the Aborigines is a complex concept: it is at once a creation myth, a whole series of fables and an entire spiritual philosophy. For the native Australians, the whole of life had its evolution in the dreamtime, and for them everything around us is brought to life by the dream. They do not perceive time as a linear process but rather see humans as existing in an eternal "now", where past, present and future exist simultaneously. The world as they see it is a magical place imbued with

supernatural forces, and we are at all times "dreaming the dream" so that it can become impossible to differentiate between the waking and the dreaming state.

AFRICAN SOCIETIES

The Bushmen of the Kalahari hold a similar viewpoint, seeing the whole of life as a dream and believing that they are the ones being "dreamed". Similarly, the Pagiboti people of Zaire consider that dreams are sent from their ancestors and believe that the spirits of the past have access to wisdom that can help with daily life. For instance, hunting is important to the survival of the Pagiboti and they believe their dreams can give them important information that can help them be successful: to dream of encountering an animal in the forest is regarded as a good sign. Many other African societies set great store by dreams, believing that they are linked to destiny. All aspects of life, from cures for sickness to political decisions, can be based on dream advice.

ABOVE According to the Aborigine creation myths we are all holders of the dreamtime.
ABOVE LEFT The Aborigines' sacred art consists of pictorial representations of the dreamtime and how the world was created.

THE DREAM SMOKE OF ULURU

The two Bell Bird Brothers were hunting emu at the rock pool near Uluru, the most sacred of all Australian Aboriginal sites (right), when their prey was disturbed by a young girl eating grubs. On her head she carried a sacred bundle which fell to the ground – the indentation is still to be seen at the base of the rock – but the brothers managed to catch the emu. They killed it and cooked it but Blue Lizard came and stole it. In punishment the Bell Bird Brothers set fire to Blue Lizard's hut and he was burned alive. The smoke from the fire can still be seen across the face of Uluru, and it is the smoke from this fire that sets us dreaming.

This story indicates one of the reasons why Uluru is so important to the Australian Aborigines. Take the rock out of their control and they lose their power of dreaming, and by implication, the power to live.

NORTH AMERICAN INDIAN TRADITIONS

Like other traditional societies, Native American cultures find it difficult to define the border between the waking and the dreaming state, and the ability to dream is highly valued. Each of the great tribes has its own understanding of dreams and a complex dream culture exists. Iroquois traditionalists, for instance, have a strong belief in dream precognition and respect the ability of a gifted dreamer to provide information vital to the survival of the people. Because Iroquois culture is built on warrior values, any sign of being taken care of in a dream is greatly feared, as it is believed that it will undermine

ABOVE LEFT Through dream journeys the shaman is able to connect with the animal world.

ABOVE RIGHT The shaman is the guide through the dream. Without the shaman our dreams are dangerous places to go.

bravery. Where a dream indicates trouble or disaster, it is believed to be possible to change its outcome by playacting the event that the community wishes to avert. In fact drama and ritual play an important part in Iroquois dream culture. Each year people travel great distances to attend a festival where dreams are acted out in a theatrical performance known as the *Ondinnonk*. According to the Iroquois, big dreams occur either because we have an out-of-body experience during sleep or because we receive an interesting "dream visitor". These are the dreams that put us in touch with our deepest spiritual source and contain vital information for health and wellbeing.

The Navajo pay particular attention to the diagnostic aspect of dreams, seeing them as tools to pinpoint illness, particular mental states and emotional disturbances. Dreams can also reveal a ritual cure for what is wrong, and if this is carried out in waking life the dreamer will return to health. For instance, there is a story of a sick girl

LEFT Ritual dances can be followed to interpret the dream in song and music. This is a valuable tool in dream interpretation but one that is specific to a culture, to those who understand the steps.

THE FOUR DIRECTIONS

Each of the four directions is associated with a particular element and quality. The element of the North is air. North is associated with the power of the mind and clear-thinking. Water belongs to the South and is associated with feelings and intuition, while the power of the West revitalizes and renews the physical body. Its element is earth. The power of the East triggers enlightenment and spiritual realization and its element is fire. This Navajo sand painting uses the four elements in its symbolic representation of abundant crops.

It is believed that positioning the bed in a particular direction allows the dreamer to "work" with the qualities of its associated element.

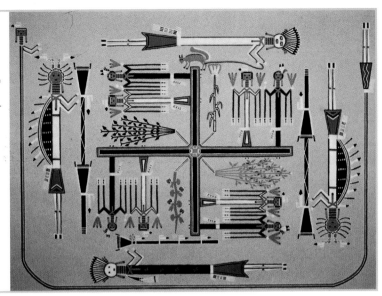

dreaming of nine feasts and being persuaded by the medicine man that if she has these feasts in reality, she would recover from her illness.

HOPI DREAM PROMPTERS

For the Hopi, a dream is viewed as a message from spirit guides who can appear in the form of an animal or other guises. Waking up and not remembering a dream is seen as losing something essential and people go to great lengths to ensure that this does not happen.

A commonly used dream prompter is a squared circle, a symbolic device used to aid dream recall. A circle is drawn on a square piece of cloth or leather. The circle is then divided into four quarters to represent each of the four directions: North, South, West and East. The square is then placed by the side of the bed. An item of symbolic value is placed in each of the four quarters – for instance, a tiny pot of water, a bunch of fresh grass, a lit candle and some burning incense – these items represent each of the four elements of water, earth, fire and air. Sleeping next to a dream prompter is believed to enhance dream recall.

THE INUIT SHAMAN

The Canadian Inuit culture is similar to those found in other northern regions, such as in Russia and the northern Scandinavian countries, where survival is challenged by the extreme climate. The Inuit believe that *anua* (souls) exist in all people and animals. Individuals, families and the tribe follow a system of taboos to ensure that animals will continue to make themselves available to the hunters, and rituals and ceremonies are performed before and after hunting expeditions to encourage success.

The shaman is the spiritual leader of each tribe. He is able to interpret causes of sickness or lack of success in hunting. In a manner similar to shamans or medicine-men in other cultures, he enters a trance-like state with the aid of drum beating and chanting. This allows him to travel out of his body, traversing great distances to determine the causes of sickness and other community problems, and to bring back solutions. In this dream-like state the shaman is imbued with magical powers and can move about outside of the dream.

CULTURAL PATTERN DREAMS

Anthropologists have suggested that the dreams of traditional societies can be broken down into four types: "big" dreams are those that possess cultural significance; prophetic dreams predict or give advance warning of events; medical dreams promote diagnosis and healing; and "little" dreams are purely personal to the dreamer. Although all dreams are valued, the ones held to be the most significant are the big dreams. These powerful dreams are also known as "cultural pattern dreams" or "official dreams".

The dream world is the real world.   SENECA INDIAN HEALER

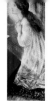

SACRED DREAMING

THROUGHOUT THE ANCIENT WORLD, THE CONNECTION BETWEEN DREAMS AND SPIRITUAL BELIEF WAS CLOSELY INTERWOVEN. DREAMS SEEM TO HAVE PLAYED A SIGNIFICANT ROLE IN THE SHAPING OF MANY OF THE WORLD'S MAJOR RELIGIONS, APPEARING AS PART OF THEIR HISTORY AND IN THEIR HOLY TEXTS. MANY OF THESE DREAMS HAVE A REVELATORY OR VISIONARY QUALITY TO THEM, WITH RICH SYMBOLIC IMAGERY AND METAPHOR. THESE EXPERIENCES ARE NOT THE SAME AS THE ORDINARY DREAMS MOST OF US HAVE MUCH OF THE TIME — ALTHOUGH IT IS POSSIBLE TO EXPERIENCE A DREAM OF SUCH PROFOUND SIGNIFICANCE THAT LIFE CAN NEVER BE THE SAME AGAIN.

BUDDHIST ENLIGHTENMENT

For a long time before the birth of Gautama Buddha (c.563-c.483 BC), many predictions had been made that a "chosen one" would arrive. While she was pregnant, Gautama's mother dreamt that she was carrying a shining, silvery white elephant with six tusks. Interpreters regarded the dream as an announcement of the chosen one's arrival. Elephants had holy status in India: the Hindu god, Ganesh, remover of obstacles, is depicted with an elephant's head, while the unusual colour and appearance of the elephant in the dream was also seen as significant. Later on in the Buddha's life, his father, a nobleman, had a dream in which his son left the family to become a monk. This came to pass when Gautama was 30 years old, when he left his family, renouncing his worldly status to seek enlightenment.

BIBLICAL VISIONS

Dreams also figure largely in both the Old and New Testaments. In the Old Testament, important dreams often coincide with critical times in the development of Judaism. For instance, while in exile in Egypt Joseph interprets the Pharaoh's dreams. The Pharaoh

BELOW Gabriel, a universal archetype who appears in several different traditions, played a significant part in the dreams of Mohammed, who dreamt that they journeyed together to the seven levels of heaven.

HINDU BELIEFS

The Hindu religion has its own interpretation of what dreams are all about and believes that some dreams come from the dreamer's own emotional nature, some from hidden fears, and some from playing back experiences in daily life. Certain dreams, however, come from the gods. These dreams only appear to very religious people, such as this sadhu (right), who live a disciplined life, or sadhana, getting up before sunrise and practising austerities.

And He said, 'Hear now my words: If there be a prophet among you, I the lord will make myself known unto him in a vision and will speak to him in a dream'.

OLD TESTAMENT, NUMBERS 12:6

dreams that seven fat cattle are eaten by seven lean ones, and then that seven ripe ears of corn are destroyed by seven blighted ones. Joseph realizes that both dreams mean the same thing: they predict seven years of plentiful harvest followed by seven years of scarcity, which will destroy the bounty of the previous seven years. The Pharaoh acts on Joseph's interpretation and during the bounteous years builds up large stores of grain. The interpretation not only saves the populace and the ruling system, but Joseph is promoted to a position of great political influence.

In the New Testament, divine messages are often relayed in dreams. The angel Gabriel appears in a vision to the pregnant Mary, announcing that she will give birth to a child of the Holy Spirit. The angel also visits Joseph in a dream, telling him to accept Mary's pregnancy and to name the baby Jesus, because he will save his people from their sins. Dreams also contain warnings. For instance, Joseph is told to take his family to Egypt in order to escape Herod's jurisdiction that all newborn male infants should be slain. Later the same angel returns to Joseph, informing him that it is safe to return after Herod is dead.

ISLAMIC DREAMS

Dreams also seem to have played an important part in the building of Islam. It is said that Mohammed (c.570-632 AD) had visions of the archangel Gabriel, who appeared to him when he was alone at night, praying and meditating. During one such

visitation, the angel dictated the first chapter, or Sura, of the Koran, the holy book of Islam. The Arabic root for the word *Koran* means "address" or "recitation". According to tradition, Mohammed could neither read nor write, but the Koran was recited word by word by him just as he had received it from Gabriel. Later Mohammed had a dream or vision that he journeyed in the company of Gabriel and other angels. He was taken to holy places and to the seven levels of heaven and hell, meeting important religious leaders and prophets from the past. This experience, referred to as the Night Journey, has inspired many writers and artists.

ABOVE Angels have appeared to many in dreams, are these dreams or visions? Moments of madness or divine communications? One of the most well known angelic dreams is Mary's, as she is told of the coming of Jesus.

THE TALMUD

The body of Jewish civil and ceremonial law, the Talmud, divides dreams into three types: dreams of prophecy, dreams of nonsense, and dreams that originate from a person's thoughts and experience during the day. The way a dream is interpreted helps determine its outcome, and actions such as fasting or reciting special prayers are recommended as atonement for a bad dream.

THE NATURE OF DREAMS

A dream is a series of pictures or events that occur in the mind. Generally dreams are experienced as we sleep, although it is possible to enter a dream-like state while awake. These images seem to be based on the dreamer's thoughts or experiences although certain dreams seem to bear little or no relation to the dreamer's normal life. Precisely how and why these images occur and what relevance they may have is a subject that has inspired a great deal of research and provokes much debate.

RIGHT One of the common factors in many dreams, is the ambiguity of images and concepts, and the way reality and fantasy become indistinguishable.

Scientific Research

THE RELATIONSHIP BETWEEN THE BODY AND MIND, THE BRAIN AND SLEEP HAS ALWAYS BEEN A PUZZLE, YET SCIENTIFIC RESEARCH INTO DREAMS IS A RELATIVELY RECENT PHENOMENON. EARLY RESEARCH IN THE 19TH CENTURY SUGGESTED THAT EXTERNAL STIMULI, SUCH AS NOISES AND SMELLS, CAN INFLUENCE DREAM CONTENT AND CERTAIN DREAM EXPERIENCES WERE GIVEN A PHYSIOLOGICAL EXPLANATION. HOWEVER IT WAS NOT UNTIL THE PHYSICS OF ELECTRICITY WAS UNDERSTOOD AND EEG (ELECTROENCEPHALOGRAM) INSTRUMENTS WERE INVENTED THAT SCIENTISTS BEGAN TO DISCOVER HOW THE BRAIN WORKS, TRANSFORMING OUR KNOWLEDGE OF SLEEP AND DREAMS.

EEG INVESTIGATIONS

In the early 1950s at the University of Chicago, Kleitman and Aserinsky made a breakthrough in sleep research using EEGs. They found that when a person was asleep the brain had periods of intense activity, demolishing the widespread idea that during sleep the brain was resting. They also found out that blind people have vivid dreams in colour.

Another important dream researcher was Kleitman's pupil, William Dement, to whom we owe the term "REM (rapid eye movement) sleep". REM occurs after periods of slow-wave or deep sleep, at regular intervals throughout the night. REM is characterized by visibly detectable movements of the eye behind closed eyelids together with a change in brainwave frequency. It is during REM sleep that we experience dreams.

Dement's research team found that if someone is woken in or immediately after REM sleep they usually have good recall of their dreams. On the other hand, if even as little as five minutes has elapsed before they wake, they usually have little or no memory of their dreams.

PHASIC AND TONIC DREAMS

We now know that REM sleep falls into two types, generating two different types of dreams. Firstly there is the phasic component. This is characterized by jerky eye movements, spasmodic limb and facial twitching and sudden breathing changes. When volunteers are woken from this sort of REM sleep, they typically describe their dreams as being strongly visual, active and "real". Phasic REM and its accompanying dreams tend to occur later on in the sleeping period. Nightmares are associated with this type of sleep.

The second type of REM sleep is known as tonic and is accompanied by muscle relaxation and

PHASIC AND TONIC DREAMS

REM sleep has two components, each having its own dream characteristics.

phasic dream I was running down a metal tunnel. It was very cold and hard and my feet made a noise on the floor as I ran. There were vibrant colours inside the tunnel and I felt I could reach out and touch them. Behind me I could hear the echoing roar of rushing water and it made me tremble. I wasn't afraid but I did feel very anxious – you know the sort of feeling, where you think the worst is going to happen at any minute. It was pretty overpowering.

tonic dream I was sitting in a temple meditating. There was a monk beside me and I could sense what he was thinking. There was a feeling of calm and peace all around and I drifted away in the swirling incense smoke. I felt weightless and insubstantial.

sometimes sexual arousal. Tonic REM takes place earlier on in the sleeping cycle. It is calmer and more restful, and tonic dreams are more passive and "feely". When woken, the dreamer typically reports such things as "I was feeling floaty" or "there was a feeling of peace".

DATA THEORIES

Although we now know much more about the brain, scientists remain divided as to the exact purpose that dreaming serves. In the 1960s, some dream researchers thought that while we are asleep the brain, like a computer, is "off-line". This does not mean it has shut down, but is that is going through a process of reassessing, filing and updating data from the day's activities. Many dreams certainly seem to fall into this category.

Some researchers took the analogy even further by suggesting that the brain, like the computer, discards redundant information through the process of dreaming. In the 1980s, Crick and Mitchison called this process "reverse learning". Dreams, they reasoned, help the mind to jettison an overload of data which could otherwise cause confusion. Dreams are like a rubbish-bin of the mind and have no particular meaning. From this perspective, we dream in order to forget.

UNDERSTANDING THE BRAIN

The brain has two hemispheres: the left side is associated with logic and language, while the right is more connected with intuition and creativity. It seems that dreaming is associated with right brain activity. Scientists have also discovered that dreams flow along visual and verbal "pathways" or nerve channels to the brain. We also know that the brain emits different types of electrical signals or waves. Of these, the following four types are of interest to sleep researchers. Beta waves (30-13 hertz) are associated with normal waking activity, with waves near the top end of the scale (30) signalling states of extreme agitation. Alpha waves (12-8 hertz) are produced during rest, while theta waves (7-5 hertz) are produced on the point of sleep. Delta waves are the longest and slowest (4-1 hertz) and are produced during deep sleep or in the womb. It is usually when alpha moves into theta that dreaming begins.

ABOVE The more we understand the function of the brain the better able we are to understand our dreams and thus not only our emotional impulses but also, perhaps, our spiritual function.

BELOW LEFT Our dreams may be a simple way of us downloading all the data we have picked up during the day and may have no meaning at all.
BELOW On the other hand dreams may be imbued with mystical importance and we would be lost without them – lesser beings indeed.

FREUDIAN PSYCHOLOGY

WHILE PEOPLE HAVE ALWAYS BEEN INTERESTED IN THE WAY THE MIND WORKS, IT WAS NOT UNTIL THE 20TH CENTURY THAT OUR UNDERSTANDING WAS REVOLUTIONIZED. THIS BREAKTHROUGH CAN BE ATTRIBUTED TO THE WORK OF SIGMUND FREUD (1856-1939), AN AUSTRIAN NEUROLOGIST AND THE FOUNDER OF PSYCHOANALYSIS. FREUD "DISCOVERED" THE UNCONSCIOUS AND DESCRIBED DREAMS AS THE "ROYAL ROAD" TO ITS UNDERSTANDING. WHEN HIS *INTERPRETATION OF DREAMS* WAS PUBLISHED IN 1900 IT WAS HIGHLY CONTROVERSIAL, YET HIS IDEAS PERMEATED ALMOST EVERY ASPECT OF WESTERN CULTURE. BECAUSE OF FREUD, DREAMS WERE ONCE AGAIN TAKEN SERIOUSLY.

THE CONSCIOUS AND THE UNCONSCIOUS MIND

According to Sigmund Freud, the conscious part of the mind represents a small fraction of the whole. It is like the tip of the iceberg, with the unconscious lying below the surface of the water. Like the iceberg, part of the unconscious is near the water's surface. Freud refers to this level as the "pre-conscious" and it is relatively easy to get in touch with. The deeper levels, however, are more difficult to access. It is a journey into the dark.

The unconscious is not static but dynamic. Freud believed that underneath our social exterior, the tip of the iceberg, at rock bottom we are a seething mass of instincts and unspeakable desires, most of which relate to sexuality and aggression, or our biological drives. He refers to this part of the psyche as the "id". Any experiences, thoughts or desires that are either too painful to allow, or that will contradict our self-image are either denied by the rational, conscious part of the personality (referred to as the "ego"), or repressed by an internal "censor" (also known as the "superego"). The unconscious is a bubbling cauldron of our personal and social taboos, yet it also provides the underlying motivations for our behaviour, of which we are largely unaware.

THE ROLE OF DREAMS

Freud believed that the unconscious cannot be studied directly but can only be inferred from clues in a person's behaviour, speech patterns and also their dreams. Dreams are symbolic representations of our unconscious needs, wishes and conflicts. Freud describes them as being in essence "the hallucinatory fulfilment of a forbidden wish". He asserts that dreams not only represent current wishes but are also the irrational expressions of infantile wishes, usually of either a sexual or an aggressive nature, that are left over in our subconscious from early childhood.

Because the wish is perceived as dangerous by the censor, it is expressed in the dream in a disguised or symbolic form. Freud believed dreams have two aspects: a latent content (the repressed desire) and a manifest content (the dream itself). So, for instance, repression of sexual desires (latent content) leads us to dream in metaphors of sexual imagery (manifest content): to dream of a chimney is to dream of an erect penis, to dream of a cave is to dream of a vagina. In other words, dream symbols are coded

BELOW Sigmund Freud was the first modern Western scientist to make a detailed attempt to understand and interpret dreams, and his legacy continues to this day.

Anyone who behaved while awake in the way the situations in the dream present him would be regarded as insane.
SIGMUND FREUD

messages, having sufficient ingenuity to slip through the tight webbing of the censor's net. Freud believed that this subversive activity was necessary because it allowed the sleeper to go on sleeping. Without such disguise techniques, the content would be so disturbing that the dreamer would be woken from sleep. This leads to Freud's description of dreams as "the guardians of sleep and not its disturbers".

APPROACH TO INTERPRETATION

Freud's approach to dream interpretation is to look for the underlying meaning, or the latent content, behind the dream. To help his patients identify the latent content of their dreams, Freud developed the technique of word association, known as "free association", where words and ideas derived from the dream are freely associated without being censored. This technique forms the basic method of psychoanalysis.

DREAM DISGUISES

Central to Freud's theory is that dreams use "disguise" techniques to hide the latent content from the internal censor. This is how he accounts for the peculiar and irrational nature of the manifest dream. These are the different disguise techniques that Freud identifies:

Condensation dreams use a kind of shorthand, coalescing or "condensing" different ideas together into a single image which is often unusual or bizarre.

Displacement dreams are when a potentially disturbing idea is redirected or "displaced" on to another person or object so that it becomes less disturbing. For instance, a young man harbours feelings of murderous rage towards his father. In his dream, he sees his father being killed by a stranger, whereby his aggressive desires are displaced on to the stranger.

Symbolization dreams are where a neutral image is used to represent a potentially disturbing, usually sexual, idea. For instance, putting a key into a keyhole is interpreted as a penis entering a vagina.

Representation dreams are when thoughts are converted into visual imagery.

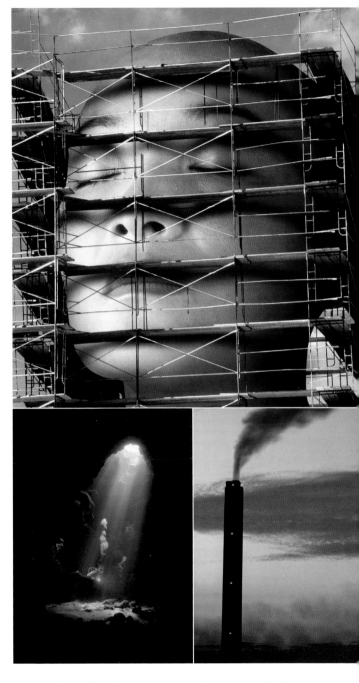

ABOVE Freud believed that all dream imagery is symbolic in content, and that the symbolism is universal rather than personal. For example if you dream of holes in the ground, tunnels or caves (above left) you are dreaming about the vagina. Similarly, if you dream of chimneys or towers (right) you are dreaming of the penis.

PSYCHOLOGY AND JUNG

For our contemporary understanding of dream interpretation we are indebted to the work of Carl Gustav Jung (1875-1961), a Swiss psychiatrist and founder of "analytical psychology", who made the study of dreams and the unconscious his lifework. Jung was a one-time pupil of Freud, and was in agreement about the importance of unconscious processes in the cause and treatment of mental illness and in the production of dreams. Gradually however, Jung became dissatisfied with Freud's theories and proposed that dreams played an important part in the healthy functioning of the psyche.

JUNG'S BASIC PHILOSOPHY

It was Freud's emphasis on sexuality and the overly biological orientation of his theories that gradually alienated his pupil, Jung. Freud's is a deterministic, and some would say, pessimistic, view of human behaviour. In a sense, he argues, we are little more than machines, driven by blind forces arising from our biological inheritance, over which we have little or no control. In contrast, Jung believed that human beings possess the capacity for growth and fulfilment and regarded sexual energy as part of a much more general, innate drive towards psychic health and wholeness. Jung calls this process individuation and describes it as the most important task any person can undertake in life – the attainment of harmony between all the aspects of the psyche, which makes us one and whole.

Essentially Jung saw life in terms of a spiritual journey and, far from being a dangerous melting pot of repressed and forbidden wishes, he saw the unconscious as a friend and guide to help us on our way. Jung applied these principles to his own life and used his dreams to help him make decisions, resolve uncertainties and move him along his path to self-realization.

THE PURPOSE OF DREAMS

Jung saw the psyche as self-adjusting, helping us to reconcile opposing parts of our nature and restore inner balance, and believed that dreams had an important part to play in this process. Dreams have a compensatory function, alerting us to imbalances in our personality and allowing us to change. They also have a teaching function, where certain aspects of the personality that need revising can be given attention. Jung believed that dreams are a way of communicating, of bringing levels of unconscious information into conscious awareness. They express the current state of the dreamer's unconscious and, Jung believed, they also provide clues as to future potential – a view that contrasts with Freud's more backward-looking perspective.

APPROACH TO INTERPRETATION

Unlike Freud, Jung never published a systematic theory of dream analysis because he believed that every dream carried its own meaning and must be interpreted individually. For Jung, the dream itself is the content and its symbols are subject to subjective interpretation. Rather than leading the person away from the dream by free association, Jung's method is to stay focused on the content of the dream itself. Through amplification or "direct association" he

BELOW During his life, Jung estimated that he interpreted around 80,000 dreams. He found that the details of a dream were not only relevant to the dreamer, but were sometimes part of a bigger picture relating to the world we live in.

JUNG'S DREAM OF HIS FATHER

Following a dream of his dead father, Jung became interested in the spiritual dimension to life.

"Six weeks after his death, my father appeared to me in a dream. Suddenly he stood before me and said that he was coming back from his holiday. He had made a good recovery and was now coming home. I thought he would be annoyed with me for having moved into his room. But not a bit of it! Nevertheless, I felt ashamed because I had imagined he was dead. Two days later the dream was repeated. My father had recovered and was coming home, and again I reproached myself because I had thought he was dead. Later I kept asking myself: 'What does it mean that my father returns in dreams and that he seems so real?' It was an unforgettable experience and it forced me for the first time to think about life after death."

The general function of dreams is to restore our psychological balance.   CARL JUNG

encourages the dreamer to explore all their associations with a particular image, returning to the image itself again and again.

THE COLLECTIVE UNCONSCIOUS

The other important area where Jung diverges from Freud is in the way he conceptualised the unconscious. Although many dreams are expressions of a personal unconscious and related to the individual psyche of the dreamer, Jung noticed that

there were other dreams that do not fit into this category. These make use of symbols which have no particular personal significance for the dreamer, but have a "universal" quality about them. Through his studies of religion, art, anthropology and mythology, he concludes that many of these symbols stem from some common source – the "collective unconscious" the largest and deepest area of the psyche. He refers to these universal symbols as "archetypes" and argues that their meaning transcends the personal.

ABOVE To understand our personal archetypes is to unlock the power of our dreams and to be truly released.
ABOVE LEFT Jung encourages the dreamer to explore their own dream, and discover its meaning for themselves.

LEFT Archetypes can be traced back thousands of generations, and traces may even be seen in the landscape, where the first human cultures in our history drew the creatures of their imaginations.

MODERN APPROACHES

FOLLOWING IN THE FOOTSTEPS OF FREUD AND JUNG, THERE HAVE BEEN MANY OTHERS WHO HAVE DEVELOPED THEIR OWN METHODS OF USING DREAMS TO GAIN INSIGHT INTO THE INNER WORKINGS OF THE MIND. TODAY A MORE ECLECTIC APPROACH TOWARDS DREAM INTERPRETATION HAS GENERALLY BECOME ESTABLISHED AND A MIXTURE OF TECHNIQUES AND IDEAS IS IN USE. IN GENERAL TERMS, THE EMPHASIS IS ON THE DREAMER RATHER THAN THE DREAM, WITH EACH PERSON LEARNING HOW TO APPRECIATE AND INTERPRET THEIR OWN DREAMS. OUR DREAMS CAN HELP US LOOK AT THINGS FROM A NEW PERSPECTIVE OR EXAMINE NEGLECTED AREAS OF OURSELVES.

ABOVE Nowadays everything in our dreams is regarded as deeply symbolic – no tiny detail gets overlooked.
ABOVE RIGHT We like to think that everything in our dream can be explained – interpreted as being connected to our waking life in some way.

DREAM THEORISTS

The 20th century saw a revival of interest in dreams and a great deal of academic and scientific research into the subject was undertaken. Calvin Hall and his associate Vernon Nordby spent most of the 1950s and 60s collecting and categorizing dreams from all over the world.

After analysing more than 50,000 dreams Hall and Nordby concluded that typical themes crop up in dreams again and again, which seemed to lend weight to Jung's theory of the collective unconscious. They also rejected Freud's distinction between the latent and manifest content of dreams, believing that the dream itself was the message.

In the 1960s, Thomas French and Erika Fromm asserted that the primary function of dreams is to work on relationship issues in the dreamer's life, an approach that has proved extremely influential. Montague Ullman took French and Fromm's ideas a stage further by making a link between dreaming and cultural and social issues, asserting that in some way our dreams are concerned with our "interconnectedness" as a species.

EXPERIENTIAL APPROACHES

In recent times, experiential approaches to dreams have been favoured over those that are theory driven. In the 1960s Frederick (Fritz) Perls, the founder of Gestalt psychotherapy, emphasized the importance of taking all aspects of the dream as a direct expression of the personal psychology of the dreamer. His greatest contribution is his use of role-playing techniques to bring the different "parts" of the dream to greater consciousness. For instance in a dream of steering a ship, you would role-play "being" the ship as well as yourself, setting up a dialogue between the two aspects of the dream.

In the 1980s, Alvin Mahrer developed a four-part experiential model for working with dreams. First tell the dream, next identify recent events, situations or experiences connected with the dream, go on to re-experience peak moments of the dream, and finish by "being" the dream.

Ann Faraday, an English dream researcher working today, encourages the use of a dream diary to record dreams, and uses the Gestalt technique to find out more about the characters in a dream.

DREAM GROUPS

Described as containing a blend of psychology, mysticism and poetry, a dream group consists of a number of individuals meeting together on a regular basis for the purpose of sharing and working with their dreams. Members of the group can offer their insights and suggestions for how to work with a dream, but are not encouraged to attempt to actually interpret anyone else's. Besides fostering a degree of self-awareness, dream groups allow people to relate to each other at a deeper level than usually occurs in most social interactions. Some groups work with a professional therapist, while others do not find this necessary.

Dream groups are becoming more popular and widespread in the US, but it is also possible to find them in other parts of the world. If such a facility does not exist in your area, it is possible for a group of like-minded people to set up their own group.

SPIRITUAL GROWTH

It is not necessary to have a religious belief to approach dreams from a spiritual perspective. Many people believe that there is more to us than physical form and see dreams as a way of connecting with that mysterious yet crucial part of the self that is often referred to as "spirit". From this perspective dreams become a tool for increased self-knowledge and personal development.

L.M. Savary developed a complex approach to dream interpretation from a Judaeo-Christian perspective, and some of his techniques can be used as a method in themselves. A useful one is the TTAQ (title, theme, affect, question) method. First give your dream a title, next identify the major theme of the dream, and consider how this affected you, noticing for instance any thoughts or feelings that it evoked. Finally explore the question that the dream is trying to help you become aware of.

ABOVE Even if we don't have any religious beliefs it isn't difficult to read a spiritual meaning into our dreams. A particular dream may be full of prosaic, everyday images, but they still have a spiritual significance for the dreamer.

In this dream ... for a timeless moment, I danced, flashed and roared with the storm and seemed to merge with the 'being' at the centre of it.

DR ANN FARADAY

DREAMS AND PREMONITIONS

TALES OF PROPHECY AND FORESEEING THE FUTURE ARE AS OLD AND DIVERSE AS HUMANITY ITSELF. WHILE ORTHODOX
SCIENCE INSISTS THAT PSYCHIC PHENOMENA DO NOT EXIST, DREAMS CONTAINING INFORMATION FROM OTHER PEOPLE OR
NEWS FROM THE FUTURE AS WELL AS DREAMS OF PROPHECY AND WARNING HAVE ALL BEEN RECORDED AT VARIOUS TIMES.
SIMILARLY THERE HAVE BEEN MANY INSTANCES OF DREAMS BEING USED AS A DIAGNOSTIC TOOL FOR HEALING PURPOSES.
HOWEVER WE ACCOUNT FOR SUCH PHENOMENA, THERE IS A BODY OF EXPERIENCE WHICH CANNOT SIMPLY BE DISCOUNTED
OR READILY BE ABSORBED BY OUR RATIONAL, SCIENTIFIC WORLD VIEW.

THE NATURE OF DREAMS

PRECOGNITIVE DREAMS

An estimated 40 per cent of reported psychic
experiences concern knowing the future in some
way, with dreams being the most common way for
premonitions (precognitions) to appear. Precognitive
dreams are ones where the dreamer somehow
receives information about the future which
subsequently turns out to be verified by events. This
information could not have been obtained or
inferred by any other means.

Traditional societies typically take precognitive
dreams seriously, believing that they may contain
information that could be vital to the survival and
wellbeing of the community. In modern society,
many precognitive dreams have been linked with
major disasters, including the sinking of the *Titanic*

BELOW Are we to take
notice of precognitive
dreams? There have been
cases where the veracity
of such dreams is utterly
convincing to the
dreamer, but does that
mean it is really possible
to dream the future?

in 1912 and the Japanese attack on Pearl Harbor in
1941. Dreams of earthquakes, volcanic eruptions,
and transport disasters on land, sea and air, as well
as the assassinations of public figures have all been
foretold in dreams. There are also instances of
particularly gifted dreamers using knowledge
gleaned in their dreams or in a dream-like state to
help the police solve crimes.

Significant historical figures have also dreamt of
their own destiny. For instance, Ghengis Khan,
Oliver Cromwell, Napoleon Bonaparte and Adolf
Hitler all had prophetic dreams of their success in
battle, while the US president Abraham Lincoln saw
his dead body laid out in a coffin two weeks before
he was assassinated. Although Lincoln took the
dream seriously he was unable to avoid its
fulfilment. On a lighter note, there are also many
instances of people dreaming racehorse winners or
lottery numbers, sometimes on a sufficiently regular
basis to make money from it.

THE SLEEPING PROPHET

Perhaps one of the most spectacular revelatory
dreamers of recent times was Edgar Cayce (1877-
1945). Known as the "sleeping prophet", Cayce was
able to diagnose illness, prescribe treatments, and
correctly describe people he had never seen while in
a sleep or trance-like state.

Cayce practised clairvoyance for 43 years and by
the time he died, he had gathered together around
30,000 diagnostic reports and case studies
containing testimonies from his patients and
doctors that vouched for the accuracy of his
diagnosis and treatments. Cayce also used his
psychic abilities to help the police identify and track
down criminals.

Dreams must be heeded and accepted, for a great many of them come true.   PARACELSUS

OTHER TYPES OF PSYCHIC DREAMS

These are also relatively common types of psychic dream phenomena.

dreams of apparitions These dreams involve the deceased, whether you know the person or not. The theory suggests that the person appears in the dream in order to convey a personal message. This message is not necessarily for the dreamer. For instance, it is common for apparitions to appear to people who didn't know them very well, giving them a message to pass on to the loved ones of the deceased.

clairaudient dreams These dreams involve sounds in which you can clearly hear information.

empathic dreams These dreams involve clear and sympathetic feelings or sensations about an event that is occurring as you dream it.

clairvoyant dreams Events occur at the same time as a dream experience of the same event. There is absolutely nothing you can do about changing or preventing anything you see in a clairvoyant dream, although the information can be used to help people.

telepathic dreams Communication is made directly from one energy source to another without any mechanical assistance of any kind. These dreams tend to show us people and events not in our immediate environment. Such dreams sometimes occur when someone is either in danger or in an unusual predicament.

SCIENTIFIC RESEARCH

The problem with premonitions is that the knowledge of the event appears to precede the cause, which in conventional science is impossible. It also raises the principle of free will. Arguments are put forward that the events could be inferred, that the dream was not specific enough, or that they are just coincidences. However research suggests that there is some evidence for foreknowledge. Tests have been conducted where participants guess which card will be shown next, or which light on a panel will come on next, and correct predictions happened surprisingly often.

RIGHT Perhaps dreams are a way for our subconscious to experiment with our hidden fears, rather than any kind of premonition of oncoming disaster that might be creeping up behind us.

NIGHT TRAVELLERS

THE QUESTION ABOUT WHAT HAPPENS TO US WHEN WE ARE ASLEEP IS ONE THAT CONTINUES TO PUZZLE US. SCIENTISTS ARE NOW ABLE TO EXPLAIN THE PHYSIOLOGICAL CHANGES THAT TAKE PLACE IN THE BODY AND ALSO TO MONITOR BRAIN WAVE PATTERNS TO INDICATE STAGES OF SLEEP. PSYCHOLOGISTS CAN EXPLAIN SLEEP AND DREAMING IN TERMS OF UNCONSCIOUS PROCESSES AND RECOGNIZE ARCHETYPAL DREAM SYMBOLS AND PATTERNS. YET NEITHER SCIENCE NOR PSYCHOLOGY CAN ACCOUNT FOR OUT-OF-BODY EXPERIENCES (OBE), WHERE A DREAMER LEAVES THEIR PHYSICAL BODY YET STILL RETAINS CONSCIOUS AWARENESS.

ASTRAL PLANES

Some people believe that dreams are our jumbled and distorted memories of our experiences in the astral kingdom, in which we have wandered while our physical body was sleeping. The astral planes are the supposed non-physical worlds that exist beyond time and space as we know it. Almost all esoteric traditions believe in the astral world in some form or another and that adepts can learn how to "astral travel", or journey into this realm at will.

The astral world is not regarded as an "imaginary" world in contrast to the physical reality of this one, but one that exists in parallel. In fact many spiritual traditions turn the argument on its head, saying that it is our present world that is illusory, and the astral world that is our spiritual home.

BELOW Many cultures believe we leave our body at night and go travelling on the astral plane – in some societies it is the job of the shaman to guide the dreamer and bring them safely back to their body.

THE ASTRAL OR DREAM BODY

In the West, the concept of astral bodies largely originated with Paracelsus, the 16th-century alchemist and healer. Paracelsus was convinced that we are influenced by the sun and moon and planetary constellations, but was not sure how. He came to the conclusion that stellar influences were exerted through what he called the "astral" or invisible energy body that surrounds the physical body. The astral body is roughly the same size and shape as the earthly one, but can detach from it and move about independently.

Psychics who are able to see the astral body maintain that it is connected to the physical body via a "silver cord". When we die, this cord is finally broken and the dream body no longer unites with the physical body.

FLYING DREAMS

During sleep, the astral or dream body lifts away from the physical body to explore other dimensions, but remains connected by the cord. The astral body can travel vast distances, but if the dream body strays too far, the physical body jerks it back again, which may register in sleep as a sense of falling, the sleeper sometimes abruptly waking from the "jolt" with feelings of disorientation and even physical symptoms, such as headaches and nausea. Some commentators believe that dreams of flying are related to psychic out-of-body experiences, the dream body floating weightless into the air, defying the laws of gravity. Such dreams are usually marked by a sense of euphoria and are rarely forgotten by those who have experienced them.

A man dreamt that he slipped out of his flesh just as a snake sheds its old skin. He died the following day. For his soul, which was about to depart from his body, provided him with these images.

ARTEMIDORUS

OUT-OF-BODY EXPERIENCES

The concept of the dream body may help to explain what is happening in an out-of-body experience (OBE). There are many well-documented instances where people have described not being "in" their bodies, but outside them, having no physical sensation but otherwise being able to see and hear what is going on. Some people have reported these experiences at the edge of falling into or out of sleep, describing themselves as "floating" near the ceiling while seeing themselves in bed. There are also many instances where people have reported OBEs while under anaesthesia. As they "float" above their physical body on the operating table, they are able to watch the proceedings and later are able to recount accurate details of what took place.

Many other people have experienced OBEs as a result of a near-death experience or shock. Such experiences are generally life transforming and seem to indicate that we have a level of consciousness that exists independently from our physical condition.

SCIENTIFIC STUDIES

Volunteers who have claimed to be able to generate out-of-body experience at will have been clinically tested. During a reported OBE, EEG readings reveal a change in brain wave patterns from a relaxed alpha rhythm to beta. Beta waves are the ones produced during normal waking activity. Similarly the breathing and heart rate both showed signs of increase, suggesting that some activity or stimulus, similar to a waking condition, was going on in the body. REM was absent, although there were more eye movements than in the usual non-dreaming (orthodox) sleep.

These findings seem to indicate that the sleeping subject was in a relaxed state but with a considerable degree of alertness. They were not, in fact, asleep. Physiological changes and changes in brain wave patterns indicate that something is happening, but more research and validated evidence is needed before science can describe something that "proves" an OBE.

ABOVE Are our dreams a tunnel from this world to the next? Or are our minds perhaps simply experimenting with fears that we avoid when we are awake but still need to confront?

ABOVE LEFT Do dreams give us a little taste of what it is like to be dead? Many claim they do and until it actually happens to us there is no way of being sure.

THE TWILIGHT ZONE

A DREAM IS AN ALTERED STATE OF CONSCIOUSNESS THAT WE FALL INTO DURING SLEEP. HOWEVER THERE ARE OTHER DREAM-LIKE STATES EXPERIENCED WHILE AWAKE OR ON THE BORDERS BETWEEN SLEEP AND WAKING. THESE INCLUDE DAYDREAMS AND HALLUCINATIONS, AS WELL AS HYPNOGOGIC STATES (OCCURRING AT THE EDGE OF SLEEP). ALL ARE CHARACTERIZED BY VIVID IMAGERY AND HEIGHTENED SENSITIVITY. THROUGH TRAINING AND DISCIPLINE, SOME PEOPLE ARE ABLE TO ENTER THESE STATES AT WILL, AND CERTAIN PLANTS AND HERBS HAVE BEEN USED TO ASSIST THE DREAMER'S ENTRY INTO A TRANCE-LIKE STATE. OTHER PEOPLE MAY EXPERIENCE THEM THROUGH MEDITATION.

HYPNOGOGIA

As we relax and drift into sleep, our brain wave pattern lengthens and slows down, changing from beta to alpha, and finally to theta. During this nodding-off stage, we can experience what is known as "hypnogogic" imagery, a series of vivid pictures or surreal imagery that bears little or no relation to waking memories. The imagery doesn't have the narrative quality of most sleeping dreams, but consists of a series of shifting and seemingly unconnected pictures that appear as if from nowhere: an animal, a face or a figure, an eye, a swirling rainbow of colours – the variety is infinite. The same process can also happen in reverse, emerging from sleep into drowsy wakefulness, where the fleeting visions may be referred to as "hypnopompic" imagery. Sometimes these persist into full consciousness when we are fully awake.

This state, also known as hypnogogia, is not only associated with sleep, but may occur in other situations where the brain wave pattern slows down sufficiently and we "switch off", such as during meditation, or even through boredom – as on a long stretch of motorway driving for instance.

HALLUCINATION

The Latin root for the word "hallucination" means "to wander in the mind", while the word "sleep" is derived from the Old English meaning "a vision". While visions, hallucinations and trance-like states are not the same as a sleep-induced dream, they nevertheless represent a dream-like experience where the boundaries between normal waking life and another dimension dissolve and merge. Within these blurred boundaries, there is a fine line between sanity and madness. For instance, people

BELOW As we begin to fall asleep, or sometimes during deep meditation, where the brain slows down, we go through a hypnogogic stage, where our mind tries to make sense of all the images in our head.

But the dreamers of the day are dangerous people, for they dream their dreams with open eyes and make them come true.

T. E. LAWRENCE

who suffer extreme states of mental illness, or who have misused certain drugs can become overpowered by hallucinations to such an extent that their grip on conventional reality breaks down, and is never really recovered.

SHAMANIC DREAMING

In many traditional cultures, the ability to enter a trance consciously and safely is a skill that is cultivated for the good of the wider community. The role of the dreamer, typically filled by the shaman or priest, is to travel "between the worlds", in search of a vision that can assist or advise his or her people. In fact the word "shaman" may be translated to mean "one who is exalted or lifted up". The shaman has the ability to step outside of their being in ecstatic trance, and is able to enter the dream world at will. While present in the other world they will be able to communicate with the "dream guides" and to bring back gifts of wisdom and healing.

BELOW LEFT Is sleep the same as an hallucination? Research on the brain suggests that the two states are very different although they share similar language, imagery and themes.
BELOW RIGHT The shaman needs to know how to explore the world of the dreamer, and this requires a rigorous and lengthy training.

SACRED HERBS

There are many plants and herbs that are known for their mind-altering effect. Some, such as fly agaric (*Amanita muscaria*) stimulate hallucinations, others such as peyote (*Lophophora williamsii*) produce out-of-body experiences, while cannabis (*C. indica*, *C. sativa*) and morning glory (*Ipomoea*) produce euphoria. Dramatic and vivid dreams can be induced by the infamous opium poppy, shown right, (*Papaver somniferum*). It was while under the influence of opium that Coleridge is alleged to have "visioned" his Kubla Khan poem. In many cultures, including our own, these plant substances have degenerated from their traditional sacred use by initiates in search of higher states of consciousness, into drugs used to escape the realities of everyday life. Most of these drugs are highly addictive and their use is illicit.

259

To become a shaman involves years of arduous training that typically involves lengthy periods of solitude, fasting and other "tests" designed to build inner strength and preserve sanity in preparation for when the ego's defences are dropped. Certain plants and herbs, as well as incense, talismans and objects of "power", are used to assist the dreamer in entering a trance-like state.

LUCID DREAMING

IN 1913, FREDERICK VAN EEDEN, A DUTCH PSYCHIATRIST, COINED THE TERM "LUCID DREAMS" TO DESCRIBE THE STATE OF BEING AWARE THAT YOU ARE DREAMING, WHILE IN THE DREAM STATE. HE BASED THIS ON HIS EXPERIENCE OF HIS OWN NUMEROUS LUCID DREAMS. CENTURIES EARLIER IN ANCIENT GREECE, ARISTOTLE HAD ALSO CONCLUDED THAT DURING SLEEP "THERE IS SOMETHING IN CONSCIOUSNESS WHICH DECLARES THAT WHAT THEN PRESENTS ITSELF IS BUT A DREAM". WHAT HAPPENS IN THE CONSCIOUSNESS OF THE DREAMER IS SOMETHING WE BARELY UNDERSTAND, BUT IT SEEMS THAT LUCID DREAMS INTRODUCE US TO THE PART OF OURSELVES THAT CREATES OUR DREAMS.

ABOVE A lucid dream is one in which we know we are dreaming. They can be very terrifying and unsettling, but if controlled can become liberating and empowering.

ABOVE There will always be clues in a lucid dream that will give the game away and become the trigger that lets us know we are in a dream – minor or major things that are utterly impossible in waking life.

DIRECTING A DREAM

Frederick Van Eeden describes a lucid dream he experienced on the night of 9th September 1904. His experience indicates that not only did he retain a level of conscious awareness in the dream, but also that he was able to direct the dream's content and action to some extent.

"I dreamt that I stood at a table before a window. On the table were different objects. I was perfectly aware that I was dreaming and I considered what sorts of experiments I could make ... I took a fine claret glass from the table and struck it with my fist, with all my might, at the same time reflecting how dangerous it would be to do this in waking life; yet the glass remained whole. But lo! When I looked at it again after some time, it was broken. It broke all right, but a little too late, like an actor who misses

his cue. This gave me a very curious impression of being in a fake world cleverly imitated but with small failures."

SPONTANEOUS LUCIDITY

In general, people who have good recall of their dreams report at least one experience of being in a lucid dream, while for those who regularly record and work with their dreams the experience seems more familiar and frequent. However, we are not really sure what it is that turns a normal dream into a lucid experience. The most common trigger seems to be that the dreamer recognizes a dream-like

People like to play around with lucid dreams as it gives us a measure of control – and that means we can direct the dream, face our deepest fears, or live our wildest fantasies in safety.

quality to the events taking place. Sometimes this is when the dreamer becomes aware of a fantastic element, such as a talking dog or being able to fly, while others come to recognize the sensation of the dream state and seem to "just know" they are dreaming. People who record their dreams regularly appear to actually incorporate their recognition of dreaming into the dialogue and action of the dream.

VIRTUAL REALITY

Many people are attracted by the notion of lucid dreams because the idea strikes us as a kind of virtual reality. Once you know that you are in a dream, perhaps you can control the action and influence the course of events – go places, do things, meet people and generally have the kind of experience you want. Because the dream world is not bound by logic or the rules of physics, it is possible to do or be anything that you desire. You can travel through the universe, turn yourself into an alligator, meet a long-lost lover or enjoy an extravagant luxury. This creates an exhilarating sense of freedom and expansion beyond everyday life.

PERSONAL DEVELOPMENT

Many Western therapists regard lucid dreaming as an essential skill on the path to inner development. Charles Tart, an American psychologist, suggests that we use the freedom in lucid dreams to seek or create a wise guide whom we can call upon for advice relating to our spiritual and psychological growth. Lucid dreams can also provide an opportunity to try out new strategies that are different to our habitual responses. By seeing all aspects of the dream as part of yourself, it is possible to stand outside of the role you are playing in the dream, analyse it and change it if you so wish. For instance, instead of fleeing in the face of a tiger, you can try turning around and facing it head on. A recent study indicates that lucid dreamers may have a stronger sense of their individuality and personal power, and may be less likely to succumb to group pressure or conform to society's expectations.

LEARNING TO LUCID DREAM

The most important key to learning how to generate lucid dreams is your level of motivation. The second is being adept at recalling your dreams, something which comes through practice. However, the following techniques may also be used to encourage lucidity:

pre-sleep suggestion As you drift to sleep, repeat a request or statement in your mind about becoming lucid in your dreams.

periodic questioning Develop a "critical-reflective attitude" to your state of consciousness while awake, asking yourself "could I be dreaming now?" at regular intervals throughout the day.

rehearse dreaming Sit down and pretend that you are dreaming. Use your imagination to create a dream.

if this were a dream Several times a day, stop and ask yourself "if this experience were a dream, what would it mean?"

meditation People who regularly practise meditation techniques seem to have more lucid dreams.

dream groups It is possible to join up with other people who are interested in exploring their dreams. People with an established forum in which to discuss their dreams tend to become regular lucid dreamers.

THE SENSE AND SUBSTANCE OF DREAMS

Every night we all dream. What we dream about can be hard to remember, or when we do remember, may be difficult to comprehend. During sleep the brain is active and our dreams are perceived through the deeper layers of the unconscious mind. The unconscious does not communicate in words or through reason, but uses visual images to stimulate intuition and feeling. When we wake we are left with a residual "sense of" something that stays with us through the day, an imprint in our memory like a footstep in the snow.

RIGHT The landscape of a dream might be an incidental detail, or may be the most significant element of it.

ARCHETYPES

IN ART OR LITERATURE, A RECURRENT SYMBOL OR MOTIF MAY BE DESCRIBED AS AN ARCHETYPE. IN JUNGIAN PSYCHOLOGY IT IS THE TERM USED TO DESCRIBE THE BASIC BUILDING BLOCKS OF THE HUMAN PSYCHE, WHICH RESIDE IN THE COLLECTIVE UNCONSCIOUS. ACCORDING TO JUNG, THE COLLECTIVE UNCONSCIOUS CONTAINS OUR INHERITED CULTURAL, ANCESTRAL AND HISTORIC MEMORIES. THESE ELEMENTS ARE DERIVED FROM THE UNIVERSAL HUMAN EXPERIENCE AND TRANSCEND THE PURELY PERSONAL. ARCHETYPES ARE THE "ORIGINAL PATTERNS", THE DEEPEST PART OF THE HUMAN SOUL THAT FEATURE IN OUR ENDURING FOLKLORE AND ART AND, NOW AND AGAIN, IN OUR DREAMS.

CULTURAL PATTERNS

The collective unconscious may be universal but the form its archetypes take are culture-specific. We see what we have been conditioned to see. For instance in Western culture, angels are celestial beings that mediate between humans and higher powers. In both the Old and New Testaments they appear in dreams and visions, bringing messages from God to the dreamer. Yet in other cultures the concept of the angel is unknown. Among the Sioux Indians of North America it is the full moon that is the heavenly messenger, holding out choices to the dreamer in its hands.

Our dreams therefore are patterned according to our culture, giving us roots deep into our ancestral

BELOW No matter what our culture, we do all seem to share certain imagery – or archetypes – that we all respond to in a similar way, even if the meaning behind the image has different shades of interpretation.

and historic past. It is these "cultural pattern" or archetypal dreams that seem to be some form of communication from the beyond, from something bigger and outside of our "little selves". They are the ones that wake us up with a start.

DREAMS BIG AND SMALL

Malinowski, a contemporary of Jung's, distinguished between two types of dream. Cultural pattern or archetypal dreams he calls "official" dreams, while "free" dreams are those that are entirely of our own making. Jung refers to these official dreams as the big or meaningful dreams as opposed to the little or everyday dreams. The little dreams are the ones where we seem to be doing our mental filing, sorting and processing all the information we receive while awake. They are the ones where we can easily identify the imagery and symbolism: "Oh, yes, I dreamed of that because I had watched a particular film just before going to bed", or "Ah, I know why I dreamed of that, it was because we were talking about it earlier in the day". The big dreams on the other hand are the ones that seem to mean something profound and defy rational explanation.

From the collective unconscious we draw images (archetypes) of extraordinary potential and power. These images present themselves to us in our big dreams. The big dreams are the ones we remember, that haunt us. They are packed with vivid imagery, symbolism and metaphor that are too powerful to be held in our mental grasp. These images are sometimes disturbing, frequently new and very often wonderful. They seem larger than life and to come from another dimension, and can provoke the question: "Am I dreaming, or being dreamed?"

We may expect to find in dreams everything that has ever been of significance in the life of humanity.

CARL JUNG

THE POWER OF ARCHETYPES

Examining these archetypes is essential if we are to
understand our dreams and the personal messages
they hold for us. The archetypes are there to
challenge us, to stretch us, to take us out of our
normal everyday life and throw us back into the
mysterious world of myths and magic. They are
there to remind us that we are more than going to
work, watching TV or eating out at the latest
restaurants. At rock bottom, we are creatures of
spirit and imagination, intuition and mystery. No
matter how "civilized" we become, like a tidal wave
an archetypal dream will suddenly appear, a
shocking reminder that we are more than the little
selves of our everyday life.

THE TIMING OF BIG DREAMS

Times of change and transition are generally
recognized as "stress points". This is because there is
a wealth of new material for us to process and
integrate into the psyche and our normal ego
defences are weakened. This may help to explain
why a powerful dream is more likely to get through
to us at such times.

Archetypal dreams often occur when we are
undergoing major life events. Typical instances
include puberty, marriage, pregnancy, death or
divorce as well as children leaving home, taking up
a new job or moving house. Major events do not
have to be personal to trigger an archetypal dream.
Dramatic global news can also affect us at a deep
soul level and there are typically many reported
incidences of big dreams after major world events,
such as the unexpected death of a public figure or
outbreaks of war and violence.

ABOVE Archetypal
dreams often occur when
we are going through
life's rites of passage –
as if they are needed
most then.
ABOVE LEFT Most
archetypes are instantly
recognizable and we
would probably associate
this character with
ancient wisdom
and nobility.

LEFT Perhaps your
dreams contain images
that your mind has taken
with it from your day's
activities. If you watch
television in bed it seems
logical that visual
elements from that will
be revisited in a dream.

ABOVE Naked in public? It's a common theme in dreams and means different things to different people, but is an indicator that the mask of the Persona has slipped. **ABOVE RIGHT** The shadow takes on many forms and has had different characterizations throughout literature, myth and folklore.

JUNGIAN ARCHETYPES

In his investigations into the collective unconscious, Jung formulated several archetypal forces or principles. These may not be definitive, but they nevertheless remain a handy and convenient tool for making sense of our dreams.

THE PERSONA

The conscious personality, the Persona, is akin to Freud's concept of the ego. It is the person we present to the outside world, the mask we wear in order to protect our most real and vulnerable self. To find the Persona in our dreams is to look for a symbolic representation of "me".

We have many guises and wear many masks depending on the social role we are playing. Responsible parent, respected professional and rebellious teenager are just a few examples. Appearing naked in a dream is an indicator that the mask has slipped, our Persona is absent and we are literally naked before others, physically, emotionally and even spiritually. If we feel the mask is tarnished we may appear as a scarecrow, a tramp, or a degenerate. If we feel the mask is too firmly in place we may wear armour or a visor.

THE SHADOW

Jung described the Shadow as a "splinter personality". Anything that does not fit with how we like to see ourselves is pushed into the background, repressed into the unconscious. Yet no matter how hard we try to keep it under control, every now and again it erupts, like a wilful and disobedient child. The Shadow is our dark side, our "sinful" nature that we judge and condemn as wrong and bad. It is our temper tantrums, black moods, anger, violence, lust, greed and unspeakable desires. It is the things we fear and hate the most.

We are very afraid of the Shadow, for it has the power to rip away the mask and reveal our true face. In our dreams it may appear as a shadowy figure, a cloaked evil-doer, a malignant force threatening to overpower us. Yet Jung did not perceive the Shadow as inherently evil, merely "somewhat inferior, primitive, unadapted and awkward". It does things in the old way, as Jung put it, and its messages are often actually for our own good.

THE ANIMA AND ANIMUS

We each wear the mask of our gender. Yet within every man and woman resides the seed of the opposite sex. "Anima" and "Animus" were the terms coined by Jung to personify the "inner woman" and the "inner man", or the feminine part of a man's personality and the masculine part of a woman's.

Both the Anima and Animus are shaped by the child's experience of his or her mother and father. Broadly speaking however, the Animus is the hero within, practical, adventurous, independent and self-assured. The Anima is the heroine, both goddess and seductress. She is sensitive, compassionate, sensual and instinctive. It must be remembered that these are psychological attributes rather than characteristics of men and women as such. When these qualities are not integrated into the psyche, we project them on to other people, particularly our partners, in our desire for that perfect person who, we believe, will make our dreams come true.

THE TRICKSTER

Hard to define because he is always one step ahead, the Trickster leads us a merry dance as we follow pipe dreams. He is the shape shifter, the joker in the pack and the jester or clown. His is the leering, jeering face in the carnival, painted and seductive. He is the Pied Piper, the Lord of the Dance who offers us delight and pleasure, but if we follow his call we will end up a laughing stock, with dust in our mouths.

Although a mischievous fraudster and saboteur, the Trickster's antics can also be corrective. With great skill he pricks the balloon of our inflated sense of self, mocking our vanities and self-obsessions, ridiculing our ambitions and desires. Not of this world, the Trickster is also the shaman, the one who can enter the realm of magic and interpret our dreams. He represents our intuitive side.

THE DIVINE CHILD

A symbol of innocence and purity, the Divine Child embodies birth and growth, potential and latent energy. The Divine Child is a link between past, present and future, a mediator who brings healing and wholeness, and possesses enormous transforming power. Symbols for the Divine Child include the changeling, the jewel, the flower and the chalice. By becoming the Divine Child ourselves we strip away all our preconceptions and judgements, as well as our ideas and goals. The Divine Child is a return to innocence, a readiness to be reborn without the mask.

THE LITTLE PRINCE

The following extract is from Antoine de Saint-Exupéry's novel *The Little Prince* in which he describes a dream-like landscape and an archetypal Divine Child figure.

"Look very carefully at the landscape so as to be sure to recognize it ... And if you should happen to come upon this spot, please do not hurry on. Wait a little, exactly under the star. Then, if a child comes towards you, if he laughs, if he has golden locks and if he refuses to answer questions, you will surely guess who he is."

ABOVE The image of the Divine Child is a very powerful one and it has inspired painters and poets for centuries. Here it is contrasted with the archetype of the hero, the youthful aspect of the Father.

LEFT The image of the Divine Child combined with that of the Great Mother is so powerful that it has inspired religions that have affected millions and filled them with awe.

THE GREAT MOTHER

From the Great Mother's loins springs all of humanity, created and birthed from her womb and her fruitfulness. This archetype has three aspects: virgin, mother and crone, each of these having a positive and a negative face. The virgin is a young bare-breasted girl garlanded with spring flowers. She dances, sings, and plays music, she is a creature of the meadows and fields. In her negative aspect she is a seductress, purposely attracting and then spurning her suitors. The round-bellied "earth" mother is the healer and nurturer, caring for the physical and emotional needs of her family. She inhabits the kitchen and bake house, the summer lodges, the woods and the glades. Or else she is the "terrible mother", possessive, demanding and devouring. The crone is the wise woman and priestess. She is intuitive and free thinking, living life according to her own rules. She possesses psychic, magical powers. Her other side is the ugly hag, a nightmare creature of the forests and caves, the underground, the underworlds. She is the evil sorceress and harpy.

THE GREAT FATHER

Parallel to the Great Mother is the Great Father. His aspects complement those of the Mother: prince, father and hermit, each with a positive and a negative side. The prince is the young man with high ideals, setting out on the quest of life. He is the dreamer and poet and is capable of greatness. In his negative aspect he is a vagabond and wastrel, the lazy lout who thinks the world owes him a living. He uses women to gratify his sexual desires.

The father is the hunter and provider. He procreates and preserves the race and represents standards and ideals to live up to. He is an authority figure and we seek his approval, but his judgements are fair. On the negative side he is the despot and ogre, an authoritarian figure who is sadistic and uncaring. The hermit excludes himself from society to nurture his soul in prayer and meditation. He is the "wise ancient", the guru, priest and spirit guide, who can help us find our inner light. He brings

FINDING YOUR ARCHETYPES

Some archetypes will have more meaning for you than others. These are the ones most likely to appear in your dreams. Draw up a list of archetypes that have the most meaning for you. This could contain characters and personalities, as well as objects and situations. Use the list to help you, adding or deleting any as appropriate.

archetypal characters

king/queen	alchemist	mythical beast	traveller
prince/princess	artist	(sphinx, unicorn,	skeleton
baby/child	monk/nun	dragon)	criminal
messenger	priest/priestess	jester	prisoner
angel	any animal	pregnant woman	ghost
devil	crows/other birds	lovers	

archetypal objects and locations

sun	rainbow	graveyard	chalice
moon	temple/church	landscape	jewels or money
stars	battlefield	sailing boat	
the four elements	clouds	cave	
lightning	maze	sword	

practical understanding to our problems and dilemmas and a sense of personal power. In his dark aspect he is the black magician who misuses his powers for personal gain.

OTHER ARCHETYPES

Archetypal themes and patterns can also appear in many other forms. For instance the journey, the eternal triangle, temptation and redemption, birth, death and disaster are all common themes that appear in myth and religion as well as in our dreams. The four elements (fire, water, earth and air) are archetypal energies, representing the natural forces of the universe that shape and sustain our lives. Animals too can be archetypal symbols. For instance, a dog may characterize loyalty, a hawk clear vision and a cat freedom and independence. Esoteric arts, such as astrology and the tarot, as well as the world's greatest myths are also based on archetypal symbols, which may help to explain their enduring fascination. Defying rational explanation they strike a chord deep within us, speaking the eternal language of the soul.

UNDERSTANDING ARCHETYPES

Archetypes permeate every facet of our lives. To begin to understand how they work and how they relate to your life, try the following questionnaire for fun. Don't think about the answers but go for the one that first comes to mind, elaborating on it as much as possible. You might be surprised at the results!

1 Choose a flower to represent yourself. What does it say about you that is hard to express in words alone?

2 What is your favourite colour and why do you like it?

3 Which is your favourite domestic animal? What qualities does it have that resonate with you?

4 Describe your favourite foods. How do you feel when you eat these foods?

5 What is your favourite tree? What is it about the tree that you especially like?

6 What kind of water do you like best: rivers, streams, lakes or the sea? Do you know what this kind of water says to you?

7 If you could shape shift, which animal would you like to become? Can you say what it is about this animal that you find so inspiring?

explanation

1 The flower represents your attitude to your soul.

2 The colour represents your emotional attitude.

3 The domestic animal represents the qualities you look for in your friends.

4 The food represents how you feel about your body and sex as a physical activity.

5 The tree represents your attitude towards life in general.

6 The water you have chosen represents your sexuality.

7 The wild animal represents the hidden you beneath the mask.

FAR LEFT AND LEFT
Archetypes help us understand ourselves and our partners, friends and family. By identifying different archetypes, such as the hero (far left) and the unicorn (left) and how they affect us, we can learn a lot about ourselves.

LEVELS OF DREAMING

THE UNCONSCIOUS IS MADE UP OF DIFFERENT LAYERS, REPRESENTING SUCCESSIVELY DEEPER STRATA OF THE MIND. FREUD CONCEPTUALIZED THESE LAYERS AT TWO LEVELS: THE PRECONSCIOUS AND THE PERSONAL UNCONSCIOUS. TO THESE JUNG ADDED A THIRD LEVEL, WHICH HE REFERRED TO AS THE COLLECTIVE UNCONSCIOUS. THERE MAY ALSO BE A DIMENSION OF THE MIND THAT CAN PRODUCE VISION-LIKE DREAMS OF EXTRAORDINARY POWER AND SIGNIFICANCE. OUR DREAMS ARISE FROM THESE DIFFERENT LEVELS, AND ALTHOUGH ANY DREAM CAN CONTAIN MATERIAL FROM MORE THAN ONE LEVEL, USUALLY ONE OR OTHER LEVEL PREDOMINATES.

BELOW Level one dreams are most often associated with the preconscious; the most accessible part of our mind. The elements within these dreams may be random mental images with no meaning.

LEVEL ONE DREAMS

These dreams are associated with the preconscious, the most accessible part of the mind. Level one dreams contain material that can be easily linked to waking life. These dreams tend to revolve around the events of the day, and opinion is divided as to whether or not they are particularly meaningful.

Sometimes dreams alter the course of an entire life.

JUDITH DUERK

Some would say that these dreams represent random, jumbled nonsense. They are a way of the mind unburdening itself and have no particular significance. Others suggest that trivial events should not necessarily be automatically dismissed: they may be used as a "way in" to deeper levels of the mind which are more difficult to access directly.

LEVEL TWO DREAMS

Dreams at this level are capable of giving us insights which we could not achieve during normal waking life. These dreams, from the personal unconscious, can include forgotten memories, repressed wishes and fears, and unacknowledged emotions and expectations. The symbolism of these dreams is uniquely personal to the dreamer and the dream scenario is usually quite different to anything in waking life. Such dreams usually have an intriguing quality to them and are not easily forgotten.

LEVEL THREE DREAMS

The collective unconscious is a storehouse of archetypal themes and symbols, forming the raw material for the deepest longings and aspirations of the human race. This level transcends the purely personal. Dreams from this level are concerned with profound issues such as life and death, love, transformation and spirituality. Dreams in this category are much less common, although people engaged in self-exploration practices such as psychotherapy or meditation, or who consciously choose to work with their dreams in some way, often report an increase in level three dreams.

COSMIC DREAMS

On very rare occasions, maybe once in a lifetime only, you may encounter an extremely important and extraordinary dream that is truly awe-inspiring. Cosmic dreams go even further than level-three type

dreams. They are ones in which the qualities of the universe itself are the major themes. They are made up of formless shapes and colours, a swirling mass of light and dark and shade with no recognizable objects or identifiable substance. Cosmic dreams are an attempt by the unconscious to make sense of the vastness of the universe and our place within it. The Moscow-born writer and mystic, P.D. Ouspensky (1878-1947) said such dreams "disclose to us the mysteries of being, show the governing laws of life, and bring us into contact with higher forces". These dreams have the capacity to change our life.

THE TUNNEL OF LIGHT

A man had the following cosmic dream when he was 41 years old, and finds that it has stayed with him through the following years:

I was rushing down this incredible tunnel of light – but it was a dark light. I had no body and was pure spirit, pure energy. There was a sound, a voice which was saying something like, "You are entering sector 16". At the end of the tunnel I came to a sudden stop and was aware that I had arrived at a sort of hole in a cliff face, but this was a cliff face a million miles high. The hole was halfway up and I was looking out over a wide plain that was completely occupied by some divine being. It was a sort of giant eye but there wasn't a physical eye – only a divine way of seeing everything. As I stood there I was aware that this eye was turning towards me, was going to look at me. I felt I wasn't worthy. This wasn't my time. I was frightened and was immediately whisked back up the tunnel. I woke up sweating and very shaken.

I have thought about this dream almost every day since having it seventeen years ago. I am determined to be "worthy" next time I go back. I think the next time will be when I die. I believe that what I was given a glimpse of was my own mortality, my own death. This dream has had a huge impact on me. Everything I do is judged against that worthiness. I can't explain what it is that would make something I do worthy, but I just know instinctively what is right and wrong."

ABOVE Each of the images in our dreams has been carefully chosen so that it means something to us, the dreamer.

LEFT Into our dream worlds we take with us the images we have accumulated through our lives.

DREAM LOGIC

LOGIC IS NOT THE FORTE OF THE DREAMING MIND. IN OUR DREAMS THE IMPOSSIBLE BECOMES POSSIBLE AND THE
NONSENSICAL APPEARS PERFECTLY NORMAL, AS PEOPLE, ANIMALS, OBJECTS AND PLACES BEHAVE IN BIZARRE AND
UNACCOUNTABLE WAYS. FREUD ONCE REMARKED THAT ANYONE WHO BEHAVED WHILE AWAKE AS THEY DO IN THEIR DREAMS
WOULD BE REGARDED AS INSANE. IN THE WORLD OF DREAMS, THE NORMAL RULES OF LOGIC, REASON AND "COMMON
SENSE" ARE THROWN TO THE WINDS AS EVENTS APPEAR TO KALEIDOSCOPE INTO A THEATRE OF THE ABSURD. YET STRANGE
THOUGH IT MAY SEEM, OUR DREAMS DO IN FACT HAVE A CURIOUS LOGIC OF THEIR OWN.

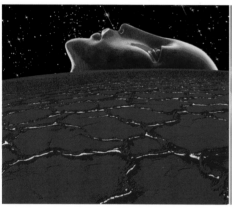 

ABOVE All our dreams have their own curious dream logic, stemming from our own personal logic. Once we crack the code all our dreams can be understood.

ABOVE RIGHT It is useful to look at other people's dream logic but bear in mind they might only match yours slightly, more likely they will bear no resemblance at all.

FREUD'S DREAM LOGIC

Intrigued by the absurdity of dreams, Freud began
his investigation into how dreams work. His work
claims that dreams express an element of logical
connection in four different ways: simultaneity,
contiguity, transformation and similarity.

When two elements in a dream are presented
close together, simultaneity suggests that an intimate
relationship exists between the two. Dream
combinations are not randomly formed but have
meaning within the dream. Contiguity is when
dream elements occur sequentially, and
transformation is when one thing turns into another.
Similarity is the direct or indirect association
between things in the dream.

The work of American psychologists Hall and
Nordby adds the idea of "relative consistency" to
Freud's ideas, noticing that dream motifs have a
certain frequency and uniformity about them.

YOUR DREAM LOGIC

Other people's ideas may be helpful when practising
dream interpretation, but they will not necessarily fit
with everyone's dreams all of the time. We all have
our own unique dream logic which may be
completely different from anyone else's. If you are
keeping a dream record, see if you can find a
consistency of pattern to your dreams. It may be
that you always appear as yourself or always as
someone else. Your dream logic is a bit like Woody
Allen films. You may see a different film each time
but the style is consistent and recognizable. You get
to know your way round as you study the subject.

MICE AND SPIDERS

Your unique dream logic invariably extends to your
dream symbolism and will most likely influence the
type of archetypes you are working with. These
represent what you need to "bring to the surface"

What is life? An illusion, a shadow, a story. And the greatest good is little enough: for all life is a
dream and dreams themselves are only dreams.
PEDRO CALDERON DE LA BARCA

emotionally and indicate the sort of imagery you feel more or less comfortable with. For even in the depths of the most awful nightmare, you will find yourself being terrorized by the sort of thing that you already know you find scary. In a sense this is a comforting thought, because you will not frighten yourself in your dreams with an image that is totally alien. If it is mice and spiders that scare you in waking life, then they are the most likely creatures to pop up and scare you in your dreams. Conversely if it is the Bogey Man, ghosts or monsters that terrify you, then that is what will stalk the nightmare corridors of your dreaming mind.

BLOOD IN THE TAPS

Your own curious dream logic is likely to remain fairly constant over the years and you will gradually come to know your dreams, and yourself, pretty well. Once you know your own dream logic you can to a certain extent ignore what is following those predictable patterns. For instance, if someone dreams that water comes out of the taps, then their logic is following a natural course. If, however, they

ABOVE Whatever scares or disturbs you in your waking life is likely to scare you just as much in your dreams. The nightmares that frighten you will carry images that you have an instant fearful reaction to.

always dream that blood comes out of the taps then that is their unique dream logic. Neither dream is good or bad, right or wrong. They are merely the unique expressions of two different dreamers whose minds are processing their unconscious material while they are asleep.

DREAMS AND EVERYDAY LIFE

There does seem to be a close relationship between what happens in our "real" lives and what happens in our dreams. The situations may change but the rules governing them tend to be the same as in everyday life. For instance if you are always concerned with what people wear, then it is likely that clothes and the way they are worn will be just as important in your dreams. If, on the other hand, you are more interested in what people say, then it is likely your dreams will follow a similar pattern.

DREAM SCENERY

DREAMS HAVE TO BE SET SOMEWHERE, TO HAVE A PHYSICAL SITUATION THAT THEY TAKE PLACE IN. THIS IS THE DREAM SCENERY, SIMILAR TO THE BACKDROP OF A THEATRE STAGE. THE LOCATION AND PROPS PROVIDE A CONTEXT FOR THE DREAM AND GIVE CLUES ABOUT THE ACTION THAT IS TAKING PLACE. FOR MOST OF US MOST OF THE TIME, THE CHARACTERISTICS OF THIS BACKDROP REMAIN MUCH THE SAME AS IN EVERYDAY LIFE. IT IS UNUSUAL FOR DREAMS TO BE SET IN A LANDSCAPE WHERE, FOR EXAMPLE, EVERYTHING IS PERMANENTLY UPSIDE DOWN. IT IS MUCH MORE LIKELY THAT THE SCENERY WILL BE THE RIGHT WAY UP AND THE DREAM ACTORS AND PROPS BEHAVE ACCORDING TO THE NATURAL LAWS OF PHYSICS.

SURREAL LANDSCAPES

Now and again of course, dream settings and characters do not obey natural laws. Trees may appear upside down, the sky may be green, the sea a brilliant shade of yellow, cats may swim and people may fly weightless above the ground. Within the context of the dream, all of these things appear perfectly normal. It is only when we wake that they strike us as odd, as the rational mind tries to make sense of the illogical and therefore impossible.

These surreal dreams are often the ones that stick in the memory and usually have particular significance for the dreamer. The landscape is what we would focus on when trying to interpret the dream, although the conclusions we reach will depend on each individual.

According to Freud, the landscape of our dreams can be interpreted, and represents the uncharted territory of the unconscious mind and our repressed sexual longings.

BELOW RIGHT Once we are immersed in the dream the landscape will appear real; it is only when we wake that it seems odd. It may be a symbolic or real place, or even both.
BELOW Interpreting the landscapes in your dreams will depend on what significance they have to you in real life. Tall buildings would have suggested the phallus to Freud, but to you they might represent anything from soaring ambition to intimidation.

> Then suddenly I ... fly slowly over the lane, over the houses, and then over the Golden Horn in the direction of Stamboul. I smell the sea, feel the wind, the warm sun. This flying gives me a wonderfully pleasant sensation... P. D. OUSPENSKY

INTERPRETING THE LANDSCAPE

In a Freudian world, soft round or curvy shapes and narrow indentations represent the female form. For instance, hills represent a woman's breasts, belly or womb, and a dark doorway or passageway, her vagina. Alternatively, hard, upright or elongated shapes represent the male form. Mountain peaks, tall buildings, a train and an aeroplane are all phallic symbols. Only you can decide if these ideas have meaning for you in the context of your dreams.

Jung did not interpret the dream landscape in the same way as Freud, yet he nevertheless believed that the place where the dream is staged makes a tremendous difference to the way the dream is interpreted. A dream that is set in a wood or forest has quite a different feel about it to one that is set in a living room or office. Some dream experts believe that dreams staged in a man-made setting are more based on the concerns of the personality, while those dreams that are set in nature come from the deeper reaches of the soul.

MOODS AND FEELINGS

It is not only the physical nature of the dream setting that is important, but the mood or atmosphere it inspires. The dream landscape has the power to provoke feelings and emotions in the dreamer. Although the scenery may look the same as it does in ordinary life, it may take on a curious surreal quality, appearing melting and hypnotic, as deeply experienced and more real than real. People in a state of hallucination have reported similar occurrences, experiencing a world where walls are sad or happy, trees can sing and dance, and crockery can throw itself at you in a fit of angry pique.

Yet dream scenery does not need to take on a life of its own for it to inspire mood and feelings. Some of the most lasting impressions of our dreams

LEFT Dream landscape not only refers to natural scenery, but to any context in which your dream takes place, inside or out. You might dream about your own living room – it would still be your dream landscape.

COMMON DREAM SETTINGS

Research indicates that the most frequent dream setting is a building, usually a domestic residence, with the living room, bedroom or kitchen being the most common place. The average number of characters in a dream is three, with strangers appearing slightly more often than friends or family members. Predominant dream activities are action-based, such as walking or running, followed by talking, sitting, socializing and playing. The most common emotions are apprehension and anger, followed by happiness and excitement.

are fragments of a landscape dimly remembered. Beautiful, awe-inspiring, tantalizing or downright peculiar, the dream setting is not only a backdrop for the action to take place, but is an integral part of the dream's content and the message it is trying to convey to the dreamer.

BELOW The dream setting allows us the freedom to imagine that anything can take place; that anything is possible, it doesn't have to be real or feasible, and it is important to examine why you have dreamt it like this.

NIGHTMARES

ALMOST EVERYONE KNOWS WHAT IT'S LIKE TO HAVE A NIGHTMARE. THE CHINESE DESCRIBE THEM AS DREAMS OF TERROR AND DREAD, WITH THE POWER TO JOLT US OUT OF SLEEP. WITNESSING ACTS OF HORROR OR BEING IN SOME KIND OF DANGER ARE THE MOST FREQUENT NIGHTMARE SCENARIOS. THESE ARE USUALLY ACCOMPANIED BY FEELINGS OF HELPLESSNESS AND PARALYSIS, OF BEING LOST OR OUT OF CONTROL AND AT THE MERCY OF AN EXTERNAL AGENT OR EVENT. FOR THOSE WHO SUFFER FROM FREQUENT NIGHTMARES GOING TO BED IS FILLED WITH FEAR. SLEEP IS NOT RENEWING AND REFRESHING, BUT IS MORE LIKE GOING INTO A STRESSFUL SITUATION, NIGHT AFTER NIGHT.

THE SUBJECTIVITY OF NIGHTMARES

Although we share a broad consensus about what is frightening, the content of our nightmares is always subjective. What is frightening in one person's dream world may seem innocuous in someone else's. What makes a nightmare upsetting is how it feels, the emotional experience, rather than the symbols or events in themselves. Consequently people who are emotionally sensitive seem to be more likely to experience nightmares than those who can shrug unwanted thoughts and feelings away. This may help explain why people with a creative bent, as well as young children, seem to suffer more frequent nightmares than other people.

WHY WE HAVE NIGHTMARES ·

Although nightmares are unpleasant, they may have a positive intention. They can be a message from the unconscious mind, a way of alerting us to something that is going on in our waking life that we need to become more aware of. When this is the case, the nightmare may recur, growing progressively more frightening until we understand what it is about and can root out the cause. Sometimes nightmares may be signs of illness and/or drug reactions, so do check with your doctor to eliminate this possibility.

CREATIVE VISUALIZATION

When nightmares become a real problem, and begin to disturb your waking life too, there are self-help measures you can take to reduce their frequency and intensity. The following suggestions are based on the techniques of creative visualization. Use them to begin to learn how to tap into the powers of your imagination in order to create change.

LEFT The more sensitive we are, the more artistic and creative, the more likely it is we are going to have nightmares. If you suffer from them, you might take some comfort from that fact.

To sleep: perchance to dream: ay, there's the rub:
For in that sleep of death what dreams may come...

WILLIAM SHAKESPEARE, HAMLET

CREATING AN IMAGINARY SCENE

Some people are able to visualize very easily; for others it might take some practice. You are trying to develop your ability to experience a mental escape from the scenes of your nightmares. Aim to make your imaginary scene such a strong image in your mind that it travels with you into your dream, and becomes your refuge over which you have control.

1 Sit in a quiet place where you feel safe and won't be disturbed. Close your eyes, breathe gently and allow yourself to relax.

2 Now imagine yourself in a beautiful place. This may be outside in nature, or indoors. It can be a real or an imaginary place. Visualize the scene as fully as possible, noticing the objects or scenery that surround you, any sounds or smells, whether it is warm or cool. Notice how you feel and what you are wearing. If you find yourself stopping at various points as you go through your imaginary scene, take notice of where you stop and then start again. It may take a few stops and starts to develop the scene in your mind's eye, but with time and regular practice it will come.

3 When you are comfortable with your scene, experiment by making small changes in it. For instance, you could change the colour of the walls, or add an animal that you like, or maybe a doorway or pathway. Continue to practise until you feel confident that the power of your own imagination has been added to your collection of skills. If at any time you start experiencing a negative reaction to what you are imagining, stop the scene and start again.

WORKING WITH NIGHTMARES

When you are able to create an imaginary scene and play about with it at will you are ready to use the technique with your nightmares. For some people, nightmares arise as a result of an actual trauma. Traumatic events can be too much for us to deal with at the time, so for the sake of preserving our sanity, they get pushed into the basement of the unconscious. Later the unexplored material may resurface in our dreams, perhaps so that any leftover memories and feelings associated with the event can be worked through and healed in relative safety. You may need to seek professional help when dealing with these sorts of nightmares.

1 Write down a recent nightmare. After you have written it down, allow yourself to change the nightmare in any way you wish, writing out a new and less threatening scenario.

2 Using your creative imagination, visualize the new dream you have written. See the scene in as much detail as possible. Let it play through your mind for 5-10 minutes, as if it is a new dream that you are actually experiencing.

3 Imagine this new dream at least once a day for a week, preferably before going to sleep. It is best to work with one dream at a time and not more than three a week.

After three months you should see some improvement in your nightmares. If no change is happening, change the dream again, creating a different scenario.

ABOVE The beautiful imaginary place that you create in your mind can take many forms. If you always return to the same place it can become more and more real, with a potency that can overcome the nightmare.

CHILDREN AND DREAMS

WE ARE BORN WITH THE CAPACITY TO DREAM. EVEN IN THE WOMB INDICATORS OF THE DREAMING STATE ARE PRESENT AND DREAMS PLAY AN IMPORTANT ROLE IN THE LIFE OF THE GROWING CHILD. THE JOURNEY OF CHILDHOOD IS THE GROWTH AND DEVELOPMENT OF INNATE CAPACITIES AS THE YOUNG PERSON LEARNS ABOUT THEMSELVES AND THE WORLD THEY LIVE IN. GROWING UP IS THE JOURNEY FROM AN INSTINCTUAL, UNCONSCIOUS STATE TO CONSCIOUS SELF-AWARENESS. CHILDREN'S DREAMS HAVE AN IMPORTANT PART TO PLAY IN THIS PROCESS. THEY ARE ONE OF THE WAYS THAT CHILDREN EXPRESS THEIR EMERGING IDENTITY AND INDICATE THEIR STATE OF MIND.

MYSTERY AND IMAGINATION

By the time we reach adulthood, we have reached some understanding about how the world is put together and our place in it. We approach the world with reason and have a sense of self or identity. For the developing child, things are not so clearly defined. The world is a place of mystery and fascination and the boundaries between fantasy and reality are blurred. It can be hard to tell where dreams end and imagination takes over. Talk to children about what happens in their dreams and

BELOW Children can be paralysed by the most intense nightmares and can be afraid to go to sleep. But without any fears children sleep with such serenity it often seems they are undisturbed by any kind of dream at all.

they will tell you of noble adventure stories where they play the hero and save the world, or else they'll tell you scary tales of monsters and demons and frightening fantasies. They also act out these fantasies in their play, both alone and when they are with other children.

Although young children may not understand their thoughts and feelings, they experience them with a rawness and intensity that as adults we may find hard to comprehend. The experience of children's daily life is much closer to the world of dreams. Children's dreams are vivid, intense and frequent. Appealing to their sense of mystery and imagination, every night they journey into a magical world of the unexpected and unexplained.

DREAM CONTENT

As we would expect, children's dreams reflect their waking lives and preoccupations. For instance, a young boy experiencing sibling rivalry may dream of quite happily killing his baby sister. To a parent, such a dream may appear alarming and shocking, but it does not mean the boy really wants to commit such an act, but is expressing his feelings of jealous outrage towards his rival, without any kind of moral inhibitions, in the dream. It is not surprising that parents and family members, rather than strangers, figure largely in children's dreams, as these are the people that fill up their waking lives. Friends and acquaintances tend to play an important role in the dreams of later childhood. Animals also feature strongly in children's dreams in various ways. Dreams tend to become longer and more complex, and more similar to the dreams of adults, as the child gets older.

If you talk to your children, you can help them to keep their lives together. If you talk to them skilfully, you can help them to build future dreams.

JIM ROHN

CHILDREN'S NIGHTMARES

Because children imagine and dream in glorious technicolour, their nightmares will be all the more frightening, all the more real. Similarly although we know there aren't really any bogey men or vampires, or monsters that are going to eat us, children don't have a cast-iron certainty about these things. As parents all we will get is a screaming child. We won't necessarily know what sparked it off, but what we do know is that the child is terrified and upset. In such a state of terror, the child needs to be reassured and to feel the comfort and safety offered by the parent. You can try telling them that if the monster appears again in a dream that it is to go away because you say so. Later you may be able to talk to the child to find out what it was all about.

However, for children to reveal shocking or disturbing dreams to their parents requires a climate of trust and sensitivity. Children won't tell their dreams if they think they will get into trouble, or that their parents will be dismissive. Sometimes children will avoid telling the truth in order to cover up what they feel their dream was really about.

AN OUT-OF-BODY EXPERIENCE

Children's nightmares are often triggered by emotional upsets. For instance, suffering disappointments, being unjustly punished, missing a favourite person, or having problems at school are some fairly common experiences. Although these problems cannot be corrected instantly, you can go a long way towards reassuring the child that they are loved and safe.

The following account is from an adult who recalls making up a dream as a child to satisfy his mother's curiosity, and reassure her. He has never told her what really happened.

"Aged about six I had a powerful experience, perhaps it was astral projection, perhaps not. But I did feel weirdly out of my body, hovering near the ceiling. I was absolutely terrified of this and screamed. My mother came rushing upstairs full of concern, but I didn't know what to tell her, it was so out of my experience, so I opted for lying. I told her that there had been a man in my room with a knife and he was going to kill me, going to kill all of us. My mother comforted me and dried my tears. For years afterwards, she talked about this 'nightmare' of mine. She told all my relatives and I never once corrected her. Even when I was grown up, I never had the heart to tell her that the content of my nightmare wasn't true, and I'd had a frightening out-of-body experience. I didn't tell her because I thought she wouldn't believe me or think it silly."

BELOW LEFT Your child may not understand or be able to articulate what they are dreaming about, so pressurizing them to tell you won't work.
BELOW Children, just like adults, are trying to make sense of the waking world in their dreams. Moments of confusion and insecurity will be reflected in their dreams and become part of the process of working out life's scary bits.

WORKING WITH DREAMS

There are many different kinds of dream. Some are at a relatively superficial level. These are largely concerned with daily trivia and seem to represent a cataloguing of the day's events. Others seem to bubble up from the deepest, darkest corners of the psyche and are not so easily understood. These are the ones that usually strike us as important in some way, even if we cannot be sure why. Learning to capture these "dreams from the deep" and finding ways to decode their meaning is what the following pages are all about.

RIGHT Working with dreams for problem-solving as well as learning to control them are two of the ways to unlock the secrets of your dreams.

UNDERSTANDING DREAMS

THERE ARE PROBABLY HUNDREDS OF WAYS OF INTERPRETING DREAMS – FROM FREUD TO JUNG, FROM MESSAGES FROM THE GODS TO DIVINATION, FROM CHEMICAL REACTIONS TO EMOTIONAL REORDERING. WHETHER WE OPT FOR A PSYCHOLOGICAL, SPIRITUAL OR SCIENTIFIC PERSPECTIVE HOWEVER, ALL OUR DREAMS STEM FROM THE DREAMER. IN YOUR DREAMS, THE IMAGERY WILL CHANGE, THE SITUATIONS AND CIRCUMSTANCES WILL CHANGE AND THE CAUSES OF THE DREAMS WILL CHANGE. THE ONLY COMMON DENOMINATOR, THE ONLY CONSTANT, IS YOU. IN WORKING OUT WHAT YOUR DREAMS MAY MEAN, THEREFORE, ULTIMATELY YOU ARE THE BEST EXPERT.

DREAMER AS THE SOURCE

It is widely believed that everything that happens in your dream is about you and not about anyone else. Once you take that on board, all your dream work starts to fall into place. No-one else can enter your inner world and interfere with your dreaming. Other people may be able to influence your thoughts and feelings, but never your dreams. They may cause you to have nightmares but the symbolism in those nightmares will all be of your own making. The key

BELOW RIGHT Dreams are a good way to monitor our emotional, mental and physical health.
BELOW Before you understand your dream you have to understand yourself, and what it is you might be trying to say to yourself.

to working with dreams is to understand what those symbols mean to you. What is it that your dreams are trying to tell you?

DREAMS AS A DIAGNOSTIC TOOL

The Greek philosopher, Aristotle, believed that dreams are a way of revealing to the dreamer what is physically wrong with the body, a sort of medical examination while you are asleep. In modern times we have been wary of paying much attention to his theory, but maybe there is something in it after all. Following in the footsteps of Freud and Jung, it is now fairly well established that dreams can be a diagnostic tool, used to determine the state of our psychological and spiritual health. When we are

A dream is the theatre in which the dreamer is himself the scene, the player, the prompter, the producer, the author, the public and the critic.

C G JUNG

THE RAT-INFESTED CAVERNS

A mother anxious about her daughter's health, experiences the following dream. It happened the night after the girl has gone for blood tests.

"That night I dreamed of boats in huge underground caverns. These boats were like barges and they were carrying vast cargoes all hidden and wrapped up in canvas, very bulky and awkward. They moved slowly and jerkily. There were thousands of them and the caverns were vast and, well, cavernous. I couldn't see what was lighting them but I had the impression of candles guttering in big candle-holders on the walls. I was standing on a sort of sidewalk which was running alive with rats.

It was obvious to me when I woke up that this was my way of trying to come to terms with my daughter's illness, which was a blood disease that had to be transported out of her system. The fact that I was an onlooker reflected my feeling of powerlessness, and the rats symbolized my secret horror of a situation I was trying hard to cope with."

going through a difficult time, such as a divorce or redundancy for instance, we would most likely expect our dreams to be disturbed, perhaps even nightmarish, containing hostile metaphors and imagery symbolic of anxiety and separation. Working with such dreams can be therapeutic, giving us an insight into what is happening at our core, beneath the veneer we present to the world.

AN EARLY WARNING SYSTEM

The unconscious mind is a storehouse of information. One way of accessing this information is through our dreams. When something is wrong for instance, our unconscious may try to bring it to our attention through a dream. In a sense, our dreams can give us a glimpse of the future; what is about to happen will first be symbolized in our dreams. The dream is like a whisper before the shouting begins. It is then up to us to heed that whisper and take action to avert the impending catastrophe.

Our dreams are like a good friend. They are always on our side and doing everything they can to help us. The only problem is that they speak a different language. To make the most of what they have to offer means learning that language.

WORKING WITH YOUR DREAMS

The unconscious is like a treasure chest, packed with revealing and important information that can help us on our journey through life. Our dreams are

a key to opening that chest, yet they are illusory and ephemeral, transient, fleeting and almost impossible to catch hold of. Dreams can't be wrestled into submission, but have to be seduced into giving up their secrets, teased into revealing their mysteries. A dream is to explore, to play with and to live with. It doesn't take too kindly to being dissected or analysed into submission. Dreams cannot be catalogued and filed away, graded and pigeonholed. They just don't operate like that. The same goes for recalling a dream. You can't demand that it be remembered. You have to sneak up on it, turn your back and wait as it shyly reveals itself. You need to half-close your eyes when you think of it and stop using your will to try and force it into the spotlight.

BELOW Our dreams are our early warning system that things are not as well as they might be; it is as well to pay heed, to listen. Our dreams are a part of us, not alien images beamed in from the outside.

DREAM RECALL

MANY PEOPLE CLAIM THAT THEY DO NOT DREAM. IT IS MUCH MORE LIKELY THAT THEY ARE UNABLE TO REMEMBER THEIR DREAMS. OUR DREAMS TEND TO SLIP AWAY, LIKE A THIEF IN THE NIGHT, BEFORE WE HAVE CHANCE TO APPREHEND THEM. YET OUR DREAMS ARE THE ONE PLACE WHERE WE CAN RELAX, WHERE WE CAN BE OURSELVES. OUR DREAMS ARE RIPPLES IN THE POOL OF OUR UNCONSCIOUS, THE PLACE WHERE THE WORRIES AND ANXIETIES THAT WE SO SUCCESSFULLY HIDE FROM THE WORLD MAY SURFACE IN SAFETY. DREAMS CAN GIVE US VALUABLE INSIGHTS INTO OUR LIVES, AND TO GET THE MOST OUT OF THEM, WE NEED TO TRAIN OURSELVES IN THE ART OF DREAM RECALL.

ABOVE Talking about dreams is a good way to defuse them, but also to begin to understand them. Women tend to talk about their dreams more than men, and express more of an interest in others' dreams.

DREAM JOURNALS

One of the best and easiest ways for remembering dreams is to keep a dream journal. It's worth keeping a special book or note pad and using it only for recording your dreams. Keep the book and a pen by your pillow and write in it as soon as you wake each morning. When you wake up, make as little physical movement as possible – even turning over can be enough for the memories to evaporate before you have had chance to record them. Lying still, in the same position as when you woke up, often increases dream recall. Keep your eyes closed. Not only will there be less distraction this way, but many people are often able to see the dream again.

If you can't remember any dreams, then just jot down feelings or thoughts that spring to mind. These may well be echoes of your last dream, a sort of dream vapour trail, and may be enough to trigger further memories of your dreams. If you wake up from a vivid dream in the middle of the night, it is a good idea to record it straightaway before going back to sleep. Some people keep a torch by the bed to save putting the bedside light on.

RECORDING DREAMS

There is no single, right way to record your dreams. You may want to jot down key words or feelings, or make a note of the people or events. Some people prefer to write a narrative of their dream while others like to include pictures or sketches. If you can't remember the start of your dream, don't give up. Don't worry about sequence; working backwards or from the middle can lead you to remember more details. Sometimes you'll be halfway through

RIGHT The more we keep a journal the more likely it is to actually influence our dreams – we begin to dream the journal. This makes analyzing and understanding our dreams much easier.

remembering a dream when you'll remember something from dreams you had previously forgotten. Even fragments of dreams are valuable and can contain useful information. Writing in the present rather than the past tense can help you re-live the dream as you record it.

You might want to record your dream on one side of the page and leave the other side blank for comments and interpretation later on. It is, however, a good idea to record the date and the place where you had the dream and to generally include as much detail as possible; some people like to include the phase of the moon for instance. If you can't write the dream in your journal immediately you wake up, then make a note of the things you remember the most. These will jog your memory later on when you do have time to continue your journal.

THEMES AND PATTERNS

As you keep your journal, images, incidents and even emotions will slowly build over time to create a picture of your unique psychic identity, but you should keep the journal for at least a month before you try to make any sense of it. When you look, you may notice recurring themes or patterns in your

dreams. Perhaps a recurring vision of being chased, or falling from a high place, or being confined in a small place for instance. Or it might be a symbol, such as a flower, a road, a boat, or a particular animal that keeps cropping up. Recurring themes often indicate there is something in your life that needs your attention, perhaps a part of you that wants expression. You could also look for links between your dreams and events that happened recently. Identifying a pattern can make us better equipped to deal with life.

LEFT Dreaming of a particular symbol and seeing it crop up repeatedly might indicate an important theme that you need to work on.

ABOVE Recurring themes often indicate recurring worries. By paying attention to what the dream is trying to say to us we can help alleviate the stress.

A dream is an answer to a question we haven't yet learned how to ask.   FOX MULDER, THE X-FILES

DREAM INVESTIGATION

HAVING LEARNED HOW TO RECALL AND RECORD YOUR DREAMS, THE NEXT STEP IS TO MAKE SOME SENSE OF THEM. BE WARY OF INSTANT INTERPRETATIONS OFFERED BY TRADITIONAL DREAM DICTIONARIES, HOWEVER USEFUL OR KNOWLEDGEABLE THEY MAY SEEM. OUR DREAMS ARE INFINITELY SUBTLE AND COMPLEX AND IT IS ALMOST IMPOSSIBLE TO ASCRIBE A CAST-IRON MEANING TO A SYMBOL. INSTEAD WE HAVE TO FIND CREATIVE WAYS OF WORKING WITH OUR DREAMS, PERHAPS USING INSIGHTS GAINED IN BOOKS OR FROM OTHERS TO HELP US, BUT ULTIMATELY DISCOVERING OUR OWN MEANING FROM DEEP WITHIN. THERE ARE MANY METHODS WE CAN ADAPT AND USE TO HELP US, SO WORK OUT THE BEST ONE FOR YOURSELF.

GESTALT TECHNIQUES

Fritz Perls was the 20th-century pioneer of Gestalt therapy. Perls said that dreams are "a message of yourself to yourself" and he saw everything in the dream as a representation of the dreamer's personal experience. The Gestalt method involves contacting different "parts" of yourself and exploring their meaning. For instance, in a recurring dream of being chased by a bear, you are both the bear and the one

BELOW RIGHT Once we wake we can calmly and quietly replay the dream and see what it means and where it comes from.
BELOW Keeping a dream journal will throw great light on the mysteries of our dreams.

being chased. You could then explore what it means for you to be the bear, considering for instance why he is chasing you. Maybe he is hungry and wants to eat you up, or perhaps he has an urgent message that he needs to give you, or it could be that he is someone else in disguise. There are many possible interpretations, but only you would know what the bear means in the context of your dream. To help you explore different aspects of yourself, it can be useful to sit in different chairs, or to use a different voice when you are "being" each of the characters. If you feel blocked and don't know what the "answer" is, make something up. You may be surprised to discover that it has some meaning. This "what part

of me and what is it saying?" approach to dreams seems to be particularly helpful for recurring dreams, or those dreams that are relatively short and uncomplicated, and which contain clear and easily recognisable symbolism.

FREE ASSOCIATION

In his therapeutic work, Freud used the technique of free association, encouraging his patient to let his or her thoughts "free wheel" from a starting point in the dream. This could be a word, feeling, object, person or symbol. To work with your dreams, take each element of the dream that you want to understand and write it down on a clean sheet of paper. Then, without thinking about it, write down whatever word comes to mind when you look at each element. Keep going until your chain of connections breaks down. You could use pictures or graphic symbols rather than words if you like.

DREAM DETECTIVE

Often the skill of dream interpretation lies in asking the right questions. You can try treating your dreams as clues to a mystery that you, the detective, are trying to solve. This means focusing particularly on those aspects of the dream that strike you as odd or disturbing in some way, and asking yourself a series of questions. For instance you could ask yourself how you feel about what is happening, if it reminds you of anything, or what your thoughts are. You may find that one question and answer leads naturally on to the next question and answer, and so on. It's rather like following a trail. When you reach a dead end with your questions, pick up on a different element of the dream and start again. You can also see if this dream detective technique works well with a partner. Someone else asking the questions can make the interpretation very different.

RIGHT Finding out what our dream is trying to say to us means we have to do some detective work – by exploring the symbolism that is unique to us we can access our subconscious desires and needs.

A dream that is not interpreted is like a letter that has not been opened. THE TALMUD

DREAM DETECTIVE

In the following dream, a young woman feels overwhelmed by emotion but can make no sense of what the dream may mean.

"I've never had a dream quite like it. I could see emotions in the air like great thick music notes. And every emotion was overwhelming. I was being played like some giant monstrous instrument. I was being plucked and strummed and fingered and drummed and thumped and blown and twanged all at once and every beat, every note was a new emotion. When I woke up I was drenched in sweat and feeling really sick, as if I had just been through the wringer. I felt limp for days unable to eat or think of anything else except this dream. It followed me round like a small insistent child that I couldn't ignore. I almost felt as if I wanted to pick it up and cuddle it, but I didn't know what it wanted."

Afterwards she played "dream detective" and asked herself a series of questions which proved quite revealing and seemed to open up the meaning of the dream.

Q: Are the emotions in the dream the same as I have been experiencing in my everyday life?

A: No, but they do seem familiar as if they are brooding just under the surface.

Q: Is there anything troubling me at the moment that is looking for emotional release?

A: I don't think so. I am quite happy at the moment, or at least I was until this dream. It has unsettled me and made me restless. Or was I restless anyway and this dream has made me focus on that?

Q: I wonder why I am restless?

A: I don't know. Since I got married six months ago I seem to have disappeared. I don't think my own thoughts anymore. I don't feel as if I exist. I am happy but I'm not thinking about things any more. Perhaps this dream is my way of getting in touch with myself, my emotions again?

PREPARE TO DREAM

PEOPLE HAVE ALWAYS SUSPECTED THAT THE INNER UNIVERSE OF OUR DREAMS IS A SOURCE OF WISDOM. THROUGHOUT HISTORY, DREAMS HAVE BEEN USED FOR HEALING, TO STIMULATE INVENTION AND DISCOVERY, AS WELL AS INSPIRE GREAT LITERATURE AND WORKS OF ART. THEY HAVE ALSO BEEN USED TO PREDICT THE FUTURE AND BRING SPIRITUAL REVELATION. FOR MOST OF US, MOST OF THE TIME, OUR DREAMS ARE NOT ON SUCH AN EPIC SCALE, BUT THEY ARE A VALUABLE SOURCE OF SELF-KNOWLEDGE. ONCE WE HAVE ACCEPTED THAT DREAMS ARE AN IMPORTANT PART OF OUR LIFE, WE WILL FIND THAT THEY BECOME MORE POTENT AND REVEALING. WE NEED, THEREFORE, TO FIND WAYS TO DREAM THE BEST POSSIBLE DREAMS.

A SHRINE FOR SLEEP

In the ancient world, dreams were "incubated" in sacred or lonely places, such as a temple or the wilderness, in order to create an ideal birth place for them. Take this principle into your own sleeping habits and transform your bedroom into a "shrine for sleep". Make sure the room is as comfortable and relaxing as possible. The temperature should be not too hot and not too cold, and there should be sufficient ventilation. Keep the space clear and free from clutter, and surround yourself with colours and objects that gently stimulate your senses in a positive way rather than depress you. Relaxing colours are lilacs, neutrals and pinks, although any shade that appeals to you is fine. Tidy away any objects that are associated with the outside world, such as shoes and clothes, and use soft lighting. Any kind of electrical equipment is best kept to a minimum in the bedroom.

BEDTIME RITUALS

In the past, societies who recognized the importance of dreaming created elaborate rituals to prepare body, mind and soul for the journey. To get the most from our dreams, we need to be in a relaxed, receptive state and approach going to sleep in a spirit of openness and enquiry. If we go to bed stressed or completely exhausted then we are unlikely to get the most from our dreams.

To get ourselves into the right frame of mind, we can create our own modern-day rituals to prepare for sleep and dreaming. One simple way of doing this is by listening to music. A little gentle classical music is a good choice, although you could experiment with other types of music to see if they have any effect on your sleep and dreaming patterns. Alternatively you could try burning incense or vaporizing essential oils in the evening. Useful scents include sandalwood as an aid to meditation and to

MEDITATION FOR DREAMS

When we meditate, we enter a state of altered consciousness. As body and mind unwind, our brain rhythms slow down to produce a relaxed alpha wave pattern, similar, yet of greater intensity, to that produced during deep sleep. In such a state, we become quiet and receptive. Try this meditation every night for a week and make a note in your dream journal of any changes to your sleep or dreams.

1 Sit in a relaxed position, close your eyes and focus on your breathing. As you breathe in, imagine a stream of golden light entering through the crown of your head.

2 Hold your breath for a few seconds, or as long as is comfortable and visualize the light circulating around your body.

3 Now breathe out, imagining the light leaving your body through the soles of your feet, taking away all the cares of the day.

4 Repeat the sequence several times.

You may want to experiment with breathing in different colours, depending on your changing needs. Pink is good for emotional healing, blue for calm, lavender for spiritual awareness, and green for fresh and original thinking.

ABOVE Creating a bedroom that is a shrine to sleep will help you to incubate dreams.
FAR LEFT Essential oils and scents can also help to create the right atmosphere for dreams and trouble-free sleep.
LEFT Bedroom rituals, such as taking a warm candlelit bath, are a good way to wind down for bed, free the mind from the day's troubles and make us more receptive to dreams.

connect with your higher self; lavender to encourage relaxation and calm; frankincense to open up to the angelic realm; and myrrh to connect with mysterious, archetypal energies. Experiment with other aromas, but make sure you choose scents that relax and soothe rather than ones that stimulate. A herb sachet placed under your pillow can also induce soothing sleep. Suitable fillers include dried hops, lavender, marjoram and passion flower.

Taking a warm, candlelit bath before bedtime is also a good way of letting go of the cares of the day in preparation for sleep. A couple of drops of essential oil can be swished into the water if you wish. Try practising a meditation technique last thing at night. It is a good way of switching off from your worldly concerns and creating a space for your unconscious to "come through" in the night without any worries and problems getting in the way.

Reach high, for stars lie hidden in your soul. Dream deep, for every dream precedes the goal.

PAMELA VAULL STARR

DREAM TOOLS

IN MANY PARTS OF THE WORLD, GREAT STORE IS SET BY DREAMS, FOR INSTANCE MANY AFRICAN SOCIETIES BELIEVE THAT DREAMS ARE LINKED TO DESTINY. DREAMS ARE SEEN AS A VEHICLE FOR THE SPIRIT WORLD TO COMMUNICATE WITH THE DREAMER, GIVING IMPORTANT INFORMATION RELATING TO HEALTH, ENEMIES OR THE FUTURE. AMONG NATIVE AMERICANS THERE IS A WIDESPREAD BELIEF THAT A "SACRED POWER" SPEAKS TO YOU IN YOUR DREAMS. THIS POWER WILL OFTEN APPEAR AS AN ANIMAL. IN SUCH SOCIETIES DREAMS ARE TAKEN SERIOUSLY AND DREAM TOOLS ARE USED TO ASSIST THE DREAMER IN A VARIETY OF WAYS, ESPECIALLY FOR PROTECTION FROM BAD DREAMS AND TO ASSIST IN DREAM PROGRAMMING AND RECALL.

ABOVE We have access to a wide range of tools to help us interpret our dreams, including those used by other cultures.

DREAM WISDOM

People have always suspected that the inner universe of our dreams is a source of infinite wisdom. Throughout history, dreams have been used for healing, to stimulate invention and discovery, as well as inspiring great literature and works of art. They have also been used to predict the future and bring spiritual revelation. For most of us most of the time, our dreams do not fall into these epic categories, yet increasingly we are recognizing them as a valuable source of self-knowledge. Once we have accepted that dreams are an important part of our life, we will find that they become more potent and revealing. This means that we should prepare ourselves for the best possible dreams that we can have.

THE DREAM DOCTOR

The Cuna Indians of Central America see dreams as having an identity or power, with bad dreams signifying an impending disaster or illness. A disturbing dream would be taken to the "dream doctor" or medicine man for interpretation and a "prescription" to make it better.

Typically the prescription is an object into which special "power" or spells have been worked. The dream tool is then taken to bed by the dreamer to work its magic through the night and nullify the bad effects of the dream. Dream dolls and spearheads are the Cuna's most common dream tools, but stones, pegs, crosses and miniature weapons, such as axes or knives, are also used.

RIGHT A Cuna Native American woman, with a young girl beside her, takes care of a dream doll. As a potent dream tool the doll will be an integral part of the owner's daily life, linking the waking and dream worlds.

The dream doctor may also make up a powder containing a special wood mixed with black date palm and rub it over the dreamer's eyes to protect them from the effects of the bad dream. Through these actions it is believed that the dream's power is negated or "earthed".

SKY AXES

The Cuna Indians live on the islands off the Atlantic coast of Panama, and their lives are very much influenced by the weather and the natural elements. Violent storms during the night frequently disturb their sleep, and a favourite dream-doctor cure is to sleep with a "sky axe". Sky axes are real axe heads that have been found at the old burial ground sites of the Cuna people. The Cuna Indians believe that these axe heads help protect their dream spirit guides from the power of thunder by making the spirit guides invisible.

As we would expect, the dream tools used by the Cuna Indians and other indigenous peoples are intimately related to a specific culture and lifestyle. However, we can adapt the principle of dream tools to suit our particular circumstances and create our own tools to assist our dreaming.

YOUR OWN DREAM TOOLS

If you want to create your own dream tools, you need to choose objects that have special meaning for you. This could be an item that has special significance in your everyday life, or a childhood toy, a memento from a lover, a gift from a friend, or a treasured photo. If it is nature that inspires you, look for natural objects such as a piece of driftwood, a pebble from a favourite beach, a piece of tree bark or a fragrant flower. Dream tools can also be chosen to tie-in with the kind of dream you are trying to have or recall, maybe in answer to a particular question or on an important theme in your life. For instance, if work is an issue, then choose an object to symbolize what it is that you do: a tool for an engineer, a mixing spoon for a chef, a pen for a writer, or a thermometer for a nurse for instance.

ABOVE Like other Native American traditions, the Fox and Sauk tribe uses costume and ritual to help people recall and interpret their dreams.

ABOVE When choosing a dream tool you might want to take one from the natural world. Stones, shells and feathers are all symbolic of the elements and therefore work well. Use your intuition to help choose an item.

EMPOWERING YOUR DREAM TOOL

Before a dream tool can work its magic, traditionally it is "empowered" by the dream doctor with special spells. You can do this yourself using colour and visualization. Use red for dreams of passion and adventure, blue or lilac for healing, green to be shown new pathways in life, and orange when looking at relationships. If you are working on communication issues, choose deep blue; for power and authority use purple; or work with yellow when seeking an answer to a health question. You could also use any other colours that intuitively spring to mind as being the ones that are most appropriate for you at the time.

To work with the colour, visualize your dream tool surrounded in coloured light, wrap the tool in a piece of the right coloured fabric or tie coloured ribbons on to the object. As you do so, spend some time visualizing the colour in your head, and mentally surround the item with it. When it is ready, take your dream object and put it under your pillow. It may help you have the sort of dream you want or else help protect you from bad dreams.

DREAM CATCHING

In Native American culture, dreams are seen as messages from sacred spirits in the night sky. Certain tribes also believe in the idea of the Great Dream. In the womb, everyone has their own great dream but this gets forgotten at birth. This dream bestows gifts

such as courage, creativity, humour or empathy upon the individual and gives a vision for the best pathway through life. From a young age, children are encouraged to "catch" and explore their dreams and young men will fast until they have a vision of their "song of life". Dream catching plays an important part in initiation ceremonies, where the initiate makes a magical or sacred circle around himself to "capture" the messages from the dream spirits in the space inside the circle. The dream catcher tool is a symbolic representation of this magical or sacred circle.

CATCH YOUR DREAMS

Dream catchers not only capture the good spirits, but also filter out any negative or unwanted powers. They consist of a cobweb-like structure on a circular frame, usually with beads or feathers attached to it. This structure symbolizes the "web of life"; in other words, it shows how all aspects of life are not separate but are intimately connected to one another. At the centre of the web sits Iktome, the spider, and keeper of dreams. Iktome is often represented by a coloured bead or shell. The dream catcher is hung near the sleeper's bed. The good dreams pass to Iktome, who holds them for the dreamer. The bad dreams are ensnared in her web and can be emptied away in the morning.

Dream catchers can be made in many shapes and sizes. They are not only useful but are also bright

---

Crying for a vision – the thirst for a dream from above – without this, you are nothing. LONE DEER and colourful and make an interesting decoration in a bedroom. Children find them especially appealing and many parents have experienced positive results with children who suffer nightmares or who are afraid of the dark. Remember to empty the dream catcher each morning by tapping any unwanted dreams into the waste bin. Do this with the child, or encourage them to do it for him or herself.

MAKING A DREAM CATCHER

A good way of protecting yourself from disturbing dreams is to make your own dream catcher. It may also help you gain more insight into where you should be going in life and show you the best choices to help you achieve your ends. A dream catcher is a very personal thing and there is plenty of scope to make it in a way that appeals to you.

YOU WILL NEED

- a thin and bendy piece of wood about 60cm (2ft) long. A freshly cut piece of bamboo or hazel is ideal.
- a length of twine, such as fishing line or strong cotton thread
- feathers, a few beads and some coloured ribbons for decoration

1 Curl the bamboo or hazel into a circle and fasten it with twine wrapped around. Some people like to cover the whole of the wood in ribbon before they start, but it is up to you.

2 Cut off any sharp ends of wood at the join and wrap some ribbon around it.

3 Tie one end of the twine onto any point on the circle and tie it to the opposite point of the circle. Cut off the long end of twine.

4 Tie another piece of twine across the middle of the circle, at right angles to the first piece.

5 Attach four shorter pieces of twine between the four tying-on points to form a square. From the middle of one of the shorter lengths, attach a piece of twine to the two tying-on-points on the other side of the circle. Repeat for the other short lengths. This gives you a sort of "cat's cradle" effect. Experiment until you have a pleasing criss-cross of lines resembling a spider's web.

6 Add a bead in the centre to represent the spider.

7 Finish by decorating the dream catcher with some ribbons hanging from the bottom of the circle. Add some feathers and beads to these downward-hanging ribbons.

When your dream catcher is finished you can empower it in the same way as with a dream tool. Hang your dream catcher at the window of your bedroom, or above the bed.

ABOVE The dream catcher is a Native American device that filters your dreams so that only the pleasant ones get through.

DREAM GUIDES

Sometimes an ally or guide will appear in our dreams. In Native American culture, animals often symbolise these guides or helpers, with each person having their own totem or "power" animal. To find your totem animal, ask to be shown in a dream, or devise a dream journey to find it. This involves a visualization in which you see in your mind a path that you begin to walk down. As you walk, take notice of the scenery and the details around you, then open your mind and call for your power animal. The animal could be anything, from a wolf to a beetle, when it arrives greet it warmly, touch it and give it love. Be aware of what it feels like and feel the love it has for you. Remember, the greater the detail the more real it will be. Your dream guide might be an animal that you feel an affinity with in real life, you might love horses, for example, or feel inspired by the traditional north American wolf or bison, but don't try and manipulate the choice, let the animal make itself known to you.

CONTROLLING DREAMS

ALTHOUGH OUR DREAMS APPEAR TO BE OUT OF OUR CONTROL, WE CAN IN FACT TAKE A MORE ACTIVE ROLE AND LEARN HOW TO INFLUENCE OR PLAN THEM. THIS MAY NOT BE SOMETHING THAT YOU THINK IS POSSIBLE, BUT IF YOU ARE WILLING TO GIVE IT A TRY YOU MAY BE SURPRISED. WE CAN ASK OUR DREAMS TO PROVIDE US WITH ADVENTURES OR SELF-KNOWLEDGE OR SHOW US CREATIVE SOLUTIONS TO OUR PROBLEMS. WHEN WE ARE FEELING LOST WE CAN ASK OUR DREAMS FOR CLARITY AND GUIDANCE, INSPIRATION AND INFORMATION. WHAT WE ARE DOING IS ASKING FOR A MESSAGE FROM DEEP WITHIN OURSELVES, CONVEYED TO US BY WAY OF METAPHOR, MOOD AND SYMBOLS, VIA OUR DREAMS.

DEVELOPING DREAM SKILLS

Dreams speak in a language of pictures and feelings rather than thoughts and words. The greater our ability to sense and visualize, the more we are able to take control of our dreams. A good place to start is in everyday life. We can begin by really starting to notice the visual impact of the world around us, observing the colours, shapes and textures more profoundly. Spend some time soaking up visual imagery that you find interesting. For instance this could include looking at paintings and works of art, tarot cards, mandalas or any other pictures that appeal to your senses. At the same time, pay more attention to your feeling state. Be aware of those things that alter your mood, noticing not only what you see, but also what you hear and maybe smell. Listening to music and reading is another way of developing your imagination and sensitivity.

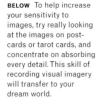

BELOW To help increase your sensitivity to images, try really looking at the images on post-cards or tarot cards, and concentrate on absorbing every detail. This skill of recording visual imagery will transfer to your dream world.

CLEAR INTENTION

In the first instance, to plan a dream means having a good idea of why you want it and what it is exactly that you expect from it. The more sincere you are, the more likely is the chance that your unconscious mind will co-operate with you. Perhaps you need to work out some aspect of a relationship, or maybe you are trying to make an important decision and are not quite sure which way to go. Drawing on information from our dreams can give us a very clear idea of where we really want to be rather than where we think we ought to be.

SETTING THE SCENE

If you want to generate a particular type of dream, first you need to be in a relaxed and open frame of mind. Next you need to focus on what it is you want to dream about. This could mean writing it out

*Don't be afraid of the space between your dreams and reality. If you can dream it,
you can make it so.*

BELVA DAVIS

LIFE DIRECTION

A young man is unsure about his direction in life so he asks for guidance in his dream.

"I really wanted to know where I was going, what I was supposed to be doing. I played some soothing music as I went to bed and let my mind go blank. I was asking for guidance as I fell asleep. I had an amazing dream in which I was riding a camel across the desert. All I really remember was the utter silence, the loneliness and isolation, but also a real feeling of peacefulness.

The message of the dream seemed very clear to me. 'Go alone and with nothing until you are ready to be with people again.' It all made perfect sense to me, and helped me a great deal."

LEFT Dreaming Bread –
an old recipe for making
your dreams come true.
Perhaps simply an old
wives' tale, but perhaps
also a method of
triggering a dream event,
the act of performing
any kind of ritual has its
own potency.

on a piece of paper and tucking it under your pillow. You could also write in your dream journal. If you have any questions, make sure they are as open-ended as possible. Repeat your requests to yourself just before going to sleep. Sometimes holding an object that is connected with the situation is helpful. Reviewing the events of the day last thing at night may also help you relate your dream to what is happening in everyday life. A good way of training your mind in this way is to add an element of ritual to your bedtime routine.

DREAMING BREAD

You might like to try this traditional ritual for generating dreams. It involves making a "dreaming bread". You can use an ordinary bread recipe but bake a round loaf. As you knead the dough concentrate on what sort of dream you want to have. When baked cut the bread into three and take a bite out of each piece. Put the remaining pieces under your pillow and that night it is said that you will dream your requested dream, as long as you don't speak between eating the bread and sleeping.

BELOW LEFT Listening to
music can also help you
to develop your
imagination and
sensitivity. But make sure
you really listen, use your
mind to process the
sounds rather than just
letting it wash over you.
BELOW By creating the
right atmosphere, and
performing simple rituals,
our dream work can
become more connected.

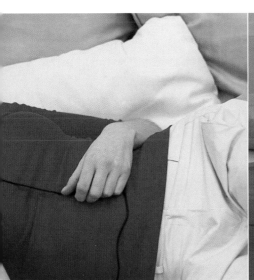

PROBLEMS AND INSPIRATION

THERE IS A TENDENCY TO SEE PROBLEMS AS A SERIES OF HAZARDS TO BE AVOIDED, OR ELSE HINDRANCES TO BE SKILFULLY NEGOTIATED. WHEN WE HAVE A PROBLEM, MOST OF US WANT TO SOLVE IT AS QUICKLY AS POSSIBLE. HOWEVER, IT IS ALSO POSSIBLE TO SEE PROBLEMS AS CHALLENGES. PROBLEMS PRESENT AN OPPORTUNITY TO LEARN AND GROW, TO CHANGE AND IMPROVE. SOMETIMES A PROBLEM IS A GATEWAY TO A BETTER FUTURE. IF WE RUSH AT SOLVING OUR PROBLEMS INSTEAD OF TRYING TO LEARN FROM THEM WE RISK NOT GROWING, NOT LEARNING. WE CAN ALSO USE OUR DREAMS TO HELP US. IF WE ARE PERCEPTIVE ENOUGH THE SOLUTION MAY BE SOMETHING WE WOULD NEVER HAVE THOUGHT OF.

SLEEP ON IT

Some of the most creative solutions to problems have not come through logic or reasoning but through dreams. For instance, in the 19th century, Dmitri Mendeleyev, a Russian chemist, was having a problem about how to organize chemical elements. Deciding to "sleep on it" he had a dream in which he saw the elements falling in the correct order. Using the information from his dream, he went on to devise the periodic table of elements, a central concept of modern inorganic chemistry.

Creative solutions do not arrive out of the blue however. They are usually preceded by plenty of "spade work", which may have taken days, weeks, months or even years before the final flash of genius. A shift in perception seems to happen more easily when the logical mind has given up on the problem. When we relax and stop trying, our innate, inner intelligence can take over and put the pieces of the puzzle together while we sleep.

DECODING THE MESSAGE

It can sometimes be the smallest detail in a dream that can provide the clue to help us solve the problem or dilemma we are working on. It might be a visual image or symbol, a smell or a sound, a mood or a feeling. It is a question of being alert and allowing intuition, rather than the conscious mind, to help us solve the riddle.

While we sleep, the mind continues to work. Freed from the restraints of logic and convention, the unconscious is free to take an unorthodox

LEFT Our dreams can expose what lies beneath the surface, thoughts or emotions that were hidden. In the same way they can help with problem solving, bringing a solution up to the surface of our consciousness.

All this inventing, this producing, takes place in a pleasing lively dream.   WOLFGANG AMADEUS MOZART

RIGHT Our mind doesn't go to sleep when our body does; it begins its most creative work. When we are awake it is to our benefit to try and decode that work, to access the creative part of ourselves.

approach to the problem and come up with a solution. It is not even necessary to be able to remember our dreams for this process to work. Most of us will have experienced being unable to solve a problem one day, but the next, after a good night's sleep, suddenly finding that either a new way of looking at the problem has appeared, or the problem itself has vanished. If you enjoy completing crossword puzzles, you could test this theory on a superficial level. Find a clue that you're unable to crack, and just before you go to sleep run it through your mind. The next day, revisit the clue and see if the answer comes to you.

DREAMS TO INSPIRE

Many writers, artists and musicians have literally "dreamed up" stories, poems, melodies and other works of art. For instance, Robert Louis Stevenson, the 19th-century Scottish writer, spent days wracking his brains for a suitable plot to explore the idea that we all have our good and bad sides. He claimed that the storyline for his novel *The Strange Case of Dr Jekyll and Mr Hyde* came to him in a dream. More recently, the famous surrealist paintings of 20th-century artists such as Salvador Dalí or René Magritte are set in dream-like landscapes, while singer-songwriter Paul McCartney says the Beatles' hit-song "Yesterday" was in his head when he woke up one morning.

BELOW Dreams have always inspired writers and artists and painters – they can still inspire us, motivate us, stimulate and encourage us. Will your dreams help to complete the jigsaw of your waking life?

DREAM DECISION

A young man is having trouble making a decision about a job offer. After a day thinking out the pros and cons, he decides to sleep on the problem, and before he falls asleep deliberately places in his mind the problem that is preoccupying him.

"I couldn't work out whether I should take the job I was being offered. On paper it seemed to be just what I was looking for, but something was holding me back. I couldn't make a decision. I went to sleep wondering about this and had a dream where I saw myself smoking a cigar. That was all. I couldn't remember anything else but the dream struck me as very evocative, very symbolic.

The cigar seemed to represent everything that was holding me back about taking that job. It represented success, winning and achievement and being like my father. I could almost smell myself in a city suit, all aftershave and cigar smoke, like a banker or a tycoon. It wasn't an image I liked and I realized it wasn't a job I really wanted, so I turned it down. The cigar made me realize that I was thinking about taking the job because it was what my father would have wanted, but it wasn't me."

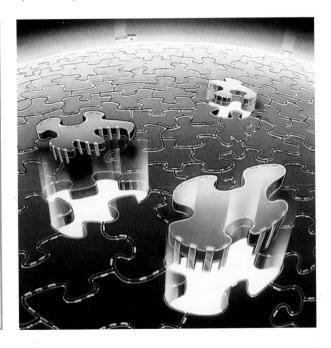

DREAMS AND RELATIONSHIPS

WE ARE SOCIAL BEINGS AND OUR INTERACTIONS WITH ONE ANOTHER AFFECT US DEEPLY. RELATIONSHIPS OF ONE KIND OR ANOTHER WEAVE THE FABRIC OF LIFE, FORMING A RICH TAPESTRY. SOME OF THESE RELATIONSHIPS ARE RELATIVELY SUPERFICIAL, WHILE OTHERS HAVE THE POWER TO AFFECT US AT A DEEP EMOTIONAL LEVEL — FOR GOOD OR BAD. OUR DREAMS CAN GIVE US GREAT INSIGHT INTO OUR RELATIONSHIPS WITH LOVERS, FRIENDS, FAMILY OR COLLEAGUES. THEY CAN HIGHLIGHT AREAS OF TENSION, REVEAL THINGS, ANSWER OUR QUESTIONS AND HELP US COME TO TERMS WITH OUR FEELINGS. WE CAN USE OUR DREAMS AS A "WAY IN" TO HELPING IMPROVE THE RELATIONSHIPS THAT MATTER TO US MOST.

ABOVE Dreams about relationships can act as a way in to understanding them more. Don't dismiss even the most banal ones, as they still could be a way of accessing how you really feel about people close to you.

MAKING SENSE OF IT ALL

Sometimes it is tricky to disentangle the messages carried in a dream. Another person appearing in a dream may be representing an aspect of the dreamer's own psyche rather than themselves. Other people may also appear in disguise as an animal or an inanimate object for instance. We also have to remember that our dreams are not our everyday lives being acted out. They are an attempt by the unconscious to comment on and try and make some sense of what is going on for us. They can reveal what is frightening or worrying us, what is making us happy or sad, jealous or angry, and what we need to further growth and development.

When using your dreams to work on relationships, avoid the temptation to come up with a quick and easy interpretation. You need to tread

carefully and keep asking yourself "have I got this right?" It may also be helpful for close friends or partners to work on their dreams together, checking the meaning of the dream with one another. This can be an exciting journey of discovery and strengthen the bond that is between you.

Of course it isn't just our lover that we might dream about. All sorts of other relationships are reflected in our dreaming – children, friends, colleagues, even enemies or mere acquaintances. How we view our relationships in our dreams can indicate how we really view them on a waking level – without the need for any social niceties. We may find that the relationships no longer sustain or support us, or that they need some care and attention. What our dreams can tell us is dependent on how honest we are with ourselves.

Personal relations are the important thing for ever and ever.
E M FORSTER

DREAM DETECTION

A good place to start doing some relationship work is to play "dream detective" and begin by asking some basic questions about the dream. By working through them, you will gain a lot of insight into what the dream is trying to tell you, which is very different from interpretation. The questions can be used to investigate any type of relationship that you wish to explore, not only sexual partnerships.

DREAM QUESTIONNAIRE

Asking the following questions may help to unlock the symbolism of your relationship dreams.

1 What exactly are you doing in the dream? How are you doing it? Describe your thoughts and feelings as you do it.

2 What aren't you doing in the dream? Is there anything specifically missing from the dream that is important, anything that you feel you should or want to be doing?

3 Imagine the dream is a play being acted out and you can rewrite any section of it. Which bits would you re-script and why? With regard to what you are doing, how would you replay the action of the dream differently?

4 Is there anything in the dream that remains unfinished or that you would like to know more about? Is there anything in the dream that brings up conflicts that you feel have not been dealt with in the dream?

5 How do your actions (and those of anyone else in the dream) parallel your actions in daily life? How far are they similar and how far are they different? If they are different, can you think of any reasons why this might be so?

6 If this dream were a film or play, what sort of film or play would it suggest to you? For instance, would it be a romance, a thriller, a comedy, a farce or an adventure story? How does this correspond with daily life? How is it different?

7 If this dream were an educational device for relationship training, what message would it be teaching? What are you learning from the dream? Does it provide any useful insights into the relationship?

8 How will you apply these insights from the dream to your everyday life? What will you do with the information you have gained from the dream?

ABOVE The relationships we have with peers are often some of the most formative and influential of our lives.
LEFT Once we become parents our emotional lives take on a whole new depth. This could well be reflected in our dreams.
BELOW Close friendships can be sustaining and supportive, but can also create angst and turmoil in our lives. Examine your dreams for clues to how you really feel about those who are closest to you.

ABOVE Acting out a dream might be impossible, and certainly impracticable. But if there is a possibility of at least recreating some part or proportion of a significant dream you are exploring, then why not try it?

WORKING WITH THE RELATIONSHIP QUESTIONNAIRE

To understand how the relationship questionnaire might be used, we can use the example of a dream had by a young man named Billy. In the dream, Billy and his girlfriend are at a railway station standing on opposite sides of the track when an express train whooshes into the station. The train doesn't stop, but when it leaves, Billy's girlfriend has disappeared.

A classic Freudian interpretation of the dream would be that the express train is a phallic symbol. It represents Billy's fear of losing his sexual prowess and the sadness he feels when his girlfriend leaves him as a result. However when Billy worked through the dream relationship questionnaire, he arrived at very different conclusions, none of which related to his sexuality. He saw the dream as a message that life was passing him by and he needed to take more risks rather than being a bystander.

WORKING WITH THE DREAM

This is how Billy works through the dream that he feels is about his relationship with his girlfriend.

"My girlfriend and I are standing on opposite sides of the railway tracks at the station. We are waving to each other. An express train comes between us and when it is going she has disappeared. I remember feeling very sad and wondering how she had got on the express train when it hadn't stopped."

Billy's answers and insights

1 I am waving at my girlfriend and I feel sad when she disappears. I am thinking about the mechanics of her disappearance as if it is a magic show at a theatre.

2 I am not going anywhere. I realize the reason I came to the station was to see her off. She was going away somewhere, not me. I am staying.

3 If I could rewrite the dream I wouldn't change anything except I wouldn't feel sad about her leaving. Now I realize that the sadness isn't about her going away but is about me not understanding how the trick was done.

4 The dream didn't bring up any conflict but it did make me realize that my girlfriend going away wasn't such a bad idea. In fact I feel our relationship isn't going anywhere but I have no idea what to do about it.

5 I think my actions in the dream are pretty similar to those in real life. I didn't behave any differently in the dream.

6 I think this would be a spy story, some sort of mystery or thriller. I guess I would like my life to be a bit more exciting and I think I'm actually a bit bored with my relationship.

7 To me the message is loud and clear. The dream teaches me that this relationship isn't going anywhere and I really ought to do something about it. It also makes me realize that it isn't just the relationship that is wrong, but my whole life is somehow over-ripe. I'm getting lazy and stuck in my ways. Deep down I think I'd like to go travelling or take up a dangerous sport or do something to wake myself up a bit.

8 The dream is trying to tell me that I have to take some action. I need to get off my backside and achieve more instead of watching other people have all the fun. I need to take some risks, make my life more exciting and enjoy being alive more.

FREE ASSOCIATION TECHNIQUE

You can take any element from a dream and use it as a starting point for free association. This means you can work with feelings as well as objects, people or places. Billy also used this technique with his express train dream, starting from the word "train". Interestingly, he arrived at a similar understanding as when he completed the dream relationship questionnaire: that he needed to take more control of his life.

TRIGGERING DREAM RECALL

Sometimes the more we look for meaning in our dreams the more such a meaning seems to elude us, or slip away. We can use techniques used in business to improve creativity and see if they might not also work with dream interpretation. For instance opening a book at random and seeing if any words that catch our eye there might trigger a memory or meaning. You could also try combining odd sequences in the dream and trying to tell a story using them. Or how about sleeping on it – using the next dream to see if it will make sense of the dream we are worrying about. It doesn't have to be a full night's sleep; try just having a quick nap and nod off thinking about your dream.

ACTING IT OUT

If you are feeling adventurous, you could try acting your dream out. This could literally mean going to a place that resembles your dream location and imagining yourself back in the dream. Alternatively, you could act it out at home, setting up a "stage" with the relevant props and characters. This exercise can be very effective when you do it with someone else. It may not always be appropriate to act out relationship dreams with the person you are dreaming about. Sometimes someone who is neutral in the relationship makes a better sounding board.

ABOVE Working with your dreams can take place at any time and in any place, all you need are a few quiet moments when you can focus your mind on your dream. Relax and allow your mind to drift.

BELOW LEFT Sitting quietly in a meditative state can often help us unlock the key to a dream's meaning.
BELOW Sometimes we need to turn our attention elsewhere and stop thinking about a dream. Try to do something completely different, and see if it rises to the surface of your mind.

USING GESTALT

A good way of understanding our dreams is to assume that everything in the dream is an aspect of ourselves. Gestalt techniques are based on this principle. Applying them to his dream, first Billy "became" the train. He discovered that this part of him moves very fast, is forging full steam ahead and has no time to stop for anything or anyone. Next he was the rail track. He thought that this showed him that the fast part of him is "on track", moving ahead to a goal. To be on this track means leaving behind a part of himself, the onlooker who is waving "goodbye". The tracks are also what keep him separate from his girlfriend. When he thought about the dream some more, he realized that his girlfriend represented the part of himself that wants to move forwards, that wants to jump on the train and go off and have adventures, but there is another part holding him back, keeping him at the station. This brought him to the wave goodbye. At first when he had the dream, he thought the wave meant he was saying "goodbye" to his girlfriend and was feeling sad because of the separation from her. Now he

wondered if the sadness was because he was separated from that vital, exciting part of himself that is prepared to jump on moving trains while he stays stuck at the station. It was like waving goodbye to his freedom and sense of adventure.

OPPOSITES

Another interesting way of working on relationship issues is to turn the Gestalt technique on its head and assume everything in the dream is the other person. In Billy's dream for instance, his girlfriend becomes the train. Looking at it like this, Billy thought it meant that she is moving too fast for him, and needed a more committed relationship than he felt he was ready for. Thinking about her as the station, he saw that she represented a stopping off point in his life. She is not the partner with whom he wants to journey through life with.

HIDDEN MESSAGES IN DREAMS

Sometimes it is not so obvious that a dream is about a relationship. However, we can rest assured that whenever we have a relationship issue, it will surface

BELOW RIGHT Our dreaming isolates us and makes us aware of the fragile and vulnerable parts of ourselves. This is nature's way of making us turn inwards and begin to question what our dreams mean.
BELOW While we sleep, doorways open in our mind, and our dreaming self takes wings and becomes capable of anything. In the world of dreams the impossible becomes achievable.

in our dreams in one guise or another. We can assume that the dream is about the problem that is worrying us, and we can try to understand it in this light. This happened to a young woman called Sandra. She was worried that her partner didn't care for her, despite the fact that he told her he loved her. She thought he wanted to leave the relationship. She then had a mysterious dream about a sailing boat with a red sail going round in circles on a lake. The person sailing the boat was a stranger, not her boyfriend. In the dream she felt worried the boat was going to capsize and there would be no one to rescue the sailor.

Using the Gestalt technique with her dream, Sandra concluded that her sense of impending disaster had nothing to do with her boyfriend but was being generated from within herself. The boat represented the relationship, and she and not her boyfriend was the one who was "rocking" it. It was as though a part of her wanted to sabotage the relationship, the part that feels claustrophobic and uneasy. She realized that in some ways she felt trapped in the relationship, that it was not going anywhere, but "round in circles". The red sail spelled danger to her, a signal to look where she was going and keep out of dangerous waters.

ABOVE In our dreams we may be faced with decisions that need to be made, choices that are reflected in our waking life. These choices may be represented by doorways or paths. Your dream is reminding you to act, not avoid.

USING MYTHS AND LEGENDS

If you enjoy and are familiar with myths and legends, you could also use these to gain insight into your relationship dreams. For instance, you could use the Arthurian legends as archetypes for dream understanding. They are a rich picking ground for all sorts of relationships, ranging from the fairly commonplace to the bizarre. You could imagine yourself in the same situation as one of the characters and notice how the story turns out. Alternatively you could consider what "message" the legend has for you.

In the Arthurian legends there are many archetypes and relationship situations that you can work with. The main characters are as follows: Arthur, a king who stands for many different aspects of the Great Father, is married to Guinevere. She meanwhile is in love with Lancelot, Arthur's closest friend. Their affair causes Lancelot to betray Arthur. Morgan le Fay, Arthur's half-sister and a powerful sorceress, has a supposedly incestuous relationship with him. Merlin, the archetypal wise old man is obsessed with a young girl, while the archetypal hero, Sir Galahad, is celibate and devoted to purity.

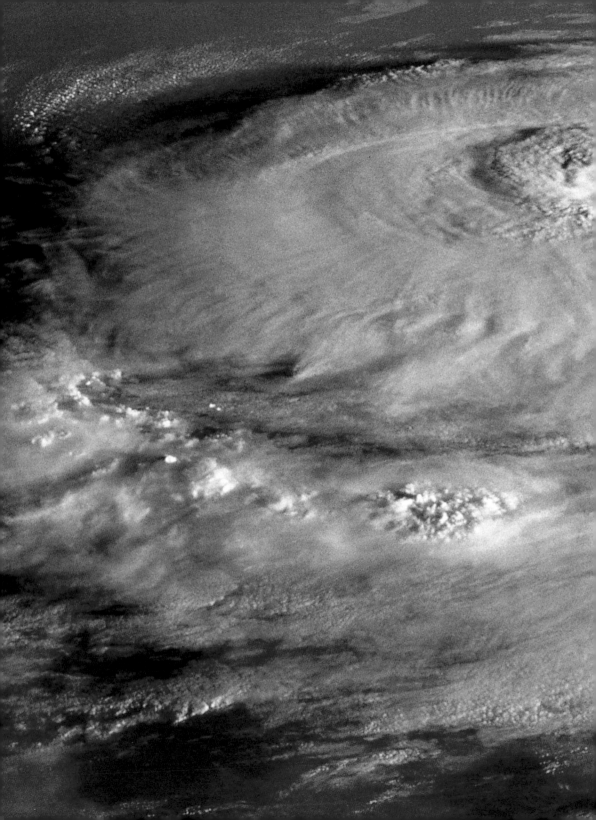

PART FOUR

THE DREAM
LEXICON

ABSTRACT QUALITIES

The properties of the countless people, objects and ideas that we encounter in our dreams can be highly significant when we are trying to work out what our dreams mean. We may focus on particular qualities because they are so dominant, or because they are distorted or unusual. Abstract concepts such as time and space, power or number, may hold a particular relevance in your dream, either pointing to a literal preoccupation or working symbolically.

RIGHT Occasionally, in our dreams, abstract concepts are so important that we divest them of all associations, then we can focus on the feelings that such dreams generate.

TIME AND SPACE

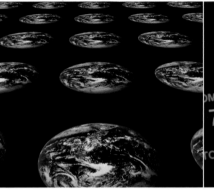

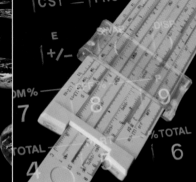

WE LIVE AS PHYSICAL BEINGS IN A PHYSICAL WORLD AND OUR LIVES UNFOLD OVER TIME. THESE TWO VERY OBVIOUS FACTS PROFOUNDLY AFFECT HOW WE LIVE OUR LIVES — AND THOSE WHO LEAD A MODERN, URBAN LIFESTYLE, WITH ITS CONSTANT ACTIVITY, RUSHING AND LIMITED SPACE, WILL BE ESPECIALLY AWARE OF THEM. DREAMS THAT FEATURE TIME AND SPACE — OUR RELATIONSHIP TO THEM, WHETHER THERE IS TOO MUCH OR TOO LITTLE OF EACH — CAN TELL US MUCH ABOUT THE QUALITY OF OUR LIVES.

ABOVE If you are in a wide open space with far-off horizons in your dreams, is this telling you something about how you feel about your waking life? Do open spaces intimidate you or do you find them stimulating?

ABOVE RIGHT Looking at how we view time and space in our dreams can reveal a lot about how we believe we fit into the universe as a whole.

ABOVE FAR RIGHT Dreaming of the tools of measurement might be an indication that we are sizing ourselves up, working out how we fit in with the things around us.

SCALE AND DISTANCE

We are affected by the amount of space we have around us and by how near to or how far we are from other people and objects. A small room may feel cosy and intimate or frustratingly restrictive. Cathedrals are built on a massive scale not only to accommodate large congregations but also to represent the power of God and to inspire awe, and perhaps feelings of insignificance.

It can be useful to look at how we feel in relationship to the spaces in which we find ourselves in our dreams, as this can point to how comfortable we are as physical beings, whether we are feeling protected or exposed, and how isolated or crowded out we are feeling. The extreme of this is found in outer space, where we are truly unconstrained by the bounds of our earthly lives or physicality.

POSITION

Where we are in relation to other objects in our dreams may also be worth noting. Being above or in front of something could indicate that we are asserting ourselves in relation to what the object is representing symbolically, feeling self-confident or dominant. Conversely, being below or behind something could point to feelings of inferiority or subser-vience, an urge to hide or be protected – or it could be that we are being invisible or "not seeing" something important.

MEASUREMENT

Rulers, weighing scales and other instruments of measurement show a particular focus on size, distance, scale or space – how near or far, how tall or long or short something is. We are

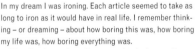

NEVER-ENDING DREAM

In my dream I was ironing. Each article seemed to take as long to iron as it would have in real life. I remember think-ing – or dreaming – about how boring this was, how boring my life was, how boring everything was.

When I woke up after what seemed to be hours of iron-ing I was almost screaming with boredom. I realized that my life was really tedious and I worried that I was a bore. I felt that I had to do something about it, and changed a lot after that.

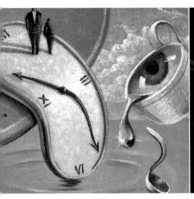

subconsciously measuring ourselves against the world we live in, especially in relation to social expectations. It may also be that we are trying to establish some kind of control over our environments, or using objective means to measure ourselves.

Dreaming of clocks may indicate a preoccupation with time, how it is regulating our lives, perhaps preventing us from having enough time to do the things we want, or having too much time on our hands. In a broader sense timepieces may be reminding us of our mortality.

ELASTICITY OF TIME AND SPACE

Time in dreams is very flexible, becoming distorted, elongated or slowed down. First there is the fact that dreams that seem to last an age might have occurred in only a second. Within the dream itself, distortions of time may relate to feeling out of control – perhaps everything is happening faster than you can cope with, or you are trying to get somewhere fast but don't seem to be moving.

As time can be stretched out or compressed in our dreams, so too can space. In a flash we can travel from one end of the universe to another, between worlds, between states of consciousness. Space can become condensed and compressed, or we become expanded, to such an extent that we can actually fill the universe. In such cosmic dreams we address our beliefs in the nature of the universe, and how we feel about our place within it.

In a dream your attention may be drawn to a preoccupation with space or time by the fact that it is distorted. *Alice in Wonderland* is a story about a dream in which the bewildered and frustrated heroine finds herself too big or small for what she wants to do or for the space in which she finds herself.

ABOVE Crowded areas full of people and activity might give you a feeling of unease, or even terror, or you might find them the most reassuring and natural places to be.

ABOVE LEFT Cosmic dreams about how planet Earth is positioned might be a way of establishing your own position in your personal universe.

ABOVE FAR LEFT Do you feel that time is slipping away from you in your waking life? Perhaps this feeling will be reflected in your dreams.

LEFT In our dreams, the boundaries between time and space can become blurred and we discover new dimensions. In dream time vast epics are played out in what seems an age but is, in real time, only seconds.

SCIENCE AND NUMBERS

SOMETIMES THE UNIVERSE APPEARS ORDERLY AND RATIONAL, AND AT OTHER TIMES IT SEEMS RANDOM AND CHAOTIC. IN DREAMS OF SCIENCE OR ONES IN WHICH NUMBERS SEEM PARTICULARLY SIGNIFICANT, WE ARE TRYING TO RESOLVE THESE CONTRADICTIONS AND MAKE SENSE OF THE WORLD AROUND US; WE WANT TO IMPOSE OUR OWN SENSE OF RATIONALITY AND CONTROL OVER OUR LIVES. SCIENCE GIVES US A MEASURE OF CONTROL OVER THE UNIVERSE AND STOPS US FEELING QUITE SO SMALL OR POWERLESS. TOGETHER WITH NUMBERS IT PUTS US ON A PAR WITH THE GODS, AND CAN GIVE US A FEELING OF CONTROL AND POWERFULNESS, WHICH CAN BE REFLECTED IN OUR DREAMS.

A SCIENTIFIC APPROACH

The discipline and rationality of science makes it a strongly intellectual activity, as we push back the boundaries of knowledge with little regard for emotional or intuitive responses. Because science is much esteemed in our society, we may seek shelter behind its authority to avoid facing our emotions or dealing with irrationality. On the other hand, the strict scientific approach to understanding may seem unnecessarily restrictive to more expressive people.

In dreams that involve science it might well also be that we are abdicating responsibility for

BELOW As children we play games with numbers. They are a part of our life from early on.
BELOW RIGHT Like all dream subjects, numbers have a personal aspect – what they signify can only mean something to us individually.

working out what makes the universe tick. We may not believe in a divine force so we hold fast to the idea that science will work it out for us.

CALCULATIONS

Numbers provide a way of quantifying aspects of our world, and we may dream of them to give us a sense of control, rationality and certainty if these are lacking in our lives. We use them in calculations, so working with figures may indicate that you are trying to take a methodical and "calculating" approach to a situation, rather than following your heart or your intuition.

NUMBERS AS SYMBOLS

Some numbers also have specific symbolic values based on cultural associations. We internalize these values and associations to some extent and may employ them in our dreams. The idea that numbers have mysterious powers has been explored in cultures around the world for millennia. In the West, numerology, as this theory is called, not only assigns particular numbers meanings but also associates them with colours and sound frequencies. If you are familiar with numerology, then such associations may reinforce the significance of the numbers, but you need to establish whether this feels true for you. Some of the values of the numbers in numerology have found their way into our cultural symbolic vocabulary and will probably seem obvious, such as One representing individualism or Two partnership, though others may not resonate particularly strongly for you.

Like all dream elements, numbers can have a personal significance as well as, in some cases, having gained symbolic value in the context of particular cultures. So for a devout Christian, Three could suggest the Holy Trinity; a musician may see it as the foundation chord of the scale, while for another

LEFT If we don't understand scientific principles, our dream symbols may present science in a negative, perhaps even intimidating, light. **MIDDLE LEFT** Doctors are part of the terrifying science dream symbolism and can appear or be used as distorted dream codes. **BOTTOM LEFT** We may use low-tech imagery such as cogs to represent time and science in our dreams.

person it may bring up the concept of the family trio of father, mother and child. Children often have strong emotional relationships to certain numbers, such as lucky Seven; a triple Six in the Christian tradition is the number of the Devil, while Thirteen has, over the centuries, come to represent bad luck so strongly that even in our modern, rational society there are streets with no house of that number. Even if you are not superstitious, the fact that these associations exist in our society is often borrowed by our mind to suggest something to us. If you relate to a given meaning on a deep and instinctive level then it is significant to you.

NUMEROLOGY

The study of the symbolic value of numbers provides a way of understanding life by studying and exploring their esoteric significance as symbols of the energy of the universe. Numerology readings use numbers that are derived from your birth date and from the letters of your name, these numbers then provide understanding of personal traits that affect how you approach life. Sometimes the system of numerology is used for prophecy.

NUMBER POWER

These are some of the basic characteristics that are assigned to each of the numbers One to Nine in numerology:

1 unity, creation, independence, assertiveness, the self

2 duality, emergence, compromise, discourse

3 power, generative force, creative self-expression

4 solidity, dullness, persistence, determination

5 sensuality, pleasure, gregariousness

6 perfection, harmony, balance, domesticity

7 mysticism, psychic powers, magic

8 materialism, success, justice, ambition

9 spirituality, mental achievement, wisdom

SIGNS AND SYMBOLS

FREUD WROTE AT LENGTH ABOUT SEXUAL SYMBOLS, OF THE MULTITUDE OF OBJECTS IN OUR ORDINARY ENVIRONMENT THAT COULD BE USED TO REPRESENT OR ATTRACT OUR ATTENTION TO SEXUALITY. JUNG EXPLORED SYMBOLIC ARCHETYPES, SUCH AS THE MASK, THE MAGICAL JOURNEY OR THE RITUAL BAPTISM, IN WHICH A PERSON, PLACE OR EVENT COMES TO REPRESENT A SHARED HUMAN EXPERIENCE. IN A SENSE, EVERYTHING DISCUSSED IN THE LEXICON FUNCTIONS AS A SYMBOL IN THE CONTEXT OF OUR DREAMS, BUT WHEN WE TALK ABOUT SIGNS AND CULTURAL OR PERSONAL SYMBOLS WE ARE TALKING ABOUT ACTUAL ICONIC OBJECTS THAT CARRY CERTAIN SIGNIFYING FACTORS.

THE COMPLEXITY OF SYMBOLS

In this context, the word "symbols" denotes icons that we use to signify allegiance, power, authority, status, belief systems and so on – such as the cross or swastika or a country's flag. It also covers alphabets and hieroglyphs – symbolic systems that have arisen in cultures around the world to communicate efficiently with others across time and distance.

The difference between these and the other symbols that we discuss in the Lexicon is that these have all been generated consciously by people to represent certain things, as a shortcut to communicating a raft of meanings, rather than evolving in a more organic way through human experience. Each of these symbols provides a complexity of meanings, which are reinforced every time we see them, much the same way that corporate or product logos are used to reinforce an image that an organization wants to project.

RELIGIOUS SYMBOLS

Our relationship with religion and spirituality in general, and with particular religions, is addressed by the manifestation of religious symbols in our dreams. These symbols evoke a highly personal response, which depends on our attitude, our own beliefs, any religious experiences we might have had, and so on. The cross, for example, is for many a revered symbol of Christ's love, but it could also be a symbol of suffering (we speak of "having a cross to bear" meaning a burden of responsibility) or even bring to mind the cruelty of religious persecution and conquest. The Star of David is a common symbol of Judaism, but it may bring associations of oppression and discrimination because of how it was used to mark out Jews in Nazi Germany.

SYMBOLS OF POWER AND AUTHORITY

National flags are associated with particular countries and their assumed or stated cultures and value systems, and so as symbols can be highly emotionally charged – think of how often the flags of certain countries are ceremonially burnt, for instance. In a general sense, they also signify allegiance to a particular country or other political or ideological body, feelings of inclusion and belonging or exclusion, pride or contempt. Flags may also bear particular symbols – the swastika, for instance, is strongly associated with the right-wing ideologies of Nazi Germany, the Holocaust, fascism, regimentation, oppression, pure evil and a host of similar negative associations – although the ancient symbol that the Nazis used as their emblem originally signified the sun, and symbolized good luck.

In an obvious way the crown is a symbol of royalty, but this in itself may mean many things,

BELOW In our dreams we will seize on any symbol and put it to virtually any use. Flags, for example, can signify a range of emotions – pride, aggression, power, belonging and alienation, to name a few.

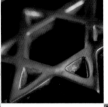

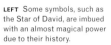

LEFT Some symbols, such as the Star of David, are imbued with an almost magical power due to their history.

LEFT Hieroglyphs are a good example of how subjective a language is. Although now an obsolete sign system, they still conjure up certain symbolic significance for us today.

ABOVE In older cultures, everything in nature held a particular meaning and was given symbolic value.

such as authority, inherited power, immense wealth, status and responsibility. A monarch, like a parent, may be either a protective, benevolent authority figure, or a threatening and despotic character who reduces our own freedom. The second kind of monarch embodies an excess of power, wealth and so on, and highlights one's own relative poverty. The scales of justice suggest balance and impartiality, as well as the authority of judges and the legal system in general.

ALPHABETS AND HIEROGLYPHS

We use symbolic systems to communicate – whether they consist of the letters of an alphabet, which represent sounds of speech, the hieroglyphs of ancient Egypt, musical notation or a code such as semaphore.

If we dream of such symbols, whether we understand them or not is crucial. The symbols may be associated with a particular nationality or culture, and understanding them may signify access to that culture, or a denial of that access. Equally, the symbols may indicate that information is being obscured or withheld, or that the dreamer has a lack of clarity, an inability to "read" or "decipher" a situation.

ABOVE Heavenly symbols, such as the sun, the stars and the moon, are a part of the richly symbolic language of religious imagery.
RIGHT Crowns, sceptres and thrones suggest the pomp and majesty of kingship and rule.
BELOW Even something simple and iconic can be given a lofty and weighty symbolism, such as the scales of justice.

Cause and Effect

For centuries, philosophers, scientists and theologians have grappled with questions of the origins of the universe, and of humankind's place within it. This is the ultimate question of cause and effect – the effect is all too visible, but the cause still a matter of great debate. On a much smaller scale, in our everyday lives, we are faced with causality all the time – our actions have consequences, which in turn have a knock-on effect, and we are often aware that our lives have taken a dramatic turn because of what seemed at the time like an insignificant or unrelated event.

BELOW AND BELOW RIGHT
How we came into being is a question that has been addressed through human history, from the creation myths of ancient Egypt (below left) to the Islamic prophets of the Middle Ages (below right). We still don't have all the answers, and our dreams will reflect this.

OUR ORIGINS

Creation myths and theories are part of every human culture. The Big Bang Theory, the Book of Genesis, the Egyptian and classical legends, the Buddhists' Seven Ages of the Universe – all attempt to address the big questions about existence, and all have entirely different starting points and conclusions in looking at the concept of our origins. Some people have a burning need to know how everything came into being and what was behind it. They may use dream time to look for the answers that will enable them to make their own sense of the universe, to formulate and test their belief systems, and to begin to conceptualize the primary force behind our creation. In fact these dreams may be an important way of revealing to us an underlying dissatisfaction with our beliefs, and a dislike of being adrift in uncertainty.

THE RHYTHMS OF THE UNIVERSE

Causation is seen in the constant interplay of the forces of the universe, and all its physical routines – the sun rising and setting, the path of the stars through the night sky, the seasons, nature, beginnings and endings, life and death, birth and growth. Dreams that tackle such fundamental questions as why we are here, where we are going and what we want from life, cause us to sit up and take notice, change direction, even change our lives.

THE FOUR SEASONS

The seasons of the year are a very potent symbol of change and the natural order of things. We use the cycle of spring, summer, autumn and winter as metaphors for the stages of our own life, and we also measure the years by the

turning of the seasons. The significance of nature in our dreams may reflect our feelings of being divorced from nature. Perhaps we live in cities and feel that we are unable to connect with the seasons visually and emotionally, but they still affect us on a very deep level, and if we don't acknowledge this it may surface in our dreams.

EVENTS IN OUR LIVES
We ourselves are agents of change. Everything we say and think and do has an effect on our own lives and on those of others, and sometimes these effects are brought forcefully to our attention. You forget something at home and go back to get it, only to hear on the news that that brief delay meant that you narrowly avoided being involved in a car pile-up. You have a conversation with a friend about your hopes and frustrations with work, and they put you in touch with someone who can make your dream of running your own business a reality.

Awake or asleep, we may turn over in our minds questions of why things happened the way they did, and what might have been if we had done something differently.

Whether you regard these little triggers as chance or fate or part of some greater plan, they all have consequences great and small, and you may turn them over in your mind again and again. If these consequences are negative, you may be plagued by regret or guilt, and these feelings are likely to be played out in dreams by your unconscious mind. You may be trying to work through the events, to find a way to absolve your guilt, to discover that the events were not after all your fault, or wishing that things had happened a different way.

I shall be telling this with a sigh
Somewhere ages and ages hence:
Two roads diverged in a wood, and I –
I took the one less travelled by,
And that has made all the difference.

ROBERT FROST, *THE ROAD NOT TAKEN*

LIFE-CHANGING DREAM
In my dream I was going to work. I was almost there when the lorry in front of me suddenly slowed to turn, and I sensed that I was going to have an accident. As I powered up the bike and overtook it, I congratulated myself on avoiding a crash. Then another lorry pulled out of a side road and I went straight into it. I could see my motorbike turning over and over in the air in slow motion. I was badly injured.

I was also badly shaken when I woke up, and as a result I gave up that job – I couldn't travel that road any more and my life changed direction completely.

STRENGTH AND WEAKNESS

IN OUR COMPETITIVE WORLD, IT IS NOT SURPRISING THAT DREAMS OF STRENGTH AND WEAKNESS TROUBLE OUR SLEEP AT TIMES. SUCH DREAMS MAY TAKE THE FORM OF CONVENTIONAL SYMBOLISM – THE STRENGTH OF A LION, A WRESTLER, IRON CHAINS OR AN ELECTRIC STORM, OR THE WEAKNESS AND FRAILTY OF A TINY CREATURE, AN OLD OR DISABLED PERSON, A DELICATE SPIDER'S WEB. OR THEY MAY HIGHLIGHT YOUR OWN PERSONAL STRENGTHS AND WEAKNESSES, EITHER LITERAL OR METAPHORIC. WHAT WE THINK OF AS STRENGTH IN OUR WAKING LIFE MAY MANIFEST COMPLETELY DIFFERENTLY IN OUR DREAMS AND WE MAY BE SURPRISED BY OUR OWN SYMBOLISM.

COSMIC STRENGTH

The universe is immense, powerful and strong, and by comparison, we humans are almost absurdly tiny, vulnerable and weak. Cosmic dreams about strength underline the fact of this terrible fragility, as our unconscious tries to come to terms with the size, power, age and complexity of the universe.

We know where we begin and end as individuals, but any similar quantification of the universe is impossible. We know that we will die at some point in time, and that when we do so this immeasurable and intricate universe will continue in all its glory without a second thought.

Our passing and fleeting presence will leave not a trace in any way.

SECURITY

Dreams about strength may be our way of investigating how safe we feel in our waking life. They may be our unconscious mind's way of getting us to do something about feeling insecure. If we live in a dangerous neighbourhood we are likely to have a constant background preoccupation with safety issues and a fear of being threatened unexpectedly; to address this our best course of action could be to learn assertiveness or how to be physically stronger, to build safe zones where we can let down our

guard, or to be more cautious about entering dangerous circumstances or places.

The insecurity that troubles us may be of a more personal nature – in our relationships rather than in the sense of our physical wellbeing – so we should look at why these relationships make us feel that way. Our dream might also be the start of a search for a guardian angel of some kind who will protect us from being overwhelmed by the strength and size of the universe.

WEAKNESS

A dream of strength could be nature's way of drawing our attention to some aspect of our

BELOW LEFT Rather than the obvious images of power or strength, images of gentleness, such as a tiny baby, may be used as a symbol for true strength.
BELOW RIGHT In our dreams, conventional metaphors for strength may appear as clear or distorted images.

defencelessness and vulnerability. If we feel threatened by stronger forces then it makes sense to seek ways of becoming stronger so we are better able to fight off the threat, or of compensating in some other way if this is not possible. The dream is flagging up the fact that we feel weak or frail or naked and we are being urged to do something about that. Where the threat comes from in our waking life is up to us to determine. It might be that we need to find a way of coming to terms with the imponderables of an immense and powerful universe, or it might be more mundane issues, such as our work or our relationships, that are threatening to overwhelm us. Either way, if we feel threatened by strength in a dream then it is likely that there is something that is making us feel threatened or vulnerable in our waking life.

PERSONAL STRENGTHS AND WEAKNESSES

It is probably physical prowess that first springs to mind when you think of strength, but just as important is the personal strength that we draw from being centred and knowing who we are. It may be that we express that centredness symbolically in an image of physical strength. We also describe as strengths and weaknesses the things that we do well or the things that we are not good at. And having a weakness for something means that we like it or are drawn to it so much that we cannot refuse it; although, say, having a weakness for chocolate may seem trivial, it could be a

signpost to some other area of your life where you lack control. It is worth bearing all possibilities in mind when you are trying to understand your dream, as your mind may be using apparently frivolous concepts as a springboard for exploring more serious issues. How power manifests in our dreams can be a reflection on how secure we feel.

A COSMIC DREAM

"I was alone in the vastness of space but I could feel the sheer size and strength of the universe closing in on me. Everything was black and I couldn't see what forces were pressing against me – it seemed as though it was the very walls of the universe that were crushing me out of existence. I couldn't fight against this sort of strength.

The dream was really quite terrifying, and I woke up feeling small and helpless. It made me realize that I was letting a lot of people walk all over me and needed to be much more assertive, to learn to say 'no' more often, especially at work."

POWER DREAMS

POWER APPEARS IN MANY GUISES – FROM THE OBVIOUS FORMS AND TRAPPINGS OF POLITICAL OR MILITARY POWER AND WEALTH, TO PHYSICAL DOMINATION, OPPRESSION, VICTIMIZATION OR BULLYING, THE AUTHORITY OF AGE OR WISDOM, OR THE PERSONAL POWER OF A TRULY CENTRED INDIVIDUAL. POWER EXERTED OVER US CAN BE A SOURCE OF INSPIRATION, RESPECT, STIMULATION, ENCOURAGEMENT, DEFERENCE AND SAFETY. ON THE OTHER HAND IT CAN PROVOKE FEAR AND HOSTILITY. HOW WE FEEL ABOUT POWER AND INFLUENCE IN REAL LIFE WILL AFFECT HOW WE DREAM OF THEM. DOES POWER EXCITE OR DISMAY YOU? DO YOU FEEL INVIGORATED BY IT OR STIFLED?

ABSTRACT QUALITIES

Power can manifest itself on a cosmic level – divine, celestial, universal, collective – and also as an attribute of an individual or organization. Dreams in which power is a dominant theme tend to be unambiguous. We are likely to respond strongly to them and to remember them because of this. In them we may be enslaved or motivated; we may even be the source of the power itself.

BELOW A dream that involves a king figure, or even a godly one may well be a reflection of a feeling you have in your waking life that you are being dominated or controlled in some way.

Our society is highly stratified, and power in a social and political sense is an inevitable part of our lives. Monarchs and presidents wield it over their citizens, bosses over employees, parents over their children. Many people are preoccupied with power, seeking it, being dissatisfied with a lack of it, feeling the effects of the power that others wield. So it is not surprising that images of power crop up in dreams quite often. We may have power thrust upon us, such as when we are promoted to a position of responsibility, and be unsure of how to handle it or of how others will react. We may have bullied

someone and now be feeling guilty. If we pay attention to how power manifests in our dreams and how we respond to it, we may learn about how to deal with the real-life situation that is preoccupying us.

NUCLEAR POWER

We have all grown up in the nuclear age, in which the possibility of being wiped out by nuclear weapons or by an accident at a nuclear power plant has seemed very real. Such power is immense, and used properly, it can enhance the quality of our lives, but if anything goes wrong, and the containment of this power fails or is breached,

---

A DREAM OF GOD

"In my dream, God was sitting on a vast, unearthly throne. But rather than paying attention to being face to face with God, I was fascinated by the throne. Its construction was really important – it was made of some kind of metal, never seen on earth, which was grey flecked with red, and had a luminous transparency like crystal.

I realised that this throne was where the real power lay: whoever sat on it would become a god, and God Himself had only got his power from having been on it for so long. If anyone else sat there, they too would acquire that sort of power. There was no power in the person, only in the throne – the material trappings of power.

I'm not religious at all so I was quite surprised to have had what seemed at first like a religious dream, but I think it was more about knowing where power lies and how to access it than about the spiritual aspect of God. I'm very concerned with power and authority in my life as I am in the police force. My uniform represents these things, but it doesn't make me feel powerful from within; it also creates a negative reaction in some people, which I don't like."

disaster is virtually inevitable. The dreams of many people are affected by such fears, and they need to come to terms with the feeling of helplessness that this kind of threat generates. Because of the "all-or-nothing" feeling that nuclear war has, we may use it to represent in a more general or metaphoric sense the end of the world as we know it, or some personal calamity.

THE POWER OF NATURE

Sometimes nature unleashes its power on a spectacular scale: lightening storms, floods, forest fires, hurricanes and avalanches all put us in our place in the universe. We try to minimize the damage done by these phenomenan, but ultimately we are powerless. An impending natural disaster in a dream – the moment before a dam bursts or a storm breaks – may show us the potential power that we have in ourselves; how we express it may make the difference between greatness and destruction.

COMING TO TERMS WITH POWER

In waking life or in our dreams, we might feel drawn irresistibly to some situation or event or person but cannot understand why. The power that draws us may be invisible and subtle but by careful analysis and observation we might begin to understand what is controlling us, and can assess what we are being manipulated or influenced by in our waking life.

By paying attention to power dreams we can literally empower ourselves in real life. Once we have pinpointed and understood the powers that we fear, find attractive or wish to develop in ourselves, then they can be tamed and put to use.

ABOVE FAR LEFT When you dream of power is it manifested on an individual basis, with a symbol of social control such as a monarch?
ABOVE LEFT Or does your dream of power involve forces such as those in large-scale industry?
ABOVE Or is it the power that might be unleashed by politicians and rulers that you fear you are unable to control?

LEFT Nature has such awesome power, such highly destructive force, that it may appear in our dreams as a frightening power indeed.

COLOUR

THE MORE AWARE WE ARE OF COLOURS IN OUR LIVES, THE MORE WE ARE LIKELY TO DREAM IN COLOUR. BUT SOMETIMES IN
A DREAM, COLOUR DEMANDS OUR ATTENTION, EITHER BECAUSE IT IS VERY STRONG OR BECAUSE IT IS UNNATURAL IN ITS
CONTEXT. IN THIS WAY IT ACQUIRES SYMBOLIC VALUE, AND YOU SHOULD CONSIDER WHAT MEANING IT HAS FOR YOU.
DO WE ALL DREAM IN COLOUR ALL OF THE TIME? THIS MAY SEEM IRRELEVANT IF YOU ALWAYS DO BUT WHAT IF YOU DREAM
IN BLACK AND WHITE? HAVE YOU EVER HAD A DREAM THAT IS IN JUST ONE COLOUR? WHAT DO THE COLOURS WE SEE IN
OUR DREAMS MEAN? ARE THEY REFLECTIONS OF OUR EMOTIONS OR OUR SPIRITUALITY?

Some colours we respond to in a very personal way, but many of the associations we have with particular colours are culturally informed – for example, white is worn by the bride on her wedding day in Western culture, but in the Far East it is the colour traditionally worn at funerals.

CREATIVE POWER OF COLOUR

We may be surprised by the intensity of colours in our dream, by the inventiveness of our imagination. But everything in our dream expresses ourselves – what we see is what we are capable of creating. These dreams can awaken in us a sense of our real power, can make us realize how impressive we really are, however much we get bogged down in our day-to-day lives.

EXPRESSING OUR INNER BEING

A dream that focuses on fantastic colour and form – whirling patterns and shifting shapes – may resemble an "acid trip", or it could be that you are making spiritual contact with your inner self. In a rainbow, all the colours are present, and are perfectly, naturally in balance. Strongly contrasting colours may signify either clear choices or a dilemma in some area of your life, while colours that merge and blend could signify an inner harmony, or, conversely, a lack of clarity.

Pay special attention if several dreams feature a particular colour, as this could be your unconscious trying to work with a particular issue that you are not addressing effectively in your waking life. Equally, if you stop focusing on this colour in your dreams then it could be that you have worked through something that was on your mind.

COLOURS BY ASSOCIATION

It is said that the colours we see in our dreams reflect the state of our unconscious mind. So if blue predominates, we may be feeling emotional, while green could suggest an interest in nature or environmental issues. These are only two possible meanings though, and it may be that your mind has randomly drawn on a catchphrase such as "feeling blue" or the Green Party of environmental politics. In the same way, blue has even been suggested as an indicator of futuristic travel because of the phrase "taking off into the blue".

COLOUR KEY

These are some associations people commonly have with particular colours. Remember though that your own personal experiences, as well as cultural differences, may mean that they do not always ring true to you – use them as a starting point to prompt your own feelings, rather than as fact.

Red: energy, fire, passion, love, sex, anger, danger

Orange/yellow: vibrancy, joy, life, sunshine, warmth, spirituality, jealousy

Green: calm, nature, illness, envy

Blue: peace, emotions, depression, space

Violet/purple: grandeur, royalty, rage

White: innocence, energy, emptiness, possibility, cleanliness, holiness

Black: death, mourning, depression, conformity, secrecy, obscurity

ABOVE Nature has her own colour symbolism which may not be for our benefit at all – flowers are coloured for the bees rather than for us.

ABOVE AND ABOVE RIGHT Natural colours, such as shades of green, have instant association with growth and renewal. If you dream of green your subconscious could be sending you a message about decisions that need to be made.
RIGHT Brightly coloured sweets attract children – do the colours have the same impact on you if you dream about them, or do they seem unpleasantly synthetic and confusing?

ABOVE The colour white in Western cultures is synonymous with purity and innocence. Dreaming of white weddings might therefore symbolize this.
LEFT Multicoloured objects in dreams may be a way for your mind to link with your emotions.
BELOW Perhaps there are no symbolic associations with colours in a dream. Vibrant shades might just be a way of your creative mind expressing itself.

The expression "seeing red", meaning to be angry, may well have come from the red mist you see before your eyes if in a severe rage, but it would be simplistic to say that this necessarily means that a dream involving the colour red always points to anger. Our conscious mind might make these easy associations of anger, violence, passion, fire and energy, but the red in your dream could also be the red of romantic love and passion, or a warning of danger. It could even be a "red herring" – perhaps before bed you saw the word "red", or a film in which colour was used for artistic emphasis. Perhaps you told your child the story of Little Red Riding Hood at bedtime. These triggers may lead your mind to cultural meanings that are commonly ascribed to the colour – the dangerous wolf is attracted by the girl's coat; her red coat may have pointed to the danger she was in.

DREAM COLOURS

"I was standing on a hilltop, and could see myself from above, turning round and round in slow motion. I was so aware of the vividness of the grass, the sky, my clothes, everything, and the colours were so bright, that I felt I was being told something. I woke up wanting to paint those colours, although I hadn't picked up a brush for years. I took up painting again because of this dream, and I'm so happy just doing it."

SHAPE, FORM, TEXTURE

LIKE COLOUR, THE SHAPE AND TEXTURE OF OBJECTS AND SPACES CAN HOLD THE KEY TO THE MEANING OF OUR DREAMS.
REGULAR GEOMETRIC FORMS CARRY ASSOCIATIONS SIMILAR TO THOSE OF THE NUMBER OF SIDES THEY HAVE, WHILE
PROPORTIONS, SUCH AS HOW LONG, TALL OR SHORT, AND HOW FAT OR THIN SOMETHING OR SOMEONE IS, MAY ALSO BE
SIGNIFICANT. YOU MAY FOCUS YOUR ATTENTION ON THE TEXTURE OF A SURFACE IN YOUR DREAM, FOCUSING ON WHETHER
IT IS SHARP OR BLUNT, SOFT OR SMOOTH, AND ALSO WHETHER IT IS WHOLE OR BROKEN. HOW MUCH DO WE DRAW ON THE
SENSE OF TOUCH? DOES EACH SURFACE HAVE TEXTURE?

Many of the above properties may be insignificant in the context of your dream, but if they particularly catch your attention or they are unusual in some way, you can be fairly certain that they are presented like this for a reason. You should ask yourself why it is that a particular shape is appearing in your dream, and if it is markedly different from what you would expect, then look at what the difference is and why your mind has formed the object in this way.

BELOW RIGHT Dreaming of pyramid shapes might have a particular mystical significance for you, or it might be a more prosaic link with your aspirations.
BELOW Dreaming of straight lines, such as a road with no turns or bends, might mean strength of purpose and clarity of vision. It might also mean predictability and lack of self-expression however.

SYMMETRY
Regular shapes have a strong connection with numbers, and because they are so basic and are found in so many aspects of our waking lives – the sides of a geometric form, the number of petals on a flower, how many points a star has – physical shapes may often be used in dreams metaphorically, to stand in for more abstract or complex concepts.

For example, a circle – whether it is a golden ring or a round room – may suggest harmony, inclusion and femininity, while a square may bring feelings of order and symmetry, masculinity, conventionality or even military precision. A triangular shape to some people may allude to a representation of the perfect balance of the Holy Trinity, the mother-father-child relationship, or the tension of a love triangle. The pyramid, often thought to have a mystical significance, has a solid base, but in its pinnacle reaches for the sky. Dreaming of this form may show that you are aspiring to greater things.

CURVES AND SPIRALS
Wavy lines are more fluid and often more random than straight lines, and in this may suggest a freedom and unpredictability not found in a more regular form. While straight lines could suggest clarity of vision or thought, twists, loops and curves may indicate obscurity or confusion. Spirals have a strong sense of movement, notice whether they are spiralling inward or outward, and feel whether they are suggestive of something in your life "spiralling out of control" or whether they give you an exhilarating sense of moving outward and upward, away from confinement. By contrast, points and angles may indicate dead ends, especially if viewed from the inside, or show a concentration of energy.

OPEN AND CLOSED FORMS

Whether the form is open or fully enclosed could also be highly significant. A box with its lid off, or an enclosed garden whose gate is open, has nothing to hide, and allows the possibility of moving out of a state of enclosure or confinement whether physical, intellectual or emotional, and of moving on to new experiences.

FAT OR THIN?

Our response to fatness and thinness in people is usually heavily influenced by widely accepted ideals and stereotypes. Your dream may use these stereotypes in a literal way, but you can also look at whether a person's size is associated metaphorically with some attitude to resources. In this way, a fat person – or object or animal – may symbolize plenty and a thin person a lack of resources; alternatively, size may point to a relationship to resources, such as whether you are hoarding or rejecting them, or using them up

faster than you can get hold of them. Fat may also have associations of cuddliness and therefore comfort, or alternatively may indicate lethargy or inaction.

PROPORTIONS

Tall people, buildings and other objects have a physical advantage in their height and can also be seen from a distance. Tall people have stature and can see farther, while from the commanding height of a tall building or hill, one has a greater perspective. Short people, on the other hand, can be looked down on both literally and figuratively, and may have difficulty in having their authority accepted. But smaller

can also mean more nimble or manoeuvrable or can offer the advantage of having an ear close to the ground.

TEXTURE

You may well have an emotional response to the texture of objects in your dream. Sharp edges and rough surfaces may be uncomfortable to the touch, or even threatening. Fuzzy surfaces may be comforting, a reminder of the cuddly toys of childhood, while smooth or reflective surfaces may be attractive but distracting or deceptive. Whether something is broken or intact is also likely to be significant, especially if it is treasured.

LEFT Dreaming of spiral shapes or movement can be an indication of how you feel about your life – is it spiralling out of control, are you on your way up and out, or are you trapped in ever-decreasing circles?

BELOW FAR LEFT Texture can feature in a dream. A feeling of roughness might be threatening but could also be attractive. **BELOW LEFT** Curves can suggest freedom and self-expression. If you dream of them perhaps you feel you need less restriction in your life. **BELOW** Formal patterns and straight lines might suggest constriction and a lack of imagination, but can bring a feeling of security and comfort if you feel life is too random and out of control.

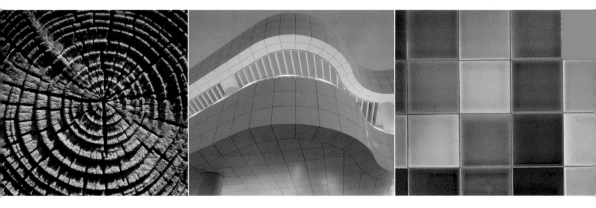

NATURE DREAMS

How we relate to the world around us and how secure we feel about being alive and part of our environment are revealed in dreams of nature. In nature we find the unspoilt, original state of our essential inner being, the truth of who we are as individuals, and a way to access the understanding of the world that we formed during childhood.

RIGHT Animals and plants reveal some of our most primitive, instinctive feelings and fears, which arise from the deepest levels of our unconscious.

DREAM LANDSCAPES

THE LANDSCAPE IS THE BACKDROP FOR THE ACTION OF THE DREAM. IT ANCHORS A DREAM IN TIME AND PLACE AND SETS THE GENERAL THEME AND MOOD, JUST AS SET DESIGN CAN ESTABLISH THE TONE OF A PLAY. CHANGING THE SET OR THE DREAMSCAPE CAN BRING ABOUT A COMPLETELY DIFFERENT EXPERIENCE FOR THE AUDIENCE OR THE DREAMER, EVEN IF THE STORY AND THE CHARACTERS REMAIN THE SAME. AS WELL AS THE PHYSICAL SCENERY ITSELF, THE QUALITY OF THE LANDSCAPE — FAMILIAR OR ALIEN, COMFORTABLE OR DISORIENTATING, OPEN OR RESTRICTED AND CLAUSTROPHOBIC — WILL HAVE EMOTIONAL SIGNIFICANCE AND AFFECT THE GENERAL FEELING OF THE DREAM.

NATURAL LANDSCAPES

Any given landscape can mean different things to different people, and you need to look at both yourself and the context of the dream to understand what it is trying to tell you. Many landscape elements, such as mountains and rivers, have very basic symbolic meanings. For instance, mountains commonly represent obstacles and rivers strong emotional currents. But even if this seems true for you, how you respond to mountains and rivers as well as how you cope with obstacles and emotions will put a personal spin on the dream images. Someone with a fear of heights will see a mountainous landscape quite differently from a mountaineer,

and their unconscious will use this image to express quite different things. Even two people who attach the same meaning to mountains may interpret the same dream quite differently if one views obstacles as frightening and daunting and the other as exciting and challenging.

Your position in relation to the landscape is also important – being on top of a mountain and gazing out over a glorious landscape of snow-covered peaks will probably give you an exhilarating sense of achievement, whereas standing at the base and needing to get to the other side may rather bring up feelings associated with challenges as yet unmet. A stream may symbolize something

relatively minor that needs to be overcome, and a bridge crossing it could give you a means of getting over that obstacle. Jungles can give rise to a feeling of being lost, alienated, emotional or fearful, but they could create a sense of being at one with the lushness and aliveness of nature in all its abundance. Being in a desert could symbolize barrenness, isolation or disorientation in some aspect of your life, or you may feel relaxed in such a vast open space if you easily feel hemmed in.

Chasms, ravines and abysses in their physical form can be frightening, as one stands on the brink, facing the possibility of falling in or losing things irretrievably over the edge. These

ABOVE What are you doing in your dream? If you are climbing a mountain you might be doing likewise symbolically in your waking life.
RIGHT If you dream of open plains and vast wildernesses then maybe you are feeling lost in your real world.
FAR RIGHT Wide open spaces in your dream could be intimidating, but perhaps means that you feel hemmed in and wish to break free from constriction and restraint.

edges of nature may represent major difficulties you are facing in your everyday waking life, issues that you are afraid to look into in a sense of no return.

Beaches provide a transition point between the solidity of terra firma and the vast sea of emotions. They are the threshold of opportunity to enter into deep emotional states, places where you have the freedom to revel in being yourself and recapture the simple joys of childhood.

THE MANUFACTURED LANDSCAPE

Not all landscapes are natural, though. Cities and big towns may symbolize complex problems that have to be negotiated, with straight streets and avenues helping to give you a clear sense of direction. Indeed how roads help or hinder your journey is very telling – if in your dream you find yourself lost in a maze of back streets and alleyways, then perhaps this dream is trying to bring to your attention a sense

of being lost and fearful, while forked paths represent decisions or choices, and twists and turns imply confusion and setbacks. Open roads could leave you feeling exposed and vulnerable on one hand or clear-sighted on the other. Or a road could be hemmed in by walls, fences, high banks or vegetation, giving a feeling of security or claustrophobia. Notice whether you stroll or feel the need to run, and how comfortable you are with the path you are on – it could be symbolizing your path through life.

Walls and fences are also ambiguous symbols. As they can close you in, they may serve as barriers, cutting you off from the rest of the world, or give a sense of security and ownership. Gates also provide openings in otherwise restricted areas, and opportunities to look outward into the unknown from a safe space. Noticing whether you look for a gate or avoid one can give you clues to your emotional state.

LONELINESS DREAM
"In my dream I was walking along a beach. This was no ordinary beach, though – it was located outside of space, a planet floating on its own. I felt unutterably sad there, like I was the last woman left in the universe and there was no one else. It made me realize how lonely I'd been and I resolved to do something about it."

ABOVE Where do you fit into the landscape? Are you part of it or an observer? This is important if you want to know what your dream means. Dreaming of cities and towns may represent complex problems in our life.

FAR LEFT If you dream of a stream try to remember its characteristics, is it bubbling and friendly, does it present an obstacle, is it flowing where you would like to go?

LEFT Are you comfortable in your dream landscape or do you feel alien and out of place; too large or too small?

THE WEATHER

LIKE LANDSCAPES, THE WEATHER COLOURS OUR DREAMS EMOTIONALLY, GIVING BROAD CLUES TO HOW WE FEEL ABOUT OUR
LIVES, AND WHAT SORT OF GENERAL MOOD WE ARE EXPERIENCING IN OUR EVERYDAY WAKING LIVES. WE GENERATE THE
WEATHER IN OUR DREAMS AS A WAY OF EXPRESSING OUR FEELINGS. BECAUSE WHEN WE ARE AWAKE OUR MOODS CAN BE
STRONGLY AFFECTED BY THE WEATHER AND THE SEASON, AND AS THERE ARE MANY WORDS THAT WE USE INTERCHANGEABLY
TO DESCRIBE BOTH THE WEATHER AND OUR MOODS AND FEELINGS (STORMY, GLOOMY, SUNNY, HAZY, TO NAME JUST A FEW),
THESE ARE RELATIVELY EASY SYMBOLS TO START WITH WHEN TRYING TO MAKE SENSE OF OUR DREAMS.

ABOVE Rain may
symbolize our problems
and worries raining down
on us – or it might just be
raining in our dream.
ABOVE RIGHT In your
dream you may be relax-
ing, taking time out to
enjoy the sunshine. Enjoy
this dream holiday.

FAIR OR FOUL?

Moods fluctuate, sometimes
unpredictably, in much the same
way as the weather. Usually the
weather in a dream is congruent
with how you are feeling, so
calm, sunny weather could
indicate a peaceful or happy
disposition, while a storm could
be expressing anger.

But it is worth taking a closer
look at weather that seems to be
at odds with your mood. You
might be raging in your dream
but if the background weather is
calm and pleasant you can be
fairly certain that your rage will
soon pass. On the other hand, if
you are being serene and
reasonable in your dream but
storm clouds are gathering and
the temperature dropping, this
could be a sign that you need to
focus your attention on feelings
that are being repressed.

RAIN AND SNOW

As water is widely considered to
be a symbol for emotions, rain
and tears alike are richly
evocative of your emotional state.
Grey skies and rain clouds cast a
gloomy shadow over your spirit,
and could indicate that your
unconscious is trying to work
with feelings of depression or
despondency. You may express
your tears as rain – the gentle
summer rain that clears the air
and feels good, the light drizzle
of a spring day, or the deluge of
the storm. The rain can be cold
and invigorating, or warm and
welcoming, and an unexpected
shower of rain could mean that
you feel your enthusiasm or
interest have suddenly been
dampened. Any kind of rain can
also have a cleansing and
rejuvenating effect. Snow can be
seen as rain in crystalline form. It

ABOVE Water represents emotions
and rain is often linked to tears – if
you dream of rain, is there
someone you are crying for? If it is
a natural expression of grief or
tension then you might find a
dream of rain is as beneficial as
a good cry.

provides another way of
expressing emotions, colder and
clearer, but also often softer and
gentler, and it dramatically
changes the appearance of the
landscape. It can mean the fun of
playtime, but it can also be
threatening – blizzards and
avalanches show the emotions
becoming overwhelming and
out of control.

STORMS

In the build-up to a storm, a
hush descends on nature along
with a feeling of anticipation of
the power to be unleashed when
the storm breaks. Dark, heavy

clouds can be oppressive and
threatening, and people who
bottle up their emotions will
recognize in the calm before the
storm the moments before an
emotional outburst.

Torrents of rain, dark, heavy
clouds, and rumbles or claps of
deep thunder all express the
charged emotional content of the
dream, whether anger or passion
or outrage. Because storms can
be dramatic, attention-grabbing
events, they are likely to be
central to the plot of the dream.
Having a stormy dream gives you
a safe opportunity to play out
powerful emotions that may be
too difficult or too dangerous to
express in real life. Lightning
gives dramatic moments of clarity
as it illuminates the landscape.
The passing of a storm parallels
the end of an emotional outburst
– you may feel relieved and
invigorated by having put out
your feelings, or you may be
surveying the damage caused.

MIST AND FOG

By contrast, dreaming of mist
and fog, drizzle and gloom, all of
which obscure the landscape,
may suggest that you are unsure
of how you feel about something.
Pay particular attention to what
you do in your dream to clear the
air, to see the way forward, as
this may give you clues to what
you can do in your waking life to
resolve a confusing issue.
Weather that obscures things can
also be hinting that you are in a
state of denial about something,
and you may need to ask yourself
what it is you are not
acknowledging.

THE SEASONS AND THEIR RHYTHMS

The rhythms of nature can be
seen in the cycle of the seasons.
As the year progresses and the
seasons change, the days
lengthen and shorten, the
weather and the landscape
changes, and plants grow, wither
and die. These patterns can also
have a profound effect on our
outlook, behaviour, and lifestyles.
The sequence of the seasons can
also symbolize the progression
from birth to death and the
experiences that we have at
different times of our lives.

THE ELEMENTS – EARTH

THE ANCIENT GREEK PHILOSOPHERS REGARDED FIRE, EARTH, AIR AND WATER AS PHYSICAL MANIFESTATIONS OF SPIRITUAL ESSENCES. THE PROPERTIES OF THESE FOUR ELEMENTS, AS THEY ARE COLLECTIVELY KNOWN, COULD BE USED TO REPRESENT ABSTRACT CONCEPTS – THE PASSION OF FIRE, THE PRACTICAL AND STABLE NATURE OF EARTH, AIR AS THE MEDIUM FOR THE COMMUNICATION OF IDEAS, AND THE DEEP EMOTIONS OF WATER – AND WERE USED TO UNDERSTAND OUR PHYSICAL AND EMOTIONAL WORLD. THROUGH THE CENTURIES AND IN DIFFERENT CULTURES AROUND THE GLOBE, THESE IDEAS HAVE A MORE OR LESS UNIVERSAL SIGNIFICANCE, AND AS SUCH ARE EXTREMELY IMPORTANT ELEMENTS IN OUR DREAMS.

Earth is where we make our impression: our boot leaves its imprint, and our hands mould and shape it. Earth symbolizes the reality of a situation; it is practical, sensible and stable, and represents conventional, traditional values, long-term goals and ambitions. It is also a powerful symbol for those aspects of our world that are timeless and unchanging. What we make from clay will become mud or dust once again when we have finished with it or discarded it and moved on in our lives. The earth provides the food that sustains us and nurtures us, but is also where we go when we have died, a dark and mysterious place where our physical being gradually disappears.

STABILITY

In our dreams, Earth usually plays a supporting rather than a starring role, and as the only one of the four elements that is solid, it represents stability and passivity. In the form of mud or dry dust, compost, clay or sand, gravel or rocks it can have different qualities; at the grand end of the scale it can even be the whole planet. How it appears as an element in our dream may say a lot about how stable we feel ourselves to be. Fields or meadows, for instance, show that we feel grounded and at peace with ourselves. Conversely, Earth may come to our attention dramatically as an earthquake, a mudslide or quicksand where we can be buried alive. Dreams of eruptions usually mean that our unconscious is troubled – we feel insecure, or fear that we are on the verge of turmoil and upheaval in otherwise stable areas of our lives. Be aware though, that stability taken to an extreme could manifest as rigidity and inflexibility, or as passivity.

MATERIALISM AND THE SENSES

The Earth element is a physical one: it is about holding energy in a material form, about creating, building and augmenting solid things or structures. Because of this, it is also about how we experience those things with our physical bodies – in Jungian terms, it is about sensation. It is likely to feature more in the dreams of people who focus on their body and their physical

LEFT Earth is a very powerful symbol – dust to dust, earth to earth, it's where we feel we come from and where our bodies are returned after our death. How does the earth figure in your own dreams?

ABOVE Flowers and meadows indicate a settled, rooted approach to life.

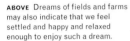

ABOVE Dreams of fields and farms may also indicate that we feel settled and happy and relaxed enough to enjoy such a dream.

surroundings, or in people who are realistic and pragmatic. We may well ask ourselves if the earth we dream of is being useful; gardening, for instance, shows that we are engaging with it in a practical and creative way, and providing the security of a food supply and a pleasant, nourishing environment.

EARTH AND THE OTHER THREE ELEMENTS

It can be revealing to see how Earth interacts with the other elements in our dreams. The heavy power of physicality found in Earth is the foil to Air's flight of the intellect. Being brought back down to earth means we must engage with reality and practical issues. Air dries out earth, turning wet mud into dust. While passionate fire burns the earth, melting the metals in it, water will turn dust back into mud, enabling seeds to germinate and grow.

By working in harmony with other elements the Earth element is creative in character – it allows the forces of the other elements to work upon it, to alter its dynamics in various ways.

ABOVE Earth is a very creative force but in our dream it may appear as barren or destroyed. We need to look closely at exactly how the Earth element appears.
BELOW Sometimes we need to be earthed, to be grounded, and our dream may be directing us to do this in our waking world.

ABOVE Working the earth in any way may indicate a need to control, to have power over our destiny and fate.
BELOW Do you feel that our planet nurtures us or that you are in control of it? Do you feel it is our mother or our servant?

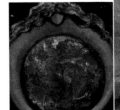

THE ELEMENTS — FIRE

THE CLASSIC SYMBOL OF PASSION AND VITALITY. FIRE IN A DREAM CAN TAKE MANY FORMS. IT CAN BE THE RAGING BLAZE OF A FOREST FIRE, THE TINY FLAME OF A CANDLE, THE HEAT OF THE MIDDAY SUN IN AFRICA, A ROARING FURNACE OR BONFIRE, AN OPEN LOG FIRE — EVEN A MATCH OR THE GLOWING END OF A LIT CIGARETTE. FIRE IS THE ELEMENT ASSOCIATED WITH OUR NERVOUS SYSTEM AND WITH MOVEMENT. IT IS OUR ENERGY, WHETHER PHYSICAL, EMOTIONAL, CREATIVE OR INTELLECTUAL. WHAT IS BEING BURNT, HOW IT IS BURNING, AND WHETHER IT IS A PRINCIPAL ASPECT OF THE DREAM OR MERELY BACKGROUND ILLUMINATION ALL AFFECT THE MEANING OF THIS SYMBOL.

SHAPES AND FORMS

Many things can produce a flame in our dream. An open log fire may represent romance and intimacy, or it could invoke feelings of comfort, of the warmth and cosiness of long, leisurely winter evenings, a warm haven protected from the cold outdoors. As a symbol of relationships, it can imply the security of a steady, warm love rather than an exciting and unpredictable new passion.

A bonfire, on the other hand, is usually livelier, more convivial and demonstrative. Bonfires are often celebratory events, and mark the purging of dead matter, of the accumulation of clutter in our lives. The ashy remains of an extinguished fire mark the end of a period of energetic activity, or of a passionate relationship.

CONTROL

Fire is a difficult element, dangerous and unpredictable. How much control you have over the fire may suggest the amount of control you have over a volatile situation or relationship in your waking life. A fire that is out of control may be pointing to a lack of constraint, or to fears about a fraught situation in your life becoming overwhelming or having devastating consequences. Tending a fire may show how we keep control over things, but it could also suggest an urge to interfere with a natural process.

Various agents may have an influence on the meaning of fire. Water quenching the flames or air being blown in to cause an inferno can change how the fire burns and the effects that it has, and so alter its symbolic value.

DESTRUCTION

Fire can often be seen as a destructive and irredeemable force; burning away or acting as a ritualized ending of some aspect or phase of your life. In its positive aspect, it purges, cleanses and purifies.

Whether what is being burned is valued or something you would like to get rid of is central to whether this is a traumatic destruction or one that gives a sense of relief and release. Your response to seeing someone burning books on an open bonfire, for instance, would say a lot about the nature of how you view learning, literature, culture, freedom of speech and so on. Many people prize books, holding them as a valuable source of information, inspiration and entertainment, and would be horrified by such destruction, but a person who cannot read may see this as a liberating dream. The destruction need not be dramatic, though – even blowing out a candle can symbolize the extinguishing of something.

ILLUMINATION

Fire also brings light and hope, dispelling darkness and revealing aspects of your life that need uncovering, bringing them to light. The steady flame of the candle gives constant

BELOW Fire is a difficult element – dangerous and unpredictable. How much control we have over it in our dream may indicate how much control we feel we have in life.
BELOW RIGHT Looking at what is burning in our fire dreams may indicate what our fears are in waking life.

illumination but little warmth, while a bonfire flares up and burns fiercely, casting great dancing shadows, then dies down again when its flames are spent. How it burns and how much attention you give it can tell you about areas of your relationships that you may need to work on.

CREATIVITY

The fire in a kiln or furnace or forge is immensely hot, and yet it is contained and controlled, and we put it to use to create things, both functional and aesthetic, that enhance our lives. We also use fire to prepare food. In these senses we can understand it as an expression of our creativity and productivity. By adding fuel to a fire we are giving our creativity greater expression.

SMOKE

A by-product of fire, smoke can be toxic or suffocating, making you ill or unable to breathe, and polluting the environment. As such it could be trying to bring to your attention the need to escape from a suffocating or unhealthy relationship before it destroys you. If there is a lot of smoke you may have difficulty seeing your way forward.

In a positive sense though, smoke signals could be giving you a message, showing you where the fire can be found or warning you away from it, and the smell of a fire or incense can bring good associations or be used deliberately to enhance your mood and bring about a feeling of stillness.

LEFT Fire can be warm and comforting as well as dangerous and unpredictable, a cosy fireside scene in your dream can be a totally unthreatening image.
MIDDLE LEFT Fire can be controlled and is also vital as a tool for our wellbeing and comfort. Dreaming of fire that is under your power and is being used in some way can indicate a level of empowerment in life.
BOTTOM LEFT Fire in the form of the small quiet fire of the candle can symbolize the tiny flame of spiritual progress.

THE ELEMENTS — AIR

AIR IS THE VERY BREATH OF LIFE: WITHOUT IT WE SUFFOCATE AND DIE. IT HAS NO FORM, SUBSTANCE, SHAPE OR TEXTURE AND YET IT SURROUNDS US, REPRESENTING FREEDOM AND SPACE AND OPENNESS, BOTH IN A LITERAL WAY AND IN THE SENSE OF FREE AND OPEN COMMUNICATION. IT FILLS OUR LUNGS, GIVING US THE CAPACITY TO BREATHE, SPEAK, SING AND SHOUT — TO EXPRESS OUR EMOTIONS. AS ONE OF THE FOUR ELEMENTS, IT RELATES TO THE MIND AND THE INTELLECT, THE GENERATION AND COMMUNICATION OF IDEAS. WE CAN'T SEE AIR OR WIND, BUT WE CAN FEEL AND SEE ITS EFFECTS — DRIFTS OF SMOKE, LEAVES STIRRING, TREES BENT IN A GALE, CLOUDS SCUDDING BY OVERHEAD, BUBBLES IN WATER.

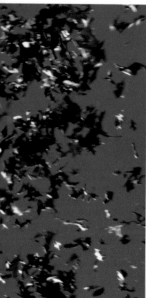

ABOVE We might not be able to see the air but we can see the creatures that use it and fly in it. If we dream of them, perhaps we are envying their soaring energy and freedom.

The current of air, whether it is a breeze or hurricane, is a vehicle for self-expression – like the air, our thoughts and emotions too are invisible but their effect is all too apparent at times. Smells are carried on the air, providing information about our environment and often generating an instant emotional response in us.

We should also look at how Air works in conjunction with the other three elements. Without air the fire cannot burn. Earth, water and air, together with the sun's

warmth and light, bring forth plants that sustain all living creatures on our planet.

THE INTELLECT
Traditionally, the element of Air symbolizes the intellect and our powers of communication. How clear the air is in our dream may show how clearly we are giving and receiving visual information and sounds. "Hot air" is a term meaning excessive verbiage, and we could see this as intellectual clutter. The mind does pick up puns, so dreams of hot air

ABOVE We can now use the air for recreational sports and doing so in our dreams could make us feel liberated and free. A dream of flying might mean we yearn for space and freedom.

ballooning, for instance, or jets of hot air, could well suggest communication overload to you – not surprising in this information age.

WIND
Air is often manifest as wind, and in our dream we should look at what effect it is having, what role

it is playing. Is it sustaining and helping us, like a cool breeze on a hot day? Do we work with it – flying, soaring or being borne aloft by it – or is it a powerful and harmful force, like the strong winds of a storm that blow us flat and bring destruction in their wake? As a symbol of intellectual and emotional direction and force, the wind in your dream is an outward manifestation of your internal life.

SUFFOCATION

The lack of air is usually more noticeable than its presence, and suffocation is an important dream theme. Suffocating, feeling short of breath, or even being in a stuffy room may show that our emotional and spiritual expression is being stifled, or that our intellect is not being

exercised sufficiently. Likewise, if we are ourselves choking someone or something, this may be pointing to unconscious guilt at choking the life out of a relationship, not allowing another person enough space and freedom, not saying what we want to say or not giving the other an opportunity to speak and be heard.

OBSCURITY

Smoke, haze or mist all obscure the view, suggesting a lack of clarity in your thinking, or being unable to see your way forward. Equally, debris flying through the air could indicate distractions, a whirl of ideas, or being caught up with other people's ideas.

HOLY BREATH

As we breathe we feel the air entering and leaving our body. The Hindus talk of *prana* – holy breath, cosmic spirit. The same is true of the Taoists of China who speak of *ch'i* – again a cosmic spirit or energy that flows like air

– and feng shui – literally "wind and water", the two cosmic forces that shape the landscape in which we live and bring us health and life. In the Bible, the Holy Spirit is said to manifest in several forms, including as a wind and a flame.

AN AIR DREAM

"I was standing on a high hill with the wind blowing all around me. Then suddenly I was being shot upwards at tremendous speed through a plastic tube on a column of air. In a flash the hill was far below me, getting smaller and smaller, more and more distant. I was aware of how important the air was. It was holding me, shooting me upwards. Without it I would fall back to the earth again and be killed.

As I realized I was reaching the top of the column I woke up and remember feeling incredibly grateful for the dream, and that I had to learn to breathe more deeply, to feel more alive."

BELOW Wind can be frightening and destructive as well as dangerous, and our dreams can reflect our fears of the untameable, wild and erratic manifestation of air.

BELOW LEFT The wind blowing through grasses is an evocative image. Are you dreaming of bending to forces that you find irresistible?
BELOW Smoke rising in misty swirls can be linked with holy breath, our spirit selves.

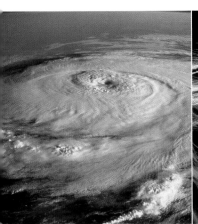

THE ELEMENTS — WATER

WATER HAS LONG BEEN THOUGHT OF AS THE SYMBOLIC VEHICLE OF EXPRESSION FOR OUR EMOTIONS, FEELINGS AND SENSITIVITY. IT IS, IN FACT, A PERFECT SYMBOL FOR THESE AS THE FORMS IT TAKES ARE SO VARIED. WATER IS THE SAME SUBSTANCE WHETHER IT IS A STILL POOL, A RAGING TORRENT, TOWERING WAVES ON THE BEACH, OR A DRIPPING TAP AT HOME. WITH THE SAME WIDE SPECTRUM, EMOTIONS CAN RANGE FROM SORROW, ANGER, JEALOUSY AND BEREAVEMENT, TO JOY, EXCITEMENT AND LOVE. ANY KIND OF WATER IMAGE IN A DREAM HOLDS THE POTENTIAL TO SYMBOLIZE OUR EMOTIONS AND OUR EMOTIONAL NEEDS, DESIRES AND CAPABILITIES.

Water represents the full range of different emotions, and it is immensely difficult to generalize when analysing the symbolism of water images. A scene that for some may be scary – say, a raging sea on a stormy night – might for someone else be exciting and exhilarating. Similarly, while for some people it is enough to feel emotionally comfortable and stable, others seek passion and new challenges.

BODIES OF WATER

Vast and deep, the sea is a particularly useful symbol for the enormity of our unplumbed, unconscious emotional depths. In some respects it is always changing, with the weather and with the ebb and flow of the tides and the constant movement of the great ocean currents – and yet it has its own rhythm and predictable aspects.

Rivers represent our emotional journey and can show us whether we let our emotions flow easily. Whether the river in your dream is strong and fast-flowing, a babbling brook or a brackish backwater could well be saying something about the strength of your emotions, and whether you are allowing them to be expressed fully and in a healthy way. Do you go with the flow, or swim against the current? Crossing a river may indicate that your emotions present some kind of obstacle, so having a means of doing so – a bridge, a raft, a ford – could be showing that there is a way forward. The stillness of a pool or pond can show the peace and tranquillity of a steady, reflective nature. A lagoon may

provide a haven of stillness from the open sea without breaking contact with your emotional nature, and the protective, enclosing nature of the lagoon suggests a feminine aspect.

QUALITY AND QUANTITY

Our lives depend on water, but it must be pure to sustain and clean us. Dreaming of muddied, stagnant or polluted water may indicate that our emotions are confused or unhealthy, even harmful, and we may need to pay special attention to looking after ourselves, giving ourselves enough space to know what we are really feeling, and not engage in self-negativity.

A deluge may be completely overwhelming, and can wipe out everything in its path, but water

BELOW Water is very evocative. It has a great power to move us, causes us to dream, and makes us reflective and contemplative. Eddying brooks and small streams are soothing, and to dream of any of these is a sign that we are relaxed and comfortable.
BELOW RIGHT The more we try to hold on to water – to our emotions and tears – the more it escapes from us; it is elusive and fluid.

also evaporates, and the lack of it can equally be traumatic. Being profoundly thirsty or in a dry, barren place can indicate that our emotional side is neglected and is in need of reviving.

RELATIONSHIP TO WATER

Where are you in relation to the water in your dream, and how do you respond to it? You may be beside a body of water trying to skirt it, crossing it in a boat, or dithering about whether to get in, or perhaps you can't wait to take a running dive and feel the rush of bubbles past your skin. If you find yourself already in the water, are you floating, sinking or swimming? You may see water as a place to have fun, a place where you can be mesmerised by the easy, rhythmical movement of your body, or a terrifying place where you feel out of your depth or fear you will drown or be eaten alive.

BELOW Water can be exhilarating; if you dream of pounding waves, perhaps you are wishing for more excitement in your life?

A WATER DREAM

"I was trying desperately to turn off a tap but the water just kept gushing out. I put my hands over the tap but the water seeped out between my fingers. I woke up crying because I recently got divorced and I miss my husband so much. The water in my dreams represented my unstoppable tears."

We use water in a very practical way. Drinking it and cooking with it are positive, embracing tasks that nourish us, while washing ourselves and our possessions in it may indicate a need to rid ourselves of negativity and emotional debris. Dissolving things in water brings about complete transformation.

BIRTH, SEX AND LOVE

We are essentially made of water, and for the first nine months of our existence, the most sheltered, protected time of our lives, we live in fluid. We may be remembering or making sense of this experience when we dream of enclosed water or of being submerged. We talk of the waters breaking just before birth, when we are ready to make our traumatic journey into the world.

Fountains, hosepipes, geysers and so on can act as symbols of sexuality – in an obvious way they represent ejaculation, but in a more general sense they can be seen as metaphors for sexual energy and release. A dream of swimming with a lover, for example, may be sensuous in a more tranquil way, and speak of the harmony of love as you move together in a slow, easy rhythm, at one in a buoyant medium.

TEARS

Dissolving in tears as salty as the sea, we express our sadness, grief, anger, tiredness, fear and insecurity, and in so doing, find emotional release. Many people have taught themselves not to cry, so dreaming of doing so may be particularly powerful if it breaks a personal taboo. If someone else is crying in your dreams consider whether this is an aspect of yourself that is trying to be expressed.

ABOVE Water dreams might contain water that has been harnessed as a resource, in the form of running taps or over-flowing bathtubs – or perhaps a lack of water, as in dry wells. All could have links with your waking life.

The Plant Kingdom

ABOVE Trees have always had the power to move us, fill us with wonder and awe.
ABOVE RIGHT Trees symbolize the power of nature and growth.

WITH ROOTS THAT SPREAD THROUGH THE DARK, FERTILE EARTH, AND LEAVES AND BRANCHES REACHING TO THE SKY FOR LIGHT AND WARMTH, PLANTS ARE PERFECT SYMBOLS OF THE RICH WORKINGS OF THE HUMAN MIND. LIKE THE UNCONSCIOUS, A PLANT'S ROOTS ARE DARK AND HIDDEN FROM VIEW, YET CAN STILL BE NURTURED WITH WATER AND FOOD, AND CAN PRODUCE A HEALTHY PLANT ABOVE GROUND. BRANCHES, LEAVES AND FLOWERS ARE THE VISIBLE MANIFESTATIONS OF OUR MINDS, AND TELL US ABOUT OUR MENTAL AND EMOTIONAL HEALTH.

TREES

Rooted deep in our unconscious and in the emotional landscape of our dreams, trees are often regarded as symbols of the past – of steady growth, age, experience, time and continuity.

Using this concept, we can see a wood as our family history and forests as the history of our society, culture, or ethnic group. Roots provide wisdom from the collective experience, and how you view trees may indicate how you feel about your own "roots".

Some tree species hold particular symbolic value, and around the world have long been valued as sacred or politically

LEFT The tree as a symbol of life, with its head in the sky and its roots buried in the earth, is deeply buried in our consciousness and permeates most cultures on earth with its resonance.

powerful icons. The oak, for instance, is seen as a symbol of longevity, strength, reliability and resilience. Down the ages the willow has had connotations of death or enchantment, and the evergreen holly with its scarlet berries has brought hope and cheer in the dark of winter. In ancient Britain certain trees were chosen as totems or symbols of tribal power – if one tribe ousted another, they uprooted a tree of the vanquished tribe and thrust it upside-down into the ground as a show of dominance. Such symbols may have lost relevance, but they are still embedded in our cultural consciousness and reappear in our dreams.

One of the key visual and conceptual symbols of the Jewish Kabbalah, used to investigate the mysteries of our spiritual life and

our relationship with God, is the complex diagram of the Tree of Life. A similar idea is used in the mythology of Native American Indian people, where the tree of life is what links heaven to earth. Shamans use this imagery in their journeys between worlds, and in their interpretation of dreams.

FLOWERS AND VINES

Associated with pleasure, beauty and relaxation, flowers also denote giving and receiving. Cultivated garden flowers imply order and the application of discipline over creativity, while wild flowers are much more intuitive and express our artistic leanings. Dead flowers may indicate a need to look at underlying unhappiness. Climbing plants may show a need to escape from a situation, or a feeling of entanglement. Some, such as honeysuckle, clematis and vines, are said to represent our ambitions.

FRUIT AND VEGETABLES

Ripe, juicy, seed-laden fruit is associated with fertility and readiness. Apples have associations of seductiveness because of the biblical temptation in the Garden of Eden, but equally they may symbolize the autumn, or the fruitfulness of our maturing unconscious. Over-ripe fruit may signify a loss of fertility, or a wasted opportunity.

Dreaming of vegetables shows a concern with nourishment, fullness and abundance – or the lack of those qualities if they are dried out or of poor quality. The shape of some vegetables may

suggest sexuality, although the context of your dream will tell you whether this is true for you.

GARDENING

Dreams about gardening may show you how you feel about work and career issues. Work and gardening alike may seem fulfilling or drudgery. We respond to gardens emotionally and the colour they bring into our lives, but weeds can choke out and destroy the life of our garden and distract us from its beauty. They may show that there are problems in our working life that need to be eliminated.

GARDEN DREAMS

If you have a gardening dream it is worth looking at what you are doing and how you are doing it, to give you clues to how you approach the practical aspects of your life.

Digging Preparing the groundwork

Weeding and pest control Removing elements, allowing desirable elements to grow unhindered

Planting Nurturing, creating opportunities

Harvesting Reaping the benefits

Grass cutting Vital maintainance work

CREATURES OF THE LAND

ANIMALS SHOW US OUR MORE INNOCENT, INSTINCTIVE AND INTUITIVE SELVES. THEY SHOW US HOW WE MIGHT BE IF THE RESTRAINTS AND TABOOS WE LEARN THROUGHOUT OUR LIVES WERE REMOVED, AND THE VENEER OF CIVILIZATION, MATURITY AND SOPHISTICATION STRIPPED AWAY. OUR PLAYFULNESS AND CURIOSITY, AGGRESSION AND SEXUALITY MAY ALL BE EXPRESSED IN OUR DREAMS THROUGH IMAGES OF ANIMALS. OF COURSE WHAT EACH ANIMAL SYMBOLIZES WILL VARY FROM CULTURE TO CULTURE. IT IS EASY FOR URBAN WESTERNERS TO SAY A LION REPRESENTS STRENGTH, WHEN TO AN AFRICAN LIVING IN THE BUSH IT MIGHT JUST SYMBOLIZE DANGER AND FEAR.

CHARACTERISTICS

If there are strong cultural associations or stereotypes around an animal's character, such as the stealth of a tiger or the cunning of the fox, you may bring the animal into your dream to stand in for such meanings, but if it is a less distinguished creature or one you don't recognize, it could be its wildness, or some characteristic or behaviour it is exhibiting in your dream, that is important. Such characteristics show you something about yourself, characteristics that you should aspire to, or avoid, or eliminate. Whether the animal is behaving normally or doing something odd

BELOW What are the animals in your dream doing? Their behaviour is as important as what kind of beast they are.

or bizarre, may say how comfortable you are with what the animal represents, or that its natural qualities are present but are being subverted.

ASSOCIATIONS

When you dream of an animal, see what associations it has for you, as well as if there are any stereotypes around that animal. Baby animals often have different associations from those of the adult, but also bear the characteristics of the adult. Use the list provided to spark off your own ideas.

WILD ANIMALS

Freud held that dreams of wild animals represent our unbridled passions – lust, greed, jealousy and the like. It is possible that the animal in your dream represents your sexual fears (a bull or a stallion the loss of prowess, a crow unfaithfulness) but such a prescriptive interpretation fails to take into account either the characteristics of the animal or the personal response you have to it. It may make more sense to extend Freud's interpretation of wild animals to mean our unbridled nature – wild animals in their natural habitat are unconstrained, so like other elements of nature, they show us some aspect of our

true selves. In a zoo or cage, farm or game reserve, the animal is to a greater or lesser extent enclosed – for display, consumption or its own protection – and its natural impulses may be curbed. If the animal in your dream has been contained like this, see whether it is content or fretting, aggressive or apathetic, to understand your own relationship with being constrained. A wild animal being hunted may suggest a threat to your natural self, while an animal stalking or hunting may have connotations of strategy, self-sufficiency or single-mindedness.

PETS

The animals in our dreams are often domestic rather than wild animals, and our familiarity with our pets is likely to give us a greater feel for their range of characteristics. If the animal is our own pet, we may relate to it more like a family member than an animal, as we know its behaviours and moods intimately and have a strong emotional bond. Your pet's playful, devoted, aloof or mysterious nature may be what you are trying to work with in your dream.

FARMING

Farm animals have qualities of both wildness and domesticity, but the relevant characteristics of

these creatures may be that they are bred and reared for slaughter; they live in vast herds or flocks or stacked up in sheds, and they are contained in a limited and sometimes very unnatural environment. This processing of animals may seem acceptable to you, or you may regard it with ambivalence or abhorrence; your attitude will influence the meaning of the dream.

SPIDERS AND INSECTS

Tiny and alien in appearance, spiders and insects have quite a different set of meanings which often have little to do with their ability to harm us by stinging or biting us or spreading disease. Many people fear or dislike them at the best of times, often apparently irrationally, and in our dreams they can be monstrous and terrifying.

ANIMAL MEANINGS

Lion Raw strength, power, danger, pride, kingship

Dog Devotion, faithfulness

Cat Independence, mystery, love of comfort, hunting

Horse Intelligence, athleticism, strength, nobility

Butterfly Beauty, capriciousness, transformation

Cow Calm, slowness, maternity

Monkey Playfulness, mischief

Mule Stubbornness, bearing of loads

Rabbit Prolific breeding

Snake Deceitfulness, venomousness

Pig Greed, dirtiness

RIGHT Most animal symbolism is fairly easy to interpret – sweet cuddly lambs are exactly that.
MIDDLE RIGHT Some animal symbolism is more complex, and carries cultural resonances – is this lion a symbol of power? Strength? Danger? Does it attract or repel you?
BOTTOM RIGHT To someone who lives where deer roam free, a dream of stags locking their antlers may denote passion and fertility, whereas to people who are divorced from the reality it might symbolize aggression and violence.

Spiders weave invisible webs to entrap their unsuspecting prey, so we may use both the spider or the web in our dreams to symbolize being trapped or betrayed in some way. Insects such as bees and ants live in colonies, and so teamwork is vital to their very survival. On its own a tiny insect may seem like nothing much, but collectively they can move large objects, build complex structures and strip a forest bare, providing powerful images for the value of co-operation and the lack of individuation. Insects also seem constantly active, so your dream may suggest a need to slow down, or to be more efficient.

ANIMALS AS FAMILIARS OR MESSENGERS

In some cultures animals are believed to come to people in their dreams as spirit messengers, and the shaman will identify a person's "familiar" – the animal most likely to communicate with them. It could be interesting to see if there is one particular animal that keeps cropping up in your dreams, and whether it communicates any message.

CREATURES OF SKY AND OCEAN

ABOVE Brightly coloured birds are used in our dreams to represent pride and conceit, power and strength.
ABOVE RIGHT The eagle is king of the birds and can therefore represent military might.
ABOVE FAR RIGHT Flocks of birds may represent how we see our own individuality – lost in such vast numbers and part of a crowd, or intact no matter what?

FLYING HIGH IN THE SKY OR SWIMMING DEEP IN THE VAST, COLD WATERS OF THE OCEAN, BIRDS AND FISH ARE CREATURES THAT ARE IN THEIR ELEMENT IN PLACES WE CANNOT EASILY GO. THEIR PHYSICAL CHARACTERISTICS – WINGS AND FINS, FEATHERS AND SCALES, BEAKS AND GILLS – TOGETHER WITH THE LAYING OF EGGS AND THE ABILITY OF BOTH BIRDS AND FISH TO MOVE APPARENTLY EFFORTLESSLY, MAY ALSO HOLD THE KEY TO THEIR APPEARANCE IN OUR DREAMS.

BIRD BEHAVIOURS

The most obvious aspect of bird behaviour, and the one that may most frequently find its way into our dreams, is flight. For us earthbound humans, the ability to fly without the assistance of any craft is as appealing as it is impossible. It represents freedom and hope – the ability to flex our muscles and feel the rush of air as we soar to great heights or cover vast distances on the wing. A "flight of ideas" alludes to a rush of intellectual creativity; on the other hand we speak of "flapping" to mean being in a panic, a feeling of loss of control. Either way, the "birds' eye view" gives us a perspective not normally available to us in which we can see the whole picture.

Back on the ground, birds are perhaps less idealized creatures – their constant pecking and scratching around in the dirt suggest fussing with details, or looking for small rewards, while a "henpecked" husband suffers the constant verbal irritation and bullying of his partner.

The fact that many phrases pertaining to birds and their behaviours have found their way into our language shows how strongly we feel about them, and means that we may incorporate them into our dreams as metaphors for our thoughts, ideas, feelings and behaviour.

NESTS AND EGGS

Birds' nests are often used to symbolize the cosiness and security of a home, and in the phrase "the nesting instinct" we suggest both the idea of settling down and preparing for a family. Nests represent a nurturing environment where the young can be kept safe until maturity, and fend for themselves. A nest may also have the less alluring meaning of a small, messy space. Birds' eggs hint at creation and conception, or more figuratively, the germ of an idea.

BIRDS OF A FEATHER

Particular species of bird have come to have specific meanings, usually by virtue of their character or appearance, or in a few cases because they have found their way into our cultural vocabulary.

Dove Peace, the Holy Spirit

Crow Death

Ostrich Being in denial, "burying your head in the sand" so as not to see important truths

Eagle King of the birds, military victory; symbol of American nationhood

Dodo Extinction

Robin Christmas

Blackbird and nightingale Joyful song

Parrot Speech, imitation

Owl Wisdom

Peacock Brilliance, pride, showing off

All birds of prey Ruthlessness, clearsightedness

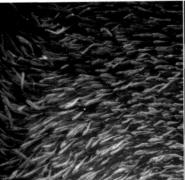

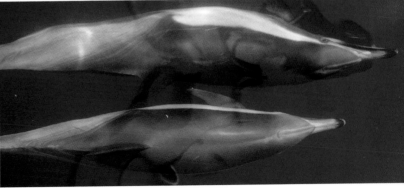

FISH

Cold and sleek and silent, fish are creatures of the water and hence are likely to be connected to our emotional states. In their silent world they have an air of mystery about them, and the deeper they reside in the sea, the more frightening and unknowable they often seem. In the murky depths we cannot see far, and we may fear the unknown monsters there as we sometimes fear the most deeply buried parts of our unconscious.

In a fish bowl, however, fish may take on a whole new meaning. Here they are on display; they have nowhere to go and nowhere to hide, and their natural characteristics are changed. In a bowl or aquarium, a fish may signify a feeling of being exposed, and possibly the boredom of a limited and monotonous environment.

The fish is a motif that appears frequently in the Christian tradition, and was used as a secret symbol of association by the early Christians; to this day it may be a sign of faith for some.

CAPTIVITY

Birds in cages and fish in aquariums or bowls are possessed, displayed, and their freedom and natural expression curtailed. Their company is decided by the person who keeps them, and they may be unable to mate. Birds may have their wings clipped, and this too is a sign of restriction and immobility.

Killing a bird may indicate that some lofty ideal is being shot down, or a freedom lost, while hooking a fish could be a sign that some deep-seated emotion has been drawn to the surface.

GROUPS AND NUMBERS

Encountering birds or fish on their own in a dream may suggest the aspirations of the individual, but often we will find birds in flocks and fish in teeming schools, where all sense of individuality is erased in favour of safety and sociability. Issues of co-operation may predominate.

A farm scene may allow for more individuality, but the existence of a pecking order may be marked. Dreaming of pairs of birds could allude to finding a mate and settling down.

ABOVE Dolphins have an extra level of meaning for many cultures. Their high intelligence and charm makes us feel they have an affinity with humans.
ABOVE LEFT What sort of fish appear in our dreams may represent how we feel emotionally about our deepest spiritual life.

BELOW Fish are creatures of the deep, the hidden and the secret, so their symbolism can be quite easy to read. A shoal of fish might indicate how you feel about your position in a social group.

THE CYCLE OF LIFE

No matter who or what we are, we all go through the same cycle of life, from birth through childhood, youth, maturity and old age to death. And no matter how we approach these different stages – whether we enjoy and welcome them or resent and try to avoid them – they are all inevitable, unless we die prematurely. How they appear in our dreams will reflect how enjoyable or difficult we find the whole experience, and dreams about the rites of passage associated with the different stages in the life cycle affect all of us and show how we are in ourselves, whether we feel secure and at ease with where we are in life, or resentful and in denial.

RIGHT Dreams that reflect the life cycle of birth and death are often the way we prepare mentally and emotionally for approaching rites of passage.

BIRTH DREAMS

BIRTH IS A HIGHLY SYMBOLIC THEME WHEN IT OCCURS IN OUR DREAMS, AND IT IS ONE WHOSE MEANING IS USUALLY QUITE EASILY INTERPRETED – IT IS ABOUT ORIGINS, NEW BEGINNINGS, LABOURING, THE STRUGGLE FOR INDIVIDUATION AND DEVELOPMENT. OUR OWN BIRTH IS PROBABLY THE MOST MOMENTOUS EVENT OF OUR LIVES, YET VIRTUALLY NO-ONE IS ABLE TO REMEMBER ANYTHING OF IT. IT IS POSSIBLE THOUGH, THAT WE DO RETAIN SOME OF THE SENSE OF IT, THAT THE EXPERIENCE OF IT STAYS WITH US SUBCONSCIOUSLY OUR WHOLE LIFE. WHAT WE ARE TOLD ABOUT IT BY OUR PARENTS OR BY OTHERS WHO WERE PRESENT MAY ALSO AFFECT US DEEPLY.

BEING BORN

In dreams of your own birth it may be that your unconscious is trying to draw your attention to some momentous event that it feels is in some way as traumatic as your birth. Often the dream will give you the clues you need to decipher what this event is – if it is not already immediately obvious. The context of the birth in your dream, together with the feelings you experience around it, will probably reflect how your unconscious feels about the event in your life – apprehensive, excited, hesitant, or reluctant, perhaps – and your unconscious is trying to encourage you to look at why these feelings are

coming up. Birth involves a momentous transition, and we may use it in our dreams to represent the shock of the new, the move into an uncertain and unsafe new world, but one that is full of potential.

As well as giving us the wherewithal to look at important events in the present, dreams about our own birth may also point to feelings or problems buried deep in our psyche. If we were abandoned at birth, or if for some reason we believe that our birth was a disappointment to our parents, we may carry this sense of being abandoned or of not being good enough with us all our lives.

OUR CHILDREN'S BIRTH

Men and women alike may feel apprehensive about their own child being born; this is a major event that brings immense change and responsibility to a person's life, and to dream of it is natural. But women in particular are visited by dreams of birth when they are expecting a child. Such dreams are a way of coming to terms with the new being that is developing inside a woman's own body, and preparing for the birth, as well as for the huge lifestyle changes that happen after the baby arrives. Fears that the unborn child will be somehow less than perfect are quite common, and this fear

BIRTH DREAM

"When I was about six months pregnant I dreamed of a space ship, all silver and spinning, with lots of portholes. It didn't land, but a ladder was lowered and a creature appeared, with spindly arms and legs and big eyes, a bit like the alien at the end of the film 'Close Encounters of the Third Kind'. The alien spoke to me and then somehow entered my belly. I think this dream was my way of accepting that something unknown was growing inside of me, and that I was approaching a new situation I had never been faced with before."

often manifests in dreams about giving birth to a monster or a changeling. Dreams of giving birth may also simply be a wish fulfilment if you want a child.

To dream of our child's birth long after the event may show we are worrying about them for some reason – perhaps they are going through transition, or we are worried about their progress.

BIRTH SYMBOLISM

Dreaming of birth or babies may have nothing to do with real life pregnancy or having babies, but can symbolize a variety of things, such as ideas, projects and plans for the future. A normal birth in a dream may symbolize new beginnings. But if the birth is premature or unnatural we should look at why events are not unfolding in the natural way. Perhaps there is some obstruction and we are too impatient for nature to take its course, forcing it to make its journey into the world prematurely. If this is the case, perhaps you are making something happen without adequate preparation, or putting pressure on someone to start something they are not ready for.

If the creature that is born is unnatural or deformed, this may well be related to stumbling blocks or problems in plans you have made; the nature of its deformity or the qualities that make it unusual are probably significant, so remember as much detail as you can. If you dream of a stillbirth you might be thinking about a project that won't come to fruition, while an abortion may be the plan's termination.

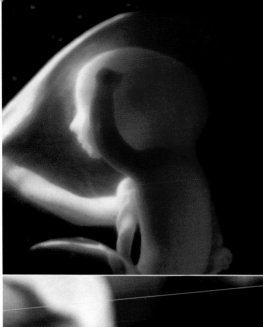

LEFT Dreaming of a baby in the womb could be reflecting your present circumstances, but might have nothing to do with babies at all. Perhaps it reflects ambitious plans and projects in your waking life that you feel need nurturing and bringing to life.

MIDDLE LEFT It is only natural to have lots of birthing dreams while pregnant – we all worry about a successful and happy delivery.

BOTTOM LEFT Dreaming of babies can mean that you are dreaming of the growth and maturing of something that is dear to your heart.

CHILDHOOD DREAMS

AS WE GROW UP WE ARE INFLUENCED BY MANY THINGS. THE PEOPLE IN OUR LIVES – ESPECIALLY OUR PARENTS AND SIBLINGS – AS WELL AS THE ENVIRONMENT WE GROW UP IN AND THE COUNTLESS EXPERIENCES WE HAVE DURING OUR CHILDHOOD YEARS, ARE ALL FORMATIVE INFLUENCES, GIVING SHAPE TO OUR PERSONALITY AND THE WAY WE APPROACH THE WORLD. HOW WE REMEMBER OUR CHILDHOOD WILL INFLUENCE HOW WE SEE· THIS STAGE OF LIFE IN OUR DREAMS. WHEN WE DREAM OF CHILDREN WE MIGHT BE DREAMING OF OUR OWN CHILDHOOD, BUT WE MIGHT ALSO BE DREAMING OF THE CHILD WE STILL ARE. DREAMS OF CHILDREN MIGHT ALSO SYMBOLIZE IDEAS AND PLANS WE HAVE THAT HAVE YET TO MATURE.

The terrifying moments of our childhood, the pain and trauma that we experience as we grow up get imprinted on our psyche and can scar us for the rest of our lives, surfacing in our dreams even when we are adults, and have "forgotten" the events. Alternatively it could be the freedom of childhood that we are yearning for in our dreams, a time when we could play to our heart's content, a time without the responsibilities and problems we face as adults. Childishness – silly, petty behaviour – may also be expressed in our dreams.

TOYS AND GAMES

Voices from our early years, familiar old toys and memories of games we used to play may all figure in our dreams as symbols of our childhood. This is a time to discover, and much of our learning is done through play, not only with toys and games but also by entering the world of make-believe through dressing-up and role play. These objects and activities are powerfully symbolic and thus easy for your unconscious to choose as representations of childhood – of fun and naivety, of curiosity, growth and development.

Particular toys or scenes may have a special meaning for you, for instance if you dream that

BELOW Dreaming that we are a child again may tell us a lot about how we feel about being grown ups,. Even if the dream is playful it may suggest feelings of unease or feeling ill equipped.

your favourite toy, from which you were inseparable as a child, is lost or taken away from you, it could be that your unconscious is using this as an analogy for possession or attachment, separation or grieving, or for a loss of security.

Games involving fantasy and role play could be a hint that we need to be more creative, see life from a different perspective, or try to change how we handle problems. Many children's games rely heavily on rules, and how the game is played can be as important as what is being played – making or breaking the rules, changing them as you go along, cheating or following them rigidly may say something about your relationship to laws and social expectations.

DREAMING OF CHILDREN

When we dream of a child or childishness we might be dreaming of the emotions we link to childhood. Young children are often more expressive than adults, and feel less constrained by what others think when they want to cry or laugh or scream. They have the time and the freedom to play actively and to explore the things they enjoy or find interesting, and may also become completely immersed in the worlds they read about. On the other hand, children may be ignored when they speak, or punished for being noisy or angry, for making a mess or not sitting still.

When we dream of children we might be recalling something in our waking life that makes us feel in a way that we associate with the state of childhood, or we may be echoing something in our everyday life that has given us the status of a child in some way.

ADULTS AS CHILDREN

If we dream about someone else as a child we might be trying to find out what makes them tick, or perhaps to get to the root of why they are the way they are. Suppose you dream of your boss as a child. You may be trying to understand what motivates them, or be attempting to reduce them to someone smaller and less powerful in order to make them less intimidating. You may equally turn an adult into a child in your dream because you want to attempt to exert some kind of control over them, or perhaps because you want to relate to them in a more direct and childlike way.

ABOVE If you dream of a teddy bear does it make you feel nostalgic for your lost childhood?
ABOVE LEFT Children are precious and usually very endearing and it is only natural to dream of such a wonderful gift.
ABOVE FAR LEFT To dream of toys can mean many things and you need to think carefully about the details of your dream, did the toy belong to you? was it broken, desirable, boring, symbolic?

A CHILDHOOD DREAM

"I was upstairs in a small room filled with sunlight, which streamed in through an open window. It was late afternoon towards the end of summer, and I was sitting on the floor, very still, very quiet. I'd been told that I had to stay here, and I had the feeling that something terrible would happen if I didn't.

I didn't understand the dream until I mentioned it to my sister. She told me that our mother would send me to my room when her parents came to visit, as they didn't know she had an illegitimate child and she was afraid they would disinherit her if they found out. She would tell me to go upstairs and stay there, and pretend that I didn't exist. When I heard this I cried and cried. Even though I hadn't remembered my mother doing this it must have made a huge impression on me, as all my life I've felt like I had to be bigger and better than anyone else – and make sure everyone knows I'm there! I like to think that the sunshine and the open window show my unstoppable outgoing nature, which existed even when I had to pretend I did not."

DREAMS OF YOUTH

ABOVE Dreaming of puberty might mean that we are working through crucial life changes in our dreams.

ABOVE RIGHT Adolescent and teenage years can represent rebellion and flux, and if we dream of this stage it may be that in our waking lives we are trying to find the right course of action to take.

YOUTH IS A TIME WHEN WE THROW OFF BOTH THE CONSTRAINTS AND THE INNOCENCE OF CHILDHOOD, TESTING AUTHORITY FIGURES AND TRYING TO FIND OUR OWN WAY IN LIFE. IN OUR TEENAGE YEARS WE EXPERIENCE THE PHYSICAL CHANGES OF PUBERTY, DISCOVER OUR SEXUALITY, HANG OUT IN GANGS, SUFFER FROM INTENSE PEER PRESSURE, AND DISCOVER OUR POWER AS YOUNG ADULTS. BUT OUR OWN EXPERIENCE AS TEENAGERS — GOOD AND BAD — WILL BE REFLECTED IN OUR DREAMS AS MUCH AS THE STEREOTYPES OF THIS LIFE STAGE, SO DREAMS OF YOUTH WILL MEAN VERY DIFFERENT THINGS TO DIFFERENT PEOPLE.

GROWING PAINS

Many people find adolescence to be a tumultuous and painful period, and some of us carry the scars for the rest of our lives. It is a time of transition from childhood to adulthood, and indeed the key take-home message of dreams about adolescence may well be metamorphosis. At this age we are not yet used to the changes in our bodies, and also often feel awkward and embarrassed at the errors we make in our quest to seem grown-up. To make things worse, we may be teased for the very mistakes we make and the changes we are going through, and withdraw as a result. Dreaming of youth later in life may mean that we are going through changes about which we feel uncertain or unconfident. We may be anticipating criticism or ridicule, or even fear that we will not be taken seriously by society. Even if your dream doesn't actually give you answers or guidance, it should be a useful way of making you aware of how you feel about the changes and what your fears are.

RIGHT The desire to be part of the "in-crowd" is probably at its most intense during youth, so if you dream about this it might reflect a feeling you have of being on the edge of things, of being not quite accepted.

PEER GROUP

At the same time as we begin to rebel against the adult world and leave our childhood ways behind, we turn instead to our peers, with whom we can identify more strongly, for ideas, support and encouragement as much as

friendship. Because the peer group becomes so important, many teenagers feel the need to conform – to adopt current fashions, have the latest gear, and even to use the right words, in order to be acceptable. In our youth we are testing out new roles, so there may be a lot of faking involved in our behaviour before we become settled in who we are. For this reason, dreams of adolescence may also be about inauthenticity, about following trends or trying to find a niche within an accepted set.

EXTREMES AND IDEALS

Because we have so many new experiences as teenagers and young adults, this period of our lives may seem to be one of extremes, especially in our feelings and behaviours. We may be more passionately in love at this time than at any other later time in our lives, or be filled with despair when things don't go our way. It is a time when we are most likely to feel prepared to step into the unknown, travel the world on a shoestring or take up

dangerous sports. This is when we are at our physical peak, and feel able to do all these things because we have a sense of being invincible, immortal. It is also a time of pushing the boundaries – partying all night long, getting very drunk or experimenting with drugs – and exploring social or political ideals. We may still do all these things or have the same feelings later in life, but as a stereotype, we are more likely to associate them with being young, and youth may be the theme of our dream to represent our desire to try new things, to step back from the mundane practicalities of life and remind ourselves of our own ideals.

LOOKING AHEAD

In our youthful explorations of the big wide world, we are in the process of finding where we belong in society and what we want to do with our lives. We leave school and have to make choices about work or further education, and begin to assert our own personal style and beliefs. While dreams about

youth may be about immaturity in yourself or others, they could also be about discovering and asserting yourself.

NOSTALGIA

Looking back at our youth, we may feel nostalgic, remembering the freedom, the fun, the passion and excitement, and forgetting the more painful moments. We may even be reconstructing a youth that we never really had, perhaps one that seems more fun and interesting than our own. If we are afraid of growing old, we may be rejecting the stereotypes of middle or old age and clinging to youthfulness, rather than embracing the positive aspects our current stage of life can offer.

ABOVE If you dream of a lack of financial freedom in youth perhaps you are admitting to a feeling that this has never really gone away, and that this is materially a real problem for you.

ABOVE LEFT The excitement and intensity of your first romance can never be matched. If you dream of young love perhaps it reflects a dissatisfaction with your love life.

ABOVE FAR LEFT Dreaming of the wilder side of youth culture might mean that you are yearning for a more exciting element in your life, whatever your age.

DREAM OF YOUTH

"In my dream I had dyed my hair red and wore a biker's jacket, and I was behaving like a teenager again. Not that I dyed my hair when I was a teenager, but in my dream it made me feel young again. Since I passed forty I've got it into my head that I must be wild, rebellious and wacky to recapture my youth and ward off middle age and all the implications of sedateness that that time of life has. I think I'm also a little jealous of my own teenage children and the fun they seem to have."

THE MIDDLE YEARS

THE PREOCCUPATIONS OF OUR MIDDLE YEARS TEND TO BE MORE PRAGMATIC THAN THOSE OF OUR ADOLESCENCE — WORK, PARTNERS, CHILDREN AND PROPERTY ARE LIKELY TO DOMINATE OUR THOUGHTS. IT IS ALSO A TIME WHEN WE COME INTO OUR OWN AS ADULTS — BECOMING ESTABLISHED IN VARIOUS WAYS, TAKING ON RESPONSIBILITIES AND MAKING DECISIONS AND JUDGEMENTS BASED ON EXPERIENCE RATHER THAN CONJECTURE. AT THE SAME TIME, WE MAY REGRET THE LOSS OF YOUTHFUL FREEDOM AND STRENGTH OR FEAR THE APPROACH OF OLD AGE. WHATEVER AGE WE ARE THERE WILL BE HAPPIER TIMES, WORSE TIMES, AND WE WILL LOOK BACK WITH REGRET OR FONDNESS. IN OUR DREAMS THIS MAY BE INTENSIFIED.

THE MATERIAL WORLD

As adults we often define ourselves by the job we have or the work we do, and others also judge us and position us in the social hierarchy accordingly. Our self-esteem may be bolstered or dented by the status of our job, or by not having any work. Changing careers can be a difficult time as we adjust our self-image, perhaps getting used to being on the bottom rung of a different career ladder.

Work also brings money, and with it the many benefits and encumbrances of the material

BELOW All of our rites of passage will become food for our dreams but probably none will be more intense than our first real love, as we move in together, set up home and start to plan a family.

world. In particular, buying our first property is a material milestone, with the implications of commitment to staying put and to being able to finance the purchase for years to come. Living in our own home also gives us the opportunity to express our personal style in the type of home we buy and in how we furnish it.

Our relationship with material things may be an aesthetic statement, and it may be about making life easier or more enjoyable, but it is often also about status and power.

Dreaming of acquiring something may be wish fulfilment around a particular object, or it could be that you want a change of lifestyle which that object represents. If it is higher social standing you are after, this could be related to your sense of self-worth rather than external issues. We also become attached to things and worry about losing them, or about being tied down by our possessions, and this may manifest itself in our dreams.

SETTLING DOWN

As well as becoming materially established and leaving youth behind, we may start actively looking for a partner, someone with whom we might settle down and perhaps start a family. But while some people feel their lives will be meaningless or unbearably insecure without these things, the idea of "settling down" may fill others with horror and they may prefer the kind of freedom that is only possible without such ties. Such preferences will influence how you read dreams in which these aspects of adulthood are significant. Dreams of 'settling down' may be a form of wish fulfilment, or a way of trying out a different lifestyle. In a less literal sense though, they could indicate a sense of being settled

in yourself and knowing what you want – even if your lifestyle doesn't seem to reflect this – or a desire for stability.

MIDDLE AGE

The stereotype of middle age that we may use symbolically in our dreams is likely to be one of settled routine and staidness. However, it can also be a time of great change and readjustment as roles alter, and these aspects may figure in a person's dreams at this time. After years of striving to establish ourselves, we may feel at a loss as to how to proceed once this is achieved. The midlife crisis that many people go through is prompted by the vision of life developing into routine. Dreams can hint at other possibilities or make us aware of exactly what is bothering us about our circumstances.

EXPERIENCE

Whatever path your life takes, the experience you gain on the way can give you maturity and insight, and it may be this aspect of adulthood that is being reflected in your dreams rather than specific rites of passage.

Although our physical form and strength gradually declines over the years, we may feel increasingly confident in ourselves and in what we do. We may come to have authority and power over others and take on increasing responsibilities. Our dreams can be a useful vehicle for coming to terms with this, and with the relationship they put us in towards others, and how we learn to handle them.

ABOVE We put our mark on our home as soon as we move in and we may well dream about it as we adapt to the newness of it all.
LEFT Dreaming of moving house might be indicative of some other kind of change in our life that we need to cope with.
BELOW Dreams of children could indicate a readiness to take on the major responsibilities of being a parent.

AGEING

WE ARE GETTING OLDER ALL THE TIME, AND GRADUALLY THE FEAR OF WHAT THIS MEANS FOR US AND OF WHAT COMES NEXT BEGINS TO PERMEATE OUR UNCONSCIOUS AND WORK ON OUR IMAGINATION. WE KNOW OR FEAR THE HORRORS OF THE FIRST GREY HAIRS, OF WRINKLES AND AN EXPANDING WAISTLINE. WE ARE AWARE THAT WE MIGHT BECOME INFIRM OR ILL, OR LOSE OUR MENTAL FACULTIES WHEN WE GROW OLD. BUT THESE FEARS CAN ALSO BE BALANCED BY THE WISDOM THAT A LIFETIME'S EXPERIENCE MAY HAVE BROUGHT US, AND OLD AGE CAN BE A TIME WHEN WE ALLOW OURSELVES TO ATTAIN A LEVEL OF PEACE AND CONTEMPLATION.

We dream of ageing for several reasons. It may be that we are worried about it, about losing our youthful looks and our physical strength and ability. It could also be that we are coming to terms with ageing, content with what we have seen and done so far in our lives and looking forward to the prospect of a comfortable and interesting retirement. A dream of old age may also be a metaphor for times past, and serve as a kind of nostalgia trip.

FEARS OF AGEING

We all react to the fear of growing old in different ways. We may face up to it, but often this is too painful and we choose instead to deny the unpleasant realities of old age, or to suppress them by ignoring them or

laughing them off. We try to reverse the ageing process by going for cosmetic surgery, dyeing our hair, applying anti-ageing creams, and wearing youthful clothes.

Our unconscious is not easily deceived though, and will deal with our fears in our dreams if we don't do so in our waking lives. It knows that we are terrified at the prospect of our lives ending and our bodies decaying, that we are afraid to confront the possibility that when we reach old age and drop the frantic activity of our younger years, we will discover that it has all been meaningless.

Dreams in which we see ourselves getting older, or already old, can be quite shocking, and act as a wake-up call for us to pay more attention to what we

are doing with our lives, to make us realise that time is passing. Sometimes these dreams mask a concern about our health, and may be taken as a cautionary note to make sure we remain as fit and active as we ought to. Recurring dreams about ageing may indicate an ongoing concern, and if you have them it is important to get to the bottom of what is bothering you.

RETIRING

Even if you are still fit and active, retiring from the working world can be the first step in starting to acknowledge that old age is not far off. You may dream about retirement in a literal way if you are approaching it in your own life, or if your partner or parents are soon to retire. This will provide you with a way to

BELOW RIGHT As time passes we can start to feel edgy, as if there are things to do that we need to concentrate on.
BELOW How we feel about our health will be shadowed in our dreams – if we are healthy while asleep it is pretty much how we will feel when we are awake.

A DREAM OF AGEING

"I was looking in a mirror and while I watched I saw my own teeth fall out and my hair turn white. The whole ageing process was immensely speeded up. I know I am getting older, but this dream really shocked me and made me feel that I wanted to hang on to my youth at all costs. But it also made me realize that I really have to enjoy what I've got because time goes so fast and I won't have it for long. And as it all slips away I have to keep reminding myself to enjoy each and every moment."

LEFT As we get older we do get more experienced, better equipped to be successful. If our dreams reflect this we can be reassured about how we fit in to the world around us.

explore possible anxieties you have around this transition.

How you see retirement will depend to a considerable extent on how well you are prepared for it, both financially and emotionally. It can be difficult to adjust to the lack of structure and activity, the loss of status, the lack of contact with your colleagues, and the sheer weight of idle time that you now have. But you may equally see it as a time to reap the benefits of your hard work, to enjoy a leisurely life or turn your hand to hobbies or other interests you have not had time for before.

WITHDRAWAL

Whatever your age, your dreams may also use retirement or old age as a metaphor for withdrawing – especially from society or from an overly active lifestyle. Indeed old age is for many a time when our contact with the outside world lessens as our ability or desire to get out decreases and our friends and siblings die. It can be a lonely time, and it may be this that your dream is trying to draw to your attention – either your own fear of becoming isolated, or guilt at not paying enough attention to an elderly relative.

WISDOM

Our stereotypes of old age are not all negative though, and while the elderly are often marginalized in Western society, we may find the archetypal figure of the wise old man or woman appearing in our dreams as a source of advice or understanding; we may even be that figure ourselves.

Grandparents or other familiar old faces may also crop up in our dreams as symbols of stability and continuity, allowing us to feel grounded and supported in our family, and giving us perspective on our lives.

BELOW FAR LEFT To dream of old or worn-out objects might point to something in our life that we feel needs to be rejuvenated.
BELOW LEFT Dreaming of possible loneliness in old age might reflect the way you feel about your life currently rather than a fear of the future.
BELOW But even when there is no hope of living forever we can rest assured that there is new life even in our dreams.

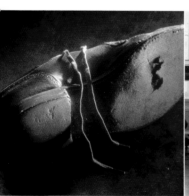

DEATH

WE ALL KNOW THAT SOONER OR LATER, DEATH WILL COME TO US, HOPEFULLY NOT PREMATURELY, BUT AS THE INEVITABLE AND INESCAPABLE LAST STAGE IN THE CYCLE OF LIFE. HOWEVER MUCH WE TRY TO AVOID THINKING ABOUT OUR OWN DEATH, OR THAT OF OUR LOVED ONES, OUR UNCONSCIOUS WILL AT SOME STAGE START TO ADDRESS THE ISSUE AND TRY TO PREPARE US FOR IT. THERE ARE MANY ISSUES ASSOCIATED WITH DEATH THAT MIGHT FEATURE IN OUR DREAMS: LOSS, LONELINESS OR RELEASE FOR EXAMPLE, AND WHETHER OR NOT THERE IS LIFE AFTER DEATH MIGHT BE ANOTHER THEME THAT WE MAY TRY TO SPECULATE ON AND EXPLORE IN OUR DREAMS.

COMING TO TERMS WITH MORTALITY

Dreams of funerals or graveyards, grief and mourning, dead bodies or skeletons may be quite literally about death and dying, and often show that we view this process in a negative light. If we are worried about death and dying then dreams of death probably happen to make us do something to try to come to terms with our own mortality. But if we dream of people celebrating, being happy,

BELOW Even if we never consciously think about our mortality it will be a source of worry to us on a deep level. We might also dream of death as a way of focusing on worries that we have of being separated from others.

remembering the dead person with pride and love, then perhaps we have made some progress in coming to terms with it. This doesn't necessarily mean we have to look forward to it, but merely that it holds no power over us to frighten us, and that we are as prepared as we can be for this event.

A LOVED ONE'S DEATH

Dreams about others dying may indicate a worry that they will die or leave us. Who we dream about may be telling us who we most fear will leave us, but it could also be that rather than a literal death, the dream represents some figurative termination of a quality that you particularly value (or dislike) in that person.

IMAGES OF DEATH

History has given us many morbid death images which our society seems to have taken eagerly on board – vaults and misty graveyards, mourners dressed in black, skeletons and gravediggers, crows, the Grim Reaper, and countless images of hell. People down the ages seem to have enjoyed frightening and torturing themselves with such images, and in your dreams they could point to disturbance and fear around death. Dreaming of being buried – especially being

buried alive – may have nothing to do with death but rather a feeling of having the life squeezed out of you, of being stifled in some way.

But death is not always disturbing – it can be very undramatic, even mundane, or very peaceful and part of the natural order. A graveyard in your dream may be a beautiful, calm place where you spend time remembering people you loved.

LIFE AFTER DEATH

Death is our biggest rite of passage, the one that takes us out of this existence and on into the next – whatever that might be. If we do believe that death is merely a transition into the next life, our unconscious may choose to show us images of change, of journeys and rebirth – which may indicate that it knows that death is not final but is indeed merely a symptom of great transformation. These dreams may be suggesting radical change or the need for such change, and not actual physical death.

How we dream about death reflects not only our views of the process but also our views of what we think happens to us afterwards. We may dream of heaven or hell as if we know what they are like, though such imagery is generally based on

LEFT Images of death don't have to be negative. They can also generate a feeling of ultimate peace and tranquillity that we may feel we need.

BELOW The religious trappings of death might suggest an awful state of nothingness, or inspire awe and acceptance. It depends on how we view death.

countless images that have been handed down to us by others. Such dreams may indicate some kind of self-judgement, seeking reward for good behaviour or fearing punishment for bad.

Whatever else it may involve, death means separation from the body, so may reveal a wish for release from ill health. It could also mean that we are coming to terms with our preoccupations with the body, or, less literally, the material world.

ABOVE Standard images of death in our dreams might actually be about some other kind of rite of passage, and perhaps something quite mundane in comparison.

LEFT Whatever religion we follow will give us plenty of imagery to fuel our dreams and visions of death and the afterlife.
RIGHT Dreaming of someone's death might mean you are reflecting on the passing of a relationship, or a phase of your friendship together.

DREAM OF DEATH

"I was in a foreign country like Egypt, being buried alive. I could feel the sand filling my mouth and my body sinking deeper and deeper into the ground. I felt I was suffocating. Just then someone uncovered my face with a spade and I could breathe. They said, 'look – some bones!' and I realized I had been dead for a long time.

I think the whole dream was about an inability to change. I felt it meant that I had to look at what was important to me, and get rid of a lot of things in my life so that I was not so stuck and held back by my possessions and rigid attitudes. I think there was also a fear that it might actually be too late to change."

MIND, BODY AND SPIRIT

Our emotional and physical experiences, together with the things we are told or learn throughout our lives, give us a framework for our beliefs, which we try, often unsuccessfully, to use to keep us safe in times of trouble and crisis. With experience we have the opportunity to develop an understanding of our limitations, to grow and change, learn and expand.

RIGHT We incorporate our experiences, our hopes and our fears into our dreams and there attempt to answer some of the questions of our existence.

EMOTIONS

ABOVE Sometimes we are not aware that we feel angry or frustrated, but such feelings can surface in our dreams.
ABOVE RIGHT Our dream symbolism may indicate painful emotions. This image could suggest isolation and loneliness.
ABOVE FAR RIGHT Holding a baby's hand is a symbol of love and tenderness. It may also mean a need to protect or be protected.

OUR EMOTIONS COVER A VAST RANGE OF EXPERIENCES, FROM ANGER AND JEALOUSY THROUGH BOREDOM AND SADNESS TO LOVE AND HAPPINESS. WHILE WE ARE ONLY TOO GLAD TO HAVE THE POSITIVE EMOTIONS, OTHERS ARE UNCOMFORTABLE AND WE MAY TRY TO PUSH THEM AWAY. BUT WE CAN'T ALWAYS CONTROL THEM, AND THEY CAN WELL UP AND OVERWHELM US, TAKING US BY SURPRISE. IN OUR DREAMS WE EXPERIENCE THE FULL RANGE OF OUR EMOTIONS, OFTEN MORE INTENSELY THAN IN OUR WAKING LIVES, AND THEY MAY HELP US COME TO GRIPS WITH THE REALLY DIFFICULT ONES.

BURIED EMOTIONS

We often hide or lose track of our emotions because we want to appear mature or civilized or in control. At times strong emotions threaten to take us over and then we may be afraid of seeming weak or vulnerable, or of doing something that we will later regret, or simply of wasting time that we think we should be spending on something else. We develop coping mechanisms to make sure that our feelings don't show, and some people are so successful at this that they lose touch with their feelings. They may also divert attention from one emotion and express it as another that may seem more

socially acceptable – for instance, men who have been brought up to believe that "boys don't cry" may express sadness as anger, and conversely many women who have had their anger curbed by social or parental disapproval may cry when angry.

When we control or divert our emotions we may delude ourselves into feeling stronger, braver, wiser, or in some other way more acceptable, but there is often a price to pay for being cut off in this way. We need to feel and express our true our emotions if we are to be well-rounded and complete human beings, to find a balance between heart and mind. Our dreams can

help us to do this by unlocking unacknowledged feelings.

FEELINGS IN DREAMS

It is always worth looking at the feelings that come up in a dream. Usually they are consistent with what you would imagine you should be feeling in the context of the dream, but sometimes the feelings and the plot may be puzzlingly at odds. Events may occur in your dream precisely to provoke a response that you will take note of, to make you think about what is really going on inside you. Sometimes this can be hard – if you always play the role of the kind and loving mother, for instance, a dream in

Dreaming permits each and every one of us to be quietly and safely insane every night of our lives.
WILLIAM DEMENT

which you sit reading a book impassively while your children are tormented will be really shocking and hard to come to terms with, but it could be a reality check on your ability to be the saint all the time, and may bring to your attention your frustrations or the fact that your own needs are not being met.

EMOTIONAL POINTERS

In some dreams the emotional content will be the take-home message rather than any events or images, and it may even be that the only thing you remember about the dream is that it was terrifying, or that in it you were extremely anxious about running out of time.

If you are not ready to deal with emotions square on, though, your mind may produce symbols to stand in for these feelings. Virtually all of your dream images can be read symbolically, or are present in your dream because they provoke some strong emotion or train of thought. Some are fairly obvious – for example a heart may stand for romantic love – while others are less clear but nevertheless

widely accepted – such as the notion that water in all its many forms represents our emotions. Many of the symbols we use to represent emotions are discussed more fully elsewhere.

The main thing is to look at the context of the symbol and your response to it in order to be able to access the emotional content. Once you understand what emotions are being brought to the surface and how they come across in your dream, you will probably have a clearer idea of how to deal with them in a useful and positive way.

ABOVE Expressing strong emotions can have a knock-on effect in our dealings with others.
ABOVE LEFT Dream imagery is often bizarre. Feeling tied-up in knots is frustrating and can make you feel like screaming.
ABOVE FAR LEFT Emotions that are held back or suppressed in your waking life may surface later in your dreams.

LEFT To dream of a macho man may suggest that it is hard for you to own your feelings as you like to appear "cool".
FAR LEFT The context of our dreams is important. A mother with her baby will mean different things for each of us, depending on our circumstances.

LOSS AND GRIEF

WHEN DEATH ENTERS OUR LIVES IT OFTEN COMES AS A COMPLETE SHOCK, AND WE ARE LEFT BEWILDERED, LOST, ANGRY AND CONFUSED. ADDED TO THE PAIN ARE FEELINGS OF REGRET AND GUILT, THE SENSE OF "IF ONLY I'D KNOWN", "IF ONLY I'D BEEN ABLE TO SAY ALL THE THINGS I WANTED TO", OR "I DIDN'T GET A CHANCE TO SAY GOODBYE". BUT IT ISN'T JUST DEATH THAT GENERATES FEELINGS OF LOSS. DIVORCE, REDUNDANCY AND EVEN THE LOSS OF PRIZED POSSESSIONS CAN BRING THEIR OWN SUDDEN SHOCKS TO OUR LIFE. HOW WE COPE CAN AFFECT HOW MUCH FINDS ITS WAY INTO OUR DREAMS, AND IT IS HERE THAT WE WILL TRY TO COME TO TERMS WITH THIS LOSS IF WE ARE NOT FACING UP TO IT IN OUR WAKING LIFE.

GRIEVING

The word "bereaved" is from an Old English word *bereafian*, which means "to plunder". And that is the feeling we have when we have lost someone or something close to us. We feel plundered, we feel that someone or something precious has been carried off without our permission or knowledge.

The experience of bereavement is not only triggered by a person's death, but other significant life events, such as divorce, separation and redundancy. The loss of such things as our health

BELOW It is very common when someone close to us dies that they continue to appear in our dreams – for months, or even years afterwards. This may be to help us work out aspects of our relationship with that person.

or our youth – or even our personal possessions – also have associations with grief and loss, and may affect us quite deeply.

Whatever the reason for our grief, we may try to work it out in our dreams. A lot of people are shocked and surprised if grieving continues in their dreams when they think they have "got over it", but the stronger the emotional tie, the longer the process is likely to go on. After someone you were close to has died, they may return to your dreams from time to time for the rest of your life.

ABOVE Although we may chide ourselves for being silly, the loss of a precious possession is likely to stir up our emotions. If you dream of your lost treasure, consider what it symbolizes for you.

FUNERALS

A funeral is an official ending. It gives us a chance to say "goodbye" and to mourn our loss. In some cultures, open displays of crying and even wailing are perfectly natural at funerals, and grieving can be expected to last, and be marked with cermonies, for months. In western society we are expected to "pull ourselves together" or "put on a brave face" and get on with our lives as quickly as possible, and far too little time or emotional energy is given to grieving. Yet if we have not fully come to terms with someone's death, they will in a sense, haunt us. Once there has been a proper grieving process, our dreams will by and large return to normal.

WORKING IT OUT

In our dreams the person or object we have lost may appear in glorious technicolour. They may seem perfectly normal and present, just as they were in life, and on waking we may feel the shock and sadness all over again when we realize it was "just a dream". This process is essential to our unconscious even if it is difficult and confusing for us. To our unconscious it is a way of working out what has happened and laying the ghost to rest. It also gives us the opportunity to say things that we feel were left unsaid, or to replay events in our unconscious mind so that we can be with our loved one once more. It is a hard and sometimes wrenching process but essential if we are to be able to get on with our lives and become as whole and as healed as possible.

DREAMS OF LOSS

Losing things in a dream may indicate that you need to mourn a loss or achieve closure on some aspect of your life. It may be something physical, such as a valuable object, or it could be more abstract, such as the loss of freedom, or of a particular phase in your life that has ended – for instance the transition from being single to being married. Even something frivolous, like having your hair cut, can be traumatic if it represents a loss of identity,

In all these cases there is a period of adjustment as you come to terms with losing something that is integral to your self-expression, or that reminds you of someone you love.

LEFT There is no easy way to mourn, but spending quiet time alone each day in reflection can help you come to terms with your loss.
MIDDLE LEFT A graveyard appearing in your dreams could be a reminder to lay the past to rest and move on with your life.
BOTTOM LEFT Piles of money in a dream may represent concerns with material security. What do you fear to lose?

GRIEF DREAM

"The year that my grandmother died I saw her in my dreams every night for months. Every morning when I woke up, I was convinced she was still alive and would run into my parents' room to tell them the good news; every morning they had to tell me she was dead. I felt the shock anew each time. It was terrible and sad, and for a good while I was frightened to go to sleep at night because I didn't want to face the shock in the morning. I even left notes to myself by my bed saying 'Granny is dead'. Each morning I woke grieving the loss. I think it helped. I feel that I can talk about her now and remember her with warmth and love."

GUILT AND BLAME

MANY PEOPLE ARE SURPRISED TO ENCOUNTER GUILT AND BLAME IN THEIR DREAMS, BUT THEY ARE AMONG THE COMMONEST OF DREAM THEMES AND PERMEATE BOTH OUR LIVES AND OUR DREAMS ON MANY LEVELS. WE MAY THINK THAT A DREAM IN WHICH WE ARE A CONVICT OR AN ADULTERER IS JUST OUR UNCONSCIOUS EXPLORING FACETS OF OUR CHARACTER THAT WE MIGHT NOT LIKE TO OWN UP TO IN OUR WAKING LIFE, BUT IT IS OFTEN GUILT THAT OUR UNCONSCIOUS IS EXPLORING. EVEN IF WE SEEM TO BE DREAMING SOMEONE ELSE'S GUILT OR BLAMING SOMEONE FOR SOMETHING, IT MAY WELL BE A DISPLACED REPRESENTATION OF OUR OWN GUILT AND SELF-BLAME.

FEELING GUILTY

Our conscious minds are very experienced at justifying our actions or blaming others so that we avoid uncomfortable feelings of guilt and self-blame. If we know we have been cruel or difficult to someone, or mishandled another person in some way, the unconscious may try to make us more aware of our behaviour so that we can see what we have done. For deep down we know what is right and wrong, and we know that we need to understand the implications of our actions and make amends for them. Part of

the role of the unconscious in our dreams is to drive us towards a greater self-awareness and understanding.

Even people who are by and large decent and honest will have the occasional lapse, and may feel disproportionately guilty and remorseful as a result. Our guilt may be misplaced too; children are often punished for being angry, and as they grow up, and even into adulthood they may continue to feel guilty when they feel anger. Adults who have this kind of problem with anger may also carry a subconscious fear of retribution as a result of anger.

CRIME AND PUNISHMENT

The greater the offence, the more intense the dream is likely to be, and we may wake feeling we have actually committed a crime, even if whatever is making us feel guilty is not the same as the dream scenario. The nature of the offence in our dream will usually give us enough clues to identify what it is we are feeling guilty about. It may be that you are being caught – or simply blamed – for a wrongdoing and you feel guilty until proven innocent. Take note of whether the punishment fits the crime – if you are given a hefty penalty for a mere peccadillo, it may be that you are feeling victimized by injustice rather than actually feeling guilty.

CONFESSION

Confessing in a dream, whether to a priest, a confidante or to the person you have wronged, also indicates that you feel guilty for something. It may also show that you are trying to purge yourself of your guilty feelings and regrets, or offload the burden of guilt on to someone else.

We treat ourselves badly at times and we may feel compelled to double the damage by "beating ourselves up" about it. Such guilt and self-blame may manifest as

BELOW Sometimes our inner voice must shout to be heard and can be symbolized in our dreams as threatening, or aggressive figures. Ask yourself what it is that you don't want to hear. Maybe you have a fear of being punished?

LEFT Fragments of our dreams are often all that we recall, but only you can decide if they make you feel guilty.

LEFT To be standing accused in your dream may tie-in with harbouring a guilty secret. Who is it that you are wronging and what is it that you fear from them?

dreams about being punished. It doesn't have to be crimes that we feel guilty for. Sometimes we feel bad about withholding love, or for not responding to someone's distress, or for failing to rise to a challenge. We may even feel guilty whenever we please ourselves rather than pleasing someone else and judge ourselves "selfish".

Guilt is one of those insidious feelings that seem to spill into every area of our lives. It has the power to go on eating away at us forever and it is often extremely hard to get rid of. But our dreams may give us a clue as to what we can do to work through such feelings, and learn from them. Ask questions of your dream and the answers will emerge.

ABOVE Feeling guilty and being a victim often go hand-in-hand. Who or what would you like to turn your back on?

DREAM OF BLAME

"I was riding a motorbike and saw my son riding towards me. We both pulled back on our handlebars and did 'wheelies'. The strange thing is my son is only five but in my dream he was a young man. I feel really guilty towards him because his mother and I separated. Even though it was his mother that left, I still feel so much of his pain at not having her there, at having to grow up ahead of his time. I feel responsible for this because I must have played a part in her decision to leave."

ABOVE To dream of a prison cell may symbolize being punished for some misdemeanour. Could it be your guilt that has imprisoned you?
RIGHT Our guilt can make us feel small and trapped. It can remind us of how it felt as children to be accused of a crime we didn't commit.

FALLING IN LOVE

MORE SONGS, POEMS AND LETTERS HAVE BEEN WRITTEN ABOUT LOVE THAN ANY OTHER SUBJECT, AND IT IS ONLY NATURAL THAT SUCH AN IMPORTANT EMOTION SHOULD FIGURE SO LARGELY IN OUR DREAMS. WE ALL NEED TO LOVE AND BE LOVED, AND WHEN WE FALL IN LOVE WE LITERALLY CAN'T STOP DAYDREAMING ABOUT OUR CHOSEN ONE, SO IT IS COMPLETELY UNDERSTANDABLE THAT THIS CARRIES ON INTO OUR SLEEPING WORLDS TOO. FALLING IN LOVE AND HOLDING THE STEADY LOVE OF A REAL PERSON ARE TWO DIFFERENT THINGS, BUT BOTH REPRESENT OR CONTAIN POWERFUL EMOTIONS, AND MAY DOMINATE OUR DREAMS FROM TIME TO TIME.

In our dreams our partner may take on a new dimension – not who they really are but who we think they are, or who we would like them to be. They may be wilder, fiercer, bossier, kinder, more or less loving, but their essence remains the same. Our unconscious may amplify an aspect of their character to draw our attention to some particular point of view so we can adjust our relationship accordingly, or in order to flag up characteristics that we don't want to see.

FIRST LOVE
For teenagers, falling in love is often a painful experience. Our first love affair can be very formative, as all our future relationships may be built on the lessons we learn in those first few soulful gazes or fumbling embraces. Likewise, that first ever love affair will probably feature prominently in our teen dreams.

It is also quite natural, especially at this young age, to fall in love with someone who is unattainable – someone we adore from afar, or who is forbidden – perhaps because they are too old for us, or are already in a partnership. This person is likely to appear in our dreams, which may have a sexual or erotic bias. Such dreams can be very realistic and make us feel confused and embarrassed, particularly when we meet the person in daily life.

ROMANCE
A kind of scene-setting for love, romance usually features more prominently at the beginning of a relationship when our feelings

are based more in fantasy than in the reality of the person on whom we have focused our attentions. At this stage it functions as wish fulfilment – we want everything to be wonderful and so we put all our effort into impressing the other person and making them feel special. We also want to be made to feel special ourselves. Romance provides a smoke screen, a context and loose set of rules and rituals in the framework of which we can get to know the other person, but it may also serve to distract us from who they really are.

The symbols and activities that we associate with romance – anything heart-shaped, candlelit dinners, sunsets on the beach, love poetry and so on – are many and wide-ranging, so dreaming of these things, whether they

BELOW RIGHT When we are in love, it can feel as if we are floating on air and our dreams may have a romantic feel to them. **BELOW** Falling in love is an exciting experience and it is most likely that our lover will keep on appearing in our dreams.

RIGHT Dreams of falling in love with someone in a very physical way might reflect something that you feel is lacking in your love life, or might recall the intense feelings that are associated with first love.

involve a particular person or not, may point to a wish for romance in our lives or the possibility that it is on the horizon. Men in particular may find themselves feeling particularly vulnerable if they show their softer side, so a romantic dream may have more to do with getting in touch with vulnerability and owning your feelings than with any kind of actual partnership.

Whether the romantic dream scenario will hold together coherently or is flawed in some way may also be taken as a hint as to how you should be approaching love and relationships. Ask yourself whether you are looking for a person to have a real relationship with or merely someone who will make you feel better by distracting you from areas of dissatisfaction in your life.

THE FOOD OF LOVE

Love and food go together in many ways, so you could consider whether food images in your dreams are linked to love. For many people food and drink are an intrinsic part of the rituals of romance and courtship, and are also the subject of fetishes. Your unconscious may make reference to expressions such as "all-consuming passion" when it dreams of eating, to suggest the nature of how you relate to a lover, and perhaps to warn you not to become too obsessive.

DREAM OF LOVE

"I was madly in love with my girlfriend's mother and dreamed of her every night for months. Every morning I would walk my girlfriend to school. Her mother would see her off, and I would barely be able to talk to her. In fact I only really went out with the daughter so I could see the mother every morning. The dreams were all quite erotic, although we never made love either in my dream or in real life. There was no way I could ever have had a relationship with her in reality for lots of different reasons, so this was my substitute."

BELOW LEFT Red roses and champagne are popular symbols of romance.

BELOW FAR LEFT Our dreams may dwell on the physical intimacy we share with our lover. This may be the actual reality or else represent some kind of wish fulfilment.

BELOW Almost everyone can remember their first kiss and what it was like to fall in love for the first time. Teenage love is an emotional roller-coaster where feelings are experienced intensely.

SEX

THE MASTER OF THE EROTIC DREAM IS UNDOUBTEDLY FREUD, WHO HELD THAT MUCH OF WHAT WE DREAM, EVEN IF IT SEEMS TO HAVE ABSOLUTELY NOTHING TO DO WITH SEX, SYMBOLIZES SUPPRESSED SEXUAL DESIRES. IN THE FREUDIAN MODEL, A SNAKE, LADDER, KNIFE, STAIRCASE, CANDLE OR PEN REPRESENT THE PENIS, AND CAVES, BOXES, TUNNELS OR DARK ROOMS ARE THE VAGINA. BUT WHILE IT IS POSSIBLE THAT SUCH OBJECTS MAY ACT AS SYMBOLS IN THIS WAY, THEY ARE NOT NECESSARILY DOING SO IN EVERY CASE, AND AS PREVIOUSLY DISCUSSED, SYMBOLS WILL HAVE DIFFERENT MEANINGS FOR DIFFERENT PEOPLE. WE MAY ALSO WORK WITH OUR SEXUALITY DIRECTLY THROUGH OVERTLY EROTIC DREAMS.

ABOVE Erotic and stylized images may appear in our dreams, but only you will understand how they relate to you.
ABOVE RIGHT The kinds of things you dream about might be symbolically, or overtly sexual.
ABOVE FAR RIGHT For both men and women, snakes are a traditional symbol of sexual power and energy. Are you comfortable with your sexuality?

Many dreams contain symbolism that only you will understand. Certain things may have become associated with sex for you by dint of your experiences – for example, if there was music playing the first time you made love, the same tune may always trigger the memory of your first sexual experience.

SEXUAL FANTASIES

Two common sexual fantasies are of having sex in a public place and having sex with a stranger. Such dreams will tend to have different meanings for men and

women because their basic sexual needs and responses differ.

Dreaming of making love in a crowded stadium, for instance, may reflect the tendency of men to boast about sex, or a woman's desire to be less inhibited. In this kind of dream a woman may be showing a need to be cheered on or encouraged by others to express her sexuality in a full and satisfying way, or she may enjoy the fact that she is capable of doing so and wants to let the world know about it.

If the dream is of having sex in a lift or on public transport, it

may highlight the fun and thrilling aspect to sex, and remind us how it feels to do something "naughty". Such a dream may bring into question your attitude to rules and social behaviour and may show a desire to break a taboo.

For men, the biological imperative to spread their seed widely is met with confusingly divergent attitudes in society – on the one hand it is frowned on as infidelity and on the other it is prized as prowess. So dreams of sex with a stranger may reveal a yearning for just this model of

People don't fall in love with what's right in front of them. People want the dream – what they can't have. The more unattainable, the more attractive.
XANDER

behaviour, either to escape social restrictions and enjoy the taste of forbidden fruit, or to reassure the man of his virility.

WISH FULFILMENT

Your sexual desires and urges do not simply go away if you are on your own, and you will probably find other ways to express them. The more cut off you are from a healthy sex life, the more likely it is that sex will appear in your dreams as a substitute for the real thing. If there is no-one special in your life you may dream of sex with a stranger, or perhaps you have met someone you desire and can't wait to be intimate with in real life. Even if you have a relationship, you may be expressing your desire for something better if your present situation is unsatisfactory. Whatever the case, these dreams are usually healthy explorations of possibilities or expressions of our needs, and we can use them as a guide to how we are feeling.

SEXUAL PROBLEMS

We may have erotic dreams that help us deal with our sexual difficulties. Our problems could be quite obvious – for example frustration at not having a sexual partner – or your unconscious might be drawing to your attention something you haven't even admitted to yourself yet. Even if you feel unable to talk about a problem, you will still need to process it and try to overcome it or come to terms with it, and your dreams can provide a useful framework for doing just this.

DISCOVERING OUR SEXUALITY

Adolescence is a time of sexual discovery and exploration, but our need to understand ourselves as sexual beings doesn't end here. Throughout our lives we may use our dreams to help work out particular aspects of sexuality of which we are unsure, or to release sexual urges that may be buried under taboo, or that we have not had the opportunity to express. We may dream of fetishes, or have homosexual fantasies, and in so doing uncover sexual impulses that are real for us, or play with ideas that we are curious about but don't want to act out in real life. Acting out the role of the opposite sex may give us an understanding of how our own sexuality may be experienced by our partner. Many people are self-conscious about their bodies, and it can be liberating to have dreams in which they can enjoy sex. Our erotic dreams can enable us to discover and fulfil our sexuality in a positive way.

ABOVE Our sexual fantasies will often be played out in our dreams. Having sex on a train is a fairly common fantasy.
ABOVE LEFT Talking about sexual problems is a sensitive area, so we may dream about them to help us work them out.
ABOVE FAR LEFT Our dreams can provide a "safe space" where we can allow and explore sexual feelings.

BELOW It may be easier to enjoy "perfect" sex in our dreams than in our actual relationships. This could be because our inhibitions don't get in the way and our partner seems to know exactly how to give us pleasure. Sharing intimate dreams with your partner can help build trust.

IMPOTENCE DREAM

"I was in a fencing tournament, and my opponent was my boss. I had already donned my mask and jacket, but while my boss was ready and waiting with his sabre raised, I couldn't find mine anywhere.

I had been unable to have an erection for some time, but this dream made me realize that it was the stress of work that was making me impotent."

HEALTHY BODY

OUR RELATIONSHIP WITH OUR BODY IS OFTEN FRAUGHT, AS OUR SOCIETY SEEMS TO BECOME MORE AND MORE OBSESSED WITH THE WAY WE LOOK RATHER THAN HOW HEALTHY WE ARE. WE HAVE MANIC SESSIONS AT THE GYM, OR GO ON FADDY DIETS AND WORRY ABOUT BEING OVERWEIGHT OR DISLIKE PARTS OF OUR BODY. THESE ANXIETIES MAY COME THROUGH INTO OUR DREAMS. ON THE OTHER HAND, A GENERAL SENSE OF HEALTH AND VITALITY IN A DREAM MAY INDICATE EMOTIONAL WELLBEING, OR AT LEAST THE DESIRE FOR IT. IN DREAMS WHERE OUR ATTENTION IS DRAWN TO A PARTICULAR PART OF THE BODY, IT COULD BE A REFERENCE TO WHAT IT ENABLES US TO DO RATHER THAN THE ORGAN OR LIMB ITSELF.

BELOW FAR RIGHT Therapeutic dreams where you are pampered and cared for might point to an absence of this in your life.
BELOW RIGHT Dreaming of a fast-moving sport might indicate that you want more action and movement in your life.
BELOW A dream in which you are enjoying the invigorating effect of exercise might simply be a dream to enjoy and nothing more.

HEALTH AND WELLBEING

Occasionally we might get dreams in which we are healthy, vibrant, and full of life. Our unconscious does throw up unexpectedly good dreams from time to time to make us realize what we do in fact possess, and although they lack drama and are easily overlooked, these dreams are just as important as dreams of pain or illness.

If we suffer from ill health, such dreams can seem cruel, but they are our unconscious mind's way of instilling hope in us, of showing us that we can overcome anything, even if only in spirit. Dreams such as this can be seen as a call to get better, to find out what is behind our condition and do something about it if possible. If, in our waking life, we are in good health then these dreams may unfold to give us clues to what our unconscious believes is our true potential.

DIET AND EXERCISE

Achieving and maintaining a beautiful, healthy body is a major preoccupation in Western society, and as such it may figure strongly in our nightly dreams if we are dissatisfied with ourselves in some way. The dissatisfaction could be an expression of low self-esteem or of control issues, as both diet and exercise involve discipline and perseverance.

While obesity may signal hanging on to comforts, dieting could suggest that you are depriving yourself in some way, and breaking a diet may be either a loss of control or a defiance of restrictions in your life. If you are exercising in your dream, this could be an indication that you are taking your own needs seriously and feeling the power of your physical being.

THE BODY

Focusing on a particular aspect of your body generally shows a preoccupation with the functionality of that body part or associations commonly made with it. So the head may symbolize your ability to think and rationalize, while the face can be seen as the front you display to the world, as well as being the most intricately expressive part of your body. The heart was long thought to be the seat of our emotions and still holds that association; it can also be thought of as our essential self, associated as it is with the

DREAM OF HEALTH

"I hadn't really noticed that my arthritis was getting worse until I had my 'jumping dream'. In this dream, I was taking vast, bounding leaps like a man on the moon. I felt so fit, so alive, so full of energy. It was an amazing dream and very inspiring. When I woke up I realized just how much pain I was in. My 'jumping dream' made me determined to get rid of it completely, and I became much more assertive and actively involved in making myself well again. I don't think I would have done anything if I hadn't had that dream."

bloodstream, the life force of the body. Hands and feet, arms and legs may be equated with action, movement and dexterity, with being able to go places and do things. Focusing your attention on the eyes, ears, nose or tongue is probably to do with the senses of sight, hearing, smell and taste, and the process of taking in information. Dreaming of the mouth or tongue might also suggest the power of speech.

We may pick up on common metaphors to do with the body when dreaming – "swallowing" information indicates gullibility, while being able to "stomach" something shows a level of tolerance for something we may not like – that we find "distasteful" or "unsavoury".

In our dreams our organs or limbs may not be in their normal state – perhaps they are injured, enlarged or shrunken, or unable to do their job properly. We may dream of having something stuck in our throat, of losing blood or seeing a pool of it. Perhaps images such as these are trying to draw our attention to some level of dysfunctionality, obstacle or imbalance in our lives.

PARALYSIS

Much like a woman who came to Freud's practice complaining of inexplicable paralysis, we are expressing our feelings of powerlessness and vulnerability in our dreams when we lose our ability to move. It may be that we are stuck in some undesirable situation and need some kind of impetus to get ourselves out of it, or that despite all the efforts we have made, we feel frustrated at getting nowhere. Dreams like this may not offer up a complete solution but might help you focus on the problem.

ABOVE Dreaming of being at one with your body and mind is a good wake-up call. Perhaps our dreams can disengage us from our obsession with weight, youth and beauty and help us value what we have.

BELOW FAR LEFT Dreams of ill health often flag an underlying worry we have in our waking lives.

BELOW LEFT Dreaming of the pleasant glow after exercise may start you on the road to a fitter life.

BELOW If you dream of healthy food perhaps you need nourishment. You might also dream of food if you are obsessed with diet and weight control.

PAIN AND ILLNESS

WHEN WE ARE ASLEEP ANY PAIN OR DISEASE WE HAVE IN OUR BODY OR MIND WILL FILTER THROUGH INTO OUR DREAMS AND BE EXPRESSED EITHER DIRECTLY OR METAPHORICALLY. CONVERSELY, EMOTIONAL DISTRESS WE MAY BE EXPERIENCING IN OUR LIVES MAY MANIFEST IN A DREAM AS PHYSICAL PAIN OR INJURY. DOCTORS AND OTHER MEDICAL STAFF THAT APPEAR IN OUR DREAMS MAY BE THERE TO HELP OR HINDER OUR PROGRESS TO HEALTH, WHILE DREAMING OF BEING IN HOSPITAL COULD BE SEEN AS AN ACKNOWLEDGEMENT OF THE SERIOUSNESS OF A CONDITION. DREAMING OF PAIN AND ILLNESS MAY ALSO BE A METAPHOR FOR SOMETHING ELSE IN YOUR LIFE, AN EMOTIONAL AILMENT FOR EXAMPLE.

RIGHT If we are suffering from pain in real life, then it wouldn't be a surprise if our dream reflected this. If we go to bed with a headache the pain might filter through into our sleep, so we dream of it.

DREAM OF ILL HEALTH

"In my dream I was ill and the doctor was applying leeches. These black slimy things were literally sucking the lifeblood out of me. I woke up feeling quite nauseous. The dream prompted me to look at my new relationship: although my new partner seemed a loving and caring person, as a doctor ought to be, I felt she was using me financially. The blood in the dream was money, and I was letting my partner bleed me dry."

PAIN

In India there is a widespread belief that dreaming about pain in any part of your body indicates that something is wrong with that part; even if a doctor finds nothing wrong it is taken as a sign that this is where pain will get to you sooner or later. But dreams are seldom prophetic, so dreaming of pain doesn't necessarily mean that an injury is going to befall you, although it is possible that your body is trying to tell you that you are ill. If you dream of pain, note what sort of pain you experience and where it is located, and consider what it could be telling you. Also look at what you do about the pain in your dream.

If dreams of pain crop up often, pay special attention to them as they are almost certainly highlighting an area of some

importance to your unconscious and may well be your mind's way of expressing emotional rather than physical pain. How we respond to painful or frightening experiences can have major repercussions – they may lead to growth and wisdom, but they can also cause us to retreat to a space that seems safe but is actually stultifying, and prevent us from growing into new awareness.

INJURIES AND ILLNESS

Your body is often symbolic of the self, so any illness or injury that affects your body in your dream is one that affects you as a person. Bruises and cuts may be symbolic of emotional bumps and scrapes, cancers of emotional malignancy, festering wounds of problems that are getting worse, blindness of not seeing or not wanting to look at something.

The fear of being seriously ill is common and we may act it out while we sleep. But the health problems in our dreams are often not life-threatening. Colds, diarrhoea, spots, rashes and warts, for instance, may be uncomfortable, embarrassing or irritating rather than painful, and suggest such discomforts in your life. You may resent being ill, perhaps being too busy to make the time or effort to look after your body. What you feel in your dream about your illness may well be what you are feeling in waking life, and your dream is a way of getting this feeling out into the open.

THE MEDICAL WORLD

If you are given medication in your dream, it is important to note how you respond to receiving it. It may seem like a gift of health, or a poison in disguise; if you don't know what it is then it may bring up control or trust issues for you. Take note of the form the medicine comes in, as well as who gives it to you, and what your relationship is to that person. Receiving an anaesthetic could suggest an emotional numbness or a kind of unconsciousness in your waking life, while surgery may indicate that drastic action is needed around some problem, or that

ABOVE How we view pain and illness – and how we would cope with being confined to bed – can be reflected in our dreams.

someone is already taking it for you. Many people may be involved in our dream illness – doctors and nurses, hospital porters and ambulance staff, to name a few. What role do these people have in your dream? Do they take charge, or are they bystanders? If medical personnel are not actually helping you, you may feel let down, and it could be useful to see if this is reflecting something you are experiencing in your life. Depending on your relationship to such figures in your own life, they may well represent the wish to be looked after, to hand over responsibility for your wellbeing to someone who you think is better qualified than you.

A dream that takes place in a hospital may suggest more significant problems in your life or more serious concerns with illness. As an environment a hospital may be alien and frightening, and one in which you have to relinquish much of your control. Many people fear that they will never leave a hospital alive, so it may also indicate that you are facing up to your mortality.

BELOW If we have real underlying fear of needles or even doctors, then our dreams may well reflect this.

ABOVE If we are taking medication that we don't really understand, or which may have side effects that we feel ill-prepared for, it will worry us in our dreams.

RIGHT Dreaming of a cold might not be a simple reflection of our physical state in real life. It might be a metaphor for something.

BELOW Medical tools can seem intimidating and invasive. If we dream of these perhaps they are symbolic of something in our lives that we feel threatened by.

Madness and Irrationality

Dreams are sometimes thought to be the workings of a mind gone temporarily insane, but actually being in the grip of insanity rarely shows any similarity to our dreams. The dreaming mind uses metaphors and allegories, images that may be quite fantastical and distorted, and operates from a different logical basis, while in madness it is rather a person's perceptions of what they see or hear or feel that may be distorted. Madness is not only used as a medical term. We may also be referring to obsession or paranoia in our dreams; even extremes of anger and emotional instability may in some cases be termed insanity.

LOGIC AND RATIONALITY

Some of our dreams may seem just like scenes from our waking lives, but at times a different logic from that of our daily lives operates, and rationality and reason seem to be suspended. But if we look more closely, within what seems to be random and meaningless nonsense there may exist a less obvious form of rationality, and within apparently demented or uncontrolled behaviour there is a degree of meaning and purpose.

Our dreams talk to us using symbols and metaphors, and we must try to understand them with our heart, not our head, to feel intuitively what these dreams

BELOW It is hard for some people to understand the fears that other people have about mental illness, fears that may surface in their dreams in the most negative ways. Try to examine these fears if you suffer from such dreams.

might mean rather than trying to reason them out. However odd they may be, they are seldom a sign of actual madness. Rather they show the unconscious mind hard at work, producing attention-grabbing images and situations that give us a new way of looking at ourselves, however strange they may seem to our rational mind.

MADNESS

It is hard for sane people to comprehend what it is to be mad, and so in their dreams they may resort to stereotypical imagery to convey the impression of it. Even still, the terms "mad" and "sane" are difficult to define absolutely, as what is right and

normal for one individual may be completely wrong or highly bizarre for another.

Madness can take many forms, and in our dreams, being insane may be showing us in an extreme way the levels of distress or confusion we are enduring in our lives and warning us to take action. If you are rather confused, dazed and incoherent in your dreams, you may need to look at how confusion may be distressing you in your waking life, or why you are unable to express yourself clearly.

ASYLUM

Finding ourselves in some kind of mental institution, or asylum, in our dreams may mean that we have acknowledged that we need help, and that we have given ourselves permission to devote our full attention to working through why we feel mad or unstable. Here we will also find ourselves thrown together with others who are insane, and this becomes the normality within the context of the asylum, and gives us a chance to benchmark our feelings and behaviours against others. By dreaming of being institutionalized, we may be showing a need to be helped or looked after, or we could be fighting against the label of madness or the norms of society.

ECCENTRICITY

Odd behaviour in a dream may be disturbing, especially if it is manifesting in someone you know well. Examine how the behaviour is different from that person's normal way of being, as it could be showing you some aspect of your own character that is asking for greater expression. For instance, dreaming of aggression in a person who is normally calm and controlled, or childish behaviour in someone you regard as mature and responsible, may be a way of letting yourself "try out" these behaviours, to see how they feel and how you respond, before you deal with them in reality.

OBSESSION AND PARANOIA

Being fixated on something or someone in our dreams is relatively common, and may reflect a naturally obsessional personal style, or it could be a signal to your conscious mind that there is something you either need to focus your attention on or have been paying too much attention to – only the contexts of your dream and your life will tell you which. The irrational fears that all too often visit our dreams may seem like paranoia, but are likely to be an accentuated form of some real fears, or an indication that we are overly concerned with other people's views of ourselves.

BEING POSSESSED

Madness can take more frightening forms though. Being possessed by devils, or wreaking

havoc in a frenzy of unbridled anger, may well affect people who have difficulty coming to terms with their own anger, or who have not found appropriate and satisfying ways of expressing their anger.

SPLIT PERSONALITY AND THE PSYCHOPATH

Sometimes a person's negative feelings can be so strong that they can only cope by cutting off from them. In a way this is what we often do in our dreams by using another character to represent an aspect of ourselves, but if we actually dream of having a split personality then it could be that reconciling two aspects of ourselves that are at odds with each other is our prime task, and it is important to find out what these are. In extreme instances, being cut off from our humanity can manifest as psychopathic behaviour: unstable and violent, the psychopath is unable to form normal personal relationships and may act in anti-social ways, indifferent to his effects on people or his obligations to society as a whole.

SPIRITUALITY AND RELIGION

ABOVE We may follow a mainstream religion in our real life, but our dreams may tell us a great deal more about our spirituality if we will look and listen to them.
ABOVE RIGHT The culture and faith we have been brought up in will dictate a lot of what our dreams will be about.

RELIGION GIVES US A FORMALIZED EXPRESSION OF OUR SPIRITUALITY AND PROVIDES A FRAMEWORK FOR OUR BELIEFS. IT IS ALSO ABOUT PRACTICE, AND IN OUR DREAMS WE MAY USE THE RITUALS AND MATERIAL TRAPPINGS OF RELIGION – PRAYER, CHURCHES AND TEMPLES, RELIGIOUS ICONS – AS POINTERS TO SPIRITUAL AND ETHICAL ISSUES. DREAMS OF RELIGION AND SPIRITUAL EXPERIENCES CAN ACT AS PROMPTS FOR US TO INVESTIGATE SOME FUNDAMENTAL QUESTIONS ABOUT OUR EXISTENCE – TO GO BEYOND THE MUNDANE BUSINESS OF OUR DAY-TO-DAY ACTIVITIES.

In a religious dream we may have an experience of true faith, of belief. We may pray to and worship our God; meet divinities face to face; meditate alone or communicate with a priest or religious leader, we may be out in the wilderness or exist in the heart of a congregation.

The Hindus call religious dreams *satsang* dreams – "words of truth" – and believe that some aspect of true divinity does actually speak words of truth to us in our dreams. But our dreams of religion are also telling us about ourselves – our beliefs, our hopes and fears, and our values. They give us the freedom to leave behind all the trappings of our material life and fling ourselves headlong into a truly spiritual way of being, and in so doing, to learn and grow.

BELIEF SYSTEMS
Our own faith, if any, will have a strong bearing on what we dream about and how we perceive the content of our dream, but while we are more likely to create a familiar faith or belief setting in our dream it doesn't necessarily mean that we will never explore and examine other belief systems in our dreams. If we do, such dreams may offer new perspectives to our own, enriching and strengthening our beliefs or challenging them and giving us new insights.

THE AFTERLIFE
The older we get the more likely we are to have religious dreams, even if we studiously avoid spiritual issues in waking life, as they are often a reminder from the unconscious mind of our

mortality. We may increasingly feel the need to explore what happens after we die, and turn to belief in the afterlife as a happier option than oblivion.

MORALITY – A BALANCING ACT
Goodness and evil, sins and forgiveness, charity and mercy – these are issues that form the focus of many a religious upbringing. While some people derive peace and comfort from religion, the abundance of these very concepts may engender rather a generalized feeling of guilt and a fear of not being good enough. Religious dreams may give us the wherewithal to feel that we are forgiven, cleansed of our faults and sins, and also to find out whether we are on the right moral track.

PRAYER

In our dreams, praying may mean many things. Prayers and sacrifices can be seen as a means of atonement or a way of bargaining with the gods; if this seems true for you, see if there is something you really want, and what you are sacrificing in order to get it. Through prayer and meditation we may be trying not only to communicate with God, but also to connect with a higher aspect of ourselves, with our own spiritual core.

THE HOUSE OF GOD

Places of worship throughout the world are usually easily recognizable, and they could figure in your dreams both as the physical representation of a particular faith, or as a place where you feel you can get in touch with your spiritual self or be closer to God. Note whether the building in your dreams provides you with an intimate environment, or if it is vast and awe-inspiring, making you feel small and insignificant in the face of a great deity.

RELIGIOUS LEADERS

Spiritual leaders can be complex figures to whom we respond in many ways. We often see them as authority figures, whether they are the kind, wise and insightful type who can guide us through spiritual and emotional turmoil, or distant ceremonial figures representing power and even material wealth. We may engage with these leaders on an individual basis, reminiscent of parent-child interaction, or receive their communication as part of a large congregation.

THE RELIGIOUS COMMUNITY

Religion can provide us with an instant community, a group of people with whom we share, to a greater or lesser extent, our spiritual beliefs and values. Socially these people can be immensely important to us, and we may define ourselves by belonging with them and by the rituals we engage in together.

Because religion and morality often go hand in hand, a congregation or other religious grouping in your dream may indicate social judgement, so it will be important to look at how you fit in with this community – if you are accepted or an outcast.

If the community is an evangelical one and you feel comfortable participating in spreading the word, it could be a sign that you have a message to get across, something that you want to tell the world at large.

ABOVE Religion can cement us to our community. Spirituality can set us free.
ABOVE LEFT Whatever religious figures we have been brought up with will often appear in our dreams as messengers.
ABOVE FAR LEFT Dreams of church buildings or icons might indicate a sense that we feel we need to atone or repent in some way.

RIGHT All faiths come complete with their own particular icons.

ENGAGING WITH PEOPLE

Of all the elements we are likely to
encounter in our dreams it is people that
will feature most often. At times in our
waking life we respond to people
strongly, falling passionately in love or
running into conflict, and without them
we can become lonely. Usually when a
person appears in a dream their
significance is unique and relevant in
the context of that dream alone,
although if you have a series of dreams
on the same theme they might become
representative of something particular –
some aspect of ourselves, or an
archetypal figure. Besides the characters
that we meet in our dreams there is
always you, the observer or participant.

RIGHT Many of the activities that fill our lives revolve around
people, and in our dreams continue to explore interpersonal
issues that are troubling us in our day-to-day lives

FAMILY

THE MEMBERS OF OUR FAMILY ARE POTENTIALLY THE CLOSEST PEOPLE TO US. THEY ARE WITH US FROM BIRTH, WE GROW UP WITH THEM, WE KNOW THEM INTIMATELY AND, HOPEFULLY, LOVE THEM DEARLY. WE SPEND A LOT OF TIME WITH OUR FAMILY, AND THIS CAN CREATE BOTH A WONDERFUL CLOSENESS AND TREMENDOUS STRESS. THERE CAN BE MORE CONFLICT BETWEEN FAMILY MEMBERS THAN ANY OTHER RELATIONSHIP. AT SOME TIMES IN OUR LIFE THE BONDS CAN BE STRETCHED TO BREAKING POINT, AND AT OTHERS THERE IS A DISTANCE THAT YOU FEEL RECONCILED TO BUT WHICH IN FACT IS SUBCONSCIOUSLY BOTHERING YOU. IT IS HARDLY SURPRISING THAT THE FAMILY FEATURES FREQUENTLY IN OUR DREAMS.

ABOVE The concept of family, and the individuals within it, is a powerful force and will figure large in our dreams. Our parents will be the most influential aspect for most of us.

Family members are irreplaceable – while friends and acquaintances may come and go, if we lose a parent or grandparent, child or sibling, or if we fall out with them irrevocably, their role can never be taken by someone else. Thus when we do get into conflict situations with them there is a lot at stake. If we are unwilling or unable to resolve issues effectively, they almost inevitably surface in our dreams.

The family can be seen as a microcosm of society, and in it we learn to understand social roles and behaviours, and establish core norms and values.

Our responses to authority, power, love, companionship and many other aspects of human behaviour and social structures will be learnt in the family and taken with us into society. Because of this, dreaming of a family member might often be pointing towards a characteristic rather than a dream about that person. For example, if you felt that your father was a forbidding and authoritarian element in your childhood, in your dream his presence might actually be a reference to a real-life bullying boss you are having difficulty with at work.

PARENTS

Our parents are probably the most influential people in our lives. We are heavily dependent on them during our early years, and they are an important source of information about the world. We also learn from them a vast array of attitudes and behaviours that may help us to integrate into society or that may be dysfunctional and present us with constant difficulties.

Our relationship with our parents evolves through childhood and changes during our adult years as we mature, and as they grow old and perhaps dependent. In dreams of our parents we are often trying to

work through unresolved childhood issues and how they continue to affect us as adults. For instance, a child that is often punished for something they haven't done may carry unjustified feelings of guilt with them for the rest of their lives. On the other hand the appearance of your parents in your dream may suggest that you are feeling a need to be loved and looked after if your parents are loving and nurturing people.

CHILDREN

Many parents expend a lot of energy on worrying about their children. They may take these worries to be bed with them, exaggerating them in their dreams, as they play out worst-case scenarios as a way of anticipating and preparing for unexpected or difficult situations. It is also quite possible that you are unconsciously aware of some difficulty with your child, and your unconscious is trying to bring this to your attention.

Dreaming about our own children after they have grown up might be an attempt to go back and change something we did, to put it to rights, and in so doing to absolve our feelings of guilt about the mistakes we made as a parent. If we can see what aspect of our parenting is

ABOVE Position and hierarchy within the family group might still affect us even when we've moved away from home.

RIGHT It is said we never really recover from our childhood and our dreams may well reflect and support this view.

LEFT If our childhood was happy then we will find any dreams of it will also be happy – and we can just enjoy them.

BELOW If on the other hand our childhood was less than safe, or we still have unresolved fears about it, our dreams may also make us feel unsafe.

disquieting us, we can to try to make amends. We can also relive the joy of our own childhood through our children, updating and perhaps improving on the experiences that we had ourselves. Our children can show us how our childhood might have been, and how we can get in touch with the child within us, giving us the opportunity to recapture the freedom and innocence of our early years. Much will depend on the nature of your own childhood and on how you relate to your children.

BROTHERS AND SISTERS
Sibling relationships are particularly complex because we may feel some ambivalence around our brothers and sisters. On the one hand they are our constant companions during childhood – we share our experiences, we play games and have jokes with each other, we have the same family situation, and so are often in a position to understand and empathize with each other more than anyone else. For a younger child, older siblings can be invaluable role models and teachers as well.

However, sibling rivalry should never be underestimated – the first-born may always at some level resent the loss of parental attention that the birth of younger siblings inevitably brings, and constant comparisons by parents and teachers can be irksome, depriving a child of their individuality and potentially bringing a sense of inadequacy.

Dreams of siblings can underscore these feelings and allow us to address buried resentments, perhaps by being more assertive. Your brother or sister may have qualities that you wish to bring out in yourself, and their presence in your dream may be an attempt to do this.

FRIENDS

THE FRIENDSHIPS WE HAVE OCCUR AT MANY LEVELS, FROM SUPERFICIAL ACQUAINTANCES TO LIFELONG COMPANIONS. CIRCUMSTANTIAL FRIENDSHIPS – SUCH AS THE COLLEAGUES WE LIKE AND WITH WHOM WE MAY OCCASIONALLY HAVE A CHAT, OR THE PEOPLE WE MEET AT NIGHT SCHOOL – MAY DEVELOP, BUT BASICALLY THEY ARE ON THE OUTSIDE OF OUR NETWORK. AT THE OTHER END OF THE SPECTRUM ARE THE PEOPLE WHO ARE OUR CLOSEST COMPANIONS, PEOPLE WE REALLY CONNECT WITH ON A DEEP LEVEL, OR WITH WHOM WE HAVE SO MUCH SHARED HISTORY THAT OUR DIFFERENCES BECOME IRRELEVANT. DREAMS OF FRIENDS MAY BE OF EITHER SORT, AND WILL HAVE SIMILARLY DIFFERENT LEVELS.

We relate to our friends on different levels, sharing deeply personal things with them and relying on them in difficult times or simply having a good time and a laugh with each other. We may have a lot in common with them, or be completely at odds with them in many ways but still value their companionship. Because our relationships with our friends are so diverse, they can mean many things to us when they appear in our dreams.

BELOW RIGHT We all need friends and companions to be a healthy part of society. We might take it for granted in our waking lives, but celebrate it in our dreams, however bizarrely.
BELOW A friendship dream doesn't have to be particularly profound, but might simply highlight the importance of a friend's presence in your life.

FRIENDS IN OUR DREAMS

We choose our friends, responding to aspects of their personality or shared experiences that we can relate to, and because of this they may sometimes be closer to us than our relatives. Friends become all the more

important if your family is not loving and supportive, and can in some cases provide a kind of substitute family. But we also befriend people with whom we share common activities or interests, and this may be the focus of the relationship rather than any deeply shared personal connection with them.

We may dream of friends for many reasons – out of love or guilt, or in order to resolve

conflict issues. If the friend you dream of is associated with an activity such as a sport or hobby, then it could be some aspect of the activity rather than the qualities of that person that you are investigating. With closer friends though, we often dream of them because they have a particular quality on which we need to focus our attention, perhaps to understand it, adopt it ourselves, or reject it.

> ### DREAM OF A FRIEND
> "I hadn't seen my friend Paul for a long time. He'd been abroad teaching and I guess I missed him. I dreamt that he was back and we were on his motorbike together. He turned to me to say something and didn't see there was a lorry coming towards us. We crashed and I woke up. I was concerned at the time because I hadn't heard from him in such a long time and I think I was worrying that something might have happened to him. I didn't know if anyone would think to let me know. On another level it could have been that I was worrying about our friendship having 'died'."

FRIENDS OR STRANGERS?

Sometimes in our dreams our friends will be transformed into unfamiliar people – so much so that we are not sure whether or not they are still the same person that we know and love. Such transformations draw our attention to the differences – so for example, if a friend who is always bouncy and jovial appears in your dream in tears, this may be a sign that you have lost touch with the positive things in life, that you need to reconnect with what makes you happy and perhaps with the people that you really enjoy being with.

LOSING A FRIEND

Such transformations may also be our unconscious mind's way of working out how we feel about relationships. Friendships are often fragile and changeable, and can easily evaporate if we don't take care of them or if our circumstances change or we develop in different ways.

Having friends can make us feel valued, and the loss of a friendship can be a heavy blow. If we do lose contact it might be no more than an accident but it still hurts, and we still feel the loss. Dreams may be a way of coming to terms with such losses, or of bringing determination to putting a friendship back on track.

LEFT A good social life is an essential part of a happy and wholesome life; it emphasizes the positive. Just as close one-to-one friendships are vital, so are groups of friends where a different dynamic exists.

BELOW LEFT We may feel the loss of friends long after they have grown away, and remember them in our dreams.
BELOW In childhood we begin to establish friendships that may last us a lifetime.

Let us learn to dream, gentlemen, and then we may perhaps find the truth.

F. A. KEKULÉ

LOVERS

FINDING AND RELATING TO A LOVER IS ONE OF THE BIG PREOCCUPATIONS OF ADULTHOOD. IF WE DON'T HAVE A LOVER WE PROBABLY WANT ONE, AND IF WE DO, WE MAY DREAM OF THEM TO REINFORCE HOW WONDERFUL IT IS TO BE IN LOVE, OR TO WORK THROUGH THE CONFLICT ISSUES THAT INEVITABLY CROP UP FROM TIME TO TIME. WE MAY DREAM NOT ONLY OF OUR CURRENT PARTNER, BUT ALSO OF PAST LOVES, OR OF PEOPLE WE ARE ATTRACTED TO BUT WHO ARE UNAVAILABLE; WE MAY EVEN HAVE FANTASIES ABOUT COMPLETELY UNATTAINABLE LOVE OBJECTS. IF WE STIFLE OUR LOVE FANTASIES OR AVOID LOOKING AT DIFFICULT RELATIONSHIP ISSUES CONSCIOUSLY, THIS MAY WELL SURFACE IN OUR DREAMS.

PAST LOVERS

It is quite common to dream of past lovers. It may mean that you are hankering after being with them again, but often it is simply your unconscious mind's way of cataloguing and storing away experiences and memories. Often it is important that you process why a relationship ended so that you don't make the same mistakes again with the next person. You may need to regain a level of self-esteem after a damaging or abusive relationship, and realize that it is alright to be just who you are.

Whatever it is you need to work through, dreams give you the opportunity to do so.

BELOW Our notions of what makes a romantic situation are often conditioned by our culture, and the standard ideals may surface in our dreams as our mind replays the images we have absorbed.

PRESENT LOVERS

Just as we dream about our friends and family on a fairly regular basis, so too do we dream of our present partner. There are many reasons for this. It can be our unconscious mind's way of reassuring ourselves that we are still loved. Even playing with notions of being unfaithful or out of love, or being cruel, hurtful, or distant may be our unconscious mind's way of checking that things are in reality alright, or of experimenting with ideas or situations without us having to try anything out for real.

Unpleasant dreams about a lover may also hint at a certain dissatisfaction in a relationship, and give you an opportunity to see how it might be to behave differently from the way you do in real life.

POTENTIAL LOVERS

Our unconscious likes to keep an open mind on what is around us. This may be unsettling if you are in a good relationship, but it is also normal and natural. Just because we dream about people we fancy doesn't mean we would do anything about it in our waking life or even that we want to. It may be just a way of experimenting with the idea without having to go there. It may also mean that unhappiness in your relationship is prompting you to see a way to finding a more satisfactory partner.

FANTASY LOVERS

The most common fantasy lovers in our dreams are real people whom we might, in an ideal world, make a play for, but with whom a relationship is at best extremely unlikely. These might be people in the public eye, like pop stars or actors, or people with whom it would be too risky to have an actual relationship, such as a boss or married person.

When we are asleep there is no limit to our imagination, and occasionally the lovers of our dreams may be really bizarre and

RIGHT Dreaming of having an affair might reflect a desire you have for the unknown.
MIDDLE RIGHT Dreaming of your love life could be a way of working through the everyday concerns of any relationship.
BOTTOM RIGHT Dreams of a romantic new affair can simply be highly enjoyable escapism.

completely unobtainable. We may also dream of breaking taboos, and have sexual dreams involving incest, or animals, for instance. Many people might be shocked by having such fantasies, and for some they may be an indication of disturbed psychological states, in which case professional help may be needed. For the most part though, our unconscious likes to slip the leash occasionally and dream of things we would simply never do – it does not mean that we would want to act these out in reality. Our dreams are a way of approaching taboos in safety, experimenting or letting off sexual steam. The meaning will depend on who we are – it could be that we are reacting to social restrictions and trying to find greater freedom of expression; in fact breaking taboos in dreams may be a liberating experience.

If you are the kind of person who worries what others think of you this may be disturbing. In our dream we may need to deal with others being judgemental, or even with our own self-condemnation, if we take unusual or inappropriate lovers. But a taboo lover may also be a companion on your journey to self-fulfilment and have qualities that you don't find elsewhere.

DREAM OF LOVERS

"I had about half a dozen dreams about my boss, who I rather fancied. They were never exactly the same, but they always involved being physically intimate, and always one or other of us was a reluctant partner in this intimacy, usually because we were afraid of discovery.

I think that this dream was my way of attaining something that in reality would never be possible. I think that the reluctance was to do with my fear that my own partner would find out that I was attracted to someone else, as well as with the fact that my boss was in reality very happily married."

PEOPLE IN OUR LIVES

IN GOING ABOUT THE DAY-TO-DAY BUSINESS OF OUR LIVES, WE ENGAGE WITH COUNTLESS PEOPLE. OUR ENCOUNTERS WITH THEM MAY BE INSIGNIFICANT OR TRIVIAL — THE FELLOW PASSENGERS YOU SIT BESIDE IN SILENCE DURING A TRAIN JOURNEY AND NEVER SEE AGAIN, THE CHECKOUT OPERATOR IN AN UNEVENTFUL VISIT TO THE SUPERMARKET — OR THEY COULD BE MORE INVOLVED, SUCH AS THE RELATIONSHIPS THAT DEVELOP WITH COLLEAGUES OR NEIGHBOURS. WE EVEN HAVE A RELATIONSHIP OF SORTS WITH FAMOUS PEOPLE WHOSE FACES ARE FAMILIAR AND WHOSE LIVES WE MIGHT READ ABOUT, BUT WHO WE MAY NEVER MEET.

RIGHT Whoever we are intimidated by in our everyday waking life is likely to "visit" us in our dreams in a similar way. If this happens repeatedly you might want to work with why this person affects you so deeply.

Any of these people could appear as characters in our dreams, whether they are playing supporting roles or taking the lead, and although at times they may simply be a necessary part of the scenery, like extras in a film, they will often appear in our dreams for a reason. Notice what role they play, as well as how you behave towards each other in the dream and how you feel during and after the interaction.

FAMILIAR FACES

In going about the routine of our lives, we get to know many faces in the places we frequent – neighbours, the people who work in the local shops or bank, the people we work and socialise with and countless others. When such people appear in a dream,

try to establish whether it is their role that seems important or their personal qualities. For instance, a neighbour may have to do with having your privacy and personal space invaded, or it may be reminding you that there are friendly people about who are always willing to help you. Dreaming of your boss is quite likely to be about issues of power, authority, status and so on, but it may be that the formal relationship you have with each other is secondary to particular personality traits that you feel he or she exhibits.

IN THE PUBLIC GAZE

Royalty and politicians, media celebrities, and others who have made it into the public arena may all feature in our dream

world. As we only know them from a distance, it will be the qualities they present to the outside world – their public face – that we probably focus on. This may be simply the fact that they have achieved fame and fortune or infamy, that they have reached the pinnacle of success on their chosen path, or it may be more specifically about what it is that they have done, or how they have gone about getting what they want. We may want their success to rub off on us, to use them as a role model, or to engage with them and turn the one-way relationship into a more personal one.

STRANGERS

What does it mean, though, if the people we encounter in our dreams are not familiar faces, but apparently arbitrary individuals? Realistically, strangers are likely to appear in our dreams as often as they do in real life, but if we do engage with them or something about them grabs our attention particularly, it may be worth looking at whether they have a particular significance to us. It may indeed be the very fact that we don't know them that is salient – we may feel uncertain or wary of them, they may behave in unpredictable or mysterious or dangerous ways, or they may be

ABOVE We might all fear crowds, especially if they are made up of strangers, but being part of a mass gathering can also be quite exhilarating.

BELOW If you dream of people who are famous in real life you are probably dreaming of what they represent to you. Alternatively, maybe there is something about fame itself that intrigues and attracts you?

ABOVE You have to look at what qualities each person brings to your dream to understand them and their impact on your life.

people we are attracted to and want to get to know. Look at the kind of interaction you have in the dream and how you feel about the contact you have with them. Obviously, a stranger chasing you with a loaded gun will bring up quite different feelings from one who shows you the way when you are lost.

In particular, see what qualities are dominant in your dream, as a stranger could present some aspect of yourself that you have yet to bring to awareness. Also look at whether the person seems to conform to any stereotypes – the tall, dark and handsome stranger who may be the lover of your dreams, or the wise old man or woman who can be your guide or angel.

Strangers who are obviously foreigners or people of different races may bring issues of difference or prejudice to the fore, and whether the person is a man, woman or child could be drawing your attention to your own personal masculine, feminine or childlike qualities that may be useful for you to focus on right now.

RIGHT Fear of getting to know people may figure in our dreams and we may seek ways to get round this in our waking life.

BELOW Work colleagues might not be our best friends but we spend a disproportionate amount of time with them, and this dominance in our lives might be reflected in our dreams.

GATHERINGS

ABOVE If you dream about a party at which you feel out of place and lonely, then analyse why this might be so. What kind of party was it? Who was there? What made you feel peripheral?
ABOVE RIGHT A gathering of lots of people in a dream can act as an indicator of how we think we fit into society.

WE GATHER BECAUSE WE ARE SOCIAL BEINGS. WE ALL BELONG TO COMMUNITIES OF VARIOUS DESCRIPTIONS – FAMILY, NEIGHBOURHOOD, WORKPLACE, NATION – AND SHARE RESOURCES, INFORMATION AND COLLECTIVE EXPERIENCES WITH EACH OTHER. WE GET TOGETHER AS A FAMILY, WE MEET COLLEAGUES TO DISCUSS BUSINESS, AND WE JOIN THOUSANDS OF STRANGERS IN PUBLIC FOR A CONCERT OR TO CELEBRATE A NATIONAL EVENT. THE GATHERINGS OF OUR DREAMS REFLECT THIS DIVERSITY, AND THEY ALSO EXPRESS HOW WE FEEL IN THE CONTEXT OF SOCIAL GROUPINGS.

HARMONY

Gatherings where people understand and support each other, and want to be together, can give a tremendous sense of belonging, and help you to feel safe, supported and sustained. If you have been struggling with such issues, dreaming of such a gathering may show that some

aspect of your personal sense of community is now being satisfied in some way.

Harmonious gatherings can also be an expression of general consensus on society's norms and values. Looking in on them from the outside, though, or being excluded from them, could indicate a rejection of these norms, or that you still have some kind of unresolved social issues – isolation, a lack of confidence about your role in your community or workplace, or uncertainty about how accepted you are by the people you value.

Unfortunately, gatherings can also be fraught with discord. Antagonism, dominance or bullying are all too present in our society and you may be using the gathering in your dream as a

metaphor for these. If this is the case, look for any signs of resolution, and also see who is present and what their dominant characteristics are. If you are involved in the dream rather than an onlooker, see what role you are playing.

ROLES

The characters in your dream gathering are probably playing particular roles, perhaps in some kind of hierarchy, or at least contributing to the group identity. They may be people you know or complete strangers – leaders and followers, teachers, diplomats trying to keep the peace and finding solutions to problems, jokers defusing situations with their humour, and the black sheep, pulling in a different direction and at odds

---

A DREAM OF REJECTION

"I was looking through a window into an expensive restaurant. All my friends were gathered together, eating and drinking and having a good time. I became very distressed at not being amongst them. Were they talking about me? Had I not been invited? Had I lost the invitation or been turned away? I banged on the window but no one could hear me. In the dream I became anxious that this was all an elaborate joke; they were pretending to ignore me, and wanted to hurt me.

I had just split up with my partner, who had been quite hurtful. I was feeling insecure and shut out, and my self-esteem had taken a blow."

with everyone. Gatherings may also speak to us of individuality, whether suppressed or given freedom. See what your own role is within the group, how others perceive you, and how you respond to that role as well as to the goals or beliefs of the group.

FORMALITY

Some people like the informality of an unstructured gathering, with its sense of companionship, freedom and youthful energy, while others prefer the more formal circumstances of an organized event. Formality can give us the safety of structure if we understand and feel comfortable with it, but it can also be intimidating if we don't feel we belong.

CROWDS

Being in a large crowd, such as at a major sports match or a New Year celebration, can be an exhilarating experience as the happy, excited mood of the people rubs off on you. But it can also be immensely stressful – even downright scary if the

crowd becomes a mob. Your relationship with the crowd in your dream is important in understanding what it means – does it give you a sense of belonging or community, a unity of purpose, a celebration, or is it threatening, in which case you may panic at the thought of getting crushed, or feel that you need to escape and be alone?

Try to relate this to your everyday life – crowd dreams could be telling you something about the amount and type of contact you are having in relation to your needs as an individual, or

about your relationship with conventions and the mass of opinions. If you tend to need time alone to recharge your batteries and aren't getting this, you may be expressing a need to get away from people for a while. Conversely you may be feeling isolated, and need people around you to make you feel human again. A crowd dream where you can't escape or where the attention of the crowd is focused entirely on you may indicate that you feel pressure to conform rather than taking your own direction in life.

ABOVE Really big crowds can be scary – but that is true in waking life as much as dreams and we shouldn't read too much into such fears.

ABOVE LEFT In a social gathering we may feel "small", which might represent that this is how we feel about ourselves in real life.

BELOW Any crowd scene can represent how we feel about being part of a group. Do you blend in or are you singled out in some way as being other than the norm? Does this please or daunt you? Do you want to conform or rebel?

CELEBRATIONS AND CEREMONIES

CELEBRATIONS CAN TAKE MANY FORMS – FROM SPONTANEOUSLY OPENING A BOTTLE OF CHAMPAGNE WITH A FEW FRIENDS, TO THE FESTIVITIES AND RITUALS OF A RELIGIOUS HOLIDAY OR A FORMAL AND HIGHLY REHEARSED NATIONAL CEREMONY. WHEN WE DREAM OF SUCH CELEBRATIONS THEY ARE LIKELY TO BE EVENTS IN WHICH WE ARE PERSONALLY INVOLVED, ALTHOUGH THE GRAND CEREMONIES OF CELEBRITIES AND LEADERS – A ROYAL WEDDING, THE FUNERAL OF A STATESMAN, OR AN INAUGURATION – MAY FEATURE TOO. OUR DREAMS MIGHT ALSO FEATURE THE SYMBOLS OF THESE CEREMONIES RATHER THAN THE GATHERINGS: A WEDDING RING, AN ELABORATE CAKE, BALLOONS OR STREAMERS MIGHT MAKE AN APPEARANCE.

ABOVE We all like to celebrate and we enjoy having our friends around us to help us party. Our dreams are no different and are to be enjoyed.
ABOVE RIGHT There are a lot of cycles in our life that need to be marked as a rite of passage. You might dream of the symbols that are linked with an event rather than the event itself.

ANTICIPATING AN EVENT

In the build-up to a major life event such as a wedding or the birth of a child, the excitement and apprehension can spill over into our dreams. In dreaming of the event our unconscious attempts to work out the fears we have around it – saying the wrong thing, forgetting something crucial, or making a fool of ourselves in some way. With weddings in particular, we are publicly entering into a social contract and may be anxious about having made the right

decision. Perhaps we are even responsible for the administration of such events, in which case it might be sheer nerves that makes us dream about them. On the positive side, such dreams give you a chance to rehearse and familiarize yourself with the event, and to anticipate things that could go wrong.

CEREMONY AS SYMBOL

Dreams of ceremonies are not necessarily about real events though. If the dream seems to spring out of nowhere we should view the ceremony as a symbol –

probably for the achievement or event that it is designed to mark, or for the feelings that the prospect of such an event evokes. So a 21st birthday party may mean that we are maturing in some way, or feeling the increased freedoms or the responsibilities of adulthood, while a wedding could be prompting us to ask ourselves about our relationship – perhaps about how committed we feel – or if we are single, to explore what kind of person we would like to settle down with.

The exact purpose or structure of the celebration may be less important than the feelings that it brings up in you, and it is worth asking yourself if you fear such events or anticipate them happily. Maybe you want to be the centre of attention but have difficulty reconciling this with being shy or modest, or perhaps you find it stressful making speeches or playing the host or hostess – roles that also put you firmly in the spotlight.

If in your waking life you are being caught up in routine and yearn to be more spontaneous, your dream celebrations could give you the opportunity to let your hair down. If you think this is true then try and create a time where you can do it for real, and live the dream.

THE PARAPHERNALIA OF CELEBRATIONS

More subtle indications or symbols of ceremonies may be present in your dream – a wedding ring standing in for the unity and commitment of marriage, a coffin for the death of a loved one, a crown or sceptre for a coronation, balloons for a festive occasion.

Clothes are an important part of many traditional ceremonies, and if in your dream the clothes are wrong for the occasion, you should look at what makes them so – wearing casual clothes to a formal occasion, for instance, may indicate your resistance to the event, or a feeling that you are not ready for it.

Gift-giving can be fraught with difficulty and evoke a strong emotional response. Look at what the gift is and how appropriate it is, the spirit in which it is given and received, who the recipient and giver are, and, if many presents are changing hands, whether they are comparable or unfairly distributed. Gifts can represent our talents and opportunities, so receiving them or being disappointed by them may hint at how you feel about broader issues in your life.

RIGHT A dream that involves a dramatic or epic celebration on a large scale might indicate that you are fretting about a real-life one you are involved with, or might be highlighting a desire you feel to live a little wildly for a time, and forget about your usual routines.
MIDDLE RIGHT By letting off steam we can release a lot of the tension that such events may induce.
BOTTOM RIGHT A symbol of celebration, such as popping corks, might be a sign or expression of happiness.

RITUAL

Many ceremonies are highly ritualized. Their stylised and formulaic nature means that everyone has a role and knows how to behave. Some rituals are extremely taxing, such as some complex and physically exacting initiation rites, which are a test of stamina, physical prowess and ultimately, of whether the initiate is ready for his or her new role.

In dreams we may try to resolve issues around a role we need to play, and so our unconscious will replay this and try to analyse our response to it. Rituals are often able to give us the comfort of predictability, but they may also be markers of change. Look at whether you are a creature of habit or if you enjoy change, and consider why change features in your dream.

DREAM WEDDING

"I was getting married and all the invitations had been sent out, but in my dream I was trying to post them and they kept turning into scorpions in my hand. The harder I tried to post them the more they fought back and tried to sting me. It was quite terrifying. Although I really wanted to get married, I had had to invite a whole bunch of people that I didn't know – my fiancé's relatives and a lot of my mother's friends and distant relations – and this was where the problem lay. I didn't want them to be there on my big day, and the dream was my way of resisting having to invite them."

SEPARATION

WHETHER IN OUR DREAMS OR IN WAKING LIFE, SEPARATION ALWAYS IMPLIES CHANGES IN OUR LIVES, LETTING GO AND STARTING ANEW. WE MAY TYPICALLY THINK OF PARTING FROM LOVED ONES, BUT THE IDEA CAN EQUALLY BE APPLIED TO LEAVING HOME, ENDING A JOB, GOING ON A JOURNEY, OR A PHASE IN LIFE DRAWING TO A CLOSE. WE MAY HAVE SADNESS AROUND THE SEPARATION AND THE LOSS OF THE LOVED AND THE FAMILIAR, BUT MANY A SEPARATION WILL INSTEAD BRING HAPPINESS, RELIEF OR EXCITEMENT AS WE LOOK AHEAD. DREAMS OF SEPARATION WILL REFLECT ALL THESE ISSUES DIRECTLY, AND CAN ALSO PINPOINT ANXIETIES WE ARE FEELING THAT AREN'T NECESSARILY OBVIOUSLY LINKED TO SEPARATION ANXIETY.

PARTING FROM OUR LOVED ONES

It is inevitable that we will at some stage be separated from people we love. As well as coping with the loss, we are afraid of being lonely and having to become self-reliant when perhaps we lack the confidence to do so, and we may give vent to these fears in our dreams. The loss of a long-term relationship is likely to affect us particularly strongly as we grow increasingly dependent on the person whose life is intimately involved with our own, although for some it may come as a relief or a blessing, a way to flourish. Either way we may use dream time to come to terms with the changes and the feelings they bring up.

LEAVING HOME

When leaving our family and home, even temporarily, we have to discover our independence, perhaps for the very first time, we need to stand on our own two feet without the support we are used to. While being a valuable and important voyage of discovery, this may also be hard to deal with.

Students often report disturbed dreams during their first year away from home. These dreams are often about their childhood, as if by dreaming it they can recapture some of the security they felt then, and are possibly missing now. Leaving the past behind in this way provides an opportunity to discover yourself as an adult, without parental constraints, and you may well use your dreams to engage with new issues and lifestyles as much as to separate from and lay to rest your childhood.

DIVORCE

Going through divorce is almost always a traumatic experience, and if you are experiencing this process your dreams will probably reflect your distress. Conflict and haggling over possessions may be scary and worrying, especially if you stand to lose a lot in the divorce. You may feel guilty about having caused your marriage to fall apart, or about not having put in enough effort to make it work – or you may blame your partner for exactly the same things. You

BELOW LEFT Separation leads to an emotion that goes very deep indeed; we may carry over such deeply held scars all of our life.
BELOW RIGHT Our dreams may reflect such feelings of separation and loneliness, and may need addressing when we are awake in order to find the source, and hopefully alleviate the pain.

DREAM OF SEPARATION

"I was at a huge fancy-dress ball, dressed in elegant clothing and a golden, feathered mask. As we danced I became aware that everyone was staring and pointing at me and making barbed, accusatory comments. I felt very vulnerable. In real life people had been very understanding and kind about me divorcing and remarrying, but this dream brought home to me what I had done. I started feeling very responsible, very accountable around the divorce."

---

may even be angry with yourself for having wasted time in the relationship. Coming to terms with our own role in a divorce is part of the long painful process to a new normality, to achieving independence for ourselves.

For many people the worst part is having to be separated from children – both the loss of their presence and guilt at abandoning them. The partner with custody may feel anxiety around having to look after them unaided. How you feel about these issues will affect the quality and content of your dreams.

Divorce is also a traumatic time for children, as they get caught in the cross-fire between the adults involved, and have immensely strong feelings that they are often not able to express or deal with fully. They may feel responsible for the split, abandoned by the parent that leaves, and in some cases fearful and unsettled around the other changes that are happening at the same time, especially if these are not explained fully to them. Children are more prone to nightmares than adults, and may be particularly affected by them at these kinds of stressful times.

MOVING ON

Long-term separation requires a major adjustment, even if there are positive spin-offs. Moving on may mean coming to terms with past issues and letting go of them, and the new start in life could provide the chance to gain or regain our freedom and sense of self. Dreams that involve objects strongly associated with your past, such as favourite childhood toys or gifts given to you by your partner, may well be showing you what you need to let go of.

LEFT Dreaming of going away somewhere, perhaps alone, might point to feelings of separation anxiety that you are trying to subdue. It might also point to a desire to get away and move on.

SEPARATION ANXIETY

At the age of around seven or eight months, a baby starts to show signs of having a strong attachment to its primary carer, and distress when separated from that person, especially when upset or ill.

At first the infant may protest by crying, but can be comforted by another. If the separation is prolonged, the child may despair, seeming calmer but becoming apathetic, no longer looking for its carer and trying to comfort itself by thumb-sucking or rocking. In the most extreme cases of separation anxiety the infant becomes detached and unresponsive, and will even ignore the return of the caregiver.

These very human reactions we have to separation might be at their most acute when we are young, but they can carry on to adulthood, and can perhaps be as traumatic and damaging. Dreams may well bring up these issues, and if you dream of them often, perhaps you need to examine where your anxieties come from.

ABOVE When it is time to move on from an unhappy relationship, the grief of separation can be hard to bear, for all concerned, even if we know it's the best course of action. If a separation you were involved with happened long ago, but is still part of your emotional baggage, you may well deal with it in dreams.

PERFORMANCE

ABOVE In our dreams, the trappings of the ballet could symbolize a desire for fame and a glamorous and "artistic" life.
ABOVE RIGHT To dream that we are taking part in a theatrical performance can reveal how we feel about being on display in the many public roles we play in life.

WHEN WE THINK OF PERFORMANCE WE PROBABLY HAVE SOME KIND OF DRAMATIC PRODUCTION IN MIND. BUT THERE IS A SENSE IN WHICH WE ARE ALL ACTORS PLAYING MANY DIFFERENT ROLES, WITH LIFE ITSELF AS A STAGED PERFORMANCE. OUR DREAMS MAY SHOW US THE STYLIZED AND PUBLIC ASPECTS OF OUR LIVES AS MUCH AS OUR PRIVATE INNER WORLDS, AND DREAMS IN WHICH PERFORMANCE FEATURES COULD WELL BE GIVING US IMPORTANT INFORMATION ABOUT THE TYPES OF ROLES WE ARE ACCUSTOMED TO PLAYING IN DAILY LIFE.

THE WORLD OF STAGE AND SCREEN

Theatrical or film productions are artificial and stylized portrayals of reality. The breakdown of a play into acts and scenes gives it a structure and predictability lacking in normal life; scenery and props are usually pared down to the essentials and actors may speak in a noticeably dramatic way for emphasis, showing and saying only what is essential to get the story or the message across. Films contain a different type of artifice, tricking us into believing that what we see is real by virtue of their detail, or abandoning any pretence at reality altogether in special effects or animation.

When theatre and film appear in our dreams, there are several aspects we need to look at.

Having a dream that features a stage or screen performance can be something of a conundrum – the entertainment is often a fictional scenario played out within the fantasy of the dream, and it can be difficult to tell where one fantasy ends and the other begins. The performers are dream characters one step further removed from reality than usual – what is being highlighted is that they are in a sense not real people even in the dream reality; they are in role, they are not what they seem. Their exaggerated movements and speech may be stressing things that we particularly need to notice. Such exaggerations, together with the fact that the actors are presenting a persona or donning a mask, may also be trying to express how ill at ease

we feel in ourselves, in that we are choosing to project an image rather than being authentic. They may also allow us to take on roles that we ordinarily cannot or will not assume – being a king or tyrant, a jester or fool, a child or even a fantasy figure.

Mime figures may be there to underscore our inability to be heard, although their exaggerated body movements could be telling us that we are more in touch with expressing ourselves physically than verbally.

PERFORMING FOR AN AUDIENCE

Asking yourself how the audience responds could give you insight into why your unconscious is using the performing metaphor. Do they like the performance, or are they chatting among

themselves, heckling or walking out? Is the performance an audition? We are constantly being assessed in our daily lives, measured against standards that may be beyond our control, and rewarded in our jobs for "performing" well. It is tempting to measure our self-worth in the light of such standards, and we will work hard towards getting a positive response. In our dreams we may be looking for this response, or may fear being challenged by others when we put ourselves forward. If the audience is ignoring you though, this could be saying something about you not getting a message across or not being noticed. If they are laughing or you are performing badly, it can reveal a fear of failure.

In a dream performance you may forget your lines – losing the thread of why you are performing, or perhaps feeling anxious or over-challenged. It may be that you are being required to say something that goes against the grain, and are having difficulty internalizing it.

CIRCUSES AND CARNIVALS

There is something intriguing about circuses and carnivals. We relish the glitz and glamour, and get an adrenalin rush from watching the daring feats of the high wire. Running away to join the circus is a classic example of escapism, and dreaming of such performances may point to a lack of adventure in our lives – we desire to be part of the show, to become a travelling player and see the world. If you do dream of a circus, look at which roles or acts dominate – the ringmaster,

lion-tamer, trapeze artist tightrope-walker, or clown, may provide clues to the issues you are trying to address.

BEING FAMOUS

In our dreams we may dream that we are playing to a packed house, that we are feted as a superstar. This may be because we desire the fame and fortune that stardom brings, or it could represent a desire for attention or recognition of our talents, or a need to be praised just for being who we are. It could also indicate something we long to achieve.

ABOVE Appearing naked in front of a laughing audience is a classic nightmare scenario. Such a dream may be about performance anxiety.
ABOVE LEFT If you have a performance dream, notice if you are a solo player or part of the chorus. Which role suits you best and what does this mean for you?

Be not afeard; the isle is full of noises,
Sounds and sweet airs, that give delight
   and hurt not.
Sometimes a thousand twangling instruments
Will hum about mine ears, and sometime voices
That, if I then had waked after long sleep,
Will make me sleep again: and then, in dreaming,
The clouds me thought would open and
   show riches
Ready to drop upon me that, when I waked,
I cried to dream again.
WILLIAM SHAKESPEARE, THE TEMPEST

CREATIVITY

EXPRESSING OUR CREATIVITY IS A VITAL PART OF THE HUMAN EXPERIENCE AND WE DO THIS IN A MULTITUDE OF WAYS, BOTH ABSTRACT AND LITERAL, THROUGH MEDIA SUCH AS MUSIC, PAINTING, HANDIWORK, POETRY, THEATRE AND DANCE. WE MAY ENGAGE IN THESE PURELY FOR OUR OWN ENJOYMENT OR FOR THE BENEFIT OF OTHERS, FOR AESTHETIC PLEASURE, PERSONAL DEVELOPMENT OR SPIRITUAL REASONS. EVEN PEOPLE WHO REGARD THEMSELVES AS LACKING IN TALENT CAN ENJOY GETTING THEIR HANDS DIRTY, SINGING IN THE SHOWER OR BOPPING TO A CATCHY TUNE. AND WE ALL SHOW TO THE WORLD ASPECTS OF OUR PERSONALITY AND OUR SENSE OF AESTHETICS IN THE CLOTHES WE WEAR AND THE WAY WE DECORATE OUR HOMES.

ABOVE In our dreams there are no restraints on our creativity. We may be able to express ourselves in ways that are not usually available to us.
ABOVE RIGHT The music in our dreams can be warm and inviting or strident and discordant. It may also tell us something about how we express our creativity.

Creative expression may be about entertainment, telling a story or giving a message, but often what we are doing is simply giving an outlet to a mood, or exploring abstract concepts of sound, colour, form or texture.

VISUAL ARTS

In graphic art we are interpreting the world around us and creating a new version that does not exist in reality. In our dreams the reality of an artwork is twice removed from that of our waking life – once by being a graphical representation (on canvas or paper) and again by being a fabrication of our unconscious. The artist may rearrange objects, distort them or place a special focus on particular features. In your dream image, distorted perspective may be an indication of too much emphasis being placed on something. Being out of focus may point to confusion, obscurity or a lack of clarity, while depth or detail in a painting can show an awareness of complexity in your life.

In creating an artwork, there is a significance or value in the subject matter, which is probably key to interpreting your dream. In photography in particular, we may be wanting to take a snapshot of life, to preserve or record something; this may suggest a yearning to hang on to things, to remember, or perhaps to dwell in the past.

In craftwork we add a practical element to creative expression, so if you dream of handcrafted items, you need to look at their function as much as their visual appearance. The presence of such objects may suggest individuality, or a strong personal touch in your environment.

MUSIC

Harmony and discord in music can signpost the same moods in your life – showing whether or not you are at one with your surroundings, your lifestyle, or the people with whom you have regular contact.

Music may be soulful, fun, energetic or restful, romantic or mathematically precise, abstract or lyrical, and these qualities may reflect your moods and feelings. Likewise, different instruments may evoke particular responses in you, or have symbolic value – playing a loud instrument such as a trumpet may enable you to be heard, while drums are used to keep in time or set the pace, and have military associations.

Orchestras, bands and choirs are useful symbols for group behaviour and co-ordination. Depending on the type of group, it may be important to blend in with the crowd, or to let your contribution stand out. Being a soloist or conductor in a dream may be about needing to "go it alone" in some venture, or take responsibility in some way that places you in a spotlight. As a soloist you may feel exposed, but you will also feel the security of having a backing group supporting and adding value to your solo performance.

Practice makes perfect – but going over something again and again can be tedious and stifle your self-expression. In your dreams it may be telling you that you are stuck in a rut or being prevented from doing other things that may be more worthwhile or enjoyable. On the positive side, though, practising is about getting things right; see how the mood of the dream ties in with your life.

CLOTHES AND DÉCOR

The way we dress and decorate our homes says a lot about our personal style – aesthetics, attitudes toward comfort, functionality, culture, prestige and so on. In our dreams and our waking lives alike, we may use colours and styles of dress in a variety of ways; to attract attention or to blend in, to impress others, to express our sexuality, or to act as camouflage. Our notions of what clothing is appropriate may be quite vague, but appearances count, and we are often judged by them.

COMMUNICATION

HUMANS ARE SOPHISTICATED COMMUNICATORS. WE HAVE EVOLVED NUMEROUS COMPLEX LANGUAGES THAT WE CAN USE TO EXPRESS THE MOST DETAILED NUANCES OF OUR FEELINGS AND EXPERIENCES. WE HAVE DEVELOPED INGENIOUS SYSTEMS OF RECORDING INFORMATION AND TRANSMITTING IT ACROSS TIME AND DISTANCE. WE ALSO COMMUNICATE WITHOUT WORDS – BODY LANGUAGE AND TONE OF VOICE SOMETIMES GIVING MORE INFORMATION THAN WHAT WE UTTER. DESPITE THIS, OR PERHAPS BECAUSE OF THE COMPLEXITY OF OUR AVAILABLE COMMUNICATION CHANNELS, WE ARE OFTEN FRUSTRATED BY MISCOMMUNICATION, A LACK OF INFORMATION, OR BY CONFUSION OVER MIXED MESSAGES.

In trying to decipher our dreams of communication, we need to pay attention to what is being said, who is saying it and in what way, as well as to what is happening at the same time. Are people shouting or whispering? Are they looking at us? Do we understand them? Is what they say compatible with what they are doing? Also consider whether the communication is happening face to face or at a distance.

BELOW Shouting in a dream can indicate that you need to speak up for yourself. Does it feel as though no one is listening to you, or that in order to make yourself heard you have to raise your voice?

SPEAKING WITH A PURPOSE

To give information and express our feelings and opinions are probably the most important reasons we communicate. But we also speak and write to change or manipulate others – to persuade them round to our point of view, by preaching or dictating to them or by using our expressions to intimidate them. We may feel uncomfortable with silence, and feel we need to fill the void with chatter to hide or deny our insecurity. And of course we talk for the pleasure of it – to make or maintain contact, or to entertain.

Get a feel for the purpose of the communication in the dream and relate it to how others speak to you in real life, as well as how you use communication yourself.

If your communication is not straightforward in the dream, try to understand why this is – perhaps you don't trust that others will accept you or agree with you if you say what you mean. If this is the case, it could be worth looking at your beliefs and checking if they are still true for you so that you can feel more confident in them or dispense with them.

LANGUAGE

We often use our dreams to try to decipher situations we don't understand, and may use language as a metaphor for our confusion – indistinct speech, riddles or foreign tongues, for example. There may be clues in the dream to why we are not communicating effectively or

---

COMMUNICATION DREAM

"I was at a noisy party where everyone was talking at the same time. I couldn't understand what anyone was saying – but I realized I could understand what they were thinking. They were thinking really rude thoughts, criticising each other's clothes, making personal comments. But their words were all jumbled as they came out. I was too embarrassed to say anything and I wanted to run out. I was afraid that someone else could understand my own thoughts – namely, that they were all animals. I woke up feeling completely lost and disoriented.

I am quite perceptive about what is going on with others, but don't always trust my intuitions and get confused by lies and subterfuge. I have also always had a problem saying what I mean and this dream was showing me my fears and frustrations around this – often I just keep quiet when I am angry with someone and really feel like being very rude. "

BELOW What would a child shouting mean in your dreams? Could it be that you are afraid to say what you think for fear of being judged as childish or rude? Or perhaps you have a child who is struggling to be heard?

LEFT We adapt the way we communicate to fit with the situation. Talking to our work colleagues is different from talking to close friends or family. How you communicate tells you a lot about how you relate to other people.

RIGHT Pay attention to body language and subtle signals as well as what is being said. Looking away while someone is talking to you could mean many different things.

understanding others, and it could be useful to see if you are in contact with people in your daily life who are hard to fathom, or who are not what they seem.

SELF-EXPRESSION

In our dreams, we may be involved in the communication process or perhaps we are onlookers seeing others interact. Watching ourselves talking can be very revealing. Are we at ease talking? Or do we find it difficult in the dream? Are we happy with what we are saying or are the words stilted and awkward? If we can't see ourselves but we are still part of the dream how do we interpret what people are saying to us? The whole secret to good

RIGHT Children love to whisper and share their secrets. Is there something private that you would like to say to someone? What is holding you back?

or accurate dream interpretation is asking questions: why are we saying this? Who are we talking to? What is their response?

SHOUTING

We cry out to make others hear, or express intensity. It is not uncommon, especially among children, to dream of shouting at the top of your voice but barely a whisper comes out. This is almost certainly to do with feeling you are not heard, that your voice doesn't count.

The meaning of every dream is the fulfilment of a wish.

SIGMUND FREUD

ENERGY AND POWER

ENERGY TAKES A MULTITUDE OF FORMS, AND IN OUR DREAMS WE ENCOUNTER IT IN THE CATACLYSMIC ERUPTIONS OF
NATURE — VOLCANOES, LIGHTNING, EARTHQUAKES — AS MUCH AS IN OURSELVES. THOUGH WE CAN EXPRESS OUR ENERGY
POSITIVELY THROUGH DANCE, SPORT AND VERY MANY OTHER ACTIVITIES, IT IS OFTEN CHANNELLED INTO AGGRESSION AND
VIOLENCE. LEARNING HOW TO CHANNEL VIOLENT, AGGRESSIVE ENERGY CAN BE A LIFELONG STRUGGLE AND WE MAY NEVER
FEEL TOTALLY CONFIDENT THAT WE HAVE IT UNDER OUR CONTROL. THE TRICK IS TO ALLOW THE FEELINGS WITHOUT
ACTING THEM OUT. IF WE SUPPRESS THEM AND TURN THEM IN OURSELVES, WE WILL DO OURSELVES HARM.

ABOVE The universe is born out of energy and our powerful responses may be much more natural than we think. To dream of nature's forces may mean that you have personal power issues to work out. How do others see you?

VIOLENT ORIGINS

Stars are born out of cosmic explosions on an unimaginable scale. Fiery forces deep within our own planet erupt as volcanoes so destructive that they can engulf entire cities and set up far-reaching tidal waves. Our entire universe was created in violent energy reactions, and continues to evolve and be transformed in this way. Even our own birth is an energetic and sometimes violent moment, a dramatic experience for mother and child alike, and the baby's first gasp of breath is a struggle.

It is not surprising, then, that we may be troubled when such images occur in our dreams. It is as though we are struggling with the violence inherent in our existence, and trying to reconcile this with the passivity and control that are in many ways esteemed in our society.

VIOLENCE CURTAILED

The struggle with energy and violence is so instinctive that it permeates our unconscious, but there are precious few socially sanctioned outlets for this in our normal waking lives. Being civilized, controlled, elegant, and sophisticated are prized at the expense of emotional expression. We still have the same instinctive reactions and negative emotions as our primitive forebears, but the "fight or flight" response is often not appropriate in our modern world. We are not allowed to be violent, no matter how incensed we are, and if we do become violent or if we have temper tantrums, we are punished, and we may feel overwhelmed, frightened and guilty at the very thought of it.

We need these dreams as safety valves for our unexpressed violence, anger and frustration, and to give us an opportunity to find alternative ways of dealing with the world so that these feelings don't well up in the first place. Sometimes our unconscious presents us with dreams of energy or violence in its raw and awesome state in order to forge a safe link between our calm outer persona and our turbulent inner self, between our civilized, rational exterior and the anger and passions that many of us tend to bottle up. In this way, having violent dreams can be a healthy experience.

The more elaborate, complex and impenetrable the mask of sophistication a person wears, the bigger the gap between feeling and response. Conversely, the more instinctual and expressive the person, the less likely they are to be troubled by such dreams, as they have already found ways of venting their energy safely in waking life.

ATTACK AND DEFENCE

If violence is a real part of your life, you may be constantly in fear and on your guard against being attacked. The trauma of even a single attack may linger for years. It can prompt feelings of anger and violence, and you may want to act these out on particular individuals. However, the feelings may be unfocused and you are simply searching for a target for them. But if you are powerless to act on your feelings in real life, you may well have these encounters in your dreams instead. You can also actively use your dreams to deal with violence in a positive way – it can be beneficial to replay the scene of an attack in your dreams in such a way that you successfully defend yourself. This can give you the strength and feeling of self-worth you need to move on.

The physical attacks of your dreams can be metaphors for many other ways in which you might be attacked. Perhaps your ideas or actions have been harshly criticized and you take this personally, or you have to bear the brunt of someone else's anger, even when you haven't deserved it. In these cases it is useful to look at the role you play – are you aggressive, taunting, or an innocent bystander, a victim of circumstances? How you respond to an attack is also important, and your dream could give you clues as to how to deal with aggression in others.

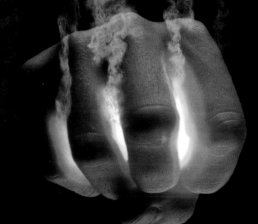

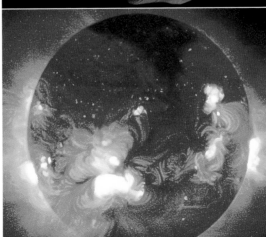

LEFT We may think ourselves cool and calm, yet our dreams may show what is bubbling beneath the surface, like a volcano waiting to erupt.
MIDDLE LEFT The tighter the grip on our natural responses, the more likely we are to "blow up".
BOTTOM LEFT Cosmic explosions are what sets the universe in motion. Powerful, violent energy is part of life – we can use this force to create or to destroy – it's up to us.

ENERGY DREAM

"I could see worlds in collision, entire galaxies erupting in fireballs and glorious colourful explosions. It was staggering, mind-blowing, and I could see how the world was made out of conflagration. It seems strange that such violent destruction can result in so much beauty.

I think that my dream was trying to tell me that I had to put more energy, more passion, into making things happen, that I had to get rid of the apathy that was holding me back."

LIVING IN THE WORLD

From the moment of our birth until we die we build up a wealth of experiences through our interactions with the "world out there". These experiences shape who we are and guide our behaviour. Often we peg our self-worth on external factors, such as our level of wealth, or our achievements or social status, and we expend a great deal of time and energy trying to gain more of these things. Our aspirations become preoccupations and we try to work out aspects of these things in our dreams. In comparing ourselves with others, we may set ourselves up for competition and conflict. But sometimes the world delivers experiences over which we have little or no control – change is part of life and accidents can happen – and our dreams can help us adjust and warn us of potential trouble.

RIGHT How we feel, how we express ourselves, how we react with the world and the people in it, combine to produce a unique experience for each of us.

AMBITIONS AND GOALS

WE ALL HAVE OUR AMBITIONS AND GOALS, HOPES AND DESIRES, AND ENJOY THE SATISFACTION OF SUCCESS WHEN WE FULFIL THEM OR DISAPPOINTMENT WHEN WE CANNOT. BUT IF WE GET TO A POINT AT WHICH WE ARE CONSUMED BY UNFULFILLED AMBITIONS, OUR UNCONSCIOUS WILL TRY TO WORK WITH THEM IN OUR DREAMS, TO SEE A WAY FORWARD OR TO ACCEPT SOMETHING DIFFERENT FOR US. IF WE FAIL TO ACHIEVE SOMETHING THAT IS REALLY IMPORTANT FOR US OR TURN OUR BACK ON A BURNING AMBITION, OUR UNCONSCIOUS WILL PRODUCE DREAMS THAT MAKE US FOCUS ON THAT GOAL AND FIND A WAY TO MAKE US SUCCEED.

REACH FOR THE SKY

We don't have to put a limit on our hopes and aspirations. If we aim for something in our dreams that we have no hope of actually achieving, it may not matter that our ambitions are unrealistic. Such fantasies can be liberating – they give us scope to stretch our self-imposed limitations, and to make possible things that might otherwise seem far-fetched.

BELOW A lock and key is a powerful symbol. Do you have an unfulfilled ambition locked away inside of you, and if so, what is the key to realizing it? Perhaps the key is just out of reach, or maybe it doesn't quite fit the lock.

If an ambition remains out of reach because we have aimed too high, however, it can cause distress. It may leave us feeling that we will never achieve what we want and make us feel like giving up. In which case we may need to take a closer look at it, at the symbolic value of what we are failing to achieve. In asking questions about a dream symbol we may find out why we are being so unrealistic and aiming too high. We can gain more insight into what makes us set ourselves up for failure and find ways to set ourselves more realistic targets.

STUMBLING BLOCKS

There may well be valid reasons for not achieving an ambition – perhaps deep down inside you know that achieving it may not be as beneficial as you might like. For example, you may have been offered a fantastic job that will mean moving abroad, but because it offers you things you really want you may well be blinded to the attendant

BELOW To dream that you are doing a tedious, repetitive task may suggest that your goals are set too low. Perhaps it's time to get your ideas in order, rather like the bottles on the assembly line, and review your ambitions.

disadvantages or dangers – your family doesn't want to go, your parents would miss you, the company is not as stable as you want to believe, or your expertise isn't up to a high-powered job.

These unconscious realizations may manifest themselves as something stopping us in our dreams. This could be a locked door or a fence that stops us going along a certain path. A guard is another common symbol; this is usually someone impassive, anonymous and immovable who bars our way. If we don't find a way past the obstacles in our dream, then perhaps we ought to reconsider our ambition. But if we do manage to get through, this may give us a clue as to what our best course of action should be. We can relate it to our waking lives and find a way of achieving our goals and ambitions. On the other hand it may show us that although achieving our goal is possible, it is going to be very difficult, so perhaps it would be better to scale back or drop what it is that we are after.

SYMBOLIC IMAGERY

Literal images of goals and targets may appear in our dream to symbolize our personal ambitions. Games involving scoring goals, or aiming accurately for a small target, such as golf or darts, can show us how focused we are and whether or not our ambitions are fixed or keep changing. As well as looking at the nature of the

goal, notice whether the game in your dream is a team effort, and if so who is helping or opposing you, or whether you are solely responsible in some way.

THE SCALE OF OUR AMBITIONS

Remember that our goals may be anything from major lifelong ambitions to relatively trivial targets, such as tidying up a messy cupboard, so if the dream does appear obviously to be about goals or ambitions but you are unable to see immediately what it could be referring to, think laterally about the nature of what you might be trying to process. Even small goals may take on greater significance than they deserve if they link into personal hang-ups – if your mother was always pestering you to tidy your room when you were a child, for instance, you may feel obsessed, angry or resistant about tidying up. Being goal oriented may also mean that you will tend to turn ordinary activities into goals, into something you can check off a list, rather than just being a regular part of daily life.

Dreams are a dress rehearsal for life. ALFRED ADLER

ACHIEVEMENT AND SUCCESS

FROM THE MOMENT WE TAKE OUR FIRST BREATH, WE ARE DRIVEN TO ACHIEVE. FOR INFANTS, LEARNING TO EAT, CRAWL, STAND UP, WALK AND SPEAK IS A MATTER OF SURVIVAL, AND OUR NATURAL INSTINCT TO ACHIEVE THESE THINGS IS SUPPORTED BY PARENTAL ENCOURAGEMENT. AS WE GROW UP, OUR ACHIEVEMENTS BECOME MORE COMPLEX AND THE WAY WE MEASURE SUCCESS CHANGES. AT SCHOOL AND COLLEGE WE ARE ENCOURAGED TO SUCCEED ACADEMICALLY AND WHEN WE ENTER THE WORLD OF WORK, ACHIEVEMENT IS LINKED WITH JOB SATISFACTION. OUR DREAMS CAN SHOW US WHERE WE FEEL PROUD OF OUR ACHIEVEMENTS AND POINT TO AREAS WHERE WE FEEL DISSATISFIED AND UNFULFILLED.

MAKING IT

You may dream of winning an award or prize of some sort to mark your achievement. Or perhaps someone claps you on the back and says "well done". You may dream that you score a goal or play the winning hand or captain your favourite team, or that you suddenly have acquired a new skill, such as being able to play the violin. Maybe you have suddenly become famous and are signing autographs and giving

BELOW What would a running child mean in your dreams? Are you still that racing child eager for success or do you have some growing up to do before you make it?

press conferences. Your dream may even give you a halo, a set of wings, a new power such as flying or walking on water. Such dreams could suggest that you are proud of your achievements. Alternatively, they may point up a glaring mis-match between your dream self and your actual experience. Perhaps you need to define what "making it" would mean for you and find an arena in which to express yourself.

SUCCESS IN OTHERS

In your dream, it may even be someone else and not you who is successful. Consider how you feel towards this person. You may feel warm and supportive and full of encouragement or you may feel jealous and competitive. But it is also worth bearing in mind that the other people in our dreams may also actually be displacements of ourselves.

Dreaming of someone else's success could be as close as we can get to admitting our own success, to being told we've done well and to knowing that we're alright. If you know the person who is successful in your dream, try to understand what they represent to you, and see what it is about their character or what they are doing that makes things go well. This may show you how you can be more successful.

TEAM EFFORT

Sometimes we dream of the success of a group – our favourite football team winning the cup or scoring lots of goals, a country finally negotiating peace after being at war for many years, or the company we work for expanding so we get that pay rise we wanted. In this kind of scenario, the group effort may be key to understanding the meaning of your dream – perhaps it is a hint not to try to do everything yourself if you want to achieve your goals, or to enable you to place some trust in the people who may help you on your way.

ACKNOWLEDGEMENT

Part of our drive for success is rooted in our desire to be acknowledged, and to be noticed and admired. Dreams of parents, friends and partners watching and cheering you on may demonstrate that you feel valued as a person, while being feted by the public, such as being cheered by a crowd or carried on their shoulders, may show a desire for public recognition. Perhaps you would like the world to see and acknowledge your status and everything that you have achieved. Prizes and medals may indicate that you need a constant reminder of your successes, and

RIGHT A silver cup is a symbol that most of us associate with successful achievement. Seeing it in a dream may mean we would like to win a prize for something that we feel proud of doing.

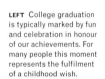

ABOVE How does it feel to be successful? Life's peak moments can pass us by in a blur because we are so caught up with speed and wanting to win.

that you are not able to rely on your own awareness of your abilities to realize what you are worth. The appearance of any of these things does, however, mean that you know within yourself that you are worthwhile and that you deserve some level of recognition.

LEFT College graduation is typically marked by fun and celebration in honour of our achievements. For many people this moment represents the fulfilment of a childhood wish.

DREAM OF SUCCESS

"I was riding in a limousine along a street lined with cheering fans; as it was a convertible, they could get really close. I looked really cool and well dressed. All these people were cheering and whistling as if I had done something really amazing. I didn't know what I had done, but it felt really good! When I woke up I thought it would be cool to be recognized like that, and since then I've been sending demos off to radio stations and record companies. I don't know if I'll get anywhere, but it feels worthwhile – if I have any moments of doubt I just have to remember that dream to spur me on. I can't wait for it to be real, to be cheered by real fans."

RIGHT When can we say we have finally reached the summit? Even in our dreams it may be difficult to plot such an exact moment, although there are times in everyone's life when we should feel proud of ourselves. When did you last feel on top of the world?

BELOW It is not always easy to measure our achievements and we may feel the need for some kind of external validation, such as more money or a certificate, to increase our self-esteem.

JOBS AND WORK

WE SPEND A LOT OF TIME AT WORK, AND EARNING A LIVING IN A SATISFYING WAY IS ONE OF LIFE'S GREATEST CHALLENGES. IT IS ONLY NATURAL FOR WORK TO OCCUPY AN IMPORTANT PART OF OUR DREAM LIFE. BUT WORK IN A DREAM IS NOT ALWAYS ABOUT AN ACTIVITY THAT WE DO — WE ENCOUNTER PEOPLE WHO ARE OPERATING IN THEIR WORK ROLES ALL THE TIME, AND OUR COLLEAGUES MAY ALSO FIGURE PROMINENTLY. ENJOYING OUR WORK MAY BE REFLECTED IN POSITIVE, HAPPY DREAMS ABOUT IT, OR DREAMS IN WHICH WE GRAPPLE WITH INTERESTING REAL-LIFE PROBLEMS THAT WE CAN'T BEAR TO LET GO OF EVEN IN OUR SLEEP. SOMETIMES STRESS AND ANXIETY RELATED TO WORK WILL ALSO SURFACE.

ABOVE When work seems like drudgery, it could be time to review your career options.
ABOVE RIGHT Your dreams may reflect what it is you really want to do with your life.
ABOVE FAR RIGHT You might dream about the work of others rather than yourself. Is this a reflection of someone in your life who has authority over you? Is the authority justified or does it worry and frustrate you?

WORK AND EMOTIONS
Unfortunately, for many people work means stress, boredom, frustration, unhappiness, and anger; we may feel unchallenged or abused or taken for granted, and our dreams may well reflect such feelings. We may say or do something extreme in the work environment of our dream, and wake worrying that we might act out such stuff in real life. But the point of these dreams may in fact be to address just that possibility – to let off steam in the safety of our dreams so that we don't cause a scene at work.

Work dreams may seem fairly realistic, but at other times our unconscious will create a memorable scenario to draw our attention to what is bothering us.

Dreaming of work might also be symbolic of more general issues, such as survival or money, how to rise to a challenge or deal with pressure, feelings of inadequacy, subservience or anger and a myriad other experiences.

PEOPLE AT WORK
We do not always dream about our own jobs, however. As in our daily lives, we are constantly in contact with or seeing images of others as they go about their work, from shopkeepers to bank managers, newsreaders to teachers, factory workers to artists and chefs. We probably hold countless attitudes about those roles – wishing we could be in the other person's shoes, or thanking our lucky stars that we

aren't. We may admire people for their work, thinking that they must be clever or talented or courageous to do what they do, and envy the satisfaction or prestige or fame that goes with their wonderful-looking jobs. Or perhaps we hate the idea of the tedium or lack of status of a particular job, the confinement of an office or the uncertainty of contract work.

Engaging with strangers in our dreams may often be in the context of their occupation, and our attitude to that occupation. Teachers, bosses and policemen, for instance, tend to be authority figures, and your experiences in real life will be crucial in forming your attitude to such figures. As a child, did you have teachers who

picked on you, inflicted corporal punishment or made you feel stupid? Or did they inspire you, understand and encourage you, satisfy and nurture your curiosity or give you a love of reading?

People at work can symbolize many different things. To dream of a cleaner, for instance, may indicate you need to get your house in order and to "clean up", while an accountant might suggest that you take stock of your affairs and get organized. An artist on the other hand may suggest that you need to relax your attitudes and think laterally or engage more with your intuitive, creative side.

COLLEAGUES

We spend much of our waking lives with colleagues, so it is not surprising if we dream about them. Often their function in our dreams will be similar to that of friends, in that they will appear because they have particular characteristics that we need to address. But in many cases their role will be more important – bosses in particular may bring up important issues relating to authority, power and status.

RIGHT Some workplaces are big and imposing. Dreaming that you are in such a building can make you feel small and insignificant, especially if you are alone.
MIDDLE RIGHT Sometimes it feels as though you are just going round and round and not getting anywhere. Your dream may be showing you that progress does not always follow a straight line.
BOTTOM RIGHT Repetitive work is not necessarily boring. Your dream may be a reminder to take a pride in all your endeavours and know that every job has its part to play.

WORKPLACES AND RESOURCES

If you find in your dream that you are unable to do things because the equipment you have for doing your job is inadequate or the work environment is unpleasant, it could be saying something general about your material wellbeing or your ability to get things done.

Do you feel that you get what you want out of life, or that there are constantly obstacles to what you want to do? Our physical environment can have a major impact on our emotional state, so it is worth noting how you feel about the workplace of your dream as much as what you are doing or the people you are with.

WORK DREAM

"I was due to go on my first business trip, to the headquarters of a major bank. In my dream I arrived at their imposing building and went up in the lift. The doors opened directly into the boardroom, which contained a massive table surrounded by middle-aged men in suits. As they looked up I realized to my horror that, although I was wearing a smart black jacket and smart black shoes, I was also wearing a frilly, homemade nightdress.

This dream was clearly to do with not feeling confident in myself or comfortable in the imposing and masculine setting of the bank. I was afraid that I couldn't pull off the meeting successfully, that I would somehow make a serious gaffe, be intimidated or not be taken seriously."

SPORTS AND GAMES

FUN, PHYSICAL WELLBEING AND A SENSE OF ACHIEVEMENT ARE JUST SOME OF THE REASONS WE TAKE PART IN SPORTS AND GAMES. THEY ALSO PROVIDE A WAY OF ENGAGING WITH OTHER PEOPLE IN A VERY ACTIVE WAY, AS BOTH TEAM MEMBERS AND OPPONENTS, AS WELL AS HELPING US RELEASE STRESS AND CHANNEL OUR AGGRESSIVE IMPULSES. FOR ARMCHAIR SPORTSMEN OR TEAM SUPPORTERS AT SPORTS FIXTURES, THERE IS THE EXCITEMENT AND CAMARADERIE OF WATCHING A FAVOURITE TEAM OR FAVOURITE SPORT IN ACTION. WITH THESE DREAMS, WE NEED TO ASK OURSELVES ABOUT THE SPORT WE ARE ENGAGED IN, HOW WE PLAY, AND OUR MOTIVATIONS AND FEELINGS, AS WELL AS WHAT ACTUALLY HAPPENS.

GAMES PEOPLE PLAY

The various forms of sporting and leisure activities represent many qualities. For instance, a violent rugby match may have more to do with aggression and teamwork than the leisurely, non-contact style of a round of golf, while an intellectually absorbing chess game is mainly concerned with strategy and has almost nothing to do with physicality. There are also many games that we play simply for fun, such as beach volleyball or the role-playing games of a child's make-believe world where the rules are made up as they go along.

SUBLIMATION OF AGGRESSION

For many people, sports and games provide a much-needed way of working through aggression and frustration. The positive effects of strenuous physical activity on the emotions are well documented, and in some sports, hitting or kicking a ball can be a great substitute for doing the same to someone who has made you very angry! By analysing how we feel and how we are behaving and reacting to others in our dream, we can try to uncover the real cause of our aggressive feelings and work through them or lay them to rest.

OPPONENTS

Who are you playing with and against in your dream? Your opponents may be real people, they may represent abstract qualities – luck, fate, challenges, opposition – or they may be an aspect of yourself that you are at odds with.

Often opponents will be people with whom we are having some kind of power struggle or conflict. Who wins is often a vital question, as it could indicate what is actually happening in an important relationship, what you wish for or what you fear. Look at how seriously you take the game – you may simply want to put your opponent in their place, to hurt them badly, or even to eliminate them altogether.

TEAMS

Being part of a team gives a great sense of belonging, going beyond our individual needs to unite in a common goal. Teams give us a place, a role, a bond with others. They show us who our friends are and how much we rely on others to achieve our goals. Sports teams can also be a

BELOW What sport are you pursuing in your dream? Is it something that you normally do? **BELOW RIGHT** What are the items of equipment associated with a game or sport? Perhaps these have a significance in your dream. **BELOW FAR RIGHT** Dreams of running a race may raise issues of winning and losing in your life.

metaphor for other social groups in our lives, such as the family or work team, and looking at how they pull together and the roles people play may be significant in relation to these units.

COMPETITION AND RESULTS

Competition is an all-pervasive feature of our society, and the games we play are often about proving who is best, who has the greatest talent, skill or intellectual ability. For many people, getting ahead gives a feeling of self-worth that they may otherwise be not capable of feeling. Winning or losing a dream game could be crucial to how you see yourself – your confidence or assertiveness, what your role is in relation to your opponent or your team, or how you view your skills and talents. If you have a relationship

where you are constantly racking up points against each other, this may show up in your dreams as a competition of some sort.

PLAYING THE GAME

Cheating or rule-breaking may hint at an unfair situation in your life, or one in which someone is being underhand with you. Rules may be about social restrictions, so check whether you know what the rules of the game are, and whether it is you or someone else who is breaking them.

COMPETITIVE DREAM

"I was playing chess against my father, using life-sized pieces. Although we laughed and joked as we played, I knew we were playing for big stakes and this created an underlying seriousness, a feeling of menace that affected my game. Behind the laughter I was in crisis: I wanted to win so badly it hurt, and I wanted to hurt him, even kill him, by winning. This was a very powerful dream and it made me realize that I had a lot to work out about my relationship with my father. We have always been competitive, and he is also very pushy, expecting me to do well, earn well, and drive myself as hard as he does. I've always felt I have a lot to live up to and although I don't like it, I've always done what he wants. In this dream I realized that I didn't have to be dominated by him forever, but that I would need to be more assertive for that to happen."

MONEY

WHAT DOES MONEY REPRESENT TO YOU? WHEN IT COMES TO WORKING WITH OUR DREAMS THE ANSWER TO THIS IS CRUCIAL. MOST PEOPLE WILL ACKNOWLEDGE THAT THEY WANT IT, AND ALMOST CERTAINLY THAT THEY NEED IT, BUT BEYOND THAT OUR RESPONSES CAN DIFFER MARKEDLY FROM PERSON TO PERSON. PERHAPS YOU SEE IT AS A MEANS TO AN END, OR AN END IN ITSELF; MAYBE YOU THINK THAT IT REPRESENTS FREEDOM AND CAN LIBERATE PEOPLE, OR YOU MIGHT SEE IT AS AN ENSLAVER. OUR OWN AND OTHERS' ATTITUDES TO MONEY IN REAL LIFE WILL INEVITABLY BE REFLECTED IN OUR DREAMS; HOW MUCH THERE IS, WHERE IT CAME FROM AND WHAT WE DO WITH IT WILL ALSO BE SIGNIFICANT.

ASSOCIATIONS

Money is generally said to point to opportunity and reward or power. Some associate it with relationships, so in this way receiving it is linked to the birth of a child, finding it could suggest benefiting from a prosperous marriage, and wasting or losing it may mean that you are wasting your love on someone unworthy.

Using a Freudian model, hoarding money implies anal fixation. Money can also be used to represent resources in general. Bear in mind that it could be denoting riches in terms of time, energy, knowledge, love and so on, rather than material or monetary wealth. Consider your relationship with these other resources too and think about how rich or poor you feel.

Some of these money associations may make sense to you and help you to understand what your dream is really about. If not, you will need to dig a bit deeper, and really try to understand what money means to you on a much more personal basis, and thus what it symbolizes in your dream.

BELOW Think about what money may symbolize to you. Love? Security? Status? Freedom? Success? It is important to understand your own reactions before you interpret your dreams on the subject.

WHAT MONEY CAN BUY

It is what we can have and do with money – as well as what is unavailable to us if we don't have it – that gives it much of its value. We may feel that it gives us the freedom to have the things we want, including leisure time and opportunities to see and do things that aren't free. But having acquired wealth, we may feel burdened by our possessions and afraid of losing them, and we may also feel trapped by the need to carry on generating it.

Dreams of money may be simple wish fulfilment, or we may find they show us how to get it, the frustrations of not having it, or the fear of being suddenly deprived of it. But we can also use money dreams as a more general symbol for greed and materialism, opportunity, the loss of something we value, or even of being trapped.

STATUS AND POWER

Money can convey power and status. We can add to this the idea that money is a reward, so having or not having it differentiates us further and makes us feel more or less worthwhile as people. These issues may well bother us, keying in to our inherent sense of self-worth, and dreams of money – especially in relation to a salary

or wage – can be about this idea of our value, of how much we are being appreciated.

GIVE AND TAKE

If you are hoarding or counting money in your dream, you may be afraid that it will run out or be feeling insecure; similarly putting

it in the bank may be to do with security,. Holding on to money can also represent holding on to ideas, rather than putting them into action. If you are giving money away, do you do so with a spirit of generosity, or because you simply want to get rid of it? Spending or giving money freely can imply a certain faith or trust in things working out, that your own needs will always be met, and this can be tremendously reassuring if you normally worry about such matters.

Owing or being owed money in a dream could be a worry about literally being burdened by debt. Looked at in a broader sense though, ask yourself if you are concerned about being indebted to someone in a more general way – perhaps they have done you a favour or you feel guilty about asking for help. You may also feel taken advantage of.

TYPES OF MONEY

The form the money takes in your dreams may hold another layer of significance. Cash is readily available, and whether it

comes in the shape of coins or notes may indicate how much you value whatever it represents to you. An IOU or cheque may signify indebtedness, delayed gratification or uncertainty around whether you will be repaid; gift vouchers may suggest generosity, but may also hint that whatever they represent has some specific value or limitation placed on it. If you dream of foreign money it could be that you are unsure of the value of something.

ABOVE Do you associate money with particular people in your life?
ABOVE LEFT If you dream of gambling in association with money perhaps you are feeling financially insecure?
ABOVE FAR LEFT To dream about saving will mean different things to different people.

BELOW Precious gold nuggets and ingots symbolize great wealth. If they appear in a dream look at the context to see what they mean.

MONEY DREAM

"I was being asked to pay admission to the cinema. I had brought a single coin in my pocket, but couldn't find it anywhere – it had slipped through a hole. A terrible grief washed over me. I couldn't understand why it should pain me so much – it was only a trip to the cinema after all.

This dream was about having given up a successful career in film-making to devote myself to my family. My children were growing up and needed me less and less, and I was aware that in the meantime my precious career seemed lost. Although I didn't regret having had children, I was experiencing pain at having let my career slip through my fingers."

AUTHORITY AND DISCIPLINE

WHEN WE ARE CHILDREN OUR PARENTS AND TEACHERS TELL US WHAT WE CAN AND CAN'T DO. OFTEN THE AIM OF THIS IS TO TEACH US SOCIAL NORMS OR PREVENT US FROM HURTING OURSELVES. BUT MUCH OF THE AUTHORITY THAT ADULTS WIELD OVER CHILDREN IS TO DO WITH THEIR OWN INTERESTS — PROTECTING THEIR BELONGINGS, THEIR NEEDS, THEIR FEELINGS. AS ADULTS WE MIGHT ASSOCIATE PUNISHMENT WITH AN ELEMENT OF UNFAIRNESS AND IMPOSITION, OR WE MIGHT SEE IT AS SOMETHING WE DESERVE MORE OF. AUTHORITY FIGURES MIGHT BE SEEN AS UNJUST AND REPRESSIVE, BUT WE MAY ALSO PRODUCE THEM IN OUR DREAMS AS A SYMBOL OF SECURITY, OR OF WISDOM AND GUIDANCE.

In punishing a child the stated aim may be to teach the child what is safe or dangerous, right and wrong, and acceptable or unacceptable, but from time to time, punishment may be meted out that has nothing to do with a child having done something "bad", but rather with an adult venting frustration or simply being a bully, and this can be frightening and perplexing.

INNER DISCIPLINE

When we grow up our attitude to authority and punishment can be quite complex, so we may use dream time to unravel how we feel, especially if we come up against problematic authority figures, moral dilemmas or confusion in our daily lives. As adults, there usually isn't the same sort of immediate authority

figure standing over us like when we were children. Hopefully we will have developed an innate sense of what is right and wrong; we have a greater understanding of the consequences of our actions and are able to exercise our own judgement and discretion. Laws and the fear of punishment keep most of us in check where our self-discipline or morality may otherwise slip.

Over the course of our lives, our unconscious takes note of the countless rules and injunctions laid down in our early years by parents, teachers and prefects; as we grow older we become aware of other authority figures and bodies of law, and we notice how others respond to these as well. We also develop subtle ways of avoiding punishment and guilt. If we are acting in a way our

unconscious thinks doesn't suit our own interests, it will let us know through the symbolism of our dreams by creating a figure who can tell us how to behave.

PUNISHMENT

Our experience of punishment and how we respond to it is also a personal one. Being given detention at school may have been immensely shameful and humiliating for one person, but for another merely irritating or even a fairly normal occurrence. Indeed for some, being punished by "the establishment" establishes "street cred". In some societies beating a child for a wrongdoing may be considered a normal – even essential – part of their growing up, whereas in others it is anathema, and thought to be damaging. So to understand what

BELOW RIGHT As children we soon learn who is in charge and this may be reflected in our dreams. Who was the dominant authority figure when you were growing up?
BELOW How we respond to authority in any of its smallest forms is very revealing. Even a red traffic light can trigger issues around sticking to or breaking the rules.

RIGHT Laws and the fear of being punished keep most of us in check. This can make us feel that we are under surveillance or living in a police state, and may show up in our dreams. Who is watching you?

punishment means in your dreams may mean coming to terms with how you view it in real life. Does it make you feel angry, guilty, submissive or humiliated, or does withstanding it give you strength? Did you feel you deserved it? If you are meting it out, look hard at what you were feeling and who you are punishing. Note what the punishment is, how severe it is, and if you feel it is deserved. Also try to discover why it is being meted out, and what it achieves.

REBELLING

What if you don't want to be told what to do, or you believe that an authority figure is wrong or evil, or you feel that someone is acting in an authoritarian way towards you but shouldn't? If your boss tells you to forge a signature or your partner dominates or controls your

relationship, you may well feel resentful but unable to be assertive or to inject a reasonable balance. If you can't deal with the matter in an adult way, you may represent the dominant person in your dreams as a teacher or parent. Your powerlessness may reduce you to a small child or even animal, or your resentment may manifest in your dreams as a symbolic rebellion or mutiny.

AUTHORITY FIGURES

The area of our lives in which we are having difficulties, together with our upbringing, social standing, beliefs and cultural background, will determine who the authority figure in our dream will be. It may be a police officer if we are in danger of breaking

the law, or a priest if religious or moral principles are at stake. For others it might be a judge, lawyer, traffic warden, headteacher, monarch, even a god. Each of these represents something different, and we need to look at what they mean to us to find out what their presence in our dream means.

> ### AUTHORITY DREAM
>
> "In my dream I couldn't find my car keys, and realized my wife had hidden them. I asked her for them back but she said no, it wasn't my turn to drive the car. She told me to go and stand in the corner for being naughty, that I'd asked for the keys before she had told me to. I stood in the corner and she was standing behind me flicking my ears and telling me I had been naughty and deserved to be punished. I felt like a small boy and was really seething inside but I couldn't do anything. In real life my wife is in control, and I guess I hate this."

BELOW LEFT Sometimes we may wonder who is pulling the strings. Our dreams can show us who is running the show and what we can do to take more charge of our lives.
BELOW It is easy for an adult to overpower a child when he wants to assert his authority. This can create a fear of authority, which we carry as adults.

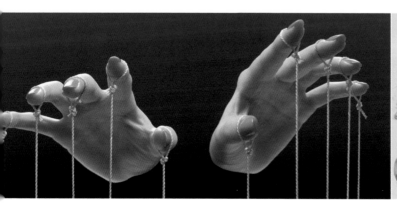

Wars and Battle

ABOVE Many societies recognize warrior values such as strength and courage. When a warrior appears in your dreams it may mean that you need to develop such qualities. **ABOVE RIGHT** If images of war haunt our dreams we may feel very shocked or disturbed. But being in conflict is something that can happen in personal relationships or you may be fighting with yourself.

ALTHOUGH NOT MANY OF US WILL HAVE ACTIVELY PARTICIPATED IN ARMED COMBAT, THERE IS ALWAYS A WAR BEING FOUGHT IN SOME PART OF THE WORLD THAT WE ARE AWARE OF AND PERHAPS CONCERNED ABOUT. ACTS OF INTERNATIONAL TERRORISM UNSETTLE US AND MAKE US ANXIOUS FOR OUR SAFETY, OR PERHAPS WE LIVE IN A NEIGHBOURHOOD BESET BY GANG CONFLICT. OUR FEARS OF DEATH AND DESTRUCTION, INJURY, INVASION, INSECURITY, HELPLESSNESS, SORROW, PAIN AND LOSS RISE TO THE SURFACE, AND IN TIMES OF WAR OUR DREAMS CAN BECOME EVEN MORE VIVID.

THE ENEMY

Dreams of war don't necessarily reflect the belligerent or defensive attitude of a nation – they are quite likely to be more to do with acting out our own private battles. Our dreams reflect why we are under attack or what we are fighting for.

Identifying the enemy and understanding what they symbolize is crucial in analysing such a dream, as is the matter of which party is the aggressor. If the war represents a power struggle or a fight over scarce resources, it is also important to understand who has the upper hand. Are you retaliating for something that has already happened, or defending yourself against an ongoing attack? Perhaps you feel invaded by a particular person or circumstance in your life, and you have to defend your "territory", or someone is bullying or abusing you and you are too frightened to fight back in real life.

It may even be that you are simply recognizing the need to be more assertive, or that you are not being taken notice of and realize that spectacular action is required in order to get through.

ALLIES AND FIGHTING STRENGTH

We also need to ask questions about our own side – whether we are fighting alone or have allies, and if so how organized and how strong they are, and what kind of tactics they use. Our own attitude and that of the people around us is important. We may feel passionately that there is a lot at stake, and that this is a war worth waging, but equally the war could be something we are forced to participate in against our will; for a pacifist, it may be complete anathema. If others seem keen, but we are not, then this could indicate some disharmony with the people we do things with in a team of some kind. A formally organized army may well bring up feelings around authority and discipline,

---

DREAM OF WAR

"I was a soldier stalking an unseen enemy, a sort of sniper in a ruined city. I followed every move of the enemy, but knew that although I was the hunter I was going to get killed. Sure enough, as I turned a corner this faceless soldier let me have it. I was blown away.

For me this was about acting aggressively because this is expected of me as a man. As a sniper I may have seemed to have the advantage, but actually I was just hiding because I was afraid that I would eventually meet my match, and didn't know when or where that might happen, or who it might be."

leadership and obedience. Being armed could signify being ready for the fight – either feeling aggressive or being prepared.

If you are not evenly matched against your opponents, though, and using bows and arrows against an enemy with firepower, you will feel the disadvantage keenly. Depending on the exact nature of the dream, actually using arms may signify either being in control of a situation or having lost it.

THE SETTING

On land, on the sea or in the air, in a jungle or a desert, or even in the streets of a city – the terrain will suggest the underlying mood of the conflict. Particularly note whether you have a clear view, and if you know where you are going, as these can indicate some clarity on the issues over which you are at war.

PERSONAL BATTLES

War in a dream is often a metaphor for the personal battles and struggles of our everyday lives. If in your dream you are

being invaded, try to feel whether there is something or someone who is invading your space. If you are waging war in your dreams, then look at conflict situations in your waking life, and whether people you have a lot of contact with are being aggressive or overbearing.

BELOW War is also about its after-effects, and the devastation that follows in its wake.

If you are defeated or outmanoeuvred in your dream, see whether you are feeling defeated or manipulated over a real issue. Also note what you are feeling in the dream – fear, anger, sadness, confusion or rebellion may all play a part and relate to events in your life. If you can identify these situations and feelings you are more likely to be able to take appropriate action.

ABOVE In our dreams, the landscape in which the conflict takes place may give us a clue as to what the dream is about.
ABOVE LEFT There are many ways of symbolizing victory. What would it look like in your dreams?
ABOVE FAR LEFT The battle for resources is one of the reasons we humans go to war.

TROUBLE AHEAD

OUR DREAMS OFTEN DROP HINTS ABOUT HOW THE FUTURE MAY UNFOLD. ALTHOUGH THERE ARE OCCASIONS WHEN PEOPLE HAVE HAD DREAMS THAT SEEMED TO PREDICT SPECIFIC EVENTS, MORE USUALLY THE INFORMATION IN OUR DREAMS IS OUR UNCONSCIOUS MIND'S WAY OF TRYING TO ALERT OUR ATTENTION TO THINGS THAT MAY HAPPEN IF WE CARRY ON DOING WHAT WE'RE DOING, RATHER THAN PREDICTING THAT SOMETHING IS DEFINITELY GOING TO HAPPEN. SYMBOLS OF WARNINGS IN OUR DREAMS MAY BE AS SIMPLE AS THE WARNINGS WE RECEIVE IN DAILY LIFE. SUCH DREAMS CAN BE TRICKY TO INTERPRET AS IT MAY NOT BE CLEAR WHAT THE SYMBOLS RELATE TO.

WARNINGS

In general, the modern Western view is that our dreams exist primarily as a means of communication between our unconscious and conscious selves. Other cultures, however, have believed that our dreams can tell us of impending trouble and have used the information as a basis for their subsequent actions. There is plenty of anecdotal evidence to support this view. Famously, the American president Abraham Lincoln dreamed of his own death, which to the great interest of dream analysts ever since, he left an account of.

Unfortunately Lincoln did not heed the warning the dream contained, and met with an early demise. Still, we have no proof that it was not mere coincidence, or evidence of what must be a common fear among those with a high political profile. While dramatic dreams such as Lincoln's are the ones that seize our imagination, part of our fascination with predictive dreams lies in how we are able to foresee such an event, and what, if anything, we should do about it. If we were to alter our behaviour to protect ourselves from the possibility that every negative dreamt experience will come true, our lives would be blighted by paranoia and become an impossible nightmare.

READING THE CLUES

Our dream warnings may be less clear than a scenario of impending death, though. More typically, the warnings we receive in dreams will be of conditions or future events of which we are already aware but are trying to ignore, or that we could foresee if we took the trouble or the courage to notice the signs. Our lives are filled with stimuli, so it is not always possible to notice everything consciously, but these dreams allow us to become aware of the fact that we are not seeing or hearing something that we need to. In fact our unconscious may remind us of this by literally making us blind or deaf in our dreams, or by giving vivid or exaggerated pictures – either symbolic or literal – of our situation.

DANGER SIGNS

In real life, dangers are often helpfully signposted using fairly universal symbols. Traffic signs warn of hazards on the road, the

LINCOLN'S DREAM

It is easy with hindsight to interpret a dream as a precognition. These are the words of Abraham Lincoln as he recounted his dream in which he had foreseen his own death at the hand of an assassin.

"There seemed to be a death-like stillness about me. I heard subdued sobs, as if many people were weeping. I feel that I left my bed and walked downstairs. I went from room to room. No living person was in sight, but the same mournful sounds of distress met me as I passed along. I kept on until I arrived at the East Room, where I met with a sickening surprise. Before me was a catafalque, on which rested a corpse wrapped in funeral vestments. Around it were guards and a throng of mourners, many weeping pitifully. 'Who is dead in the White House?' I demanded of one of the soldiers. 'The President,' was his answer. 'He was killed by an assassin.'"

stylized image of the skull and crossbones is used to signify poison and other similar dangers, while "keep out" signs warn you that you are about to trespass on private property. If such symbols appear in your dreams, you can take them as an indication of some danger or difficulty you are headed for, given your present circumstances or actions.

An alarm fitted to your house or car may point to feelings of insecurity or vulnerability, either around your physical being or possessions, or around your sense of self. You may feel that you need to protect yourself from attack, or from losing things that are significant. If the alarm is ringing, there may be more of a sense of urgency in these feelings, as though you are already in danger, it is important to take such a clear warning seriously.

DECODING A SITUATION

Sometimes the benefit of heeding a warning lies in the process of working out what it is about. The next step is to actively take on board the significance and implications of a situation, and in such cases our unconscious may present us with more obscure signs. If we can decode them, we will understand how to adjust our lives. For instance, you may dream of a realistic situation in your present life getting out of control. From this you may conclude that you need to make some adjustments about how you relate to the people in that situation; or that your life is going too fast and you must slow down; or that you need to take control of this aspect of your life.

RECURRING DREAMS

If you repeatedly dream of something that worries you, take whatever action you feel necessary to set your mind at rest. It doesn't mean that your dreams are foretelling things that will definitely go wrong, they are merely drawing your attention to a possible problem.

Recurring dreams can be an attempt by our unconscious to point out when we are ignoring danger; the dream may be repeated over and over again until we do something about it.

ABOVE Sometimes the mood or atmosphere in a dream can make us feel uneasy and could be a warning of trouble ahead. **ABOVE LEFT** Warning dreams are not easy to interpret. It may not be clear whether the warning is of an event about to happen or is a metaphor for personal issues.

BELOW When life is not going our way it is easy to feel a victim. Perhaps your dream is about improving your own circumstances. Maybe you need to take more control and stop blaming the "hand of fate"?

DANGERS

EVERY NOW AND AGAIN OUR DREAMS SEEM TO COME TO US SPECIFICALLY TO TELL US OF DANGER, USING METAPHORS FOR WHATEVER DIFFICULTIES OUR UNCONSCIOUS BELIEVES WE MIGHT BE IN. WHEN PLANE CRASHES, NATURAL DISASTERS, OR ACCIDENTS IN THE HOME FIGURE IN OUR DREAM NARRATIVE THEY MAY SIGNAL SPECIFIC PROBLEMS IN OUR LIVES THAT COULD LEAD US INTO TROUBLED TIMES. THEY MAY BE TELLING YOU ABOUT SPECIFIC FEARS THAT HAVE ARISEN BECAUSE OF THE SUPPOSED DANGERS THEY MAY PRESENT, OR TIE IN TO EVENTS THAT HAVE ALREADY OCCURRED IN YOUR LIFE AND WHICH YOU ARE AFRAID MIGHT HAPPEN AGAIN. THEY MAY EVEN BE COMPLETELY IRRATIONAL.

DANGEROUS PEOPLE

Threatening behaviour by other people is a common sign of social or emotional trouble. We might dream of being attacked – an intruder with a knife, a crazed lunatic rushing at us out of nowhere, someone grabbing us from behind. The attack may represent a personal threat rather than a physical one, for example if you have a bullying or critical boss or a domineering partner. Such scenarios may well be warnings, indications that our unconscious actively believes we are under attack or being overwhelmed by someone, and it is best to take notice of what such dreams are telling us.

NATURAL DISASTERS

In some dreams we might be threatened by dramatic events of nature – lightning, avalanche, storm, flood, earthquake, meteor strike – and again we should take note of these dreams. They have a symbolic intent, to warn us that we may feel insecure, out of control and at the mercy of fate, or overwhelmed. Different types of disaster are likely to place emphasis on different aspects of our being – for instance flooding can relate to the emotions, fire to passion or anger, an avalanche or earthquake to the stability of our lives – although the details will vary from person to person. All are disruptive, but in their upheaval they may also suggest a purging of some central aspect of our lives, sweeping away all that has gone before so that we can start afresh.

DANGER IN THE HOME

The dangers of our dreams can be minor domestic mishaps like getting an electric shock from a faulty plug, losing or breaking something we value, or the kitchen being flooded due to a blocked drain. Such dreams could be warnings of real dangers

---

DREAM OF DANGER

"I was walking along a dark, rural lane. It had been raining and the trees were dripping black water. Suddenly I felt myself grabbed from behind and thrown to the ground. I remember, in my dream, worrying more about my coat getting wet than about what was to happen to me. I felt I knew the person who had attacked me, even though I couldn't see his face. He stood over me in a very threatening attitude with his fists clenched. This dream seemed so real that I didn't feel I could ignore it, and I spent ages trying to work out who my attacker was. I came to the conclusion that he represented a colleague I worked very closely with but had never really trusted. I had a quick look at his work later that day and found he had been taking my ideas and passing them off as his, and I had been literally 'in the dark' about his behaviour for some time."

that could actually occur in our waking lives. We may have seen but ignored the signs of an "accident waiting to happen" – a frayed wire, a blocked drain – and this is our unconscious mind's way of bringing these defects to our notice and making sure that more serious mishaps don't happen. But they may also be symbolic rather than literal – pointing to discord in the home or fears around a multitude of issues to do with loss or damage or danger.

A more calamitous event, such as the house falling down, could indicate difficulties around your security, stability or domestic situation, while a dream of being trapped in a house on fire may be a powerful metaphor for how you feel about some central aspect of your life.

EMOTIONAL OUTCOMES

The accident or disaster in your dream may be intended as a catalyst for some behaviour or emotion rather than a sign of danger. For instance, you may have feelings of guilt or blame around some completely different scenario in your life where things are not working out – maybe you need to express these feelings and work with them. Or you may be contemplating failure, especially of something that you see as being very important – perhaps your plans or dreams for the future are going awry and the life journey you had envisaged for yourself is being abruptly curtailed. But in every disaster a hero emerges, and it could be that you are seeking to take on this role – to gain recognition for strength or bravery, or love.

ABOVE Our unconscious is infinitely creative in the way it produces its dream images. Being in a precarious situation is highlighted by this image. It may indicate things slipping out of control.

LEFT In dreams, as in waking life, danger can come at us from any direction and from where we least expect it.

CHANGE AND IMPERMANENCE

WHEN THINGS ARE GOING WELL IT IS FAIRLY NATURAL TO WANT THEM TO LAST THAT WAY FOREVER. BUT CHANGE IS ACTUALLY ONE OF THE FEW CERTAINTIES WE HAVE IN LIFE AND OUR DREAMS OFTEN DROP HINTS ABOUT HOW THE FUTURE MAY UNFOLD. WHATEVER OUR SITUATION IS NOW, IT IS SURE TO BE DIFFERENT SOON. WE MIGHT BE ENERGIZED BY THIS PROSPECT AND FIND IT EXCITING, OR WE MAY FIND IT THREATENING AND SCARY. WE MAY EVEN REFUSE TO BELIEVE IT COULD BE TRUE. BUT NO MATTER WHAT OUR ATTITUDE, THERE IS NO GETTING AWAY FROM THE FACT THAT CHANGE IS A NATURAL AND INEVITABLE PART OF LIFE AND OUR SUBCONSCIOUS MIND WILL BE DEALING WITH IT IN OUR DREAMS.

CONSTANT CHANGE

There is a story of a king who asked his advisers to come up with a saying that would be true for all time, no matter what situation we find ourselves in. The advisers thought long and hard but were defeated, so the king turned to a Buddhist monk who said, "This too shall pass." This was the phrase the king had been looking for.

This story illustrates the point that change is inevitable. The changes we experience may be more or less noticeable at different points in our lives.

Some, such as having a baby, getting married or divorced, or leaving school, will be major and will alter the course of our lives and the roles we play. Other changes will be more subtle and may have more to do with our inner world – our feelings and perceptions change over time and affect the way we relate to others.

RESPONDING TO CHANGE

Some changes are self-generated, and we have some control over them. We are able to decide what happens and when. But often change is out of our control and can take us on a journey that we didn't intend. These sorts of changes, such as losing a partner or a job redundancy, may be scary as we have to adjust to an unknown that is not of our choosing. Changes that are forced on us can be useful and welcome or they can provide setbacks – whether we resist or "go with the flow" will make a huge difference as to how well we cope.

How we respond to change is reflected in our dreams. If we cope well, then change may be symbolized by something that is fluid or flowing, such as a running brook or clouds moving across an open sky. If the change is dramatic or important, then an image of transformation, like that of a caterpillar turning into a butterfly, or a chicken hatching from an egg, may appear. If we are finding it difficult to cope with change, then the symbolism may be more intimidating, such as dreaming that our teeth are falling out. Our unconscious will always provide the clues about what is happening.

TRANSITION

As we move through life, we leave behind the behaviours and attitudes of one phase to move into something new: when one door closes another opens. Such

BELOW Our dreams will reflect how we view change and how we adjust to the unknown. Do we hanker for the past, or are we able to move with the times? Consider what an image like this steam train could mean in your dreams.

times of transition are not always easy. We may find it hard to adjust to losing our youth for instance, or when we discover that our thoughts and feelings are outdated. Like a bird learning to fly, we have to find new ways of coping with life as we settle into each different phase.

At such times, our dreams may be filled with images of running away, travelling or exploring; in such activities we may be searching for the energy of more youthful pursuits; trying to escape from the narrowing of focus that often goes with the ageing process; or, in a more positive light, we may be discovering the value of our present lives and looking forward to some kind of transition.

TRANSFORMATION

Some dream images can be frustratingly fluid. In a second our surroundings may have transformed, through the shapes and colours of objects, the size or layout of a room, or a person's character. We are more flexible than we imagine, and often it is a matter of courage or imagination to see how wonderful change can be. On the other hand, we may use our dreams to confront or justify our fears of change and difference, or of uncertainty about the stability of a situation. Transformation in our dreams can guide us in how to make positive changes in our lives and overcome our resistance to things being different.

RIGHT Whether we find change easy or difficult will depend to some extent on our attitude. Our dreams may show us scenes from nature to remind us that every ending also contains the seeds of a new beginning.

ABOVE All change is a metamorphosis of one sort or another – things changing from what they were to what they will become. Some of these changes will feel weird or unsettling in our dreams. **ABOVE LEFT** Change lies hidden beneath the surface of what we can already see, and is something of a mystery.

DREAM OF CHANGE

"I was chasing mice, trying to get them back into their cage, but each time I caught one it suddenly rotted in my hand. I was panicking and running everywhere trying to keep these mice in. I wanted to scream at them 'Stay in the cage or you'll go to pieces'.

My children were leaving home, and it was very unsettling; I didn't know what to do with myself and I felt left behind. Each mouse in the dream was a child. I wanted them to stay in the cage with me. If I have to stay why shouldn't they have to as well? I also worried about how they would cope in the big wide world and wanted to stop them from leaving, but I suppose in my heart I knew that this was a change they needed to make whatever I felt about it ."

MOVEMENT, MACHINES AND STRUCTURES

Our dreams are often signals of change and progress, and movement, machinery and structures can be connected with these things. We all use machinery of one kind or another. It enables us to effect changes, and mould our environment to our needs and taste. Technology means that both the machinery and the things we can do with it are constantly evolving. This evolution may be challenging and exciting, but for many it is stressful and bewildering. It is easy to feel lost as if in a maze of new ideas. Alternatively we seek security in the structures we create – the comfort and safety of our homes or other buildings.

RIGHT Movement, whether of ourselves or of things in our surroundings, can signify change and show us how at ease we are with ourselves and our environment.

FLYING AND FALLING

OUR DREAMS RELEASE US FROM THE CONSTRAINTS OF OUR EARTHBOUND LIVES, AND SO IT IS NOT UNCOMMON IN OUR UNCONSCIOUS FANTASIES TO FIND THAT WE CAN FLY. AS WELL AS A SENSE OF RELEASE AND FREEDOM, FLIGHT MAY GIVE US A DIFFERENT PERSPECTIVE ON OUR WORLD, THOUGH IN MANY DREAMS IT INVOLVES LITTLE MORE THAN SKIMMING OVER THE SURFACE OF THE GROUND. DREAMING OF FALLING IS LESS LIKELY TO BE A PLEASANT EXPERIENCE, BOTH IN THE PHYSICAL SENSATIONS IT MIGHT CAUSE, AND ALSO BECAUSE FALLING OFTEN POINTS TO THE PRESENCE OF TROUBLES AND A SENSE OF BEING OUT OF CONTROL THAT WE MIGHT BE CARRYING IN OUR WAKING LIVES.

CONFRONTING OUR INNER FEARS

For some people dreams of flying and falling may be an attempt to confront a fear of heights or to deal with vertigo – the dizziness we experience when our sense of balance has been disturbed. You can actually reprogramme your subconscious before you go to sleep with an instruction like "if I dream of flying or falling I will have wings and come to no harm". If you repeat this instruction to yourself often enough, then in your dreams you will indeed develop wings and cope better with the sensations in the dream.

There have been cases of people so terrified of having dreams of flying or falling that they resist the onset of sleep. For some, learning to sleep with a

BELOW RIGHT Flying in our dreams can be a positive experience and we can learn a lot from it. It can feel very liberating to find ourselves free from the constraints of the everyday world.
BELOW Dreams of flying or falling can be so scary and realistic that some people are too afraid to go to sleep in case they have such a dream.

pillow or cushion pressed up against the soles of their feet helps, as this stimulates the sensors in the feet and the sense of balance is restored, so there is no unconscious worry about being in freefall.

THEORETICAL INTERPRETATIONS

Freud and his followers maintain that for men dreams of flying are often associated with sex, while for women falling dreams may indicate succumbing to sexual temptation. Another school of thought says that flying and falling dreams point to the existence of a soul which can leave the body while we are asleep, and that such dreams are merely echoes or memories of these out-of-body experiences. Others still have said that falling

dreams indicate the presence of internalized fears around our ambitions – the fear of falling from power or position.

PERSONAL INTERPRETATIONS

Any of these interpretations may be true in some circumstances, but since our dreams are personal to us, we also need to take into account our situation, experience and feelings, together with the details of the dream itself, before we can try to understand what it means.

Flying in our dreams is often quite a positive and liberating experience, as it suggests that we have shed the physical limitations of being earthbound. Flying high can be aspirational – think of the concept of "soaring to new heights" – or it could suggest that

we are seeking a new perspective on some aspect of our lives. We may find ourselves "flying in the face of something", trying to escape from the narrowness of social conventions or the dull routine of daily life perhaps, or it could be something more urgent or threatening that we are trying to escape from. Our dream flight could just be the frustrating business of not being able to get airborne, despite a monumental effort to do so, in which case you should look closely at what is holding you back; similarly see if there are any obstructions or other difficulties in flying, as these could indicate things that are hindering you in your life.

Falling may be liberating, but it is more likely to be linked to a loss or reduction of some kind, such as falling from power or from grace. It may represent loss of control – hence the expression "falling in love" – or it may be about getting into trouble. We talk of "falling out of favour" or even just "falling out" with someone, and any of these could be suggested in your dreams. The

RIGHT Dreams of falling may jolt us awake with a start as we come to "land". Notice what it is in your dream that breaks your fall – is it something soft and safe or is it more precarious? What does this mean to you?

feeling of falling into an abyss may point to the actual process of falling asleep, losing consciousness, or losing awareness or sensation. In any case, note whether you catch on to something while you fall, which could indicate a reprieve or point to something that might help you. Also see whether the landing – if it happens – is hard or soft, and what you land on – you may land in a safety net or plunge into a pool of water.

FLIGHTS OF FANCY

If you lie down and close your eyes, the resulting loss of visual stimulation means that you concentrate much more on your other senses. Physical sensations are particularly intense. But within a few minutes your body will probably be so relaxed that you will feel little other than your breathing. Concentrating on the

rhythm of your breathing in this way gives a sensation of movement. Add to this the lack of visual stimulation, the relaxed bodily posture, plus sleepiness, darkness and quiet, and you have pretty well all you need to imagine you are flying. The same goes for falling. If you lie down, close your eyes and roll your eyes upwards, the sensors in your feet that tell your brain about your spatial orientation and position get turned off, and your brain assumes that you are in freefall. The feelings of flying and falling that the brain generates may get translated into dream material.

BELOW LEFT The desire for flight has always been a source of fascination for us. Until we invented machines to help us fly, we could only experience it in our dreams.
BELOW It is not by chance that we use the phrase "falling asleep". The physical sensations are similar to falling, which may explain where some of our falling dreams come from.

PURSUIT

WE DO NOT ALWAYS KNOW WHAT WE ARE RUNNING FROM IN OUR DREAMS. OUR PURSUER MAY BE SOME UNKNOWN FORCE OR TERRIFYING POWER, AND IT IS IMPORTANT TO ESTABLISH WHAT IT SYMBOLIZES. IT IS OFTEN THOUGHT TO BE OUR FEARS IN SOME FORM OR ANOTHER, BUT IT MAY EQUALLY BE ASSOCIATED WITH CONFLICT. TO COME TO TERMS WITH THE CONFLICTS IN OUR LIVES WE NEED TO ACCEPT OR CONFRONT THEM RATHER THAN AVOID THEM, HOWEVER FRIGHTENING THEY MAY BE, AND PURSUIT DREAMS CAN HELP US TO DO THIS. BY ASKING OURSELVES THE QUESTION "WHAT AM I RUNNING AWAY FROM IN MY WAKING LIFE?" WE MAY FIND THE KEY TO WHAT OUR PURSUIT DREAMS ARE ALL ABOUT.

LEFT Are you being pursued or are you watching a chase unfold? Perhaps you are the pursuer? You might, of course, be all the elements of the chase, all this needs to be assessed as you try to interpret what this feeling of pursuit means to you.

representing our hidden inner conflicts. But in some dreams we may have the courage to turn around and confront our pursuer, to face issues that we need to face, to challenge and stand up to the people who are causing us misery. In these cases, the dreams may be about dealing with conflict in our lives.

Conflicts can come at us from all sorts of sources – work, love, sex, money, children and countless others – and often have no easy solution. How we handle the chase in our dreams will

BELOW Pursuit does not have to mean a physical chase. It is possible to feel we are under scrutiny, or pursued by threats or feelings. Look closely at your dream symbolism to discover what is happening to you.

RUNNING FROM FEAR

Often in our dreams we are running from people, things or situations that make us frightened or anxious. We may not know what it is we are running from, although we may

have strong feelings around it or a clear sense of its qualities. It could even be that we are running away from some aspect of ourselves that we dislike or feel uncomfortable with, and we can see this type of dream as

show us something important about how we are handling the conflict we are trying to address.

If the pursuit dream is a recurring one we do have the ability to reprogramme ourselves so that we can, in our dream, stop and turn around and see what is pursuing us. We could also use techniques such as gestalt to work with the material. But if it is a one-off dream and we don't have that opportunity, then we should investigate the underlying fears or conflicts that it presents.

Feeling that your legs are tied, or that you are unable to move no matter how hard you try is quite common in pursuit dreams. This may be associated with the REM stage of sleep where we relax so deeply that we cannot move a muscle. When we go to sleep our brain shuts down our physical movements and we go into a kind of natural paralysis – perhaps to make sure that our dreams don't literally run away with us. But it can also symbolize

RIGHT We may feel threatened in a dream by vague fears or a shadowy figure but not have a clear sense of what it really is that is making us feel uneasy.
MIDDLE RIGHT The threat of pursuit may become more tangible as our fears grow monstrous.
BOTTOM RIGHT Another way of approaching pursuit dreams is to view the pursuer as an aspect of yourself that wants your attention.

feeling helpless, trapped or tied down to something when you want to be able to escape.

GIVING CHASE

There may of course be dreams in which we are the ones doing the chasing. To interpret these dreams we should look at who or what we are pursuing and what they mean to us. Then we need to examine our lives to see what dreams we chase, what ambitions remain unfulfilled, what goals we have yet to satisfy. The dreams we chase may be nebulous, dark, unspoken, unshaped, but once we turn the spotlight on them and think about what they may mean, they do in the end tend to become recognizable.

RUNNING FROM A PROBLEM

"I had this dream in which I was being chased by what seemed to be a patch of darkness. I felt there was something or someone within the darkness; I couldn't see it, but it seemed big and powerful and dangerous, and I felt that it could hurt me emotionally in some way. I was running but not getting anywhere because my feet were tied up with rope. The patch of darkness was almost upon me when I woke up.

When I was awake I went through my life to try and find out what my deepest concerns are. It wasn't difficult to work out. My husband has been offered an excellent opportunity in the city and wants us all to move, but I am happy where we are and feel the children's schooling is better here and that being settled and happy should take priority over his career move. This is causing me a lot of upset at the moment. In my dream I think the patch of darkness represented the forces of fate that were about to overwhelm me. The dream stimulated me into being less passive, though, I am not a victim to fate, and I have become more assertive since."

MAZES AND BEING LOST

ABOVE A maze is a kind of puzzle that is designed to get us lost and it can be fun to find ourselves going round in circles. See what being in a maze means for you.

ABOVE RIGHT Any dream about getting lost has been given to help us find a way out of a confusing situation in our waking life. It would be foolish to overlook the opportunity.

BEING LOST IN OUR DREAMS MAY BE AS SIMPLE AS FEELING LOST IN OUR WAKING LIFE. CERTAINLY THE SYMBOLIC VALUE OF MAZES AND LABYRINTHS IN OUR DREAMS IS ABOUT BEING LOST. WE MAY BE LOST THROUGH PHYSICAL DISORIENTATION, CONFUSION OR MISUNDERSTANDING, LOSS OR LONELINESS OR THROUGH OTHER DIFFICULTIES. THE THEME OF BEING LOST COULD ALSO POINT TO A MORE COMPLEX ISSUE, HOWEVER, AND IT IS BEST NOT TO JUMP TO QUICK AND EASY CONCLUSIONS, BUT TAKE SOME TIME TO WORK OUT THE DETAILS OF THE DREAM AND WHAT THEY MIGHT MEAN.

Mazes and labyrinths both consist of a network of pathways, but while a maze is designed to get you lost, a labyrinth has a definite goal at its heart. There may be a whole system of forked paths and dead ends but they are there to steer you towards the centre, to stop you retracing your steps and finding your way out.

A maze will often take you round in circles before spitting you out where you first began. It isn't designed to take you inward and indeed may deliberately keep you from the centre.

BEING LOST

When we dream of mazes and labyrinths, what is important is finding out why we are lost, what it is that we are turning away from. We all encounter difficulties and fears from time to time, but while some of us get on with trying to work them out, others feel unable to address them immediately and prefer to set them aside until they feel strong or clear-headed enough to do so. For the latter, this may manifest as dreams in which we are lost or misled, where we can't find our way out of a situation or to a place of safety. We struggle in the maze, held captive by our confusion. The reason we are being given the dream is not necessarily to spur us on – although that may be part of it – but rather to give us some insight into how to get out simply and easily. The dream is like a map written in code, and we can

DREAM OF BEING LOST

"I was underground, caving in a series of potholes with a friend. He had the map but it fell into a pool of deep water. We were lost and the light from our helmet torches began to fade. We were standing in a cave with many exits. We were concerned that there were underground lakes we would fall into so we felt we had to go up. Suddenly a bat flew out of nowhere and disappeared up one of the shafts. We knew which way we had to go: the bat had shown us the way.

Later on I realized that I was feeling bad about my job. I had wanted to study biology but had done accounts because it seemed a more practical career choice. I guess the bat was telling me to start again, to be true to myself. Once I did this the whole of my life seemed to improve."

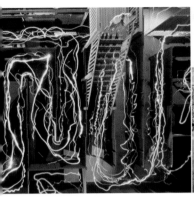

study our dream to see if we were helped through the dream maze by something or someone. This may be someone we know or a stranger; it may be some sort of angelic being or even an animal, wild or domestic.

THE CONFUSION OF CHOICE

Mazes and labyrinths often involve making a series of choices. If we make the right decisions we get to where we want to be, achieving a goal or clarity. If we make the wrong choices we remain lost, or land up where we began. It can be hard to remain clear-headed in such a situation, and if we are confused, making choices becomes a difficult process, and one in which we may easily make mistakes. The dream may well be helping us to make the choice based on intuition or on information that hasn't been accessible to our conscious mind.

The fact that we are in a maze in our dreams may even simply be warning us that some aspect of our lives is more complicated

than we thought, and that we should pay attention to the complexity of the choices we have to make. In your dream, look at the nature of your decision-making process – whether it is impulsive or random, or calm and rational, based on carefully weighed up factors. Notice whether it is

effective, and whether you are alone in the maze, and if not, does your companion help you or distract or mislead you? The answer to these questions may reveal the extent to which you can rely on others in your decision-making, how much trust you feel, or whether you want and are able to "go it alone".

ABOVE The symbolism of the stylized maze is a very powerful one, and one that your dream self will love to explore.
ABOVE LEFT Notice your surroundings in your dream. Are you where you want to be?
ABOVE FAR LEFT When we get our wires crossed, things get confusing. Our dreams may show us how to untangle the obstacles.

LEFT Are you lost and alone in your dream or is there someone who can lend you a helping hand? See if you can relate this to your life. Do you tend to struggle on alone because you find it hard to ask for support?

Exits and Entrances

Physically, an entrance and an exit are simply two sides of the same opening, whether it is a doorway or some other kind of opening. Although they are physically identical, what differentiates one from the other is your viewpoint and which way you pass through. Doorways might also symbolize a whole variety of different things in your life; an entrance or an exit might represent an escape from a problem or an unpleasant circumstance, or it might be a temptation to escape from responsibility and reality. When you dream of portals your interpretation will depend on the circumstances around you.

Freud would no doubt have attributed some sexual meaning to exits and entrances, while others suggest, for instance, that doors opening outward indicate a need to express yourself more and those opening inward a need to explore some aspect of your inner being. Each of these interpretations may fit in some circumstances, depending on the context in which the door appears in the dream and on your own circumstances. But even if they do fit, it is also important to find out more about the dream and how and why the doorway features – the kind of

BELOW Every exit is also an entrance and vice versa – it depends on which way we look at it.
BELOW RIGHT Dreams about exits and entrances may be trying to tell us something about the transitions that are going on in our waking life.

entrance, whether it is you or someone else who is opening the door, and whether you are going in or out, for instance. It may be a small doorway, a huge gateway, or a cleft in a mountainside, and you should take note of the kind of structure it is part of as this may also be significant.

TRANSITIONS

An entrance or exit marks a transition from one space to another – spaces that may be similar, such as two rooms in a house, or quite different from each other, like an interior space and a garden. This could suggest

being at some kind of threshold or making an adjustment in your life, so look at how the transition works in your dream. Perhaps you make a grand entrance to the applause of a crowd, or you have to squeeze through, or maybe you slip between one dream scene and another without really noticing how you do so. These scenarios may all say something about how comfortable you are with the transition, whether or not you look forward to it, and how easy or difficult it is.

Every time you move from one space to another you are making an entrance and an exit at the

same time, so it is worth looking at which aspect of the movement draws your attention – leaving or arriving, getting out of a place or going in. Sometimes you may be poised on the threshold itself, in a sort of limbo. How you feel about the space you are leaving behind as well as the one you are entering may also give important clues about the meaning of the transition – say, whether you have any regrets, or are relieved to be moving on. Whether or not you can retrace your steps will have a bearing on how easy it is to make your entrance or exit.

Transitions in your life may be physical ones, such as moving house, starting a new job, or going to live in a new country. But the entrances and exits in your dream can also be about emotional or spiritual thresholds, such as starting a brand new relationship or ending an existing one, or about the transition between consciousness and unconsciousness, or many others.

CLOSURE

Exits can be about achieving closure, about ending a period in your life or a way of being so that you can move on. You may need to start something afresh or begin a new venture, and it may be important for you to be able to leave behind any "baggage" you may have been carrying.

EXCLUSION

Sometimes the entrance in your dream is tantalizingly or frustratingly impassable; perhaps it's something that is perfectly visible but just beyond your reach. It may be a locked door, or a skylight up in the roof, or a barred window; if you encounter one of these, ask yourself if there are situations in your life from which you feel barred or excluded. Or perhaps you can see a way forward to something you want but are not sure how to get to it because there are obstacles in the way; if this is the case, see whether there was any

alternative route to the place you were trying to get to in your dream, or someone who could help you unlock the door or reach the skylight. These could suggest alternative ways of achieving what you are after in your waking life.

ABOVE Our dreams can show us that we have an opportunity to step out into new terrain.
ABOVE LEFT Sometimes the exits and entrances in our dreams are out of reach. We may want to go there, but it is impossible or too dangerous just now.

EXITS AND ENTRANCES DREAM

"There was a cocktail party going on in a large room that was accessed by a large door off a long corridor. There were lots of people standing around talking, smoking, eating and drinking. I kept walking in and out of this big doorway, I was the only one that was coming and going. Each time I came in I fell over, more and more drunk, and people kept turning round to look at me, but I didn't care. As soon as I went out and was standing in the corridor I was quite sober again.

For me, a cocktail party is the kind of boring, formal, old-fashioned function that older people like my parents would go to. The people at the party were all drinking, but they could handle it while I just got really drunk. But I was deliberately playing the fool each time I came in, perhaps as a way of rebelling against the older people.

I think the dream was actually about the prospect of joining my parents' business. I thought I'd come round to the idea but the dream showed that I haven't really – I actually find the business boring, and I think I'm too young to be getting into something like that! I'd rather find my own way through life, and do the kind of things my friends are doing."

BUILDINGS

Like us, buildings have a lifespan – they degenerate, decay and fall into disuse. In our dreams they could represent us and we may need to look at what point in our own life the building is trying to be. Some dream interpretations suggest that buildings represent the dreamer's body, and this does seem to fit with such expressions as "my body is a temple". But if the structure in your dream isn't a temple but an art deco cinema showing old gangster movies, or a disused tin mine, or high-rise city office blocks, you may need to explore more deeply what the structure means to you. It is also possible that only part of a building is relevant.

In some cases you can take the buildings in your dreams at face value – as nothing more than a literal part of the scenery. Your unconscious has to set the dream somewhere and a building you know well may be used because it is a familiar and appropriate setting for the events of the dream. If the surroundings fit then you can probably discount them, but if the building is strange or unusual or disjointed in any way though, you need to look closer.

TYPES OF BUILDING
The function of the building in your dream could be a big clue to its meaning. For example, churches or temples are likely to

be associated with your spiritual side or your relationship to religion, while a bridge may signify that you need to cross some obstacle or forge a link between two people or things or ideas. Underground structures, such as basements, mines or cellars, may be particularly relevant if you are currently in the process of exploring and uncovering deeply rooted personal issues. And you are likely to have quite different feelings around an industrial building such as a factory or power plant from those connected with a little cottage.

Different people will also have different responses to the same setting – for instance, you may find a factory a noisy, smelly and confusing or overwhelming place to be, but for someone else its salient feature could be that it is to do with mass-production or innovation and newness, in which case it could be to do with innovation or progress in some important aspect of their life.

APPEARANCE
Particular qualities of the building may come to your attention and have specific

relevance – either the materials or the style, the state of repair, or perhaps some element such as a chimney or staircase.

The clean lines and cold, reflective materials of a modern building may suggest orderliness or control in your life, forward-thinking or a detachment from your heritage, while a rustic cottage with rough wooden beams and a lived-in feel could indicate a feeling of comfort or security. Since our response to styles and materials is highly personal, however, you will need to see the building in the context of your own personal feelings and tastes.

The state of the buildings or other structures can provide another layer of significance to the basic meaning of the building. Clean and orderly or dirty, well maintained or falling apart – if you see the building as some aspect of your own being then the state of repair and cleanliness could indicate how you view yourself. A shabby or neglected building may be hinting that you need to look after yourself more, that you don't value yourself enough or suffer from low self-esteem.

BELOW There are probably as many different kinds of building as there are people. How you feel about them and what they represent in your dreams will be a matter of personal taste and association.

> The dream is an involuntary kind of poetry.
> JEAN PAUL RICHTER

ABOVE Some buildings will take on an otherworldly quality in our dreams, as though they are trying to tell us something very deep and instinctive.

ABOVE A staircase is how we go up or down and traditionally has been linked to a man's sexual prowess. What would you make of such an image in your dreams?

STAIRCASES

It is often said that a staircase is symbolic of a man's sexual prowess, ambition or career progress. It could mean any or none of these things, but notice how important it is in your dream – as in life, it could just have a practical function and simply be a means of getting about between floors in your dream narrative. If your unconscious wants to draw your attention to your sexual prowess, it may well choose a more obvious symbol.

In any case, it is worth considering that staircases allow you access to higher places, and that you may be using the stairs as a symbol for your ability to progress or achieve greater status; conversely descending a staircase may show a loss of these things. A staircase may also transport you between different states of consciousness or the higher and lower aspects of your being. Elevators and escalators may act in the same way as staircases, and help you on your way, but bear in mind that you are taking an "easy ride" by using them.

ABOVE A tall, upright building may represent a desire to be seen. Notice how the buildings appear in your dreams – are they new or old, clean or dirty?

ABOVE Buildings get old and fall into disuse. What would a dream of a ruined building mean for you? Is there something you have been neglecting and would like to repair?
RIGHT Factory buildings can appear alien and overpowering, although they may also represent work and progress.

BELOW How we view buildings in our dreams can tell us a lot about how we see ourselves. Here a city landscape towers above an area of domestic housing.

HOMES AND DWELLINGS

OUR HOUSES AND HOMES ARE EXTREMELY IMPORTANT TO US. EVEN BEFORE WE MOVE INTO A NEW PLACE, WE OFTEN MAKE ELABORATE PLANS ABOUT HOW TO MAKE IT OURS. WE DECORATE, RE-ORGANIZE THE ROOMS AND BUILD EXTENSIONS IN AN ATTEMPT TO PUT OUR PERSONAL STAMP ON IT. OUR AIM IS TO HAVE A HOME THAT IS SAFE, WARM, AND COMFORTABLE. IN OUR DREAMS A HOUSE IS OFTEN A MARK OF THESE THINGS AND CAN SHOW US ABOUT OUR SENSE OF SELF AND HOW SECURE WE FEEL. IF A HOUSE OR OUR HOME BECOMES A SCARY, THREATENING PLACE IN OUR DREAMS, THEN THAT MAY BE HOW WE VIEW IT IN OUR WAKING LIFE AND IT COULD BE SOMETHING WE NEED TO LOOK AT MORE CLOSELY.

A SAFE HAVEN

When we are at home we feel secure and more able to cope with the difficulties in our lives and the things that we find threatening. In our lives and our dreams alike, it can be a base to return to from our forays into a potentially dangerous and unpredictable world, and for many of us, the home is the centre of our life, our heart. The houses in our dreams are often familiar to us, and an obvious line of questioning you should pursue concerns the person who lives there, what they are like and what your relationship to them is. The home you grew up in or the house of a favourite aunt or grandparent is likely to be filled with a great many memories and reminders of your childhood, and could signify a nostalgia for these times, or perhaps be bringing to your attention an issue that arose at the time you were living there or visiting often.

ATTRIBUTES

If you dream of an unfamiliar house, it is the qualities of the building that are important. It is more likely to represent some aspect of yourself – your body, your personality, or your sense of who you are. You should ask yourself what it is about this particular building that has made you represent yourself in this way.

A big, grand house may show a need to expand your horizons or capabilities, to establish yourself more solidly, or to make a bolder statement to the world about yourself; on the other hand if you find in your dream, for instance, that you live in a mansion but are stressed by the upkeep, it may indicate that you feel you have taken on something that is bigger than you can handle. Equally, a small cottage may be cosy and comfortable or cramped and mean. If the house or furnishings are shabby, ask yourself if there is something you have done that would generate such a feeling. A tidy and well-maintained house may show a healthy self-regard or clarity of mind.

ROOMS

The rooms in a house allow us to compartmentalize aspects of our lives. Different areas of our lives may be represented by the function of particular rooms – the bedroom for sleep, sex and relaxation, the dining room for nourishment, the living room for leisure and sociability. So how you feel and what you are doing in each of these rooms could be

BELOW Our dreams often have a fairytale quality to them and can surprise us. Opening the kitchen cupboard to find fluffy white clouds inside could suggest a desire to be transported from the humdrum routine of domestic life.

RIGHT Colour and style create an impact. Do you feel at ease in your dream house or are you an uninvited guest?

key to understanding how comfortable you are with these different aspects of your life.

Rooms are also said to represent your potential. If a room is familiar it signals your current or past capabilities, whereas an unfamiliar room could be showing you your unfulfilled potential; whether you are eager to explore it or back out and close the door may show how ready you are to realize that potential. Sometimes the houses in our dreams have hidden rooms or rooms that we are forbidden to enter. These may represent unexplored parts of ourselves or parts that we feel are taboo.

BUILDING A HOUSE

To dream of building a house might mean that you are interested in building greater security or turning an increase in prosperity into something concrete, though you will have to decide for yourself whether this type of interpretation seems correct. Different aspects of the building process may carry particular meanings as well. For instance, laying foundations may indicate establishing yourself, or creating a stable base for some project or aspect of your life.

Dreaming about a building project going awry could be about unforeseen problems or obstacles. Notice what building materials are being used and see what this means for you.

BELOW LEFT Most of us aspire to owning our own home. Your dreams can show you how realistic your expectations are.
MIDDLE LEFT We all have a stylized, idyllic image of perfect living. We may visit this place in our dreams for reassurance.
BOTTOM LEFT To dream of a stately home or a large house may mean that we need to expand our horizons and "think big".

DREAM OF A ROOM

"My mother was driving me mad. I fled upstairs, but although there are only two flights of stairs in my house in real life, I ran up three flights of stairs in my dream. At the top I found myself in a lovely attic room, full of warmth and light and nice comfy chairs. It was decorated in wonderful lush fabrics and rich colours, and there was a smell of incense in the air. This seemed to be the happiest room I had ever been in and I felt so safe and comfortable here.

This was my own space, which I created in my dream as a refuge, a place where my troubles – in the form of my mother – could not follow me, and it was a place where I felt I could really be myself."

TOOLS AND MACHINES

THE DEVELOPMENT OF TOOLS AND MACHINES IS PART OF WHAT IT MEANS TO BE HUMAN. FROM THE EARLIEST TIMES, WE HAVE DEVELOPED TOOLS TO HELP US WORK MORE EFFECTIVELY AND TO INCREASE THE RANGE OF TASKS WE ARE CAPABLE OF PERFORMING. TOOLS AND MACHINES ENABLE US TO DO A MULTITUDE OF THINGS. THEY RANGE IN SIZE AND COMPLEXITY FROM THE SIMPLE PAPERCLIP TO THE VAST AND COMPLICATED STRUCTURE OF AN OIL-RIG OR SPACESHIP. OUR QUEST FOR PROGRESS AND IMPROVEMENT MEANS THAT TECHNOLOGY, WHICH BRINGS ABOUT THE CHANGES TO OUR TOOLS, OUR MACHINES AND MANY ASPECTS OF OUR ENVIRONMENT, IS AN EVER-PRESENT PART OF OUR LIVES.

TOOLS

When we think of tools the first thing that springs to mind may be carpentry or gardening equipment, but in fact we use all sorts of objects and even employ abstract ideas to manipulate our environment or to help us do a task – so a stick becomes a tool when we use it to draw in the sand or prop open a gate, and we can use our dreams as tools for understanding those issues in our lives to which we need to pay more attention.

In your dreams look for tools being used inappropriately or ones that are malformed or malfunctioning. If the person using the tool is right and the tool fits the purpose, then you could look beyond it to the job of work that is being done. Bear in mind though, that "rightness of fit" may in fact be just what your unconscious mind is trying to demonstrate: you need to use the right tool for the job.

MACHINES

There are also complex tools that enable us to undertake bigger and more complicated tasks. Machines do not require the same effort from us as hand tools as they have their own source of energy. This gives them a more human quality – they need fuel to work just as we need food; they emit waste; and some also look vaguely human. Sometimes we even give them names and refer to them fondly as "she" or "he". Because of this affinity to machines and the fact that we use them constantly, they may appear in our dreams as symbols for our own efforts and abilities.

MACHINE DREAM

"I was inside some sort of giant machine with cogs and wheels made of brightly coloured plastic, and a lot of wires and sparking electrical connections. I couldn't work out what this machine did, or what part of it I was in. I helped make it run but I had no idea how.

I had recently become a father, and the dream confirmed for me that however wonderful our baby was, I was extremely worried about my new role, about how to cope with the baby and how to understand his needs. The clue that linked the dream to my life situation was the plastic parts which reminded me of the Lego I played with as a child."

BELOW MIDDLE Simple tools can symbolize complex issues: what do you need to sweep away? **BELOW RIGHT** Being able to assemble things in a logical way is a skill that you may need to develop. **BELOW** Computers are an integral part of modern life and can appear in our dreams in unusual ways.

TECHNOLOGY DREAM

"I dreamt that I was trying to get my cash card into an ATM, but the card kept bending and slipping away; the more I pushed the softer it became and the less I could insert it. I suppose if I had been a man this dream would easily have been interpreted as being about impotence, but in my case I was anxious about some exams that were looming. I was worried that when I got into the exam room my brain would go soft and everything I had studied so hard to remember would slip out of my mind at the time when I most needed it. "

MACHINES IN DREAMS

Not all machines have a human quality. Sometimes they are big and impersonal, even menacing. Machines can be immensely powerful and unyielding – they can crush us if we get in the way, they tower over us and we can feel intimidated. They may even chase us, or simply have a dark and brooding presence. These qualities may mean the machines in our dreams become symbols of intimidation, of powerful forces or inevitability in the face of our powerlessness. Not knowing how to use a machine may also make us feel disadvantaged and we may employ this scenario in a dream to represent our frustrations or limitations.

FUNCTIONS

Often it is the function of the tool or machine that is important in our dreams. A dredger, for example, easily symbolizes the process of drawing up and bringing to light the contents of the murky depths. We might just have chosen a simple bucket and spade to dig up mud, but a full-size dredger is a more captivating and obvious image. In looking at the function of the tool or machine, also consider what it is the machine is acting on – what it is uncovering or burying, neatening off, transporting, shattering or moulding. Each of these actions may relate to something that is happening to you in your waking life.

TECHNOLOGY

In our dreams, technology may represent a threat to traditional values and ways of doing things, and may bring up feelings of fear or anxiety. For technology is a powerful symbol of movement and unstoppable change. This may leave us feeling left behind, confused or alienated, and it could also be a symbol for us to slow down. Technology can also represent cool efficiency and be tremendously empowering and exciting. It makes our lives easier and enables us to do a wider range of things more quickly and with less effort. Computers, mobile phones and DVD players as well as washing machines, cars and countless other devices are all part of modern technology and can appear in our dreams.

ABOVE Large machinery can symbolize a menacing and inhuman presence in our dreams. Check to see who or what is intimidating you and revisit the dream to see if it offers a clue about how to deal with the problem.

BELOW New technology allows us to bring the past into the present. Is there anything you need to update in your life?
BELOW LEFT A tool that doesn't work properly hinders progress. Use your dream to check what isn't working in your life.

Travel

In difficult times we often wish we could escape, get right away and leave our troubles behind us rather than struggle on with trying to solve them. We may dream of travel, of being on the road or flying off into the blue yonder. But travel dreams are not always escapist; they may represent our journey through life and the paths we take, or perhaps they reflect an eagerness to broaden our horizons. They are also important symbols of transition and change — our desire for some kind of change in ourselves or our circumstances, our fears around change, or our need to change.

ABOVE Travel dreams can show us where we are going in life. Notice if you are alone or with others, moving or stationary?
ABOVE RIGHT Seen from above, a complex network of roads may not look so confusing. Maybe a fresh perspective is called for?

THE JOURNEY

Because dream travels can be so varied, you will need to ask a number of questions about the nature of the journey in your dream – where you were going, the purpose of the journey, whether you were on foot or in a vehicle, travelling at speed or dawdling along. What the journey and the terrain were like and who your travelling companions were, if any, are also worth considering.

MAPS

If there was a plan or route involved in your travelling dream it is worth examining what they were like and what help they gave you. Maps can give you an overview of your journey and help you to plan a route or see where you are, but if they are unclear or misleading, don't

relate to the places you pass through, or you simply can't decipher them, this may suggest you are lacking direction in life.

DEPARTURES AND DESTINATIONS

Many a dream journey has no real starting point or end point. Instead you may simply have a

sense of being on the road to nowhere or needing to be on the move, or you may be exploring a place and seeing what it has to offer. These types of journey may have very different meanings. Not knowing where you are going can be highly significant, as it could show that you need to explore what you want out of

RIGHT Paths wind and diverge as we tread our way through life, and a dream may reflect this.

life, where you want your life journey to lead. On the other hand, it may be that getting left behind or being late may be the key issues, rather than where you are coming from or going to. If you do remember the beginning of your dream journey, it is worth looking at the starting point closely. It may represent something you are trying to run away from, or it could be a part of your past that you are ready to leave behind. The kind of departure may give a clue to which meaning is true for you.

Destinations are likely to be about goals and desires if you have chosen them, although they could equally be about situations that you are afraid of getting into if you don't seem to have control over where you are going.

TRAVELLING COMPANIONS

For the solo traveller, the journey may be a lonely one, but one in which you can be in charge,

make all the decisions and take responsibility for whatever happens along the way. If you do have travel companions, though, ask yourself what they are like, whether they are people you know or not, and how they behave on the journey. A loving, supportive companion may indicate that there is someone

you can take with you on your journey through life, while a person who hijacks your plans, dogs your footsteps, or insists on leading the way or having the best seat may be pointing to issues around people who are in some way interfering with your own plans.

People you meet along the way may help or hinder your journey, rescuing you from difficult situations or misleading you. These may be archetypal figures or may relate to actual people in your life who may be helping or obstructing your plans or goals.

LEFT Maps help us pinpoint where we are going. Is your map easy or hard to decipher?
MIDDLE LEFT Notice if your fellow travellers are good to be with or if they are annoying you.
FAR LEFT If your life feels like a long desert trek, remember that deserts also have their beauty and you can adapt to survive.

TRAVEL DREAM

"I had a dream in which travel was very prominent and obviously meant something important but I didn't know immediately what it was. I was crossing the Nevada desert in a red sports car, heading towards Las Vegas, where I was going to go gambling. Although I was alone, I could feel the presence of a blonde woman who may have just got out of the car.

I don't normally gamble in my waking life, but in relationships I can sail pretty close to the wind. I recently had a relationship with someone I was very fond of, and I now really regret messing her about. She was right to dump me. I guess I was gambling with her life and her future, and I lost. Maybe she was the woman who had just got out of my car in my dream. I think it's quite revealing that it was a red sports car as well. Although I don't own one it does symbolize the freedom and energy of youth to me."

VEHICLES

IF THE TRAVELS IN OUR DREAMS ARE ABOUT ESCAPING OR ABOUT OUR LIFE JOURNEY, VEHICLES ARE THE MACHINES THAT MOVE US FROM ONE PLACE TO ANOTHER, PROVIDING OUR MEANS OF ESCAPE OR PROGRESS. THE TYPE OF VEHICLE WE CHOOSE TO REPRESENT IN OUR DREAMS MAY GIVE US CLUES TO THE NATURE OF OUR JOURNEY, AND ITS STATE OF REPAIR CAN SHOW US HOW OUR JOURNEY IS PROGRESSING. DIFFERENT KINDS OF FEAR OR UNEASE WILL PROBABLY SURFACE IN YOUR DREAMS; DO YOU HAVE A FEAR OF FLYING OR A TERROR OF BEING LOST AT SEA? PERHAPS EVERYDAY MEANS OF TRANSPORT, SUCH AS BUSES OR TRAINS MAKE YOU FEEL UNEASY, PACKED FULL AS THEY ARE WITH OTHER TRAVELLERS.

MEANS AND MEDIUM OF TRANSPORT

In looking at the kind of vehicle in which we are travelling in our dreams, it is useful to consider how and where the vehicle usually travels as well as its speed and if we have control over it.

Travelling on the ground may have quite different implications to flying or going by boat, as earth, air and water have their own complex sets of symbolic meanings that also need to be considered. So road travel could indicate groundedness and practicality, while flying may suggest ideas and fancies, and water an emotional journey. Getting airborne could be an allusion to our ideas or plans taking off and coming to fruition.

We also have preferences and feelings around different means

of transport – for instance, catching a bus when we are used to travelling in a chauffeur-driven car may have implications of loss of status, of reliance on public services instead of self-sufficiency, of having to wait, of being part of an anonymous crowd instead of having individual attention. Depending on whether or not the journey goes smoothly, the dream may be allaying fears around these issues or confirming your worst nightmares. Meandering down a lane on a bicycle can take a long time, and you may be frustrated at the slow pace or choose to enjoy the countryside as you go; it could also give you a sense of being in control as you can decide your route as well as where you stop. Space travel, by contrast, may suggest exploration of the unknown, and as we

hurtle at an incredible speed into the vast emptiness of space, away from everything and everyone that we know and love, we may feel lonely and isolated. We may also use a space ship to represent the pinnacle of technology, change and progress.

Many people are afraid of flying or boats, so dreams of travelling in these may well be bringing to the fore some of the insecurities you may have around not being on terra firma.

CARS AND DRIVING

As they are such an integral part of our lives, cars often feature in our dreams. We attach meanings to owning or being seen in certain kinds of car, and may use these meanings to represent certain things in our dreams. So a sports car implies power and

BELOW There are many types of vehicle. The ones we choose in our dreams can say a lot about us.
BELOW RIGHT Dreams of driving a car are quite common. Are you in control or is disaster looming ahead?

success – material, personal and sexual – while a sedan can be associated with families and stability, an off-road vehicle with adventure and exploration, and a truck with carrying a load. The condition of the vehicle may say a lot about how we are in relation to these aspects of our lives, while whether we own it or have borrowed or stolen it could be telling us about whether we feel we deserve them.

ACCIDENTS AND BREAKDOWNS

Derailment, car crashes or sinking boats are all powerful symbols of things going wrong in our lives, especially if we are involved in the accident, and can be taken as a warning. The scale of the accident can be used as an indicator for the seriousness of the problem – so a scrape in a parking lot may be a gentle warning, but a full passenger plane exploding in mid-air over the sea could be a more urgent message. Unlike accidents, hijackings are deliberate, and may be warning you that someone wants to take over your life or is holding you to ransom.

A vehicle that breaks down may be saying that your life is running into difficulties, or that you need to call a halt to ideas of escape. If this is the case, looking at exactly how it malfunctioned could give you a more precise picture of the area of your life that has broken down. Brake failure could show that you are unable to slow down or stop; running out of power is likely to be about your lack of energy.

ABOVE Some vehicles are very complex and need great knowledge and expertise to operate.
LEFT There is a simplicity and freedom about riding a bicycle. It is low maintenance and you are self-sufficient.
BELOW Launching into outer space could be thrilling or frightening. You would have to check how it is for you.

MAGIC AND FANTASY

Magical, mystical people, mythical
beasts, heroes and demons parade
through our dreams, inspired by the
fictions and superstitions of our culture
and brought to life by our imagination
as metaphors for our hopes and desires,
for the irrational terrors of our early
years, and even for the tricksters and
con artists we meet as we go about our
daily lives. These dreams can be
tremendously challenging as we can take
nothing for granted in this fantasy
reality, removed from the context of the
here and now, and in them we confront
our fears and demons head-on.

RIGHT Fantastical dreams can be used to access possibilities
beyond the mundane reality of everyday life, to help us shed
conventional boundaries.

FANTASTICAL DREAMS

DREAMS IN WHICH LANDSCAPES, CHARACTERS, MOTIFS AND PLOTS ARE FANTASTICAL OR SURREAL ARE AMONG THE MOST DIFFICULT TO INTERPRET AS THEY ARE NOT BASED IN OUR EVERYDAY EXPERIENCES AND WE HAVE NONE OF THE USUAL REFERENCE POINTS TO HELP US. FANTASY DREAMS CAN BE VERY UNSETTLING, SHAKING US OUT OF ROUTINE OR COMPLACENCY. THEY RETURN TO HAUNT OUR WAKING THOUGHTS AND DEMAND THAT WE STRIVE TO UNDERSTAND THEM – SWEEPING THEM UNDER THE CARPET OR IGNORING THEM SIMPLY DOESN'T WORK. THEY MAY LINGER FOR A LONG TIME AND BE QUITE HARD TO PURGE FROM OUR CONSCIOUSNESS.

FANTASY CHARACTERS

Dreams sometimes feature fantastical creatures – gentle, dreamy unicorns and ferocious dragons, seductive mermaids, fairies and elves, talking animals and a myriad others we may have created with or without the assistance of literature or legend. The creatures of our fantasies are part of our desire for things to be beyond the real world.

These creations may return us to our childhood where monsters lurked under the bed and the line between reality and fantasy was much more indistinct. They may be frightening or disturbing, forcing us to address our fears head-on, but sometimes they are wonderful, joyful creatures that show us new possibilities or have unimaginable love or wisdom. They may have exceptional powers, or take us to places that we can literally only dream of.

Creatures that we fabricate in our own minds, that are not found in myths or in the books we read as children, may have features that we take from several sources and combine into one character as a kind of catch-all for how we want to be or what we are most afraid of. It may be some idealized figure who will empower us, or a demon who threatens to destroy us.

FANTASY WORLDS

Dreams of fantasy may consist of unusual events or creatures set in surroundings that seem natural or familiar, or they may take place in weird and wonderful settings – a vast cavern that stretches upward as far as the eye can see, or the strange landscape of another planet; we may be floating in nothingness or surrounded by permeable membranes that melt away, leaving us in a new setting. In fantastical environments even the laws of nature may be different – gravity may be stronger or weaker, we may be able to do things we can't normally do, such as flying – and social structures may be incomprehensible. Great battles or forces of good and evil confronting each other directly strip away the mundane detail of our real lives, along with the rules of politics and diplomacy.

The fictitious worlds of literature are as varied as they are fantastical. Some, such as Tolkien's Middle Earth or C.S. Lewis's Narnia, may look like places we could visit, but the creatures that inhabit them and

BELOW Our dreams are very close to the hidden, magical world of the unconscious and many dreams have a fairy-tale quality about them. **BELOW RIGHT** In fantasy dreams, unusual or mythical creatures are the products of a rich and fertile imagination.

key elements of the plot could only be found in fantasy. Alice in Wonderland has an explicitly surreal dream setting, although it has realistic elements alongside its talking animals, mutations, and spatial distortions. Or the infamous world of Harry Potter shows us ordinary boys and girls who are able to slip out of family life into a world where they have magical powers: people walk through walls and play games in mid-air; cars can fly and animals have special powers. Perhaps part of the reason that all these stories are so popular is that they each explore archetypal themes, such as the use of power or the struggle between good and evil.

TRANSFORMATION

Like the hybrid animals of mythology, fantastical elements may involve the coming together of objects or beings that are normally quite distinct, or the transformation of one thing into another. Material objects may take on unusual properties or space and time may be distorted. These transformations and mutations draw your attention to both the normal and the unusual properties of the objects or creatures, and you should try to reconcile both and notice what it is that is being distorted.

Fantasy dreams may represent all that we find exceptional about the world. They are our unconscious mind's way of being inventive and unconventional and can help us work through some very human issues. Fantastical or magical dreams also remind us that we are much more than logic and reasoning. We are creatures with a powerful imagination and have the ability to devise creative solutions to our problems and answers to some of the big questions about our very existence.

ABOVE Art and literature can provide a stimulus for the unconscious in its nightly dream production. Check the landscape of your dreams to see if there is anything you recognize. Is the narrative running as it should or has the story changed?

I suspect that there are more things in heaven and earth than are dreamed of, or can be dreamed of, in any philosophy.   J. B. S. HALDANE

LEFT Children are usually fascinated by magic and fantasy, perhaps because they are much closer to their instinctive feelings than most adults.
FAR LEFT The fantasy images we produce in our dreams will have a cultural emphasis. Traditionally, fairies are magical creatures who use their powers to either help or hinder us.

MYTHS AND LEGENDS

OUR DISTANT ANCESTORS TRIED TO FIND EXPLANATIONS FOR THE MANY PHENOMENA OF NATURE IN THE WORLD AROUND THEM – THE SUN RISING, THE CHANGING SEASONS, AND CYCLES OF LIFE AND DEATH. BECAUSE THEIR KNOWLEDGE WAS LIMITED, THEY DEVISED EXPLANATIONS BASED ON THE EXISTENCE OF SUPERHUMAN BEINGS, GODS AND GODDESSES WHO NOT ONLY OFFERED AN EXPLANATION FOR WHY THINGS WERE THE WAY THEY WERE, BUT ALSO CREATED THE POSSIBILITY OF INFLUENCING NATURE BY MEANS OF SACRIFICES, PRAYERS AND OFFERINGS. OTHER CREATURES PERFORMED SIMILAR ROLES – FIRE-BREATHING DRAGONS, THE PHOENIX RISING FROM THE ASHES, GIANTS AND MERMAIDS.

TIMELESS, UNIVERSAL TALES

In preliterate societies, the most common way of passing on these understandings, values and beliefs was in memorable stories that could be told and retold. Their significance was easy to understand, and the characters, creatures and events that were portrayed had a universal relevance. In this way, stories became part of the cultural vocabulary of any society, and the creatures of myth and legend are deeply embedded in our psyche; in our dreams we use them as signposts to the qualities that they embody, as icons.

ENTERING THE WORLD OF MYTH

In our dreams we are free to enter mythical worlds. We can don a mask or join a procession, engage with the king or the fool, the warrior priest or the god of winter. We can even become that character – try out its role, take on its greatness.

These dreams put us in touch with our instinctive and intuitive selves – a side of us that may need attention. They may be an

LEFT Our dreams are a way of entering the world of myths and legends. By identifying with the characters in our dreams we may learn something about ourselves.

emotive plea from our unconscious mind to dance in the moonlight, to worship the corn, to make a sacrifice or an offering. But we are also fragile beings who are subject to all sorts of fears; myths both allay those fears and add to them.

GODS AND GODDESSES

Mythical figures probably appear in our dreams in much the same way as they did to our ancestors. In our dreams, making an offering to calm a raging god makes sense to us just as it did in real life to our forebears. Our unconscious processes have not changed, although just as our own personal experiences affect how we understand any dream element, our relationship with these figures will be based on how we respond to what they typically represent to us.

We create gods and goddesses so that we can feel safe and protected, so that we can absolve ourselves of responsibility for something; but in their creation we also unleash the terrible aspects of such deities – death and destruction, their capricious nature, their awesome powers. We create them to protect us but we may also come to fear them, and we learn to deal with this dichotomy in dreams of myths. We are shown that the qualities

and powers these supernatural beings have in abundance exist within us if we have the courage to acknowledge them.

HYBRID CREATURES

Myths and legends from around the world and through the ages are filled with creatures that are part animal and part human, or that are a mixture of two or three different creatures, and have an element of danger. Mermaids – half fish and half beautiful woman – have been blamed for many a shipwreck, as they lure sailors on to the rocks, while the sphinx, with the head of a woman and the body of a lion, is notorious for strangling travellers who cannot answer her riddles.

Minotaurs, griffins, satyrs and centaurs join the line-up of hybrid creatures from the realm of myth and legend. All have particular associations from the tales in which they feature, but they also embody qualities of the creatures they comprise. In this way, the sphinx may have qualities of femininity but also

the ferocious, uncompromising strength of a lion, and by virtue of her behaviour in the Greek legend could represent any threatening and somewhat enigmatic character, particularly if associated with knowledge and learning, such as a punitive teacher. In a sense, by dreaming of a hybrid creature we are hedging our bets, or efficiently representing several qualities in a single character, trying to resolve anomalies in our lives.

PEOPLE

Not all the characters in myth and legend are fantastical. People appear throughout these tales, sometimes in elevated roles as kings and queens, other times as ordinary mortals who are caught up in greater things. Either way, they could be used to illustrate the ideals and extremes of human nature – heroism, bravery, love, power and so on. Such tales also illustrate some timeless human quandaries and problems, such as the tragedy of Oedipus, who unknowingly kills his father and

marries his mother; the agony of the endless task of Sisyphus, who is obliged to push a rock up a hill, only to have it roll down as he has almost reached the brow. By working with these characters in our dreams, we work with the qualities that they embody and the battles that they fight.

ABOVE The mythical figures in our dreams usually have something very profound to convey. **ABOVE LEFT** Hybrid creatures can remind us of the beast within us all. **ABOVE FAR LEFT** Giant figures may assume the status of gods with the power to create or destroy life.

MYTHICAL DREAM

"In my dream I was walking through a forest. I could hear the birds singing and could feel the warmth of the sun on my skin. A soft breeze was blowing. As I walked, I came to a tiny cottage – it might sound far-fetched but it really did look like a gingerbread house, the kind you read about in fairy-tale stories. The house looked so inviting and I was tired and hot from walking, so I went up to the door and walked inside. I remember walking up a few stairs and going into a bedroom. It wasn't a room I had ever seen before. As I went in, I heard the front door downstairs click shut and the room I was in became shadowy. I started to feel afraid. There was a dark-haired man at the window and he was trying to get into the room. I tried to run away, but my legs wouldn't move. I woke up shouting.

At first it was difficult to revisit this dream or nightmare, but I decided to focus on what the man at the window represented. As I worked with the dream, to my amazement he turned into a golden-haired Apollo kind of figure, a sort of sun-god. I interpreted this to mean that I am afraid of my own power. I see it as something dark or "bad", so I try to run from it, but actually it radiates light."

ALIENS AND UFOs

WHEN FACED WITH THE UNKNOWN WE OFTEN TRY TO MAKE SENSE OF IT – IN THE FIRST INSTANCE IN TERMS OF WHAT WE ALREADY KNOW WELL, AND THEN PERHAPS IN TERMS OF CONCEPTS FROM THE REALM OF FANTASY OR SPECULATION, OF WHICH WE COULDN'T POSSIBLY HAVE ANY REAL EXPERIENCE. DREAMING OF ALIENS, SPACE SHIPS, FLYING SAUCERS AND SO ON MAY BE OUR WAY OF EXPLAINING AND VISUALIZING THE INEXPLICABLE SITUATIONS OR PHENOMENA THAT WE ARE TRYING TO UNDERSTAND AND COME TO TERMS WITH. WHEN WE HAVE TO FACE THE UNKNOWN WE TRY TO GIVE IT A FACE, A PERSONALITY. THE CREATURES FROM OUTER SPACE SERVE THIS PURPOSE WELL; THEY ARE, BY DEFINITION, ALIEN.

ALIENS

It is surprising how the aliens in our dreams are often very similar. How much this is due to us all watching the same films, and how much it is the manifestation of a new archetype that has developed in our collective unconscious, is difficult to tell. Indeed both could be true, and it is simply that the film-makers are the ones that give shape in a visual way to the archetype.

THE ALIEN WITHIN

Everything in a dream comes from within yourself – you create all of it for your own personal consumption, and there is nothing in it that is actually alien.

If you are creating images of aliens then they represent some part of you that feels alienated or frightened of the unknown – or exhilarated by it. Some part of you is acknowledging an aspect of your life that is manifesting as alien or foreign, that has not been incorporated into your self-image, your lifestyle or your personal environment.

Aliens are often represented as scary, unpredictable creatures that seem bent on threatening our existence and invading our planet. In this way they provide an easy metaphor for situations in our own lives where we feel threatened or invaded by something or someone over

which we have little or no control. It is also significant that we have little understanding of these creatures – we cannot comprehend or anticipate their motives or intentions, and we often have no way of communicating with them. They are unknown and unknowable, and consequently we have no idea of the scale of the threat. Dreaming of aliens is often our way of working through situations that make us feel anxious – perhaps confronting head-on the source of our anxiety and allowing us to try out ways of dealing with it.

Many people feel that they do not fit into society; they feel

BELOW RIGHT Some of the most mysterious phenomena on Earth have been connected with aliens from outer space. **BELOW** When it comes to dreams of aliens and UFOs, there does seem to be some form of universal symbolism that we all understand.

different from most other people they meet, and an encounter with aliens may be a positive, life-affirming experience. Being abducted by aliens may show a yearning for an alternative society where they feel they belong, or it could be an expression of belief in the existence of a society where they are valued.

SPACE TRAVEL

If aliens use UFOs as their vehicle for accessing or invading us, flying saucers, space ships and rockets might well also offer a dramatic avenue of escape for us. It may be that we actually want to break out of our limited world, and such craft offer us a way of literally reaching for the stars, exploring the unknown, having adventures not normally possible in real life. Seeing Earth receding into the distance may help us to stand back and see our world in perspective, in the context of the vastness of space.

ABOVE The concept of UFOs is fascinating. In our dreams they could represent a dramatic way of leaving the everyday world behind.
LEFT To dream the aliens are landing may mean that we should be prepared to encounter something new or strange in our lives.
BELOW When we break out in our dreams we may be trying to break out in our waking life. Spiralling weightless in the galaxy could suggest a spiritual, enlightening experience.

SPACE DREAM

"The sky was full of glowing space ships, full of smoking beings. We were firing guns and bullets at the space ships and the aliens were falling down dead everywhere, bleeping as they died. But there were more of them than I could count and they didn't all die – some were landing. Then I woke up."

This was the dream of a six-year-old child who was worried about starting in a new class at school. In his dream the aliens represented the threatening situation he was having to face and his lack of control over it.

PROPHECY

ABOVE Some people have dreamt about plane crashes and other disasters before they have happened, but prophetic dreams are actually quite rare.
ABOVE RIGHT What looks like a prophetic dream may have a metaphorical meaning: are you living on a knife edge?

WE USUALLY FIND PROPHECY MANIFESTING IN DREAMS IN TWO DIFFERENT WAYS — FIRSTLY AS DREAMS IN WHICH WE FORESEE FUTURE EVENTS (OR FEEL THAT WE DO SO), AND SECONDLY AS DREAMS IN WHICH WE, OR OTHER CHARACTERS IN THE DREAM, ARE TRYING TO LOOK INTO THE FUTURE. WHETHER OR NOT YOU BELIEVE IT IS ACTUALLY POSSIBLE TO SEE INTO THE FUTURE, BOTH THESE KINDS OF DREAMS MIGHT SUGGEST THAT YOU FEEL A NEED TO DO SO; WHETHER IT IS THROUGH INSECURITY OR CURIOSITY IT IS WORTH ANALYSING WHY, OR WHAT IT IS YOU WANT TO FORESEE.

PROPHETIC DREAMS

There have been countless reports of people having a dream that changed their life. They saw an elevator accident, so the next day they took the stairs and the elevator plunged to the ground, killing everybody in it. Or they saw a ship sinking and cancelled their cruise holiday, although hundreds of other passengers perished. Or perhaps they may have dreamt of a car crash and saved their lives by catching the train the next day.

Perhaps we should be a little sceptical of these many urban legends. Only the success stories survive – we do not get to hear of those who took a different course of action than planned and this subsequently turned out to be the wrong thing to do. Nor do we hear of people who change their plans because of a dream and find that it made no significant difference in their lives. Dreams of prophecy are actually very rare. And yet in those cases that actually do turn out to be prophetic we are dealing with something outside of the normal, something

mysterious and inexplicable. It's only when we have had a dream that came true ourselves that we can judge whether such a thing is possible. Once it has happened to us we believe, we know, we don't doubt.

It may also be that we dream how we want the future to be, and having already created the desired scenario, we find we are more able to make it happen. In this way the dream may seem prophetic, but it might be more accurate to think of it as a prompt or suggestion.

GAZING INTO THE FUTURE

Wanting to know what the future holds in store seems to be universal – no matter what society or what period in history you look at, you will find seers

---

PROPHECY DREAM

"I'm a keen tarot reader, so I'm not surprised when I find myself doing this in my dreams. In this dream I was with a female friend of mine who is single. She and I were having a glass of wine together, sitting on purple cushions. We started playing with the tarot, and she turned up the card of the Lovers. I remember thinking that I must remember to tell her, that it looked like she would meet someone special very soon.

I actually had forgotten the dream until a couple of months later, when sure enough my friend started a new relationship! Then the memory of the dream came flooding back and I told her what had happened. I think I need more practice in recalling my dreams if they are to be any use!"

and prophets, in addition to numerous tools or methods employed, often by ordinary people, to foretell events that have yet to happen.

In your dream the kind of person who is foretelling the future may be significant – is it one of the great prophets (a biblical figure, perhaps, or Nostradamus) whose predictions may hold the authority of their fame and greatness, or is it a fairground "gypsy" in fancy dress, who gazes into a crystal ball and puts on something of a performance for you, and may just be pulling the wool over your eyes? How credible they are and whether you believe in prediction is critical to how much you believe what you hear.

Some kinds of prediction rely on a kind of sixth sense, while others make use of consistent and well-established methods, such as tarot reading, palmistry, astrology or numerology, and to some extent make their projections on the basis of existing trends or patterns. Either way there may still be a leap of

faith. Much of our desire to see into the future is an expression of our desire for certainty and clarity in a world that is so uncertain and so complex that clarity is hard to find.

We turn to prophecy to help us make decisions we are faced with, or to reassure us that we

are on the right path. Dreaming of prophecy could be showing you that you need to make some choices, or clarify what the issues are before you can do so. You may fear something is going to happen, and express your anxiety by trying to find out what you are going to be faced with.

ABOVE Our desire to know what the future has in store is universal. The symbolism of tarot cards can be interpreted in a similar way to dreams.
ABOVE LEFT Whether or not we can see into the future is open to debate. To dream of gazing into a crystal ball may mean you are looking for direction.

LEFT Traditionally, virgin priestesses were attributed with the power of "second sight". If such a figure appears in your dreams pay particular attention to what she is trying to communicate – it could be very important.

MAGIC

IN ESSENCE, MAGIC IS ABOUT TWO THINGS – CHANGE AND POWER. WITH MAGIC, DRAMATIC TRANSFORMATION CAN BE BROUGHT ABOUT IN OUR LIVES, WHETHER WE ARE THE AGENTS OF CHANGE OR WHETHER SOME OTHER MAGICAL FIGURE IS ABLE TO PERFORM HIS OR HER ART ON US. WHOEVER HAS THE ABILITY TO PERFORM MAGIC HOLDS GREAT POWER, ESPECIALLY OVER THOSE ORDINARY MORTALS WHO DO NOT. WITH MAGIC WE CAN DO THINGS THAT WE ARE NOT NORMALLY ABLE TO DO, AND WE FEEL BOTH THE JOY AND THE DANGER OF HAVING THIS IMMENSE POWER. MAGIC CAN ALSO MEAN TRICKERY, HOWEVER, AND IT MIGHT BE THIS CHARACTERISTIC THAT WE ARE DREAMING OF.

ABOVE Animals often take on supernatural characteristics. If you dream of an unearthly creature you need to explore your dream fully to find out what it means. In some cultures a black cat is said to symbolize good luck.

TRANSFORMATION AND CHANGE

Dreams about magic may be a sign that we need to make changes, within ourselves or in our environment. They can be about movement or the lack of it, about being stuck and needing to make effort and expend energy in order to move on, to free ourselves from stagnation and from feeling stuck in a rut. Magic gives us an extra boost to get us to see things differently and get us moving again.

MAGIC AND POWER

In our dreams we can perhaps move objects, conjure up demons, raise a storm or calm a sea. We can kill or heal from a distance, transform people into other creatures with the wave of a wand, and become invisible.

We have probably all wished occasionally that we could do these things in our waking lives. This would give us tremendous power and perhaps it is this that we are after when we dream about magic. Sometimes it would be wonderful to wave a magic wand and make everything better, to change things that are in reality beyond our control – even to subjugate those who normally hold us in their power. We may take great delight for instance, in being able to turn a bullying boss into a tiny mouse, or an unfriendly neighbour into a puff of smoke.

Conversely, having magic performed on us, particularly if it is done against our will, or if it is done by characters who have bad intentions or who in our waking lives have authority over us, can be immensely disempowering and could be drawing our attention to a lack of power or control in our lives. A dream of losing powers that we felt we previously had can also have a similar effect.

HOPES AND FANTASIES

In a more general sense, though, dreaming of magic allows us to work out our fantasies – in our dreams nothing is impossible if we want it to come true, and we have the power to live out our hopes and desires. Dreams also prompt us to look at certain areas of our life that may be lacking in some way, and teach us what we need to do to make things happen. While in a literal way the tricks of magic in our dreams may only be possible in a dream world, their underlying truth can be carried into our daily lives and give us something to work with.

PURVEYORS OF MAGIC

In our dreams it is important to look at the nature and intentions of those who hold the magical powers – whether they are our allies or are threatening and potentially harmful characters is vital to understanding why we are dreaming of magic.

Witches and wizards, as well as magicians and sorcerers, may be sources of good or evil alike. Magicians enthral us with their sleight-of-hand performances, but such trickery may also be more than entertainment, prompting us to look at people in our lives who deceive and trick us, who are trying to pull the wool over our eyes. We need to

look at how we might be living a lie, lulled into a false sense of security by our own illusions or those put out by others. In Jungian thought the archetype of the Magician is also known as the Fool, whose surface folly disguises hidden depths of wisdom. Being outside the normal order of society he can say things that no one else would dare to, and thereby shows us things we might otherwise avoid looking at.

THE TRICKS OF THE TRADE

Spells, potions and magic wands are the typical tools of witches and wizards and their presence is another indicator of magic dreams. Being "spellbound" in a dream is akin to being in the thrall of an influential person in waking life, and indeed the lesson to be learnt from such dreams could be to look at whether you are overly impressed by someone, being taken in or manipulated by them, or attracted to something in them which is not real.

If you think the dream character does seem to correspond to someone in your waking life, take note of your gut response to them, notice how trustworthy they are, and try to see beyond any surface appeal.

THE SUPERNATURAL

THE MYSTERIOUS WORLD OF THE SUPERNATURAL IS INHABITED BY GHOSTLY FIGURES, VAMPIRES, WEREWOLVES AND A HOST OF OTHER CREATURES. MANY OF US LIKE THE COMFORT OF FAMILIARITY, AND FIND THE IDEA OF THE SUPERNATURAL DISTURBING AND TERRIFYING. BY AND LARGE WE AVOID CONTACT WITH THIS WORLD, BUT SOME SEEK IT OUT AND LINK UP WITH IT IN SÉANCES OR BY EXTRA-SENSORY PERCEPTION (ESP). DREAMS OF THE SUPERNATURAL CAN IMPLY THAT OUR PSYCHE WANTS US TO SPEND MORE TIME AND EFFORT INVESTIGATING SUCH MATTERS AS ACKNOWLEDGING OUR SHADOW SELF. ALTERNATIVELY, WE MAY NEED TO MAKE A RADICAL CHANGE OF DIRECTION IN OUR LIVES.

GHOSTS

When ghosts appear in our dreams they can represent unfinished business. Ghosts are the unsettled spirits of the dead who haven't yet found their place in the hereafter, perhaps because they still have some tie to earthly matters. As ghosts are neither fully present nor fully absent, they raise questions about uncertainty and lack of clarity, perhaps about who we are or what we are doing in our lives.

In ghostly figures we are confronted with our own mortality. They give us some sneak preview of the afterlife, without really offering any explanations. Perhaps they offer some hope as well that our existence does not terminate with our death. We can also see them as shadows of ourselves –

personifications of our own dark nature, the shadowy side of our selves that we often dare not face.

How the ghosts behave in our dream and how we respond to them is important in discovering what they mean. Some are invisible, others may be shadowy translucent figures. They may be noisy poltergeists or silent figures that only betray their presence by moving things, pointing to our lack of control over our own environment. They may interact with us, but often don't do so directly. You may feel terrified or stressed, or be comforted by their presence. They may be recognizable as strangers, deceased friends or relatives, or famous people. Your relationship to them as such will also affect what they mean in your dream – for instance the ghost may be

BELOW RIGHT Ghosts and phantoms may haunt us in our dreams and this can feel very unnerving. Try to find out what the ghostly visitation is about.
BELOW Strange unearthly figures may appear in our dreams, but these are usually the products of our dreaming psyche.

GHOSTLY DREAM

"I was sitting in a graveyard surrounded by pale, ghoulish figures. I knew they were out to devour me – it was as if I were destined to be a victim, to have my life drawn from me. There was nothing I could do as these ghastly, ghostly shapes crowded around me. But the horror that woke me wasn't them – it was the feeling of my own quiet acquiescence.

When I was thinking about this dream I realized this was exactly how I was behaving in my relationship, allowing my partner to make all the decisions, and it was burying my personality. On going back over the dream in my mind, I knew that I had to return to that graveyard and shout 'No!' and make them retreat, not just sit there and let them eat my soul."

your nagging mother-in-law who is very much alive but casts a shadow over you and is forever interfering with your life.

Ghosts may be all that remain to us of people who have already died, and seeing one may provide a welcome opportunity to have contact with a loved one who has died but whose death you may not yet have come to terms with.

SUPERNATURAL PARASITES

Vampires are the infamous figures of the dead who leave the grave after dark and suck the blood of the living, drawing with it their life-force, or energy, which they need to survive, and often killing their victims in the process. These are the parasites of the supernatural world, and they share this dubious distinction with other ghostly figures such as ghouls, who prey on the dead, and the succubi and incubi, demons who take human form to suck the sexual energy out of sleeping people. In more superstitious times the Catholic Church blamed many a nocturnal

RIGHT A wolf baying at full moon is often associated with supernatural forces. Full moon is when the forces of nature are at their strongest, and traditionally has strong associations with lunacy.

sexual awakening on such apparitions, while in China ghosts are said to be "hungry".

Vampires are defeated by daylight or the simple but powerful icon of the wooden cross, showing us that even such basic forms of protection can give us an escape route from the horror. Indeed, dreams of parasitic ghosts and vampires are often about self-protection. If you dream of these creatures you should look at those aspects of your own life where you feel you are being devoured or having the life sucked out of you. Perhaps you are feeling either used or dominated by your partner, or you have an exploitative boss who makes you work long hours so that you don't have the life or energy to do the things you enjoy. More unusually you may be acting parasitically and have some kind of disturbance around

this. These dreams are our unconscious mind's way of working out such relationships, as well as making us aware that something is wrong.

BATS AND WEREWOLVES

Like vampires, werewolves and bats are nocturnal creatures that suck their victim's blood. A vampire can "shape shift" into a bat, while a werewolf is a human who becomes a vicious beast at full moon. If these creatures appear in your dreams it may be to draw attention to something going on in your life that is frightening or tricky to deal with.

BELOW LEFT Be wary of bewitching figures, as vampires in particular often appear seductive. Who is trying to suck your blood?
BELOW The spirits of the dead come to life at night. A disused building can appear very spooky.

PART FIVE

DIRECTORY
OF SIGNS

A The first letter of the alphabet, used to signify the best, first.

ACTIVE INTELLECT Unknown origin, also one of the signs for water.

ADINKRAHENE Most important of the Ghanaian adinkra symbols, signifying the importance of playing a leading role.

ADONI Hebrew word meaning a lord who is not God.

AEROPLANE Spiritual aspiration, and the transcendence of human limitations.

AIR The element. Kabbalistic sign.

AIR The element. Old chemistry symbol.

AKOBEN Ghanaian adinkra symbol meaning vigilance and wariness. The akoben is a horn used to sound a battle cry.

AKOKONAN "Leg of the hen", Ghanaian adinkra symbol meaning mercy, nurturing. Inspired by the hen's habit of treading on her chicks without hurting them, being a protective but also corrective parent.

AKOMA NTOSO Ghanaian adinkra symbol meaning understanding and agreement.

ALCHEMY, the art of. The sun sign is at the centre, surrounded by the four elemental triangles, crowned with the Christian cross, and then placed in a circle representing the eternal or spiritual dimension.

ALCHEMY, the art of, variation. Used in the 17th century, this sign was created under the influence of Pythagorean geometry mysticism.

ALCHEMY, the art of, variation. This symbol is also engraved on rock faces dating from 1000 BC in Uxmal,
Central America. The symbol was adopted by Rudolf Steiner and is associated with Steiner's anthroposophy.

ALCOHOL Alchemistic sign.

ALCOHOL Early chemical sign.

ALEMBIC Alchemistic sign for distillation flask or still. Also used in early chemistry.

ALGOL The fixed star, used in some Kabbalistic mysticist contexts on magical amulet seals.

ALGORAB The fixed star, used in Kabbalistic magical amulet seals.

ALINEA Typographical sign used in printed texts, meaning the beginning of a new train of thought.

ALL IS WELL Ground to air emergency code.

ALMOND An important symbol with pagan and Christian roots associated with purity and virgin birth. Its juice was associated with semen in the ancient world. Biblical tradition says that Aaron's priestly status was shown by his rod blossoming and producing almonds. Western art often shows Mary and Jesus enclosed in an almond-shaped aureole.

ALPHA The first letter of the Greek alphabet, associated with beginnings. Linked with God, who is said to be the alpha and omega – the beginning and the end. Also once a secret sign of the Christian faith.

ALPHECCA The fixed star, used as a Kabbalistic magical amulet seal.

ALUM Alchemistic sign.

AMALGAM Alchemistic sign.

AMALGAMATION Alchemistic sign.

traditions, heavenly creatures in Jewish, Christian and Islamic traditions, thought to be evolved from Semitic and Egyptian winged deities. Seen as messengers, warriors, guardians or protectors.

ANT Hard work, organized community. The anthill is a symbol of industrious life in Tibetan Buddhism; in parts of Africa it is associated with fertility and creativity.

ANTI-CLOCKWISE SPIRAL Dynamic symbol of life force, cosmic and earthly.

APHRODITE Sign of the goddess.

APRICOT In China, the apricot is a symbol for a beautiful woman; the Japanese plum (*ume*) is sometimes called an apricot.

AMPERSAND Typographical sign meaning "and".

ANIMALIA The animal kingdom, 18th century.

ANTARES The fixed star, Kabbalistic magical amulet seal.

APOLLO This symbol of the god is based on the shape of the lyre, which was Apollo's instrument.

AQUA REGIA Alchemistic sign for "king's water".

ANARCHISM Synonym for the political movement.

ANKH A cross topped with a loop; ancient Egyptian symbol of immortal life. Later adopted as a Christian symbol by the Egyptian Coptic Church.

ANTELOPE In Africa associated with the moon and fecundity; for the Bambara (Mali) the animal was sent by the creator god to teach humans agriculture.

ANTIMONY Alchemistic, also used in medicine.

APPLE Symbol of bliss, especially sexual; emblem of love, marriage, spring, youth, fertility and immortality. Linked with the forbidden fruit of the Garden of Eden and so a Christian symbol of temptation and original sin.

AQUA REGIA Alchemistic sign for king's water, variation.

ANCHOR In early Christianity, a secret sign for the cross; hope, salvation. Also a symbol of the sea; of steadfastness and safety; and of the self.

ANSUR Rune for A

ANVIL In Polynesia and parts of Africa, associated with the female principle and fertility; in Scottish folklore, linked with magical powers of the blacksmith.

APE Respected in ancient Egypt, Africa, India and China, but distrusted in the Christian tradition, where it is a symbol of vice and lust.

APPROXIMATELY EQUAL TO Mathematical sign.

AQUARIUS Zodiac sign.

ANGEL Symbol of divine will in several

ANTI NUCLEAR CAMPAIGN The emblem of the Campaign for Nuclear Disarmament, made up of the semaphore signs for the letters "N" and "D".

ARATHRON Planet, mystical Kabbalistic sign for the first Olympic spirit.

ARCH Triumph and victory; grand human achievements.

ARIES Zodiac sign.

Hindu gods symbolize their complexity and power. An upraised arm can suggest either a threat or a blessing. The arm also has protective connotations.

ARROW, WAVY Sea currents.

ATOM, less common variation than above.

ARROW, WEAPON In Islam stands for the wrath of Allah, in Christianity for martyrdom and death. Bundled or broken in Native American symbolism, arrows stand for peace.

ARSENIC Alchemistic sign, variation.

ARCTURUS The fixed star, Kabbalistic magic amulet seal.

ARK OF THE COVENANT One of the symbols of the Jewish faith, a chest that was God's pledge of divine protection. The ark was kept in another symbol of Judaism, the Tabernacle.

ARMOUR In medieval Europe, armour symbolized the knightly virtues of courage, protection, honour and strength; symbol of warrior class in China and Japan.

AUDI Corporate emblem of the car manufacturers, symbol of unity and togetherness.

ASS The god, later oss, rune for rapids or waterfall.

ASS See Donkey

ARES Sign of the god.

ARSENIC Alchemistic sign.

AUROCH The rune Ur, sign for auroch.

ARROW As directional sign.

ASTERISK Typographical sign for footnote.

ARK OR BOAT A symbol of salvation and preservation found in the mythology of peoples all around the world. In Christianity the ark stands for the Church, for Mary or for Christ; in secular symbolism it is a symbol of the Earth adrift in space.

ARSENIC Alchemistic sign, variation.

AUTUMN Old Germanic time sign.

ARES Sign of the god, variation.

ARROW/ARROW HEAD Penetration – by light, death, love or perception. Linked to sun symbols and the piercing darts of love.

ATOM Also uranium, nuclear reactor (on maps), nuclear research, nuclear physics.

ARES Sign of the god, variation.

ARSENIC Alchemistic sign, variation.

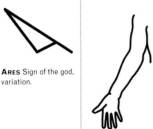

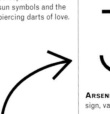

ARROW, CURVED Ancient sign found in prehistoric cave art in Western Europe.

ARM Symbol of power and strength; the many arms given to

AUTUMN Old Germanic time sign, variation.

AXE Almost universal symbol of decisive power and authority. Associated with the creative force of the thunderbolt. Linked with ancient sun and storm gods. Used to invoke thunder and rain in West Africa; symbol of the union of families in Chinese marriage.

BADGER Linked with playfulness in China; in Celtic tradition with slyness, deceit.

BALL Symbol of childhood games; in China, associated with the sun and the yin/yang symbol.

BAMBOO Chinese symbol of resilience, longevity, happiness

and spiritual truth; Japanese symbol of truth and devotion.

BANANA Freudian phallic symbol.

BASILISK A medieval symbol of lust and disease.

BASKET Womb symbol; in the Americas, stories about baskets and basket-making are related to women.

BASS CLEF Music notation.

BAT Associated with death, symbol of fear and superstition, linked with witchcraft and the occult in Western folklore. In Africa and ancient Greece it was a symbol of perspicuity. Can signify madness. Underworld divinity in Central American and Brazilian mythology.

BATH Associated with bathing and thus with purification, both spiritual and physical.

BEANS Symbol of fecundity, used as love charms in India and to ward off evil spirits in Japan.

BEAR Emblem of masculine courage and primeval force; while she-bears symbolize care and warmth – although Jung linked them with dangerous aspects of the unconscious. In Christian and Islamic traditions the bear is cruel and lustful.

BEARD Important aspect of male symbolism, representing dignity, sovereignty, virility and wisdom. Sign of a king; in ancient Egypt beardless rulers, including women, were depicted with false beards to proclaim their status.

BEE/BEEHIVE Society, industry and working together; honeybees are also linked with romantic love in European, Chinese and Hindu traditions. Bees are linked with death and the otherworld in European folklore.

BELL The voice that proclaims the truth, especially in Buddhist, Hindu, Islamic and Christian traditions. In China it symbolizes obedience and cosmic harmony. Small tinkling bells can represent happiness and sexual pleasure. Worn on Hebrew dresses as a sign of virginity. Linked with the

feminine principle, also protective. Marks the passing of time and proclaims good news, warns of danger and tolls for death.

BELT OR GIRDLE Female chastity, marital fidelity or seductiveness. Magic girdles appear in myth as emblems of strength and became a symbol of honour in England. The rope girdles of monks allude to the scourging of Christ. The Hindu girdle is an emblem of the cycles of time.

BEORC Rune for B.

BETHOR The planet; mystical Kabbalistic sign for the second Olympic spirit.

BIOHAZARD Warning, USA.

BIRCH Beneficial, protective, sacred to Germanic gods. Cosmic tree of Central Asia. In shamanic rites it symbolized human ascent to the spirit world.

BIRDS Symbol of the human soul, representing goodness and joy, standing for wisdom, intelligence and the swift power of thought. Aboriginal stories suggest they bear information. In Western art birds can symbolize air and touch.

BIRTH CHART Elizabethan England, 17th century.

BISON/BUFFALO
High-status animal in India and South-east Asia. In China the domestic buffalo is associated with the contemplative life. For North American Indians it symbolizes strength, prosperity, plenty and supernatural power.

BJARKAN Rune associated with new life and growth.

BLESSED SIGN One of the blessed signs that appears, among other places, in the early symbolism of the Buddha's footprints in India. In the West this symbol stands for the hexachord, and for harmonics in general.

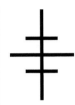

BLESSING/HARMLESS A variation of the pope's cross.

BLINDFOLD/BLIND Spiritual blindness; in Masonic ritual, removing the blindfold symbolizes spiritual illumination. In classical antiquity, Fortuna (goddess of fortune) is blindfolded to show that she favours none above any other.

BMW Corporate emblem of the car manufacturer, a variation of the sun cross, the ancient structure for the sun's energy.

BOAR Primordial symbol of strength, aggression and resolute courage

across the northern and the Celtic worlds. Sacred as a sun symbol in Iran, and a moon symbol in Japan. It became a Christian symbol for tyranny and lust.

BOAT Symbol of womb-like protection, also linked to the salvation and regeneration symbolism of the ark.

BOIL/ABCESS Alchemical sign.

BOIL (verb). Old Germanic.

BOIL (verb). Alchemistic sign.

BONES Symbol of possible reincarnation or bodily resurrection for ancient societies. Ancient beliefs held that the essence of a person was contained in the bones, a connection that is echoed in the phrase "felt in the bones".

BOOK Symbol of knowledge and wisdom in many sacred traditions (Judaic, Christian, Islam); in ancient Egypt, the Book of the Dead was a collection of sacred charms buried with the dead to assist them in the afterlife.

BORAX Alchemistic sign.

BORAX/TINKAL Alchemistic sign.

BOW Symbol of stored energy, willpower, aspiration, love, divine power and tension. Emblem of war and hunting. In Oriental thought it also represented spiritual discipline.

BOWL/VESSEL Alchemistic.

BOX Symbol of womb and female unconscious, associated with secrets and hiding. In classical myth, Pandora's box is a symbol of what must not be opened.

BRACELET As jewellery can denote rank. May also be used as identity tags.

BRASS Alchemistic.

BREAD A staple of life, associated with hope in the Hebrew tradition, unleavened bread symbolizes purification and sacrifice. Christian metaphor for the food of the spirit, and the body of Christ.

BRIDGE Spans two distinct realms (Heaven and Earth, matter and spirit, the visible and the invisible); transition symbol, the crossing of one state to another.

BRIDLE In classical antiquity, said to have been invented by Athena, goddess of peace and war; associated with temperance and restraint, as in "bridling" or the reining in of passions.

BROOM Associated with magical powers from ancient times. A symbol of removal. Western folklore links brooms with witches due to the belief that evil spirits could bewitch the implement used to drive them out.

BUBBLE Symbol of illusion (Buddhism, Taoism); the transient and ephemeral.

BUCKLE OF ISIS Ancient Egyptian protection sign.

BUDDHA The seated Buddha is a symbol of enlightenment.

BUFFALO See Bison

BULL Hugely symbolic animal representing moon, sun, earth, sky, rain, heat, feminine procreation, male ardour, matriarch and patriarch, death, regeneration. In cave art the bull is a symbol of vital energy. The bull's bellowing stamping energy is linked with thunder and earthquakes, especially in Crete.

BULL ROARER Musical instrument and cult object common to indigenous peoples

(Americas, Australia); when whirled in the air, it makes an otherworldly roaring sound, similar to the sound of thunder. Used in shamanic ritual and initiation ceremonies to communicate with the spirit world and with the ancestors.

BULL'S HORNS Linked with the crescent moon.

BUTTERFLY Symbol of the soul and resurrection as far apart as Congo, Mexico and Polynesia. Also a symbol of life and its cycle; in Western art Christ is sometimes depicted as holding a butterfly.

CADUCEUS The staff of the snake, the attribute of the Greek god Hermes, and the Roman equivalent Mercury, symbolizes the mediation between opposing forces and has been interpreted as an

emblem of homeopathic medicine. The caduceus is also a symbol of commerce.

CALCINATIONS Alchemistic sign.

CALF Associated with feasting, hospitality and celebration (as in "the fatted calf") and also with sacrifice (Judaism).

CALTRAP Heraldic device, originally spiked objects used in battle to bring down cavalry horses.

CAMEL Traditional symbol of wealth and status in the Middle East; in medieval Europe a symbol of temperance; in Christianity the camel is associated with humility and obedience.

CAMELLIA A Chinese symbol of health and fortitude. Associated in Japan with sudden death.

CANCER Zodiac sign.

CANCER Zodiac sign, variation.

CANDLE A symbol of spiritual illumination, witness and joy. Its short-lived flame is a metaphor for the solitary, aspiring human soul.

CANNABIS LEAF Symbol of Rastafarianism,

whose followers believe it is a "holy herb" whose use is grounded in scripture; a symbol of protest against white mainstream society; also a symbol of youth culture in Western society.

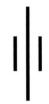

CANNON/GUN Also iron in early chemistry.

CANOPY Shade and protection, also associated with royal power, symbol of heavenly protection.

CAPRICORN Zodiac sign.

CAPRICORN Zodiac sign, variation.

CAPRICORN Zodiac sign, variation.

Middle East; used to mark and beautify holy and domestic spaces. In Europe, carpets have symbolized status, with a red carpet having ritual use in public ceremonies involving high-ranking dignitaries, royalty and celebrities.

harmful djins in Islam and with bad luck in Japan. Associated irrevocably with witchcraft and the Devil in the west.

CHAIN A symbol of attachment and connection, the relationship between two things. Gold chains signify honour and status. A modern symbol of slavery and captivity. Broken chains symbolize the fight for freedom, and the achievement of liberty from oppression.

CAPRICORN Zodiac sign, variation.

CASTLE/FORTRESS Archetypal symbol of protection and a place of refuge (spiritual and temporal); a place that is set apart and hard to enter, containing the heart's desire.

CATERPILLAR In India, a symbol of the transmigration of souls; for the ancient Romans, it was an emblem of greed and ugliness.

CAVE Very old ideogram for cave, farm, village or fortress, also used on modern maps for cave.

CENTAUR A mythical hybrid creature, half man and half horse, became a symbol of duality, of man trapped by his physical or sensual impulses, especially lust and violence.

CARDS, PLAYING Associated with gaming, gambling and fortune-telling in Europe and Asia. The cards themselves contain symbolic imagery (the court cards, joker, the four suits) and numbers.

CAT Symbol of transformation, clairvoyance, agility, watchfulness, sensual beauty, mystery and female malice. In Rome seen as emblem of liberty. Their nocturnal habits and powers of transformation were distrusted.

CAULDRON Linked with magic, symbol of transformation, germination, plenty, and the possibility of rebirth or rejuvenation. Also linked with torture, trial or punishment.

CEDAR Symbol of power and immortality.

CERBERUS Guardian of the entrance to the Greek underworld, symbol of the fearful uncertainties of death.

CHAIR Universal symbol of authority and superior rank, linked to the throne. Among the Swahili (Zanzibar) the "chair of power" is for visitors and the most important members of the family.

CARP In China an emblem of longevity, virility and scholarly success. Images of carp were used on ship's masts or roofs to ward off fire.

CAVE Most primal symbol of shelter, linked with the womb, birth, rebirth, origin and the centre. Darker meanings include the entrance to Hell or the unconscious.

CELTIC HARP Symbol of the bardic tradition, but also has links with the underworld. Used as a symbol for Ireland.

CERES Asteroid.

CARPET/RUG Sacred and secular use in the

CAT, BLACK Linked with evil cunning in the Celtic world, with

CELTIC KNOT Symbol of the universe, because it was drawn in a continuous line, and therefore used as a protective sign.

CHAI The Hebrew word for "life", commonly used on necklaces and other ornaments.

CHALICE/CUP A vessel of plenty and also of immortality; in Christianity, the chalice is a ritual cup used at Eucharist; in Medieval Europe, this cup was associated with the Holy Grail. In Japan, exchanging cups is a symbol of faithfulness and forms part of the marriage ceremony.

CHARIOT A dynamic symbol of rulership in ancient iconography; a symbol of spiritual authority and the mastery of gods and heroes. Hindu mysticism associates charioteering as a symbol of the Self, and in moral allegory it is an image of the triumphant journey of the spirit.

CHERUB A type of angelic being in Islamic, Judaic and Christian traditions; in Christian art cherubim are shown as winged children representing innocence, with blue wings that symbolize the sky.

CHILDBIRTH Child is born, genealogy.

CHIMERA A mythological snake-lion-goat hybrid creature, symbol of the victory of spirit over matter.

CHRIST A monogram formed by the initials of Christ in their Greek form, PX. In this variation the X is turned 45 degrees to form a cross.

CHRIST Monogram, variation, combined with the Greek letters alpha and (lower case) omega, the first and last letters of the Greek alphabet to symbolize Christ as first and last.

a cross above the letters alpha and omega, signifying that Christ is the first and the last.

CHER Rune for harvest. Also known as Jara.

CHEVRON A symbol of rank in military and heraldic contexts.

CHIMNEY A phallic symbol in Freudian psychology.

CHRIST Monogram, variation.

CHRIST Monogram, variation, the triangle at the base is a symbol of divinity meaning that Christ is the centre of the Holy Trinity.

CHRONOS God.

CHRONOS God, variation.

CHEVRON A heraldic variation.

CHINA Used from the earliest Chinese writings as a symbol of how they viewed their civilization, as the "empire of the Middle", set between Heaven and Earth, and in the centre of an otherwise uncivilized world.

CHRIST Monogram, variation.

CHRIST Monogram, variation.

CHRONOS God, variation.

CHERRY A Samurai emblem in Japan, the fruit is a symbol of virginity in China, and its blossom is highly auspicious. In Christian iconography the cherry is an alternative to the apple as the fruit of paradise.

CHICKEN In parts of South America (Makumba cult), the Caribbean (Voodoo) and Africa, a cult animal; a guide of souls in initiation rites, sacrificial animal. Tenth sign of the Chinese zodiac.

CHRIST Monogram, variation.

CHRIST Another monogram symbolizing Christ, this one is built up by

CHRYSANTHEMUM A solar and imperial symbol in Japan, linked with longevity and joy; a Chinese Taoist symbol; and in Western art it is used as a symbol of autumn.

CHRYSLER Corporate emblem of the car manufacturer, a variation of the pentagon combined with the pentagram.

CHURCH In Christianity an image of the world; also associated with the Bride of Christ and the Mother of Christians, and therefore with motherhood.

CINNABAR Alchemistic sign.

CIRCLE Intersected with diagonal cross, modern sign for zero position on machines.

CIRCLE Intersected with diagonal line, Greek letter phi, commonly used in computer programs for zero. In other contexts it signifies diameter or average number.

CIRCLE Intersected with horizontal line, another of humankind's earliest ideograms, found on rock paintings in the inner Sahara and many early systems of writing. Used in modern contexts to mean open. On ships it is the main part of the plimsoll mark.

CIRCLE Intersected with upright cross, a rare sign sometimes used in alchemy for oil or wax. In musical notation it signifies "to be repeated".

CIRCLE AND ARROW One of the most common ideograms in Western culture. Sign for the planet Mars. Also for iron and zinc, and morning.

CIRCLE On horizontal line, ancient ideogram perhaps signifying greatness and power.

CIRCLE On several decreasing horizontal lines, meaning unknown; appears in several prehistoric European caves.

CIRCLE On vertical line, ancient ideogram; in ancient Greece it was a sign for Aphrodite; in alchemy a sign for night.

CIRCLE With vertical line continuing downwards, one of the oldest ideograms, it also appeared in the runic alphabet where for a while it stood for the m-sound.

CIRCLE Divided by horizontal line, often found on rock carvings. In early Chinese calligraphy it denoted the sun; in the Greek alphabet it is the letter theta.

CIRCLE Divided by vertical line, an ancient sign in early alphabets from the Near East. Alchemistic sign for nitrogen.

CIRCLE Empty, one of the oldest ideograms. Sometimes represents the sun or the moon, and also openings such as eyes or the mouth. Used in ideographic writing for up to 5000 years.

CIRCLE Filled, perhaps the most common of the ancient ideograms found in many ancient cultures.

CIRCLE Semi, on vertical line, iconic sign for rising sun, used for dew in meteorology.

CIRCLE Another very early ideogram, associated with the divine or powerful. In Buddhist and Christian art it is used to denote charisma or halo.

CIRCLES Small, connected by straight lines, very old structure found in ancient China and in Nordic rock carvings. In Kabbalistic mystical contexts, similar signs are used for stars and sounds.

CIRCLES Three, filled, known as bowl hollows, these have been found in Nordic rock carvings; also used in modern maps to indicate ruins or sights worth seeing. Used in meteorology for rain. In mathematics and geometry it means therefore. Used upside down, the sign means because.

CITROËN Corporate emblem of the car manufacturer, inspired by the V symbol for victory and military superiority.

CLAY Alchemistic sign.

CLOUD Symbol of fecundity and revelation; in China pink clouds are signs of happiness. Cloud nine is mystical bliss. Modern associations are with gloom, obscurity or depression.

CLOAK Its symbolism of metamorphosis and concealment is due to the instant change it makes to the wearer's appearance. In Teutonic and Celtic legends, magic cloaks are associated with invisibility and forgetfulness. The cloak also symbolizes intrigue, and the world of espionage.

CLOCK Symbol of time and of the transience of life; a stopped clock can symbolize death, and in South America they are placed on graves to symbolize the transition between life and death.

CLOUD Symbol of fecundity and revelation; in China pink clouds are signs of happiness. Cloud nine is mystical bliss. Modern associations are with gloom, obscurity or depression.

CLOVES Represent health and sweetness in Japan and China; in Japanese art, they were one of the Myriad Treasures carried by the Seven Deities of Good Fortune.

CLUB Has a dual role representing either primitive brutality or heroism in art.

CLUBS Suit of playing cards.

COAGULATE/FIX Alchemistic sign.

COBRA. In India cobra divinities, (nagas) were guardian symbols, generally benevolent. The Hindu cobra has a jewel in its hood and symbolizes spiritual treasure. The erect, hooded cobra is the protective serpent emblem of royal power, used by the pharaohs as an emblem to strike down enemies. There is a general link between snakes and wisdom or prophecy.

COBRA On ancient Egyptian headdresses the cobra was a protective sign and a symbol of royal power.

COLUMN/PILLAR Symbols of temporal and spiritual aspiration and power; God appeared to the Israelites in the wilderness as a pillar of fire. Two columns appear outside Masonic temples, representing force and form.

COCK Generally positive symbolic links with the dawn, the sun and illumination. In China the cock was a funerary emblem warding off evil. In Japan it is a sacred creature. In Islam the cock was seen by Mohammed in the First Heaven. Cocks also symbolize lust.

COCONUT Extensive use in Hindu rituals; "sacrificed" as a replica for the human head and is also associated with Shiva, because its three "eyes" symbolize the eyes of Shiva. Also associated with fertility.

COMB Sacred and protected in Maori tradition.

COMET A change in the heavens; in many cultures a portent of war and disaster. Also a symbol of hope and new beginnings.

COMET Variation.

COMET Variation.

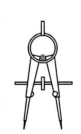

COMPASSES Associated with architecture during the Renaissance; in European art it can symbolize the rational mind. Together with the set square it is one of the most important symbols of Freemasonry.

COMPOSE Alchemistic sign.

CONCH SHELL Buddhists, the Maya and the Aztecs used the conch as a ceremonial horn. Its shape associates it with the symbolism of the spiral. In Hinduism the sound of the conch symbolizes the origin of existence. An emblem of Vishnu.

CONDOR A solar symbol in South America.

CONFERENCE Modern sign, similar to older signs meaning togetherness.

CONFUSED MENTAL STATE Used in modern comic strips.

CONSTELLATIONS OF FIXED STARS Chinese.

COPYRIGHT SYMBOL Used to denote lawful ownership of text or images.

CORAL Its red colour links it with blood in many traditions: for Christians it symbolizes Christ's Passion; in Greek myth, it was formed from the drops of Medusa's blood. In ancient Rome, coral necklaces were worn to ward off disease.

CORN In European cultures, associated with summer, harvest and fertility.

CORNUCOPIA Roman horn of plenty that cannot be emptied; it is used to denote abundance and prosperity in Western art, and is a feminine symbol of maternal nourishment and love. Attribute of Dionysus, god of wine, Demeter and Priapus, also of the allegorical figures of Earth, Autumn, Hospitality, Peace, Fortune and Concord in Western art.

COSMIC TREE The "tree of life" reversed so that its roots draw spiritual strength from the sky.

COW Ancient symbol of maternal nourishment, often personified as mother earth, and the moon.

To Hindus and Buddhists the cow's quiet, patient rhythms of life present a parallel with holiness.

COW Hindu, the symbolism of the cow is taken to its highest for Hindus, who view it as sacred. Its image everywhere is one of happiness.

COWRIE SHELL Symbol of wealth and rank in parts of Africa, appearing on costumes and artefacts; Freudian symbol for female sexual organs, also associated with fertility and good luck.

COYOTE A divinatory symbol or culture hero in North America and Africa.

CROCODILE Major symbol of destructive voracity, bringer of divine punishment, and archetypal devourer. Treated with fearful respect as a creature of primordial

CRADLE Womb symbol; associated with security, protection and safety. Its traditional boat-like shape also links it with travel; a symbol for a safe journey through life.

CRANE Linked by the Chinese to immortality; in Africa with the gift of speech, and widely with the ability to communicate with the gods. Christian symbolism sometimes links it with resurrection.

CRICKET Linked with death and resurrection in China; also a good luck symbol.

and occult power over water, earth and the underworld. The ancient Egyptians had a crocodile fecundity god called Sebek. It has more positive connections in parts of Asia, where it appears as the inventor of the drum and of song.

CROSS OF CHRIST.

CROSS OF ENDLESSNESS A symbol for eternity.

CROSS OF GOLGOTHA Similar to the cross of the Crusaders.

CROSS OF LAZARUS Ancient symbol for holiness and divinity.

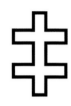

CROSS OF LORAINE Used in heraldry.

CROSS OF PALESTINE Used as a symbol for the kingdom of Jerusalem after the city was captured by the Crusaders.

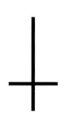

CROSS OF PETER An upside-down Latin cross that commemorates the martyrdom of St Peter, who was crucified upside down.

CROSS OF PHILIP Associated with Nordic countries, some of which use it in their flags.

CROSS OF ST ANDREW'S Named after the apostle Andrew, who was crucified on a diagonal cross.

CROSS OF ST ANTHONY Named after a hermit in Egypt, who was said to have chased away a pack of demons with a cross of this type. Also known as the Tau cross, T-cross, Egyptian cross, Crux commissa and the robber's cross.

CROSS OF ST BIRGITTA Set with five precious stones representing the five wounds of Christ.

CROSS OF ST GEORGE

CROSS OF ST HAN/ CROSS OF ST JOHN Also a magic ideogram from the Viking era, possibly also used in Kabbalism.

CROSS OF ST JOHN

CROSS OF THE ARCHANGELS Also known as the Golgata cross.

CROSS OF THE ARCHANGELS Variation.

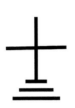

CROSS OF THE EVANGELISTS

CROSS OF THE HOLY CHURCH Also used in alchemy for crucible.

CROSS OF THE PATRIARCH

CROSS OF THE POPE

CROSS OF THE ROBBERS

CROSS, ANCHORED One of the disguised crosses used by early Christians.

CROSS, ANGLED

CROSS, ARROWED Meaning expansion in all directions and for that reason a favoured symbol of fascists.

CROSS, ARROWED Variation.

CROSS, CELTIC

CROSS, CELTIC Variation.

CROSS, COPTIC

CROSS, DIAGONAL Equal-length arms, an extremely old sign found in prehistoric caves. Egyptian hieroglyph meaning divide, count. Signifies multiplication, confrontation, annulment, cancellation, opposition, obstruction, mistake and undecided.

CROSS, DISSIMULATA Variation of the disguised form of the cross used by early Christians.

CROSS, DISSIMULATA Variation, also used on the seal of the Prince of Byblos, a Phoenician city, in the year 2000 BC.

CROSS, EASTERN ORTHODOX

CROSS, EGYPTIAN/ COPTIC

CROSS With equal length arms, an old ideogram from most cultures found in every part of the world, often associated with the four elements. Used in mathematics as the sign for addition.

CROSS With filled or closed, short arms, common in ancient Greece, pre-Columbian America and the Near East up to 1000 years before the birth of Christ, associated with the sun and power.

CROSS, FITCHEE Originated in the times of the crusades when knights took crosses with them that could be thrust into the ground during worship in the field of battle or encampment.

CROSS, GREEK

CROSS, HOLY ROMAN Has a swastika in the centre, a possible allusion to the return of Christ.

CROSS, IRON/ MANTUAN CROSS Used as a German order medal.

CROSS, LABARUM/ CHI-RHO A monogram formed with the two initial Greek letters of the word Christ.

CROSS, LILY

CROSS, MALTESE Also known as the Cross of Promise. Used as the emblem of the Order of St John, based on old Assyrian symbols.

CROSS, MALTESE Variation.

CROSS Open with closed arms, an ancient symbol that seems to have been linked with the weather, the four winds or the four directions.

CROSS Sitting over a globe. Sign for world evangelization.

CROSS, PORTALE

CROSS, RESTORATION Used in the 15th century in heraldry and in European coinage. Also used by the Inca as a sign for sun.

CROSS, TAU/ EGYPTIAN

CROSS, TAU Variation with snake.

CROSS, SQUARE Representing the Earth with its four corners.

CROSS, WHEEL/SUN CROSS First appeared at the dawn of the Bronze Age, appearing in ancient Egypt, China, pre-Columbian America and the Near East. Associated with the wheel.

CROSS, WHEEL, DIAGONAL Suggests a cancelling or neutralizing characteristic.

CROSS, WITH GARMENT A symbol of the crucifixion.

CROSS, WITH ORB A symbol of the final triumph of Christ over the world.

CROSSROADS A symbol of decision-making, life changes and journeys.

CROW Emblem of war, death, solitude, evil and bad luck in Europe and India, but in the Americas and Australia has positive symbolism as a solar bird that is a creative, civilizing bird.

CROWN Identified with power, glory and consecration. Originating as wreaths, crowns draw on the celestial symbolism of the circle – representing perfection and the ring – representing continuity.

CROWN OF THORNS Originally mocking the symbolism of a crown (by the Roman soldiers who crucified Christ) it has now become a symbol in itself of sacrifice and consecration.

CROZIER Originated as a masculine fertility symbol, it implies royal or spiritual power to administer justice. Linked with the sceptre, the staff and the rod. One of the signs of a bishop's religious authority is his crozier.

CRUCIBLE OR MELTING POT Alchemistic sign, also old chemistry.

CRUCIBLE Old chemistry, variation.

CRUX DISSIMULATA Christian symbol of hope.

CRYSTAL Modern New Age symbol.

CUBE Linked to symbolism of the square, hence associated with the physical manifest world. A symbol of wisdom and perfection; for example in Freemasonry, ashlar (a smooth cube) represents the perfected person; one of Islam's most holy structures, the Ka'ba, is cube-shaped.

CUPID/EROS With his bow and arrows of desire, Cupid is a symbol of love and romance.

CURVED LINE A segment of a circle, appears in many ideographic systems, ancient and modern.

CYPRESS Western symbol of death and mourning, but in Asia and elsewhere a symbol of longevity and endurance.

DAEG Rune for D.

DAGGER/KNIFE Sacred symbol in Buddhist and Sikh religions. For Sikhs, it symbolizes courage and dignity. In Tibetan Buddhism a ritual dagger with a three-sided blade is used to protect sacred buildings. In European traditional lore, daggers are linked to treachery.

DAISY Christian symbol of innocence associated with the Virgin Mary, and the rays of the sun; also sacred to Freya, the Germanic sky goddess.

DANGER Energy, the symbol for heat combined with an arrow.

DANGER Energy, heat, variation.

DANGER Poisonous, used in botany. Also stands for checkmate in chess.

DAY Rune associated with light, breakthrough and success.

DEATH The moment of/passing out, used in modern comic strips.

DECOCTION Alchemistic sign.

DEER Universally benevolent symbol associated with dawn, light, purity, regeneration, creativity and magic.

DENEB ALGEDI Magical amulet seal.

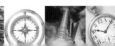

474

DENKYEM The crocodile, Ghanaian adinkra symbol meaning ability to adapt to circumstances, just as the crocodile adapts from water to land.

DHARMACHAKRA The Buddhist eight-spoked wheel.

DIED IN BATTLE Military expression, also used on maps to denote a battle site.

DIGGING STICK Aboriginal, traditional tool used to gather roots and vegetables now used in modern art to represent ancestral being.

DISTAFF Used to prepare flax for spinning, a symbol of Athena/Minerva, Greco-Roman goddess of wisdom and inventor of spinning and weaving; also associated with the passing of time.

DISTANCE Modern technical symbol.

DISTILLATION Alchemistic sign.

DISTILLED OIL Alchemistic sign.

DIVINE POWER Ancient Nordic/Anglo Saxon sign; also logo for Mitsubishi Group.

DIVISION Mathematical sign.

DIVISION Mathematical sign, variation.

DIVORCED Genealogy.

DIVORCED Genealogy, variation.

DOG Symbol of loyalty; protective vigilance in Celtic and Christian traditions; in ancient thought associated with the underworld, where it acted as guide and guardian. Dogs are guardian symbols in Japan and China, but in China they also have demonic links.

DOLL Used in religion, ritual and magic as surrogates for people and deities.

DOLLAR SIGN USA currency.

DOLPHIN Widespread symbol of salvation, transformation and love. Emblem of Christ as saviour. In ancient Greek mythology the dolphin is the bearer of the gods, saviour of heroes and carrier of souls to the Islands of the Blessed. Attribute of Poseidon, Aphrodite, Eros, Demeter and Dionysus. Entwined with an anchor, the dolphin can symbolize prudence.

DOME Symbol of the heavens, frequently appearing in sacred or important civic buildings, such as mosques, Byzantine churches or the Roman pantheon.

DONKEY/ASS Well-entrenched modern symbol of foolishness, but earlier connotations were much more positive (humility, poverty and patience), or sinister in both Egyptian and Indian mythology.

DOOR/ENTRANCE A place of transition seen in many cultures as an opportunity for good or evil forces to enter or leave, hence doorways are often guarded.

DOSE OF MEDICINE Large pill or bolus, old pharmacology; also Japanese Buddhism, also in alchemy for orichalcum or dissolvent.

DOT, SINGLE One of the most common ancient Western ideograms in existence since the era of cave paintings and rock carvings.

DOTS, THREE IN TRIANGLE Sign for therefore (modern).

DOTS IN A LINE Sign for something left out (modern). Several dots in a line was the sign for rain for the Anglo Saxons.

DOVE Universal symbol of peace, particularly when holding an olive branch – this is an allusion to the story of Noah, when the flood began to recede and land became visible. The dove is also a personification of the Holy Spirit and a symbol of baptism.

DOWN WITH! Sign of popular dissent, formed by the sign for "viva!" upside down.

DRAGON Benevolent symbol in the East, malevolent in the West, and containing a wealth of symbolism for each.

DRUM Primeval means of communication, symbol of creative power in India, the voice of Heaven in China, used to promote trance and ecstasy in shamanistic societies. In modern Western symbolism the drum is linked to war and warning.

DUCK Symbol of happiness in Japan and China, with a pair of mandarin ducks symbolizing marriage and domestic harmony.

DWELLING Egyptian hieroglyph.

EAGLE An unambiguous and universal symbol of power, speed and perception. Attribute of the greatest gods, adopted much later as a symbol of imperial power. Also appears in carvings in Christian churches, usually on fonts, pulpits and lecterns, as one of the attributes of St John.

EAR Receptivity; in Africa, ears symbolize humans' animal nature. In the East, long earlobes are a symbol of wisdom and longevity. Ear piercing was traditionally an ancient sign of a pledge.

EARTH Element.

EARTH Element, Kabbalistic.

EARTH The planet, used as early as 500 BC. Used today on maps to signify a chapel. Alchemy sign for antinomy.

EARTH The planet, modern.

EARTH The planet, modern variation.

EARTH The planet, variation.

ECLIPSE OF THE MOON Astronomy.

EGG A universal symbol for creation, often the thing that life sprang from, whether vegetative, godly or elemental. A propitious symbol all over the world symbolizing luck, wealth, health, birth and resurrection. Also associated with spring. In Jewish tradition the egg is a symbol of promise.

EHWAZ Rune for E.

EIGHT Symbol of cosmic equilibrium and renewal. A lucky number in China.

EIGHTH HOUSE Astrology.

ELECTRICITY Thunder, lightning.

ELEPHANT Ancient symbol of sovereign power in India, China and Africa, and by this association linked with dignity, intelligence, prudence, peace. The mount of Indian rulers, and of the thunder and rain god, Indra. Ancient Rome associated the elephant with victory. Medieval Europe believed the male refrained from sex with its mate during her pregnancy, which made it an emblem of chastity, fidelity and love. The white elephant of Burma, Thailand and Cambodia is a symbol of fertility and rainfall.

ELEVENTH HOUSE Astrology.

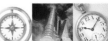

ELHAZ Rune for Z, meaning an elk.

ELLIPSIS Nothing, zero, absence.

EMPEDOCLES' ELEMENTS, AIR Pre-Socratian ancient Greek geometrical symbols of the elements.

EMPEDOCLES' ELEMENTS, EARTH Pre-Socratian ancient Greek geometrical symbols of the elements.

EMPEDOCLES' ELEMENTS, FIRE Pre-Socratian ancient Greek geometrical symbols of the elements.

EMPEDOCLES' ELEMENTS, WATER Pre-Socratian ancient Greek geometrical symbols of the elements.

EMPEROR Jesus, first, only one, self.

EMU Appears in Australian Aboriginal creation stories; therefore killing an emu is associated with bad luck.

ENCLOSED SPACE Tank or closed room, also buried in genealogy.

ENNEAGRAM Nine-pointed star, Christian, nine gifts of spirit.

ENTRANCE See Door

EOH Rune for Y, meaning yew tree.

EPA Ghanaian adinkra symbol, meaning handcuffs, symbol of slavery and captivity.

ERMINE Heraldry.

ESSENCE Alchemistic sign.

ETHERIC OIL Alchemistic sign.

EVAPORATION Modern.

EXCLAMATION MARK Modern, denoting surprise or emphasis in text.

EYE OF FIRE Ancient Germanic, four elements in alchemy.

EYE OF HORUS Symbol of cosmic wholeness, and of the all-seeing power of the ancient Egyptian god Horus. Also known as the wedjat.

EYE OF THE DRAGON Ancient Germanic sign for threat, danger.

EYE/EYEBROW The ability to see, vision (literal and metaphorical), associated with magic or spiritual power in many traditions. In Chinese Buddhism long eyebrows are a sign of wisdom and old age.

EYE, THE THIRD Also called the "eye of the heart", a symbol of the eye of spiritual perception in Hinduism, and of clairvoyance in Islam. Adopted by the Freemasons as one of their society's signs.

FAITH Early Christian symbol, one of those found inscribed in the catacombs where the Christians hid from Roman persecution. Fish are associated with hope in Hebrew tradition.

FALCON Identical symbolism to the hawk; a solar emblem of victory, superiority, aspiration, spirit, light and liberty. Many Egyptian gods are depicted with the head of a falcon. The eye of a falcon symbolizes sharp vision. In Western tradition the falcon is an emblem of the hunter, and in Nordic mythology of the sky god, Woden.

FAMILY A sign combining the sign for woman, the sign for man, and the sign for woman with child.

FE Rune, meaning cattle or livestock, also a Viking symbol for moveable property.

FERN Koru fern, Polynesian.

FIG Symbol of fecundity, also in Buddhism of moral teaching and immortality.

FIRE Masculine symbol of creation, destruction, purification, revelation, transformation, regeneration and spiritual or sexual ardour.

FIRST HOUSE Astrology.

FAN Symbol of goodness (Chinese); an attribute of one of the Japanese Seven Deities of Good Fortune, and of Vishnu (Hindu god). Emblem of kingship in Africa, Asia and the Far East.

FEATHER Symbol of Maat, ancient Egyptian goddess of justice. In Native American traditions, feathers hold the spirit of the bird and are highly prized.

FIAT Corporate emblem of the car manufacturer, derived from the sun cross.

FILTER (VERB) Alchemistic sign.

FIRE Alchemistic sign.

FISH Phallic symbol of sexual happiness and fecundity. In China the fish is an emblem of plenty and good luck. The letters of the Greek word for fish – *icthus* – form an acronym for Jesus Christ, and so the fish became an early secret Christian sign. In Hebrew tradition fish represent the true and faithful. Fish appear as saviours in Hindu myth.

FASCES Pictorial representation of an axe wrapped around with rods and bound with leather, which Roman officials carried as a symbol of their authority. Later the fasces became a Roman punitive emblem of state power, and was later adopted by fascism.

FEMALE

FIFTH ELEMENT The quintessence or ether. The best.

FINGERS/ FINGERNAILS Connection with spiritual power (India), and with the five tenets of Islam. Long fingernails are traditionally a sign of wealth and status; long, claw-like nails are attributes of the kings of the Dahomey in Africa.

FIRE Kabbalism.

FIREPLACE See Hearth.

FISH A simplified icon that was used by early Christians as the first emblem of Christ.

FEOH Rune for F.

FIFTH HOUSE Astrology.

FIRE Very old ideogram, also used for lunar halo.

FIREWORK In the modern world associated with festivals and celebration, the more lavish the spectacle, the bigger the occasion; also associated with other symbolism, for example rocket, wheel, star, spiral.

FISH HOOK Symbol of fishing and helpless entrapment.

FAST MOVEMENT Modern.

FIVE ELEMENTS OF WESTERN IDEOGRAPHY, THE DOT Almost all Western ideography is based upon five basic shapes, the dot, the line, the semi circle and the two spirals.

FIVE Associated with the human microcosm and the hand; important symbol of totality in China, Japan and Celtic tradition. Also associated with love, health, sensuality, meditation, analysis, criticism and the heart.

FLASK/BOTTLE Alchemistic sign for a flask that is not transparent.

FLOWER Culmination or crowning achievement; feminine beauty; also a sign of impermanence and transience. Specific flowers also have their own symbolism, and, in some cultures, language. Widespread use in rituals all over the world (birth, marriage, death, celebrations).

FLY WHISK Symbol of royalty in many cultures, in Polynesia a mark of rank, for Buddhists a sign of compassion.

FOUR ELEMENTS Medieval.

FIVE ELEMENTS OF WESTERN IDEOGRAPHY, THE LINE

FIXATION Alchemistic.

FLASK Alchemistic sign for a flask made of glass.

FOOT Bare feet are often a sign of humility. In the East, foot washing is an act of hospitality and a sign of love; Christ washing the feet of his disciples was a symbolic gesture of his love and service.

FOUR EVANGELISTS

FIVE ELEMENTS OF WESTERN IDEOGRAPHY, THE SEMI-CIRCLE Also known as the section.

FLEUR-DE-LIS A stylized lily with three flowers used as the emblem of France.

FLUTE/PAN PIPES Associated with Pan (Greek god of the woods and fields), hence linked with nature and sexuality; bamboo flutes are associated with Zen Buddhist monks.

FOUR EVANGELISTS Variation.

FIVE ELEMENTS OF WESTERN IDEOGRAPHY, THE SPIRAL Also depicted in reverse.

FLAG Emblem of rulership and identity at many levels (international, national, local); in war, a symbol of military honour, with a white flag representing surrender; a fluttering flag can suggest new beginnings.

FLOW/MELT Alchemistic sign.

FLY Associated with sickness, death and the devil in many traditions.

FOUNTAIN A source of water and therefore of life. Drinking from a fountain can symbolize spiritual refreshment or immortality. In Islamic tradition fountains represent the connection between humans and God.

FOUR Solidity, organization, power, intellect, justice and omnipotence.

FIVE ELEMENTS OF WESTERN IDEOGRAPHY, THE SPIRAL Variation.

FLAMING HEART See Heart of fire.

FOURTH HOUSE Astrology.

Fox In European traditions, associated with cunning and slyness, appearing in medieval art as a symbol of the devil. In China and Japan the fox is a bringer of wealth.

Frog Foetal symbol especially in Egypt, associated with magic, germination, evolution, the moon's phases, water and rain. Good luck emblem in Japan.

Fu Authority, Chinese.

Fulfoot Swedish variation of the swastika.

Fumes Alchemistic.

Funtunfunefu The Ghanaian adinkra symbol of Siamese crocodiles, who share one stomach but still fight over food. A warning against infighting and tribal conflict.

Gargoyle A carved waterspout, typically seen on the gutters of church or cathedral parapets. During the Middle Ages gargoyles were mostly grotesque or demonic, symbolizing the power of the Church to wash away evil.

Garlic Associated with strength and protection from evil spirits in many traditions. In antiquity garlic was associated

---

with the moon and magic and was regarded as a powerful aphrodisiac.

Gate A transitional symbol marking the movement from one place, time, spiritual or psychological state to another. Gates can also symbolize spiritual and/or secular power.

Gemini Zodiac sign.

Geofu Rune for G.

Giants An ancient ideogram probably first drawn 10,000 years ago, used in the Nordic runic alphabet

---

as a sign for giants or Titans. Also used as an expression of power.

Glass/arsenic Alchemistic sign, also unmarried in genealogy.

Globe/orb Power emblem of gods or imperial rulers, symbol of totality.

Glove Powerful symbol of rank used as an acknowledgement of superiority or fealty, also as a love pledge.

Goat Ambiguous symbol meaning virility, lust, cunning and destructiveness in the male, and fecundity and nourishment in the female. Sign for

---

Capricorn, one of the signs of the zodiac. In Roman myth the cornucopia derives from the horn of the goat, Amaltheia, the revered wet-nurse of the baby Zeus.

Goddess Of morning or evening, Greek and Byzantium.

Goddess

Gohei Sacred wands topped with zigzag streamers of white paper used in Shinto rituals.

Gold leaf/gold foil, Alchemistic sign.

Gold Alchemistic, variation.

Gold Alchemistic, variation.

Gold Alchemistic, variation.

Golden number 17 From the medieval clog almanacs for calculating the phases of the moon.

Golden number 18 From the medieval clog almanacs for calculating the phases of the moon.

GONG Widespread use in sacred rituals in China and Japan. In Chinese temples they are beaten to gain the attention of the spirits, while Zen Buddhists use gongs as part of liturgical chanting and meditation. Sounding a gong can indicate arrivals or departures.

GOOSE Medieval bestiaries compared geese to the devout, although white geese were linked to fancy dressing and malicious gossip. The domestic goose is a symbol of the home, women, fidelity and married life. The wild goose is associated with cooperation, interdependence and vigilance. Because wild geese are said to stay with a sick goose, they are also symbols of loyalty.

GORGONS Snake-haired mythological winged women-hybrids of ancient Greece, embodiments of adversarial evil.

GOURD/CALABASH Pre-eminent symbol for many traditional African societies, where it appears in creation myths, representing the world egg or the womb.

GRAIL In European traditions the grail is a sacred object (typically a chalice or stone) whose wondrous powers confer the elixir of life and eternal youth; in medieval legend, particularly linked with King Arthur and his knights, it was believed to be the cup used by Christ at the Last Supper and used to catch his blood at the crucifixion.

GRAIN A central symbol of growth, rebirth and fertility, together with rice, corn, barley and wheat. Often an attribute of earth gods and goddesses. Ancient fertility symbol, used at weddings to sprinkle over the married couple.

GRAPES Complex ancient symbol of natural fecundity and of spiritual life in both pagan and Christian traditions.

GRASS The victory over barrenness, a fertile land; as a dream symbol, can represent new growth, new ideas and new enterprises.

GRAVE Related literally and symbolically to a place of residence for the dead and where the dead can be remembered. As a barrow or tumulus, it may be a symbolic allusion to holy mountains.

GRAVEL/SAND Alchemistic sign.

GRIFFIN Lion-eagle hybrid symbol of dominion over land and sky, evolved from an aggressive emblem of power into a protective symbol.

GRIND/CRUSH Alchemistic sign.

GROWING Also rebirth and genesis, Egyptian hieroglyphs for woman and female sex.

GYE NYAME Ubiquitous Ghanaian adinkra symbol, meaning "except for God", which is by far the most popular for use in decoration.

HAGALL Rune for H.

HAGITH Kabbalism.

HAIL Rune associated with accidents and misfortune.

HAIR A complex symbol with many meanings, most associated with the life force; can be a sign of holiness and strength, royal power, freedom, virility, virginity or permissiveness.

HALO Symbol of divinity or sanctity, originally based on the nimbus that surrounds the sun. Used particularly in Christian art, the halo is thought to have been first used on pagan sun gods, such as Mithras. Halos also appear in Buddhist spiritual traditions.

HAMMER As a weapon the hammer is a symbol of male strength, linked with the power of the sun and the gods of war. As a tool the hammer can appear as a symbol of protection or of divine skill.

HAMMER AND SICKLE Symbol of communism's unification of the working classes, combing the sickle as a symbol of agricultural workers, and the hammer, symbol of industrial workers.

HAND Symbol of temporal and spiritual power, action, strength and protection.

HAND OF FATIMA A symbol of the hand of God and of the five fundamentals of Islam: faith, prayer, pilgrimage, fasting and charity. Used extensively in Islamic countries as a protective and good luck charm.

HAPPINESS Rune.

HARE A lunar animal linked with divinity, menstruation and fertility. Because of its links with divinity it has sometimes been a forbidden food.

HARP Widespread use in ritual and sacred ceremony; in the Old Testament associated with Jewish nationhood. The magical harp of the Dagda (Celtic) could play music suitable for every occasion and had the power to send its enemies to sleep. The three-stringed harp used in ancient Egypt symbolized the three seasons of flood, growth and dryness.

HAWK Solar emblem of victory, superiority, aspiration, spirit, light and liberty.

HAZEL Symbol of divinity, wisdom, fertility and rain. A hazel wand was the instrument of northern European magicians and wizards.

HEAD In some traditions the location of the soul, associated with fertility and phallic symbolism, instrument of reason and thought.

HEART An ancient symbol whose original meaning is not known. Graphically related to fire. Signifies love; also appears with religious meaning among the Aztecs, Hindus, Buddhists, Muslims, Jews, Celts and Taoists.

HEART ON FIRE/FLAMING HEART Symbol of an ardent Christian, but also, in art, an attribute of charity and profane passion.

HEARTH/FIREPLACE Symbol of the home, of comfort, security and human community. For the Romans, it was the site of the household guardian spirits (lares), for the Aztecs the sacred place of Ometecuhtli, who was believed to live at the heart of the universe and in the heart of all people.

HEDGEHOG A symbol of wealth in China and Japan; in medieval Europe associated with greed and gluttony. In parts of Central Asia and Africa it is associated with the sun (because of the ray pattern made by its spines) and the invention of fire.

HELMET Symbol of protection, but also linked with invisible power.

HEMESH HAND A Jewish variation of the hand of Fatima with similar protective symbolism.

HEPTAGRAM This star contains all the symbolism of the number 7.

HERALDIC DAGGER Used in printed text as a sign for note.

HERMAPHRODITE Used in botany for double-sexed plants.

HERMES Sign of the god.

HERMES Sign of the god, variation.

HERMES Sign of the god, variation.

HERON Emblem of the morning sun.

HEXAGON Geometric shape, important in Islam as a directional.

482

HEXAGRAM Based on the triangle, an ancient sign for the Jewish kingdom.

HINDU/HINDUISM

HIEROGLYPH Symbolizing the unification of Egypt.

HIPPOPOTAMUS In ancient Egypt, a female hippo was a fertility symbol and worshipped as an upright hippopotamus goddess. In the Old Testament, the hippo is a symbol of brute force.

HIGH Spiritual dignity.

HNEFATAFL A design for a games board used by the Vikings.

HIJAB An Islamic item of clothing that carries various symbolic interpretations, including liberation and oppression. For many of those who wear it, it is an expression of their love for God.

HOLLY A symbol of hope and joy.

HOLY SIGN From India around 4,000 years ago. Also found on Japanese Buddha statues from the 8th century.

HOLY SPIRIT According to some sources this Christian sign is derived from a stylized dove. This sign was also used in alchemy to signify the spirit of a substance.

HOLY SPIRIT An early Christian symbol, one of those found inscribed in the catacombs of Roman Palestine in the years of Christian persecution.

HOLY TRINITY This shape, denoting the unity of three, is used extensively in the architecture of churches and cathedrals. The sign itself, however, is ancient, and has been

found as far back as 3000 BC inscribed on the statue of an Indian priest king.

HOLY TRINITY A triquetras variation.

HOLY TRINITY Another triquetras variation.

HOLY TRINITY Variation.

HOLY TRINITY A Spanish variation.

HOMECOMINGS A sign from the Hopi Indians of Arizona, also symbolizes several returns or tribal migration.

HOMOSEXUAL See Male

HONEY Linked with the gods, purity, inspiration, eloquence and plenty.

HONEY Alchemistic sign.

HONEY Alchemistic, variation.

HONEY Alchemistic, variation.

HOOD Associated with magic and the power to make its wearer invisible. Freudian phallic symbol.

HORN Symbol of power and strength associated with the animals that have them. A bull's horn is a female lunar symbol (the crescent moon is horn-shaped), and associated with fertility; a ram's horn is a male, solar symbol, associated with virility.

HORSE Symbol of animal vitality, velocity and beauty, also associated with the power of wind, storm, fire, waves and running water.

HORSESHOE Ancient protective symbol, with heel uppermost it is used in magic to call on the protection of the moon.

HORUS Ancient Egyptian solar god, symbol of cosmic wholeness.

HOUR Time sign, alchemistic.

HOUR Time sign, alchemistic, representation of hourglass.

HOURGLASS Symbol of time, and its inevitable passing.

HWEMUDUA Measuring stick, Ghanaian adinkra sign, meaning the need to strive for the best quality, whether in production of goods or in human endeavours.

HYDRA The many-headed dragon serpent of Greek myth symbolizes the difficulty in conquering our vices.

HYE WON HYE Ghanaian adinkra sign meaning "that which cannot be burnt". This symbol

gets its meaning from traditional priests that were able to walk on fire without burning their feet, an inspiration to others to endure and overcome difficulties.

IBIS A sacred symbol of wisdom for the ancient Egyptians.

ICE GRANULES Hail, meteorology

IGLOO Inuit symbol of their culture and way of life.

INFINITE Modern mathematical sign for infinitely great sum or number or indefinite number.

INFINITY Referring to time, distance or numbers.

ING Rune for Ng.

INGZ Rune, associated with fertility.

IRON Alchemistic sign.

IRON Alchemistic sign, variation.

IS Rune for I.

ISHTAR Goddess, queen of the heavens for the Babylonians and Assyrians, also god of childbirth.

ISLAM Made up of the morning star and the morning moon.

ISLAND A symbol of non-celestial heaven, a magical other place set apart from the real world.

ISOMORPH/ CONGRUENT In mathematical and geometrical systems.

IVY Symbol of immortality and also friendship; in the classical world also associated with vegetative abundance and sensuality, hence Dionysus/Bacchus (god of wine) is often depicted wearing an ivy crown.

JACKAL Symbol of destructiveness or evil in India, but in ancient Egypt worshipped as Anubis, god of embalming.

JAGUAR Linked with divination, royalty, magic, the spirit world, the earth, the moon and fertility. An important icon in shamanic traditions.

JARA Rune for J.

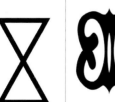

JESUS CHRIST

JUNO Asteroid.

KANGAROO A symbol of modern-day Australia, traditionally associated with powerful mothering instincts (it carries its young in its pouch and is a fierce fighter) and with ancestor spirits.

to heaven and earth, while in West Africa, a bunch of gold keys on a ring are part of court regalia, symbolizing the wealth of the state. In Japan, the key is a symbol of happiness because of its power to unlock the rice pantry.

the knot of Isis (a type of Ankh with arms folded down) was the emblem of life and immortality. Knots can be used to symbolize love and marriage, A recurring motif in Celtic art, its symbolism linked to the ouroboros, the perpetual moving and joining together of human and cosmic activities. A loose interwoven knot symbolizes infinity or longevity. Tight knots symbolize union, but also blockage or protection.

LADDER OF TRANSMIGRATION Medieval Christian sign for the soul's pilgrimage from earthly existence to paradise.

JEUNE BRETAGNE The Celtic separatist movement in Brittany, France. The symbol was originally a Celtic one associated with migration.

JUNO Asteroid, archaic variation.

KAUN Rune meaning boil or pustule.

KINTINKANTAN Ghanain adinkra sign for puffed-up extravagance.

LAGU Rune for L, meaning water or sea.

JEWELS Symbols of purity, refinement and superiority. In Eastern traditions they embody spiritual knowledge.

JUNO Asteroid, variation.

KEN Rune for K.

KITE Used as an oracular device in China and Japan; the Japanese flew kites for good health and to secure a good harvest. Chinese kites decorated with butterflies symbolized prayers for the souls of the dead and the living.

KU KLUX KLAN The symbol of the racist organization of USA.

LABYRINTH See Maze

LAMB One of the earliest symbols for Christ, emblem of purity, sacrifice, renewal, redemption, innocence and gentleness. Important sacrificial and redemptive symbol for Islam and Judaism.

JUICE/SAP Alchemistic sign.

JUPITER The planet.

KEY Through its power to lock and unlock doors, the key is a symbol of spiritual and secular authority, of access to sacred and temporal wealth. In Christianity for example, Christ gave St Peter the keys

KNOT In art, literature and sacred tradition, knots symbolize the power to bind and to set free; in ancient Egypt

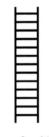

LADDER One of the symbolic links to mountains, also a symbol of ascension, aspiration and success.

LAMP/LANTERN
Symbol of spirit, truth and life. In shrines or on altars symbol of devotion and the presence of divinity. In art personification of vigilance. A Chinese lantern is a fertility symbol, used in Chinese and Japanese festivals to attract the souls of dead ancestors.

LANCE Associated with Christ's Passion, also with chivalry, symbol of masculine, phallic, earthly power. A broken lance symbolizes the experienced soldier

LAND OF EGYPT
Associated with symbol for return or homecoming.

LANTERN See Lamp

LAPIS LAZULI
Alchemistic sign.

LAPIS PHILOSOPHORUM
Stone of wisdom, alchemistic.

LAUREL The leaves of the laurel or bay tree were, for the Greco-Roman world, symbols of victory, peace, purification, divination and immortality. Laurel also had talismanic significance in North Africa, and in China it is the tree under which the lunar hare produces the elixir of immortality.

LAUREL LEAF WREATH
Linked to Apollo, Greco-Roman victory crown for both warriors and poets.

LEAD Alchemistic sign.

LEAD Alchemistic, variation.

LEAD Early chemistry.

LEAD Old chemists sign.

LEAD Alchemistic, variation also musical notation meaning to raise a half tone. In old pharmacology it was used to mean

"take in God's name". In modern use it is called the hash sign and is used on telephones.

LEAD SULPHATE
Alchemistic sign.

LEMON Symbol of bitterness, failure or disappointment, in Christian art can represent faithfulness.

LEO Zodiac sign.

LEO Zodiac sign, variation.

LEOPARD Often associated with wildness, aggression and battle; in antiquity, a symbol of strength and fertility and an attribute of Dionysus; a symbol of the supreme judicial authority of the Kings of Benin (West Africa).

LESBIANISM See Love between women

LIBRA Zodiac sign.

LIGHTHOUSE Symbol of safety and protection in the face of danger; in Early Christian art, associated with Christ, also the heavenly harbour into which the soul sails after the dangerous journey through life. Freudian phallic symbol.

LIGHTNING Modern western sign for lightening made from the two signs for danger, heat together with the arrow sign for directed movement.

LIGHTNING Variation, linked with Fascism, also rune for 's'.

LILY Identified with Christian piety, purity and innocence. In older traditions associated with fertility and erotic love and the fertility of the Earth Goddess. Symbol of fecundity in ancient Greece and Egypt.

LIME Alchemistic.

oneness, the self, authority, power. Also symbol for yang, the active, powerful, warm, extrovert and masculine dimensions of the universe.

LIME Early chemistry.

LINE Straight, diagonal, in modern iconography signifies forbidden or cancelled when over another sign.

LINE Straight, horizontal, represents the base, the earth, or land. Can also mean to link, increase or decrease when placed over or under another sign.

LINE Straight, vertical, one of the basic elements in western ideography. Stands for unity,

LINES Three identical parallel and vertical, signifies three units, also active intellect.

LINES Three identical, parallel and horizontal, similarity in one dimension, used in meteorology to indicate mist.

LINES Two identical, parallel and horizontal, equals, a doubling of the uniting and linking quality of a single horizontal line.

LINES Two identical, parallel and vertical, symbol for yin, the passive, receptive, material dimension of the universe.

LINGA A sculpted upright phallus common throughout India. A cult image and sacred symbol of the male, creative principle (Hindu), associated with Shiva, the divine power of creation, and the "world axis". The feminine counterpart of the linga is the yoni.

LION Solar animal invested with divine qualities; symbol of royal power and dominion, military victory, bravery, vigilance and fortitude. Royal emblem of England and Scotland and of British imperial power in the 19th century. In China and Japan the lion is protective.

LIZARD Symbol of evil (Greco-Roman, Christianity, Maori). Among Native American tribes, associated with shamanic powers and vision quests as well as strength (the Plains Dakota). For Aboriginal Australians the

frill-necked lizard (kendi) is a powerful rainmaker. A symbol of a peaceful household for the Babanki (Cameroon).

LOGR Rune for onion or water, stream or sea.

LOOSEN/UNSCREW Modern.

LOTUS FLOWER Ancient and prolific symbol in Egypt, India, China and Japan. Symbol of birth, cosmic life, the divine, human spiritual growth and the soul's potential to achieve perfection.

LOTUS FLOWER An ancient Egyptian mystical symbol used to signify the Earth.

LOVE BETWEEN WOMEN Lesbianism, modern ideogram.

LOZENGE The rhombus or diamond shape – one of the Chinese Eight Treasures, representing good fortune.

LUTE In China symbol of the scholar and of harmony in marriage and government. In Renaissance art popular emblem of the lover; if shown with strings broken can be a symbol of discord.

LYE Alchemistic sign.

LYRE Symbol of divine harmony, musical inspiration and divination. Linked with Orpheus. In myth it was invented by Hermes, who gave it to Apollo, whose attribute it became.

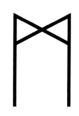

MADR Rune for M, meaning, man or human. Also known as mann.

MAGNESIUM Early chemistry.

MALE HOMOSEXUAL LOVE Modern.

MAP OF THE WORLD Ideogram from the Middle Ages, the vertical line signified the Mediterranean sea, the horizontal line to the left was the Nile, that to the right the Don River, the upper right section was Europe, the left Africa, the bottom Asia. The full point in Asia was Jerusalem.

MARS The planet, variation, also sign for iron.

MAZE/LABYRINTH Possibly linking back to the cave systems in which humanity once lived; ambivalent symbolism includes protection, initiation, death or rebirth, choices and life direction.

MERCURY Alchemistic, variation.

MERCURY Sign of the planet, ancient Greek variation.

MAN/THE MALE There is no one symbol that represents the male principle, but this is a symbolic theme that underlies most of the world's cultures: the principle of the patriarch. Less potent today, it is still important, and carries associations such as the sun, law, authority and the warlike spirit.

MARCASITE/FOOL'S GOLD Also iron sulphate, alchemistic.

MASK Dramatic means of projecting symbolism in religion, ritual and theatre. Symbol of concealment or illusion, in Western art an attribute of deceit personified, of vice and of night.

MELTING OVEN/ FORGE Alchemistic.

MERCURY Alchemistic, variation.

MERCURY Sign of the planet, variation.

MANDRAKE Believed in the Middle Ages to have magical powers; a symbol for sorcery and witchcraft.

MARS The planet, named after the Roman god of war, in Greece known as Ares. Became the sign for iron (the metal used for weapons) due to Mars' link with war.

MAYPOLE European folkloric phallic symbol, spring emblem of fertility and solar renewal, linked to classical spring rites.

MENORAH The nine-candelabra of Judaism, symbol of the nation of Israel.

MERCURY Sign of the planet.

MERCURY Sign of the planet, variation.

MERMAID See Siren

MERCURY Alchemistic.

MERCURY Sign of the planet, variation; also for mercury, metal, also poison in early chemistry.

METAL Alchemistic.

488

MIGRATION A Hopi Indian sign centred around the idea of several returns, or homecoming.

MIGRATION Variation, Celtic, more recently adopted by Jeune Bretagne, a French separatist movement.

MIHRAB Islamic, niche in the wall of a mosque indicating the direction of Mecca, decorated with geometric motifs and text from the Qur'an.

MINARET A slim tower connected to an Islamic mosque. Derived from an Arabic word meaning

"to give off light", the minaret acts as a beacon of illumination to the surrounding community – it is from here that the muezzin calls the faithful to prayer.

MIRAGE

MIRROR Symbol of veracity, self-knowledge, purity, enlightenment and divination. Sometimes in Western art seen as symbol of pride, vanity or lust. Linked with magic, especially divination.

MISTLETOE Sacred to the Celtic druids as a fertility and regeneration symbol, has since been attributed with fire, lightning and rebirth. The berries were once credited with healing properties.

MITSUBISHI Corporate emblem of the Japanese firm.

MIX/MIXTURE Alchemistic.

MIX Alchemistic, variation.

MONKEY Its imitative skills make it a symbol of human vanity and other folly.

MOON Egyptian hieroglyph.

MOON/MONTH Hittite hieroglyphic system.

MOON, NEW In astrology symbolizes human receptivity, instinct, subconscious, emotional life and ability to react. Also used as a symbol for the mother, or women in general. Alchemical sign for silver.

MOON (WANING) Used, together with a star, as the symbol for the Roman province of Illyricum and then for Constantinople. Later it developed into the sign for the Islamic faith.

MOTHER AND CHILD Appears on pre-Columbian engravings and rock

paintings in Arizona, and on an Etruscan vase from around 550 BC. Also found in medieval churches throughout Europe, and in ancient stone structures in Sweden.

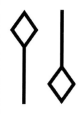

MOUNTAIN Symbol of transcendence, eternity, purity and spiritual ascent. Associated with immortals, heroes, sanctified prophets and gods.

MOUSE Associated with female sexuality, lechery and voracity (Greco-Roman), although a white mouse is a good luck symbol (Roman). Also associated with destructive, dark forces, stealth and cunning (Celtic) in European folklore during the Middle Ages; mice were associated with witches and the souls of the dead; infestations of mice were considered a divine punishment.

MOUTH An open mouth associated with the power of the

spirit to speak, the inspiration of the soul; alternatively it can symbolize destructive forces, things being "eaten" and "devoured".

MUSHROOM Symbol of life arising from death, longevity and happiness in China; souls of the reborn in some parts of central Europe and Africa. Folklore links it with the supernatural.

MUSICAL NOTE In the Middle Ages, also (reversed) used as ideogram by the Sumerians around 3000 BC.

NANNAN Very ancient sign for moon god later known as Sin in the Euphrates-Tigris region. For the Babylonians the sign was linked with Venus and the sun.

NAUDH Rune for N meaning need, misery.

NAVEL The centre of creative and psychic energy, the source of life, linked to fertility.

NAZI SS Logo of the Nazi special police unit known as the Schutz Staffeln, or SS.

NEPTUNE Sign for the planet, rare variation.

NET Symbol of catching and gathering; in the East, deities sometimes shown with a net that they use to draw people closer to them; in Christianity, it is associated with the apostles as "fishers of men". In Jungian psychology, fishing with a net can signify connecting with the unconscious.

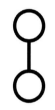

NICKEL Calcinated copper, alchemistic.

NIED Rune for N.

NIGHT Time sign, alchemistic.

NIKE Corporate logo.

NINE As the triple triad, nine is a supremely powerful number, the most auspicious Chinese number, the most potent yang number. In mysticism it represents the triple synthesis of mind, body and spirit. Hebrew symbol of truth, Christian symbol of order within order.

NKONSONKONSON Chain links, Ghanaian adinkra symbol meaning strength within unity, used as a reminder to contribute to the community.

NOOSE A masonic symbol of the cord that binds one to life and in initiation rituals, of being born into a new life. As hangman's noose, a symbol of death and the end of life.

NOSE Associated with intuitive discernment, hence expressions such as "sniffing out the truth". In Maori culture, rubbing noses is not only a way of kissing, but symbolizes the gods breathing life into humans and is a sign of peace. In Japan, people point to their nose rather than their heart to indicate themselves.

NSORAN Sorrow or lament, Ghanian adinkra symbol.

NSOROMMA Child of the heavens, Ghanaian adinkra symbol used as a reminder that God is father and watches over all people.

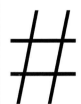

NUMBER In modern Western systems. In musical notation it is called a sharp and is an instruction to raise a half tone. Also used in early chemistry to denote air.

NUMBER 10 From the medieval clog almanacs to calculate the moon's phases.

NUT Highly symbolic in the Jewish tradition, the nut is the symbol of the scholar, and represents virtue in that the beginning and end, seed and fruit are one and the same. The Romans considered the nut a fertility symbol in both humans and animals.

NYAME BIRIBI WO SORO God is in the heavens. Ghanaian adinkra symbol.

NYAME NNWU NA MAWU God never dies, therefore I cannot die. Ghanaian adinkra symbol reminding people of immortality.

OAK Linked with nobility and endurance, sacred to thunder gods of the Celts, Greeks and Germanic tribes, symbol of male potency and wisdom but linked to mother goddesses and the Dryads, oak nymphs.

OBELISK Rectangular, tapering pillar, Egyptian symbol of the sun god, Ra, topped by a reflective pyramid that caught the light.

OCTAGON Draws on the symbolism of the number eight, emblem of renewal, and combining the symbolism of the square and the circle.

OCTAGRAM OF CREATION Gnostic, also Nordic invocation of magic and protection.

OIL Alchemistic.

OLYMPIC GAMES Five linked rings symbolizing the five continents of the world that participate in the sporting event.

OM SYMBOL (Aum), the greeting of peace in India. The symbol represents the four states of consciousness: awake, dreaming, sleeping, without dreams and the transcendental state.

OMEGA The last letter of the Greek alphabet.

ONE A symbol of God, emblem of primordial unity, could also stand for the sun or light, and the origin of life. Confucian perfect entity. Symbol of beginning, the self and loneliness.

ONE Roman numeral, singular, individual, emperor, Jesus. Used in English speaking world to signify the first person.

OPEL For their corporate logo this car manufacturer used the ancient sign for victory.

ORANGE Commonly a symbol of fertility.

ORB See Globe

OSTRICH In ancient Egypt an ostrich feather was a symbol of justice and truth. The burying of its head in the sand is a modern symbol of avoiding the truth.

OTHEL Rune for O.

OTTER Often associated with lunar symbolism from its periodic nature of diving and rising in water. A Romanian folk song tells of otters guiding the souls of the dead. The otter often also symbolizes laughter, playfulness and mischievousness.

OUROBOROS A serpent in circular formation with tail in its mouth, symbol of cyclic time, eternity and the indivisible, self-sustaining character of Nature.

OWL Associated with magic, the otherworld, wisdom and prophecy in many traditions.

OX Universally benevolent symbol of strength, patience, submissiveness and steady toil. Christian emblem of sacrificial Christ. Sacrificial animal in the ancient world. Taoist and Buddhist symbol of the sage.

PACHUCO CROSS An identifying sign, often used as a tattoo, by Hispanic-American street gangs.

PAGODA Sacred building in the Buddhist tradition, the diminishing tiers symbolize spiritual ascent.

PALLAS Sign of the asteroid.

PANTHER The panther commonly depicts desire and power. However, in ancient Christian symbolism the panther was one of three animals representing chastity. The black panther is a feminine symbol of the night, death and rebirth.

PARASOL/UMBRELLA Symbol for the dome of Heaven in ancient China. The parasol was Vishnu's symbol and also an emblem of the Buddha himself. The parasol is often also a solar symbol suggesting the rank, authority and even the halo of the king who is shaded by it. In an everyday sense the parasol represents protection.

PARROT A symbol of the sun and the coming of the rainy season in Native American lore. In Hinduism, Kama – god of love – rides a parrot across three worlds spreading love and desire.

PARZ A very early rune, later came to mean secret, mystery, initiation in Anglo-Saxon literature.

PAWNSHOP Originally part of the Medici family arms, who were rich money lenders.

PEACE Christian.

PEACH A very important symbol in Chinese culture with many meanings; associated with immortality, an emblem of marriage, a fertility symbol.

PEAR The pear is a mother, or love, symbol with erotic associations that are probably due to its shape. Associated with Aphrodite and Hera in classical mythology. A longevity symbol in China.

PELICAN Christian symbol of self-sacrificial love, based on the medieval misconception that the birds tore their own breasts to feed their young. This link with shedding its own blood led to its use to represent Christ.

PEN A Freudian phallic symbol, also associated with the executive function and the power of reason. In the Sufi tradition the Supreme Pen represents Universal Intelligence.

PENTAGON Associated with the planet Venus, used in a few established Western ideographic systems.

PENTAGRAM/ PENTACLE Used since 4000 BC with unknown significance, especially by the Sumerians, until Pythagorean mysticism defined it as a symbol of the human being. Known as Solomon's Seal in medieval Jewish mysticism.

PEORTH Rune for P.

PER CENT Modern.

PHALEC Used in Kabbalistic mysticism for the spirit of Mars.

PHILOSOPHER'S STONE Alchemistic.

PHOENIX The legendary bird that renews itself in fire became the most famous of all rebirth symbols, a resurrection emblem and eventually the symbol of the indomitable human spirit.

PIG Ambiguous symbolism of gluttony, selfishness, lust, obstinacy and ignorance, but also motherhood, fertility, prosperity and happiness.

PIPE In Native American culture tobacco was a sacred herb. Smoking shared pipes was a social activity based around religious ceremony or tribal alliances.

PISCES Zodiac sign.

PISCES Zodiac sign, ancient Greek variation.

PLAITED SIGN Nordic design pattern.

PLATINUM A metal discovered in the mid-1800s, its sign is a combination of those for gold and silver.

PLEIADES Magical amulet seal.

PLIMSOLL MARK Named after its inventor, printed on the sides of cargo ships to give visible checks as to the safety of the cargo's weight, depending on which waters the ship was sailing in.

PLOUGH Symbol of peace, also a male fertility symbol, the male plough entering the female earth. Also a thematic symbol of man's farming activity, pushing back the wilderness and taming it to produce food. Counter-balance to the sword, as an anti-war concept.

PLUTO Sign of the planet, the most common variation.

PLUTO Sign of the planet, variation.

POSEIDON Sign of the god.

PRAYER BEADS Used in religious contexts, such as Catholicism and Buddhism, as an aid to remembering specific prayers or sequences of prayers. The number of beads in the string usually has symbolic meaning.

PRECIPITATION Alchemistic.

PURIFICATION Alchemistic.

QUINCUNX Astrology, the inconjunct aspect: a 150-degree angle between planets as seen from Earth.

POTASH Alchemistic.

PROCYON Astrological sign for the star procyon.

PYRAMID Carrying the same symbolism as the triangle, one of the most powerful and versatile geometric symbols.

QUINTESSENCE Alchemistic.

PLUTO Sign of the planet, variation.

POTASSIUM CARBONATE Late alchemy and early chemistry.

PRAYER STICK An aid to prayer in shamanic traditions, and a link with God.

PROTECTION An example of several similar structures that were drawn on barns and houses for protection or good fortune.

QUAIL Chinese symbol of light, also warmth, ardour and courage. In Greek and Hindu traditions the quail is a symbol of renewal of life and return of the sun.

QUINTILE Astrology.

POLARIS Fixed star, magical amulet seal, Kabbalism.

PRAYER WHEEL Tibetan, an aid to prayer for Buddhists and Hindus that is spun round as the prayer unfolds. Its turning movement therefore is a symbol in itself of the cycles of birth, death and rebirth.

POMEGRANATE Strongly identified with sexual temptation, also with unity, linked to fertility, love and marriage.

POUND STERLING British currency.

PUMPKIN In China, and in feng shui the pumpkin symbolizes prosperity and abundance. A pumpkin with a face carved out of it is known as a Jack O' Lantern, which is a symbol of Halloween.

QUESTION MARK Modern, denoting a question in written text.

RABBIT Strong moon association and therefore linked with menstruation and fertility in most traditions. Folkloric symbol of harmless guile.

RAD Rune for R.

RADIATION Used since antiquity for radiation of light, in modern usage release of energy or radiation, in comic strips fistfights and explosions.

RAIDO Rune associated with raiding, journey.

RAIN Vital symbol of fecundity linked to divine blessings or punishments. Emblem of purity.

RAM Symbol of solar energy, as first sign of the zodiac represents

renewal of fertility and return of spring. Also symbolizes virility, ardour and obstinacy.

RAPHAEL Symbol of the archangel.

RAT Symbol of fecundity, also destructiveness and avarice. Generally negative associations but in folkloric traditions it is a symbol of knowingness, and in Asian traditions it is associated with gods of wisdom, success or prosperity.

RATTLE Used in shamanic rituals, and a symbol of the shaman him/herself and their position as a mediator between Earth and the otherworld.

RAVEN A symbol of loss, death and war in western Europe, but venerated elsewhere

as a solar and oracular symbol; the messenger bird of the god Apollo in the Greek world and linked with the Roman cult of Mithras. In Africa the raven is a guide, and to Native Americans a culture hero. The Inuits have a creator god called the Raven Father, and they believed that killing a raven would bring bad weather.

RECYCLING A modern sign for the recycling of household or industrial waste.

REEDS Japanese and Celtic symbol of purification. Fertility symbol in Mesoamerica. In classical tradition it is an emblem of Pan (he made his pipes from reeds), and in Christian symbolism it is linked to Christ's Passion from the vinegar-soaked sponge that was offered to him on the end of a reed. In Western folklore tradition, reeds were believed to protect from witchcraft.

REGULUS Star, medieval magical amulet seal.

REINDEER In cultures of the far north reindeer have lunar significance as funerary symbols, and are said to be conductors of dead souls. The flight of reindeer associated with Christmas probably originates in the flight of the Lapp shaman.

REPETITION Musical notation.

REVERSED FOUR Ancient and widespread structure found in prehistoric caves in Western Europe, meaning unknown.

RHINOCEROS An astrological symbol of the ancient Indus Calendar (3100 BC), the rhinoceros is one of four animals that surround Brahma, the Hindu god of creation.

RIBBON The symbolism of the ribbon depends more upon colour or context. Ribbons are often worn to indicate the wearer identifies with a particular cause or memory.

RICE Central emblem of growth, rebirth and fertility. Staple food in India and China and therefore has particular significance in these cultures, with links to divine nourishment. In Asia rice is used as a fecundity symbol at Indian weddings and appears in mythology as the gift of the gods to the first humans. In China rice wine was a sacred drink, and grains of rice were placed in the mouths of the dead. The Japanese god, Inari is the god of prosperity and of rice.

RING Circular symbol of eternity and therefore a prime binding symbol, also symbol of completion, continuity, strength and protection. Used as an emblem of authority, occult protective power, and as the sign of a personal pledge.

ROCK The rock commonly symbolizes that which is unchanging, enduring and motionless. In Chinese Taoist thought, rocks, as seen in landscape paintings, are associated with the qualities of the active principle, yang. Similarly in Hindu tradition rocks are embued with this same active principle. Sisyphus' rock is a symbol of the earthly desires of humans.

ROCK SALT Alchemistic.

ROD/WAND, ancient symbol of supernatural power associated with the tree, the phallus and the snake.

ROSE Mystic symbol of the heart; centre of the cosmic wheel; of sacred, romantic and sensual love, and of perfection.

ROSETTE The eight-leaf rosette is an ancient and global symbol representing birth, death and rebirth, specifically in relation to the sun or the planet Venus. In modern times rosettes made from ribbons are used to mark a victory.

RUBBER Alchemistic.

SAFFRON Alchemistic.

SAGITTARIUS Zodiac sign.

SALMON Symbol of virility, fecundity, courage, wisdom and foresight. To the Celts the salmon was linked to transformation and virility. To the people of northern Europe the salmon's migration upriver made it a totem of nature's bounty and wisdom.

SALT Alchemistic sign.

SALT WATER Alchemistic sign.

SANDAL Removal of sandals represents the connection between the human and the Earth: this is seen in the Masonic ritual of removing sandals, and in Moses making contact with holy ground on Mount Sinai. To the ancient Taoists winged sandals enabled the immortals to move through the air, symbolism seen also in the winged sandals of Hermes and Perseus.

SANFOKA Ghanaian adinkra symbol meaning "return and get it", signifying the importance of learning from the past.

SAP See Juice

SATURN Sign for the god.

SATURN Sign for the god, variation.

SATURN Sign for the planet.

SAUVASTIKA Reversed swastika, Greek variation from around 500 BC.

SAUVASTIKA Reversed swastika, associated with misfortune and bad luck.

SCALES Common representation of justice, truth, balance and prudence; the weighing up of decisions and actions. In ancient Egyptian mythology, scales were used to weigh the souls of the dead, and in Christian iconography angels are often depicted with scales as the symbol of divine judgement.

SCALLOP SHELL Associated with Aphrodite, and therefore with love.

SCARAB BEETLE Ancient Egyptian solar symbol.

SCEPTRE/STAFF Originally a male fertility symbol, implies royal or divine power and has been used as a symbol of imperial or kingly position, especially in Western art.

SCISSORS Ceremonial tool whose action of cutting marks the culmination and opening of a new project, as in the opening of a building. Scissors were associated with Atropos, the Fate who cut the thread of life.

SCORPIO Zodiac sign.

SCORPIO Zodiac sign, variation.

SCORPIO Zodiac sign, variation.

SEAL OF LOA-TZU Taoist sage.

African myths the rainbow snake links the earth with the heavens; the Aztec bird-snake divinity Quetzalcoatl does the same, and in Egypt the barge that carries the dead to the underworld enters a serpent. The snake also has sexual and agricultural fertility symbolism.

Apollo, Osiris, Mithras and the Buddha. Symbol of perfection for Islam.

SHEAF OF WHEAT Fertility symbol, also associated with abundance, plenty, with daily bread and with harvest time.

SHIELD Symbol of protection and deliverance. In the medieval chivalric period, the shield was part of a knight's badge of honour and identification. In Aboriginal myth, the shield is associated with the moon.

SCROLL Symbol of learning and law.

SEAL OF SOLOMON Also known as the pentagram, and the Star of David.

SERPENT COILED AROUND EGG Sometimes referred to as the cosmic egg, Greek symbol of the world being protected by a cosmic serpent.

SEXUAL LOVE Modern, composed of heart sign and the arrow of Eros, one of the most widely used contemporary icons.

SHEEP Meekness and a helpless need for leadership and protection.

SCYTHE Farm implement used for cutting crops, associated with Roman god Saturn. In medieval iconography, an attribute of the Grim Reaper (Death).

SEED OF THE UNIVERSE This is the Tibetan sign for the origins of the universe, also found in the coat of arms of the Aztec god Quetzalcoatl.

SESA WORUBAN Ghanaian adinkra symbol, meaning the ability to change or transform life.

SHAMROCK Emblem of Ireland, supposedly from the time when St Patrick, patron saint of Ireland, used the shamrock to explain the three elements of the Holy Trinity to his congregation.

SHEPHERD Symbol of protection and care. Jesus Christ is portrayed in the Bible as the Good Shepherd, and this image has been widely used in Western art.

SHOE The shoe is commonly a symbol of possession. It is an Islamic tradition to remove one's shoes when crossing the threshold of another's house, showing one claims no possession of the property. Shoes can also signify that an individual is his or her own master.

SEA HORSE Can symbolize the male role in the birthing process, as the male animal carries its young within its own body.

SERPENT/SNAKE Most significant and complex animal, symbol of primeval life force and divine self-sufficiency. Often part of creation myths; Vishnu, the Hindu creator god, rests on the coils of a great snake; in

SEVEN Sacred, mystical and magical number; symbol of cosmic and spiritual order; sacred to

SHARK Modern associations with terror and violence.

SHOFAR A symbol of the Jewish faith, a ram's horn that is blown like a trumpet on Jewish new year.

SHOU The Chinese character for long life, used in the decoration of ceramics and textiles.

SICKLE One of the tools of the Grim Reaper, associated with death, also with harvest and agriculture. One of the parts of the sign for communism.

SIEVE Commonly symbolizes the separation of good and evil. The sieve is also used as a sifting tool of divine justice or satanic judgement.

SIGEL Rune for S.

SIGRUNE Rune linked with victory.

SIKHISM Sign of the Sikh faith.

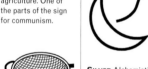

SILVER Alchemistic.

SILVER Alchemistic, variation.

SIREN/MERMAID Seen as the embodiment of the sexual side of the female, symbol of temptation, beauty and otherness.

SIRIUS Star, magical amulet seal, Kabbalism.

SIX Symbol of union and equilibrium.

SKULL Potent symbol of death, used as a sign warning that a substance is poison. As part of the skull and crossbones motif is also a symbol of piratism.

SLING From the biblical story of David and Goliath, the sling has been used as a symbol of the triumph of the weak.

SMA Egyptian, union.

SMOKE An ascension symbol; means of communication on cosmic and mundane level for Native Americans. Also a symbol of concealment.

SNAIL Usually a lunar symbol associated with cyclical or periodic processes in nature. In coming out and returning to its shell the snail is indicative of an eternal homecoming. The snail is also associated with the sexual symbolism of the vulva; the Aztecs

considered it to be a symbol of conception, pregnancy and birth.

SNOW Six-pointed crystal; modern sign for freezing.

SOLAR ECLIPSE Symbol of cosmic danger; in ancient cultures was a symbol of fear.

SPACE ROCKET Symbol of human endeavour and soaring ambition.

SPADES Suit of cards, associated with fighting, destiny, logical thinking, and death. Originally iconic sign for sword.

SPEAR As the lance, a symbol of masculine, phallic and earthly power. Associated with chivalry and with the Passion of Christ, from the spear that pierced his side. The broken lance is an attribute of St George, patron saint of England, and symbolizes the experienced soldier.

SPHINX In ancient Egypt, a monument of a human-headed lion, symbol of the sun. In ancient Greece, a riddle-spinning hybrid with wings, female human head and breasts, which Jung saw as a symbol of the devouring mother.

SPICA Sign of the star.

SPIDER Folkloric links with oncoming rain, also with gifts from Heaven.

SPIRAL The clockwise spiral starts from the middle, symbolizes water, power, independent movement and migration. One of the most important and ancient symbols; most common of all decorative motifs throughout cultures. As an open and flowing line it suggests extension, evolution and continuity.

SPIRAL Maori Koru, the Polynesian spiral has sexual symbolism and is based on the uncurling fern leaf. It shows the close link between spiral motifs and natural phenomena.

SPIRAL OF LIFE Found in the Bronze Age in Ireland, this sign is drawn in one single line without beginning or end.

SPLIT/CLEAVE Appears in earliest Chinese and other ancient writing systems.

SPRING Time sign, alchemistic.

SPRING Time sign, Germanic.

SQUARE An expression of the two dimensions that constitute a surface; symbol of land, field, ground, or the earth element. Thought to mean realization or materialization in Egyptian hieroglyphs.

SQUARE WITHIN A CIRCLE In Chinese symbolism this represents Earth. In Beijing the temple of Earth is constructed on this principle, whereas the temple of Heaven is a circle within a square.

SQUARE, WITH CROSS In China and Japan symbolizes field or ground, not common in Western ideography.

SQUARE, WITH DOT Village in Chinese writing; urine in alchemistic; wet ground in meteorology.

SQUARE, WITHIN A SQUARE Keep, retain, keep inside or close in. Modern sign for manhole.

STAFF See Sceptre

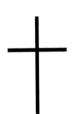

STAFF OF APOLLO Also known as the Latin cross; in pre-Christian times it represented the god Apollo and appeared on ancient coins. Also used in pre-Columbian America and the Euphrates–Tigris region as a sun sign.

STAFF OF THE DEVIL

STAFF OF JUPITER/ZEUS

STAFF OF ODIN

STAFF OF POSEIDON

STAFF Egyptian.

STAFF Phoenician.

STAG Solar emblem of fertility, the antlers symbolize the tree of life, the sun's rays, longevity and rebirth. Antlers have been used as headdresses for dieties; on the Celtic antlered god Cerunnus they represented spring and fecundity.

STAIRCASE Symbol of ascent and descent; in the acquisition of knowledge of the divine when rising, or of the unconscious or the occult when descending.

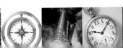

STAR Three-pointed, known as an Ethiopian emblem, a rare three-pointed star symbol.

STAR Four-pointed, also known as the sun star, denotes serious and solemn warning.

STAR Five-pointed, one of the most common and important Western ideograms; used on 35 national flags; widely used as a military and law enforcement symbol. Denotes the Bethlehem star. Used to indicate top quality.

STAR Six-pointed; rare in Western ideography but used in some United States as a policeman's badge.

STAR Eight-pointed, an ancient symbol for the goddess, or the planet, Venus, and for the Morning or Evening Star.

STAR, EASTERN Sign for the planet Venus. Common among tribal peoples in Africa and the Americas.

STAR Gnostic.

STAR OF DAVID Most well known of Jewish symbols, is supposed to be based on the shape of King David's shield, but is almost certainly more modern. Also known as the seal of Solomon, and in mystic traditions as the pentagram.

STAR OF LAKSHMI

STAR OF VENUS

STAR OF VENUS Phoenician variation.

STARFISH With its five-fold symmetry, the starfish is an esoteric symbol associated with five-pointed stars and the spiral of life.

STEEL Alchemistic.

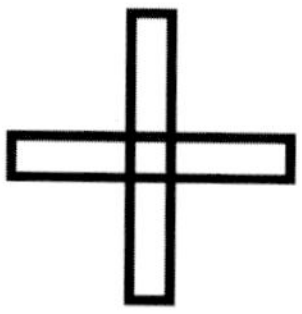

STONES/PEBBLES Alchemistic.

STORK Symbol of longevity and filial devotion. Sacred to Greek goddess Hera. Linked to purity, piety and resurrection for Christians.

STUPA Graphical representation of a stupa symbolizing the organization of the universe: square for earth, circle for water, triangle for fire, crescent for air and droplet for ether.

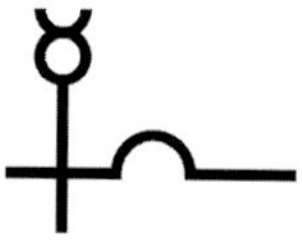

SUBLIMATE Alchemistic.

SUCCESS Protection against evil, Sumerian; also Viking.

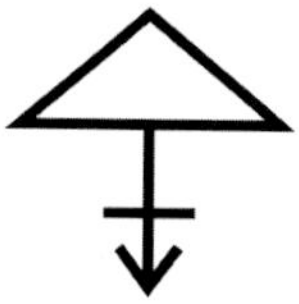

SULPHUR Alchemistic.

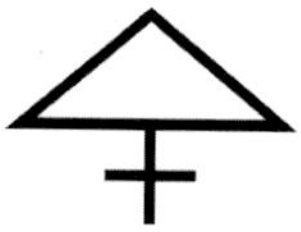

SULPHUR Alchemistic, variation.

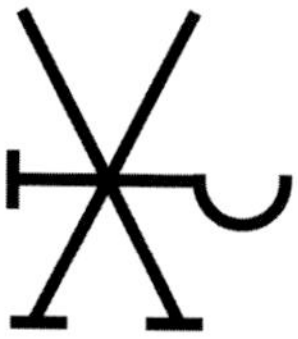

SUMMER Time sign, alchemistic.

vitality, passion, courage and eternally renewed youth, knowledge, intellect and truth. Emblem of royalty and imperial splendour.

SUN Variation, also gold in pre-Christian Greece.

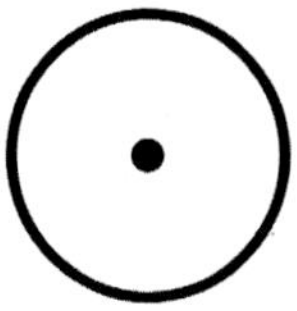

SUN Most ancient ideogram for the sun, seems to have been used in every cultural sphere on earth.

SUN Bronze Age Nordic, also prehistoric Egyptian.

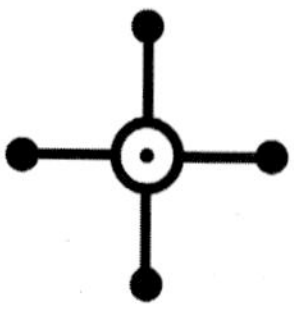

SUN Dominant symbol of creative energy in most traditions; symbol of

SUN CROSS Danish Bronze age.

SUN CROSS Variation found in excavation of 4000 year-old Cretan city of Troy.

SUN WHEEL Used in Gaul, also sign of Taranis, Celtic god of thunder.

is usually associated with sun and power, with the life force and cyclic regeneration – often extended to signify the Supreme Being. In modern times the swastika was monopolized by Hitler as sign of the Nazi party in 1930s.

had been a positive sign of cosmic regeneration was degraded into a political emblem of repression and violence.

TAMBOURINE/ TIMBREL An important ritual object to the Israelites and a Jewish symbol of victory and jubilee.

TARTRATE Alchemistic.

SUN GOD The archetypal ancient Egyptian sign, known as the Eye of Horus, and as the *wedjat*. Symbol of cosmic wholeness, and of the all-seeing power of the god Horus.

SUNRISE New day, earliest Chinese writing systems.

SWASTIKA Ancient Greek variation.

SWASTIKA Pre-Columbian America variation.

TAMFOA BEBRE Ghanaian adinkra symbol meaning the importance of learning from the past.

TASSELS In 17th-century France the tassel came to represent wealth, prestige and power. As Masonic symbols, the four tassels represent the cardinal virtues. In Catholicism and other religious traditions, the wearing of tassels can symbolize rank.

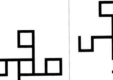
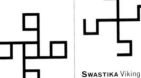

SUN/SUNLIGHT/ STARS Japanese.

SWAN Romantic and ambiguous symbol of masculine light and feminine beauty in Western music and ballet. Attribute of Aphrodite and Apollo.

SWASTIKA Celtic variation.

SWASTIKA Viking variation.

TARGET Modern.

SUN WHEEL Also known as the ring cross; common in the Nordic countries, pre-Columbian America, and throughout the Mediterranean about 3,500 years ago.

SWASTIKA Ancient ideogram first found in Sumeria about 3000 BC. Its name comes from the Sanskrit *su*, "well", and *asti* "being". Used in India, Japan and Southern Europe with various meanings, all of them positive, including as one of the symbols of the Buddha. The swastika

SWASTIKA Christian variation.

SWASTIKA Nazi variation, in which an ancient symbol that for thousands of years

SWORD Important and ancient symbol of authority, justice, intellect and light. Emblem of magic. Linked to exceptional virtue and cults of the sword, particularly in Japan and in the religious rituals of the crusades. Carries a ceremonial role, especially to confer knighthoods. Symbol of constancy, and wrath personified, in religious thought it is often equated with wisdom and knowledge.

TARTAR Alchemistic, also found on South American rock carvings.

TAURUS Zodiac sign.

TEARS Symbols of grief or sadness.

TEETH Primordial symbols of aggressive-defensive power.

TEFILLIN Jewish, leather pouch containing quote from the Torah, strapped to the arm and head.

TEN Symbol of perfection, especially in Jewish tradition; symbol for whole of creation for Pythagoreans; and for perfect balance for Chinese.

TEN COMMANDMENTS Jewish.

TEST Alchemistic.

TET OF OSIRIS Also known as the Djed Pillar, is a stylized tree, symbolic of the tamarisk tree that held Osiris's body. It symbolizes sturdiness, stability and the ability of the spirit to break from its earthly bonds and rise towards the heavens. It is equated with the backbone, and possibly also with the penis.

TETRAGRAMMATON The four Hebrew letters used to represent the name of God, Yahweh, a name that must not be spoken aloud in the Jewish faith.

THEOSOPHICAL SOCIETY A society founded in the 19th century and still in existence today, whose primary objective is Universal Brotherhood based on the idea that life and all its forms is indivisibly One.

THISTLE Symbol of retaliation; also healing or talismanic powers. Emblem of martyrdom and of Scotland.

THORN Commonly associated with blocks and barriers, whether internal or external. Christ's crown of thorns can be understood as a crown of suffering or as a solar symbol with the thorns representing the rays of the sun emanating outwards. Flying thorns in China were weapons that drove out evil. "A land of thorn and thistles" in the Jewish and Christian traditions referred to soil that was untilled and therefore virginal.

THORN Rune for Th.

THREAD A linking symbol that connects many different states of being to one another, and to a unifying origin. Ariadne's thread linked Theseus between the underworld and the everyday world. Puppet strings link the puppet to the puppet master.

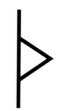

THREE The most positive number in symbolism, religious thought, legend, mythology and folklore. The lucky three is a very ancient concept. In Christian thought it has central importance as the doctrine of the Trinity, God the Father, God the Son and God the Holy Spirit, a theology that has forerunners in classical, Celtic and Hindu traditions.

THRONE Traditional symbol of kingship, divine authority and power.

THUNDERBOLT Linked with Nazism, and with the rune for yew, Viking.

TIGER In Asia and India the tiger replaces the lion as the symbol of all that is great and terrible in nature.

TOAD Symbol of death; linked to witchcraft in European traditions; a good luck lunar symbol in China; associated with rain and riches.

TODESRUNE Rune of death.

TODESRUNE Rune of death, variation.

TOMAHAWK Pipe tomahawks were used to seal treaties between different Native American groups. The Algonquian tamahak was ceremonial and a symbol of leadership.

TOMATO The Bambara associate tomato juice with blood, and thus the tomato is considered to have the blood of life, and is the bearer of the foetus.

TORCH A symbol of illumination. Its light is born to illuminate passage on a journey. The concept of the flame that is never extinguished is a potent one.

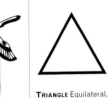

TOTEM POLE A symbolic carved pole representing totem animal and guardian spirits of an individual or clan.

TREASURE Abundant riches, found rather than earned, have always been a symbol of attainment, and feature in mythologies as reward for the just, or the means to punishment for the wrong-doer.

TREE OF LIFE Universal symbol of creation, the tree of life has its roots in the waters of the underworld, its trunk in the earthly world, and its branches in the heavens. Seen as a way of accessing other worlds.

TRIANGLE Equilateral, associated with the divine number three, symbol for power, success, prosperity and safety. The Hittites used it for well, good or healthy.

TRIANGLE Single axis symmetric, variation of equilateral triangle.

TRIANGLE Pythagorean.

TRIANGLE With horizontal line, element of fire in the Middle Ages.

TRIANGLE Upside down, element of water. Also negative spectrum of meaning.

TRIANGLE Upside down, with horizontal line, element of earth in the Middle Ages.

TRIANGLE With a vertical line, in Hittite hieroglyphics this sign represented the king, the vertical line signifying the unique being inside the triangle, which stood for power and divinity.

TRIDENT Symbol of sea power; emblem of Neptune; of ancient Minoan civilization; and later of Britannia.

TRIQUETRA A tripartate symbol composed of three interlocked vesica pisces, most commonly used for the Holy Trinity but predates Christianity and was likely a Celtic symbol of the triple goddess or Odin.

TRISKELION Greek word for three-leg, this was found on an Athenian shield used as a competition prize in 500 BC.

TRUMPET Instrument of portent, momentous news or action, used in military, ritualistic and state occasions.

TUDOR ROSE Emblem of the Tudor royal dynasty created by combining the white rose of York with the red rose of Lancaster.

TURTLE/TORTOISE Symbol of the whole universe, its shell representing the heavens, and its flat base, earth. Chinese and Amerindian tradition link penile erection with the way the head emerges from its shell.

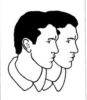

TWINS Sign of Gemini, twins are generally symbols of the nature of dualism.

TWO Symbol of duality: division but synthesis, attraction but repulsion, equilibrium but conflict. Thought of as unlucky in China.

TYR Rune for T.

UMBRELLA See Parasol

UNDERWORLD Egyptian hieroglyph.

UNICORN Ultimate symbol of chastity, courtly symbol of sublimated desire, Christian symbol of the incarnation.

UR/URUZ Rune, meaning strength, sacrificial animal.

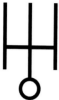

URANUS The planet.

URANUS The planet, variation, also morning.

URN/VASE Female symbol, often appearing as emblems of eternal life in art or in funeral rituals.

VENUS The planet.

VENUS The planet, variation.

VESCIA PISCIS Also known as the fish bladder or mystical almond, adopted by Christians from pagan sources to symbolize purity and virginity.

VESSEL/BOWL Alchemical; also ancient Germanic time sign for summer.

VICTORY Christian.

VINEGAR Alchemistic.

VIRGIN MARY A symbol used by the Christian Church to represent the mother of Jesus.

VIRGO Zodiac sign.

VISHNU The Hindu god holds this sign in one of his four hands as a symbol of the whole universe.

VITRIOL Alchemistic.

VITRIOL Early chemistry.

VIVA! See Down with!

VOLKSWAGEN Emblem of the car manufacturer.

WALNUT Judeo-Christian symbol of fertility and longevity.

WAND See Rod

WATER Alchemistic, also modern.

WATER In all times and all cultures; among the earliest Egyptian hieroglyphs; also adopted to signify resistence.

WATER Kabbalism.

WATER Early chemistry.

WATER ELEMENT See Triangle, upside down.

WATER Common in ancient Greece as decoration.

WAX Alchemistic.

WEEK Time sign in alchemy.

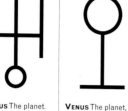

WELL The symbolism of the well is commonly associated with qualities of the sacred or of the unconscious; wells are places of knowledge; the source of life; places of healing; wishes or good luck.

WHALE Ark or womb symbol of regeneration, linked with initiation in Africa and Polynesia.

WHEEL Solar image of cosmic momentum, ceaseless change and cyclic repetition; later of power and dominion. Linked with the progress of mankind. Hindu and Buddhist emblem of reincarnation. Western image of fortune and fate.

WHIP Symbol of rulership, judgement and fertility; the flail replaced the whip in Egypt, and the fly whisk in Africa, China and India.

WOLF Ambivalent symbol of cruelty, cunning and greed but in other cultures of courage, victory or nourishing care (Roman). Sacred to Apollo and Odin.

WOOD Alchemistic.

WREATH The first crown – symbol of spiritual or temporal authority – drawing on the symbolism of the circle (perfection) and the ring (continuity).

YIN YANG Chinese symbol for the duality of the universe.

ZEUS God, variation.

WHITE ARSENIC Alchemistic.

WOOD Alchemistic, variation.

ZEUS God, variation.

WHITE LEAD Early chemistry.

WOMAN A common sign in both ancient and modern systems.

WORLD Tibetan.

WYNN Rune for W.

YIN YANG Earliest ideogram for yin yang. Ideogram in the West for the number 10 from latin X; also signifies hourglass.

WIND FURNACE Alchemistic.

WOMAN/FEMALE SEX Egyptian hieroglyphs; also found widely in cave art; associated with growing and genesis implying that woman is the originator of life.

WOW FORO ADOBE Ghanaian adinkra symbol for persistence and prudence.

YANTRA STRUCTURE Indian, also sorting in computer usage.

YOKE Symbol of oppression from Roman times.

ZIGZAG

ZINC Alchemistic.

WINTER Old Germanic time sign.

YEAR Time sign, alchemistic.

YONI Buddhist symbol of the vulva.

ZODIAC Also known as the ecliptic, the via solis or the way of the sun.

ZEUS Sign of the god.

ACKNOWLEDGEMENTS

504

Unless specified, images used in the book belong to Anness Publishing Ltd. With thanks to the following agencies for additional images:

Art Archive: p12t Musée des Antiquités St Germain en Laye/Dagli Orti; p14t British Museum/Dagli Orti; p14b Musée du Louvre, Paris/Dagli Orti; p15t Musée du Louvre Paris/Dagli Orti; p15m Abbey of Novacella or Neustift/Dagli Orti; p16tm Luxor Museum, Egypt/Dagli Orti; p17b Egyptian Museum Cairo/Dagli Orti; p18b Musée du Louvre Paris/Dagli Orti; p19tl National Archaeological Museum Athens/ Dagli Orti; p21 Chateau de Malmaison, France/Dagli Orti; p23t National Museum of Prague/ Dagli Orti; p23b Bibliothèque des Arts Décoratifs Paris/Dagli Orti; p29t Taj Mahal, India, Dagli Orti; p40 from George Catlin's illustrations; p46t Buddha, Musée Guimet, Paris/Dagli Orti; p49t Palatine Library Parma/Dagli Orti; p50tr Museo San Marco Florence/ Dagli Orti; p50br Musée des Beaux Arts Tours/Dagli Orti; p52t Turkish and Islamic Art Museum Istanbul/Dagli Orti; p53b British Library; p59tl Palazzo Barberini Rome/ Dagli Orti; p58tr, p66t British Museum; p72b British Library; p74t Venus of Willendorf; p75 Peggy Guggenheim Collection Venice/Dagli Orti; p85t Palazzo Arco Mantua Italy/Dagli Orti; p88bl Cathedral Museum Ferrara/Dagli Orti; p91t Dagli Orti; p92t (Douce OR.a3 fol 30), Bodleian Library Oxford; p93b Stadelisches Kunstinstitut Frankfurt; p96tr Russian Historical Museum Moscow/Dagli Orti; p98tm Archaeological Museum Aleppo, Syria/Dagli Orti; p99b Old Kingdom Egyptian, Saqqarah, Egypt (B.49) Musée du Louvre Paris/Dagli Orti; p100b Médiathèque François Mitterand, Poitiers/ Dagli Orti; p101bl Warburg Institute London/Eileen Tweedy; p109t Scrovegni Chapel Padua/Dagli Orti; p114br Newgrange, Ireland/Dagli Orti; p122 Musée des Beaux Arts Tours /Dagli Orti; p123t Ragab Papyrus Institute Cairo/Dagli Orti; p125t Galleria Sabauda Turin/ Dagli Orti; p126 Queretaro Museum Mexico/Dagli Orti; p128tl Galleria Sabauda, Turin/ Dagli Orti; p130br

Victoria and Albert Museum London/ Eileen Tweedy; p131tm British Library; p133t Dagli Orti; p133b British Library; p134t Musée d'Orsay, Paris/ Dagli Orti; p134b British Library; p135t Musée des Arts Africains et Océaniens/Dagli Orti; p135b Prehistoric Museum Moesgard Højbjerg, Denmark/ Dagli Orti; p137t Dagli Orti; p137b British Museum/ Eileen Tweedy; p138br Victoria and Albert Museum London/Graham Brandon; p139 Museo Civico Padua/ Dagli Orti; p141t (Pers b1 Folio 15a) Farrukhabad, Bodleian Library Oxford; p142t Museo del Prado Madrid/Dagli Orti; p142b Galleria d'Arte Moderna, Rome/ Dagli Orti; p144t Canto XIII, Dante's Divine Comedy, by Gustave Dore; p145tl Musée Condé Chantilly/ Dagli Orti; p145tr Ashmole 1511 folio 68r, Bodleian Library Oxford; p146tr Museum Recklinghausen/ Harper Collins Publishers; p147b Mexican National Libary/Mireille Vautier; p158b Lucien Biton Collection Paris/Dagli Orti; p161t Dagli Orti; p165t Musée Thomas Dobrée, Nantes/ Dagli Orti; p165b Palazzo Pitti Florence/Dagli Orti; p166t Tate Gallery London/Eileen Tweedy; p169tr Médiathèque François Mitterand, Poitiers/ Dagli Orti; p170tr National Gallery, London/Eileen Tweedy; p172t National Gallery London/Joseph Martin; p184t Buonconsiglio Castle Trento/Dagli Orti; p190t Burnley Art Gallery/Dagli Orti; p191t British Library; p192t Culver Pictures/Dagli Orti; p193tl Galleria Borghese, Rome/Dagli Orti; p198b Museo del Prado, Madrid/Dagli Orti; p199t Dagli Orti; p203t Archaeological Museum Merida Spain/ Dagli Orti; p206t (Arch Bb9 plate 98), Bodleian Library Oxford; p220–1 *The Dream of Aescupalius,* Accademia Venice/Dagli Orti; p222t Musée du Louvre/Dagli Orti; p223t Eileen Tweedy, p224l Egyptian Museum/Dagli Orti; p224r *Ruins of Thebes* by Carl Richard Lepsius, Musée du Louvre/Dagli Orti; p227t National Archaeological Museum, Athens/Dagli Orti; p229 *The Death of Julius Caesar* by Vincenzo Camuccini, Galleria d'Arte Moderna, Rome/Dagli Orti; p230 V&A Museum, London/Eileen Tweedy; p233 British Library; p236 *The Dream of Tartini,* National Museum Budapest/

Dagli Orti; p237b Bibliothèque Municipale Poitiers/Dagli Orti; p242r Turkish and Islamic Art Museum, Istanbul/Harper Collins Publishers; p243t *Joseph explaining the dreams of Pharoah* by Jean Adrien Guignet, Musèe des Beaux Arts, Rouen/Dagli Orti; p254 Ocean Memorabilia Collection; p265tr *The Guest of Stone* by Marco Marcola, Museo Civico Sartorio Trieste/ Dagli Orti; p276 *Dulle Griet*, detail, by Pieter Breughel the Elder, Mayer van den Bergh Museum; pp280–1 *Ossian's Lament* by Karoly Kisfaludy, National Gallery, Budapest/Dagli Orti; p314l Ragab Papyrus Institute/Dagli Orti; p417tr Musèe Carnavalet, Paris/Dagli Orti; pp444–5 *Queen of the Night,* Mozarteum, Salzburg/Dagli Orti; p446l *The Wild Swans* by Otto Svend, Dagli Orti; p447t *The Tower of Babel* by Pieter Breughel the Younger, Dagli Orti; p448 *The Depths of the Sea* by Sir Edward Burne Jones, Private Collection; p449c *Mount Helicon with Pegasus and centaur Chiron* by Giovanni Falconetto, Palazzo Arco, Mantua, Italy; p453b *Libuse* by Vitezlav Karl Masek, Musèe National d'Art Moderne, Paris/Dagli Orti.

The Bridgeman Art Library: p21tl Museo e Gallerie Nazionali di Capodimonte, Naples, Italy; p21b Louvre, Paris, France, Lauros/ Giraudon; p22tl Musee des Antiquites Nationales, St. Germain-en-Laye, France; p28t, Nottingham City Museums and Galleries (Nottingham Castle); p32b Museo Nacional de Antropologia, Mexico City, Mexico, Sean Sprague/Mexicolore; p41t Bibliotheque des Arts Decoratifs, Paris, France, Archives Charmet; p42b Bibliotheque Nationale, Paris, France/ Archives Charmet; p44b Private Collection/Ann & Bury Peerless Picture Library; p51 Prado, Madrid, Spain, Giraudon; p56t Freud Museum, London, UK; p57tr Archives Larousse, Paris, France; p58b Fogg Art Museum/ Harvard University Art Museums, USA, Bequest of Grenville L. Winthrop; p60b Private Collection; p61 Private Collection/Chris Beetles, London, UK; p70br Private Collection/Chris Beetles, London, UK; p72t Bristol City Museum and Art Gallery, UK; p73t Musee Gustave Moreau, Paris, France; p85b Private Collection/Archives Charmet; p94t Private Collection; p102b The Illustrated London News Picture Library, London, UK; p103tl Private Collection/Paul Freeman; p103tr Institut National des Jeunes Sourds, Paris, France/ Archives Charmet; p104b Museo de America, Madrid, Spain; p108tr Private Collection/ Richard Philp, London; p111t Walker

Art Gallery, National Museums, Liverpool; p113tr Palazzo Ducale, Urbino, Italy; p115t British Museum, London, UK; p116b Private Collection/ The Fine Art Society, London, UK; p117t Private Collection/Christopher Wood Gallery, London, UK; p118t Private Collection; p119tr Leighton House Museum and Art Gallery, London, UK; p132t Private Collection/ Lawrence Steigrad Fine Arts, New York; p136 Private Collection; p138bl Bibliotheque de L'Arsenal, Paris, France, Archives Charmet; p140t Musee d'Art Thomas Henry, Cherbourg, France, Giraudon; p140b Nationalmuseum, Stockholm, Sweden; p141 Bibliotheque des Arts Decoratifs, Paris, France, Archives Charmet; p143t Bibliotheque des Arts Decoratifs, Paris, France, Archives Charmet; p144b Royal Asiatic Society, London, UK; p145b The Marsden Archive, UK; p154t Bibliotheque de L'Arsenal, Paris, France/Archives Charmet; p155t/ Private Collection/Stapleton Collection; p155b Private Collection/Stapleton Collection; p156bl Private Collection/ Stapleton Collection; p157 Musee des Beaux-Arts, Rouen, France, Lauros/ Giraudon; p160b Ms Add 24189 fol.15 Library, London, UK; p169tl Ashmolean Museum, University of Oxford, UK; p171b Private Collection/ Stapleton Collection; p175t Lady Lever Art Gallery, National Museums Liverpool; p179t Trustees of the Watts Gallery, Compton, Surrey, UK; p186b Private Collection/Ann & Bury Peerless Picture Library; p188t Johnny van Haeften Gallery, London, UK; 189t Galleria degli Uffizi, Florence, Italy, Alinari; p194t Archaeological Museum of Heraklion, Crete, Greece; p194b Giraudon; p196t Musee Girodet, Montargis, France/Peter Willi; p198t/ p204b 28681 f.9 Psalter Map, British Library, London, UK; p205 Hotel Dieu, Beaune, France/Paul Maeyaert; p208b Ms 386 fol.25r Bibliotheque Municipale, Cambrai, France, Giraudon; p210b Palazzo Pitti, Florence, Italy; 211t Louvre, Paris, France; p213t Nationalmuseum, Stockholm, Sweden; p213b Louvre, Paris, France; p215b Private Collection/ Index; p216b Private Collection/ Bonhams, London; p217tr Musee de la Chartreuse, France/Giraudon.

Corbis: p22b Richard T. Nowitz; p24bl; p24br Charles & Josette Lenars; p25t DiMaggio/Kalish; p25m Kevin Fleming; p26 Paul Almasy; p27l Charles & Josette Lenars; p27r Margaret Courtney-Clarke; p30t Wolfgang Kaehler; p30b Chris Rainier; p31t Charles & Josette Lenars; p31bl

Michael & Patricia Fogden; p34b; p35t; p36t John Noble; p36b Peter Harholdt; p37b Tiziana and Gianni Baldizzone; p43t Brian A. Vikander; p45t Reuters; p47t Christine Kolisch; p52b Nevada Wier; p58t Close Murray/Corbis Sygma; p59b Elke Stolzenberg; p64t Hulton-Deutsch Collection; p66b Archivo Iconografico, S.A.; p67t Anthony Bannister; Gallo Images; p69tl Matthew McKee; Eye Ubiquitous; p69tr; p74m Charles & Josette Lenars; p74b Christie's Images; p76b Murray Andrew/Corbis Sygma; p77b Leonard de Selva; p78b 1661-Drawing of Copernicus' world system, Bettmann; p79t Galileo Galilei before the Inquisition (ca. 1632) by Robert-Fleury, Bettmann; p86t David Muench; p87tl Nik Wheeler; p87tr Dean Conger; p87b Jose Luis Pelaez, Inc.; p88bm Bob Krist; p88br Carl & Ann Purcell; p89t Michael S. Yamashita; p90t Roger Antrobus; p93t Jim Zuckerman; p95t; p96tl Anthony Bannister; Gallo Images; p98tr Carmen Redondo; p101t early print shop workers at their trade, c.1800s, Bettmann; p104t Jeffrey L. Rotman; p105t Bettmann; p105b William Whitehurst; p112t Farrell Grehan; p113tl Penny Tweedie; p126 Greenhalf Photography; p127 Tranquility Base, the Moon: Apollo 11 commander Neil Armstrong takes first step on lunar surface, Bettmann; p129 Matthias Kulka; p150b Tiziana and Gianni Baldizzone; p151t Sheldan Collins; p151m Werner Forman; p153tl Jonathan Blair; p153tr Brian A. Vikander; p153b Michael S. Lewis; p156br; p159t Alison Wright; p159b Bob Krist; p167b Michael Freeman; p174t Rose Hartman; p175bl Adam Woolfitt; p176b Lindsay Hebberd; p177t Mark Cooper; p177b Norbert Schaefer; p178t Lindsay Hebberd; p179b George Huey; p182tl Lindsay Hebberd; p182tr; p186t Fabrizio Bensch; p187b Catherine Karnow; p191 Jim Zuckerman; p193 Lindsay Hebberd; p196b Werner H. Müller; p199b Michael & Patricia Fogden; p202t Archivo Icono-grafico; p203b Reuters; p206b Werner Forman; p209tr Galen Rowell; p212b Hubert Stadler; p217tl Clayton J. Price; pp304–5 Julie Lemberger; p222b Gianni Dagli Orti; p225r Marc Garanger; p226 Calliope and Homer by Antonio Canova, Archivo Iconografico, SA; p227b Ruggero Vanni; p228l Raphael, School of Athens, detail, Ted Spiegel; p228r Araldo de Luca; p232tl Richard A. Cooke; p232tr Dallas & John Heaton; p232b Craig Lovell; p234br Elio Ciol; p235t Greenhalf Photography; p235b Richard Hamilton Smith; p237t The Witch by David

Ryckaert III, Ali Meyer; p238 Penny Tweedie; p239tl Ralph A. Clevenger; p239tr Otto Rogge; p240tl Tom Bean; p240tr Dave Bartruff; p240b Bob Rowan/Progressive Image; p241 Geoffrey Clements; p242l Chris Lisle; p243b The Annunciation by Edward Burne Jones, Christie's Images; pp244–5 David Pu'u; p246 Charles Gupton; p247tl Ron Lowery; p247bl Ryszard Horowitz; p247br Richard Cummins; p248 Sigmund Freud by Bettmann; p249t John Lund; p249bl Larry Williams; p250bl Carl Jung by Bettmann; p251t Rick Gayle; p251tr Ron Lowery; p252l Benjamin Rondel; p252r David Pu'u; p253 Mark Cooper; p255t; p255b James Nazz; p256 Chris Lisle; p257l William Whitehurst; p257r David Aubrey; p258r Dale O'Dell; p259t Chris Hellier; p259br Chris Rainer; p260l Phil Banko; p260r Firefly Productions; p261 Shutter & Mouse; pp262–3 Destruction of Jerusalem by Ercole de'Roberti, Historical Picture Archive; p265tl Stapleton Collection; p265b Roy McMahon; p266r Todd A. Gipstein; p268 O Holy night by Henry Raymond, Christie's Images; p269r Maiden and Unicorn, Araldo de Luca; p270 Art Becker Photo; p271t Ron Lowery; p272l Jim Zuckerman; p272r Jose Luis Pelaez, Inc.; p273t Douglas Kirkland; p275br Dale O'Dell; p278, Richard T. Nowitz; p279l Ron Lowery; p279r Norbert Schaefer; p282l George Shelley; p282r Denis Scott; p283 Dale O'Dell; p286l LWA-JDC; p287 Pete Saloutos; p289t Denis Anthony Valentine; p290 Ron Watts; p291t Danny Lehman; p291c Lindsay Hebberd; p296 Denis Scott; p297b Mendola/Jeff Mangiat; p300 Thomas Schweizer; p301t LWA/Stephen Welstead; p302r Mauro Panci; p308b Art Becker Photo; p309b Digital Art; p311t Mug Shots; p311c Firefly Productions; p313tl Gianni Dagli Orti; p313 Adam Woolfitt; p313br Charlemagne Receiving the Monk Alcuino by Jean Victor Schnetz, Archivo Iconografico; p314r Portrai of Ibn Rushd by Andrea di Buonaioto, Archivo Iconografico; p315cl Mug Shots; p318 Michael Boys; p319tl Alfred Ko; p323bc B.S.P.I; p327t Bill Ross; p330

Julie Meech/Ecoscene; p331cl Ted Spiegel; p334r Galen Rowell; pp344–5 Markku Lahdesmaki; p346 Dale O'Dell; p347t Al Francekevich; p347c Layne Kennedy; p348 David Woods; p349l Mendola/Doug Chezem; p349r Rick Gayle; p350tl Edward Holub; p350b Ted Horowitz; p351l Lawrence Manning; p351c Rick Gomez; p353t L. Clarke; p353c Joe Baraban; p354l LWA/Dann Tardif; p354r Paul Hardy; p355bl Jim Erickson; p355bc LWA/Dann Tardif; p355br Randy M. Ury; p356 Mark L. Stephenson; p357tl Markku Lahdesmaki; p357tr Benjamin Rondel; p357c John Heseltine; p357br Elizabeth Opalenik; pp358–9 Fairies Dancing by Blake, Bettmann; p360l Myron Jay Dorf; p360c Michael Pole; p360r Jon Feingersh; p361tl Bo Zaunders; p361tc Anthony Redpath; p361tr Strauss/Curtis; p361bl Ariel Skelley; p361br Pete Saloutos; p362l Jose Luis Pelaez,Inc.; p362r James Noble; p363t Steve Prezant; p363c Ron Slenzak; p364 Roy Morsch; p365tl Mark Garten;p365tr John Acurso; p365c Terry W. Eggers; p365b Bill Binzen; p366l Norbert Schaefer; p366r Nancy Brown; p367bl Ronnie Kaufman; p367bc Westlight Stock; p367br Jose Luis Pelaez, Inc.; p368l Elena Segatini Bloom; p368c Jon Feingersh; p368r Douglas Kirkland; p369tl Trinette Reed; p369tc Gianfranco Benvenuto; p369tr Patrik Giardino; p369b Cheque; p372 Oddo & Sinibaldi; p373tr Lester Lefkowitz; p373c L. Clarke; p373bl Michael Barley; p373br LWA/Stephen Welstead; p374 LWA/Dann Tardif; p375t Mark Tuschman; p375c 2 Face; p375b David Woods; pp378–9; p381tl Joe Bator; p381tr Roy Morsch; p381b C. Moore; p382r Markku Lahdesmaki; p383bl Don Mason; p383br Brian Bailey; p385t Bill Varie; p385c Jose Luis Pelaez, Inc.; p385b Paul Barton; p386 LWA/Dann Tardif; p387tl Alan Schein Photography; p387tr Anthony Redpath; p387c Jose Luis Pelaez, Inc.; p387br Mauro Panci; pp388l Roy Morsch; p388r Robert Sememiuk; p389tl Shutter & Mouse; p389tr Tony Arruza; p389b Kevin Muggleton/Tim Bird; p390l Javier Pierini; p391t Steve Starr; p391b Rick Gayle; p392r Joel Sartore; p393 Andrea Pizzi; p394l Arthur Beck; p394r Julie Lemberger; p395l Robbie Jack; p395r Chuck Savage; p396l George Disario; p398 Franco Vogt; p399tr Roy McMahon; p399b Chris Carroll; p400 Chiselvision; p401t Robert Cassel; p401c Sandford/Agliolo; pp402–3 Christie's Images; p404l David Chmielewski; p405t Ron Lowery; p405c Steve Chenn; p407c Chuck Savage; p408l Markku

Lahdesmaki; p409t Dale O'Dell; p410r Firefly Productions; p411t Jim Cummins; p414r Tim Davis; p415bl Myron Jay Dorf; p416r Philip Wallick; p417b The Triumph of Death by Pieter Brueghel the Elder, Archivo Iconografico, S.A.; p419tl Sanford/Agliolo; p419tr Al Francekevich; p420l Bob Witkowski; p420r Roy Morsch; p421t Robert Bowen & Ryszard Horowitz; p421b Masahiro Sano; p422 Herrmann/ Starke; p423tl Bill Ross; p423tr Markku Lahdesmaki; p423b Grafton Marshall Smith; pp424–5 Swim Ink/Griff Teller; p426l Bruno; p426r Ed Bock; p427t Sandford/Agliolo; p427bl Tom & Dee Ann McCarthy; p428t 2 Face; p428b Jeff Vanuga; p429t David H. Wells; p429b David Audrey; p430l Denis Scott; p430r Firefly Productions; p431tl Roger Ressmeyer; p431tc Jim Erickson; p431tr Third Eye Images; p431b Galen Rowell; p432l Michael Setboun; p432r Philip Harvey; p433l David Raymer; p433r Lester Lefkowitz; p434 Derek Trask; p435tc Mark L. Stephenson; p435br Joe Bator; p436l Cynthia Diane Pringle; p436r Tom Young; p437t Marianne Haas; p437ct T. Kevin Smyth; p437cb Kelly-Mooney Photography; p439t Larry Lee Photography; p439bl John Lund; p439br Dale O'Dell; p440tl Lawrence Manning; p440b Firefly Productions; p441t Ed Bock; p441bl Ronnie Kaufman; p441br Jon Feingersh; p442r & p443t Firefly Productions; p443c Carl Schneider; p447br Chiselvision; p449l Chris Hellier; p449r Araldo de Luca; p450r Stocktrek; p451t Jim Zuckerman; p451b Dale O'Dell; p452r John Lund; p453tr Paul Barton; p454 Peter Steiner; p455tl KJ Historical; p455c The Love Potion by Evelyn De Morgan, Massimo Listri; p455b Strauss/Curtis; p456l Douglas Kirkland; p456r Mark Kessell; p457t Jeff Vanuga; p457bl Gerhard Steiner; p457br J Richardson.

Fine Art Photographic Library: pp218–19 & p304–5 Dolce Far Niente, John William Godward; p231 Bathing in the Ganges, India by Valentine Cameron Princep; p264 The Angel's Message by George Hillyard Swinstead; p267 The Rescue by Arthur Hughes; p269l Hermia and Lysander by John Simmons; p271b Spirit of the Night by John Atkinson Grimshaw; p303b Galahad and his Angel by Payton; p357bl A Bright and Happy Christmas, Anon; p447bl The Lily Fairy by Falero.

The Kobal Collection: p76t Warner Bros/The Kobal Collection.

INDEX